About IFPRI

The International Food Policy Research Institute (IFPRI), established in 1975, provides research-based policy solutions to sustainably reduce poverty and end hunger and malnutrition. The Institute conducts research, communicates results, optimizes partnerships, and builds capacity to ensure sustainable food production, promote healthy food systems, improve markets and trade, transform agriculture, build resilience, and strengthen institutions and governance. Gender is considered in all of the Institute's work. IFPRI collaborates with partners around the world, including development implementers, public institutions, the private sector, and farmers' organizations.

About IFPRI's Peer Review Process

IFPRI books are policy-relevant publications based on original and innovative research conducted at IFPRI. All manuscripts submitted for publication as IFPRI books undergo an extensive review procedure that is managed by IFPRI's Publications Review Committee (PRC). Upon submission to the PRC, the manuscript is reviewed by a PRC member. Once the manuscript is considered ready for external review, the PRC submits it to at least two external reviewers who are chosen for their familiarity with the subject matter and the country setting. Upon receipt of these blind external peer reviews, the PRC provides the author with an editorial decision and, when necessary, instructions for revision based on the external reviews. The PRC reassesses the revised manuscript and makes a recommendation regarding publication to the director general of IFPRI. With the director general's approval, the manuscript enters the editorial and production phase to become an IFPRI book.

Agriculture, Development, and the Global Trading System: 2000–2015

Edited by Antoine Bouët and David Laborde

A Peer-Reviewed Publication

International Food Policy Research Institute
Washington, DC

International Food Policy Research Institute, 1201 Eye Street NW, Washington, DC 20005, USA Telephone: 202-862-5600

DOI: http://dx.doi.org/10.2499/9780896292499

Library of Congress Cataloging-in-Publication Data may be found on page vi.

Cover Design: Jason Chow/IFPRI
Project Manager: John Whitehead/IFPRI
Book Layout: BookMatters

Abstract

This book is devoted to the complex relationship between the global trading system and food security, focusing on two important elements: the Doha Development Agenda (DDA) and how food price volatility can be managed, or not, through trade instruments. The first section of the book is based on the premise that more trade integration can fight poverty and alleviate hunger. The second section examines whether managing price volatility is doable through more or less trade integration. This section deals in particular with policy instruments available for policy makers to cope with price volatility: food stocks, crop insurance, and export restrictions. Analysis concludes that without a strong and efficient World Trade Organization (WTO) capable of conducting ambitious trade negotiations, the food security target will be much more difficult to hit.

Library of Congress Cataloging-in-Publication Data

Names: Bouët, Antoine, editor. | Laborde Debucquet, David, 1977– editor.
Title: Agriculture, development, and the global trading system : 2000-2015 / edited by Antoine Bouët and David Laborde.
Description: Washington, DC : International Food Policy Research Institute, [2017] | Includes bibliographical references and index.
Identifiers: LCCN 2017026301 (print) | LCCN 2017024798 (ebook) | ISBN 9780896292499 (pbk. : alk. paper) | ISBN 9780896292505 (ebook)
Subjects: LCSH: World Trade Organization. | Doha Development Agenda (2001–) | International trade. | Commercial policy. | Food security. | Food prices.
Classification: LCC HF1379 .A35 2017 (ebook) | LCC HF1379 (print) | DDC 382/.41—dc23
LC record available at https://lccn.loc.gov/2017026301

Contents

Figures and Tables

Figures

Tables

Acronyms and Abbreviations

ACP	African, Caribbean, Pacific countries
AMA	agricultural market access
AMIS	Agricultural Market Information System
AMS	aggregate measurement of support
AoA	Agreement on Agriculture
ATF	Agreement on Trade Facilitation
BRIC	Brazil, the Russian Federation, India, China
CAP	Common Agricultural Policy
CGE	Computable General Equilibrium
CTAMS	current total aggregate measurement of support
DDA	Doha Development Agenda
DFQF	duty-free quota-free
DSU	Dispute Settlement Unit
EPAs	Economic Partnership Agreements
FERP	fixed external reference price
FTA	free trade agreement
GATT	General Agreement on Tariffs and Trade
GDP	gross domestic product
GHG	greenhouse gas
GTAP	Global Trade Analysis Project

LDC	least developed country
LDP	loan deficiency payments
MFN	most favored nation
MIC	middle-income country
MPS	market price support
NAMA	nonagricultural market access
NFIDCs	Net Food-Importing Developing Countries
NGO	nongovernmental organization
OECD	Organisation for Economic Co-operation and Development
OTDS	overall trade-distorting support
PSE	producer support estimate
R&D	research and development
RAM	recently acceded member
RTA	regional trade agreement
SDRs	Special Drawing Rights
SDT	special and differential treatment
SSM	special safeguard mechanism
SVE	small and vulnerable economies
TPP	Trans-Pacific Partnership Agreement
TRQ	tariff-rate quota
VRAM	very recently acceded member
WACIP	West Africa Cotton Improvement Program
WTO	World Trade Organization

Foreword

In 2017, free trade proponents and protectionists still fiercely debate whether international trade has a positive impact on alleviating hunger and malnutrition worldwide. The authors of this book argue that free trade associated with strong and fair institutions can play a positive and important role in the fight against hunger. Free trade reduces the level and volatility of agricultural and food prices, diversifies the sources of supply and nutritional contents of dietary regimes, and expands the size of markets in which efficient farmers can sell their products.

During 2000–2015, however, there were severe failures of cooperation in the field of international trade. This book, which builds on continuous efforts by IFPRI to generate transparent and evidence-based information for different stakeholders, provides an in-depth analysis of two of these failures.

The first one concerns multilateral trade negotiations and the Doha Development Round, launched in 2001. After more than 15 years of negotiation, this round is not yet completed. This book offers a thorough analysis of the reasons for this failure: the level and distribution, across sectors and countries, of trade distortions; and the political economy of the negotiations.

The other failure of international trade cooperation the authors examine is the poor response to high agricultural prices and price volatility. Between 2006 and 2008, international agricultural commodity prices skyrocketed and price volatility substantially increased. Many governments have reacted by adopting inefficient trade and agricultural policies or even policies that increased price volatility: food stocks, crop insurance, and export restrictions. In this book, the authors precisely evaluate these failures and present policy recommendations.

In a time of emerging protectionist forces, it is of great importance to emphasize the positive and active role that international cooperation and a freer and fair trading system can play in terms of economic development and alleviation of hunger and malnutrition. It is also crucial to highlight the key role that multilateral institutions can play in the global trading system. Such institutions offer a framework for collective action and also protect small and poor countries from the non-cooperative trade policies of large countries. The World Trade Organization (WTO) in particular must remain a strong and active multilateral institution. This book offers a convincing argument for such a role for the WTO and other multilateral institutions.

Shenggen Fan
Director General, IFPRI

Acknowledgments

We thank Maximo Torero for the recommendations he has provided since the beginning of this project as well as for the constant support given to the research conducted by the trade team of the International Food Policy Research Institute (IFPRI) since 2005. That research forms the core of this book. His leadership has been inspiring.

We thank Eugenio Díaz-Bonilla, Joseph W. Glauber, Will Martin, and David Orden for their suggestions on an earlier version of the book. We also thank the IFPRI Publications Review Committee, chaired by Gershon Feder, and two anonymous referees whose recommendations have improved the storyline of the current book. We are also very grateful to Sara Gustafson for her editing and proofreading efforts. All remaining errors and/or omissions are ours.

This book was undertaken as part of the CGIAR Research Program on Policies, Institutions, and Markets (PIM) led by IFPRI. Funding support for this study was provided by the European Union's Seventh Framework program FP7/2007–2011 under Grant Agreement number 290693 FOODSECURE—Exploring the Future of Global Food and Nutrition Security and the CGIAR Research Program on Policies, Institutions, and Markets. PIM is in turn supported by donations from Australia, Belgium, the Bill & Melinda Gates Foundation, Canada, China, Denmark, the European Commission, the Indian Council of Agricultural Research, the International Fund for Agricultural Development, Irish Aid, the Netherlands, the Russian Federation, South Africa, Sweden, Switzerland, the United Kingdom's Department for International Development, and the United States Agency for International Development. The views and opinions presented do not necessarily reflect those of the European Commission, PIM, IFPRI, or CGIAR. The authors are solely responsible for the contents of this book.

Chapter 1

INTRODUCTION: SETTING THE STAGE

Antoine Bouët and David Laborde

While food security has long been recognized as a universal human right, there are still 795 million undernourished people across the globe (FAO 2015). This unacceptably high number, along with the recent series of global food security and food price crises, has mobilized many international institutions, national governments, and nongovernmental organizations (NGOs) and made the worldwide alleviation of hunger and undernutrition a top international priority. Food and nutrition security is a multidimensional objective and, as such, requires policy interventions at many stages: investment in agricultural systems and rural areas, investment in health and education, improvements in market access, implementation of social protection mechanisms and safety nets, and improvements in governance. International trade also forms a key element.

However, there remains a long-standing and intense debate regarding the role that international trade can play in improving food security, specifically the appropriate global policy orientation. Although the conversation involves many complexities, the following are the *main* terms of the debate. On one side, many think that countries must pursue the goal of food self-sufficiency to secure local production of agricultural items and local populations' access to food. In this line of thinking, "self-sufficiency" implies import restrictions to support local production. On the other side are those who believe that the best way to secure populations' access to food is to remove all barriers to trade. In this line of thinking, free trade will more effectively increase the global production of agricultural and food products and secure the cheapest access to these items for all consumers.

This book is devoted to the complex and controversial relationship between the global trading system and food security. In particular, it aims to answer the question of why trade and the World Trade Organization (WTO) matter for food security. While this relationship has been debated for a long time, the 2001–2015 period saw some major changes to the global trading system that changed the terms, and the intensity, of that debate. This period, which coincides with the twenty-year anniversary of the establishment of the WTO, presents a good opportunity to examine the impacts of the integration of agriculture into the global rules–based trading system, initiated with the Uruguay Round in 1995 and implemented gradually until 2004.

In particular, it aims to answer the question of why trade and the WTO matter for food security. This question is quite relevant at the time when the global community defines new ambitious development goals, especially the Sustainable Development Goal 2, "Zero Hunger" by 2030, and policy makers around the world and public opinion forget the value of a healthy trading system and lean toward isolationist approaches (UNDP 2017). As shown in Figure 1.1, the appeal of "free trade" has varied over time. The issue was first raised during the nineteenth century and was fed by political and economic debate, culminating in 1890 with the first peak of effective liberalization before being smashed by a wave of protectionist measures (for example, the McKinley Tariff Act in the United States, the Méline tariff in 1892 in France, and so on). After this harsh history lesson, free trade was resurrected at the end of World War II, and a keen interest in the topic emerged between the mid-1980s and 1995, culminating in the creation of the WTO. Unfortunately, since then, it seems that a new period of doubt has emerged.[1] Understanding why we face such a reversal and what it means for our collective future is important.

Some Preliminary Definitions

The basic definition of *food security* is well known. According to the Food and Agricultural Organization of the United Nations (FAO), food security is reached "when all people have physical and economic access at all times to adequate food or the means for its procurement, without discrimination of any kind" (FAO 2015). In Chapter 8 of this book, Eugenio Díaz-Bonilla reminds us of the more multidimensional definition of food security: (1) availability; (2) access; (3) utilization; and (4) stability. Looking at this more complex definition, it becomes clear that attaining food security is a major challenge. Food availability depends on domestic production, stocks, and trade. Access to food is influenced by income and employment, and thus by economic growth and development. Utilization of food depends on the quality of food, health services, water and sanitation infrastructure, education, and women's

1 In 2016, trade skepticism is shared by many politicians in the United States, the United Kingdom, France, Germany, and other OECD countries.

FIGURE 1.1 The popularity of free trade, measured in word frequency analysis

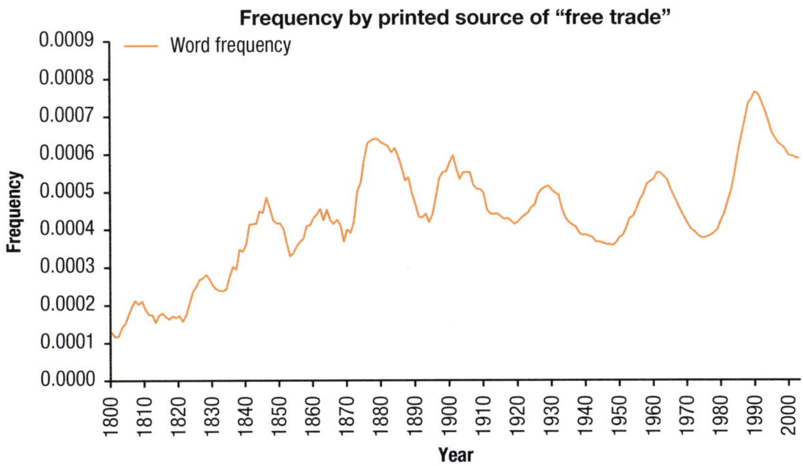

Source: Google (2016).

Note: Google Ngram is an online search engine that calculates and charts the frequency of any sequence of words in sources printed between 1500 and 2008 available in the Google book library. Similar terms like "trade liberalization" display a similar pattern in the recent years, but have appeared only after 1947 when with the GATT, the idea of removing trade previously constrained became popular.

empowerment, among other factors. Finally, stability in food security means that physical and economic access to and proper utilization of food must take place "at all times."

It is particularly important to add the *quality* dimension to our understanding of food security, going beyond the *quantitative* challenge of ensuring a certain number of calories consumed every day. The nutritional aspect of the world's diets has gained increased attention from policy makers and development practitioners in recent years. Developing countries can suffer from both undernutrition and overnutrition at the same time; thus, increased income and food consumption will not be sufficient to achieve the world's ultimate nutrition and health goals. Consequently, it is important to also assess the role that international trade can play in people's access to food items of higher nutritional quality and in dietary diversification. As for products other than food products, a key contribution of trade to food consumers' welfare is not only access to goods at lower prices, but also access to wider varieties of products (food from new origins, new cereals or vegetables, fruits all year long, and so on). Recently it was estimated that the number of imported product varieties available in the United States increased by a factor of three between 1972 and 2001; the value to US consumers of this expanded import variety was evaluated to be 2.6 percent of GDP (Broda and Weinstein 2006). Finally, fully understanding food security also requires an understanding of poverty. As demonstrated in Chapter 8, these two multidimensional concepts are strongly correlated. Poverty is particularly associated with such "damaging fluctuations" (Sinha, Lipton, and Yaqub 2002) as violence, natural disasters, harvest failure, disease or injury, unemployment or underemployment, and the augmentation of relative food prices. During the 2007–2008 episode of higher and volatile global food prices, many experts emphasized the ensuing risk of increased poverty and food insecurity.

Comprehensively defining food security is complex; defining the global trading system is even harder. We see this system as the set of rules and institutions upon which international trade is based. The system heavily involves the WTO. Three of the WTO's activities are particularly important for international trade. First, the WTO establishes a certain number of clauses and rules (most favored nation status, national treatment, transparency, etc.) that member countries must follow when they trade with others. Second, the WTO organizes periodic multilateral trade negotiations. In 2001 the WTO launched a new round of trade negotiations, with development set as a main objective. These negotiations were called the Doha Development Agenda (DDA) and highlighted the importance of international trade liberalization to economic and welfare gains in developing countries. The Doha Ministerial Declaration stated that "international trade can play a major role in the promotion of economic development and the alleviation of poverty. We recognize the need for all our peoples to benefit from the increased opportunities and welfare gains that the multilateral trading system generates. The majority of WTO members are developing countries. We seek to place their needs and interests at the heart of the Work Programme adopted in this Declaration" (WTO 2001).

The Doha talks represented the first time that a multilateral trade negotiation focused on the objective of development; however, thus far, the WTO appears to be failing in the delivery of successful new trade liberalization. Chapters 2, 3, 4, and 6 of this book discuss why the Doha Round has failed to come to fruition—and what this means for future negotiations. These chapters also highlight the critical importance of agricultural issues in ongoing trade talks and how the different faces of food security impact global negotiations. For instance, discussions on food security were among the two most important topics during the Bali Ministerial (2013).

The third aspect of the WTO's activities is the Dispute Settlement Unit (DSU), which provides a framework for litigating trade disputes. This makes up a key aspect of the global trading system since the absence of such a mechanism would certainly imply the multiplication of trade wars, with rounds of costly retaliation and counterretaliation. Since 1995, the DSU has litigated (or is currently litigating) 82 agricultural trade disputes out of a total of 485 cases, meaning that agricultural trade disputes account for 17 percent of all disputes. In contrast, international agricultural trade represents only 8 percent of total global trade. This disparity highlights the sensitive, sometimes contentious nature of agricultural trade.[2]

In addition to the WTO, the global trading system includes various regional agreements and preferential trading regimes. Regional trade agreements result in reciprocal trade between signatory countries, while preferential trade agreements are nonreciprocal, giving developing countries unilateral better access to rich economies' markets. Compatibility between multilateral regimes like the WTO and regional and preferential agreements is one of the major successes of the global trading system. Let us now focus on the relationship between the global trading system and food security. We first try to understand how trade can help in promoting food security and improving nutrition. Then we assess the impact of various trade policy instruments on food security.

How Can Trade Promote Food Security and Improve Nutrition?

It is generally understood that improvements to the global trading system can facilitate trade, which can in turn help to alleviate hunger and improve food security. The theoretical and empirical justifications for this positive relationship between an open trading system and increased food security are well known. However, in different countries the various political and social configurations make this relationship more complex due to market failures, inefficient policy interventions, and political economy constraints. Modern trade economy theory has its roots deeply anchored in the policy debate surrounding the degree of trade openness desired for food products. In his *Essay on the Influence of a Low Price of Corn on the Profits of Stock*, Ricardo (1815) introduced the key rationales for free trade in food products and formulated the notion of "comparative costs" for the first time. Two years later, he exposed the theory of comparative advantage in *On the Principles of Political Economy and Taxation* (1817).

2 Authors' calculation based on WTO statistics.

In the 1910s, 1920s, and 1930s, Heckscher (1919) and Ohlin (1933) from the Stockholm School of Economics generalized Ricardo's theory and stated that a country has a comparative advantage in goods that intensively use its abundant factors and a comparative disadvantage in goods that intensively use its scarce factors. This theory forms the basis of the pro–free trade vision of classical economists and shows that worldwide production (of food in particular) is more efficient if free trade is implemented. Free trade supports countries' specialization according to the comparative advantage principle, meaning that global food production is increased and average production costs are reduced. At the same time, trade liberalization improves average incomes, ensuring real income gains for the average consumer.

Trade openness alone, however, is not sufficient to ensure improved food security. In the line of the neoclassical theory of international trade, Stolper and Samuelson (1941) offer a precise evaluation of how trade openness can affect remunerations of productive factors. Specifically, international trade benefits the abundant factor of production and hurts the scarce one. In that sense, this theory clearly demonstrates that trade openness could hurt the incomes of the poor in some cases, and in each nation there will be winners and losers. Without explicit redistributive policies, trade liberalization may not be inclusive and the food security of some vulnerable groups may be compromised.

International trade also has varied impacts on the relative price of consumption goods. On one side, the relative price of goods in which a nation has a comparative disadvantage and which it imports decreases with the implementation of free trade. On the other side, the relative price of goods in which a nation has a comparative advantage and which it exports augments with the implementation of free trade. In other words, under a more open trade regime the relative price of food items may either increase or decrease depending on where a country's comparative advantage lies for those items.

These static elements are not the only ones that should be taken into account; when it comes to free trade, there are also dynamic elements that we must consider. For example, since free trade augments the real remuneration of abundant productive factors, it should also accelerate those factors' accumulation. In countries that have a comparative advantage in agricultural goods (products that are intensive in land), the real remuneration of this productive factor should increase, implying an extension of the land area under agricultural cultivation. This in turn increases the specialization of those countries' economies, as well as a more concentrated international supply of food. Further trade integration is also needed from a dynamic point of view to facilitate the transportation and exchange of food and agricultural commodities from countries with excess supply to countries with excess demand. There is a simple reason for this: while national food demand remains stable over time, national food supplies are uncertain, or even unstable, particularly due to changing weather conditions. It is dangerous to think that local food production alone will always be able to satisfy local food demand. Trade is needed to diversify a country's food sources and decrease the risk of a food crisis.

Finally, the demand for food and nutrient diversity is much better satisfied by an open trading system, since international trade offers consumers more varieties of food. This was demonstrated theoretically by Krugman (1979) and Lancaster (1980) and empirically by Deason and Laborde (2015). The latter study calculates the macronutrients (calories/protein/fat) contents of agricultural trade flows over a long period of time and shows that the nutritional content of international trade has been increasing since 1996, especially for developing countries. Despite its complexities, international trade has thus become an important feature of the global food system, as shown in Figure 1.2. As of 2015, nearly 20 percent of the calories produced in the world crossed an international border before being consumed. This share was only 12 percent in 1975. It is interesting to note that this share has only marginally increased since 2005, the year that represents the final period of the implementation of the WTO's Uruguay Round and the last major effort to improve the global food trading system.

While the growth of trade in manufactures since 1975 has been explosive, trade in agriculture has progressed more slowly. This point is clearly confirmed by Aksoy (2004), who compares average annual real export growth rates in agriculture (4.9 percent in the 1980s versus 3.4 percent in the 1990s) and in manufactures (5.7 percent and 6.7 percent, respectively), and more recently by Xu (2015). Using an FAO database, Xu estimates that while world trade in manufactures was more than 8 times larger than agricultural trade in 1997, world production of manufactures was only 3.8 larger than production of agricultural goods. Finally, from the WTO website, we confirm that between 1990 and 2014, exports (in value) of manufactures have increased much more rapidly (multiplying by more than 5) than exports of agricultural products (which have multiplied by only 4.2), even with the recent rise in global agricultural prices. This illustrates the huge potential that exists to use agricultural trade as an instrument to enhance food security.

International trade allows consumers in different parts of the world to access nutritious commodities and improved dietary regimes. One example is the worldwide adoption of quinoa, a nutrient-rich traditional cereal. The

FIGURE 1.2 Worldwide share of produced calories crossing an international border before final consumption (%)

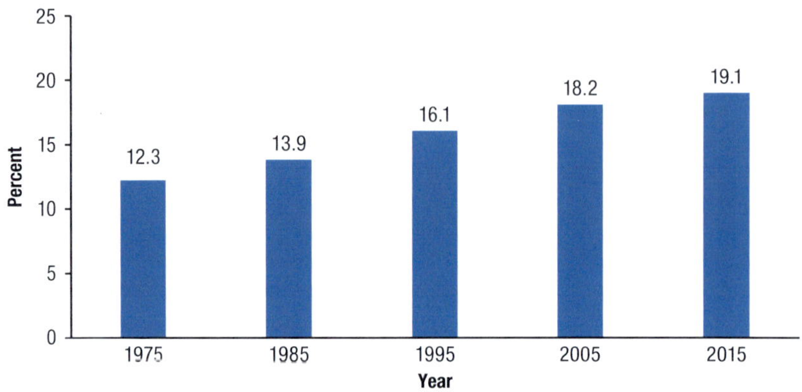

Source: Authors' computation based on Deason and Laborde (2015).

story of quinoa may be emblematic of the potential role of international trade in improving food security and nutrition, connecting poor producers in specific regions to global demand through international value chains. Quinoa is a highly nutritious crop rich in protein, dietary fiber, several B vitamins, and essential amino acids and lower in fats than most other crops (Johnson and Ward 1993). Quinoa is also recognized for its adaptability to various agroenvironmental conditions (FAO n.d.). Initially quinoa was cultivated only in the Andean region. In the early 1990s, however, the National Aeronautics and Space Administration (NASA) began "evaluating growth and productivity of several crops in a controlled-environment culture, with the goal of selecting those meeting nutritional needs and exhibiting a manageable growth habit" (Schlick and Bubenheim 1993, 1) for its long-term human space program. At the time, quinoa became recognized as very close to the best standards in terms of nutritional content designed by the FAO.

This launched quinoa on a successful growth trajectory in terms of world trade and consumption. Global trade in quinoa (in volume) multiplied by more than 96—from 590 metric tons to 57,000 metric tons between 1996 and 2014 (Figure 1.3a). This explosion in trade was driven by rapidly increasing imports in many developed countries, mainly the United States but also in middle-income countries like Brazil or the Russian Federation, where consumers with increased purchasing power can now access a more diversified food basket (Figure 1.3b). The international price of quinoa exploded during this

FIGURE 1.3 A snapshot of the global quinoa market

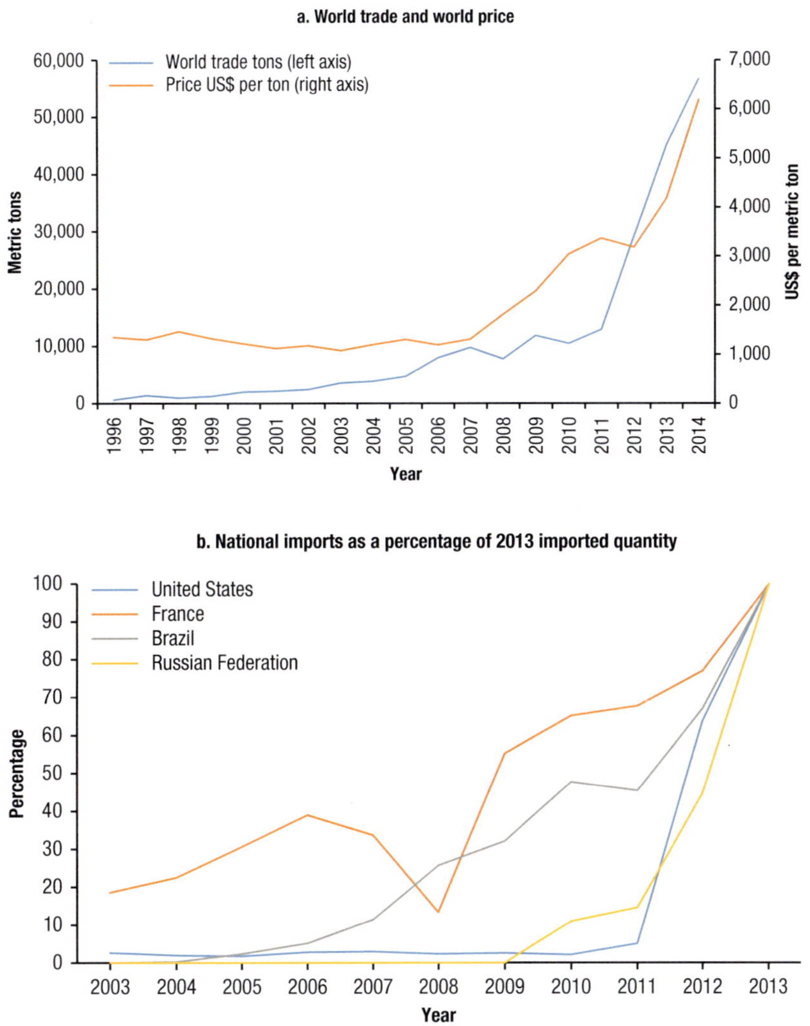

Source: Authors' computation based on Deason and Laborde (2015).

period, from US$1,299 per metric ton in 1996 to US$6,185 per metric ton in 2014 (Figure 1.3a).[3]

Although quinoa is now cultivated in more than 70 countries, the production of quinoa remains highly concentrated in its traditional region—Bolivia, Ecuador, and Peru—and tripled in this area between 1992 and 2010, while the area dedicated to quinoa doubled (FAO n.d.). Simultaneously, the domestic price of quinoa drastically increased in this region; FAOSTAT indicates that the local producer price of a ton of quinoa increased from $444 in 2004 to $1,163 in 2014 in Bolivia and from $299 to $2,774 in Peru (FAO 2016). The growth in quinoa's popularity and trade volume has several effects for both regional economies and local stakeholders (Romero and Shahriari 2011; *Economist* 2012). The huge augmentation of quinoa exports has substantially raised local farmers' incomes in a region considered to be very poor. Bellemare, Fajardo-Gonzalez, and Gitter (2016) find evidence of a positive general equilibrium effect on the Peruvian economy as a whole as a result of rising quinoa prices. However, the expansion in quinoa exports has penalized local consumers, especially poor ones, as a result of the increase of domestic prices. Since quinoa has traditionally formed an important element of local diets in the region, concerns about increasing local malnutrition have emerged alongside quinoa's global growth (Romero and Shahriari 2011). In addition, with the massive increase of local cultivation has come fear of local environmental damage (Jacobsen 2011).

The case of quinoa shows how the impacts of international trade on food security can be relatively complex. A boost in national exports to the rest of the world has increased local production and prices. This benefits local producers and global consumers but can hurt domestic consumers if targeted policy responses are not delivered. Let us examine the potential impacts of various trade policy instruments on food security.

What Are the Potential Impacts of Trade Policy Instruments on Food Security?

The concept of food security is complex, implying a combination of food availability, access, and utilization. *Availability* means low food prices and increased local consumption; *access* means sufficient incomes and increased purchasing power; and *utilization* means sufficient health services, water and sanitation infrastructure, and education, among other factors. Table 1.1

3 All dollar amounts in this chapter are in US dollars.

TABLE 1.1 Short-term impact of various trade policy instruments on prices, surpluses, and public revenues

Policy instrument	Impact on local price	Impact on local consumption	Impact on local production	Impact on public revenues	Impact on world price
Import duty	+	–	+	+	–
Import quota	+	–	+	?	–
Import subsidy	–	+	–	–	+
Export subsidy	+	–	+	–	–
Export tax	–	+	–	+	+
Export restriction	–	+	–	?	+

Source: Authors.
Note: ? = undetermined.

summarizes the short-term impact of six trade policy instruments on local prices, local consumption, local production, public revenues, and world prices. We do not capture the impact of these six instruments on food security itself because food security can be impacted in many different ways by changes in domestic prices, consumption, production, employment, and public revenues and public expenses.

In the case of an *import duty*, there is less local competition from foreign producers; this implies higher local prices, which support domestic producers but hurt domestic consumers. Import duties also increase public revenues. Thus the impact of an import duty on food security is not clear-cut. Increased local production may support farmers' incomes, and augmented public revenues may improve and expand local infrastructure. These are positive outcomes for food security. Reduced local consumption with increased food prices, however, may hurt food security—particularly for poor populations. Is the effect on producers larger than the effect on consumers? Since the agricultural sector is characterized by net imports, local consumption is greater than local production and the impact of an import duty on food security is thus generally considered to be globally negative. Import duties also decrease demand on world markets, which tends to drive world prices down. This is positive for net buyers abroad and negative for net sellers.

The case of an *import quota* is similar, except that a quota may or may not generate public revenues depending on how import licenses are distributed. This policy may be considered even more damaging to food security than an import duty because it implies a quantitative restriction to trade, creating shortages without providing additional financial resources to help governments supporting poor consumers.[4] An import subsidy is an unconventional trade policy instrument, and it is seldom applied in its simplest form. However, its effects are quite interesting. When imports are subsidized, there is more local competition between local and foreign producers. More competition from abroad means reduced prices and decreased local production but increased consumption and less public revenue. The impact of an import subsidy on consumers is large, and subsidies tend to support food security. Import subsidies also augment both demand and prices on the global market.

If exports are subsidized, local producers become more interested in exporting than in supplying their production on the domestic market. Thus, while production increases under this policy, the *export subsidy* supports exports, not the local food supply. In this case, domestic prices increase and the effect on consumption is negative. So although an export subsidy is beneficial to farmers' incomes, it is detrimental not only to local consumption but also to public revenues. Globally, we may consider export subsidies negative for food security since this instrument supports selling food items abroad and not locally.

An *export tax*, alternatively, may be positive for food security; this is why export taxes are often implemented in times of food crisis (see Chapters 11 and 12 in this book for a complete discussion of export taxes). When exports are taxed, local farmers become more interested in selling their commodities locally than abroad. This increased supply on the domestic market makes domestic prices go down. While an export tax penalizes domestic producers and could lower farmers' incomes, it benefits both domestic consumers and public revenues. An *export restriction* (for example, an export ban) has the same consequences as an export tax, except that it may not increase public revenues if export licenses are given freely to domestic producers.

It is important to note that all these policy instruments do not have a single clear-cut, straightforward impact on food security, which is to be expected, as they are primarily aimed at trade, not at food security. On the one hand, import subsidies and export taxes/restrictions can help improve food security, at least in the short term. On the other hand, import duties/quotas and export subsidies are policy instruments that hurt food security. Four remarks are worthwhile here:

4 Because of their cost and inefficiency, these instruments were banned during the Uruguay Round and replaced by tariff-rate quotas combining a reduced tariff on a given imported quantity (that is, the quota) and a high tariff beyond these quantities.

1. We have focused only on short-term impacts; in the long term, several effects may take place that cancel out or even reverse these short-term impacts. For example, an export tax decreases domestic prices in the short term, but if it is a long-term policy, it may discourage investment in the agricultural sector and substantially reduce long-term supply, which may in turn augment long-term domestic prices.

2. We have also focused only on the impact of a policy instrument on the sector in which it is applied rather than on other sectors. As an example of how a policy may impact additional sectors, take again the case of an export tax and consider that it is applied on a raw agricultural commodity that is used as an input for a food product. The export tax on the raw commodity may stimulate the production of the food product since the price of its input is decreased; thus, in this case, the export tax plays the role of an input subsidy. In Argentina, for example, the government has long implemented an export tax on soybeans, which has decreased the domestic price of a good that is used as an input by the crushing industry (see Bouët, Estrades, and Laborde 2014). Thus the production of the manufactured goods (meals and vegetable oil, biodiesel) is increased thanks to this export taxation.

3. Thus far, we have focused only on the impact of one unique policy instrument. The implementation of one of the six policy instruments presented in Table 1.1 coupled with another policy instrument may have a different impact on food security than the implementation of a single policy alone. For example, consider a case in which the government uses the receipts generated by an import duty to finance cash transfers to the poor. In this case, this policy may have positive, not negative, effects on food security.

4. We have not discussed the underlying redistributive impacts of these policies within each category of agents. For instance, trade policies are not targeted by nature: a price increase will always benefit large producers with a high share of marketed production more than smallholders. Since the latter group is the one that most policy makers want to support when aiming to reduce poverty and hunger, this represents a serious limitation of these policy instruments.

Clearly, food security is a complex objective to attain, requiring both increased incomes for poor people and lower prices for food items. International trade can boost farmers' incomes in poor countries and can benefit global consumers through lower food prices and enriched diets. However, an expansion of trade may also hurt consumers in the exporting country (by increasing domestic prices) and producers in the importing country. Therefore, assessing the net effects of trade policies on food security requires complex and detailed qualitative assessments. For example, restricting imports is negative as far as food security is concerned because it increases consumption prices for food items. Thus, while an import duty has a positive impact on public revenues and local production, this should not be considered a first-best instrument to achieve these objectives. To increase public revenues, a government should consider the implementation of a direct tax on incomes, taxes on value-added, and so on rather than an import duty that impacts a large share of poor people's expenditures. Similarly, to increase local agricultural production, governments should consider measures to facilitate better market access for local farmers, better access to credit and fertilizers, the expansion of transportation infrastructure, investment in research and development, and other measures to target the real bottlenecks and challenges faced by the country's agricultural value chains.

Overall, there is a cost associated with protectionist policies aimed at achieving food self-sufficiency. Consumers lose more than producers under these policy regimes, while governments gain in profits and taxes. Several studies have evaluated these costs. Beghin, Bureau, and Park (2003) have estimated the cost of food self-sufficiency and agricultural protection in South Korea (Republic of Korea). At the launch of the Doha Development Agenda the Republic of Korea's government had promoted food security as its main objective and was relying on a combination of trade, domestic production, and self-sufficiency to reach that goal. The government massively subsidized local production (at a level corresponding to 75 percent of the value of production in 1999) and imposed nearly prohibitive tariffs in the rice, meat, and dairy sectors. Beghin, Bureau, and Park (2003) have estimated that this subsidization resulted in 15.8 Korean wons in lost consumer incomes for every 10 wons-increase in farmers' incomes. Globally, this policy cost $4.76 billion annually in resource misallocation.

Warr (2005) estimates the impact of a rice import ban in Indonesia, implemented in 2006 to assist poor farmers and reduce poverty. The study uses a general equilibrium model of the Indonesian economy with household disaggregation and a top-down microsimulation. Warr concludes that the rice import ban is equivalent to a 125 percent tariff in terms of incidence on domestic price; this is six times the pre-2004 tariff. Under this ban the incidence of poverty rises by almost 1 percent of the population, and poverty increases in both rural and urban areas. In rural areas only the richest farmers gain from the ban. This seems to be an important effect of many food self-sufficiency policies: the poorest households are harmed more since domestic food prices rise under these policies and because the share that poor populations spend on food is higher.

As this literature illustrates, the objective of food self-sufficiency is costly and may have an antipoor bias. It is also a misleading policy objective, as it is difficult to guarantee that the local food supply will be sufficient to meet local food demand every year. National demand for food is stable because food is a first-necessity good. However, domestic production is clearly not stable. As Chapter 8 highlights, "domestic production in individual countries is far more volatile than global and regional aggregates." Hazell, Shields, and Shields (2005) conclude that domestic food prices show higher volatility than respective world prices. Díaz-Bonilla, Thomas, and Robinson (2003) show that food trade significantly helps to reduce the volatility of food consumption in developing countries. Minot (2012) examines trends in food price volatility using a database of African staple food prices and finds that price volatility is lower for processed and tradable foods than for nontradable foods. The issue of volatile national agricultural production is further exacerbated by the threat of climate change, including increasing global temperatures and more frequent extreme weather events. International trade certainly has an important role to play in mitigating these negative consequences of climate change (see Chapter 8).

It is important to note that while some trade policies, such as export taxes, may have positive short-term impacts on food security, this positive impact is local. Impacts on these countries' trading partners may be drastically different. An export tax, for example, reduces the food supply on international markets and tends to increase world prices, particularly if the exporting country is large. In other words, countries may try to reduce domestic food prices by increasing the world prices of these goods, consequently increasing prices (other things being equal) at which consumers in other countries can buy these goods. This is typically a beggar-thy-neighbor policy (that is, a policy that is implemented by a government to correct a distortion and improve the national situation but that deteriorates the economic situation of other countries; see Chapters 11 and 12 for further discussion).

Along the same line of thinking, while an export subsidy may increase domestic prices in the country implementing the subsidy, it may also contribute to food security abroad by easing access to food and reducing local prices in food-importing countries. Of course, the same subsidy has a vastly different impact on foreign food-exporting countries since it induces a contraction of their export revenues. The analysis presented here is preliminary, but it helps provide a framework for the rest of this book to examine the complex relationship between trade and food security in more detail. With this framework in place, we now paint a picture of the state of the world's distortionary trade policies today. First we look at traditional distortionary policies, such as import duties, export subsidies, and domestic support measures (policies that tend to decrease world prices); then we look at such policies as export taxes/restrictions, food reserves, and biofuel mandates, which tend to increase world prices and have become more favored by countries worldwide since the 2007–2008 food crisis.

Trade and Agricultural Policies Today: A *Tour d'horizon* of Traditional Distortionary Policies

Under the category of traditional distortionary policies, we include protection at the border, particularly import duties, and measures of domestic support. These distortionary policies have traditionally been the object of negotiations at the WTO or in other trade agreements. Chapters 2, 4, and 6 present a global picture of trade policies today. Chapter 6 shows that based on the MAcMapHS6v2.1 database, the average duty on imports in 2004 was at 4.6 percent. This level is slightly lower today (Bureau, Guimbard, and Jean 2016), clearly indicating that tariff protection is currently low—on average reaching 4.2 percent in 2013. However, this finding hides high levels of protection in some sectors and some countries. For example, the average global duty on imports of agricultural products is estimated at 16.4 percent; the average global duty on imports on industrial products is estimated at 3.9 percent. Tariff protection is particularly high in the sugar, meat, dairy, cereal, and vegetable and fruit sectors. This fact is of course especially important for this book's focus on the relationship between international trade and food security.

Average overall protection is also close to 10 percent in least developed countries (LDCs), which is higher than in middle-income countries (8.6 percent) and much higher than in high-income countries (3 percent). It is worth mentioning, however, that the average tariff protection on agricultural goods is higher in middle-income countries (18.3 percent) than in LDCs (11.6 percent). These findings give a more accurate picture of the current state of global trade policies: a world with average low import duties but with high protection remaining in agricultural sectors and in LDCs. If we define trade policies as the set of policies at the border—that is, import duties and other import restrictions, exports subsidies and taxes, and so on—we consider agricultural policies to include all other types of policies that affect agriculture. These consist of policies that support domestic demand for agricultural commodities, such as nutrition programs and biofuel mandates; direct market price supports that raise market prices; direct payments that raise farmers' incomes through income transfers; input subsidies; and loss compensation programs such as crop insurance and disaster assistance (Glauber and Effland forthcoming).

Under the WTO's Agreement on Agriculture (AoA), signed in 1995, all WTO members are obliged to report two categories of domestic support in order to measure the distortionary impact of these policies on global trade: notifications related to the calculation of the current total aggregate measurement of support (AMS), considered to be major sources of distortions and for which spending is disciplined (the Amber Box category); and notifications related to new or modified domestic support measures for which exemption from reduction is claimed. The latter category is mainly constituted by the Green Box category and is considered to have minimal trade-distorting impacts. Green Box measures include measures of support not tied to production or market prices, such as agricultural research and training programs or payments to farmers related to environmental practices. Other exempted policies include Blue Box measures, which are trade-distorting programs that include conditions to reduce those distortions (for example, a Blue Box measure may have a condition that limits production); developmental measures (the Development Box—for example, investment subsidies in developing countries, agricultural input subsidies for resource-poor producers, and so on); or other distortionary payments up to 5 percent of the total value of production (the de minimis; this threshold is increased to 10 percent for a developing country).

At the beginning of the Doha Round, trade-distorting policy instruments were heavily used by advanced economies to support their farmers. The European Union has traditionally been thought of as the WTO member with the most important Amber Box program. However, the European AMS fell from 81 billion euros in 1995 to 5.9 billion euros in 2012–2013; the WTO's cap on this program is 72.2 billion euros per year. This means that today the European Union is complying with its WTO obligation on domestic support. Simultaneously, the EU's Green Box program has expanded and stood at 71.1 billion euros in 2012–2013. Thus it can be concluded that the European Union's agricultural policy has a significantly less distortionary impact on world markets than it did 20 years ago, not only because of the adoption of less distortionary policy instruments but also because the EU is a less powerful agricultural economy today (Matthews 2014).

Concerning the United States, the AMS cap on Amber Box program subsidies is currently at $19.1 billion. The country's total agricultural support programs, conservation programs, and crop insurance programs are estimated to be more than $200 billion for fiscal years 2016–2025 (Glauber and Effland forthcoming). It is often concluded that US domestic support has moved away from direct interventions like price support programs to measures more decoupled from actual production and to insurance programs. Consequently, many argue that today's US agricultural policy is less distortionary to trade (Orden and Zulauf 2015). However, its high cost and resilience is also underlined (Glauber and Effland forthcoming).

Agricultural insurance programs have often been motivated by the desire to provide incentives for expanded agricultural production, thereby improving food security. The use of insurance programs has increased drastically since the end of the 1980s. One reason for this growth could be the potential exemption of insurance programs from WTO reduction commitments and a regime of higher but more volatile world prices since 2005. Chapter 10 presents the evolution of these insurance programs in developed and developing countries and examines their treatment under the WTO, noting that insurance subsidies could come under increased WTO scrutiny and challenge in the future. In emerging economies such as Brazil, China, India, and the Russian Federation, notifications of domestic support for agriculture point to increasing levels of support (see Chapter 5). However, as shown in Chapter 5, there are significant differences between these four economies. While agriculture and food account for an important share of Brazilian exports, this share is relatively low in China, India, and the Russian Federation. There are also strong differences in the participation of these countries in WTO governance and negotiations. Since 1995, Brazil's participation in the WTO Dispute Settlement Unit has been forceful; this country has been demanding freer agricultural trade and was very active in the G20 group that requested substantial cuts in agricultural tariffs by developed countries.[5] India's position, however, has been drastically different: its government has given priority to

5 This G20 group in the WTO agricultural negotiations is distinct from the G20 group of major economies brought together regularly to address global economic issues. In 2012 the 23 members of the G20 in the WTO comprised Argentina, Bolivia, Brazil, Chile, China, Cuba, Ecuador, Egypt, Guatemala, India, Indonesia, Mexico, Nigeria, Pakistan, Paraguay, Peru, Philippines, South Africa, United Republic of Tanzania, Thailand, Uruguay, Venezuela, and Zimbabwe.

a food security agenda with "special" products exempted from liberalization and a "special safeguard mechanism" aimed at handling price variations and import surges (see Chapter 2).

While Organisation for Economic Co-operation and Development (OECD) countries have significantly cut their domestic support to agriculture over the past 30 years, this support has markedly increased in emerging economies (see Chapters 2 and 5). However, as far as support to agriculture is concerned, emerging countries make up a heterogeneous group. Brazil, Chile, Colombia, Israel, Kazakhstan, South Africa, Ukraine, and Viet Nam have relatively low levels of support, while China, the Russian Federation, and Turkey have support levels closer to the OECD average, and Indonesia has levels much higher than that average (OECD 2016).

Overall, between 2001 and 2015, trade-distorting policies (traditionally tariffs and domestic support) evolved significantly. Even without the conclusion of the Doha Round, tariff liberalization has continued, not only through the conclusion of regional trade agreements but also, and maybe more important, thanks to the end of the completion of the Uruguay Round and unilateral liberalization. In the European Union and the United States, domestic support has moved away from trade-distorting policies toward Green Box policies (that is, nondistortionary or less distortionary measures). In emerging economies, meanwhile, domestic and market price support has clearly been augmented, particularly in China and Indonesia. All of these policies are supposed to put downward pressure on the world price of agricultural commodities. For the past 10 years, however, several countries, including key exporters, have given priority to policies that instead put upward pressure on world prices.

Trade and Agricultural Policies Today: New Issues

Since 2005, a new issue has emerged in the debate regarding trade policies. While traditional trade talks were focused on measures reducing world prices (such as import restrictions and export subsidies), both at-the-border and beyond-the-border policies were contributing to higher world prices by reducing supply or strengthening demand. Many countries now use policies such as export taxes and export restrictions. Piermartini (2004) noted that approximately one-third of WTO members imposed export duties. More recent research (Bouët, Estrades, and Laborde 2013) has shown that the average export tax on global merchandise trade was 0.48 percent in 2007. The same study found that export taxes are concentrated on raw agricultural products, minerals, processed oilseeds, aluminum and iron, and timber, with the bulk of these taxes imposed on energy products. Finally, using a Computable General Equilibrium (CGE) estimation, it is concluded that removal of all export taxes leads to an overall gain of 0.24 percent in world real income, or $133 billion per year by 2020, and expands world trade volumes by 2.8 percent compared to their 2020 levels in the baseline.

Two factors help explain the growing importance of export restrictions. First, as stated earlier, export taxes or export restrictions may help fight food insecurity by decreasing local food prices. Second, the WTO does not prohibit export taxes and other forms of export restrictions. More precisely, as Crosby (2008, 3) has stated: "General WTO rules do not discipline Members' application of export taxes," but "they can agree—and several recently acceded countries, including China, have agreed—to legally binding commitments in this regard." Chapters 11 and 12 analyze the use of export restrictions during the 2007–2008 food crisis and show that these were typically beggar-thy-neighbor policies, intended to improve food security at home at the cost of food security abroad.

Even if the growth of biofuel markets over 2000–2009 is an important evolution of agricultural markets, this book does not include a specific chapter on this topic, for several reasons. First, biofuel programs represent a policy-driven demand shock on world agricultural prices, and as such they have no specific implications about how the world trading system rules should be revised or adjusted to deal with external shocks or policy reforms. Of course, biofuel mandates influence international trade, but they are not trade policy instruments and their indirect impacts have contrasting impacts among trade partners. Aside from food security issues, these policies have certainly caused a significant shock that influences the production and trade of other goods—for example, such substitutes as palm oil may have been expanded due to the contraction of rapeseed oil availability. However, this remains a demand shock, like the increase of demand for food from Asia, a food stamp program, or the increase in world population. All these shocks affect the world trading system, and demand-driving policies are difficult to discipline, especially when they operate at market prices (see in Chapter 9 for an important discussion of this issue). To guide policies, the key issue is to understand how the world trading system and its rules, as they are designed today, may react to these shocks. Seen in this light, export taxes/restrictions are a primary aspect of the world trading system, since they belong to the set of trade policy instruments and their implementation clearly amplifies an initial shock (for example, a biofuel mandate) on world agricultural markets (see Chapters 11 and 12).

Second, although the support for biofuel production has intensified after 2001, this support is starting to wane and rapid growth of the recent years will not continue. Raising interest in biofuels was certainly related to the spikes in oil price seen in 2005–2008 and 2010–2014, the initial expectations in terms of carbon emissions reductions, and the goals of promoting energy security based on domestic supply.[6] In particular, the United States and the EU implemented significant programs to support the domestic production of biofuel. In the United States two programs have historically been important: the Renewable Fuel Standard (RFS), which imposed a floor on the demand for ethanol and biodiesel, and the blender tax credit, which increased the market value of ethanol. The blender tax credit for ethanol and duties on ethanol imports were recently eliminated, and the RFS mandates established in 2007 have been relaxed (Glauber and Effland forthcoming).

In Europe biofuel policies were implemented through the Renewable Energy Directive (RED), which included a (percentage) target for the use of renewable energy in road transport fuels by 2020. In 2009 this target was fixed at 10 percent. The RED also established biofuel sustainability criteria with which all biofuels produced or consumed in the EU have to comply. After considering environmental and food price externalities (Laborde 2011) during several years of debate, the EU significantly reshaped its policy in 2016 by capping the share of energy consumption in road transportation made from food-crop feedstocks at 7 percent. In recent years this policy change has curbed Europe's biofuel demand while a similar movement took place in the United States, driven by both the blend wall (the upper bound technical limit on the blending rate tolerated by most of the cars currently used) and the shift of Renewable Fuel Standard 2 (RFS 2) legislation away from corn ethanol to favor advanced biofuels. Other countries have implemented programs aimed at supporting the local production of biofuel, including Argentina, Brazil, China, Japan, and the Republic of Korea. In the case of Brazil, some argue that consumption of biofuel is driven by relative prices between ethanol and gasoline (due in particular to Brazil's large and growing fleet of flex fuel cars) rather than by government policies (Al-Riffai, Dimaranan, and Laborde 2010).

A review of the literature on biofuels shows that strong conclusions in terms of policy recommendations are difficult to support, since the impact of

---

6 In the United States the replacement of methyl tertiary butyl ether (MTBE) as an oxygenator in the gasoline by ethanol has played an important role in the accelerated growth of ethanol production and consumption in 2005–2006. In this case the ethanol was not a substitute to gasoline but a complement.

biofuel programs on agricultural prices is uncertain. On the one hand, a substantial part of the literature concludes that biofuels policies have played a significant role in the food price spike. De Gorter, Drabik, and Just (2013) show that US and other OECD countries' biofuel policies have played a prominent role in linking food-grain commodity prices and biofuel prices, as well as in the price spike for corn, oilseeds, wheat, and rice between 2006 and 2012. Wright (2014, 75) clearly blames biofuel policies for increased agricultural price volatility: "The cause of [the rise in food prices] was no perfect storm. Far from being a natural catastrophe, it was the result of new policies to allow and require new use of grain and oilseed for production of biofuels." Condon, Klemick, and Wolverton (2015) conclude that increased ethanol production explains about one-third of the increase in corn prices from 2007 to 2010. Using the IFPRI IMPACT model, Rosegrant (2008) estimates that 30 percent of the 2000–2007 increase in weighted average grain prices was due to biofuel production. He even concludes that biofuels explain almost 40 percent of the 2000–2007 increase of the price of maize. However, this is no consensus.

On the other hand, Babcock (2011) affirms that from 2005 to 2009 the impact of US ethanol subsidies on food prices and food quantities was "quite modest." Based on a time-series analysis linking food and fuel prices, Zilberman et al. (2012) show (1) that changes in biofuel prices have little impact on food prices, (2) that the impact varies across crops and locations, and (3) that biofuels have not been the most important factor of increasing food prices. Hochman et al. (2014) underline the role of a declining stock-to-use ratio since 1985. Similarly, all simulations conducted at IFPRI with MIRAGE-BioF conclude that biofuel mandates have only a small impact on food prices. Dimaranan, Valin, and Bouët (2010) develop a biofuel version of the MIRAGE model to evaluate the environmental benefits of ethanol policies in the United States and the EU under different trade policy options and show that ethanol production has environmental benefits only under certain restrictive assumptions.

Using the same model plus modifications concerning improved data and coproducts, Al-Riffai, Dimaranan, and Laborde (2010) evaluate the impact of EU and US biofuel mandates on global agricultural and biofuel markets. They conclude that these mandates have a positive impact on agricultural value-added and greenhouse gas (GHG) emissions and a limited impact on food prices (less than 1 percent impact on the consumer food price index for all regions in the world), although some commodities can see higher impacts (up to +20 percent for some oilseeds). Brazil is found to benefit from increased biofuel production and exports; in addition, the use of cropland for biofuel production significantly increases in this country. Laborde and Valin (2012) improve the sector database and the modeling of the agricultural supply function and land-use change to study the environmental implications of the EU biofuel mandate. They question the sustainability of the EU biofuel program, particularly its biodiesel component and therefore the cost-benefit advantage for the EU and the world to achieve greenhouse gas savings through this instrument.[7]

While the literature is unanimous in concluding that biofuel mandates play a role in increasing agricultural prices, it is not consensual on the magnitude of the impact and even more uncertain on the food security implications. Indeed, higher food prices will support agricultural investments, R&D, and so on. Most of the literature considers that a key issue was the quick increase in biofuel consumption, which fostered the price peaks, while long-term effects will be milder. As discussed earlier, the future will not see a similar pattern affecting the biofuel markets again. Although an interesting discussion, sparked by the biofuels example, would be to analyze how the global trading system should be adjusted to support a sustainable bioeconomic pathway in future decades, it goes beyond the scope of this book, which is primarily focused on ongoing trade negotiation challenges.

Another policy instrument is at the heart of today's WTO debate. Food stocks are a final factor receiving increased attention in the trade and agricultural policy debate, thanks to the 2007–2008 global food crisis and the growing international concern regarding food security. As explained in Chapters 8 and 9, there are different types of food stocks: *emergency food stocks,* which cope with disruptions in domestic or international food supply; *food redistribution stocks,* which support the distribution of food through a variety of programs; and *buffer stocks,* which aim to stabilize prices. Emergency food stocks and food redistribution stocks may be needed for a global policy targeting food security. Buffer stocks are more difficult to justify, however, and research has concluded that they are costly and often inefficient at stabilizing prices (see Chapters 8 and 9). At the WTO Bali Ministerial Conference in

7 As already stated, we are starting to see a stagnation or even a shift away from biofuel policies, especially first-generation, crop-based biofuel. The United States has relaxed several of its biofuel mandates, while the EU now gives priority to renewable energy rather than to biofuel specifically. This point is worth mentioning, even if it does not constitute a solid reason for not specifically studying biofuels policies.

2008 the issue of food stocks derailed talks until a peace clause was signed (see Chapter 9).

Where Does This Book Fit into the Debate?

In the context of the framework and historical timeline laid out in this introduction, the rest of the book focuses on two important elements of the relationship between the global trading system and food security: the Doha Development Agenda (DDA) and whether food price volatility can be managed through trade instruments. The DDA has placed international priority on development, an objective upon which every nation should agree. In 2001, when the DDA was launched, it was expected that trade liberalization could help support development and fight poverty and food insecurity worldwide. Fifteen years after the start of these negotiations, however, the round is still not yet completed.[8] Are the reasons for this failure political or economic? What are the policy instruments and/or sectors on which progress or failure hinges? What are the costs associated with a non–Doha Round? A successful DDA would lead to substantial gains for the world in general and for developing countries in particular by continuing the reduction in global distortions and limiting policy uncertainties.

While agriculture has been a part of the rules-based global trading system since the implementation of the Uruguay Round, the 2000s brought new concerns in terms of global food security. During the second part of that decade, the world experienced a significant increase of food price levels. Chapter 9 illustrates that today's nominal food prices in US dollars are above those seen in previous decades. Many observers are also seeing an increase in food price volatility; this refers to variation over time in the price of food rather than to the level of these prices. For example, Minot (2012) compares price volatility in international markets during 1980–2006 with price volatility during 2007–2010 and finds a significant increase in the volatility of the price of rice, wheat, and maize as well as of the International Monetary Fund Food Price Index.[9]

However, a close look at a more sophisticated measure of volatility, such as the extreme volatility method proposed by Martins-Filho and Torero (2016),

8 In Nairobi, in December 2015, WTO trade ministers agreed to eliminate agricultural export subsidies. This is a modest result as compared to the initial level of ambition.

9 However, he also finds that in African countries, only 7 of the 67 prices studied showed a significant increase in volatility between 2003–2006 and 2007–2010 (see Minot 2012).

shows that while episodes of extreme international price volatility existed for several crops (maize and wheat in particular) in the summer of 2002 and again in 2006–2011, such events have remained limited over the past 15 years. In addition, price volatility was higher in the 1970s. Specific efforts have been made to improve the information surrounding these events, such as the Agricultural Market Information System (AMIS) initiative supported by the G20, to help prevent future instances of extreme price volatility. Many countries responded to high international food price levels and increased international food price volatility through the use of trade policy instruments, either by restricting exports or by decreasing import duties. However, this book concludes that these policies are not the appropriate response for several reasons: (1) although export taxes/restrictions decrease domestic prices, they contribute to higher world prices; (2) trade policies should be used for treating trade issues (which food price volatility is not); (3) in terms of economic theory, there are more direct instruments (such as investments in food supply and research and development) with which to address supply-side problems, while safety nets and cash/in-kind transfers can help poor households cope with augmented food prices.

This book does not cover all aspects of the global trading system. For instance, norms and other nontariff barriers to trade are not discussed in this book. Nontariff barriers are important impediments to the free circulation of merchandise in general and of agricultural goods in particular. Kee, Nicita, and Olarreaga (2009) estimate that in the early 2000s, the simple average *ad valorem* equivalent of all worldwide nontariff barriers was 12 percent. Disdier, Fontagné, and Mimouni (2008) study the impact of sanitary and phytosanitary (SPS) barriers and technical barriers to trade (TBT). They indicate that in 2004, among the 154 importing countries in their database, only 92 notified SPS and TBT measures. In addition, of more than 690 agricultural and food products in their database, only 4 of these products did not face any barrier in any importing country. They also show that SPS and TBT measures significantly reduce agricultural imports to the OECD from developing countries. However, norms and other nontariff barriers to trade are not at the center of the DDA talks, nor do they contribute actively to the price volatity issue. As these are the two main axes of this book, the issue of these barriers are not discussed.

This book is the first in a series coming out of the Markets, Trade, and Institution Division of the International Food Policy Research Institute. It is composed of research conducted at IFPRI by a group of researchers studying trade issues. It consists of thirteen chapters, six of which have recently been published in academic journals; seven chapters are new. The first section of the book, "What Can the Doha Development Agenda Deliver, and How Can It Fail?" is based on the premise that more trade integration can fight poverty and alleviate hunger. This section shows the advantages for the world and developing countries offered by a successful DDA (see Chapters 3 and 6). However, it also provides a more unconventional view: more liberalization of trade under the auspices of the WTO may protect the world against the adverse consequences of protectionist policies, to the benefit of developing countries in particular (see Chapter 6). Why could the DDA fail? There are many reasons for this potential, if not probable, failure. First, the number of participants in the negotiations has significantly increased since the start of the talks, making it difficult to find a solution that is acceptable for every country. In addition, the issues being treated are much more complex than those discussed during previous rounds (see Chapters 2 and 3). Moreover, these multilateral trade negotiations are no longer a confrontation between a group of rich countries specialized in industry and services and a group of poor countries specialized in agriculture. The latter group of countries in particular has developed more heterogeneous preferences in terms of the potential outcomes of the round (see Chapters 2 and 5). Finally, it is likely that the negotiators of the Doha Agenda have selected tariff-cutting formulas that are efficient from an economic viewpoint but that may imply very high political costs; such political reasons matter even if more economic efficiency is to be reached (see Chapter 4).

In "The Doha Round: Virtuous Circle or Infinite Loop?" (Chapter 2), David Laborde analyzes the ongoing process of the Doha Round—from its inception in December 2001 to the current deadlock. The chapter provides a short history of the past 15 years of trade negotiations and a political-institutional explanation of their failure. In "Why Is the Doha Development Agenda Failing? And What Can Be Done?" (Chapter 3), Antoine Bouët and David Laborde make an intensive utilization of the MIRAGE model of the world economy to provide a strategic analysis of the failure of this round of negotiations based on game theory. The analysis states that there is no outcome that can increase the payment of all players simultaneously. While game theory offers potential ways to escape this stalemate (such as establishing international transfers, extending the domain of negotiations, or excluding some countries from the negotiations), no solution appears implementable for the Doha Round. This raises the question: Is there all the reason in the world to be pessimistic?

In "Formulas for Failure? Were the Doha Tariff Formulas Too Ambitious for Success?" (Chapter 4), David Laborde and Will Martin focus on tariff-cutting formulas, a key element of the trade negotiations. They explain that the DDA's tariff-cutting formulas were selected based on economic efficiency, meaning these formulas sharply reduce the highest tariffs. However, this approach may also generate very high political costs, which could pose a challenge to the desired economic efficiency. The agricultural policies of Brazil, the Russian Federation, India, and China (BRIC) are scrutinized by Lars Brink, David Orden, and Giselle Datz in Chapter 5 ("BRIC Agricultural Policies through a WTO Lens"), with particular attention paid to their compatibility with WTO rules. The chapter stresses that although the BRIC countries are often referred to as a unified group, their interests concerning the agricultural sector greatly differ. What are the gains expected from a Doha Round? This issue has often been studied in the economic literature, particularly with the use of multicountry, multisector Computable General Equilibrium (CGE) models such as MIRAGE. This type of modeling exercise is used to compare the world economy with and without a DDA; the economic model simulations with DDA usually lead to small worldwide gains. In "Assessing the Potential Cost of a Failed Doha Round" (Chapter 6), Antoine Bouët and David Laborde offer a new way to evaluate the DDA by comparing a resort to protectionism when the DDA is implemented with a resort to protectionism when the DDA is not implemented. Their results see greater economic benefits from the potential agreement.

One sector is emblematic of the nexus between agriculture and development in the global trade system and the difficulties of current trade negotiations: the cotton sector. At the beginning of the DDA, four African countries (Benin, Burkina Faso, Chad, and Mali) denounced the support given by rich countries' governments to those countries' own local cotton producers, a support that is thought to depress world cotton prices, reduce production in developing countries by limiting farmers' access to inputs, and consequently decrease the income of tens of millions of poor households. In Chapter 7 ("Domestic and Trade Policies Affecting the World Cotton Market"), Fousseini Traoré provides a thorough analysis of the world's cotton sector, with particular focus on how this sector has been treated during the DDA negotiations. Cotton is important for food security since its production makes up the main source of income for many poor people in West African economies. The cotton sector is also emblematic of the political economy of trade negotiations: how a sector of small importance for rich economies, but with highly concentrated interests, can lead to a failure of negotiations even though the potential benefits of liberalization for some poor developing countries are high.

The second part of the book, "Successful and Failed Trade Instruments for Managing Price Volatility," examines whether the management of price volatility is achievable through more or less trade integration. This section deals in particular with the instruments available for policy makers to cope with price volatility: food stocks, crop insurance, and export restrictions. All of these instruments are topics of discussion within the WTO since they all affect international trade. Similarly, all of these policy instruments were used by various countries during the recent food crisis (2007–2008) to preserve domestic food security. From a general point of view, this section aims to demonstrate that the use of such instruments is not necessarily the best way to react to increased global price volatility. In two consecutive chapters, Eugenio Díaz-Bonilla offers an extensive view on food security stocks. In "Food Security Stocks: Economic and Operational Issues" (Chapter 8), Díaz-Bonilla discusses several economic and operational aspects of the constitution and use of public stocks for food security in developing countries. The chapter proposes a policy approach that would limit the active role of trade policy and would support improved land and water access for small producers as well as substantial investment in human capital, infrastructure, and agricultural R&D. Chapter 9, "Food Security Stocks and the WTO Legal Framework," studies the legal issues posed by the WTO texts on public stockholding for food security purposes. It provides the background of the debate and gives two interpretations of the interim solution agreed upon at Bali in 2013.

A less well-known policy instrument aimed at supporting farmers against price instability is crop insurance. In "Agricultural Insurance and the WTO" (Chapter 10), Joseph W. Glauber describes the increasing popularity of these programs, particularly in developed countries. One key explanation for this growth in popularity is the fact that these policies are supposed to be exempt from reduction since they are being classified in the Green Box. However, Glauber examines in detail the treatment of agricultural insurance under the WTO and shows that some of these policies have recently been challenged. This implies that such programs may become less effective as an instrument to countervail price volatility. Another popular policy instrument in times of higher food price volatility is export restriction. This policy was particularly common during the 2007–2008 food crisis and was often used at the same time that food-importing countries were decreasing their import duties. Both policies—raising export restrictions and decreasing import duties—aim to help consumers rather than producers. The last two chapters of the book evaluate the economic consequences of such policies.

The first evaluation of export restrictions is conducted using a series of partial-equilibrium models. In Chapter 11, "A Quantitative Analysis of Trade Policy Responses to Higher World Agricultural Commodity Prices," T. Edward Yu, Simla Tokgoz, Eric Wailes, and Eddie C. Chavez conclude that "trade policies implemented by those major trading countries will usually create more price pressure on the poorer food-deficit countries/regions that are less capable of manipulating their trade policies." In Chapter 12, "Food Crisis and Export Taxation: The Cost of Noncooperative Trade Policies," Antoine Bouët and David Laborde use the MIRAGE model of the world economy to explore the trade and economic consequences of these policies. The chapter illustrates how increased export taxes in large net food-exporting countries and reduced import tariffs in large net food-importing countries, in the dynamics of retaliation and counterretaliation, can contribute to successive increases of global agricultural prices and can thus harm small net food-importing countries. The path to the objective of worldwide food security remains long. Reaching this objective will require not only the implementation of policy instruments in different dimensions of economic policy but also international coordination of these policies.

Bibliography

Aksoy, M. A. 2004. "The Evolution of Agricultural Trade Flows." In *Global Agricultural Trade and Developing Countries*, edited by M. A. Aksoy and J. C. Beghin, 17–35. Washington, DC: World Bank.

Al-Riffai, P., B. Dimaranan, and D. Laborde. 2010. "European Union and United States Biofuel Mandates: Impact on World Markets." Inter-American Development Bank, Technical Notes IDB-TN-191, December, Washington, DC.

Babcock, B. A. 2011. "The Impact of US Biofuel Policies on Agricultural Price Levels and Volatility." ICTSD Issue Paper 35. International Centre for Trade and Sustainable Development, Geneva.

Beghin, J., J.-C. Bureau, and S. J. Park. 2003. "Food Security and Protection of Agriculture in Korea." *American Journal of Agricultural Economics* 85 (3): 618–632.

Bellemare, M. F., J. Fajardo-Gonzalez, and S. R. Gitter. 2016. "Foods and Fads: The Welfare Impact of Rising Quinoa Price in Peru." Towson University Department of Economics Working Paper Series 2016-06, Towson University, Towson, MD, US.

Bouët, A., C. Estrades, and D. Laborde. 2013. "A Global Assessment of the Economic Effects of Export Taxes." *The World Economy* 36 (10): 1333–1354.

———. 2014. "Differential Export Taxes along the Oilseeds Value Chain: A Partial Equilibrium Analysis." *American Journal of Agricultural Economics* 96 (3): 924–938.

Broda, C., and D. E. Weinstein. 2006. "Globalization and the Gains from Variety." *Quarterly Journal of Economics* 121 (2): 541–585.

Bureau, J.-C., H. Guimbard, and S. Jean. 2016. "Competing Liberalizations: Tariffs and Trade in the 21st Century." CEPII Working Paper. Centre d'Études Prospectives et d'Informations Internationales, Paris.

Condon, N., H. Klemick, and A. Wolverton. 2015. "Impacts of Ethanol Policy on Corn Prices: A Review and Meta-Analysis of Recent Evidence." Selected paper prepared for presentation at the Agricultural and Applied Economics Association's and College of Agricultural and Environmental Sciences Joint Annual Meeting, Washington, DC, August 4–6, 2015.

Crosby, D. 2008. "WTO Legal Status and Evolving Practice of Export Taxes." *Bridges* 12 (5): 3–4.

Deason, L., and D. Laborde. 2015. "Trade and Nutritional Contents." Unpublished, International Food Policy Research Institute, Washington, DC.

De Gorter, H., D. Drabik, and D. R. Just. 2013. "Biofuel Policies and Food Grain Commodity Prices 2006–2012: All Boom and No Bust?" *AgBioForum* 16 (1/1). Accessed February 22, 2017. http://agbioforum.org/v16n1/v16n1a01-degorter.htm.

Díaz-Bonilla, E., M. Thomas, and S. Robinson. 2003. "Trade, Food Security, and the WTO Negotiations: Some Reflections on Boxes and Their Contents." In *Agricultural Trade and Poverty: Making Policy Analysis Count*. Proceedings of the OECD Global Forum, Paris, May 23–24, 2002.

Dimaranan, B., H. Valin, and A. Bouët. 2010. "Evaluating the Environmental Cost of Biofuel Policy: An Illustration with Bioethanol." *International Economics* 122: 57–88.

Disdier, A.-C., L. Fontagné, and M. Mimouni. 2008. "The Impact of Regulations on Agricultural Trade: Evidence from the SPS and TBT Agreements." *American Journal of Agricultural Economics* 90 (2): 336–350.

Economist. 2012. "Foreign Interest Grows in an Old Highland Staple." May 12.

FAO (Food and Agricultural Organization of the United Nations). 2015. "Sustainable Development Goals." Accessed January 8, 2017. www.fao.org/post-2015-mdg/14-themes/food-security-and-the-right-to-food/en/.

———. 2016. FAOSTAT database. Accessed July 2016. http://faostat.fao.org.

———. n.d. "Quinoa." Accessed January 8, 2017. www.fao.org/quinoa/en/.

Glauber, J. W., and A. Effland. Forthcoming. *US Agricultural Policy: Its Evolution and Impact.* IFPRI Discussion Paper. Washington, DC: International Food Policy Research Institute.

Google. 2016. Google Ngram services. Accessed September 20, 2016. https://books.google.com/ngrams.

Hazell, P., G. Shields, and D. Shields. 2005. *The Nature and Extent of Domestic Sources of Food Price Instability and Risk.* Vol. 25. Washington, DC: World Bank.

Heckscher, E. 1919. "The Effect of Foreign Trade on the Distribution of Income." *Ekonomisk Tidskrift* 21: 497–512.

Hochman, G., D. Rajagopal, G. R. Timilsina, and D. Zilberman. 2014. "Impacts of Biofuel on Food Prices." In *The Impacts of Biofuel on the Economy, Environment, and Poverty: A Global Perspective,* edited by G. R. Timilsina and D. Zilberman. New York: Springer.

Jacobsen, S. E. 2011. "The Situation for Quinoa and Its Production in Southern Bolivia: From Economic Success to Environmental Disaster." *Journal of Agronomy and Crop Science* 197 (5): 390–399.

Johnson, D. L., and S. M. Ward. 1993. "Quinoa." In *New Crops,* edited by J. Janick and J. E. Simon, 219–221. New York: Wiley.

Kee, H. L., A. Nicita, and M. Olarreaga. 2009. "Estimating Trade Restrictiveness Indices." *The Economic Journal* 119: 172–199.

Krugman, P. R. 1979. "Increasing Returns, Monopolistic Competition and International Trade." *Journal of International Economics* 9: 369–379.

Laborde, D. 2011. "Assessing the Land Use Change Consequences of European Biofuel Policies." Unpublished, International Food Policy Research Institute, Washington, DC.

Laborde, D., and H. Valin. 2012. "Modeling Land-Use Changes in a Global CGE: Assessing the EU Biofuel Mandates with the MIRAGE-BioF Model." *Climate Change Economics* 3 (3): 1–39.

Lancaster, K. 1980. "Intra-Industry Trade under Perfect Monopolistic Competition." *Journal of International Economics* 10: 151–176.

Martins-Filho, C., and M. Torero. 2016. "Relative Prices of Food and the Volatility of Agricultural Commodities: Evidence for a Panel of Developing Economies." In *Food Price Volatility and Its Implications for Food Security and Policy,* edited by M. Kalkuhl, J. von Braun, and M. Torero, 239–267. Switzerland: Springer.

Matthews, A. 2014. "An Updated Look at the Impact of the EU's Common Agricultural Policy on Developing Countries." IIIS Discussion Paper 454. Institute for International Integration Studies, Dublin.

Minot, N. 2012. *Food Price Volatility in Africa: Has It Really Increased?* IFPRI Discussion Paper 1239. Washington, DC: International Food Policy Research Institute.

OECD (Organisation for Economic Co-operation and Development). 2016. *Agricultural Policy Monitoring and Evaluation 2016*. Paris: OECD.

Ohlin, B. 1933. *Interregional and International Trade*. Cambridge, MA, US: Harvard University Press.

Orden, D., and C. Zulauf. 2015. "The 2014 Farm Bill in Historical Perspective." In *The Economic Welfare and Trade Relations Implications of the 2014 Farm Bill*, edited by V. H. Smith, 11–24. Bingley, UK: Emerald Group.

Piermartini, R. 2004. *The Role of Export Taxes in the Field of Primary Commodities*. WTO Discussion Paper. Geneva: World Trade Organization.

Ricardo, D. 1815. *Essay on the Influence of a Low Price of Corn on the Profits of Stock*. London: Printed for John Murray, Albemarle Street.

———. 1817. *On the Principles of Political Economy and Taxation*. London: Printed for John Murray, Albemarle Street.

Romero, S., and S. Shahriari. 2011. "Quinoa's Global Success Creates Quandary at Home." *New York Times*, March 19.

Rosegrant, M. W. 2008. "Biofuels and Grain Prices: Impacts and Policy Responses." Testimony for the US Senate Committee on Homeland Security and Governmental Affairs, May 7.

Schlick, G., and D. L. Bubenheim. 1993. "Quinoa: An Emerging 'New' Crop with Potential for CELSS." NASA Technical Paper 3422. Unpublished, National Aeronautics and Space Administration, Ames Research Center, Moffett Field, CA, US.

Sinha, S., M. Lipton, and S. Yaqub. 2002. "Poverty and Damaging Fluctuations: How Do They Relate?" *Journal of Asian and African Studies* 37 (2): 186–243.

Stolper, W. F., and P. A. Samuelson. 1941. "Protection and Real Wages." *Review of Economic Studies* 9 (1): 58–73. http://dx.doi.org/10.2307/2967638.

UNDP (United Nations Development Programme). 2017. "Sustainable Development Goals." Accessed February 14, 2017. http://www.undp.org/content/undp/en/home/sustainable-development-goals.html.

Warr, P. 2005. "Food Policy and Poverty in Indonesia: A General Equilibrium Analysis." *Australian Journal of Agricultural and Resource Economics* 49: 429–451.

Wright, B. 2014. "Global Biofuels: Key to the Puzzle of Grain Market Behavior." *Journal of Economic Perspectives* 28 (1): 73–98.

WTO (World Trade Organization). 2001. "Doha WTO Ministerial 2001: Ministerial Declaration." Adopted November 14, 2001. Accessed January 8, 2017. https://www.wto.org/english/thewto_e/minist_e/min01_e/mindecl_e.htm.

Xu, K. 2015. "Why Are Agricultural Goods Not Traded More Intensively: High Trade Costs or Low Productivity Variation?" *World Economy* 38 (11): 1722–1743.

Zilberman, D., G. Hochman, D. Rajagopal, S. Sexton, and G. Timilsina. 2012. "The Impact of Biofuels on Commodity Food Prices: Assessment of Findings." *American Journal of Agricultural Economics* (aas037), 95 (2): 275–281.

SECTION 1

What Can the Doha Development Agenda Deliver, and How Can It Fail?

Chapter 2

THE DOHA ROUND: VIRTUOUS CIRCLE OR INFINITE LOOP?

David Laborde

In November 2001, while the world was still reeling from the attacks of September 11, 143 countries launched the first round of trade negotiations under the aegis of the World Trade Organization (WTO) in Doha. While the events of recent months had awoken the United States' unilateralist instincts, the international community felt that it had to demonstrate its unity and its desire to strengthen multilateral approaches. The idea still prevailed that economic development and the fight against poverty were the best ways to promote understanding between peoples and nations: if poverty is the root of violence, it is essential to fight it. Thus the Doha Round, which should have only been the next step in the slow process of trade liberalization initiated in 1947 by the General Agreement on Tariffs and Trade (GATT), automatically carried disproportionate expectations as the "Development Round."

A World in Need of a Development Round?

At the same time, the WTO was a victim of its own success. As the only international institution that seemed capable of operating quickly and fairly, the institution was expected to address more and more issues. Thus, in addition to the standard topics—customs duties, subsidies for production or exports, technical and health standards, and so on—issues regarding technology transfer, labor law, competition policy, public procurement, climate change, and food security began to pervade the discussion. The WTO was starting to become *the* global governance solution, taking the place of slower UN agencies and being expected to deliver global prosperity. Associating the Doha Round with development also addressed the expectations of developing countries who felt that their concerns had been largely ignored up until that point. However, the association carried with it some major political risks. Only a consistent set of trade- and non-trade-related measures, including domestic policy reforms, can truly address major development challenges. Removing barriers to trade and exchange is not enough to ensure economic development. But a trade round such as Doha has neither the vocation nor the means to improve, or damage, the situation of hundreds of millions of poor people on its own—contrary to what the most vocal stakeholders claim. Thus it was (or should have been) obvious that these exaggerated expectations would end in disappointment. Last but not least, in Doha in November 2001, WTO members approved China's accession to the institution, adding an unknown variable to an already complex equation. While the negotiation designs were inherited from an era in which global trade was dominated by OECD members, China's addition to the ranks of WTO members showed that the global trade pattern and the balance of powers was continuing to evolve.

This chapter aims to provide a narrative of the 15 years of the Doha Round negotiations and to quantitatively illustrate how these negotiations have tried to reach a compromise regarding the market access pillar of the agricultural talks.[1] While the Doha Round itself involved more than 20 topics (not just agriculture) and although agricultural trade makes up less than 10 percent of global trade, the issue of agriculture remains key for both developed and developing countries, particularly regarding the goal of ending poverty and hunger worldwide. In addition, while five decades of GATT negotiations liberalized the industrial sector, especially for developed countries, agriculture remained largely outside the trade policy reform trend for a long time and was included in the global trade discipline only starting with the Uruguay Round's conclusion in 1994. At this time, the use of agricultural distortions around the world appeared relatively straightforward. In terms of border protection, applied tariffs (including tariff-rate quotas) were equal to 19.2 percent in agriculture (Boumellassa, Laborde, and Mitaritonna 2009), with a higher level of protection in middle-income countries (24.1 percent) compared to the rest of the world (17.1 percent in high-income countries, 16.5 percent in least developed countries). However, this apparently homogenous level of protection across the globe hides two key features. Developed countries displayed an overprotection of agriculture compared to other sectors; in these markets, average

1 The Doha Round talks on agriculture covered three main aspects, or "pillars," of agricultural protection: border protection, domestic support, and export subsidies. The *border protection* takes the form of customs duties (*ad valorem*, specific, mixed, or compound), tariff quotas (quotas associated with different levels of customs duties), and sanitary and phytosanitary standards. *Domestic support* combines price support measures, subsidies for production, and direct payments. These support measures are grouped into different "boxes"—Amber, Blue, and Green—based on their harmfulness for trade. The *export subsidies* range from European Union refunds (monetary payments) to some countries' food aid policies and export credits at subsidized rates. The variety and complexity of agricultural support measures complicate the negotiations and make it difficult to quantify individual efforts.

industrial tariffs were only about 2.6 percent, seven times lower than agricultural tariffs. This ratio was much smaller for other groups of countries: about 2.2 for middle-income countries and 1.4 for least developed countries. The asymmetry regarding how agriculture was, and still is, considered by developed economies explains important frictions that have come up repeatedly during the Doha negotiations.

The imbalance in tariff protection shows how relative and effective rates of agricultural protection have been higher in developed economies than in developing economies; however, there is another important element that has undermined the performance of farmers in developing countries. Historically, key exportable products were significantly taxed by developing-country governments, leading to an effective net taxation of this sector. To fully capture this mechanism, it is useful to look at another indicator focusing on the average price distortions farmers face. The World Bank study of agricultural protection from 1955 to 2007 led by Kym Anderson (2009) finds that the situation regarding agricultural protection, on both exports and imports, has changed dramatically within the space of a generation. As shown in Figure 2.1, net agricultural protection in developing countries was generally negative in the early years of the sample. In contrast, in industrial countries, agricultural protection was close to 20 percent at the start of the study period and only rose from there.

As can also been seen from Figure 2.1, the dynamics of agricultural protection in developed and developing countries have been quite different. Agricultural protection in developing countries has continued to trend upward, albeit with some variations over time. By the end of the sample period, net agricultural protection in developing countries averaged around 7 percent. In contrast, in industrial countries, protection peaked in the late 1980s and has since fallen by one-third. This decline correlates with the prospect—and the reality—of the Uruguay Round Agreement's disciplines on developed-country agriculture. In developing countries, where the disciplines resulting from the Uruguay Round were considerably weaker, the apparent underlying trend of agricultural protection increasing as incomes rise appears to have continued. The tendency for agricultural protection to rise as countries develop was historically very strong in industrial countries and seems likely to be repeated in today's developing countries in the absence of effective WTO disciplines. As discussed in Anderson and Nelgen (2011), this trend has strong behavioral underpinnings, including the decline in the share of urban expenditures on food, the increasingly commercial orientation of farmers, and farmers' increasing reliance on purchased inputs. Using the counterfactual

FIGURE 2.1 Nominal rate of assistance from border measures in developed and developing countries (%)

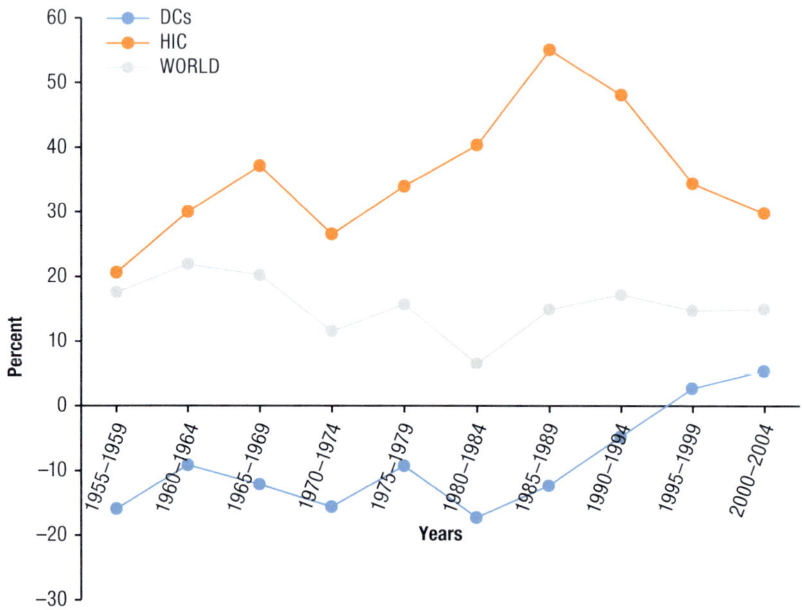

Source: Anderson (2009).

Note: DCs = developing countries, including South Korea (Republic of Korea) and Taiwan, China. HICs = high-income countries, including Eastern Europe and Central Asia.

protection rates arising from a simple political-economy model sharply increases the average tariff equivalents in developing-country agriculture and dramatically increases the value of a Doha agreement. However, these strong structural trends may have been only partially understood at the beginning of the round; and, the issue of binding agricultural support in middle-income countries should have been identified earlier.

Of course, agricultural policies are not limited to tariffs and price support instruments. This has been properly acknowledged during the Uruguay Round negotiations, and disciplines on subsidies and other farm support programs constitute the second pillar of the negotiations. The Uruguay Round imposed some disciplines on the most distortive policies, particularly to try to prevent the uncooperative and costly subsidies race seen in the 1980s between the United States and the EU. Meanwhile, disciplines on subsidies and farm support in developing countries were nearly nonexistent under the Uruguay Round; however, many of these countries did not have financial

FIGURE 2.2 Producer support estimates in developed and developing countries (% and US$ millions)

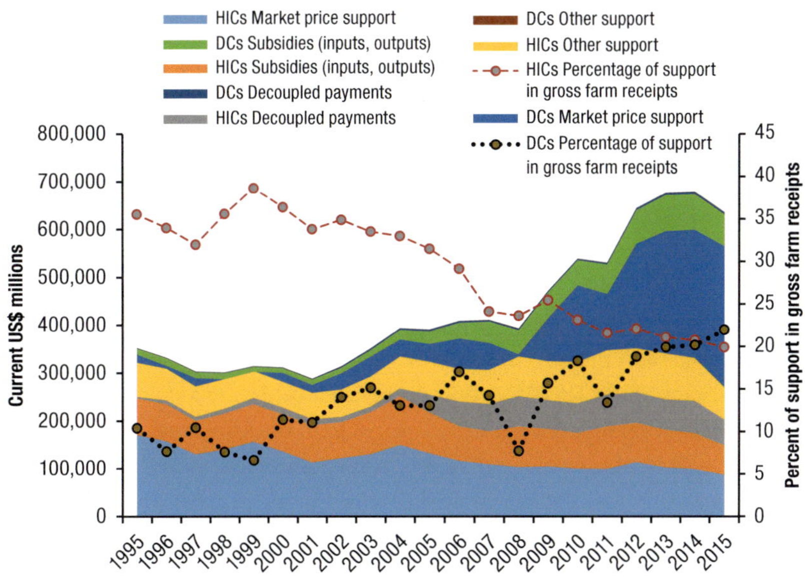

Source: Author's computation based on OECD Producer Support Estimate database (OECD 2016).

Note: DCs = developing countries; HICs = high-income countries. The HICs aggregate includes all high-income Organisation for Economic Co-operation and Development (OECD) countries, and the developing countries aggregate includes all developing countries monitored by OECD, either OECD members (Chile and Mexico), or non-OECD members (for example, Indonesia and Viet Nam). The developing countries aggregate includes only one African country (South Africa) and does not include India, a large producer.

means to take advantage of the lack of WTO disciplines on domestic agricultural support.

Here, significant transformations have occurred since 1995, as illustrated in Figure 2.2 based on the OECD Producer Support Estimate database (OECD 2016). From 1995 to 2015, policy support to farmers has been reduced in developing countries in both real and relative terms (from 36 percent of developed-country farm receipts to 20 percent); the reverse trend has been observed in emerging economies (from 10 percent to 22 percent). This inversion of the hierarchy has occurred both in relative and in absolute terms (current US$). In addition, the structure of the support provided in developed countries has evolved to accommodate WTO disciplines: the use of decoupled payments has increased, particularly in the EU (see Bureau, Laborde, and Orden 2013). This evolution can be summarized by a few statistics. In 1995 farm support in high-income countries represented 88 percent of the total support from OECD and major emerging economies (such as

India); this ratio fell to 40 percent in 2015 for the same sample of countries. Also, 53 percent of farm support in developed economies was provided through price support instruments and therefore linked to border protection in 1995; price support instruments represented only 32 percent of developed-country farm support in 2015. Meanwhile, these figures moved from 40 percent to 72 percent for the emerging countries group. So while developed countries have reformed their policies to follow the WTO disciplines, emerging countries have started to use the policy space they have thanks to higher level incomes and budgetary capacity. The distortions in emerging economy markets have moved from net taxations to net protection, with increasingly large domestic markets leading to an explosion of their market price support distortions.

This discussion helps us to understand where WTO negotiators stood in 2001: still caught in the "old" world dominated by developed countries' policies, while new challenges were emerging due to the structural evolution of the world and the induced rebalancing in economic powers and influences. While it may not have been clear at that time, trying to adapt the rules inherited from the Uruguay Round to a changing world and to new expectations of a "development" round could lead only to a deadlock. Before entering into the intricacies of the Doha Round, it is useful to show its similarities to and differences from its predecessor, the Uruguay Round.

Many Similarities with the Uruguay Round

Several overarching principles have guided each round of WTO negotiations. First, any agreement reached must be global and inclusive following the "single undertaking" principle: "Nothing is agreed until everything is agreed." However, the different topics of negotiation cannot be explicitly linked, as the work of the various committees is independent. Thus the negotiations on nonagricultural market access (NAMA) are unrelated to what is happening in the negotiations on agriculture, at least formally. The merit of this approach is that a lack of progress in one area does not delay progress in another. However, it can also prove dangerous if, after making substantial concessions in several areas, some countries never receive any compensation or are unable to balance their efforts during the negotiation cycle. The second principle is the unanimous acceptance of the final agreement; such consensus is difficult to obtain because of the increased number of participants. To solve this problem, there must be flexibilities, or "liberalization modalities," in place to prevent one country from being especially exposed to the movement toward liberalization due to its trade specialization. Starting from a single rule that applies to all, should there be flexibility for each country that will be managed unilaterally, or should exceptional cases be considered one by one through the adoption of a discretionary approach involving potential requests and offers? The first solution was preferred in the 2008 modalities; as it appears impossible to combine the need for high flexibility for some countries and the need to maintain safeguards to ensure that this flexibility is not misused by other countries, the second option seems to be more appealing, even if it is not clear whether it can be practically implemented among 161 WTO members.[2]

The third principle states that trade liberalization should harmonize tariff structures and should reduce the largest distortions the most. Thus the highest tariffs and the largest subsidies should be cut more sharply. A fourth and final principle is that it is acknowledged by all that developing countries, especially the least developed countries (LDCs), are authorized to make less effort than developed countries to reduce trade-distorting tariffs and subsidies. This is the notion of special and differential treatment (SDT). However, the nature of the criterion used to compare the efforts of different countries remains unclear. Is it in the ex-ante rules or their consequences? Should countries be compared to each other or to an "absolute" standard? In addition, the last two principles (progressivity of tariff reduction and SDT) may be in conflict. As developing countries are typically the most protectionist, they should be forced to make the most significant cuts, according to the tariff principle; yet, because of their greater economic vulnerability, it is accepted, according to the SDT principle, that they put forth less effort than rich countries. A last important issue is the lack of clarity about the "graduation" between categories—that is, when does a developing country become a developed country? For instance, the Republic of Korea has started the agricultural negotiations of the Doha Round as a developing country, even though its income per capita exceeds many EU countries.[3] All of these issues were already part of previous negotiations, but several new elements make the present task more difficult.

2 This issue is discussed in Chapter 4.

3 Similar issues arise with other "categories" that are required to provide reduced commitments, such as the recent or very recent WTO members. How long will China be treated as a "recently" acceded WTO member?

Key Differences

The modalities of liberalization should impose a different timing from previous cycles. For instance, in agriculture, the trend is to diverge from a simple goal of cutting duties by an average of 36 percent, as under the Marrakesh Agreement, to a more binding approach based on formulas.[4] This would provide enough freedom for individual countries and their technical staff to accommodate their own specificities and the most sensitive products. As determined quite early in the Doha Round, the modalities will define "formulas" for tariff reduction. Once the formula and the mathematical parameters are decided, the reduction applied to each tariff line is deduced mechanically. For this reason, a degree of flexibility has been introduced, leading to additional negotiations on a full range of additional parameters (number of sensitive products, tariff cutting rates for sensitive products, and so on). This approach has reinforced the technical dimension of the negotiations. Each country must now estimate the impact on its own tariffs and the impact on those of its partners. In their mercantilist approach, some negotiators want to reduce their concessions (reduction of tariffs and subsidies) while still maximizing the gains for their exporters. In this scenario, defining liberalization modalities is a long process; it is not enough to confine the ambassadors in a room overnight to obtain the miraculous figure that will unlock the cycle.

The second notable difference between the Doha Round and previous negotiations is the sheer number of participants. The number of members increased from 23 countries during the GATT negotiations in 1947 to 123 members during the Uruguay Round; this complicates the discussions because countries have different economic structures and comparative advantages, potentially conflicting national preferences, and unequal negotiating capacities. Thus it will be a challenge to reach a "fair" outcome that is acceptable to all WTO members. Naturally, groups of convergent interests have formed under these conditions: the G10 for protectionist wealthy countries, the G20, the G90, and so on. In this way, countries are strengthening their political weight and pooling their expertise. The multitude and complexity of topics, as well as the parallel workflow, can make the situation unmanageable at the country level for many developing countries, leading many to accept the need to delegate to a third party on a particular point. However, this delegation does not always go smoothly; even within the European Union, despite

4 Here we discuss only the tariff reduction formula. Of course, the Uruguay Round negotiators who tackled the agricultural issue for the first time had to struggle with many complex issues, such as the tariffication of quantitative measures and the domestic support classification and commitments.

50 years of political and economic integration, member states have not hesitated to publicly announce their disagreement with the positions of the commissioner and to weaken the commissioner's position in the negotiations.

Another aspect of the Doha Round's second difference is that the number, role, and bargaining power of key players have evolved. Throughout previous decades, different configurations have taken place within the Quad—a group comprised of the United States, the EU, Japan, and Canada. The group of the so-called five interested parties (the United States, the EU, Brazil, India, and Australia) was instrumental in working out the details of the July Framework Agreement of 2004. In 2006 the round was suspended due to a mini-ministerial meeting of the G6 (the United States, the EU, Australia, Japan, Brazil, and India); attempts at reviving the round took place in the spring of 2007, following the meetings of the G4 (the United States, the EU, India, and Brazil). However, all these initiatives have not led to significant progress, and hope for successful negotiation lies around the current WTO table, involving 161 countries. Beyond the numbers, the nature of the countries involved in the negotiations themselves has changed. The old clashes between two advanced economies such as the European Union and the United States have been replaced by more complex discussions in which developing countries play an increasing role. The main dividing lines now seem to contrast the rich North with the poor South. But while this portrayal is not without merit, it is a naïve approximation of reality. There is not one homogenous South but several, with countries that are at different stages of development and have very unequal capabilities to participate in international trade. The WTO *de jure* recognizes three categories of countries, each subject to different disciplines according to its ability to support the liberalization process. However, between the two extreme groups formed by developed countries and LDCs, developing countries form a disparate set; it is here where we find China alongside Honduras, and Brazil competing with Cameroon. In the current context, all developing countries are subject to the same disciplines, and the same privileges should be granted to them.

The question of creating an additional category *de jure* arises. Should major emerging countries be asked to put forth more effort in reducing trade-distorting policies since they will be the main winners of the round, or should the current cohesion among developing countries be maintained? It is likely that any proposal to separate emerging countries would be denied by countries like Brazil and Argentina because their developing-country position would be weakened. Wealthy countries, meanwhile, frown upon the idea of countries hiding behind pictures of poor African farmers in order to penetrate their markets. Finally, small and medium developing countries waver between the interest they may have in the constitution of a distinct class of "emerging" countries, that would not receive as many preferences as they, and the need to have champions among these emerging countries that would be able to bend rich countries on subjects important to all developing countries.

The latest addition to the cycle, and perhaps the most discrete, is the participation of China, the world's foremost largest exporter. While China has carefully avoided any conflicting position, the nation's strategy has been first to come closer to the positions of developing countries and then to come closer to the positions of developed countries, according to its own interests. It is true that as a new member of the WTO, and because of the significant efforts made upon its accession, China will only be subjected to a milder version of the liberalization rules applied to others. As an exporter, it will fully benefit from lower tariff barriers from its trading partners, both developed and developing. In the area of industrial goods, both developed countries and developing countries fear making concessions that will benefit China. For many developing countries, American or European industrial products are not direct competitors, while such products from China clearly are. New commitments requested by developed economies regarding domestic support in agriculture and the delicate issue of capping overall farm subsidies will be strongly opposed by China, where domestic support has grown significantly alongside development. China will likely aim to keep significant policy space for these issues available in the future, even though its absolute level of agricultural support could have global implications due to its size (see Chapter 5 for a more detailed discussion of this issue).

China has obvious interests, as far as market access and compliance with international rules (intellectual property), that it can pursue as a WTO member; however, in the short term, China is a major governance challenge for an institution that provides unique measures for all developing countries—whether the size of China or the size of Gabon. Moreover, when China is taken into account, the complexity of delivering global development within the WTO is even more acute. A cycle that would improve the situation for millions of Chinese workers or Brazilian agricultural workers would reduce poverty on the planet significantly, but would this situation be acceptable if this same cycle led to no improvement or even a deterioration in the situation for other countries, especially some of the least developed ones? And if the cycle offers compensation to those neglected countries, should this compensation come from the main winners, regardless of whether they are poor or rich countries, even though the latter group believes it has already had to sacrifice its own interests to promote the growth of emerging countries? From the beginning of the negotiations, all of the elements that would lead to 15 years of vicissitudes in the cycle were in place. This chapter aims to provide a summary of this long process and quantifies the different proposals made during the negotiations.

From Seattle to Bali: Much Ado about Nothing?

This section discusses the different steps leading to the current stalemate in the Doha Round, focusing on major events, especially WTO ministerial conferences, and actions by key countries. It is an extended and updated version of Laborde (2008).

From Seattle (1999) to Doha (2001): Difficult Beginnings

The origins of the Doha Round, and its expectations, were set a couple of years before its official launch. Originally planned to be the Millennium Round, the round got a false start in Seattle in December 1999. While the press was mainly interested in what was happening in the streets—the "antiglobalization" activists besieging the conference center—the real revolution took place in the conference room. Developing-country representatives refused to sign the declaration that should have launched the cycle, believing that their aspirations were not taken into account. Despite this setback, working groups were set up in 2000 to advance the liberalization of services and agriculture, two new and complex topics introduced by the Marrakesh Agreement that concluded the Uruguay Round in 1994. Agriculture, a politically sensitive sector in most countries, had escaped trade liberalization for almost 50 years and, despite the success of the Uruguay Round in bringing it under trade disciplines, it remained protected by a set of complex and opaque measures.

The Declaration of the Fourth Ministerial Conference in Doha in November 2001 (WT/MIN(01)/DEC/1, November 20, 2001) aimed to erase the memory of Seattle. WTO members were able to agree unanimously on a negotiating mandate for the round. Recognizing that trade and development were interrelated and that the interests of developing countries could not be ignored, the emphasis was put, at least in letter if not in spirit, on the "development" dimension. In practice, the round was to continue the negotiations on agriculture and services launched in 2000 and would establish a new stage in the liberalization of goods while still respecting the specificities of developing countries, especially the most vulnerable, and implementing current WTO agreements. From the point of view of many developing countries, the Doha negotiations were needed to better balance what they considered the excessive concessions that industrialized countries received during the Uruguay Round. These concessions related not only to new topics (such as intellectual property rights and services) but also to the legal room given to protect and subsidize industrialized countries' agriculture, which included permission to use export subsidies for agricultural products (such subsidies are prohibited for industrial products under the GATT and WTO frameworks).

Therefore, the negotiating package discussed in Doha was named the Doha Development Agenda. Overall, the Doha Ministerial Declaration laid out an ambitious negotiating program with specific instructions for different topics, including agriculture, services, market access for nonagricultural products, intellectual property, investment, competition policy, government procurement, trade facilitation, WTO rules for regional trade agreements, the Dispute Settlement Understanding, environmental issues, and electronic commerce. Under these conditions it was hoped that the Doha Round would deliver a new package ensuring global cooperation and development. The end of the round was scheduled for January 1, 2005; negotiators were optimistic that three years of discussions would be enough, even though it took nine years to conclude the Uruguay Round. However, the negotiating arrangements were stopped on March 31, 2003, and an agreement on these terms has still not been found.

Hangover in Cancun (2003): A First Wake-Up Call

The fifth WTO Ministerial Conference was held in Cancun, Mexico, in September 2003. This meeting needed to assess the situation, validate the methods defined earlier in the year, and agree on how to conclude the round. Although the question of the modalities was not resolved before Cancun, a strong sign preceded the meeting: a consensus text between the European Union and the United States on the agricultural issue had appeared during the July 2003 Mini Ministerial in Montreal.[5] The EU could maintain some tariff peaks in agriculture due to limited exemptions (what became the "sensitive products" concept) and could maintain a limited number of export subsidies, while the United States received a new and extended concept for the Blue Box, giving them enough policy space to accommodate the innovations of the

5 Breaching the gap between the US and the EU positions on agriculture was essential to conclude the Uruguay Round and was embodied by the Blair House Agreement (1992).

2002 US Farm Bill. Yet the meeting skidded and agriculture, which should have been liberalized, only crystallized tensions.

Developing countries overwhelmingly rejected the document submitted to negotiators as a basis for multilateral consensus. This document matched almost word for word the text prepared by the European Union and the United States at the Montreal meeting. The dynamics of negotiation cycles that had prevailed for 50 years (that is, reaching an agreement between the members of the quad—the EU, the United States, Canada, and Japan—and then foisting the agreement on others) came to an end. Other WTO members wanted to have their say, particularly the major emerging countries such as India and Brazil, as head of the G20 negotiation groups. African countries, the G33, grouped in the G90, also took center stage over the cotton issue. With the support of NGOs, four LDCs (Benin, Mali, Burkina Faso, and Chad) decided to denounce what they saw as a major injustice: the support that northern countries—the United States being the first among them—provide to their cotton producers leads to a depression in world prices, depriving millions of farmers in Africa and Asia of an important source of income.

No compromise was reached on the issue of agriculture, and the so-called Singapore issues (trade facilitation, transparency in government procurement, investment, and competition) that the European Union considered priorities were removed from the negotiating mandate. The agenda was overloaded, and developing countries did not want to make commitments on new topics. Only the issue of trade facilitation, the source of gains for both exporters and importers, survived. The Cancun conference ended in failure, but the issue of development, as well as its complexity, was clearly illustrated. Developing countries had taken a more active role and compensated for their individual technical or political weaknesses by building coalitions such as the G20 (emerging countries that adopted an offensive trade strategy) or G90 (African-Caribbean-Pacific [ACP] countries that adopted a defensive trade strategy). However, while developing countries found it easy to come together to say no to proposals they did not want, it proved much more difficult for these countries to overcome their inherent differences, develop their own proposals, and build consensus among themselves as to what they *do* want. In addition, the question of whether northern countries should make sacrifices to achieve certain development objectives was evidently posed. For instance, were US negotiators prepared to abandon their country's cotton subsidies in order to improve the lives of African farmers, at the risk of the current presidential administration losing congressional support from the southern cotton-producing states?

The consequences of the failure of Cancun were straightforward. The weakening of the multilateral sphere led to greater preference for regional agreements, initiating a move that is perfectly embodied in mega-trade deals, such as the ongoing negotiations of the Trans-Pacific Partnership Agreement (initiated in 2008) or the Transatlantic Trade and Investment Partnership between the EU and the United States (started in 2013).[6] In the three months following Cancun, the United States and the EU launched or updated nearly a dozen bilateral negotiations with countries in Latin America or Asia. Essentially, rich countries decided that if some developing countries were willing to slow the trade integration process, they would trade only with those who showed goodwill. But although such bilateral negotiations go faster, they are much more perverse in terms of global governance and inclusiveness. They allow the strongest country to impose its will based on its bargaining power, while peripheral countries and areas, already marginalized, are put aside. In addition, and from a purely economic point of view, bilateral and regional agreements create trade diversion (imports, rather than coming from efficient countries, come from "preferred" countries).

Hong Kong (2005): A New Start

To avoid the premature death of the WTO, member countries decided to come back to the negotiating table. In July 2004 they agreed to a framework agreement that incorporated the Doha mandate, highlighted the importance of the cotton issue, and relaunched negotiations on the question of modalities. Although the text remained hopelessly vague regarding what liberalization efforts would actually entail, a key element began to emerge. To facilitate the difficult trade-off between national constraints and the ambition of a multilateral agreement in agriculture, a *degree of flexibility* was admitted. This flexibility would take the form of lists of sensitive and special products that are excepted from the rule that would define liberalization in the sector. In April 2005, on the occasion of the Ministerial meeting of WTO members, a practical but crucial step took place. A system of guidelines was developed to convert specific agricultural tariffs (for example, dollars per ton) to *ad valorem* equivalents (percent on the Cost Insurance Freight [CIF] price). Four years after the beginning of the cycle and five years after the start of talks on

6 On January 23, 2017, President Donald Trump signed a presidential memorandum to withdraw the United States from the Trans-Pacific Partnership Agreement. However, the negotiations still continued.

agriculture, member countries finally agreed on how to measure the starting point for negotiations.

The sixth Hong Kong Ministerial Conference, held in December 2005, aimed to consolidate the potential progress of the past 18 months and to avoid a second Cancun at all costs. The scope of this conference's ambition was much smaller than previous rounds: rather than aiming for sweeping success, members instead focused on agreeing on a common declaration to show that the engines of the negotiations were restarting. These lowered ambitions were due in part to a new shadow cast on the horizon by the US domestic electoral cycle. The US's Trade Promotion Authority, the legal provision allowing the president to negotiate trade agreements directly without congressional approval, was coming to an end in the first half of 2007, and the expected victory of the Democrats in the November 2006 midterm elections reduced the likelihood that the Bush administration would obtain an extension of its negotiating mandate.

Meanwhile, the US strategy had largely changed after Cancun. Widespread calls for the United States to reduce its domestic support programs were unpopular among the American electorate. US negotiators felt that the only way to sell such cuts domestically would be to simultaneously push for larger tariff cuts from the EU, despite knowing that the EU would not accept concessions beyond what the G20 (especially Brazil) was asking. If the EU had accepted larger tariff cuts, American negotiators would have been able to use that success at home to compensate for any cuts in domestic support programs; as the EU did not accept these cuts, the United States was able to place the blame for the stalemate at the feet of the EU. For US negotiators it was absolutely necessary to focus attention on an issue in which the United States had little to give (tariffs) and to avoid discussions about the country's highly sensitive domestic support programs, for cotton in particular.

Hong Kong did end on a positive note, however, despite these challenges. Several problems saw notable advances, such as the commitment to end export subsidies by 2013. In addition, a tight schedule was adopted to complete the round by the end of 2006 and so avoid the pitfalls of the US political agenda. With this new schedule the issue of modalities for tariff reduction and domestic support discipline would become the priority and would be able to be completed by July 2006. Another positive point of the conference was that developing countries were unable to overcome their heterogeneity to make joint proposals. The cotton issue was beginning to be addressed with constructive dialogue between the United States and African countries. The case of bananas on the European market—a source of conflict between Latin

America on the one hand and the Caribbean and Africa on the other—was carefully avoided, despite the fact that it was symptomatic of the problem of preference erosion.[7] The ACP countries, and more generally the least developed countries, receive preferential access to the European market. They pay hardly any customs duty and thus benefit from preferential margins that allow them either to export the products for which they are not competitive or to sell on the European market at much higher market prices and to collect the associated rents. In this context, any decline in European protection results in a reduction in EU domestic prices and, for partners who have a trade preference, a financial loss: this process is what is known as *preference erosion*. This shows that the interests of developing countries are conflicted, and it is difficult to help both the poorest (the LDCs), which include Caribbean and African nations, and the more efficient (emerging economies), which include Latin American nations, at the same time. Moreover, countries from which no effort is asked, such as the LDCs, are still affected by the negotiations.

Despite these positive developments, the negotiations remained stalled. On July 24, 2006, the Director-General of the WTO, Pascal Lamy, decided to suspend the cycle sine die. The stalemate came from the three main participants. The European Union refused to further cut its agricultural tariffs if the United States did not do the same with their domestic support and if emerging countries did not accept an ambitious tariff reduction formula in the industrial sector. The United States explained that they would not make concessions on the issue of farm subsidies as long as the EU continued to apply high tariffs and as long as emerging countries would not open their markets to imported manufactured goods. The G20, representing the latter group of emerging countries, asked for increased agricultural liberalization in the North before making any effort on the industrial side. Some developing countries, led by India, were also upset that their concerns regarding their food security agenda (reduced liberalization for "special" products, new instruments to handle price variation and import surges through a "special safeguard mechanism") were not properly considered. This latest issue will become more and more important in the incoming negotiation phases.

Even as Hong Kong came to a stalemate, exchanges of views continued, and during the Davos Forum in January 2007, representatives of the main

7 The banana issue and the ACP preferences were also a stumbling block for the launch of the Doha Round. In November 2001 an agreement was achieved between the ACP, the EC, and the Latin America countries where the EU-ACP preferences benefited from a waiver until December 31, 2007, while nine LAC MFN (most favored nation) banana suppliers get extended tariff-rate quotas (TRQs) access and the promise of further trade regime reform.

countries reiterated their commitment to conclude the cycle and reach an agreement. In early 2007 quiet negotiations began between the so-called G4 countries (the United States, the European Union, India, and Brazil) to try to reach an agreement on broad modalities; this effort ended in another failure at a summit in Potsdam in June 2007, although much of the progress made in those negotiations was reflected in the chair's negotiating text of August 2007. Active negotiations resumed again in Geneva in the fall of 2007. Based on all of these efforts, new technical documents presenting the modalities were proposed in December 2007 and again in April 2008 to pave the way to a "mini–ministerial meeting" in Geneva in July 2008. The third revision of these modalities were gathered in the so-called July package, while some revised versions disseminated in December 2008 and known as Rev.4 were the most advanced and detailed materials generated by the round thus far.

The negotiations again failed, however, in part due to a dispute between the United States and India regarding safeguard mechanisms in agriculture. This highlighted the important issue of food security in the round, but other serious issues were also pending, such as the level of ambition in terms of NAMA (nonagricultural market access) concessions that emerging countries will face. Responding to this failure, Lamy said: "Looking at what is on the table now, members believe that the Doha Round is still worth fighting for." After the mid-2008 failure, the negotiations fell into a coma for several years. A new momentum started to emerge with the appointment of the sixth Director-General of the WTO, Roberto Azevêdo, in September 2013. The subsequent Bali Ministerial was seen as a potential rebirth of the round, building on a series of meetings and postconference agreements regarding several issues. Given the difficulties in pushing through negotiations on all of the Doha Round topics, WTO members decided to refocus their talks on a more limited number of issues that seemed to have a better chance of leading to a general agreement. On December 7, 2013, after several days of work and the usual posturing and drama, members managed to close the ninth Ministerial Conference in Bali with an agreement on the WTO's first comprehensive multilateral trade package. Until that point the trade agreements completed since the WTO's creation in 1995 had been mainly regional and plurilateral agreements that included some, but not all, WTO members.[8]

---

8 Plurilateral agreements involve commitments by a subgroup of WTO countries on specific issues. If the disciplines only apply to the signatory parties, the benefits should apply to all WTO members thanks to the MFN clause.

The work in Bali can be divided into three groups of decisions that needed to be made. The main group includes the decisions and agreements related to the subset of components of the Doha Round (sometimes called the "Bali Package") that were ready for ministers to decide upon at the Bali Ministerial. Then there are the decisions about the WTO work program post-Bali; these decisions focused on future trade negotiating activities. Finally, there was another group of decisions in which the Ministerial Conference took note about the regular work of the General Council, issued further Ministerial decisions, and gave instructions for future regular work. For instance, the adoption of the Decision on the Accession of the Republic of Yemen, an LDC, by which Yemen became the 160th member of the WTO, can be noted under this third group. These different issues are discussed in detail, in terms of both legal framework and implications for developing countries, in Díaz-Bonilla and Laborde (2015).

The Bali Package can be divided into three topics: (1) trade facilitation, (2) agriculture and cotton, and (3) specific issues related to the special treatment of developing countries and LDCs under WTO rules. The Agreement on Trade Facilitation (ATF) was seen as the major success of the Ministerial and was mostly sought by developed countries (they were the "demandeurs," in trade diplomacy jargon), but it can be argued that there are also potential benefits for all categories of developing countries in the reduction of red tape and trade costs. The problem with trade facilitation for developing countries and LDCs is that building customs machinery takes money and effort, and these countries often face more pressing needs. For developing countries, especially India, the main achievement of the Ministerial was the establishment of a "peace clause" on the topic of agricultural public stockholding for the purpose of food security (for more information on this peace clause, see Chapter 9 of this book).

An important step included in the Bali Ministerial Declaration was the instruction for WTO members to define a post-Bali work program during 2014. Crucially, a specific component of the Bali Package, the ATF, required a final review of the wording and the completion of some legal steps in order for the agreement to be sent to WTO members for final approval by their legislatures. Those issues were scheduled to be completed during a meeting of the WTO General Council in July 2014.

The Bali outcome was ambiguous. On the one hand, it demonstrated that many countries were still ready to commit to the multilateral approach, look for an agreement, and make concessions, as the United States showed by accommodating India's request regarding their food security objective.

On the other hand, the most significant and difficult aspects of the Doha Round, such as market access modalities and commitments on domestic support, remained unsolved. The July 2014 meeting broke down in disarray when India made the implementation of those final legal steps contingent on clarifications regarding the "peace clause" and decided to hold up negotiations of the ATF until the text was clarified. From July to November, there was a flurry of negotiations to try to work out a compromise, until a final agreement on the wording was achieved during the WTO General Council meeting on November 27, 2014.

Almost a year after the original Bali Ministerial, WTO members managed to patch up their differences (Azevêdo 2013). This recent agreement allows for the implementation of the different decisions that were supposed to have been settled at Bali but that were held up by the dispute on public food stocks and puts back on track the post-Bali work program. However, the twentieth anniversary of the WTO did not bring significant changes despite the Director-General's call to members: "2015 is going to be a big year for the WTO. We have important work to do and real deadlines to meet." The July 2015 deadline for the post-Bali work program was missed, leaving open the possibility to conclude the Doha Round during the tenth Ministerial Conference in Nairobi, Kenya. Countries are still divided about which strategy to use to save the round, assuming it can, or should, be saved. Some players consider that the 2008 modalities are still relevant and the main basis for any agreements in a near future. Others are calling for "recalibration" and/or "simplification" to achieve a quick and intelligible outcome.

Quantifying the Different Proposals

As discussed, the Doha Round has been characterized by a lengthy process, where different and sometimes conflicting points of view have been exchanged. Technical proposals regarding the modalities have been elaborated and consolidated by the negotiation chairs to sketch a potential outcome for the round. These efforts took place mainly between 2001 and 2008, when the most advanced texts were proposed. Using these different proposals, and based on Bouët and Laborde (2010), we can propose a systematic quantification of these proposals to see how the various positions have evolved and how the balance between sectors and countries has changed. These quantification efforts help to summarize the complexities of the proposals using a few metrics (average tariffs, global trade changes, real income variations), to assess the gaps existing between the expectations of the different players, and to determine why, with so much time devoted to finding a balance between a formula approach and the need for flexibility, negotiators are still missing key factors needed to reach an agreement (the topic of Chapter 4).[9]

An Overview of the Main Proposals

The Doha Round was a "broad" cycle, initially including 21 bargaining topics. Regarding market access, the issue of tariffs did not seem to face major difficulty, as it was to be negotiated using an easily quantifiable variable and as negotiators enjoyed the benefit of experience from eight previous GATT rounds. Services or intellectual property promised to be much more sensitive topics. Yet after seven years of discussions, tariffs and reduction modalities remain a major sticking point, so that the debates on this issue have overshadowed other issues. In 2003 two proposals (the Harbinson and Girard proposals) were submitted to WTO members.[10] The Harbinson proposal focused on agriculture and included a tiered formula that was supposed to reflect a potential consensus. The Girard proposal, however, focused on industry and included a "modified Swiss formula," under which tariffs were harmonized by using a corrective parameter that depended on the initial average (this formula was particularly favored by India, which had especially high tariffs at the time).

Just before the Hong Kong Ministerial Conference in December 2005, the main negotiating parties submitted their own proposals, which had different versions of the tiered formula for agriculture concerning import tariffs and domestic subsidies and of the Swiss formula for industry with special and differential treatment. The United States made the most aggressive proposal, while the G20 proposal included an ambitious liberalization program for developed countries and a more limited one for developing countries. The EU proposal included a more protectionist approach for developed countries, while preserving the main objectives of the Harbinson proposal. During eight years of negotiations the various positions have evolved and converged, as represented by the December 2008 chairs' proposals. These modalities are discussed at length in Chapter 4. Market access modalities have reached a high level of sophistication, although the general philosophy is simple, with progressive tariff-cut formulas for both agricultural and nonagricultural goods. Much flexibility has been introduced, however, with different degrees of

9 As discussed in Chapter 3, appreciating these different expectations is a key element to understanding the difficulties in finding a cooperative outcome.

10 For a presentation of these proposals, see Bouet and Laborde (2010).

special and differential treatment and special provisions for tariff escalation, tropical products, and long-standing preferences. Under the chairs' proposals, developed countries provide a duty-free, quota-free market access initiative for LDCs, with a 3 percent exemption clause in terms of products. Export subsidies should have been phased out by 2013 for developed countries. Regarding domestic support, this package includes a harmonizing cut on overall trade-distorting support as well as product-specific disciplines.

It is especially important to compare the December 2008 package with various proposals that were put on the table either by Harbinson and Girard or by the EU, the G20, and the United States. Such a comparison shows in which direction the negotiations have gone, and especially whether they have evolved toward a specific proposal put forward years ago. Such a comparison also helps us evaluate the initial degree of ambition in these proposals. This chapter focuses on the impact both at the world level and on developing countries, since development was the initial goal of negotiators. Five negotiating proposals are assessed: (1) a combination of the Harbinson proposal in agriculture and the Girard proposal in industry, both submitted in 2003 (called the Harbinson and Girard scenario); (2) the G20 proposal submitted in 2005 at the Hong Kong Ministerial (called the G20 scenario); (3) the proposal submitted by the European Union in 2005 at the Hong Kong Ministerial (called the EU scenario); (4) the US proposal at the time of the 2005 Hong Kong Ministerial (called the US scenario); and (5) the December 2008 package (called the 2008 scenario). Tariff reductions are applied at the six-digit level of the Harmonized System on a country-by-country basis using the MAcMapHS6 version 2 database (Boumellassa, Laborde, and Mitaritonna 2009). Differences between bound, applied most favored nation (MFN), and preferential tariffs are explicitly taken into account. *Ad valorem* equivalents of specific tariffs are computed based on the WTO guidelines for the implementation of tariff cut formulas. All sensitive and special products are selected using the political economy criterion of Jean, Laborde, and Martin (2008).

The first scenario (Harbinson and Girard) is based on 2003 proposals from the WTO chairs: the Harbinson proposal for AMA (agricultural market access) (TN/AG/W/1) and the Girard proposal (TN/MA/W/35) for NAMA (nonagricultural market access). The AMA tariff reduction includes a tiered formula with three bands for developed countries and four bands for developing countries. Flexibility is allowed inside each band. For each tariff line, negotiators can choose the cut rate under two constraints: a minimal cut rate specific to each band and the simple average cut over all products for each band. The Jean, Laborde, and Martin (2008) criterion is used to define the optimal behavior of each country inside each band. Also, 10 percent special products for developing countries is assumed, for which the cut rate is limited to 5 percent. The NAMA proposal (which supposedly reflects the Girard proposal) is based on a Swiss-like formula in which the "Swiss coefficient" is equal to the simple average base rate times a scale coefficient (equal to 1 for developed countries and 1.5 for developing countries). For unbound lines, the base rate is equal to the MFN rate times 2, with a minimum of 5 percent. Countries that have a binding coverage below 35 percent do not reduce their tariffs.

The second scenario is the G20 proposal. For agricultural market access, the G20 proposal on market access of October 2005 is relied on. This includes a tiered formula (four bands for both developed and developing countries) with differentiated thresholds and coefficients, and a capping for highest tariffs (100 percent for developed countries, 150 percent for developing countries). Also, 4 percent sensitive products for developed countries and 6 percent for developing countries is allowed for, with a 30 percent deviation from the formula cut (45 percent deviation for developing countries). In addition, 5 percent special products for developing countries with no cut is included. The nonagricultural market access component is based on the 2005 Argentina, Brazil, and India communication (TN/MA/W/54). It is similar to the Girard formula but includes a differentiated formula for bound and unbound lines. The same scale coefficients are assumed as in the Harbinson and Girard scenario, as well as the binding markup to compute the base rate on unbound lines. In addition, 5 percent of tariff lines (maximum 5 percent of imports) with no cut is considered.

The third scenario represents the European Union's contribution from October 2005. Agricultural market access is described by a tiered formula (four bands) similar to that of the G20 proposal but with a lower reduction target for developed countries. In addition, the lower band (0–30 percent) allows for flexibility by defining a simple average cut target and lower and upper bound tariff reductions. Here the criterion from Jean, Laborde, and Martin (2008) is used to define each country's optimal behavior inside the first band. Also, 8 percent sensitive products (50 percent deviation from the formula) are authorized for developed countries (one-third additional sensitive products are allowed for developing countries). For nonagricultural market access, a Swiss formula is used with coefficient 10 for developed countries and 15 for developing countries. The base rate of unbound tariff lines is equal to the applied MFN rate plus 10 percent. A clause of 5 percent sensitive products (maximum 5 percent of imports) with no cut is implemented. A 100 percent duty-free, quota-free initiative is granted by developed countries to developing countries.

The fourth scenario is the US proposal. It includes stronger tariff reduction in agriculture with the same formula approach as the G20 proposal (Scenario 2) and smaller tariff caps (for example, 75 percent for developed countries). Only 1 percent sensitive products are authorized for developed countries (1.33 percent for developing countries). The same discipline is applied in nonagricultural market access as in the EU proposal (Scenario 3).

Scenarios 2–4 are based on pre–Hong Kong 2005 Ministerial proposals, with elements from the July 2004 package incorporated when needed. The fifth scenario (the 2008 scenario) is based on December 2008 modalities. An extensive discussion of this scenario is available in Laborde, Martin, and van der Mensbrugghe (2012) as well as in Laborde and Martin (2015; also Chapter 4 in this book). The agricultural market access pillar (TN/AG/W/4/Rev.4) includes a tiered formula with four bands and differentiated coefficients for developed and developing countries. Taken into account are provisions for sensitive and special products as well as the additional cuts that deliver special access for tropical products and reduce tariff escalation. For the nonagricultural market access pillar (TN/MA/W/103/Rev.3), a Swiss formula with coefficient 8 is applied for developed countries and a menu of options including sensitive products combined with a Swiss formula using coefficients ranging from 20 to 25. Also considered are the special cases of the recently acceded members (RAMs), the small and vulnerable economies (SVEs), and the countries with low binding coverage as defined by the document TN/MA/W/103/Rev.3. A 97 percent duty-free, quota-free initiative is included for OECD countries, as well as for Brazil and India. In all cases, developing countries as well as countries with low binding coverage are free from any tariff reduction in nonagricultural market access. Always implemented are the consequences of the EU–Turkey customs union for nonagricultural market access for countries with low binding coverage. All export subsidies are removed in all scenarios. A tiered formula is used to reduce overall trade-distorting support (OTDS) (Scenario 5) or the total aggregate measurement of support (Scenarios 1–4).

To sum up: in Scenario 1 all countries belong to the same band and the reduction rate is 50 percent. For other scenarios the EU is in the last band and the reduction rate applied to its support is 80 percent under the G20 proposal and 2008 modalities, 70 percent under the EU proposal, and 83 percent under the US proposal. For the United States (second band) the cut rate is 70 percent under the G20 proposal and 2008 modalities and 60 percent under the EU and US proposals. Domestic support reductions are applied in a dynamic way, as described in Bouët and Laborde (2010), with an additional assumption of a 2 percent annual rate of augmentation. The OTDS capping in the dynamic Computable General Equilibrium model MIRAGE is introduced.[11]

Market Access Implications

This section evaluates these scenarios first in terms of the impact on the protection applied and faced by each group of countries and second in terms of trade and real income. The next section focuses on the potential impact of these trade reforms on developing countries.

Table 2.1 shows the impact of these different proposals on protection. The latest modalities scenario (the column labeled "2008") would reduce world protection by 26 percent, from 4.5 percent to 3.3 percent. In comparison, the US proposal (the column labeled "United States") would have cut this world average by 50 percent, while the EU proposal would have resulted in a reduction of only 37 percent.[12] Given numerous flexibilities, global agricultural protection would decrease by 25 percent (that is, by less than industrial protection) if the December 2008 package were to be implemented, whereas it would decrease by 73 percent under the US proposal. Concerning agricultural market access, the latest modalities scenario would cut applied protection by a little more than one-third for high-income countries (from 17.6 percent to 11.6 percent) and by less than 3 percent for middle-income countries (from

11 Under the standard approach, domestic support is computed from base-year levels and converted into an *ad valorem* equivalent. This approach is unrealistic because of the WTO constraint on overall support and because taking into account the growth of production value in the agricultural sector will lead to a reduction in the subsidy rate to meet the new WTO commitments. Focusing on agricultural production and exports, the following is evident: (1) US agricultural production is directly affected by domestic support reduction (−1.5 percent in agricultural and agribusiness production instead of +0.1 percent). (2) EU agricultural production is nearly unaffected by subsidy reduction thanks to the recent Common Agricultural Policy (CAP) reform and the large share of Green Box payments in the overall EU domestic support. (3) On the other hand, the OTDS limits applied to US farmers will benefit EU producers and exporters. Overall, EU production is reduced less when the Doha Development Agenda tariff reduction is combined with the OTDS treatment than when it is not combined with the OTDS treatment (−1.17 percent versus −1.27 percent). Finally, (4) the situation of Brazil is magnified compared to that of the EU. In this case, Brazilian production increases more with the OTDS treatment (+4.03 percent to +3.78 percent).

12 The reader may notice a few differences between these figures and those presented in Chapter 4 by Laborde and Martin or Chapter 6 by Bouët and Laborde. However, these differences are limited, especially when considering relative changes, and are the consequences of differences in the base year for the trade data used for tariff aggregation.

TABLE 2.1 Impact of five liberalization proposals on applied tariffs (%)

Category	Baseline	Harbinson and Girard	G20	EU	United States	2008
All goods						
All countries	4.5	3.2	2.8	2.9	2.3	3.3
High-income countries	3.3	1.8	1.5	2.0	1.5	2.1
Middle-income countries	8.6	7.5	7.2	5.7	4.8	7.5
Developing countries	12.2	12.2	12.2	12.2	12.2	12.2
Agricultural market access (AMA)						
All countries	17.8	13.4	11.0	12.3	7.6	13.4
High-income countries	17.6	11.9	8.7	10.9	5.2	11.6
Middle-income countries	18.7	17.7	17.5	16.5	14.0	18.2
Developing countries	13.6	13.6	13.6	13.6	13.6	13.6
Nonagricultural market access (NAMA)						
All countries	3.6	2.4	2.2	2.2	2.2	2.6
High-income countries	2.3	1.1	1.0	1.4	1.4	1.4
Middle-income countries	7.7	6.6	6.3	4.8	4.8	6.6
Developing countries	12.0	12.0	12.0	12.0	12.0	12.0

Source: Bouët and Laborde (2010).

18.7 percent to 18.2 percent). This should boost developing-country exports to developed countries.

Table 2.2 illustrates to what extent foreign market access would be improved under each scenario. The latest modalities (2008) scenario would improve market access for high-income countries by 25 percent, for middle-income countries by 29 percent, and for developing countries by 37 percent. In agriculture the gains would be equivalent for the three groups of countries: around 25 percent. Therefore, under the Doha Development Agenda, developing countries would improve their access to foreign markets but would also suffer an erosion of preferences, especially in agriculture; the protection faced by their agricultural exports would decline by 2.3 percentage points, compared with a 4.5 percentage point decline for high-income countries and a 4.3 percentage point decline for middle-income countries.

Economic Impacts

The economic impacts of these trade policy and domestic support scenarios are simulated using the Modelling International Relationships in Applied General Equilibrium (MIRAGE) Computable General Equilibrium

TABLE 2.2 Impact of five liberalization proposals on tariffs faced on exports

Exports	Baseline	Harbinson and Girard	G20	EU	United States	2008
All goods						
All countries	4.5	3.2	2.8	2.9	2.5	3.3
High-income countries	4.7	3.3	3.0	2.9	2.6	3.5
Middle-income countries	4.2	2.8	2.5	2.7	2.4	3.0
Developing countries	3.0	1.9	1.4	1.3	1.3	1.9
Agricultural market access (AMA)						
All countries	17.8	13.4	11.0	12.3	7.6	13.4
High-income countries	17.6	13.2	10.9	12.1	7.4	13.1
Middle-income countries	18.4	13.9	11.3	13.0	7.9	14.1
Developing countries	9.3	8.3	7.0	6.6	6.4	7.0
Nonagricultural market access (NAMA)						
All countries	3.6	2.4	2.2	2.2	2.2	2.6
High-income countries	3.8	2.7	2.4	2.3	2.3	2.9
Middle-income countries	3.1	1.9	1.8	1.9	1.9	2.1
Developing countries	2.2	1.2	0.8	0.7	0.7	1.3

Source: Bouët and Laborde (2010).

(CGE) model of the world economy, as explained in Bouët and Laborde (2010). Table 2.3 indicates the potential impact of the various scenarios on the volume of exports and real income by groups of countries. Also evaluated is the potential impact of full liberalization—complete removal of all import duties, export subsidies, and domestic support—as a point of reference; finally, the unevenness of gains across countries by reporting standard errors (in US$ billions) of these real income gains is evaluated. Global real income would improve by a mere 0.09 percent—about US$70 billion as annual gain in 2025—under the 2008 scenario and by 0.24 percent under the US scenario.

Overall global exports would increase by 2 percent under the 2008 scenario. This reflects the modest but positive ambition of the current market access modalities. Interestingly, the welfare outcome would be close to the 2003 starting point. Although the 2008 tiered formula in agriculture is more aggressive than that of the Harbinson proposal, its additional flexibilities would more than compensate for the stringent coefficients (agriculture exports would increase by 5.4 percent compared to 5.6 percent in the Harbinson and Girard case). This illustrates the dilemma of the negotiations:

TABLE 2.3 Impact of six liberalization proposals on trade and real welfare by 2025

Indicator	Full liberalization	Harbinson and Girard	G20	EU	United States	2008
World exports of goods and services						
US$ billions	1,934	400	502	527	621	326
Changes (%)	11.6	2.4	3	3.2	3.7	2
World exports of agriculture and agrifood products						
US$ billions	409	47	92	60	152	45
Changes (%)	49	5.6	11	7.2	18.1	5.4
World exports of manufacturing goods						
US$ billions	1,517	350	405	465	466	276
Changes (%)	11.6	2.7	3.1	3.6	3.6	2.1
Real income						
US$ billions	384	66	134	126	190	69
Changes (%)	0.49	0.08	0.17	0.16	0.24	0.09
High-income countries (%)	0.51	0.08	0.17	0.19	0.25	0.09
Middle-income countries (%)	0.43	0.1	0.17	0.09	0.22	0.09
Developing countries (%)	−0.67	−0.32	0.29	0.01	−0.27	−0.1
Standard deviation of the real income gains	0.98	0.29	0.45	0.35	0.51	0.22

Source: Bouët and Laborde (2010); MIRAGE model simulations.

trying to reach a high degree of ambition with a challenging formula but still undermining it with flexibilities to make it politically acceptable.

The modeling assumptions are conservative and do not take into account some nontariff barriers, liberalization in services, and some dynamic aspects of trade liberalization; nevertheless, these gains are at least positive for the majority of countries and equal about 20 percent of the gains from total trade liberalization. In addition, they lay the foundation for future liberalization by reducing the existing binding overhang—that is, the gap between bound tariffs and applied tariffs. A much more politically challenging approach based on the US proposal would lead to gains equaling half of what would result from full trade liberalization. These results illustrate how far trade negotiations have evolved, constrained by defensive interests. For example, in terms of applied protection, the implementation of the December 2008 package would decrease agricultural protection in rich countries by about as much as the Harbinson and Girard scenario and even less than the 2005 European proposal. The application of the US proposal in this domain would result in a

TABLE 2.4 Impact of five liberalization proposals on developing countries' exports by 2025

Exports in value (% change)	Harbinson and Girard	G20	EU	United States	2008
India	0.7	1.9	6.6	9.8	1.7
Cambodia, Bangladesh	–4.9	–4.2	–1.6	–2.2	–3.5
Mexico	–0.1	–0.1	1.8	2.1	0.8
Middle East and North Africa	0.3	0.8	1.0	1.3	0.6
Nigeria	–0.1	–0.2	–0.7	–0.4	–0.1
Pakistan	2.4	3.0	10.7	11.5	1.1
Rest of Oceania and of Southeast and East Asia	2.5	2.8	4.9	5.3	1.4
Former Soviet Union countries	0.3	0.5	0.3	0.7	0.1
Rest of Latin America	0.6	1.3	2.1	3.3	0.9
Rest of southern Africa	0.1	2.2	0.5	2.9	0.3
Rest of South Asia	1.0	0.7	1.3	–0.5	–0.5
Rest of Africa south of the Sahara	–0.5	–0.2	–0.3	–0.2	0.0
Selected LDCs of Africa south of the Sahara	–0.9	–1.2	–0.1	–2.0	0.2
South Africa	2.2	3.2	4.2	4.5	1.2
Sri Lanka	5.7	5.8	5.2	5.8	4.8
Thailand	4.4	5.2	8.5	9.1	4.5
Turkey	0.3	0.4	0.8	1.2	0.5

Source: Bouët and Laborde (2010); MIRAGE model simulations.

much more ambitious liberalization of world agriculture. Regarding nonagricultural market access, a Doha agreement defined by these modalities would result in the liberalization of the economies of middle-income countries by about as much as was expected under the Harbinson and Girard and the G20 scenarios, while the application of the 2005 European proposal would have liberalized these sectors much more. Again, defensive interests are respected. This selection of the smaller common denominator is translated into the trade changes: the highest increases in nonagricultural exports (EU and US proposals, about 3.6 percent) and in agricultural trade (US and G20 proposals, between 11 and 19 percent) are avoided, and smaller increases are achieved (2.1 percent for manufactured goods and 5.4 percent for agriculture and the agrifood sector).

Table 2.4 presents the potential impact of these five trade reforms on developing countries' exports in 2025. The potential impact of these trade reforms on exports varies: unlike some middle-income countries, such as Sri Lanka and Thailand, that can substantially benefit from new access to foreign

TABLE 2.5 **Impact of five liberalization proposals on developing countries' real welfare by 2025**

Real income (% change)	Harbinson and Girard	G20	EU	United States	2008
India	0.1	0.2	0.2	0.5	0.1
Cambodia, Bangladesh	−0.5	−0.4	−0.1	−0.2	−0.3
Mexico	0.0	−0.1	0.0	0.0	−0.1
Middle East and North Africa	0.1	0.2	0.0	0.1	0.1
Nigeria	−0.1	−0.2	−0.5	−0.4	−0.1
Pakistan	0.2	0.5	0.7	0.7	0.2
Rest of Oceania and of Southeast and East Asia	0.3	0.4	0.4	0.6	0.2
Former Soviet Union countries	0.1	0.2	0.1	0.3	0.1
Rest of Latin America	0.2	0.3	0.1	0.4	0.2
Rest of southern Africa	0.2	1.2	0.5	1.6	0.2
Rest of South Asia	−0.2	−0.3	0.0	−0.2	0.0
Rest of Africa south of the Sahara	−0.1	0.0	−0.1	0.0	0.1
Selected LDCs of Africa south of the Sahara	−0.1	−0.1	0.2	−0.3	0.2
South Africa	0.1	0.1	0.0	0.1	0.1
Sri Lanka	0.5	0.5	0.6	0.7	0.4
Thailand	1.1	1.8	1.2	1.9	0.9
Turkey	−0.1	−0.1	0.1	0.1	0.0

Source: Bouët and Laborde (2010); MIRAGE model simulations.

markets, developing countries, such as those in Africa, do not increase their exports substantially. In fact, their exports may even be negatively affected; in 2025 exports from Cambodia and Bangladesh will be 3.5 percent lower if the 2008 modalities are implemented. And it could be worse, since all other scenarios imply a decrease in exports for developing countries by 2025. Obviously, the inclusion of a duty-free, quota-free clause for developing countries in their exports to OECD countries (also implemented in the EU scenario) can compensate for these eroded preferences.

Table 2.5 gives the results on real income for the same group of countries and confirms that the potential gains for developing countries are meager, if not negative. As a result, more is needed to address developing countries' concerns. Even considering that this modeling exercise underestimates the impact of the Doha agreement on developing countries, potential gains are small. Indeed, different scenarios imply losses for developing countries, especially LDCs, reflecting eroded preferences as a result of a multilateral agreement and rising terms of trade for imported commodities, including food products. While these losses are significant in the case of the Harbinson and Girard, G20, and US proposals, they are almost nonexistent as far as the EU proposal is concerned and are quite small under the December 2008 proposal. It is important to remember that the last two scenarios include a duty-free, quota-free initiative given by OECD countries to least developed countries, while the other scenarios do not. Finally, by reducing the losses of the weakest economies and limiting the gains of the main winners, the long negotiation process has reduced the unevenness of the gains (see the simple standard deviation in the last row of Table 2.3). These results illustrate the conflicting triumvirate that has led the Doha Round to its dead end: ambition, fairness, and domestic political feasibility.

Conclusion

Achieving the completion of the Doha Round would have been a nice gift for the WTO's twentieth birthday. However, in 2015, a positive outcome seems even more difficult to reach than it did in 2008. Each development designed to give a little more flexibility in the hopes of reaching an agreement has in fact reduced the effectiveness of liberalization and expected gains, eroding the appetite of trading powers to reach an agreement. Of course, we should not ignore that the round's ups and downs are merely a reflection of the difficulty of articulating the political and technical dimensions of the negotiations; however, the reasons to be pessimistic are accumulating. The global framework has significantly changed since 2001, and the mismatch between the foundations of the round and the current situation is increasing. First, the world trade and the world economy have changed profoundly since 2001. WTO members such as Brazil, India, and the recently integrated China have emerged as major trading and economic powers. Their share in world merchandise exports jumped from 4.1 percent in 1993 to 7.7 percent in 2003 to 11.5 percent in 2008. Total developing economies accounted for 43 percent of global merchandise trade in 2013 (WTO 2014). The emerging countries, gathered into the G20 coalition, have become a major player in the WTO negotiations. Thus the negotiations are no longer the reserved domain of the European Union and the United States, and the burden of the concessions may need to be redistributed.

Second, global agricultural markets have gone through significant turmoil since 2001, with episodes of very high prices (2008–2009 and 2011–2012) reducing the need for export subsidies but fostering other unilateral policies intended to insulate markets and achieve strong price reduction (2015). In this context, political pressure to establish more active farm policies has emerged. In the United States we have witnessed a trend toward the recoupling of farm support since the 2002 Farm Bill; this move was confirmed in the 2008 and 2014 Farm Bills, making it increasingly difficult for the United States to accept new constraints, especially when looking at the 2008 proposed modalities. Similarly, the development of fiscal capacity in emerging countries has allowed them to significantly increase their domestic support; at the same time, some of these countries have become leading exporters (for example, India) for some commodities, bringing into question their impact on world markets and the need for increased disciplines, despite their remaining desire for enough policy space to implement their own development policies. To illustrate this evolution, even a simple narrative such as the cotton case (see Chapter 7 in this book) has become much more complex. The evolution of the cotton market has made the scenario for low-income, cotton-producing countries in Africa, Asia, and Latin America much more complicated than the original characterization of small, poor cotton producers pitted against subsidized production in the United States. Now domestic and trade policies in some large developing countries (for example, stockholding and interventions in China) may have to be considered, leading to a significantly modified political economy of the agricultural negotiations in general. Thus, finding an agreement on agricultural issues, always a highly complex topic and so emblematic of the development dimension of the negotiations, seems as far away as ever.

However, it is dangerous to just discard any hope for a successful round, even if the negotiation's ambition has to be reduced. First, it should be remembered that negotiations take time. The Uruguay Round lasted *nine* years while dealing with a reduced number of countries and topics. Fifteen years is a long period of time, but it may not be unreasonable, especially during a period that has been marked by a rebalancing of nations' economic sizes and roles at the global level and important economic turmoil and financial and economic crisis. Even if a WTO agreement could contribute to global stability and improved global governance, we may have to accept that countries may want more clarity regarding the future and the new world equilibrium before making commitments that will bind their border, and in some cases beyond-the-border, policies for the decade to come.

Second, a nonagreement would be a pretty dangerous solution. Even if some NGOs or advocates of unilateralism would welcome the death of the WTO, many countries, especially the weakest, would strongly suffer from this failure. If the WTO fails to provide a negotiating space, it will be transformed into an arena of conflict. Major trading powers will compete via the Dispute Settlement Unit (DSU), while reaching bilateral or plurilateral agreements, including megadeals that will forget, or be biased against, the smallest and most vulnerable countries. Also, each additional agreement will increase the complexity of trade policy and will undermine the incentives of the major countries to resume the multilateral approach. So beyond the gains of trade liberalization, the global public good of a very much alive and healthy global trading system is at stake (see Bouët and Laborde 2010).

Third, and on a thoroughly pragmatic level, the round can still bring concrete, low-hanging fruits by consolidating many concessions already made. While the round may not deliver on the high expectations regarding development issues or mercantilist gains, a small success will not mean the end of the negotiations but rather a new step on a longer road. Even using conservative assumptions, quantifications of the round show that it will accomplish between one-fourth and one-third of the goal of reaching global free trade (see Laborde, Martin, and van der Mensbrugghe 2012). This is a very significant achievement, and it may be the upper bound that the different economics can digest at this time. Political economy and adjustment costs should not be neglected, and any future rounds will have to learn from the difficulties met during the first global trade negotiations occurring in a multipolar, twenty-first-century world.

Bibliography

Anderson, K. 2009. *Distortions to Agricultural Incentives: A Global Perspective, 1955–2007.* London: Palgrave-Macmillan; Washington, DC: World Bank.

Anderson, K., and S. Nelgen. 2011. "What's the Appropriate Agricultural Protection Counterfactual for Trade Analysis?" In *Unfinished Business? The WTO's Doha Agenda,* edited by W. Martin and A. Mattoo, 325–354. London: Centre for Economic Policy Research; Washington, DC: World Bank.

Azevêdo, R. 2013. "The WTO Has Truly Delivered." Speech delivered at the ninth WTO Ministerial Conference, Bali, December 7, 2013. Accessed 2013. www.wto.org/english/news_e/spra_e/spra16_e.htm.

Bouët, A., and D. Laborde. 2010. "Eight Years of Doha Trade Talks: Where Do We Stand?" *The Estey Centre Journal of International Law* 11 (2): 349–370.

Boumellassa, H., D. Laborde, and C. Mitaritonna. 2009. *A Picture of Tariff Protection across the World in 2004: MAcMap-HS6, Version 2.* IFPRI Discussion Paper 903. Washington, DC: International Food Policy Research Institute.

Bureau, J.-C., D. Laborde, and D. Orden. 2013. "US and EU Farm Policies: The Subsidy Habit." In *2012 Global Food Policy Report,* chapter 6, 58–67. Washington, DC: International Food Policy Research Institute.

Díaz-Bonilla, E., and D. Laborde. 2015. *The Bali Agreement: An Assessment from the Perspective of Developing Countries.* IFPRI Discussion Paper 1444. Washington, DC: International Food Policy Research Institute.

Jean, S., D. Laborde, and W. Martin. 2008. "Choosing Sensitive Agricultural Products in Trade Negotiations." IFPRI Discussion Paper 788. Washington, DC: International Food Policy Research Institute.

Laborde, D. 2008. "Doha: Un Cycle en Developpement." In *L'Economie Mondiale 2008.* Paris: Centre d'Etudes Prospectives et d'Information Internationale.

Laborde, D., and W. Martin. 2015. "Formulas for Failure? Were the Doha Tariff Formulas Too Ambitious for Success?" *World Trade Review* 14 (1): 45–65.

Laborde, D., W. Martin, and D. van der Mensbrugghe. 2012. "Implications of the Doha Market Access Proposals for Developing Countries." *World Trade Review* 11: 1–25.

OECD (Organisation for Economic Co-operation and Development). 2016. OECD Producer Support Estimate database. Accessed July 12, 2016. www.oecd.org/agriculture/agricultural-policies/producerandconsumersupportestimatesdatabase.htm.

WTO (World Trade Organization). 2014. *International Trade Statistics 2014.* Accessed 2016. https://www.wto.org/english/res_e/statis_e/its2014_e/its2014_e.pdf.

Chapter 3

WHY IS THE DOHA DEVELOPMENT AGENDA FAILING? AND WHAT CAN BE DONE? A COMPUTABLE GENERAL EQUILIBRIUM-GAME THEORETICAL APPROACH

Antoine Bouët and David Laborde

The trade negotiations led under the banner of the Doha Development Agenda (DDA) are complex, as highlighted by the Cancun summit in September 2003 and the Geneva meeting in July 2008.[1] This last meeting largely confirmed the perception of the DDA as a failure (*Economist* 2008). In 2012 and 2013, trade officials tried to give a new impulse to Doha negotiations, but in 2015 they were not yet completed even if in December 2013, in Bali, the new WTO director, Roberto Azevêdo, announced the Bali package concerning in particular implementation of trade facilitation. During the Geneva meeting in 2008, Pascal Lamy tried to cut a deal among seven countries (Australia, Brazil, China, the European Union, India, Japan, and the United States). This initiative has been criticized due to the fact that the WTO rules call for consensus.[2] Another distinctive feature of these negotiations is the emergence of countries' coalitions (such as the G20, the G90, or the G10), which play an active role in the bargaining process.[3] A new characteristic is also present in the "Aid for Trade" package, which according to the WTO, means further assistance for developing countries "to increase

1 This chapter was originally published in Bouët and Laborde (2010). We thank Jean-Christophe Bureau, Lionel Fontagné, Gaspar Frontini, Tom Hertel, Sébastien Jean, Will Martin, participants of the 2004 Global Trade Analysis Project (GTAP) conference in Washington, DC, and the September 2004 Association Française de Sciences Economiques (AFSE) Congress in Paris, and two anonymous referees who provided comments on an earlier version of this paper.

2 The July 2008 Geneva group was supposed to identify a compromise representing interests well beyond those of group members.

3 The G20 gathers together 20 emerging countries and least developed countries (LDCs), is led by Brazil and India, and also includes China and South Africa. It generally plays an active role in favor of agricultural liberalization. The G90 is a set of 90 poor countries with a more defensive trade strategy aimed to advance pro-poor policies (most African countries are members of this group). The G10 includes 10 countries, mainly from the Organisation for Economic Co-operation and Development (OECD); these include Iceland, Japan, Norway, South Korea (Republic of Korea), Switzerland, and Taiwan, China. The G10 primarily seeks to impede agricultural liberalization.

their capacity to take advantage of more open markets" (WTO 2016). Some observers, however, describe this initiative as financial compensation for countries that are expected to suffer losses under the agreement (see Stiglitz and Charlton 2006; Evenett 2005b).

The objective of this chapter is to provide a strategic analysis of these negotiations. In particular, we examine whether these trade negotiations can reach a pro-liberalization outcome, and if so, which packages may be approved. If no pro-liberalization outcome is possible, we ask the following questions: Which countries are preventing the achievement of an agreement, and why? Is there any way to change the negotiation rules to achieve a pro-liberalization outcome? How can we explain the creation of coalitions, and do they thwart the success of the negotiations?

Strategic analysis of international trade negotiations is common in the economic literature. Johnson (1953) studies tariff equilibrium between two big countries. In a later work (Johnson 1965) he examines an international trade framework where trading partners exchange reduced production in import-competing sectors for increased production in exporting sectors. Mayer (1981) shows that a domestic conflict of interest may prevent the negotiation of free trade between two big countries. The Prisoners' dilemma is used by Riezman (1982) to show that the outcome of a noncooperative game between big countries is tariff equilibrium. Baldwin and Clarke (1988) analyze the Tokyo Round as a bargaining process between the European Union and the United States, where both trading partners try to minimize an overall welfare loss function. Tyers (1990) identifies policy preferences that are implicit in European and Japanese actual tariff patterns and uses these derived weights and the associated objective function to assess which tariff reforms could be negotiated by both countries. Grossman and Helpman (1995) have demonstrated that trade agreements allow governments to escape the well-known terms of a trade prisoners' dilemma even when those governments are subject to domestic political pressure. Turning to the precise rules of those agreements, Bagwell and Staiger (1999, 2002) have established that reciprocity and nondiscrimination might act as commitments toward efficiency under a broad set of assumptions on the underlying domestic political games.

We think that the strategic context of the DDA is far different from that of previous rounds. The large number of players (from 23 in 1947 up to 160 countries in June 2015) and the diversity of economic situations are especially important considering that the WTO rules call for consensus. More important, while the outcomes of previous rounds were largely expected to be negotiated between the EU and the United States, the number of active participants (Australia, Brazil, and India, for example) in the current bargaining process has increased. The immediate question that comes to mind, therefore, is whether these new features explain the stalemate in which these negotiations seem to have been since the second half of 2008. Recent methodological developments allow for a more systematic study of this bargaining process. Thanks to improvements in computation ability, the availability of databases on world macroeconomic variables (for example, the GTAP database; Dimaranan and McDougall 2005) and market access (for example, the MAcMapHS6 database; Bouët et al. 2008), and the development of multicountry and multisector Computable General Equilibrium (CGE) models, it is possible to simulate numerous scenarios of trade reform and evaluate their impacts on each WTO member. This may be done against the economic theories of negotiation developed by Nash (1953), Shapley (1953), and Kalai and Smorodinsky (1975). Hence, the combination of theoretical developments and modeling capacities allows us to model negotiations among numerous countries and regions with microeconomic foundations.

To analyze the potential outcome of the DDA, we use the MIRAGE (Modelling International Relationships in Applied General Equilibrium) model of the world economy and recent databases covering market access and domestic support.[4] Unlike traditional studies that begin with a particular scenario, we herein study a set of agreements representative of discussions at the time of the beginning of the negotiations. These include 143 trade shocks that are expected to represent the whole set of negotiations. These shocks are studied with the help of the MIRAGE model. Inside the domain defined by all these potential outcomes, the Nash solution, as defined by the theory of axiomatic bargaining, is selected. The Nash solution defines an efficient and rational solution to any bargaining problem.

We find that a pro-liberalization agreement is very difficult to achieve due to the heterogeneity of WTO members. There are, however, several possible solutions. First, the exclusion of small countries improves the efficiency of the negotiation process, regardless of the governments' objectives. Second, the creation of coalitions potentially allows developing countries to act against the solutions selected by rich countries. Third, it may be possible and useful to expand the domain of trade negotiations. Fourth, game theory indicates that side payments may be effective, in that actors can maximize the "size of

4 The MIRAGE model was developed at the Centre d'Etudes Prospectives et d'Informations Internationales (CEPII) in Paris. A full description of the model is available in Decreux and Valin (2007).

the cake" for their purposes by using side payments to compensate losers and buy the agreement of each player. The chapter first explains our methodology. Next, the economic impacts of all scenarios are broadly characterized. We then apply the theory of cooperative games and introduce three mechanisms for improving the efficiency of the negotiations. We look at the possibility of coalitions, and finally we offer conclusions.

Methodology

Model and Data

This study uses the MIRAGE model of the world economy to assess economic consequences of various trade reforms. The MIRAGE model is a multinational multisector CGE model (see Decreux and Valin 2007). In this study the MIRAGE model is used under its static version, with a perfect competition hypothesis and without modeling foreign direct investment. The main purpose of this modeling scenario is to simulate many potential trade reforms and to represent as exhaustively as possible the entire domain of negotiation. We use *perfect competition* instead of *imperfect competition* as the latter framework necessitates supplementary data (number of firms, mark-up, and magnitude-of-scale economies) for calibration purposes, which are difficult to gather for many regions. At the same time, this theoretical option can deeply affect the impact of a trade reform (see van Tongeren, van Meijl, and Surry 2001). The use of the static version is also justified by the fact that we are not interested in the dynamics of the reform but only in the long-term impact on various regions.

The first source of data is GTAP6.1 (Dimaranan and McDougall 2005), which provides world macroeconomic accounts and trade flows for the year 2001. Notably, we seek to describe the complexity of the negotiations *at the beginning of the process*. Of course it would be worthwhile to study whether the current trade features have made the negotiations even more difficult than they were at the beginning of the process. However, we contend that the main reasons for the present stalemate are:

1. the large number of participants with heterogeneous economic and trade characteristics;
2. the dispersion of protection and other distortions across sectors; and
3. the existence of trade preferences and regional agreements that generate preferential access.

These three features still characterize the world trading system in 2015, even if new policies have been put in place (for example, the US Farm Bills implemented in 2002 and 2008, the Economic Partnership Agreements implemented or still in negotiation, the recent developments in the European Common Agricultural Policies, and so on): in fact, these new policies may further complicate the intricacy of international trade relations.[5] On the other hand, from 2004 to 2014 the negotiations have focused on narrow issues. Starting with the 2004 July Package, the broad features of the modalities have been defined and the remaining controversial issues are connected more to the flexibilities to be given to rich and developing countries, including sensitive and special products and special safeguard mechanisms. Since they address very particular political economy problems, introducing them into the analytical framework presented here will bring limited insights.

The market access data comes from the MAcMapHS6 version 1 database (Bouët et al. 2008), which measures protection in 2001 and includes all regional agreements and trade preferences existing to this date. A database on bound duties (Bchir, Jean, and Laborde 2006) has also been developed to apply tariff formulae on bound duties instead of applied duties. Accounting for the binding overhang effect is particularly important in the case of developing countries, for which binding overhang is often large. A database on domestic support has also been constructed from OECD's data on the production subsidy equivalent, as the traditional aggregate measure of support (AMS) relies on old world prices data. This database takes into account trends in agricultural policies established by the US Farm Bill in place in 2001 and the CAP Agenda 2000. Existing databases on market access in services (Francois and Hoekman 1999; Hoekman 1996; Kalirajan et al. 2000; Trewin 2000) are incomplete and not reliable enough to be the basis of a systematic analysis of WTO negotiation. In the GTAP database, protection in services is insufficiently assessed. Frequency indexes are much more informative but do not fully account for the complexity of trade barriers in this sector. To cope with this lack of data, we impose a uniform *ad valorem* tax of 20 percent in all countries and in all business service activities. It is a transaction cost that generates rents for economic agents in the importing country. Since we acknowledge that using a homogenous 20 percent tax on business services is a very crude modeling approach, we present results with and without this modeling element to check how it affects results.

5 Our baseline takes into consideration the US Farm Bill in place in 2001 and the Everything But Arms (EBA) Initiative.

Our initial expectation is that the heterogeneity of negotiating countries could lead to a DDA failure. Therefore, when selecting the strategy of geographical decomposition to be used for this work, we give priority to analyzing the structural diversity of the various WTO members. Of course, the geographic decomposition is a key element of the methodological design of the study. We think that the main elements that determine a country's stance in the negotiations are (1) the average level of trade-related distortions that affect its imports and its exports; (2) the sector and partner dispersion of its protection; (3) its economic size and dependence on trade; and (4) its product and geographic concentration of imports and exports.

On the basis of the GTAP6.1 database, we select countries that are specific either in terms of trade specialization (Brazil and Argentina [agriculture] versus China and Bangladesh [industry] versus India [services]), or in terms of preferential access received (Bangladesh, which is beneficiary of the Everything But Arms Initiative versus China, India, Indonesia, and Thailand, which are not; Mexico and Canada with their preferential access to the United States versus all other OECD countries), or preferential access given (the EU versus Japan and Australia), or geographic structure of trade flows (all the continents are represented). Another element is the structure of protection, in terms of average level (OECD versus middle-income countries versus low-income countries) and of sector dispersion of protection (the EU, Japan, Korea, Taiwan versus the United States). We also account for the diversity in economic size and dependence on trade (Bangladesh versus China and India, New Zealand and Chile versus the United States and the EU).

Table 3.1 presents the geographic decomposition. Considering the intercountry and inter-region trade and protection, this decomposition captures 95.5 percent of the world tariff revenue (which can be considered as a measure of the global distortion in play) and 71.3 percent of world trade (which is the macroeconomic variable affected by the distortion).[6] It appears to be a solid basis for our modeling exercise. The sector decomposition focuses on agriculture and identifies 23 sectors, 10 of which are agricultural (Table 3.2). In agriculture, sectors where distortions are large are rice, sugar, cereals nec (not elsewhere classified), livestock and meat, meat products, milk and dairy products. In industry, these are mainly textile and wearing.

6 These calculations have been realized using the MAcMapHS6 database.

TABLE 3.1 Geographic decomposition

Country or region	GTAP code	Coalition
Argentina	arg = Argentina	G22/Cairns
Australia	aus = Australia	Cairns
Bangladesh	bgd = Bangladesh	G90
Brazil	bra = Brazil	G22/Cairns
Canada	can = Canada	Cairns
Chile	chl = Chile	G22/Cairns
China	chn = China	G22
CIS (Commonwealth of Independent States)	rus = Russian Federation; xsu = rest of Former Soviet Union	
EFTA (European Free Trade Association)	che = Switzerland; xef = rest of EFTA	G10
European Union (25 countries)	aut, bel, dnk, fin, fra, deu, gbr, grc, irl, ita, lux, nld, prt, esp, swe, cyp, cze, hun, mlt, pol, svk, svn, est, lva, ltu = 25 countries of the European Union	
India	ind = India	G22
Indonesia	idn = Indonesia	Cairns
Japan	jpn = Japan	G10
Republic of Korea; Taiwan	kor = Republic of Korea; twn = Taiwan	G10
Mediterranean Countries	tur = Turkey; xme = rest of Middle East; mar = Morocco; xnf = rest of North Africa	G90
Mexico	mex = Mexico	G22
New Zealand	nzl = New Zealand	Cairns
Rest of Asia	xea = rest of East Asia; mys = Malaysia; phl = Philippines; vnm = Viet Nam; xse = rest of Southeast Asia; lka = Sri Lanka; xsa = rest of Asia	
Rest of Central America	xca, xcb = Rest of Central America and of the Caribbean	G22
Rest of South America	xsm = Rest of South America	G22
Rest of the world	xoc = rest of Oceania; hkg = Hong Kong; sgp = Singapore; xna = rest of North America; col = Colombia; per = Peru; ven = Venezuela; ury = Uruguay; xsm = rest of South America; xer = rest of Europe; alb = Albania; bgr = Bulgaria; hrv = Croatia; rom = Romania	
South Africa	bwa = Botswana; zaf = South Africa; xsc = Rest of South Africa Custom Union	G90/G22/Cairns
Africa south of the Sahara	mwi = Malawi; moz = Mozambique; tza = United Republic of Tanzania; zmb = Zambia; zwe = Zimbabwe; mdg = Madagascar; uga = Uganda; xss = rest of Africa south of the Sahara	G90
Thailand	tha = Thailand	G22/Cairns
United States	usa = United States	

Source: Authors.

TABLE 3.2 Sector decomposition

Sector code	Description	GTAP code
Agri_ind	Food products, not elsewhere classified	ofd, vol
Bev_Tob	Beverages and Tobacco	b_t
Bus_serv	Business services	isr, obs, ofi
Cereals nec	Cereals, not elsewhere classified	gro, wht
Chim_ind	Chemical industry	crp, p_c
Dairy_prod	Milk and Dairy Products	mil, rmk
Electronic	Electronic	ome
Lvst_Meat	Livestock and Meat	ctl, oap
Mach_ind	Equipment goods	omf
Meat	Meat products	cmt, omt
Metal_ind	Metal industry	fmp, i_s, nfm
OthCrop	Other crops, not elsewhere classified	ocr, osd, pfb
OthInd	Other industries	ely, nmm
OthPrim	Other primary products	coa, frs, fsh, gas, oil, omn, wol
OthServ	Other services	cns, dwe, gdt, osg, ros, trd, wtr, ele
Rice	Rice	pcr, pdi
Sugar	Sugar	c_b, sgr
Textiles	Textile	tex
Tran_ind	Transportation industry	mvh, otn
Trans_com	Transportation and Telecommunication	atp, cmn, otp, wtp
Veg_fruit	Vegetable and Fruit	v_f
Wearing	Wearing, apparel	lea, wap
Wood_paper	Wood and paper	lum, ppp

Source: Authors.

Note: See the GTAP website for a full description of GTAP sectors and GTAP code.

The Objective of Trade Negotiators

A strict definition of national objectives is necessary for analytical purposes. Those objectives have to represent the elements taken into account by negotiators. It leads us to consider four indicators in this study: (1) the Hicksian equivalent variation of the representative agent; (2) real gross domestic product (GDP); (3) maximization of exports; and (4) terms of trade. The *Hicksian equivalent indicator* has often been adopted in the literature and has robust microeconomic foundations. Also, using this indicator means that consumers' interests are as weighted in the government's objective as producers' interests and public receipts. The *real GDP* is often cited as an objective by negotiators, but it lacks microeconomic foundations. *Maximization of exports* is a mercantilist objective, frequently quoted by negotiators, and the *terms of trade* is another mercantilist objective. These objectives appear to be gross approximations, but we limit our analysis to these four objectives as it would be unviable to design a political model adapted to every WTO member. It could be argued that real GDP and welfare are very close objectives. In fact, if trade is initially balanced, the change in Hicksian variation as a share of initial expenditure is the change in nominal GDP deflated by the change in the cost of expenditure. However, trade is not initially balanced in our modeling exercise. Moreover, we define real GDP here by deflating nominal GDP by production prices, and not the cost of expenditure.

Optimizing terms of trade is a key objective and is considered politically important by authors such as Bagwell and Staiger (1999). Terms of trade are usually improved when trading partners liberalize. When only one country liberalizes and others do not, its terms of trade deteriorate, while a country that does not liberalize while others do may experience deterioration of its terms of trade due to its initial free access to foreign markets (such a situation would be an example of eroded preferences). In this sense, optimizing terms of trade can accurately characterize the mercantilist spirit of trade negotiators. It is possible to consider a trade reform wherein all WTO members receive improved terms of trade, in that the WTO does not comprise all countries in the world. Of course, this case is less conceivable given an international organization composed of 153 countries rather than the 23 present at the first negotiation.

Scenarios

A set of trade shocks is simulated in order to give a fairly correct representation of what could be negotiated under the DDA at the time of the launching of this negotiation and what the fundamental interests of WTO members are. From this point of view, it would not be correct to design numerous scenarios around the last modalities published in 2008, since that would not reflect the real problems associated with these negotiations since the beginning of the process. On the contrary, we have to design scenarios around the main dimensions that were discussed during the first years of the round. Five key dimensions of the negotiation are emphasized through the design of these shocks: (1) the extent to which import duties are cut; (2) the degree of harmonization (progressivity) adopted in the tariff-reduction formulae; (3) the provision of special and differential treatment (SDT); (4) global or sector-level negotiation; and (5) a cut in export subsidies.

We consider services, industry (NAMA for nonagricultural market access), agriculture (AMA for agricultural market access), and reduction of export subsidies (Table 3.3). We suppose that liberalization in services takes the form of a reduction by 50 percent in the transaction cost previously defined. As far as industry is concerned, on the one hand, two Swiss formulae are simulated with coefficients a = 5 percent and a = 10 percent. The agreement may include an SDT in some cases. In the case of SDT, the coefficient of the Swiss formula is doubled for developing countries and tripled for least developed countries (LDCs), implying that market access is improved in those countries to only a reduced extent. Finally, a complete liberalization in the textile-apparel sector is tested. This "0 for 0 option" is added to a scenario with a 5 percent Swiss formula in other industrial sectors and without SDT. In agriculture, two Swiss formulae are also considered, with less harmonizing coefficients (a = 15 percent and a = 30 percent). SDT is also tested in the same way as for industry. As the EU proposed a linear reduction of import duties, by a 33 percent coefficient, this nonharmonizing formula is simulated. In this case, the coefficient is 25 percent for developing countries, 15 percent for LDCs. Finally, concerning export subsidies, a cut by 75 percent is considered.

In all trade shocks, duties less than 3 percent are annulled. From a global point of view, 143 trade shocks are simulated. To facilitate identification, the following code is adopted (Table 3.3). A trade shock is notified sABCD with A,B,C and D an integer that belongs to {0,1,2,3,4,5}. For instance, the trade shock s0121 means (see Table 3.3): (1) the status-quo in services; (2) a Swiss formula in NAMA with a 10 percent coefficient and no SDT; (3) a Swiss formula in AMA with a 25 percent coefficient and with SDT; and (4) a reduction in export subsidies by 75 percent.

Assessing Economic Impacts of Potential Reforms

The impact of the five modalities on protection applied is shown in Table 3.4 with the split between agricultural sector (AMA) and nonagricultural sector (NAMA).

The trade reforms that maximize world gains in terms of Hicksian equivalent variation or GDP are presented on Table 3.5: s1531 is a liberalization in services, a very harmonizing Swiss formula without SDT in industry and agriculture, with a "0 for 0" option in textile and apparel, and a 75 percent

TABLE 3.3 Definition of scenarios

Indicator	A	B	C	D
		Domain		
Value	Services	NAMA (nonagricultural market access)	AMA (agricultural market access)	Export subsidies
0	Status quo	Status quo	Status quo	Status quo
1	Reduction by 50%	a = 10%	a = 25%	Reduction by 75%
2	n.a.	a = 10% + SDT	a = 25% + SDT	n.a.
3	n.a.	a = 5%	a = 15%	n.a.
4	n.a.	a = 5% + SDT	a = 15% + SDT	n.a.
5	n.a.	0 for 0	Linear formula + SDT	n.a.

Source: Authors.
Note: n.a. = not applicable.

reduction in exports subsidies. It implies the largest increase in world welfare. This optimum is s0531, when excluding negotiation in services. If the criterion is the augmentation of exports, the best scenario is s1530 under which export subsidies are not cut. These gains are comparable with those obtained in similar studies (Bchir, Fontagné, and Jean 2005): US$105 billion if the most liberalizing scenario is adopted.

The examination of results implied by each scenario leads to several conclusions.

- A major part of world gains come from agricultural liberalization, due to the high level of initial protection. This confirms conclusions of other studies, like van der Mensbrugghe and Beghin (2004), Francois, van Meijl, and van Tongeren (2005), or Hertel and Keeney (2006).
- Gains coming from liberalizing industry are smaller. In the best case scenario, they add up to US$14 billion. It corresponds to a very harmonizing Swiss formula, without SDT and with a "0 for 0" option in textile and apparel. A smaller initial protection explains these limited gains. Moreover, tariff peaks are less frequent.
- Gains are overadditive; the sum of gains coming from elementary shocks is inferior to that derived from the scenario in which all these shocks are combined.
- A cut in export subsidies is all the more fruitful as it is combined with a reduction in agricultural tariffs.

TABLE 3.4 Impact of various tariff cuts on applied import duties (%)

	Initial level		Case 1		Case 2		Case 3		Case 4		Case 5	
Country or region	AMA	NAMA	AMA	NAMA	AMA	NAMA	AMA	NAMA	AMA	NAMA	AMA	NAMA
Argentina	11.8	12.7	10.6	6.9	11.7	10.0	8.8	4.3	11.0	6.9	11.8	0.0
Australia	3.1	5.4	2.2	3.0	2.2	3.0	1.9	2.1	1.9	2.1	2.2	0.0
Bangladesh	19.4	15.7	13.4	1.8	18.8	2.2	9.5	1.5	18.1	2.2	19.3	0.0
Brazil	11.1	12.5	9.6	6.5	10.9	9.4	7.8	4.0	10.1	6.5	11.1	0.0
Canada	23.2	2.9	6.0	1.7	6.0	1.7	4.3	1.3	4.3	1.3	15.7	0.0
Chile	7.0	6.8	7.0	6.8	7.0	6.8	7.0	4.3	7.0	6.8	7.0	0.0
China	23.5	7.4	9.9	3.7	12.9	4.8	7.7	2.7	10.7	3.7	18.5	0.0
CIS (Commonwealth of Independent States)	16.9	8.8	16.8	8.8	16.9	8.8	16.8	8.8	16.9	8.8	16.9	0.0
EFTA (European Free Trade Association)	60.0	1.5	11.9	0.6	11.9	0.6	8.2	0.4	8.2	0.4	50.9	0.0
European Union (25 countries)	24.4	2.4	7.7	1.3	7.7	1.3	5.6	0.9	5.6	0.9	17.2	0.0
India	57.2	30.0	19.8	6.9	31.1	10.4	13.8	4.5	22.5	7.0	48.6	0.0
Indonesia	11.4	6.0	5.9	3.2	6.9	3.9	4.8	2.3	6.2	3.2	9.9	0.0
Japan	49.9	1.7	11.0	0.9	11.0	0.9	7.8	0.7	7.8	0.7	43.0	0.0
Mediterranean countries	28.3	7.6	12.4	5.3	14.6	5.7	10.0	4.8	12.0	5.2	26.4	0.0
Mexico	41.1	10.4	14.2	5.3	19.5	7.6	10.7	3.5	15.6	5.3	34.3	0.0
New Zealand	2.3	2.8	1.9	2.5	1.9	2.5	1.9	1.9	1.9	1.9	2.1	0.0
Rest of Asia	16.0	9.6	8.2	3.4	9.3	4.1	7.5	2.9	8.6	3.5	15.4	0.0
Rest of world	5.2	1.9	3.7	1.2	3.9	1.4	3.2	1.0	3.5	1.2	4.9	0.0
Rest of Central America	16.8	4.7	9.2	3.0	11.6	3.7	7.2	2.1	9.9	3.0	14.8	0.0
Rest of South America	15.7	11.0	11.7	8.6	13.5	9.7	9.7	7.4	12.0	8.5	15.2	0.0
South Africa	21.8	7.3	7.9	3.1	10.1	4.3	6.2	2.0	8.6	3.1	21.6	0.0
South Korea–Taiwan	41.8	7.8	11.2	3.3	11.2	3.3	8.2	2.3	8.2	2.3	29.7	0.0
African countries south of the Sahara	17.9	12.2	13.0	2.5	15.6	3.0	9.9	2.1	14.6	2.7	17.9	0.0
Thailand	27.1	11.5	14.0	3.8	19.1	5.2	10.4	2.6	15.4	3.8	23.4	0.0
United States	5.5	2.2	3.1	1.0	3.1	1.0	2.5	0.7	2.5	0.7	4.3	0.0

Source: MAcMapHS6v1; authors' calculations.

Note: AMA = agricultural market access; NAMA = nonagricultural market access. Reference group weights. Cases 1 to 5 correspond to the lines in Table 3.3. For example, case 1 combines a Swiss formula with coefficient a = 10% in NAMA and a Swiss formula with coefficient a = 25% in AMA.

TABLE 3.5 World optimum

Category	With liberalization in services	Without liberalization in services
Optimal scenario	s1531	s0531
Equivalent variation	US$105.05 billion or 0.33%	US$93.8 billion or 0.29%
Real GDP	US$127.21 billion or 0.41%	US$114.99 billion or 0.37%

Source: Authors' calculation.

Note: s1531 implies liberalization in services (1), the strongest liberalization (a = 5 percent) in NAMA including the 0 for 0 in textile and wearing (5), the strongest liberalization (a = 15 percent) in AMA (3), and the reduction of export subsidies. s0531 is the same scenario without services liberalization.

Figure 3.1 shows each scenario according to two characteristics: the unweighted average welfare gain in percentage of initial real income (horizontal axis), and the standard error of the welfare gains in the countries/regions (vertical axis). In the lower left corner of Figure 3.1, we see a set of 47 trade reforms characterized by negative or low unweighted average gains and low standard deviations. One common characteristic of these scenarios is that they yield a relatively small global gain for the world economy (the maximum is US$41.2 billion). In contrast, the minimum global gain predicted for the set of trade reforms located in the upper right corner is US$68.5 billion. Thus we see that the larger the world gain, the more unequal its distribution.

All of the trade reforms in the lower left corner of the figure are characterized not only by relatively low global gains for the world economy but also by relatively small standard deviations and small unweighted average gains. Reforms leading to negative unweighted average gains are projected to hurt many countries/regions through losses and/or hurt some countries with large relative losses. All of these reforms lack liberalization in agriculture or include a linear tariff reduction in this sector. The distribution of welfare gains varies according to the modalities of each liberalization scenario. For instance, while generating the same increase in world welfare (US$14 billion—that is, a growth rate of 0.04 percent), the scenarios of agricultural liberalization under a linear formula (s0050) or a large industrial liberalization (s0500) give contrasting pictures in terms of distribution. In the first case, total real income gain is more evenly shared out among players (whatever their economic size), the percentage of unweighted average gain is greater than the world gain, and the standard deviation is somewhat low. In the second case, industrial liberalization benefits the richest countries/regions, such that the percentage of unweighted average gain is negative, while the world gain is positive. The standard deviation is about fourfold higher.

FIGURE 3.1 Distribution of scenarios by unweighted global average and standard deviation of country gains

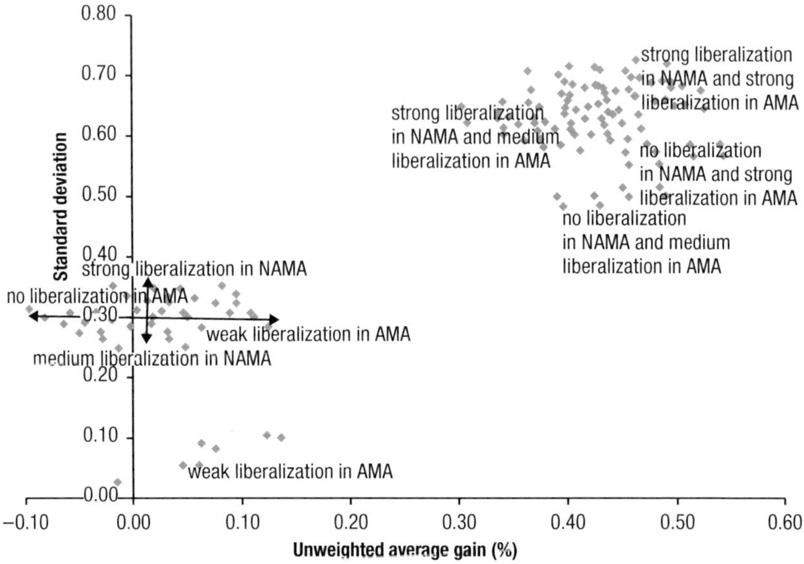

Source: Authors' calculation.
Note: AMA = agricultural market access; NAMA = nonagricultural market access.

Conversely, all reforms located in the upper right corner of the figure are characterized by a Swiss formula in agriculture, with or without SDT. For all scenarios in the upper right corner of the figure where a Swiss formula is applied on agricultural tariffs, the standard deviation of gains is high, but the unweighted average gain (in percentage) is greater than the global gain for the world economy, implying that these reforms are supported by numerous countries/regions and large countries/regions do not capture most of the gains.

The uneven distribution of the gains is understandable if we consider that the main effects are driven by agricultural liberalization. The cost of protection is quadratic for importing countries/regions. Therefore, we expect the gains to be concentrated in regions where the distortions were initially high. Also, for exporters, two complementary effects are in play, particularly for agricultural liberalization. First, the elimination of tariff peaks creates strong losses for exporters who initially enjoyed preferential access but strong gains for nonpreferred exporters; in this sense, developing countries/regions have contrasting interests. Furthermore, if agricultural liberalization drives the majority of the gains, such gains will be concentrated in countries/regions with stronger comparative advantages in this sector (for example, the Cairns Group). Second, in addition, the terms of trade will affect food prices, thereby creating opposite effects on net importers and net exporters of food products. Thus liberalization of industry alone yields an unfair distribution of gains, while liberalization of agriculture alone confers large gains to numerous countries/regions, but these are more unequally distributed. Combining the two options increases the size of the cake, but with an even more unequal distribution (s1530). Therefore, agricultural liberalization is crucial to make the game politically acceptable.

Modeling the Bargaining Process

Based on game theory, this section describes trade negotiations as a cooperative bargaining process between players. The Nash solution is presented according to several hypotheses about bargaining powers.

The Nash Solution

The Nash solution is characterized by the following features: the outcome is individually rational (no player is losing compared to the pre-negotiation situation, called the *threat point*); the outcome is Pareto-optimal (there is no negotiable outcome unanimously preferred); the outcome may be democratic or may reflect a given distribution of power between players (*bargaining powers*); unlike other axiomatic approaches (egalitarian solution, utilitarian solution, Kalai Smorodinsky solution), the Nash solution fulfils a set of other properties: independence of irrelevant alternatives, independence to a change of units, weak Pareto constraint, symmetry (Mas-Colell, Whinston, and Green 1995).

The Nash solution should not be confused with the concept of Nash equilibrium: (1) the *Nash equilibrium* applies to *noncooperative games* and states that the outcome of a game where players do not cooperate is a situation where nobody has any interest to change his or her strategy as long as all other players do not change their own strategy; (2) the *Nash solution* applies to *cooperative games* and states that the issue of a negotiation should be individually rational and Pareto-optimal, as just defined. Let us consider that the trade negotiation is a bargaining process between 25 zones on 143 potential outcomes. Let W_0^m be the region *m*'s initial "payment" in the case nonagreement is reached, $W^m(s)$ its payment when the outcome *s* is adopted. *S* is the set of the 143 feasible outcomes. We assume that in case of failure of the bargaining game, the outcome (that is, the threat point) is the status quo—that is, $W^m(s) = W_0^m, \forall m$. However, we can also imagine other cases, as follows:

1. Countries/regions start trade wars, increasing their applied duties to the maximum allowed by their bound duties (or even further). This alternative would require us to model and solve the Nash noncooperative game across the 25 countries/regions.
2. Countries/regions decide to negotiate preferential agreements. In this case, we would have to define an optimal trade agreement for each of the 25 countries/regions with any combinations of the 24 other countries/regions, as well as potential agreements with third parties.

These two alternatives would require strenuous calculations that are beyond the scope of the current analysis. Here we seek to understand, within a simple framework, the stalemate in which the trade negotiations have been stalled since 2001. Bouët and Laborde (2010) investigate the potential outcome of Doha Development Agenda (DDA) failure, but the alternative scenarios they used are ad hoc and inconsistent with the game-theory approach discussed herein.

The Nash Solution without Bargaining Power

In a first stage, we consider that all regions m participate in negotiations and have an identical bargaining power, whatever their geographical, population, and economic size are.[7] The Nash solution is:

$$s^* \in Arg_{s \in S} Max G(s) = \prod_m (W^m(s) - W_0^m) \quad (1)$$

$$\text{with } W^m(s^*) - W_0^m \geq 0, \forall m \quad (2)$$

Condition 2 ensures that the solution will be individually rational.

Table 3.6 shows the different Nash solutions according to the objective adopted by governments and to the negotiation rule defined by equations 1 and 2. The first row gives the Nash solutions when the 25 zones have identical bargaining power, the second row when each country has the same power (democratic weights—see next subsection), and the third row when zones have

7 The objective function defined by (1) is a product of regions' changes in welfare; each element can be weighted either by the population of the region, the number of countries composing the region, or economic size of the region (see next subsection). If we do not weigh these differences, regions have identical bargaining power.

TABLE 3.6 Nash solutions of the cooperative game

Category	Equivalent variation	Real GDP	Exports	Terms of trade
1 region, 1 voice	s1000	s1520	s1530	No solution
1 country, 1 voice	s1000	s1510	s1530	No solution
Economic weight	s1000	s1551	s1530	No solution

Source: Authors' calculation.

Note: s1000 is a status quo with only a liberalization in services (a net gain for everyone in our modeling). s1510 implies liberalization in services, the strongest liberalization (a = 5 percent) in NAMA including the 0 for 0 option in textile, a moderate liberalization (a = 25 percent + SDT) in AMA and no export subsidies reduction. s1520 differs from s1510 by the introduction of SDT in agriculture. On the opposite, s1530 is the same scenario but the AMA liberalization is the strongest (a = 15 percent, no SDT). s1551 implies liberalization in services, the strongest liberalization (a = 5 percent) in NAMA including the 0-0 in textile and wearing, the weakest liberalization (linear reduction) in AMA and the reduction of export subsidies. s0531 is the same scenario without services liberalization.

bargaining power (see next subsection) proportional to their economic size (GDP-CHELEM database 2001; CEPII 2016). When maximizing exports, the Nash solution represents a very ambitious degree of liberalization (s1530) that benefits all players. Optimizing terms of trade is not a sustainable objective, as this objective features a purely mercantilist world where international liberalization is a constant-sum game and where no Paretian improvement is feasible. In our study, the only possible solution under this objective would be a situation in which all WTO members agree on a reform that improves their terms of trade while deteriorating those of non-WTO members. When maximizing equivalent variation, the outcome is the status quo, except for liberalization of services, which gives every player a welfare gain. Considering that our modeling of services is relatively limited, we can focus on the result without services. In this case, negotiation reaches a stalemate. If governments maximize GDP, it is likely that industry will be hugely liberalized but market access in agriculture will be only slightly improved.

As far as the objective of equivalent variation is concerned, Bangladesh clearly plays a key role in trade negotiations, as this country does not see improvement of its equivalent variation under numerous scenarios, due to deterioration of terms of trade and erosion of preferential margins. This illustrates the position of numerous developing countries/regions that have been granted significant preferences in rich and large markets and are highly specialized in a few products. Thus our results suggest that the position of such countries forms the underlying basis for the stalemate of trade negotiations. In the absence of bargaining power, each player has the same influence.

However, our definition of a player follows the countries/regions modeled herein, meaning that our disaggregation scheme introduces a bias into the structure of the game. By introducing bargaining power based on measurable country/region features, we can correct for the arbitrary choices inherent in our disaggregation.

The Nash Solution with Bargaining Power

The cooperative game theory allows for taking into account bargaining powers. It is possible to introduce differentiated bargaining powers in the Nash axiomatic approach. We modify equation 1 by weighting each player's surplus by α_m. The Nash solution is given by:

$$s^* \in Arg_{s \in S} Max G(s) = \prod_m (W^m(s) - W_0{}^m(s))^{\alpha_m} \qquad (3)$$

under the same individual rationality constraint expressed by equation (2).

Two alternative weights are considered:

- α_m equals the number of voices at WTO for each zone (1 voice for United States, the European Union, 2 for the Korea/Taiwan zone, 11 for the Mediterranean countries, and so on). This weighting structure is qualified as a *democratic* system.[8]
- α_m equals the share of the zone in the world GDP. This is the economic power.

Several elements justify giving larger countries a larger bargaining power: (1) multilateral trade negotiation is a bargaining process about market access, and opening the access to large and rich countries is a real priority for all players; (2) big countries have a strong bargaining power since their threat of retaliation is potentially detrimental; (3) big countries have a higher capacity to understand the impact of the various reforms, and they can more easily influence other WTO members on nontrade issues.

The last two rows of Table 3.6 present the results when we use these weights. Only the Nash solution under real GDP criterion is modified when weights are included. In a democratic context, the same solution is adopted, except that it does not include SDT in agriculture. This option has a restrictive impact on South-South trade. When they have a greater decisional power, it is abandoned. On the contrary, when an economic weighting

---

8 "Democratic" must be interpreted as a relative concept.

system is adopted, the s1551 is agreed. This is clearly a compromise between the European Union, Japan, and other industrialized countries. The United States maximizes GDP when s1500—that is, large openness of industry and services—is adopted. If exports and GDP are not consistent objectives for trade negotiators, the main conclusion of this section is that a status quo is highly probable. In the next subsections, three ways out are considered: the exclusion of some players, the implementation of side payments, and the extension of the domain of negotiation.

Excluding Some Players

A key reason for the Doha stalemate is obviously the number of negotiating members, which adds constraints to the bargaining program. As a consequence, a solution would be to exclude some members from the negotiating process. Several points support this view: (1) trade negotiation between more than 150 countries is an extremely difficult task as countries' preferences are quite different; (2) trade negotiations require human and technical resources, which only rich countries have; (3) an interpretation of the current situation, when considering the fact that neither LDCs nor small and vulnerable economies (SVEs) have to liberalize, is that they are not officially excluded from the negotiation but have no obligations (so this situation is very close to an exclusion of these countries from the negotiation process); (4) observers often describe past trade negotiations as a bargaining process between a few rich countries (see, for example, the Blair House agreement between the EU and the United States; Messerlin 1995).

To go further, we examine how the exclusion of poor countries—that is, eliminating some of the m players of the optimization program, affects the negotiation. Until the end of this chapter we call *IR*-set the set of scenarios that respect the individual rationality constraint in each program (see equation 2). Table 3.7 indicates the number of solutions in the IR-set, according to various degrees of exclusion of poor countries (the criterion being a share in world GDP). For example, when the equivalent variation is the objective of all negotiators, excluding countries the GDP of which is less than 2 percent of the world GDP implies that the IR-set is 59 instead of 1. Excluding countries always expands the IR-set of the game. When terms of trade are the objective, exclusion has to be large: the 4 percent threshold implies that India does not take part in the bargaining process such that some agreements may be reached: s1311 with economic weights, s1351 in other cases. When negotiators

TABLE 3.7 Cardinal of the set of feasible and individually rational (IR) scenarios when player exclusion is allowed

Exclusion threshold	Equivalent variation	Real GDP	Exports	Terms of trade
None	1	31	39	0
< 2% of world GDP	59	47	142	0
< 3% of world GDP	60	47	142	0
< 4% of world GDP	87	47	142	112

Source: Authors' calculation.

Note: The exclusion threshold is applied to the GDP of the player (region in the model) and not to each country belonging to the region. IR is the set of scenarios where all players have no negative payoff (individual rationality constraints).

maximize equivalent variation, even the first threshold which excludes only small countries is efficient. The s1510 outcome is adopted under bargaining weights based on economic size except when the interests of all zones with less than 4 percent of world GDP are excluded: the United States, the EU, and Japan are the only negotiators (these are the Triad countries) and s1551 should be chosen (see above). With democratic weights the outcome of trade negotiations is (1) s1530 for a 2 percent threshold; (2) s1230 for a 3 percent threshold; (3) s1511 for a 4 percent threshold. Democracy undermines the influence of the United States and the EU, while improving the position of Mediterranean countries.

From a global point of view, restricting negotiation to richer countries implies the adoption of a less harmonizing tariff reduction formula in agriculture. Moreover, when only Bangladesh does not participate in the bargaining process, an outcome may be reached under the equivalent variation criterion. Thus we find that the exclusion of WTO members is efficient. However, this is quite opposite to the essence of multilateralism. Excluding poorer countries/regions is particularly inconsistent with the developmental objective of this round. Therefore, the following section addresses a more cooperative solution: the inception of side payments among countries/regions.

Setting Up Side Payments

In a cooperative framework a worldwide Pareto-optimum should be agreed on when countries/regions are allowed to redistribute the benefits obtained from trade liberalization. Setting up side payments provides a supplementary degree of freedom, and all outcomes are then feasible as long as total welfare increases.

The "Aid for Trade" package cements this idea into a workable strategy (see Evenett 2005a). From an institutional point of view, these international transfers may take several shapes: aid for development, financing of facilities, adjustment packages (see the proposal of the International Monetary Fund's Anne Krueger in Cancun [Krueger 2003]). For example, various proposals have been put forth regarding the compensation of African-Caribbean-Pacific (ACP) countries for preference erosion as part of the tentative banana deal reached between Latin American producers, the EU, and the United States. Equivalent variation is the criterion that best fits these international financial transfers; for this reason we study implementation of side payments under this objective function.

From a mathematical point of view, the program of the cooperative game with side payments is defined by the equations:

$$s^* \in Arg_{s \in S} Max G(s) = \prod_m (W^m(s) + T^m - W_0^{\ m})^{\alpha_m} \quad (4)$$

$$\text{With: } W^m(s^*) + T^m \geq W_0^{\ m}, \forall m \quad (5)$$

$$\text{And: } \sum_m T^m = 0 \quad (6)$$

T^m represents the payments received/paid by m. The objective function to be maximized (equation 4) indicates that each country's real income variation, thanks to the trade reform, is augmented by the side payment when it is positive and is decreased when it is negative. Equation 5 expresses individual rationality and slightly differs from equation 2 as the side payment is included. Equation 6 means that the sum of the international transfers is balanced. It can be shown that the optimal solution is defined by

$$W^m(s^*) + T^m - W_0^{\ m} = \alpha_m . \sum_m (W^m(s^*) - W_0^{\ m})$$

At the optimum, a player should get a share α^m—its bargaining power—of the total gain. If all players have the same power (the unweighted situation), the final distribution of gains has to be even. Otherwise, a player will use its veto power to block the outcome. Therefore the more uneven the initial distribution, the larger will be the redistribution.

The Nash bargaining game set-up describes a redistribution process on absolute level of gains. Therefore attributing the same bargaining power to different players will lead them to try to get the same share of the overall gain. But the same share represents very different outcomes in terms of relative gains. Adopting a weighting scheme that provides the same bargaining power to a big country and to a small one may be quite quixotic since an even distribution of absolute gains will lead to a very extreme distribution of relative gains. Using GDP weights allows us to correct for such a problem. However, a development-friendly outcome of the DDA may aim for the reduction of world inequalities; such a reduction entails that developing countries' gains should be more than proportional to their initial GDP. The "unweighted" and the "democratic" weighting schemes have such properties. When setting up side payments, the first-best solution to be agreed on is the one associated with the largest overall gain: s1531. It is the most ambitious scenario in terms of liberalization. When services are excluded from negotiation, the solution is s0531.

The total amount of side payments is shown in Table 3.8. Notably, the international transfers are very large. As discussed earlier, the more efficient the reform, the larger the global gain and the higher its dispersion. So in a sense these large transfers are due to the consensus rule and the right of veto given to each WTO member. They are much larger than the amount countries need to make up for their losses induced by the negotiated outcome: between 20 and 30 times larger. In fact, countries have to be compensated not only for losses (difference between equivalent variation implied by reform and initial equivalent variation) but also for not getting the average gain. These transfers add up to between 40 percent and 80 percent of total welfare gain, which represents a considerable financial payment. Moreover, the more power rich countries have, the smaller the transfers. For a similar reason, the "democratic" weighting scheme induces a large redistribution because most WTO members are small economies that have limited or no gains. The liberalization of services, by increasing the size of the cake, leads to more redistribution of gains except in the case of bargaining power based on economic size, due to the specific situation of the United States (see earlier).

Figure 3.2 shows the distribution of transfers under side payments. Services are included in the liberalization process and the Nash solution is defined with and without bargaining powers. This solution defines three net payers that are among the main beneficiaries from the liberalization process: the European Union, the European Free Trade Association (EFTA), and Japan. It is obviously related to a tariff structure with numerous peaks. Japan pays US$40 billion to other countries upon a total gain of US$45 billion. For some LDCs, side payments obtained are the only source of gain (Bangladesh and Africa south of the Sahara) and are quite significant (about 2.5 percent of the income of Africa south of the Sahara). The GDP-weighted case is obviously more advantageous for rich countries. For example, the EU does not pay anything, and Japan's payment is reduced by about 25 percent. The United States benefits from large payments (US$34 billion). Previously, countries'

TABLE 3.8 Nash solutions with side payments (US$ billions)

Global transfers	Unweighted	Democratic	Economic weights (GDP)
With liberalization in services	66.4	80.7	44.0
Without liberalization in services	63.2	78.8	44.1

Source: Authors' calculation.

FIGURE 3.2 Distribution of transfers among players (US$ billions)

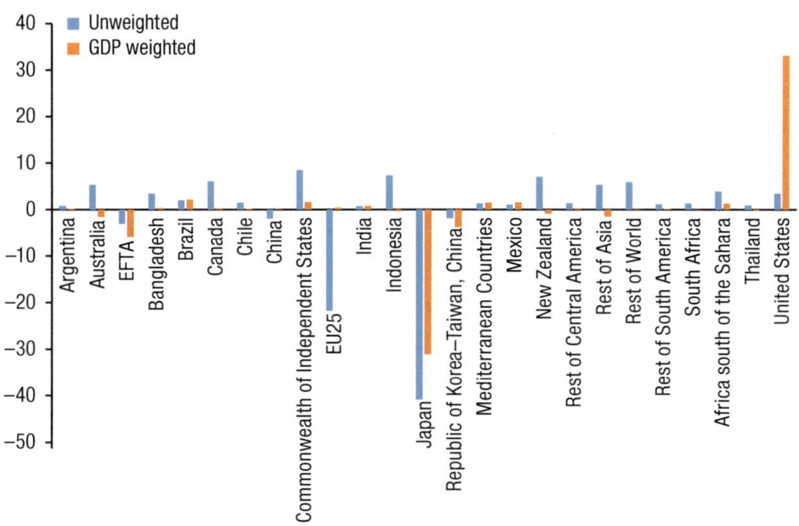

Source: Authors' calculation.

Note: EFTA = European Free Trade Association; EU25 = European Union 25 countries.

The most ambitious scenario is the optimal outcome with transfers (s1531) when transfers are allowed. A negative transfer is a payment done, a positive one is a payment received.

gain did not reflect their economic size. When services are excluded, the profile of the distribution is similar. But larger side payments received by the United States are noteworthy due to its gains related to trade liberalization in services.

Extending the Domain of Negotiation

Another possible solution is to extend the domain of the negotiation. For example, the introduction of the Singapore issues, such as trade facilitation, or more generally, the inclusion of services in the negotiation might be viewed as an extension of the domain of negotiation: countries that lose due to the liberalization of agriculture and industry could offset these losses by gains from the liberalization of this sector. As it is not possible to extend the domain of negotiation from the situation depicted in the previous sections, we consider a restriction of this domain and evaluate the IR-set of the game when the negotiation takes place either only in agriculture, or only in industry, or only in services, or only about export subsidies.

Results are illustrated on Table 3.9. For each criterion (Equivalent variation/Real GDP/Terms of trade), we indicate the number of scenarios in the set of feasible issues (column Domain), then the number of scenarios in the IR-set (column IR-set). Since a negotiation between all players gives birth to a quasi-stalemate when players maximize equivalent variation (the IR set consists of only the liberalization of services), and complete stalemate when the objective is terms of trade, we also consider an exclusion of countries/zones representing less than 2 percent of the world GDP, and then a situation where countries/zones of which GDP is less than 4 percent of the world GDP are excluded. For example, when the objective is equivalent variation and in the case of an exclusion of countries/zones of less than 2 percent of world GDP, a negotiation in all dimensions is especially beneficial as the IR-set consists of 59 potential agreements instead of 0 if the negotiation takes place only in agriculture or industry.

It appears from Table 3.9 that an extension of the domain of negotiation systematically increases the number of trade reforms that countries can potentially agree on. The agricultural sector appears once again at the cornerstone of the trade negotiations. Whatever the negotiators' objective is and in any scheme of country participation (all players/exclusion at 2 percent of world GDP/exclusion at 4 percent of world GDP), it is impossible to find a solution other than the status quo if a negotiation takes place only in agriculture: the IR-set of the game is systematically empty.

Analyzing Coalitions

Since 1995, the functioning of WTO is clearly affected by coalitions whose life span is more or less long and whose raison d'être is not evident. The G20 case clearly illustrates this point. This coalition gathers countries with heterogeneous trade characteristics. In this context it is useful to examine the role and the impact of such coalitions. We suppose that a coalition is justified when small players have been excluded from a negotiation and form a

TABLE 3.9 Impact of an extension of the negotiation domain (IR)

		IR-set		
Criteria	Domain	All players	Exclusion at 2% of world GDP	Exclusion at 4% of world GDP
Equivalent variation				
Services	1	1	1	1
Industry	5	0	0	5
Agriculture	5	0	0	0
Export subsidies	1	0	0	1
All dimensions	**143**	**1**	**59**	**87**
Real GDP				
Services	1	1	1	1
Industry	5	5	5	5
Agriculture	5	0	0	0
Export subsidies	1	1	1	1
All dimensions	**143**	**47**	**47**	**47**
Terms of trade				
Services	1	0	0	0
Industry	5	0	0	2
Agriculture	5	0	0	0
Exports subsidies	1	0	0	1
All dimensions	**143**	**0**	**0**	**112**

Source: Authors' calculation.

Note: The results for the "all dimensions" rows mimic the information of Table 3.7. IR is the set of scenarios where all players have non-negative payoff (individual rationality constraints).

coalition as a means to continue participating. The presence of small countries/regions in a negotiation that is supposedly taking place only among large countries deeply affects the cooperative game. To exemplify this, we examine the situation in which a 4 percent threshold has been applied; in this case, if no coalition is introduced, the Nash solution is determined by taking into account only gains for the Triad countries (that is, the United States, the EU, and Japan).

Numerous coalitions of countries appeared during the eight years of the Doha negotiations. Among them, the G90, G20, and G10 have been especially effective and are studied herein. Assuming that each WTO country has veto power under the principle of unanimity, it is difficult to justify the appearance of coalitions. However, we feel that coalitions allow small countries to gather in order to participate in negotiations from which they would otherwise be excluded. As far as the consequences of coalition formation, we compare the gain obtained by each country/region in the presence and absence of a coalition. For a country/region, participation in the coalition implies that its interests are taken into account, while such interests are not accounted for in the absence of the coalition, because the formation of this coalition entails a change in the set of agreeable reforms and in the solution of the cooperative game. Moreover, we assume that the bargaining power of a coalition equals the sum of its members' bargaining powers.[9] Table 3.10 through Table 3.13 show these comparisons for different countries/regions in different game configurations—that is, with or without other coalitions, with or without bargaining power.

Table 3.10 provides the results for the G10 coalition, which provides gains to all its members. The situation of Japan is strongly improved (+US$44 billion) when the other G10 members' participation constraints are introduced, especially in case of GDP weights. The G10 is worthwhile for its members only if they have to face the United States and the EU. In the presence of other coalitions (G20 and G90), the G10 does not manage to influence the final outcome of the game.

The situation for G20 members is displayed in Table 3.11. This coalition improves the welfare of all of its members, especially when bargaining powers are based on GDP size. In this case, seven of the ten G20 countries/regions modeled herein move from net losses to net gains when we switch from the s1551 (weighted case) outcome selected by the Triad to the s1210 situation.[10] In the s1210 situation, NAMA liberalization is limited, SDT is introduced, and the AMA tariff reduction is deepened with a moderate Swiss formula coefficient instead of the linear formula chosen by the Triad. In the presence of the G10, the G20 still has incentives to appear. In all configurations, India benefits the most from the G20 implementation. However, the presence of the G90 eliminates the incentives for the G20 to appear. Indeed, the G90 allows small economies to step back in the arena and enforce their participation constraints; they empty the core of the game, meaning that there is only one possible outcome (that is, s1000, which is either the status quo or the unique liberalization of services, depending on the possibility of negotiating in this sector). The presence or absence of other players cannot modify the outcome.

9 An existing coalition with the sum of its members' GDP shares larger than the fixed threshold uses its right of veto as long as the individual rationality of each of its members is not satisfied.

10 We consider that s1551 is the scenario closest to the US-EU agreement that preceded the Cancun meeting.

TABLE 3.10 Effects of the apparition of the G10 coalition on its members (US$ billions)

Country	Unweighted	GDP weights	Democratic weights
EFTA (European Free Trade Association)	0	4.6	0.3
Japan	0	44.4	1.2
Republic of Korea–Taiwan	0	4.2	0.2

Source: Authors' calculation.

Note: G10 = A group of 10 countries mainly from the Organisation for Economic Co-operation and Development (OECD), including Japan, the Republic of Korea, and Taiwan, China. This table represents the change in real income for the different members of the G10 if this coalition appears. The exclusion threshold is set to 4 percent of world GDP, thus the reference situation is the case where only the United States, the EU, and Japan participate in the negotiations. The presence of the G90 and/or G20 does not allow the G10 to modify the outcome of the game and these cases are not represented here.

TABLE 3.11 Effects of the apparition of the G20 coalition on its members (US$ billions)

	G20 facing the Triad (United States, EU, Japan)			G20 facing the Triad and the G10		
Country or Region	Unweighted	GDP weights	Democratic weights	Unweighted	GDP weights	Democratic weights
Argentina	0.6	**1.0**	0.6	0.6	0.4	0.4
Brazil	**0.9**	**0.8**	**0.9**	**0.9**	**0.9**	**0.9**
Chile	**0.1**	**0.1**	**0.1**	**0.1**	**0.1**	**0.1**
China	1.1	3.9	1.1	1.1	0.8	0.8
India	1.6	**3.6**	1.6	1.6	1.0	1.1
Mexico	1.4	**2.5**	1.4	1.4	1.0	1.0
Rest of Central America	0.1	**0.3**	0.1	0.1	0.1	0.1
Rest of South America	0.2	**0.5**	0.2	0.2	0.1	0.2
South Africa	0.1	0.3	0.1	0.1	0.1	0.1
Thailand	0.1	0.3	0.1	0.1	0.1	0.1

Source: Authors' calculation.

Note: G10 = A group of 10 countries mainly from the Organisation for Economic Co-operation and Development (OECD), including Japan, the Republic of Korea, and Taiwan, China; G20 = A group of 20 emerging countries and least developed countries that is led by Brazil and India and also includes China and South Africa. This table represents the change in real income for the different members of the G20 if this coalition appears. The exclusion threshold is set to 4 percent of world GDP. The presence of the G90, a group of 90 poor countries, does not allow the G20 to modify the outcome of the game and this case is not represented here. Figures in bold indicate countries that move from losses to positive gains with the implementation of the coalition.

TABLE 3.12 Effects on G90 coalition for its members of other coalitions (US$ billions)

G90 facing other coalition	Bangladesh	Mediterranean countries	Africa south of the Sahara
Triad			
Unweighted	**0.3**	−1.3	**1.1**
GDP weighted	**0.3**	0.8	**1.5**
Democratic weights	**0.3**	−1.3	**1.1**
Triad + G10			
Unweighted	**0.3**	−1.3	**1.1**
GDP weighted	**0.3**	−1.7	**0.9**
Democratic weights	**0.3**	−1.6	**1.0**
Triad + G20			
Unweighted	**0.2**	−2.5	**0.6**
GDP weighted	**0.3**	−2.3	**0.7**
Democratic weights	**0.2**	−2.5	**0.6**
Triad + G10 + G20			
Unweighted	**0.2**	−2.5	**0.6**
GDP weighted	**0.3**	−2.3	**0.7**
Democratic weights	**0.2**	−2.5	**0.6**

Source: Authors' calculation.

Note: G90 = A group of 90 poor countries with a more defensive trade strategy aimed to advance pro-poor policies (most African countries are members of this group). This table represents the change in real income for the different members of the G90 if this coalition appears. The exclusion threshold is set to 4 percent of world GDP. South Africa is not represented here but the existence of the G90 always reduces its gains. Figures in bold indicate countries that move from losses to positive gains with the implementation of the coalition.

The G90 (Table 3.12) is the most interesting coalition. By allowing Bangladesh to reenter the negotiation, the presence of this coalition empties the core of the game. The G90 improves the situation of both African countries south of the Sahara and Bangladesh by maintaining the status quo. For the Mediterranean countries, in contrast, status quo in AMA and NAMA is not the best outcome. These countries would prefer a liberalization scheme that is agreed upon by the largest players. For this reason the G90 brings them net losses. Finally, the G90 is never useful for South Africa; this country is always better off when playing with the G20. These two last remarks illustrate the heterogeneity of the interests inside the G90 coalition. We conclude by looking at the consequences for the EU and US gains of the implementation of these different coalitions (Table 3.13). As expected, in most situations,

TABLE 3.13 Effects of the coalitions on the EU and US gains (US$ billions)

	Unweighted		GDP weights		Democratic weights	
Game configuration	EU25	US	EU25	US	EU25	US
Triad + G10	0.0	0.0	1.9	–2.8	1.4	–0.4
Triad + G20	–11.4	–2.0	–3.0	–5.1	–11.4	–2.0
Triad + G90	–27.5	0.1	–18.3	–3.3	–27.5	0.1
Triad + G10 + G20	–11.4	–2.0	–3.0	–5.1	–11.4	–2.0
Triad + G10 + G90	–27.5	0.1	–18.3	–3.3	–27.5	0.1
Triad + G20 + G90	–27.5	0.1	–18.3	–3.3	–27.5	0.1
Triad + G10 + G20 + G90	–27.5	0.1	–18.3	–3.3	–27.5	0.1

Source: Authors' calculation.

Note: EU25 = European Union 25 countries; the Triad is composed of the EU, the United States, and Japan—the three countries for which GDP is above 4 percent of world GDP; 4 percent of world GDP is the threshold we have chosen for participating in the negotiations. The reference situation is the scenario when only the Triad participates in the negotiations.

the gains of the two major players are negatively impacted by the formation of counterpowers.

Conclusion

In this chapter the simultaneous use of CGE analysis and game theory allows us to explain some strategic features of the DDA trade negotiations. In particular, we see that AMA talks play a crucial role: they increase the overall gain but also reduce the inequalities driven by NAMA liberalization. Simultaneously, trade negotiation cannot take place if only liberalization in agriculture is negotiated, as the core of the game would be empty. Moreover, the adoption of tariff-harmonizing formulae (more cuts in higher import tariffs) leads to greatly increased global gains. Finally, the dramatic complexity in the current structure of protection and market access convincingly explains why trade negotiations are so difficult today. Thus it does not seem surprising that our game-theoretic CGE approach concludes with a rather pessimistic statement: the Nash solution is often the status quo.

Obviously, the number of negotiating members adds constraints to the bargaining program. We show that the exclusion of countries/regions with GDPs below a certain threshold drastically improves the efficiency of the negotiation process, regardless of the governments' objective. We also demonstrate that the formation of coalitions is a potential means through which developing countries/regions may block solutions imposed by rich countries/regions. The G20 coalition is successful with the inclusion of the SDT clause and with less liberalization of the industrial sector. Moreover, the G10 is always beneficial for its members. We also consider the expansion of the domain of trade negotiation. Negotiating in services, industry, and agriculture is more efficient than negotiating in only industry and agriculture, which is itself more efficient than negotiating in agriculture alone. Side payments may also be a workable solution, as they allow large agents to maximize the size of the cake, while compensating losers. When we implement a cooperative solution of the game with side payments, we find that these international payments represent a significant share of global income gain. Notably, however, in one solution side payments are used to remunerate very rich countries/regions (for example, the United States). Both characteristics of this cooperative solution make it implausible.

An illustration of the realistic aspect of our conclusions is that previously WTO Director-General Pascal Lamy combined the three solutions that we propose herein, in the hopes of breaking the stalemate: (1) He has sought to expand the coverage of the negotiations. We feel that more could be done in this regard, especially with the inclusion of the Singapore issues.[11] (2) He has tried to reach an agreement between a limited number of WTO members (most of the WTO Geneva meetings in July 2008 took place among seven countries). (3) He has sought to implement side payments ("Aid for Trade" can be interpreted along these lines). There may be other means to compensate for losses related to erosion of preferences, such as granting new preferences (for example, see the duty-free quota-free regime given by rich countries to LDCs at the Hong Kong Ministerial). Given the complexity of the current trade and protection structures, negotiators must be highly creative when designing a final trade agreement that could be accepted by all WTO members.

Bibliography

Bagwell, K., and R. Staiger. 1999. "An Economic Theory of GATT." *American Economic Review* 89: 215–248.

———. 2002. *The Economics of the World Trading System*. Boston, MA, US: Massachusetts Institute of Technology Press.

Baldwin, R., and R. Clarke. 1988. "Game Modeling Multilateral Trade Negotiations." *Journal of Policy Modeling* 9 (2): 257–284.

11 The Singapore issues (trade and investment, trade and competition policy, transparency in government procurement, and trade facilitation) were introduced to the WTO agenda at the December 1996 Ministerial Conference in Singapore.

Bchir, M., L. Fontagné, and S. Jean. 2005. *From Bound Duties to Actual Protection: Industrial Liberalisation in the Doha Round.* CEPII Working Papers 2005-12. Paris: CEPII (Centre d'Etudes Prospectives et d'Informations Internationales).

Bchir, M., S. Jean, and D. Laborde. 2006. "Binding Overhang and Tariff-Cutting Formulas." *Review of World Economics* 142 (2): 207–232.

Bouët, A., Y. Decreux, L. Fontagné, S. Jean, and D. Laborde. 2008. "Assessing Applied Protection across the World." *Review of International Economics* 16 (5): 850–863.

Bouët, A., and D. Laborde. 2010. "Assessing the Potential Cost of a Failed Doha Round." *World Trade Review* 9: 319–351.

CEPII (Centre d'Etudes Prospectives et d'Informations Internationales). 2001. "Chelem on the Net." Accessed 2001. www.cepii.fr/anglaisgraph/bdd/chelem.htm.

Decreux, Y., and H. Valin. 2007. *MIRAGE, Updated Version of the Model for Trade Policy Analysis Focus on Agriculture and Dynamics.* CEPII Working Paper 2007-15. October. Paris: Centre d'Etudes Prospectives et d'Informations Internationales.

Dimaranan, B. V., and R. A. McDougall. 2005. *Global Trade, Assistance, and Production: The GTAP 6 DataBase.* Center for Global Trade Analysis. West Lafayette, IN, US: Purdue University.

Economist. 2008. "So Near and Yet So Far." May 8.

Evenett, S. J. 2005a. "From 'Trade versus Aid' to 'Aid for Trade'?" Accessed 2008. https://www.alexandria.unisg.ch/22674/1/EvenettWTOnews2September2005.pdf.

———. 2005b. "Some Tough Love on 'Aid for Trade.'" *Intereconomics* 40 (6): 326–329.

Francois, J., and B. Hoekman. 1999. *Market Access in the Service Sectors.* Amsterdam: Tinbergen Institute.

Francois, J., H. van Meijl, and F. van Tongeren. 2005. "Trade Liberalization in the Doha Development Round." *Economic Policy* 20 (42): 349–391.

Grossman, G., and E. Helpman. 1995. "Trade Wars and Trade Talks." *Journal of Political Economy* 103: 675–708.

Hertel, T. W., and R. Keeney. 2006. "Assessing the Impact of WTO Reforms on World Agricultural Markets: A New Approach." In *Agricultural Commodity Markets and Trade: New Approaches to Analyzing Market Structure and Instability,* edited by A. Sarris and D. Hallam, 402–425. Rome: FAO (Food and Agriculture Organization of the United Nations), Edward Elgar.

Hoekman, B. 1996. "Assessing the General Agreement on Trade in Services." In *The Uruguay Round and the Developing Countries,* edited by W. Martin and A. Winters, 88–124. Cambridge, UK: Cambridge University Press for the World Bank.

Johnson, H. 1953. "Optimum Tariffs and Retaliation." *Review of Economic Studies* 21 (2): 142–153.

———. 1965. "An Economic Theory of Protectionism, Tariff Bargaining, and the Formation of Customs Unions." *Journal of Political Economy* 73 (3): 256–283.

Kalai, E., and M. Smorodinsky. 1975. "Other Solutions to Nash's Bargaining Problem." *Econometrica* 43 (3): 513–518.

Kalirajan, K., G. McGuire, D. Nguyen-Hong, and M. Schuele. 2000. "The Price Impact of Restrictions on Banking Services." In *Impediments to Trade in Services: Measurement and Policy Implications,* edited by C. Findlay and T. Warre, 215–230. London and New York: Routledge.

Krueger, A. 2003. Speech presented at the Fifth WTO Ministerial Conference, Cancun, September 10. Accessed 2004. www.imf.org/external/np/speeches/2003/091003.htm.

Mas-Colell, A., M. Whinston, and J. Green. 1995. *Microeconomic Theory.* New York: Oxford University Press.

Mayer, W. 1981. "Theoretical Considerations on Negotiated Tariff Adjustments." *Oxford Economic Papers* 33 (1): 135–153.

Messerlin, P. 1995. *La Nouvelle Organisation Mondiale du Commerce.* Paris: Dunod.

Nash, J. 1953. "Two-person Cooperative Games." *Econometrica* 21 (1): 128–140.

Riezman, R. 1982. "Tariff Retaliation from a Strategic Viewpoint." *Southern Economic Journal* 48 (3): 583–593.

Shapley, L. 1953. "A Value for N-Person Games." In *The Shapley Value: Essays in Honor of Lloyd S. Shapley*, edited by A. Roth, 307–317. London: Cambridge University Press.

Stiglitz, J., and A. Charlton. 2006. "Aid for Trade: A Report for the Commonwealth Secretariat." Columbia University Academic Commons. Accessed February 22, 2017. https://academic commons.columbia.edu/catalog/ac:126953.

Trewin, R. 2000. "A Price-Impact Measure of Impediments to Trade in Telecommunications Services." In *Impediments to Trade in Services: Measurement and Policy Implications,* edited by C. Findlay and T. Warre, 101–118. London and New York: Routledge.

Tyers, R. 1990. "Implicit Policy Preferences and the Assessment of Negotiable Trade Policy Reforms." *European Economic Review* 34 (7): 1399–1426.

van Tongeren, F., H. van Meijl, and Y. Surry. 2001. "Global Models Applied to Agricultural and Trade Policies: A Review and Assessment." *Agricultural Economics* 26 (2): 149–172.

Van der Mensbrugghe, D., and J. Beghin. 2004. *Global Agricultural Liberalization: An In-depth Assessment of What Is at Stake.* CARD Working Paper. Ames, IA, US: Center for Agricultural and Rural Development, Iowa State University.

WTO (World Trade Organization). 2004. "The Doha Declaration Explained." Accessed 2004. https://www.wto.org/english/tratop_e/dda_e/dohaexplained_e.htm.

Chapter 4

FORMULAS FOR FAILURE? WERE THE DOHA TARIFF FORMULAS TOO AMBITIOUS FOR SUCCESS?

David Laborde and Will Martin

Determining the size of tariff reductions to be undertaken on particular tariff lines is central in any tariff negotiation.[1] One approach to doing this is the "request and offer" principle that was used in General Agreement on Tariffs and Trade (GATT) negotiations prior to the Kennedy Round.[2] This has the enormous advantage of allowing countries to choose the products they liberalize and the extent to which they liberalize trade in them. Unfortunately, as demonstrated by Baldwin and Lage (1971) and Baldwin (1986), it is likely to be unsuccessful in obtaining many agreements on tariff reductions that would ex post be regarded as improvements over the status quo. This problem arises because the benefit to the *demandeur* of any tariff cut by its partner is diluted by the subsequent extension of access on a nondiscriminatory basis. This view was consistent with the outcome of the first five GATT negotiations which, after initially encouraging progress in the first Geneva Round, yielded only small reductions in applied tariffs.

The approach adopted in the Kennedy and Tokyo Rounds, and attempted in the Doha Development Agenda, was to specify a formula for tariff reductions for each member. In principle, this overcomes the free-rider problem involved with bilateral negotiations. Every member can see what is on offer and can take this into account in its evaluation of the proposal. There are many possible formula approaches available for use in trade negotiations (Francois and Martin 2003), but there is neither clarity about the objectives of the negotiators nor any obvious link between the formula chosen and the objectives of negotiators. While we have some broad guidance from economic theory about the approaches to reform that are likely to yield Pareto improvements in economic welfare, we have essentially no guidance on what will

1 This chapter was originally published as Laborde and Martin (2015).

2 The Kennedy Round was the sixth round of negotiations under the GATT era from 1964 to 1967.

generate the greatest political resistance. Key questions include whether negotiators are seeking to increase the efficiency of their economies subject to the limited political capital provided by market access gains, or whether they seek to offer just enough expansion in market access to bring about an agreement, while minimizing the political costs at home in achieving this outcome.

The Doha Agenda approach ultimately involved formulas that make deeper cuts in the higher tariffs. This is particularly the case in nonagricultural market access (NAMA), where the famous "Swiss formula" used in the Tokyo Round is proposed for tariff cutting. In agriculture, the formula used is a less-aggressive compromise—the "tiered formula"—which places tariffs in tiers, with progressively higher reductions in higher tariffs. These approaches are highly desirable from an economic point of view because higher tariffs generate much higher efficiency costs in the imposing country than do lower tariffs. A key problem with the formula approach, however, is that some tariffs—protected by particularly strong interest groups—are likely to need to be exempted from the general formula treatment for political reasons. In the Kennedy and Tokyo Rounds members sought to keep the number of exceptions to a minimum. This proved an insufficiently rigorous constraint, with the addition of exceptions threatening to spiral, putting the goal of liberalization at risk. In the Doha Agenda negotiators tried a different approach, by specifying constraints on the range of products that could be exempted from the formula treatment, while leaving the specific products to be given less-than-formula cuts to the discretion of each country's policy makers.

Although this was an important new approach to trade reform, it encountered several difficulties that may have contributed to the travails of the negotiations. The first was that the formulas chosen were particularly progressive in their application—cutting the highest tariffs by the largest percentage. This appears to have contributed to pressure for what we see as a particularly comprehensive and complex set of exceptions. This pressure for exceptions, and the poorly defined nature of some of the exception rules, resulted in the loss of the transparency about benefits that is meant to be one of the key advantages of a formula-based negotiation over one based on request and offer procedures. When the negotiations collapsed in 2008, the chief negotiator for the United States—the most experienced country in the negotiations and perhaps the one with access to the greatest analytical capacity—expressed concern that the draft agreement was a "Black Box" in terms of its impacts on market access (see Schwab 2011).

Given this lack of transparency, analysis of the proposals offered in the negotiations required very careful analysis of the likely ways in which countries would choose to use the numerous flexibilities available to them (see, for example, Jean, Laborde, Martin 2011) and careful use of aggregation (Laborde, Martin, and van der Mensbrugghe 2011) to allow for the sharp changes in tariff profiles resulting from the use of the formulas and exceptions. Only with this analysis did it become clear that the proposed agreements, despite their flaws, offered substantial improvements in market access and economic welfare (Martin and Mattoo 2011). The political costs of reform are particularly important in the context of the Doha Agenda, because of the difficult landscape on which the Doha Round is taking place, with low tariffs on the industrial product tariffs that have provided the traditional fuel for negotiations (Martin and Messerlin 2007). Bouët and Laborde (2010) explored this background using a game-theoretic approach and found that given the heterogeneity of WTO members, careful design of formulas and flexibilities would be needed to achieve an outcome that was welfare-improving for all countries.

In this chapter we outline the nature of the tariff-cutting rules and exceptions under consideration in the Doha Round and their implications for market access. Because they are very different in their details, we outline the agricultural proposals first and then those for nonagricultural market access. We focus on the December 2008 proposals that were under discussion when the negotiations collapsed and have not subsequently been modified, although negotiators could choose an alternative starting point if the negotiations were renegotiated. We consider the political costs of securing agreement under proportional tariff cuts and the key tariff-cutting approaches in the latest Doha proposals.

The Agricultural Formula Proposals

Agricultural markets remain highly distorted by border measures in both developed and developing countries. A central feature of the draft agreement for agriculture is a tiered formula for cutting agricultural tariffs, which provides for larger proportional cuts on higher—and hence more economically costly—tariff rates. The Modalities (WTO 2008a) involve four bands, with the boundaries for developed and developing countries given in Table 4.1, together with the proportional cuts to be made in *bound* agricultural tariffs in each band. The cuts for developing countries are two-thirds of those for developed countries because of the long-standing view in the WTO that special and differential treatment for developing countries implies smaller tariff cuts than for the industrial countries. The bands for developing countries are

TABLE 4.1 The tiered formula for cuts in agricultural tariff bindings

	Developed		Developing	
Band	Range (%)	Cut (%)	Range (%)	Cut (%)
A	$t_0 \leq 20$	50	$t_0 \leq 30$	33.3
B	$20 < t_0 \leq 50$	57	$30 < t_0 \leq 80$	38
C	$50 < t_0 \leq 75$	64	$80 < t_0 \leq 130$	42.7
D	$t_0 > 75$	70	$t_0 > 130$	46.7
Average cut	Min	54	Max	36

Source: Authors' summary based on WTO (2008a).

wider partly for this reason, and partly because the higher average tariffs in developing countries means they might otherwise face higher average cuts in their tariffs than the industrial countries.

Unlike the Swiss formula used in the nonagricultural market access negotiations, this formula does not provide a smooth mapping from initial to final tariffs. The larger cuts applying to tariffs in the higher bands mean that tariffs just above the boundaries between the bands end up somewhat lower than some tariffs in the lower bands, resulting in the surprising saw-tooth tariff mapping depicted in Figure 4.1.

To address the interests of particular groups of countries, the modalities also include a wide range of special features, such as deeper cuts on tropical and tariff-escalation products, and flexibilities that allow countries to make smaller cuts on "sensitive" products and zero cuts on "special" products.[3] Some groups of countries, such as recently acceded countries, are also able to make smaller or zero cuts in their agricultural tariffs. The details of these exceptions, and the approaches used to model their impacts, are summarized in Table 4.2 and discussed in Laborde and Martin (2011a). Another important factor also discussed in Laborde and Martin (2011a) is the impact of the many gaps between bound and applied tariff rates: The formula is applied to bound tariffs, so how the formula ultimately affects applied tariffs is a complicated issue.

3 In addition, for products covered by tariff-rate quotas (TRQ), flexibilities will be mitigated by an increase of existing quotas. It is noteworthy to underline that beyond the tariffs and the size of the quota, the administration method of TRQs is critical to measure the final market access delivered by this instrument, and the 2013 Bali Package (see WT/L/914) ensures effective market access.

FIGURE 4.1 **The pattern of tariff cuts under the tiered formula**

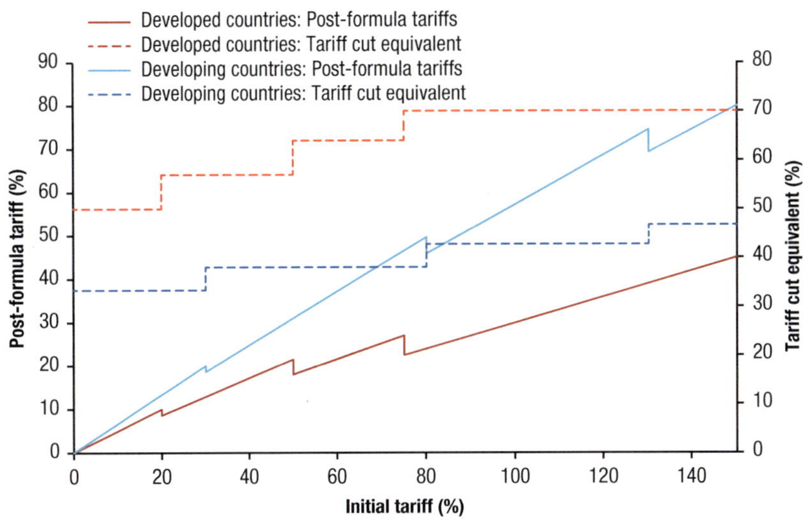

Source: Authors' summary based on WTO (2008a).

The scenarios for which we provide results are:

- **Baseline:** Tariffs that would apply in the absence of a DDA agreement in 2025. These estimates are based on 2004 tariffs, with adjustments for internationally binding commitments to reform.
- **B:** Tariffs following implementation of the DDA formula without flexibilities.
- **C:** Tariffs following implementation of the formula with country exceptions, such as those for least developed countries (LDCs), small and vulnerable economies (SVEs), and recently acceded members (RAMs).
- **D:** Tariffs after the tariff-cutting formulas with flexibilities for countries and products.

In Table 4.3, we see that the formulas applied *without exceptions* (scenario B) would result in a decline from 14.6 to 9 percent in average *applied* agricultural tariffs worldwide. In the WTO developed countries, the result is a cut of more than 50 percent in applied rates, from 15.4 to 7.0 percent. In WTO developing countries other than the LDCs, the reduction is from 13.7 percent to 11.2 percent, a cut that is smaller than in the industrial countries partly

TABLE 4.2 Key elements of the agricultural tariff cuts used in the analysis for agriculture

Element of negotiation	Developed Countries	Developing Countries	Least Developed Countries (LDCs)	Small and Vulnerable Economies (SVEs)	Very Recently Acceded Members (VRAMs)	Recently Acceded Members (RAMs)
Bands	0/20/50/75	0/30/80/130	no liberal-ization	as developing countries	no liberal-ization	
Proportional cut	50/57/64/70	33.3/38/42.7/46.7	no liberal-ization	Developing countries' cut reduced by 10 points.	no liberal-ization	developing countries' cut reduced by 8 points
	Scaled proportionately if the average cut (including sensitive, tropical, and tariff escalation products) < 54% in industrial countries; if > 36% in developing countries					
Sensitive products	5% of lines	6.7% of lines	no liberal-ization	as developing countries with cut reduced by 10 points	no liberal-ization	
	If > 30% in top tier, 2 percentage points more					
Special products		14% of lines; 40% no cut and 60% with 15% cut	no liberal-ization		no liberal-ization	
Tariff escalation products	Cut from next higher tier applied. In top tier add 6 per-centage points to the cut		no liberal-ization		no liberal-ization	
Tropical products	t ≤ 10, cut to zero; 10 < t ≤ 75, 70% cut; t > 75, 78%		no liberal-ization		no liberal-ization	
Cotton	Duty-free access by developed and those developing countries able to do so to LDCs		no liberal-ization		no liberal-ization	

Source: Laborde and Martin (2011a).

Note: Republic of Korea is treated as a developing country for agriculture. Economies treated as SVEs were: Antigua and Barbuda, Barbados, Belize, Bolivia, Botswana, Brunei Darussalam, Cameroon, Democratic Republic of the Congo, Côte d'Ivoire, Cuba, Dominica, Dominican Republic, Ecuador, El Salvador, Fiji, Gabon, Georgia, Ghana, Grenada, Guatemala, Guyana, Honduras, Jamaica, Jordan, Kenya, Macau, Mauritius, Mongolia, Namibia, Nicaragua, Nigeria, Panama, Papua New Guinea, Paraguay, Saint Kitts and Nevis, Saint Lucia, Saint Vincent and the Grenadines, Sri Lanka, Trinidad and Tobago, Uruguay, and Zimbabwe. RAMs treatment includes China, Croatia, Ecuador, Jordan, Mongolia, Oman, Panama, and Taiwan, China. VRAM treatment (no cuts) include Albania, Armenia, Georgia, Kyrgyz Republic, Republic of Moldova, the former Yugoslav Republic of Macedonia, Saudi Arabia, Tonga, Ukraine, and Viet Nam. The "special" product percentages are higher than in the December 2008 modalities because of the "serious objections" of some developing countries.

TABLE 4.3 Average applied tariffs levied on World Trade Organization (WTO) agricultural products by scenario (%)

	Scenario			
Country or region	Baseline	B	C	D
Brazil	4.8	4.7	4.7	4.8
China	7.8	5.3	6.3	7.5
EU27	15.9	6.6	6.6	10.2
India	59.2	54.6	54.6	59.2
Japan	29.8	14.0	14.0	20.4
United States	4.8	2.1	2.1	3.0
World Bank classification				
All countries	14.6	9.0	9.2	11.9
Developing countries (non-LDCs)	13.3	11.3	11.7	13.2
High-income countries	15.5	7.5	7.6	11.1
Least developed countries (LDCs)	12.5	12.2	12.5	12.5
WTO Classification				
Developed WTO	15.4	7.0	7.0	10.4
Developing WTO (non-LDCs)	13.7	11.2	11.6	13.6
Normal developing WTO	15.1	12.3	12.3	15.0
Recently acceded member (RAM) WTO	13.4	12.8	13.0	13.4
Small and vulnerable economies (SVE) WTO	10.7	7.8	9.5	10.5

Source: Laborde and Martin (2011a).

because of key features of the formula—the smaller cuts and higher-tier boundaries laid out in Table 4.1—and the greater binding overhang in many developing countries. Indeed, the cut on bound tariffs is about 61 percent for high-income countries and 38 percent for low- and middle-income countries, while applied tariffs are reduced by 52 and 15 percent respectively.

Without exceptions, the cut in the EU27 applied agricultural tariff is from 15.9 to 6.6 percent—a cut of almost 60 percent of its initial value. In the United States the corresponding cut is from 4.8 to 2.1 percent—a reduction of 56 percent from its initial value. The cut in Japan's average applied agricultural tariff is almost 16 percentage points, from 29.8 percent to 14 percent—a reduction of over 50 percent. In Canada the cut would be from 10.7 to 5.1 percent, a reduction of more than 53 percent. The flexibilities for commodities—sensitive and special products—included in Scenario D more than halve the worldwide cut in tariffs, from 5.4 percent with only country flexibilities to 2.7 percent with country and commodity flexibilities. Interestingly, it is in the industrial countries that the cut in applied tariffs is reduced the most—with the tariff after flexibilities declining from 7.4 percentage points to 5 percentage points. In low- and middle-income (non-LDC) countries, these flexibilities reduce the cut from 1.6 percentage points to 0.1 percentage points—a larger proportional reduction than for high-income countries but a smaller one in percentage point terms.

Nonagricultural Market Access Proposals

The central feature of the modalities for nonagricultural market access (NAMA) is the use of a nonlinear tariff-cutting formula. The formula is applied on base rates equal to existing bound tariffs or average applied most favored nation (MFN) rates (period 1999–2001) plus 25 percent for currently unbound tariff lines. The tariff formula in this case is the highly nonlinear Swiss formula, which reduces the highest tariffs by the most. The Swiss formula requires tariffs in *ad valorem* terms, and all tariffs are to be converted into *ad valorem* terms and bound in those terms.

The Swiss formula is defined as:

$$t_1 = \frac{a_i t_0}{a_i + t_0} \qquad (1)$$

where t_1 is the tariff after application of the formula; t_0 is the tariff rate before application of the formula; and a_i is a coefficient for group *i,* which differs between developed and developing countries, and in line with the decisions of each developing country about the number of products it would like to subject to smaller tariff cuts.

The operation of the formula is perhaps most easily seen graphically, as in Figure 4.2, where the upper line shows the tariff after a formula with a coefficient of 20 percent, while the lower line shows the results of the formula with a coefficient of 8 percent. As is clear, the Swiss formula cuts the highest tariffs by the most, with tariffs of 100 percent being cut to 16.7 percent when using the coefficient of 20 percent and to 7.4 percent with a coefficient of 8 percent. In contrast, tariffs of 1 percent are barely cut in either case. Since the highest tariffs generate the largest economic costs, the Swiss formula is highly desirable from an economic efficiency viewpoint. Politically, it is much more challenging, because it involves cutting high tariffs on products for which policy makers receive strong support for protection (Jean, Laborde, and Martin 2011). When it was used in the Tokyo Round of the GATT (1974–1979), it proved difficult to avoid substantial numbers of exceptions (Baldwin 1986),

FIGURE 4.2 The Swiss formula for tariff cutting (%)

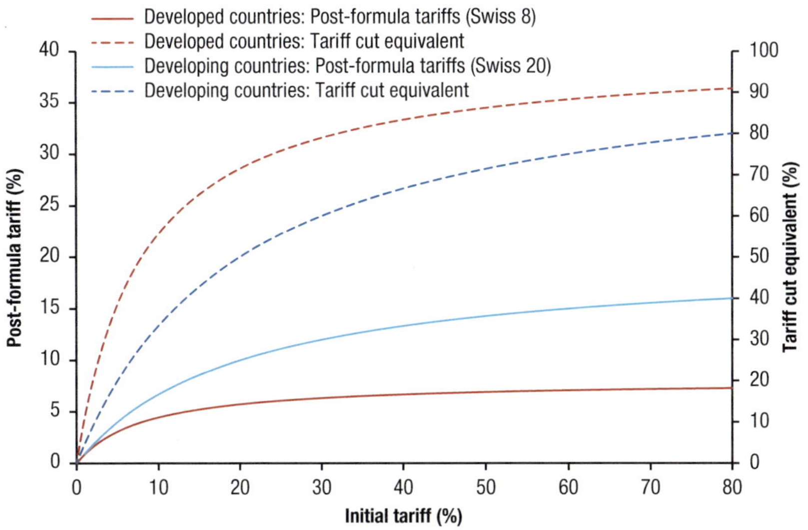

Source: Authors.

a problem that has recurred for developing countries in the Doha negotiations (Falconer 2008; Schwab 2011), although the industrial countries have been willing to consider its use without exceptions. The modalities provide for a single value of a_i of 8 percent for industrial countries and three different choices for developing countries: 20 percent, 22 percent, or 25 percent. With a coefficient of 25, no flexibilities would be available. Choosing lower coefficients allows members more access to flexibilities, as specified in Table 4.4.

Although the formula was originally intended to apply to all developing countries, many exceptions were made with the result that only around 20 developing countries would actually apply the formula. Details of these exceptions—which applied to SVEs, LDCs, and countries with less than 35 percent binding coverage (so-called Para 6 countries)—are given in Laborde and Martin (2011b), together with a discussion of the impact of the tariff cuts being implemented for bound rates given the frequent, large gaps between bound and applied tariffs. Where the modalities offered a choice of approaches, we followed the approach of Jean, Laborde, and Martin (2011, 2014) by using a political welfare function: identifying a policy maker's objective function to identify the option that would minimize the loss of policy makers' welfare. The political welfare function was also used to allocate the 22 developing countries undertaking NAMA tariff reductions with the Swiss formula to the

TABLE 4.4 Tariff-cutting formula menu for the NAMA negotiations

Elements of negotiation	Developed countries	Developing countries	Least developed countries (LDCs)	Paragraph 6 countries
Formula	Swiss 8	20 (i): No cuts on 6.5%/7.5% of lines/imports; 20 (ii): ½ cuts on 14%/16% of lines/imports; 22 (i): No cuts on 5%/5% of lines/imports; 22 (ii) ½ cuts on 10%/10% of lines/imports; 25: No flexibilities	No liberalization	No liberalization
Flexibility	None			
Unbound	Most favored nations (MFN) 2001 + 25%			

Source: Laborde and Martin (2011b).

Note: NAMA = nonagricultural market access. Members self-selected developing- or developed-country status. Members likely selecting developed-country status include members of the European Union, plus Australia, Canada, Iceland, New Zealand, Norway, Switzerland, and the United States. The Republic of Korea is a developed country for NAMA. LDCs are identified in the UN list of least developed countries. Economies treated as SVEs for NAMA were Antigua and Barbuda, Barbados, Belize, Bolivia, Botswana, Brunei Darussalam, Cameroon, Cuba, Dominica, Dominican Republic, Ecuador, El Salvador, Fiji, Gabon, Georgia, Ghana, Grenada, Guatemala, Guyana, Honduras, Jamaica, Jordan, Kenya, Macau, Mauritius, Mongolia, Namibia, Nicaragua, Panama, Papua New Guinea, Paraguay, Saint Kitts and Nevis, Saint Lucia, Saint Vincent and the Grenadines, Sri Lanka, Trinidad and Tobago, Uruguay, and Zimbabwe. Paragraph 6 economies (those with less than 35 percent of tariffs bound) were identified as Cameroon, China, Democratic Republic of the Congo, Cuba, Ghana, Kenya, Macau, Mauritius, Nigeria, Sri Lanka, Suriname, and Zimbabwe. The following VRAMs are not required to make any tariff cuts beyond their accession commitments: Albania, Armenia, Cape Verde, Kyrgyz Republic, the former Yugoslav Republic of Macedonia, Republic of Moldova, Mongolia, Saudi Arabia, Tonga, Viet Nam, and Ukraine.

option that minimized the political cost of NAMA tariff cuts. A summary of the way the tariff-cutting menu was implemented is given in Table 4.4.

The tariff scenarios reported are:

- **Baseline:** Tariffs that would apply in the absence of a DDA agreement in 2025. These are based on tariffs in 2004, with adjustments for internationally binding commitments to reform.
- **B:** Tariffs following implementation of the DDA formula without flexibilities.
- **C:** Tariffs following implementation of the formula with country exceptions, such as those for LDCs, SVEs, and RAMs.
- **D:** Tariffs after the tariff-cutting formulas with flexibilities for countries and products.

The tariff-cutting formulas are applied to bound tariffs rather than to applied tariffs, and hence it is useful to first examine the implications of the formula and exceptions for the level of bound tariffs. We use the standard assumption in this literature that the applied rate at the finest available level is cut only when, and to the extent that, the new bound tariff falls below the initial applied tariff rate.

TABLE 4.5 Average (trade-weighted) applied tariffs levied on World Trade Organization (WTO) nonagricultural products by scenario (%)

	Scenario			
Country or region	Baseline	B	C	D
Brazil	8.5	7.4	7.4	7.8
China	5.6	3.9	3.9	4.4
EU27	1.8	1.0	1.0	1.0
India	12.9	11.7	11.7	12.0
Japan	1.3	0.7	0.7	0.7
United States	1.5	0.8	0.8	0.8
World Bank Classification				
All countries	2.9	2.0	2.2	2.3
Low- and middle-income countries	6.1	4.6	5.0	5.3
High-income countries	1.6	1.0	1.0	1.0
Least developed countries (LDCs)	10.9	8.0	10.9	10.9
WTO Classification				
Developed WTO	1.7	1.0	1.0	1.0
Developing WTO non-LDCs	4.8	3.6	3.8	4.2
Normal Developing WTO	3.9	3.1	3.1	3.4
Recently acceded members (RAMs) WTO	9.5	7.1	9.5	9.5
Small and vulnerable economies (SVEs) WTO	5.3	3.9	4.0	4.4

Source: Laborde and Martin (2011b).

Moving to the reductions in applied tariff rates in Table 4.5, we see that, if the formulas were applied without exceptions, average tariffs would fall from 2.9 percent to 2.0 percent.[4] In the high-income countries, the reduction is from 1.6 percent to 1.0 percent, a reduction of 0.6 percentage points. Interestingly, the effect of the Swiss formula is strongly dampened by the existing trade and tariff structure: for developed economies, the average cut on bound tariffs will be below 50 percent due to the fact that 53 percent of their products—75 percent of their MFN imports—have tariffs of below 4 percent. In non-LDC low- and middle-income countries, the reduction is estimated to be from 6.1 percent to 4.6 percent: 2.5 percentage points, a cut of four-tenths of the original tariff. In some developing countries (such as Bangladesh, Pakistan, and Thailand), application of the formula alone would appear to result in

4 Under this no-flexibilities scenario, a coefficient of 25 is chosen for all developing countries.

substantial cuts in average tariffs.[5] When we consider the group of countries that would apply the standard developing-country formula, the reduction in tariffs is from 3.9 percent to 3.1 percent, a cut of 0.8 percentage points—a much smaller cut than would apply were this formula applied to the RAMs and SVEs. For low- and middle-income countries, the overall limited effect of the formula is driven by an average large binding overhang (an average reduction of 41 percent in bound tariffs translates to a 25 percent cut in applied tariffs).

Why So Much Political Resistance?

The formulas used in both the agricultural and nonagricultural negotiations were highly progressive, in terms of cutting the highest tariffs by the most. From an economic point of view, these are outstandingly good approaches to tariff reform, because the economic costs of a tariff rise with the square of the rate. But this economic virtue may have an associated downside. High tariffs are that way because there is strong political support for the beneficiaries of this high protection. If, as Falconer (2008) has suggested, the aggressive nature of these tariff-cutting formulas resulted in intense pressure for exceptions, excessive zeal in the tariff-cutting formulas may have contributed to the problems created by the exceptions—including the loss of market access liberalization, reduced efficiency of tariff cutting, and a lack of transparency about the implications of the reform.

A Political Economy Framework for Trade Reform

A fundamental challenge in choosing tariff-reduction formulas is a lack of clarity in the objectives of the formula. Trade theory provides little guidance on which specific forms to pick other than that progressive tariff cuts and proportional cuts are likely to result in Pareto improvements (Vousden 1990, Chapter 10)—but there is no guarantee that these will be politically acceptable. Anderson and Neary (2007) show that reducing multiple tariffs may lead to a "policy dilemma" since market access and welfare gains evolve differently when tariff dispersion is changed. They show that reforms that increase both welfare and market access may exist, but identifying them requires more information about the structure of the economy (for example, relative prices and cross-price effects) than is usually assumed.

In order to study the effects of the market access options proposed in the Doha Round, Jean, Laborde, and Martin (2011) used a political economy

5 In this scenario no duty-free quota-free (DFQF) initiative for LDCs is considered.

framework inspired by Grossman and Helpman (1994). The resulting political welfare function in (1) takes into account the political benefits resulting from a set of domestic prices and the economic costs of the trade barriers needed to sustain those prices.

$$G(\mathbf{p},u) = \frac{1}{a}\iota\mathbf{C}(\mathbf{p}) + (-z(\mathbf{p},u) + \mathbf{z}_{\mathbf{p}}'(\mathbf{p} - \mathbf{p}^{*})) \qquad (2)$$

where C(p) is the vector of benefits accruing to politicians at domestic prices, $\mathbf{p}$; ι is a vector of ones; a is the weight that politicians place on aggregate welfare relative to political support provided to them, $z(\mathbf{p},u) = e(\mathbf{p},u) - g(\mathbf{p})$ is the balance of trade measure of economic welfare, defined as the difference between the expenditure function $e(\mathbf{p},u)$ for utility level of the representative household, u, and a net revenue function defined to include revenue from production g(p), and tariff revenues, $\mathbf{z}_{\mathrm{p}}(\mathbf{p} - \mathbf{p}^{*})$; where $\mathbf{p}$ is a vector of domestic prices; $\mathbf{p}^{*}$ is the vector of world prices; so that $(\mathbf{p} - \mathbf{p}^{*})$ is a vector of specific tariff rates. $\mathbf{z}_{\mathrm{p}} = \mathbf{e}_{\mathrm{p}} - \mathbf{g}_{\mathrm{p}}$ is a vector of net imports, and $\mathbf{z}_{\mathrm{p}}'(\mathbf{p} - \mathbf{p}^{*})$ is tariff revenues, which are assumed to be redistributed to households.[6]

Assuming that the initial situation reflects a political-economy optimum, the initial tariff structure can be used to characterize the column sums of $\mathbf{C}$, which are the perceived net impacts of changes in the price of one product on political support. Writing these column sums divided by a as a row vector $\mathbf{h}$, and setting $\frac{dG}{dp} = 0$, yields a potentially observable expression for $\mathbf{h}$ at the initial domestic price vector. The resulting equation reveals politicians' preferences at the margin by equating the marginal political benefits to politicians of providing protection with the marginal economic costs they are willing to incur in order to provide this support:

$$\mathbf{h} = -(\mathbf{p}^{0} - \mathbf{p}^{*})'\mathbf{z}^{0}_{\mathrm{pp}} \qquad (3)$$

Here, we focus on the short-run case where the political influence of a given sector (or product) is assumed to be constant over the relevant political cycle.

Figure 4.3 considers the case of a single tariff. The marginal political benefits, 1/a . MC, rise with the level of the tariff, but less rapidly than the social costs, or the protection rate would be infinite. The short-run contribution function is represented by the line h because, as shown by Hillman (1982), short-run political support from firms is likely related to current output rather than the output after adjustment to a price change.

---

6 Throughout, bold characters refer to vectors or matrices while lower case characters refer to scalars.

FIGURE 4.3 Marginal political benefits and economic costs of a tariff

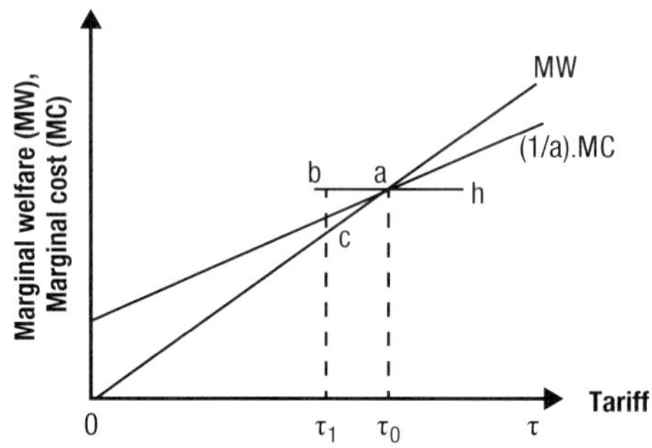

Source: Authors.

This analytical framework extended by Jean, Laborde, and Martin (2014) allows us to define the trade-off in terms of the political cost, welfare, and market access impacts of any trade policy reform. It also provides some potentially very helpful guidelines for reform in the particular case where cross-price effects in the demand matrix can be ignored, demand curves are linear, and small tariff changes are considered. For example, under these specific assumptions, it shows that a *benevolent policy maker* attempting to maximize the efficiency gains per unit of political cost will choose a proportional cut in all applied tariffs. In contrast, a *negotiator* seeking to minimize the political cost of achieving a given level of market access expansion will tend to reduce all *ad valorem* tariffs by a constant absolute amount. Finally, a *social planner* seeking to maximize the change in the economic efficiency to market access ratio will move toward a uniform tariff.

Even if these rules assume specific restrictions on the demand system, and assume that tariff-cutting formulas are imposed on applied tariffs, rather than bound tariffs, they provide essential insights. The traditional recommendation of the literature about harmonizing formulas aimed to reduce tariff heterogeneity and increase the efficiency of any trade reform no longer appears to be a first best choice when political constraints are considered. Indeed, the political cost of an aggressive formula may exhaust the political capital available during trade talks quickly, reducing strongly the capacity of the negotiation cycle to deliver large market access or welfare gains. At the opposite end, softer formulae such as proportional cuts may be a better compromise, where political capital is limited, to deliver either market access or welfare.

The problem of high political costs with the initially considered formula approach might be addressed by changing the formula or by considering alternative formulas. The second approach was floated by Falconer (2008), who suggested moving from the tiered-formula approach to an average-cut approach. A difficulty with this approach is that it might have prejudiced the negotiations by putting at risk their market access goal. Members who were free to choose their tariff cuts—even if subject to minimal constraints, such as a minimum cut in each tariff line—might use the smallest cuts on products that had high import-demand elasticities, high initial import volumes, or both in such a way that the market access opportunities created would not generate sufficient interest for the negotiations to proceed.

However, if discretionary exceptions to tariff-cutting formulas are to be allowed—as they have been in the Doha proposals—the design of these exceptions is important and should take into account political-economy considerations as well as the implications of the proposed exceptions for the market access of partner countries. The product exceptions allowed in the Doha proposals for agriculture involved only limits on the number of tariff lines, a totally inadequate discipline. As shown by Jean, Laborde, and Martin (2011), this approach allows members to apply small cuts to products that are important and for which large cuts in applied tariff rates would be required by the formula. As we have seen, this resulted in the cuts in applied tariffs being reduced dramatically relative to the formula cuts—particularly in high-income countries. As they showed, moving to disciplines on the share of trade covered would have sharply reduced the adverse consequences of exceptions for the negotiations. Constraining the impact of flexibilities by limiting the trade volume on which they could be applied was shown by Jean, Laborde, and Martin (2011) to be very helpful in reducing their adverse impacts on market access. Perhaps a better—but still potentially feasible—approach would be to constrain the use of flexibilities: the greater the flexibilities' impact, as measured on a mercantilist trade restrictiveness index of the type proposed by Anderson and Neary (2003), the greater the constraints on their use. Alternatively, a cost for flexibilities might be incorporated by requiring countries to negotiate exceptions from the general tariff formula via request-and-offer negotiations.

What Might Make an Agreement Feasible?

Using the AMA proposals and the Jean, Laborde, and Martin (2011, 2014) framework, we examine the implications of the formula relative to welfare and market gains versus political costs. For this analysis we assume that consumer preferences can be represented using a CES function covering all goods, and that policy makers ignore any impacts of their tariff changes on world prices.

Table 4.6 displays for all WTO members as a group, and for selected countries, the expected effects of the formula (Scenario C in Table 4.3), and of the formula plus flexibilities (Scenario D in Table 4.3) relative to a proportional cut in bound tariffs leading to the same market access outcomes. All relevant variables for policy makers (welfare gains, market access concessions—that is, import increases—and political costs) are expressed as a percentage of the Scenario C effects (the strongest market opening, before introducing product flexibilities). We characterize each scenario using the ratios that characterize different policy makers: efficiency gain per unit of political cost for the *benevolent policy maker*, welfare gain per unit of market access for the *social planner*, and political cost per unit of market access for the *negotiator*. Market access changes are measured in terms of changes in imports. At the global level the overall market access also represents the overall improvement in market access for all exporters.

The results in Table 4.6 provide a number of insights. Looking at the criterion of welfare and efficiency gains per unit of market access granted, we generally find declines as we move from the tiered formula (C) to a proportional cut (C1). This is consistent with the economically high-quality nature of the tiered formula, which imposes larger cuts on the higher tariffs. Now, focusing on the criterion of the benevolent policy maker, the welfare gains per unit of political cost incurred rise when we move from the formula cuts to a proportional cut with the same level of market access. In the all-members case, the increase is from 1.59 to 1.63. For individual countries, the increases are generally in the same order of magnitude. The political costs per unit of import access provided also decline as we move to the proportional formula. While these results are consistent with the Jean, Laborde, and Martin (2014) finding that proportional cuts are optimal for a benevolent policy maker, they cannot be taken for granted since both the formula and the proportional cut are applied to bound tariffs, and this analysis takes into account cross-price effects in the demand system. The proportional cut approach lowers the political cost per unit of market access given—the criterion of the pure negotiator—in all cases.

Overall, the flexibilities (Scenario C to Scenario D) cut by half the magnitude of the welfare and market access gains at the global level. When we turn to Formula Scenario D, with product flexibilities, we find that the efficiency of the reform per unit of market access is reduced: increased flexibilities reduce welfare gains more rapidly than market access due to the increase in tariff heterogeneity. Looking at the political economy of the reform, a more complex situation arises. The political costs per unit of market access provided

TABLE 4.6 Welfare, market access, and political costs of formulae and flexibilities: AMA

	Efficiency gains per unit of additional imports (%)	Efficiency gains per unit of political cost (%)	Political cost per unit of additional imports (%)
Total WTO members with effective market access concessions			
Formula Scenario C	0.84	1.59	0.53
Proportional cut equivalent to C1	0.80	1.63	0.49
Formula and Flexibilities Scenario D	0.77	1.63	0.48
Proportional cut equivalent to D1	0.80	1.53	0.52
Brazil			
Formula Scenario C	0.58	3.52	0.16
Proportional cut equivalent to C1	0.58	3.68	0.16
China			
Formula Scenario C	0.62	2.61	0.24
Proportional cut equivalent to C1	0.60	2.97	0.20
Formula and Flexibilities Scenario D	0.59	3.32	0.18
Proportional cut equivalent to D1	0.61	2.85	0.21
European Union			
Formula Scenario C	0.79	1.70	0.47
Proportional cut equivalent to C1	0.78	1.72	0.45
Formula and Flexibilities Scenario D	0.80	1.54	0.52
Proportional cut equivalent to D1	0.82	1.47	0.56
India			
Formula Scenario C	0.81	1.43	0.57
Proportional cut equivalent to C1	0.80	1.47	0.54
Formula and Flexibilities Scenario D	0.67	2.04	0.33
Proportional cut equivalent to D1	0.85	1.25	0.68
Japan			
Formula Scenario C	0.81	1.64	0.49
Proportional cut equivalent to C1	0.75	1.69	0.44
Formula and Flexibilities Scenario D	0.74	1.68	0.44
Proportional cut equivalent to D1	0.74	1.64	0.45
United States			
Formula Scenario C	0.61	2.61	0.24
Proportional cut equivalent to C1	0.61	2.71	0.22
Formula and Flexibilities Scenario D	0.62	2.55	0.24
Proportional cut equivalent to D1	0.62	2.55	0.24

Source: Authors' computation.

Note: The Flexibilities Scenario reduces effective agricultural trade liberalization in Brazil to nearly 0. AMA = agricultural market access.

to trading partners—the sine qua non of political success—is unchanged for WTO members as a whole. The flexibilities reduce the overall political cost in the same proportion as the market access gains. However, for WTO members such as India, the political costs per unit of trade expansion fall sharply. For all the other members represented in Table 4.6, however, the political costs per unit of market access rise, substantially in the case of the European Union. The welfare gains per unit of political cost decline slightly for WTO members as a whole, while rising substantially for India. This outcome would not arise in the textbook case where tariff cuts are imposed on applied rates and cross-price effects are absent. It arises because of the complex relationship between the applied and bound tariff schedules and the selective nature of the flexibilities. In the final row of each block, we move from Scenario D to a proportional cut that yields the same market access outcome. In each case except the United States, this increases the political costs per unit of market access, reducing the scope for agreement among negotiators focused on mercantilist goals. It does, however, increase the economic welfare gains per unit of political cost expended.

When we turn to NAMA in Table 4.7, we find results that are broadly similar for WTO members as a group. As we move from the Swiss formula to the proportional cut, the political costs of concern to the negotiator fall quite sharply, and the welfare gains per unit of political cost rise, even though the welfare gains per unit of market access fall as we move away from the Swiss formula. The political costs per unit of market access fall further as exceptions are introduced. In this case, however, these political costs are the same when a proportional cut calibrated to the market access gains of the formula plus flexibilities is introduced.

For each of the industrial countries considered, the political cost per unit of market access falls quite sharply as we move from the tiered formula to a proportional cut, while the efficiency gains per unit of political cost rise. This reflects both the sharp reduction in political costs incurred and the increase in market access as goods that are both high volume and relatively low tariff face larger tariff cuts. The picture is more complex in developing countries, where flexibilities are allowed. In Brazil the political cost per unit of market access rises as the flexibilities are introduced, and the efficiency gains per unit of political cost fall. In contrast, in India and China the formula with flexibilities minimizes the political costs per unit of market access provided and maximizes the efficiency gains per unit of political cost.

A key feature of the current impasse is the fact that the combination of initial low tariffs in developed economies, high binding overhang in developing

TABLE 4.7 Welfare, market access, and political costs: NAMA

	Welfare per unit of political cost (%)	Welfare per unit of market access (%)	Political cost per unit of additional imports (%)
All WTO countries			
Formula without Flexibilities (Scenario C)	4.17	0.63	0.15
Proportional cut (calibrated market access on Scenario C)	4.94	0.61	0.12
Formula with Flexibilities (Scenario D)	5.41	0.60	0.11
Proportional cut (calibrated market access on Scenario D)	5.48	0.60	0.11
All WTO countries with effective opening			
Formula without Flexibilities (Scenario C)	4.18	0.63	0.15
Proportional cut (calibrated market access on Scenario C)	4.94	0.61	0.12
Formula with Flexibilities (Scenario D)	5.42	0.60	0.11
Proportional cut (calibrated market access on Scenario D)	5.48	0.60	0.11
Brazil			
Formula without Flexibilities (Scenario C)	3.71	0.63	0.17
Proportional cut (calibrated Market Access on Scenario C)	3.87	0.63	0.16
Formula with Flexibilities (Scenario D)	3.77	0.63	0.17
Proportional cut (calibrated market access on Scenario D)	3.79	0.63	0.17
China			
Formula without Flexibilities (Scenario C)	3.77	0.66	0.17
Proportional cut (calibrated market access on Scenario C)	5.05	0.62	0.12
Formula with Flexibilities (Scenario D)	5.93	0.61	0.10
Proportional cut (calibrated market access on Scenario D)	5.00	0.62	0.12
European Union			
Formula without Flexibilities (Scenario C)	8.21	0.57	0.07
Proportional cut (calibrated market access on Scenario C)	9.39	0.56	0.06
India			
Formula without Flexibilities (Scenario C)	2.38	0.73	0.31
Proportional cut (calibrated market access on Scenario C)	2.63	0.70	0.27
Formula with Flexibilities (Scenario D)	4.18	0.64	0.15
Proportional cut (calibrated market access on Scenario D)	2.46	0.72	0.29

(continued)

TABLE 4.7 *(continued)*

	Welfare per unit of political cost (%)	Welfare per unit of market access (%)	Political cost per unit of additional imports (%)
Japan			
Formula without Flexibilities (Scenario C)	4.98	0.59	0.12
Proportional cut (calibrated market access on Scenario C)	5.94	0.58	0.10
United States			
Formula without Flexibilities (Scenario C)	6.72	0.59	0.09
Proportional cut (calibrated market access on Scenario C)	8.76	0.58	0.07

Source: Authors' computations.
Note: NAMA = nonagricultural market access. The industrial countries are allowed no flexibilities.

economies, and flexibilities have led to limited gains in the nonagricultural sector. With limited possibilities for gain in the manufacturing sectors, the fuel that drove previous rounds of negotiation is running perilously close to dry, as noted in Martin and Messerlin (2007). This makes it difficult for policy makers in developed economies to engage the export interests whose support, and even enthusiasm, was critical in reaching earlier multilateral agreements. Without engaging these interest groups, it is difficult for policy makers to find a solution to counterbalance the pressure from agricultural interests to retain their protection.

Beyond solving the basic domestic political-economy equation, the Doha Round embodies a paradigm shift in global trade negotiations and their governance. Agreement between the EU and the United States is no longer sufficient for a global agreement. Emerging countries—in particular Brazil, China, and India—have become key players in terms of commercial and diplomatic strength. Obviously, increasing the number of players increases the difficulty of finding a positive outcome to the bargaining game (Bouët and Laborde 2010). It has also resulted in concerns about the traditional GATT practice of treating all developing countries other than the LDCs in the same way in terms of special and differential treatment.

Although initially less protected than agriculture, due to its size and role in world trade of goods and services (91 percent of trade in goods, 78 percent of all trade in 2010), any concessions on NAMA could potentially have large-scale effects. In this context the sectoral initiatives (that is, developing countries engaging in tariff elimination or tariff capping at a very low level for a subset of products, negotiated on a plurilateral basis and at the industry level) appear to be a potentially important complement to the formula approach. Laborde (2011) proposes an extensive discussion and quantification of these initiatives. They appear as another circumvention of a rigid harmonizing formula approach, in order to push the scope of liberalization while still respecting the political constraints and incentives of policy makers.

Indeed, the Swiss formula approach proposed in the modalities and discussed earlier fails to deliver significant market access gains for two reasons: for developed countries, the Swiss formula with a coefficient of 8 performs poorly on market access because many products with large trade volumes are subject to relatively low tariffs. With 53 percent of HS-6 products, and more than 75 percent of MFN imports of these countries, being subject to tariffs of 4 percent or lower, the cuts in average tariffs are modest. For developing countries, higher binding overhang and the inclusion of flexibilities to address their political constraints water down the liberalization. At the same time, aggressiveness of the Swiss formula leads to high political costs, in particular for tariff peaks (see Table 4.7 and its discussion). In contrast, the sectoral initiatives could deliver large and effective cuts to applied rates—and hence increases in market access—of value to almost all members in the very short run (Laborde 2011). The seven main initiatives (that is, those supported by countries who account for more than one-third of NAMA imports) would increase overall market access concessions in NAMA by one-third and eliminate the asymmetry among WTO members in terms of concessions and gains.

Conclusion

The Doha proposals involve tariff formulas that cut high tariffs much more sharply than lower tariffs. From an economic point of view, this is highly desirable and has potential to yield Pareto improvements (Turunen-Red and Woodland 1991; Vousden 1990). However, it is far from clear that this approach is politically achievable. As observed by one of the key negotiators (Falconer 2008), as soon as it was adopted, the pressure for flexibilities and exceptions became intense. Another key feature of the tariff-cut proposals is a wide range of exceptions. Many of these are extremely badly designed in allowing countries excessive flexibility to impose very small tariffs on products that are collectively important to exporters. In the agricultural agreement in particular, these flexibilities are constrained only by the number of products that can be included—a criterion that provides insufficient discipline since only a very small share of tariff lines account for most of the imports and trade restrictiveness.

A simple model based on the political-economy framework developed by Grossman and Helpman (1994) provides powerful insights into the political costs associated with movements from the political-economy equilibrium that underlies the initial tariff regime. Just as the economic costs of raising protection from its initial level are quadratic in the tariff, the political costs of lowering the tariff from its initial level are also quadratic. This suggests that attempts to use formulas that sharply reduce the highest tariffs are likely to incur political costs that put achieving international agreement at risk. A tariff formula that comes closer to reducing tariffs proportionally seems likely to provide a better balance between the political costs of reform and the desirability of achieving improvements in economic efficiency.

A detailed examination of the formulas proposed under the Doha Agenda shows that the political costs of an agreement to increase market access could have been reduced substantially by using a proportional-cut approach rather than progressive tariff-cutting formulas. Returning to a proportional-cut approach at the same level of market access concessions would generally raise the welfare gains per unit of political costs incurred. However, this approach is likely to be difficult because exceptions tend to lower the political costs associated with the level of market access provided. This suggests that the combination of ambitious formulas with deep exceptions customized to the specific situation of applied and bound tariffs frequently has more political appeal than might have been expected. While this approach compromises the economic efficiency goals of the negotiations, the results in this chapter suggest that it has probably not been the cause of the political stalemate that has becalmed the Doha negotiations.

Bibliography

Anderson, J., and P. Neary. 2003. "The Mercantilist Index of Trade Policy." *International Economic Review* 44 (2): 627–649.

———. 2007. "Welfare versus Market Access: The Implications of Tariff Structure for Tariff Reform." *Journal of International Economics* 71: 187–205.

Baldwin, R. E. 1986. "Toward More Efficient Procedures for Multilateral Trade Negotiations." *Aussenwirtschaft* 41 (Heft II/III): 379–394.

Baldwin, R., and G. Lage. 1971. "A Multilateral Model of Trade-Balancing Tariff Concessions." *Review of Economics and Statistics* 53: 237–245.

Bouët, A., and D. Laborde. 2010. "Why Is the Doha Development Agenda Failing? And What Can Be Done? A Computable General Equilibrium-Game Theoretical Approach." *The World Economy* 33 (11): 1486–1516.

Falconer, C. 2008. "Communication from the Committee on Agriculture." Special Session, World Trade Organization (WTO), April 30. Accessed 2009. www.wto.org/english/tratop_e/agric_e/chair_texts07_e.htm.

Francois, J., and W. Martin. 2003. "Formula Approaches for Market Access Negotiations." *The World Economy* 26 (1): 1–28.

———. 2004. "Commercial Policy, Bindings, and Market Access." *European Economic Review* 48 (June): 665–679.

Grossman, G., and E. Helpman. 1994. "Protection for Sale." *American Economic Review* 84 (4): 833–850.

Hillman, A. 1982. "Declining Industries and Political-Support Protectionist Motives." *American Economic Review* 72 (5): 1180–1187.

Jean, S., D. Laborde, and W. Martin. 2011. "Formulas and Flexibility in Trade Negotiations: Sensitive Agricultural Products in the World Trade Organization's Doha Agenda." *World Bank Economic Review* 24 (3): 500–519.

———. 2014. "The Political Costs of Policy Reform." Unpublished manuscript. World Bank, Washington, DC.

Laborde, D. 2011. "Sectoral Initiatives in the Doha Round." In *Unfinished Business? The WTO's Doha Development Agenda*, edited by A. Mattoo and W. Martin, 277–298. London: Center for Economic Policy Research; Washington, DC: World Bank.

Laborde, D., and W. Martin. 2011a. "Agricultural Market Access." In *Unfinished Business? The WTO's Doha Agenda*, edited by A. Mattoo and W. Martin, 35–54. London: Center for Economic Policy Research; Washington, DC: World Bank.

———. 2011b. "Non-agricultural Market Access." In *Unfinished Business? The WTO's Doha Agenda*, edited by A. Mattoo and W. Martin, 55–68. London: Center for Economic Policy Research; Washington, DC: World Bank.

———. 2015. "Formulas for Failure? Were the Doha Tariff Formulas Too Ambitious for Success?" *World Trade Review* 14 (1): 45–65.

Laborde, D., W. Martin, and D. van der Mensbrugghe. 2011. *Measuring the Benefits of Global Liberalization with Optimal Aggregators of Trade Distortions*. World Bank Policy Research Working Paper 5665. Washington, DC: World Bank.

Martin, W., and A. Mattoo. 2011. *Unfinished Business: The WTO's Doha Agenda*. London: CEPR; Washington, DC: World Bank.

Martin, W., and P. Messerlin. 2007. "Why Is It So Difficult? Trade Liberalization under the Doha Agenda." *Oxford Review of Economic Policy* 23 (3): 347–366.

Schwab, S. 2011. "After Doha: Why the Negotiations Are Doomed and What We Should Do About It." *Foreign Affairs* 90 (3): 104–117.

Turunen-Red, A., and A. Woodland. 1991. "Strict Pareto-improving Multilateral Reforms of Tariffs." *Econometrica* 59 (4): 1127–1152.

Vousden, N. 1990. *The Economics of Trade Protection.* Cambridge, UK: Cambridge University Press.

WTO (World Trade Organization). 2008a. Revised Draft Modalities for Agriculture, TN/AG/W/4/Rev.4, December 6. World Trade Organization, Geneva.

———. 2008b. Draft Modalities for Non-agricultural Market Access, TN/MA/W/103/Rev.3, December 6. World Trade Organization, Geneva.

Chapter 5

BRIC AGRICULTURAL POLICIES THROUGH A WTO LENS

Lars Brink, David Orden, and Giselle Datz

This chapter examines agricultural policies of the BRIC (Brazil, the Russian Federation, India, China) through the prism of the disciplines on domestic support under the Agreement on Agriculture (AoA) of the World Trade Organization (WTO).[1] The effects of agricultural policies of the BRIC on production and trade have implications for their own domestic (and also global) food security as well as for world agricultural markets. As the BRIC have emerged as global economic powers, and their per capita incomes rise, questions intensify in a historical context about their governments' future treatment of agriculture. We examine the obligations in the WTO of the BIC (Brazil and India, members since 1995, and China, which acceded in 2001) and how they have notified their agricultural support to demonstrate compliance with the rules and their commitments. The inclusion of the Russian Federation under the WTO disciplines in 2012 demonstrates the disciplines' relevance even in the absence of a new agreement, and we discuss the disciplines on agricultural support established for the Russian Federation in its accession. We also assess the new rules that were negotiated in the Doha Round before it faltered at the end of 2008 as they would apply to the BRIC. While the prospect for adoption of new Doha disciplines has become remote, the negotiated provisions are informative about the future policy space the BRIC and other countries sought to maintain.

Until the Uruguay Round, it had proved impossible to achieve multilateral disciplines on the protection of and support for agriculture. The 1994 Agreement on Agriculture set forth the first such rules with the objective over time of achieving substantial and progressive reductions in distortions to

1 This chapter was originally published as an article in the *Journal of Agricultural Economics* 64, no. 1 (February 2013): 197–216. The authors have benefited from the earlier work of Fuzhi Cheng (2011), Munisamy Gopinath (2011, 2012), and André Nassar (2011) and from comments of the participants in the 2011 Leibniz Institute of Agricultural Development in Transition Economies (IAMO) forum titled "Will the 'BRICs Decade' Continue?—Prospects for Trade and Growth."

world markets. Eighteen years of experience have subsequently demonstrated how difficult this task remains. In the area of agricultural domestic support, countries have largely shown compliance with their legal obligations, and their WTO notifications track various changes in policies and expenditures. However, difficulties arise over whether the notifications to the WTO provide timely, accurate, and meaningful measurement of economic support and whether the disciplines have contributed to reducing trade distortions.

These analytical issues arise in evaluating the agricultural policies of the BRIC through the WTO lens. The situation of agriculture within their economies differs, leading to differences in their policy initiatives and an absence of a coordinated international stance. In addition, the details of the WTO rules apply differently to each one of the BRIC countries. The differences in the provisions applying to the four BRIC derive from a combination of several underlying differences. One is the difference in the rules for developing and developed countries. Special and differential treatment for developing countries is a principle in the WTO framework. However, developing-country status essentially results from self-declaration and has over time become less associated with economic criteria. Several members of the OECD (Organisation for Economic Co-operation and Development) use the developing-country provisions of the WTO Agreement on Agriculture (Chile, Israel, Mexico, South Korea [Republic of Korea], and Turkey). As developing countries in the WTO, Brazil, India, and China enjoy certain flexibilities on the level and type of agricultural support that is subject to WTO limits. The Russian Federation, as a developed country, does not enjoy the same flexibilities.

Another difference relates to the level and type of the support the BRIC provided in earlier years, which form the base for their WTO ceiling commitments on support. This gives Brazil and the Russian Federation latitude for a certain amount of subsidies within their ceiling commitments—they have a Bound Total Aggregate Measurement of Support (Bound Total AMS) greater than nil.[2] India and China do not have that particular latitude—their Bound Total AMS is nil. A third difference results from the processes used to establish the rules and commitments of the BRIC: negotiations in the Uruguay Round for Brazil and India, negotiations on WTO accession for the Russian Federation and China. For example, under a rule negotiated in China's accession, which deviated from earlier practice in developing-country accessions, China cannot exempt certain input subsides from WTO disciplines. Also

2 Bound Total AMS is a ceiling commitment, above which WTO members are not authorized to allow their Current Total AMS (see further discussion below).

under the 2008 Doha draft disciplines, the four BRIC would enjoy large but different degrees of flexibility to provide distorting support. The flexibilities would result from the particular Doha rules applying to developing countries (Brazil, India, and China) and to members that have acceded to the WTO after 1995 (the Russian Federation and China).

Thus, for the BRIC as a group, there is little substantial commonality of circumstance under the WTO disciplines on agricultural domestic support, except that the existing or possible future constraints allow considerable flexibility. Nevertheless, the WTO rules and their commitments will play some role in determining the extent and form of any distortionary policies the BRIC individually or collectively pursue as their incomes rise and they transform over the coming decades into economies in which agriculture accounts for a smaller share of national incomes.

Agriculture in the BRIC Economies

The levels of real GDP (gross domestic product) of the BRIC are shown for 1995–2010 in Figure 5.1a (constant 2000 US dollars). The rapid growth of China's economy relative to the others is evident as it more than tripled in size over 15 years. India also shows substantial growth, essentially doubling in size from a lower initial level. By comparison, Brazil and the Russian Federation show much slower growth. The 1995 per capita real GDP (not shown) was only US$372 in India and US$657 in China, compared to US$1,618 in the Russian Federation and US$3,609 in Brazil. By 2009, per capita GDP had risen to US$766 in India and US$2,206 in China, compared to US$2,805 in the Russian Federation and US$4,399 in Brazil. The per capita income comparisons go a long way toward explaining differences in levels of agricultural income (value-added) relative to total GDP among the BRIC. The percentage of GDP accounted for by agriculture was initially far higher in India and China than in the Russian Federation and Brazil (Figure 5.1b). The share of GDP accounted for by agriculture dropped sharply in China (by half) as its economy grew; likewise, agriculture's share of the Indian economy dropped by 30 percent as the economy doubled.

The economic importance of agriculture in Brazil is more evident in its international trade. Agriculture and food accounted for one-third of Brazil's merchandise exports throughout the 15 years, fluctuating with highs and lows of world prices and other factors (Figure 5.1c). In contrast, the Russian Federation's agriculture and food exports were only 5 percent of merchandise exports. Agriculture and food exports declined as a share of the total

FIGURE 5.1 Growth and agriculture among the BRICs

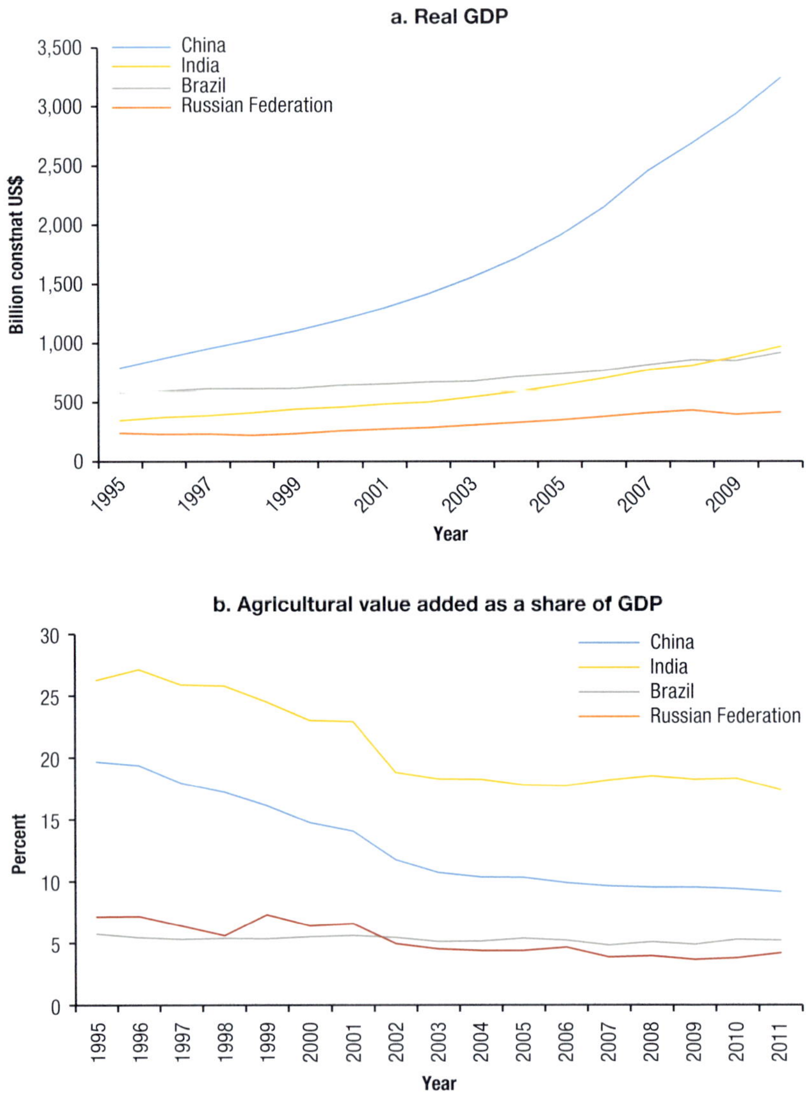

c. Agricultural and food exports as a share of merchandise total

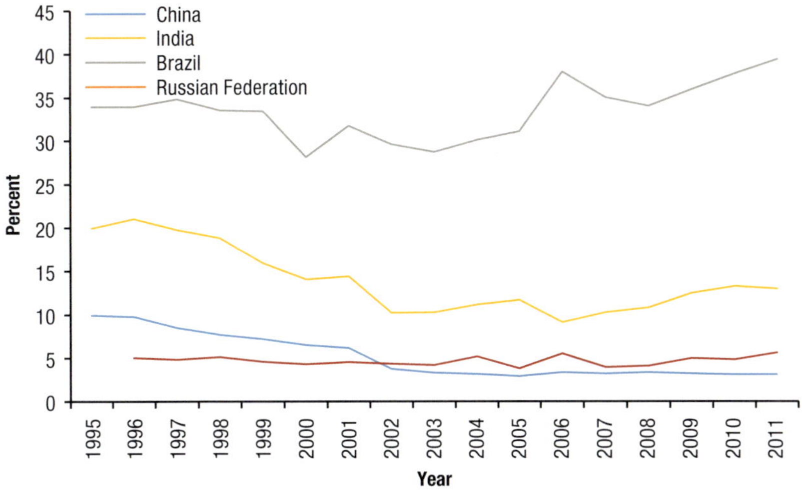

d. Agricultural and food imports as a share of merchandise total

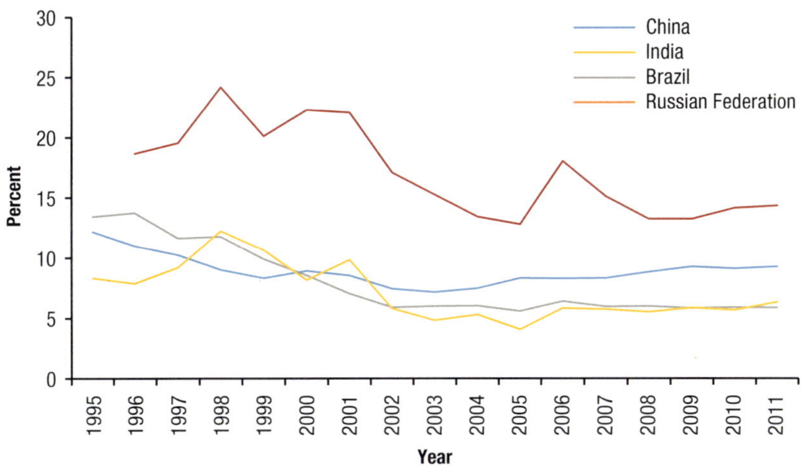

Source: Authors' calculations from IMF and World Bank data.

Note: BRICs = A group of emerging economies consisting of Brazil, the Russian Federation, India, and China.

exports of China and India and by 2010 were closer to the share in the Russian Federation than in Brazil. The share of agriculture and food in merchandise imports is higher for the Russian Federation than the other BRICs (Figure 5.1d). There is a downward trend in the share of merchandise imports accounted for by agriculture and food in all four countries, not just for China and India, where overall growth has been highest.

Participation in WTO Agricultural Governance

Given the differences in their agriculture and agricultural trade, the BIC have played quite different roles in WTO governance processes for agriculture. Brazil has been forceful in using the WTO's dispute settlement process to discipline support for agriculture in developed countries.[3] In *US–Agriculture Subsidies*, a case that is still pending but not actively under adjudication, Brazil contends (similar to a case first brought by Canada) that the United States violated its WTO support commitment in almost every year between 1999 and 2005. In *US–Upland Cotton* the WTO Appellate Body found under the Agreement on Subsidies and Countervailing Measures that numerous price-contingent US subsidies gave rise to serious prejudice to the interests of Brazil. In *EC–Sugar*, brought by Australia, Brazil, and Thailand, the Appellate Body expressed the view that domestic support was the source of the export subsidy that was found to exist. These cases demonstrate that a country can be challenged for violating the WTO rules because of the size and nature of its agricultural support. However, it has proven relatively easy for countries to meet their commitments under the domestic support disciplines of the WTO's Agreement on Agriculture.

Like many other countries, the BIC have notified their agricultural domestic support to the WTO Committee on Agriculture only with substantial delays, and notifications for recent years are still outstanding. The delays may in some situations, for the BIC as for other countries, be explained by difficulties in gathering the necessary data in a timely fashion, resulting from, for example, inadequate data collection procedures or allocation of too few resources to the task. However, the absence of a country's notifications for many years is more difficult to explain. Some countries may perceive gaining a strategic advantage from not revealing details on their farm support in the WTO notification format, whether for the regular work of the Committee on Agriculture or for the Doha negotiations initiated in 2001. The individual BIC countries have differed in their notification approaches (the Russian Federation's 2012 accession is too recent for delays in annual domestic support notification yet to have been incurred).

Brazil provided relatively prompt notifications in the early years of the WTO, but its notifications became delayed once the Doha Round began. No annual notifications were submitted by Brazil between 2000 and 2004,

3 Contentious issues are also addressed in bilateral negotiations and through the WTO Committee on Agriculture, as evidenced in the Committee's meeting reports. See Brink (2011) for elaboration on dispute settlement.

followed by notifications of support through 2008–2009 in February 2012. China provided notification information for 1996–1998 in 2001 as it acceded to the WTO, provided additional notifications through 2001 in October 2006, but notified support through 2008 only in October 2011. A more extreme case of failing to submit timely notifications is India. As late as in May 2011, its notifications of domestic support covered only three years, 1995/1996–1997/1998. In June 2011 domestic support notifications from India were circulated, but only going as far as 2003–2004. Delays such as these mean that timely information was not available during the Doha negotiations and have made it difficult for the WTO Committee on Agriculture to carry out its mandate to review the implementation of commitments. In contrast, regular up-to-date reviews of agricultural policies and support are prepared by the OECD but only for its limited membership and certain emerging economies, including Brazil, the Russian Federation, and China but not India.

All three BIC countries are members of the G20 WTO negotiation group of developing countries that argued in the Doha negotiations for deep cuts to agricultural support in the developed countries (WTO 2011a).[4] Brazil has been particularly forceful in pressing this case. On other agricultural issues, sharp differences have divided the BIC. India has sought rules for agricultural tariff safeguard mechanisms that Brazil has vigorously opposed. Cohesion among the BIC goes only so far—it prevails mainly when it comes to seeking concessions from developed countries, but not to initiatives that affect their diverse individual trade interests. It is unclear how the Russian Federation will seek to pursue its interests in the WTO and how its chosen approaches might affect the governance and accomplishments of the organization. Kerr (2012) espouses a pessimistic view, based on an assessment that the characteristics of the Russian Federation economy are antipathetic to WTO membership, including the idea that the Russian Federation would not be interested in an ambitious Doha outcome. This contrasts with the optimistic view that, based on the rule of trade law, the Russian Federation's membership will cement its integration into the global economy (Lamy 2011). The aims of each BRIC country concerning domestic support in the Doha Round would not be expected to differ from the usual apparent aims of other WTO members, which tend not to be driven by a purely economic rationale. Any BRIC country might thus want to preserve its

4 This G20 group in the WTO agricultural negotiations is distinct from the G20 group of major economies brought together regularly to address global economic issues. In 2012 the 23 members of the G20 in the WTO comprised Argentina, Bolivia, Brazil, Chile, China, Cuba, Ecuador, Egypt, Guatemala, India, Indonesia, Mexico, Nigeria, Pakistan, Paraguay, Peru, Philippines, South Africa, the United Republic of Tanzania, Thailand, Uruguay, Venezuela, and Zimbabwe.

own entitlements to provide distorting support while also wanting to constrain such room in countries to which it exports, from which it imports, and with which it competes in third-country export markets. While it may be difficult to pursue domestic support interests on a product-by-product basis, the balance between the constraints on product-specific and non-product-specific support could be the subject of divergent priorities among BRIC countries.[5]

WTO Disciplines on BRIC Agricultural Support

The WTO rules for domestic support are complicated (WTO 1995b).[6] Those countries that provided significant levels of support in the 1986–1988 base period established a ceiling commitment (Bound Total AMS) on certain production-related support, such as budgetary outlays and support through administered prices. Such support was summed across all basic agricultural products and a non-product-specific category. Most developing countries had no or only low levels of support in 1986–1988 and consequently they have a nil Bound Total AMS.[7] Brazil is one of the exceptions. Applied support counting toward the limit is measured in an annual Current Total AMS (CTAMS). There are de minimis thresholds below which product-specific and non-product-specific AMS support can be exempted from counting in the CTAMS. These thresholds are 10 percent of value of production for Brazil and India (as developing countries), 8.5 percent for China (as negotiated during its accession), and 5 percent for the Russian Federation (as a developed country). For India and China, the de minimis thresholds are the effective limits on AMS support: an AMS that exceeds the threshold is counted in its entirety in CTAMS, which is not allowed to exceed these countries' nil Bound Total AMS. Three categories of support are exempt from the limits on AMS support. Support through measures that "have no, or at most minimal,

5 As an exporter of, for example, wheat, the Russian Federation's domestic support interests with respect to this commodity may differ not only from those of China, an increasing importer of wheat, and India, whose wheat imports have dwindled, but also from those of Brazil, whose wheat exports are growing while it remains a net importer. As an importer of meats, while also in the process of developing its own livestock industry, the Russian Federation's interests may diverge from those of meat-exporting Brazil. Kiselev and Romashkin (2012) discuss the Russian Federation's agricultural trade with developing countries.

6 Brink (2009, 2011) provides detailed and comprehensive descriptions.

7 Anderson (2009, 2012) shows that developing countries as a group from the 1950s on effectively taxed agriculture: the nominal rate of assistance was negative albeit rising. By the late 1990s the nominal rate of assistance for agriculture in developing countries as a group had turned positive, and it remained positive in 2000–2004 and 2005–2010.

trade-distorting effects or effects on production" and that meet certain specific criteria is exempt as what is usually called Green Box support. Certain payments associated with production-limiting programs are exempt as Blue Box support. A third exempt category excludes, for developing countries only, general investment support for agriculture and input subsidies to low-income or resource-poor producers. It is sometimes called the Development Box.

The product-specific AMS includes price-related payments to producers, certain other types of product support and levies, and an indicator of market price support (MPS). The MPS is calculated "using the gap between a fixed external reference price [from the 1986–1988 base period] and the applied administered price multiplied by the quantity of production eligible to receive the applied administered price" (WTO 1995b). The WTO indicator of MPS differs from an economic measurement that uses the gap between contemporaneous domestic and world market prices and the total quantity of production to gauge the size of the transfer to producers resulting from policies that maintain that gap.[8] The method for calculating WTO MPS is enshrined in the text of the Agreement on Agriculture and has not been considered for change in the Doha negotiations. Some countries, while following this method and also referring to policy changes concerning applied administrative prices and eligible quantities of production, have notified significantly reduced amounts of WTO MPS.

BIC Agricultural Support and Support Notifications

Agricultural policies among the BIC have differed in the type and level of support provided.[9] In Brazil a distinction is drawn between commercial farmers and family farmers. Support is delivered primarily through credit programs (including debt rescheduling), directed to both commercial and

---

8 The use of administered prices in the WTO MPS results from designing it to account only for domestic measures, to the exclusion of border measures, such as tariffs. It was also designed as an indicator whose size could be entirely controlled through policy decisions, meeting some governments' concern about taking commitments on a variable outside their control. This led to the use of fixed reference prices and eligible production, as distinct from current reference prices and total production, which are beyond government control. Recognizing that the WTO MPS does not, despite its name, measure market price support in an economic sense, economic analysts exercise caution when introducing the WTO MPS in their work. The OECD, in contrast to the WTO, uses an economic measurement in the producer support estimate (PSE); see, for example, OECD (2012). The World Bank also uses an economic approach to examine agricultural protection and support since the mid-1950s (Anderson 2009).

9 This section draws from and updates the chapters by Nassar, Cheng, and Gopinath and the conclusion chapter by the editors in Orden, Blandford, and Josling (2011).

family farmers. Price and income support programs for certain commodities—including edible beans, maize, wheat, rice, and soybeans—are oriented to commercial farmers. For India, self-sufficiency in production has been a goal of agricultural policy since independence. This has largely been achieved for staple grains but less so for pulses and vegetable oils. India maintains programs of administered prices (minimum support prices) for cereals, pulses, oilseeds, sugar, and cotton and makes extensive use of tariffs and tariff-rate quotas to protect its domestic agriculture. Its output price policies are administered countercyclically (at times of high world prices, India has lowered tariffs and imposed export restrictions to put downward pressure on domestic prices). India has provided substantial subsidies for inputs such as fertilizer, electricity, and irrigation.

In China various policies have discriminated against agriculture historically, for example, through agriculture-specific taxes or by maintaining commodity prices below market-determined levels. The discrimination against agriculture has been reversed and farmers are now supported through input subsidies, direct payments, and price support. China reports most of this support as AMS support, which, although increasing, is accommodated within the de minimis thresholds (some direct payments are reported as Green Box support). Investment in agriculture-related infrastructure projects is a large component of government budgetary support for agriculture.

Summaries of the BIC domestic support notifications are given in Figure 5.2 for 1995–2008. Brazil and India notify their support in US dollars, and China (from 1996) notifies in its own currency (the average 1996–2008 exchange rate was around 8 Chinese renminbi per US dollar). Since India's notifications were available only through 2003–2004 by October 2012, Gopinath's (2011) estimated (shadow) notifications are used for the years 2004–2005 through 2008–2009. Brazil is the only BIC that has a nonzero, though small, Bound Total AMS. Brazil notifies MPS and some other support (primarily certain credit subsidies and price support payments) as product-specific AMS. The AMS for one or more products (cotton or wheat) has exceeded the de minimis threshold in a few years in Brazil as shown in Figure 5.2a. Thus Brazil has used the policy space for specific crops that results from having a nonzero Bound Total AMS. The resulting sum of AMS support counted in Brazil's CTAMS has always been well below the Bound Total AMS. The small magnitude of Brazil's product-specific AMS support is given perspective in Figure 5.2b. The rightmost bar for each year shows 10 percent of the value of total agricultural production. Brazil's product-specific AMS support summed across all commodities is always less than 1 percent of total production value.

India's and China's product-specific AMS support has completely (India) or primarily (China) consisted of WTO MPS. The de minimis thresholds are effectively these countries' constraints on such support. The WTO MPS for India (calculated using reference prices and administered prices converted to US dollars) and China has been or is estimated to have been negative or zero for many years (Figure 5.2c and Figure 5.2d. This occurs when administered prices were below external reference prices for key food staples (rice and wheat) or no quantity was indicated as production eligible for the price support.[10] Because of the methodological issues relating to prices and eligible production, the notified WTO MPS does not correspond to the economic market price support provided in either country. Farmers growing rice or wheat in India and China have been "disprotected" (effectively taxed) by output pricing policies in certain years since 1995, but mostly they received positive economic market price support after 2000. Disprotection occurred again in India and China when world prices rose sharply in 2008 and policy interventions were used to insulate domestic markets from the increase.

Support under the other notified categories is also shown in Figure 5.2b, Figure 5.2c, and Figure 5.2d. No BIC has notified Blue Box support. Green Box support has increased quite regularly in nominal value and as a percentage of the total value of agricultural production in India and China, but it has fluctuated in Brazil. The level of Green Box support as a percentage of total production value, the explanation for growth in support, and the composition of the Green Box support (not broken down in Figure 5.2) differ among the three countries.[11] Green Box support is nearly 10 percent of the total value of production in India and China, but for Brazil, Green Box support falls to its

10 The increases in administered prices in India since the last notified year (2003–2004) have raised them to significantly higher levels than the external reference prices in rupees. Gopinath's (2011, 2012) estimates of MPS closely match India's notifications for the years 1998/1999–2003/2004 and indicate a positive price gap in US dollars for rice and wheat from around 2008/2009. A US industry report (DTB Associates 2011) takes issue with the use of only actual procurement by the government as the eligible quantity rather than total production. As a commodity's administered price is being raised, using total production would make its AMS exceed the de minimis threshold at an earlier point in time than if only procurement were used.

11 Caution is appropriate in making cross-country comparisons of levels of support in the notifications. Each country exercises substantial discretion in the measures it notifies to the WTO and in the measurement of levels of support. Although scrutiny of the notifications occurs through the WTO Committee on Agriculture and through dispute proceedings, no systematic corroboration is undertaken to ensure comparability of the notified support.

FIGURE 5.2 Notified agricultural support of Brazil, India, and China

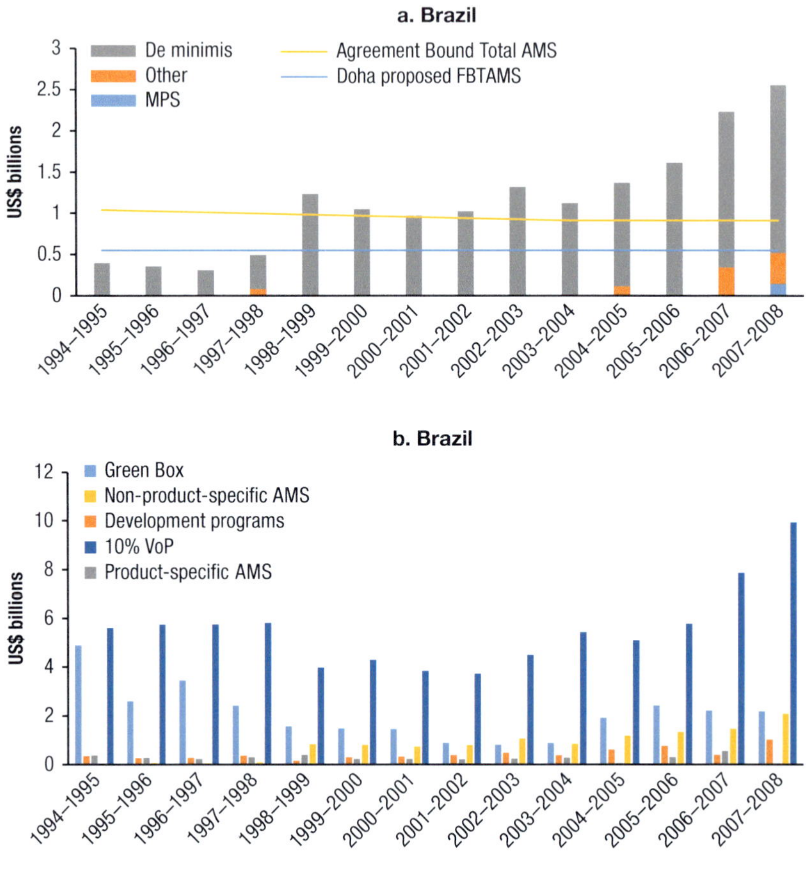

lowest value in 2002–2003, and remains only about 2–4 percent in later years. India's Green Box support is primarily composed of expenditures directed toward subsidizing low-income food consumers. If this public stockholding for food security is set aside, India's Green Box support is only about 2 percent of the total value of production in 2008–2009, less than in Brazil. China notified Green Box support of 593 billion renminbi in 2008 (US$87 billion), a large component of which consists of infrastructure investments. Such investments are not included to the same extent in the notifications of the other countries. China's Green Box support also includes direct payments to grain

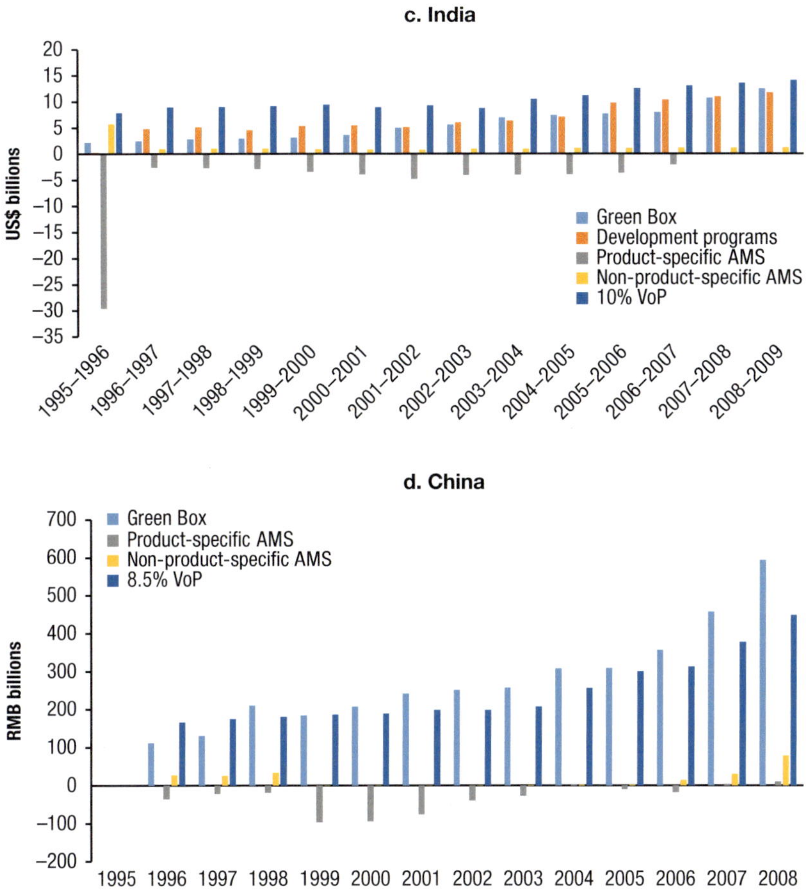

Source: Domestic support notifications submitted to the WTO Committee on Agriculture (series G/AG/N), various notifications by each country and estimated by Gopinath (2011).

Note: MPS = market price support; AMS = Aggregate Measurement of Support; FBTAMS = Final Bound Total AMS; VoP = value of protection.

producers notified as decoupled income support since 2004; these have been less than 1 percent of total agricultural production value.[12]

The BIC have notified various types of input and investment subsidies. India has notified this support primarily under the exemption for development programs. India's development program support averages a relatively high level of about 8 percent of the total value of production, in part because

12 Huang et al. (2011) argue that China's support policies have caused few distortions to grain acreages or input use.

it notifies significant subsidies for electricity and irrigation.[13] Brazil has notified smaller amounts of support under the development program exemption (averaging less than 1 percent of production value) and as non-product-specific AMS support: these values increase in later years due to investment credit subsidies and debt rescheduling. The level of China's non-product-specific AMS support, comprising mainly input subsidies, increased rapidly from 2006 but remained less than 1.5 percent of the value of production in 2008, before increasing sharply (not shown) in later years. China has not notified subsidies for irrigation or electricity, a potentially important omission.

Overall, the BIC have notified less support than the developed countries, but the levels of support in India and China have increased over time both nominally and relative to total agricultural production value. Because of its fluctuating Green Box support, Brazil's notified support is seen to have increased only in the more recent years. The estimated total of all notified support for agriculture (including nonexempt and exempt support under the WTO rules) was of a similar order of magnitude relative to the total value of agricultural production in China and India as in the United States in 2008.[14] This was a year of low US price-linked subsidies because world market prices for agricultural products were relatively high. With a porous international Agreement on Agriculture, domestic support policies remain heterogeneous across the BIC.

Domestic Support Disciplines under the Russian Federation's WTO Accession

The Russian Federation became a developed-country member of the WTO in August 2012 after the conclusion of an accession process that had been under

---

13 In its notifications for 1996–1997 and 1997–1998, 80 percent of India's notified subsidies for fertilizer, electricity, and irrigation were included in the development program category, based apparently on the share of small farms in the total number of farms (Gopinath 2011). Subsequently, in its notification made in 2011, India notified all such input subsidies from 1998–1999 through 2003–2004 under the development program exemption, noting that close to 100 percent of farm holdings are those of low-income, resource-poor farmers (WTO 2011b). Gopinath's shadow notification estimates in Figure 5.2c follow India's earlier notification practice and thus continue to divide the non-product-specific support between development programs and non-product-specific AMS using the 80 percent calculation. For the years 1998–1999 through 2003–2004, the sum of non-product-specific support Gopinath estimates under development programs and as AMS averages about US$1.4 billion less than notified by India. See Gopinath (2012) for further discussion of India's 2011 notification.

14 In this calculation of total support, public stockholding for food security programs in India and domestic food aid in the United States are deducted from the notified Green Box support (see Orden, Blandford, and Josling 2011, Chapter 11).

way from before the formation of the WTO in 1995. In the final stages of the accession negotiations, the size of the Russian Federation's Bound Total AMS became one of the contentious issues. One reason for this was the rising levels of agricultural support in the Russian Federation since around the year 2000, which made agricultural exporting countries concerned about potentially having to compete with heavily supported Russian producers both in the Russian Federation and in third-country markets. The increasing levels of support in the Russian Federation were documented in, for example, the policy monitoring carried out by the OECD, and they were also apparent in the base data provided by the Russian Federation over the years in line with the requirements of the WTO accession process. According to those requirements, the Russian Federation provided data for a rolling series of three-year periods in formats similar to those members use to notify their yearly support levels to the WTO Committee on Agriculture (WTO 1995a).[15] Moreover, senior Russian Federation officials, including the minister of agriculture, repeatedly expressed the view that the Russian Federation's room to provide farm support should be of a certain size, even stating the desired large levels.

Support as measured by the OECD (but excluding market price support) declined from 1991–1993 to its lowest point in 1999–2001 (Table 5.1). From there it increased to US$6.1 billion in 2008–2010, about the same level as in 1991–1993. The Russian Federation is reported to have originally submitted WTO domestic support data for 1991–1993 and proposed a Bound Total AMS of US$16.2 billion (OECD 2007). Subsequently the Russian Federation provided data for 1993–1995 and proposed a Bound Total AMS of US$9 billion (OECD 2007, 2009). This was followed by data for 2001–2003 and 2004–2006 (Ministry of Economic Development 2008). Eventually the idea of a Bound Total AMS starting at US$9 billion and then declining to US$4.4 billion a few years later was introduced in the negotiations (RIA Novosti 2010).

The Russian Federation's Bound Total AMS as agreed in its accession is US$9.0 billion in 2012 and 2013, declining in equal steps to reach US$4.4 billion in 2018 and then staying at that level.[16] The data underlying

15 For acceding countries, a more recent base period than 1986–1988 is conventionally used for domestic support. For example, China's base period is 1996–1998.

16 In agriculture, the Russian Federation also has market access commitments and a nil export subsidy commitment. The final bound tariff in agriculture averages 10.8 percent, compared to an average applied tariff ranging between 13.2 percent and 14.6 percent in the years 2007–2011, and tariff-rate quotas apply to beef, pork, and pork trimmings (until 2020), some poultry products and some whey products (Kiselev and Romashkin 2012; WTO 2011d).

TABLE 5.1 The Russian Federation's support for agriculture (OECD Producer Support Estimate excluding market price support) (US$ billions)

	1991–1993	1992–1994	1993–1995	1994–1996	1995–1997	1996–1998	1997–1999	1998–2000	1999–2001
Three-year average	**5.8**	6.4	**7.6**	7.6	5.2	3.6	2.3	1.7	1.4
	2000–2002	2001–2003	2002–2004	2003–2005	2004–2006	2005–2007	2006–2008	2007–2009	2008–2010
Three-year average	1.4	**1.4**	1.5	1.8	**2.0**	2.6	**4.0**	5.2	6.0

Source: OECD (2011).

Note: The Russian Federation's representation of any WTO MPS (market price support) in its accession documents for most of these years does not appear to have been made public. The Organisation for Economic Co-operation and Development (OECD) MPS is calculated very differently from the WTO MPS. The OECD MPS is therefore simply subtracted from the PSE levels, generating essentially an indicator of budgetary support only. Averages are calculated from annual data, converted to US dollars using yearly exchange rates, in OECD (2011). Amounts in bold refer to years for which the Russian Federation is reported to have submitted data in line with WTO methodology.

the final value of the commitment refer to the 2006–2008 period. As shown in Table 5.2, the Russian Federation's AMS support increased significantly in 2008 over the 2006 and 2007 levels. It can be conjectured, based on the OECD data series, that a larger Bound Total AMS would have resulted if support data for 2007–2009 had been used to determine its level, since budgetary support in the OECD data was larger in 2009 than in 2006. As a developed country, the Russian Federation's de minimis percentage is 5 percent and it does not have access to the developing-country exemption for certain development programs. The Russian Federation expresses its commitment in US dollars. This gives the Russian Federation some protection against a drop in the value of its currency relative to the US dollar: having a nominal Bound Total AMS in a depreciating domestic currency reduces the real amount of distorting support the country can provide without violating its WTO obligation.[17]

The Russian Federation's accession commitments in domestic support are unusual because they start at a negotiated level higher than in its base period and then decline in five steps to the final bound level. Some other acceding members have taken reductions over a transition period, but the starting point has been an amount calculated from the data for the base period, not an

17 The Agreement and the WTO requirements (WTO 1995a, 1995b) are silent on what currency to use for the Total AMS commitment. Brazil's data underlying the commitment level are in US dollars only; India's and China's are in their own currencies. The Russian Federation expresses its underlying data in both roubles and US dollars, along with an exchange rate. This provides for greater transparency than if only US dollars were used.

TABLE 5.2 Calculation of the Russian Federation's Current Total AMS in base years 2006–2008

	2006			2007			2008		
	AMS (US$ millions)	% of value of production		AMS (US$ millions)	% of value of production		AMS (US$ millions)	% of value of production	
Product-specific AMSs									
Hemp and flax	5.5	45.3		7.3	41.3		14.5	60.8	
Sheep	8.8	5.1		15.1	2.5	dm	27.0	3.4	dm
Reindeer	17.0	70.0		30.0	117.4		35.0	65.7	
Horse	—	—		1.2	0.7	dm	8.3	5.3	
Milk	155.6	1.9	dm	231.6	2.0	dm	362.2	2.4	dm
Meat	33.9	0.4	dm	67.3	0.3	dm	69.2	0.5	dm
Eggs	11.3	0.5	dm	13.8	0.5	dm	18.8	0.5	dm
Wool	0.4	1.0	dm	1.2	2.4	dm	0.3	0.4	dm
Non-product-specific AMS	3,744.9	6.3		3,827.2	5.1		5,596.1	5.6	
Subsidies for operating inputs	1,455.5			756.6			1,969.3		
Subsidies for capital inputs	482.3			560.3			647.8		
Credit concessions	1,318.9			1,618.8			1,858.6		
Subsidies for crop insurance	245.4			143.1			174.7		
Rail freight rates	94.2			101.5			63.0		
Production subsidies	148.7			196.0			338.6		
Other subsidies	—			450.8			544.2		
Current Total AMS	**3,776.2**			**3,864.4**			**5,653.9**		
2006–2008 average Current Total AMS = 4,389.4									

Source: WTO (2012).

Note: dm = de minimis (no more than 5% of the product's or agriculture sector's value of production). — = not reported. AMS = aggregate measurement of support.

Current Total AMS is the sum of all non-de minimis AMSs. Non-product-specific AMS subcategories are based on interpretation by Brink of 23 programs reported in the source document.

amount unrelated to past support in that period.[18] In the Russian Federation's case, the US$4.4 billion support level in the 2006–2008 period corresponds to the end point of the reductions, not the starting point. A unique and possibly significant element of the provisions that apply to the Russian Federation

18 The members who have taken such reductions include Croatia, Lithuania, the Republic of Moldova, and Taiwan; China, who reduced their commitments by the 20 percent used by developed countries in the Uruguay Round; and Jordan and Saudi Arabia, who reduced by the corresponding 13.3 percent for developing countries. Only Bulgaria, which reduced by 79 percent, is similar to the Russian Federation in the extent of reduction undertaken after accession (Brink [2003] discusses the Bulgaria case).

is a rule regarding product-specific AMS support. Although applying only through 2017, it requires the sum of all product-specific AMS support to be no more than 30 percent of the non-product-specific AMS (WTO 2011c, paragraph 1187). This constraint on product-specific AMS support echoes the initiatives in the Doha negotiations to set product-specific limits. For the Russian Federation the rule prevents an early large shift from non-product-specific to product-specific AMS support.

According to the OECD, market price support makes up a large share of policy support to agricultural producers in the Russian Federation—some 65 percent of the producer support estimate (PSE) consists of market price support. The main instruments of price support are border measures, such as tariffs and nontariff measures, which do not enter the calculation of the WTO MPS. In the WTO base data for 2006–2008, the Russian Federation does not report any administered price larger than the fixed external reference price (FERP) and hence reports no market price support. Apart from other differences in policy coverage between PSE and AMS support, the 2006–2008 amounts calculated with the WTO methodology, and which correspond to the Russian Federation's final Bound Total AMS of US$4.4 billion, are therefore significantly smaller than the support measured by the OECD PSEs for the Russian Federation in 2006–2008.

The Russian Federation's budgetary agricultural support is provided mainly through measures within multiyear frameworks. The support reported by the Russian Federation for 2006 and 2007 included support provided through programs under the 2006–2007 National Priority Project for Development of the Agro-Industrial Complex (OECD 2007). The 2008 support was delivered mainly through instruments under the State Program for Development of Agriculture 2008–2012. The support programs were very similar under the two frameworks. A large part of support, whether Green Box or AMS support, is provided by regional authorities. This is particularly the case for recent initiatives to modernize livestock production. The Russian Federation claimed significant amounts of support (average of US$2.1 billion in 2006–2008) as eligible for the Green Box exemption. Most of this support was in the form of general services such as research, training, inspection, pest and disease control, and enhancement of soil fertility. Only very small amounts were claimed under the direct payment clauses of the Green Box.

As shown in Table 5.2, during the base years 2006–2008 product-specific AMS support, mainly for livestock products, was generally small enough to fall below the de minimis threshold, except in the very small production sectors of flax, hemp, reindeer, and horses. The non-product-specific AMS accounted for almost all of the Russian Federation's AMS support. It included subsidies for fertilizer, chemicals, fuel, feed, seed, machinery leasing, breeding animals, and crop insurance, as well as credit and other concessions. The dominance of non-product-specific AMS support is unusual among developed countries, although non-product-specific support does make up a large share of non–Green Box support in the BIC, as discussed above. As a developed country, the Russian Federation cannot exempt any of its non-product-specific support as development program support. If the Russian Federation had reported only slightly less support as non-product-specific AMS, it would not have exceeded the de minimis threshold (especially in 2007), and the resulting base-period CTAMS would have amounted to almost nothing, leading to a much smaller Bound Total AMS.

The Russian Federation's final Bound Total AMS of US$4.4 billion is of some significance in relation to the size of the agriculture sector. It corresponds to 5.7 percent of the Russian Federation's 2006–2008 value of production of some US$78 billion. However, the value of production has been increasing rapidly: US$59 billion, US$76 billion, and US$99 billion in 2006, 2007, and 2008, respectively. Even in the very poor harvest year of 2010 the value of production remained around US$99 billion (Federal State Statistics Service 2011), making the final Bound Total AMS correspond to around 4.5 percent of the 2010 value of production. By comparison, Brazil's Bound Total AMS of US$0.9 billion was only 1.1 percent of its production value of US$82 billion. On the other hand, the United States's Bound Total AMS of US$19.1 billion was 6.7 percent of the 2009 notified value of production of US$285 billion, and the EU27 Bound Total AMS of 72.2 billion euros was 21 percent of the 2008–2009 notified value of production of 344 billion euros. Although Russian Federation's 2013 Bound Total AMS (US$9 billion) corresponds to 9 percent of the 2010 value of production, the relative size of the Russian Federation's final Bound Total AMS in 2018 would appear to be more constraining than is the case for the United States and the European Union. The contrast will become sharper if the value of production in Russian Federation agriculture continues to increase rapidly in the future.[19]

The Russian Federation could ease the constraint of its Bound Total AMS to some extent by introducing product-specific AMS support within the de minimis thresholds for each product, at least after the expiration in 2017 of its unique transition rule on such support. In the longer term it may also be possible for the Russian Federation to change the specifics of some of its

19 Liefert and Liefert (2012) discuss the potential for such a development to materialize.

non-product-specific AMS programs in order to make the revised programs qualify for the Green Box exemption. Bringing non-product-specific AMS support below the de minimis threshold would free up room for additional product-specific AMS support above de minimis levels within the Russian Federation's Bound Total AMS.

These considerations begin to arise with the 2008–2012 State Program coming to an end. The Russian Federation's cabinet approved in July 2012 a new long-term plan to support agriculture in 2013–2020. Media reports indicate that subsidies for fuel and fertilizers would be terminated, while other subsidies would be introduced. The new subsidies would be paid per hectare of farm land and per liter of milk (Medetsky 2012). Details are scarce and it is not clear when legislation will pass. Without details it is not possible to judge in which category the Russian Federation might be able to place any future hectare-based support—AMS, Blue Box, or Green Box. However, if the Russian Federation were to report significantly less support as non-product-specific AMS, it would more easily stay below the Bound Total AMS as this limit declines from 2013 to 2018. The Russian Federation authorities have long emphasized a need to increase the production of livestock. If more support were put in place toward this goal, such as MPS relying on administered prices, some of it could be reported within the larger flexibility for product-specific AMS available after the expiration of the special rule in 2017. The presence of the Bound Total AMS means, however, that the Russian Federation's AMS support will be limited by international commitments, which was not the case before its WTO accession.

Continued Support Latitude under the Doha Round Proposals

One of the aims of the Doha agricultural negotiations is a substantial reduction in trade-distorting support. Strengthened and improved rules and commitments for domestic support were part of the framework agreed upon in 2004, but the negotiations stalled in December 2008. The Doha draft modalities (WTO 2008) remain indicative of both the tightening of the provisions governing trade-distorting domestic support that could (and perhaps eventually will) result from Doha and the space for future policies that countries are currently seeking to maintain. Bound ceiling levels on domestic support would be tightened and extended for certain countries under the Doha proposals. Doha would sharply reduce the Bound Total AMS, lower the de minimis percentages for a number of countries, and introduce a limit on overall

Blue Box support. Doha would place a ceiling on a new indicator of overall trade-distorting support (OTDS), calculated as the sum of the CTAMS, de minimis AMS support, and overall payments in the Blue Box. The proposals would also impose product-specific limits on AMS support and Blue Box payments.

The Doha domestic support provisions would have a major impact on the levels allowed for some developed countries, but less so for the BRIC. The proposed final commitments of the BRIC (after phase-in periods over eight years) are shown in Table 5.3, with the proposed US final commitments (after phase-in over five years) given for comparison. The Doha proposals encompass a harmonizing approach, in which the countries that provided the largest support in the past would make the largest percentage cuts to their commitments. For the United States, the OTDS limit would decline from a base level of US$48.5 billion to a Final Bound OTDS commitment of US$14.5 billion, which corresponds to 7.4 percent of its base-period total production value. The existing US Bound Total AMS of US$19.1 billion would drop to US$7.6 billion. Further constraint would come from reducing the de minimis percentages for the United States and most other developed countries from 5 percent to 2.5 percent. Total Blue Box support would be limited to 2.5 percent of the 1995–2000 value of production.

The commitments for Brazil follow a pattern similar to those of the United States but the reductions reflect the more lenient treatment for developing countries. Brazil's OTDS limit would decline by 37 percent from its base to a final bound level of US$8.3 billion. Its Bound Total AMS would be reduced by 30 percent and its de minimis thresholds by one-third. No reductions are required from Base OTDS or in the de minimis thresholds for India or China. Overall, Blue Box support would be capped at 5 percent of base-period production value for the BIC.

One consequence of the Doha proposals is that the Final Bound OTDS of India and China (at 25 percent of base-period total value of production) would be larger than that of the United States. The OTDS support that India and China could provide (on a dollar basis at 2009 exchange rates) would be nearly US$26 billion and US$86 billion, respectively.[20] However, India and China face the constraint within this OTDS scope that each product-specific AMS be kept within its de minimis threshold. This allows less AMS support

20 Under proposals for recently acceded members (RAMs), China's, and possibly the Russian Federation's, allowed trade-distorting support could even exceed the OTDS limit as long as the excess consists only of de minimis support (see Brink 2011).

TABLE 5.3 Proposed Doha commitments and de minimis percentages

Domestic support category	United States	Brazil	India	China	Russian Federation: If Recently Acceded Member (RAM)	Russian Federation: If Very Recently Acceded Member (VRAM)
	US$ billions	US$ billions	US$ billions	RMB billion (US$ billions)[a]	US$ billions	US$ billions
Base Overall Trade-Distorting Support (OTDS)[b]	48.5	13.1	25.6	584.4 (85.5)	10.2	10.2
Full reduction percentage from Base OTDS	70	37	—	—	37	—
Final Bound OTDS	14.5	8.3	25.6	584.4 (85.5)	6.5	10.2
Pre-Doha Bound Total AMS	19.1	0.9	—	—	4.4	4.4
Full reduction percentage from pre-Doha level	60	30	—	—	30	—
Final Bound Total AMS after reduction	7.6	0.6	—	—	3.1	4.4
Overall Blue Box limit	4.9	2.4	5.1	116.9 (17.1)	1.9	1.9
De minimis percentage	2.5	6.7	10.0	8.5	4.2	5.0
	Commitment as share of base-period value of production					
Final Bound OTDS	7.4	17.0	25.0	25.0	16.8	26.4
Final Bound Total AMS	3.9	1.3	—	—	8.0	11.4
Overall Blue Box limit	2.5	5.0	5.0	5.0	5.0	5.0

Source: Authors' calculations for the Russian Federation; see Orden, Blandford, and Josling (2011) for the other countries.
Note: [a]Based on 2009 IMF average yearly exchange rates; [b]base period for OTDS is 1995–2000 for the United States and the Russian Federation (the Russian Federation's value of production was larger in 1995–2000 than in 1995–2004) and 1995–2004 for Brazil, India, and China. — = zero.

for each product relative to production value than some developed countries (and Brazil and the Russian Federation among the BRIC) have provided in the past for certain products. The Russian Federation's provision of product-specific AMS support within its OTDS scope might also be constrained. This would result from the product-specific AMS limits being based only on some earlier years' de minimis thresholds, expressed in monetary terms, in the absence of large product-specific AMS support in earlier years.

The Doha draft modalities of 2008 introduced different provisions for recently acceded members (RAMs) and very recently acceded members (VRAMs). It is commonly assumed that all those that have acceded under the WTO accession rules since 1995 (some 30 countries, including China) are recently acceded members. The draft modalities identify four VRAMs by name, but that list naturally goes only up to 2008.[21] It is thus not clear whether RAM or VRAM provisions would apply to the Russian Federation under a continuation of Doha. As a WTO member, the Russian Federation is now in a position where it can influence that identification. Because a developed-country VRAM (such as Ukraine) would enjoy greater flexibilities than a developed-country RAM (such as Taiwan, China), the Russian Federation would be expected to argue for VRAM status. As a RAM, the Russian Federation would take a 37 percent reduction from its Base OTDS, while as a VRAM, it would not reduce from Base (Table 5.3). As a RAM, it would reduce its Bound Total AMS by 30 percent to US$3.1 billion, while as a VRAM, it would not reduce. Likewise, as a RAM, it would reduce the de minimis percentage to 4.2 percent, but as a VRAM, it would keep it at 5 percent. Thus, if the Russian Federation were to be treated as a VRAM, Doha would not impose any reductions on the domestic support constraints the Russian Federation negotiated when acceding to the WTO, and some of the Russian Federation's new limits under Doha (such as overall Blue Box) would be set as for developing countries.[22]

Conclusion

This chapter has examined BRIC agriculture policies through the lens of the WTO's rules and ceiling commitments on domestic support. The BRIC have emerged collectively as a key set of players in the global economy, but their interests are not always convergent. The agricultural interests differ among the BRIC and the stance toward the WTO governance of agriculture policy differs among its members (Brazil, the Russian Federation, India, and China). As incomes have increased in India and China, agriculture support seems to be growing. The BIC domestic support notifications reflect increasing levels of support to an extent, but support as notified under the WTO rules can differ significantly from support measured in standard economic terms. The MPS as measured by the WTO may turn positive for India and China if administered

21 The four named VRAM countries are Saudi Arabia, the former Yugoslav Republic of Macedonia, Viet Nam, and Ukraine (WTO 2008). It is not clear whether VRAM is a subset of RAM or they are mutually exclusive categories.

22 The Russian Federation's overall Blue Box limit, whether a RAM or a VRAM, would be twice as large as it would have been if the Russian Federation were not recently acceded. If Doha provisions were to apply as soon as in the next few years, which is unlikely, the Russian Federation's ongoing reduction of the Bound Total AMS until 2018 would need to be considered when starting the implementation of any Doha reductions over time.

prices are raised. The difference between using government procurement or total production as eligible production (which would hinge on specific policy details concerning the applied administered price) could then prove important in determining the scope these countries have for providing support while remaining in compliance with the WTO rules and commitments. In addition, for India and Brazil the development program exemption could prove important for future compliance with support limitations. The Russian Federation's ceiling commitment upon accession in 2012 declines through 2018, albeit from a high level, and a special rule applies to product-specific support in the short run. This accommodates the non-product-specific policy emphasis in the Russian Federation's past support. In the longer run, should it choose to do so, the Russian Federation will be able to provide sizeable non-product-specific AMS support within the relevant de minimis threshold while also increasing product-specific AMS support beyond the de minimis thresholds for many products—a pattern of support seen in some other developed countries.

With the Russian Federation as a member, the BRIC divides into two groups in terms of constraints on product-specific AMS support under the WTO disciplines. In one group are Brazil and the Russian Federation. Despite their very different agricultural trade positions, both these countries have an established Bound Total AMS commitment under the WTO rules, which gives them some latitude in offering support for certain products. Brazil would, and the Russian Federation might, also face tighter constraints under the proposed Doha rules. India and China, in contrast, lack the latitude for product-specific AMS support that a nonzero Bound Total AMS commitment offers. Both they and possibly the Russian Federation would experience a milder tightening of the constraints on trade-distorting support than would Brazil under a Doha agreement. This contrast illustrates a more general point. Agriculture is likely to remain a component of the BRIC economies for which evaluating differences among the individual countries will remain at least as important as thinking of them collectively as a rising force in the world economy.

Bibliography

Anderson, K., ed. 2009. *Distortions to Agricultural Incentives: A Global Perspective 1955–2007.* London: Palgrave Macmillan; Washington, DC: World Bank.

———. 2012. "Agricultural Price Distortions: Trends and Volatility, Past and Prospective." Plenary paper, International Conference of Agricultural Economists, Foz do Iguaçu, Brazil, August 18–24.

Brink, L. 2003. "New Members of the WTO: Their Commitments in Agriculture and Provisions Proposed in the Doha Negotiations." Paper presented at the Conference on Agricultural Policy Reform and the WTO: Where Are We Heading? Capri, Italy, June 23–26. Accessed September 2012. www.ecostat.unical.it/2003agtradeconf/Contributed%20papers/brink.pdf.

———. 2009. "WTO Constraints on Domestic Support in Agriculture: Past and Future." *Canadian Journal of Agricultural Economics* 57: 1–21.

———. 2011. "The WTO Disciplines on Domestic Support." In *WTO Disciplines on Agricultural Support*, edited by D. Orden, D. Blandford, and T. Josling, 23–58. Cambridge, UK: Cambridge University Press.

Cheng, F. 2011. "China." In *WTO Disciplines on Agricultural Support*, edited by D. Orden, D. Blandford, and T. Josling, 310–352. Cambridge, UK: Cambridge University Press.

DTB Associates. 2011. "Domestic Support and WTO Obligations in Key Developing Countries." Unpublished, DTB Associates, Washington, DC.

Federal State Statistics Service. 2011. "Agricultural Production Output by Type of Agricultural Farms." Accessed August 2011. www.gks.ru/bgd/regl/b11_12/IssWWW.exe/stg/d01/15-01.htm.

Gopinath, M. 2011. "India." In *WTO Disciplines on Agricultural Support*, edited by D. Orden, D. Blandford, and T. Josling, 277–309. Cambridge, UK: Cambridge University Press.

———. 2012. "WTO Disciplines on Agricultural Support Update: A Comparison of India's WTO Domestic Support Notifications with Shadow Measurements." WTO Domestic Support Notification Update. Unpublished, Oregon State University, Corvallis, OR, US. Accessed September 2012. http://ebrary.ifpri.org/cdm/ref/collection/p15738coll5/id/3566.

Huang, J., X. Wang, H. Zhi, Z. Huang, and S. Rozelle. 2011. "Subsidies and Distortions in China's Agriculture: Evidence from Producer-Level Data." *Australian Journal of Agricultural and Resource Economics* 55: 53–71.

Kerr, W. 2012. "Taming the Bear: The WTO after the Accession of Russia." *The Estey Centre Journal of International Law and Trade Policy* 13: 150–159.

Kiselev, S., and R. Romashkin. 2012. *Possible Effects of Russia's WTO Accession on Agricultural Trade and Production*. ICTSD Issue Paper 40. Geneva: International Centre for Trade and Sustainable Development (ICTSD).

Lamy, P. 2011. "Director-General's Statement on Russia's Accession." World Trade Organization (WTO), December 16. Accessed September 2012. www.wto.org/english/news_e/sppl_e/sppl213_e.htm.

Liefert, W. M., and O. Liefert. 2012. "Russian Agriculture during Transition: Performance, Global Impact, and Outlook." *Applied Economic Perspectives and Policy* 34: 37–75.

Medetsky, A. 2012. "Cabinet Tweaking Agricultural Subsidies under WTO." *Moscow Times*, July 15. Accessed September 2012. www.themoscowtimes.com/business/article/cabinet-tweaking-agricultural-subsidies-under-wto/462109.html.

Ministry of Economic Development. 2008. "On the Current State of Russia's WTO Accession Negotiations." December, World Trade Organization, Geneva.

Nassar, A. 2011. "Brazil." In *WTO Disciplines on Agricultural Support*, edited by D. Orden, D. Blandford, and T. Josling, 223–276. Cambridge, UK: Cambridge University Press.

OECD (Organisation for Economic Co-operation and Development). 2007. *Agricultural Policies in Non-OECD Countries—Monitoring and Evaluation 2007.* Paris: OECD.

———. 2009. *Agricultural Policies in Emerging Economies 2009—Monitoring and Evaluation.* Paris: OECD.

———. 2011. Producer and Consumer Support Estimates database. Accessed September 2012. www.oecd.org/tad/agricultural-policies/producerandconsumersupportestimatesdatabase.htm.

———. 2012. *Agricultural Policy Monitoring and Evaluation 2012: OECD Countries.* Paris: OECD.

Orden, D., D. Blandford, and T. Josling, eds. 2011. *WTO Disciplines on Agricultural Support: Seeking a Fair Basis for Trade.* Cambridge, UK: Cambridge University Press.

RIA Novosti. 2010. "Russian Agricultural Minister Boosts WTO Accession—Paper." September 28. Accessed September 2012. http://en.rian.ru/business/20100928/160749576.html.

USDA (US Department of Agriculture). 2011. "Agricultural Exchange Rate Data Set, Nominal Annual Country Exchange Rates." Accessed September 2012. http://ers.usda.gov/Data/ExchangeRates/.

WTO (World Trade Organization). 1995a. "Accession to the World Trade Organization—Information to Be Provided on Domestic Support and Subsidies in Agriculture." WT/ACC/4, WTO, Geneva.

———. 1995b. *Results of the Uruguay Round of Multilateral Trade Negotiations—The Legal Texts.* Geneva: WTO.

———. 2008. "Revised Draft Modalities for Agriculture." TN/AG/W/4/Rev.4, WTO, Geneva.

———. 2011a. "Groups in the Agriculture Negotiations." Accessed September 2012. www.wto.org/english/tratop_e/agric_e/negoti_groups_e.htm.

———. 2011b. "Notification of Domestic Support, India." G/AG/N/IND/7, June 9. WTO, Geneva.

———. 2011c. "Report of the Working Party on the Accession of the Russian Federation to the World Trade Organization." WT/ACC/RUS/70; WT/MIN(11)/2, WTO, Geneva.

———. 2011d. "Working Party Seals the Deal on Russia's Membership Negotiations." Accessed September 2012. www.wto.org/english/news_e/news11_e/acc_rus_10nov11_e.htm.

———. 2012. Domestic Support and Export Subsidies in the Agricultural Sector. WT/ACC/SPEC/RUS/39, August 23. WTO, Geneva.

Chapter 6

ASSESSING THE POTENTIAL COST OF A FAILED DOHA ROUND

Antoine Bouët and David Laborde

After 15 years of negotiations, WTO members have not reached a final agreement on the Doha Round liberalization modalities.[1] Conflicts still exist on several issues regarding the commitments that both developed and developing countries should make. For instance, the United States is still reluctant to tackle the issue of domestic support to the cotton sector, and India and other developing countries wish to avoid restrictions, such as the anti-concentration clause, on their ability to use flexibility in nonagricultural market access (NAMA) negotiations. Beyond these very specific elements of disagreement, it seems that the incentives to conclude the Doha Round are weak. Because large market access gains have already been achieved in the manufacturing sectors of developed-country markets (Martin and Messerlin 2007), the impetus that existed in previous multilateral negotiations has vanished. In addition, the remaining issues are not only more difficult to negotiate, but the political costs are high and the gains are more difficult to assess. For developed countries, liberalizing agricultural markets remains a very complex issue. At the same time, developing countries want to maintain protection in manufacturing and, based on nascent industry considerations, to avoid making new commitments regarding services. Last, regional and bilateral liberalizations have reduced the market access gains expected by key players and have fostered resistance to multilateral liberalization that will erode existing preferences. Therefore, the longer the negotiations last, the weaker are the incentives to conclude a successful round.

In parallel, impact assessments using a Computable General Equilibrium (CGE) model have provided increasingly accurate quantitative information concerning the gains and losses associated with the DDA in particular, thanks

1 This chapter was originally published as an article in *World Trade Review* (Bouët and Laborde 2010).

to the improved quality of data.[2] Great improvements have been achieved since the Uruguay Round assessment, where a lack of information on tariffs led to an overestimation of potential gains. However, improved information has shown that the gains from the Doha Round are lower than expected (Bouët 2008), since the models now capture the fact that applied tariffs are in most cases lower than their most favored nation (MFN) bound level, due to both binding overhang (the gap between MFN bound and applied rates) and preferences (the gap between MFN and bilateral applied rates). In addition, the implementation of trade scenarios has become more and more precise, adding details and including numerous flexibilities and exceptions that exist, limiting the scope of liberalization (Jean, Laborde, and Martin 2008).

The shrinking gains associated with the DDA (see Anderson, Martin, and van der Mensbrugghe 2005; Decreux and Fontagné 2006; Bouët, Mevel, and Orden 2006) have led both economists and policy makers to state that the real gains go far beyond tariff-reduction effects and can be found outside the standard model. For example, gains in productivity, the liberalization of services, and trade facilitation are still weakly represented in CGE exercises but may account for a large share of the positive effects of a successful round. Moreover, even if applied tariffs are not cut, the simple fact that tariff lines are bound and that the existing binding overhang is reduced has a significant value because it provides a more stable trade environment.

The goal of this chapter is not to uncover additional benefits associated with the DDA, but to reexamine the value of an agreement by considering potential gains and losses in a moving landscape of trade policies. Traditional impact studies have assessed the potential gains of the Doha negotiations by comparing the consequences of the negotiation modalities to the status quo baseline. Therefore, the cost of failed negotiations has been seen as just an opportunity cost representing the unrealized gains. This approach, however, may have underestimated the real costs associated with the failure of the DDA. Such a drastic event would make the business-as-usual scenario uncertain because the status quo is not a long-term perspective for trade policies. The current trend of multilateral trade liberalization may not survive this failure, and the global public good provided by the WTO that helps to free trade in a stable and less-distorted environment may vanish. Therefore this chapter compares the effects of a DDA scenario with other relevant alternatives.

---

2 It is more questionable whether the CGE models themselves have improved significantly in terms of incorporation of new theory.

Aside from the DDA scenario, we study four protectionist scenarios that are characterized by different orders of magnitude and different approaches. Throughout the chapter we take into account the commitments enforced through the current trading system that limit WTO members' capacity to impede international trade—in particular, through binding border protection. We develop a new database of historical world protection that prevailed from 1995 to 2006. This allows us to examine by how much tariff barriers have decreased since the creation of the WTO and to determine the maximum tariff during this period of time that will be the basis of a protectionist scenario. We also use the MAcMapHS6v2 database (Laborde 2008) on applied and bound protection in 2004 to define another protectionist scenario characterized by the implementation of the highest protection authorized by the current multilateral system. We implement these different tariff scenarios in the MIRAGE model of the world economy in order to evaluate the economic consequences of these cooperative and protectionist outcomes.[3] The difference between cooperative and protectionist scenarios represents a potential reduction of US$2,261 billion in trade (in constant terms) if we refer to bound tariffs, and US$1,170 billion if we refer to maximum tariffs implemented between 1995 and 2006.[4]

Another point of view is to consider the WTO agreement as a "preventive" scheme against potential trade wars. This is why we undertake a comparison between a resort to protectionism when the DDA is implemented and a resort to protectionism when the DDA is not implemented. The comparison shows that this trade agreement could prevent the potential reduction of trade by US$809 billion. Therefore it acts as an efficient multilateral "preventive" scheme against the adverse consequences of trade "beggar-thy-neighbor" policies. The reference scenario for this figure is a situation where countries adopt bound duties, whereas if we consider a situation where countries adopt the highest tariffs implemented between 1995 and 2006, world trade would be reduced by a supplement of US$581 billion. These new findings clearly demonstrate the potential cost of a failed Doha Round. As stated by WTO Director-General Pascal Lamy in his speech at the Lowy Institute in Sydney on March 2, 2009: "The Doha Round is the most effective way to further

3 MIRAGE (Modelling International Relationships in Applied General Equilibrium) is a multicountry, multisector dynamic CGE model, developed initially at the Centre d'Etudes Prospectives et d'Informations Internationales (CEPII) in Paris. A full description of the model is available in Decreux and Valin (2007).

4 Throughout this chapter, we evaluate one scenario by the deviation from the baseline for the 2020 horizon. We compare two scenarios by comparing these two deviations.

constrain protectionist pressures by reducing the gap between bound commitments and applied policies" (Lamy 2009).

The chapter is structured as follows. The first section details the motivation of this study. Next, the methodology is described. The chapter then presents the results of all scenarios, both in terms of level of border protection and in terms of economic impact. The final section concludes.

Background

This section provides a detailed background of this study. If we undertake a new assessment of the Doha scenario, based on the last draft modalities discussed next, we also evaluate completely different trade scenarios that are aimed to estimate the potential cost of a worldwide resort to protectionism. Are these latter scenarios realistic? First, we consider the wave of protectionist and "beggar-thy-neighbor" policies adopted since early 2008 and conclude that there is no straightforward evidence that the threat of trade wars has increased. Second, we examine historical data on world protectionism and point out that trade policies offer a moving landscape, in the long-term as well as in the medium-term. Third, we proceed to a review of the economic literature in order to understand the rationale for these up-and-down variations in applied protection.

Has Protectionism Recently Increased?

It has often been stated that since September 2008, rising protectionism has occurred among WTO members, mixing increases in MFN duties, nontariff barriers, and the proliferation of antidumping duties (see, for example, Baldwin and Evenett 2008, 2009). Border measures, like nonautomatic licensing requirements by Argentina or tariffs on steel products by India, have recently been implemented. Numerous bailout measures, apparently related to the banking and financial crisis, have also been adopted and contain protectionist measures like the "Buy American" provision included in the US stimulus package agreed on in February 2009.[5] All these measures that in one way or another subsidize domestic firms are questionable in terms of their compatibility to the WTO law (see Bhagwati and Panagarya, in Baldwin and Evenett

5 On September, 16, 2009, the Global Trade Alert (2009) website listed 573 "red" measures adopted throughout the world during the 2008–2009 global downturn: that is to say, measures that have been implemented and that are *almost certainly* discriminating against foreign trading interests.

2008), especially if they survive the crisis. The WTO authorizes domestic subsidies when aimed at restructuring businesses, promoting innovation, and/or assisting displaced workers (Hufbauer and Schott 2009). However, some of these measures are weakly linked to the financial crisis, especially some trade policy modifications that were initiated in early 2008 and fully implemented at the end of the year. Regarding the WTO, all border measures are compatible since tariff increases respect the bound commitments. Some bailout measures may be WTO-compatible, if temporary. The US "Buy American" provision violates the WTO Government Procurement Agreement under which Canada, the 27 European Union (EU) countries, Hong Kong, Iceland, Israel, Japan, Korea, Liechtenstein, Norway, Singapore, Switzerland, and the United States have to open procurement to competition from firms based in the signatory countries (Hufbauer and Schott 2009). This obligation is not extended to all WTO members; firms from Brazil, China, and India cannot complain about this provision.

While bailout and restructuring measures may be understood as an attempt to circumvent the disastrous economic impact of the banking and financial crisis, the recently increasing adoption of beggar-thy-neighbor protectionist policies is not obvious. Most of the figures pointing out a multiplication of increased import tariffs or antidumping procedures do not make any temporal comparisons (like a report to the Trade Policy Review Body [TPRB] by the WTO staff; WTO 2009) or compare it with 2007 as a year of reference. The *Recession and Protectionism 'Within the Rules': Risks to the Multilateral Trade System*—a monthly newsletter of the Institute for the Integration of Latin America and the Caribbean (INTAL 2009)—states that "according to the information from the International Trade Centre (ITC) and the WTO, during the first half of 2008 the number of antidumping cases rose by 40%." The newsletter, however, does not specify if the reference is the first half of 2007, and it does not provide medium-term references. Gamberoni and Newfarmer (2009) affirm that "after a period of slowdown, the number of antidumping cases (both investigations initiated and imposition of duties) surged in 2008, especially in the second half of 2008. Compared to 2007, antidumping initiations grew by 15% and findings with imposition of duties grew by 22%." Again, we do not know if 2007 is the right comparison. In addition, during a period of economic crisis, exporting firms are prone to reduce their prices to support demand. This leads mechanically to an increase of antidumping investigations without requiring a more protectionist attitude by policy makers.

Figure 6.1 indicates trade disputes handled by WTO from 1995 (first quarter) to 2009 (second quarter). As seasonal variations are large, they are cumulated on four consecutive quarters. Of course, there is a lag between the time when a protectionist measure is implemented and the time when a complaint is filed. Therefore the observed increase in the number of trade disputes during the last quarter of 2008 might reflect the increase of antidumping procedures noted in early 2008. In that case, this is not unique as the same phenomenon occurred in 2000 and 2002. Moreover the cumulated number of trade disputes in four consecutive quarters has decreased in the first quarter of 2009 and is under the level attained in the same quarter in 2007 and 2005. There is no indication of a recent surge in protectionism. It should be noted, however, that reliable information is difficult to gather. For example, the WTO staff makes references to protectionist measures but concedes that "the information on changes in trade policies and trade-related policies contained in this report has been collected by the Secretariat from a variety of public and official sources. In some cases it has been possible to verify the information through formal channels, but in most cases it has not" (WTO 2009).

The Moving Landscape of Trade Policies

It is often stated that pressure for protectionism is cyclical. Although this statement is rather difficult to support with concrete evidence, it can be easily demonstrated that protectionism has been cyclical in rich countries from the end of the eighteenth century to the mid-twentieth century. Figure 6.2 points out this "cyclicity" in the United States from 1891 to 1940. The US tariff has followed a liberalizing path from 1940 until now. This trend can be found in France (see Messerlin 1985) and other European countries (Bairoch 1995 or Irwin 1992, among others).

Does this conclusion apply to all countries throughout the world? It is difficult to say because no historical database on applied protection exists at the world level. In addition, a decreasing national average can hide increases in tariffs at the product level. This is why we examine the frequency of tariff increases at the HS6 (Harmonized System–6 digit) level from one year to the other in 164 countries between 1995 and 2006 using the TRAINS (Trade Analysis and Information System) database (Table 6.1).[6] We calculate the *ad valorem* equivalent (AVE) of MFN applied protection (*ad valorem* duties and

6 TRAINS is an information system developed by UNCTAD (2016) at the HS-based tariff line level covering tariff, para-tariff, and nontariff measures as well as import flows by origin for more than 160 countries.

FIGURE 6.1 Trade disputes handled at the World Trade Organization (WTO) Dispute Settlement Body, 1995–2009 (first quarter 1995–second quarter 2009, cumulated on four consecutive quarters)

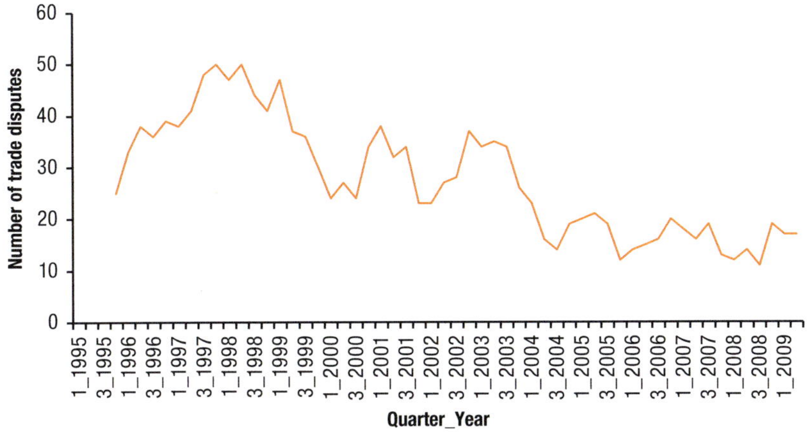

Source: WTO (2008).

FIGURE 6.2 Amount of import duties divided by dutiable imports, United States, 1891–2001

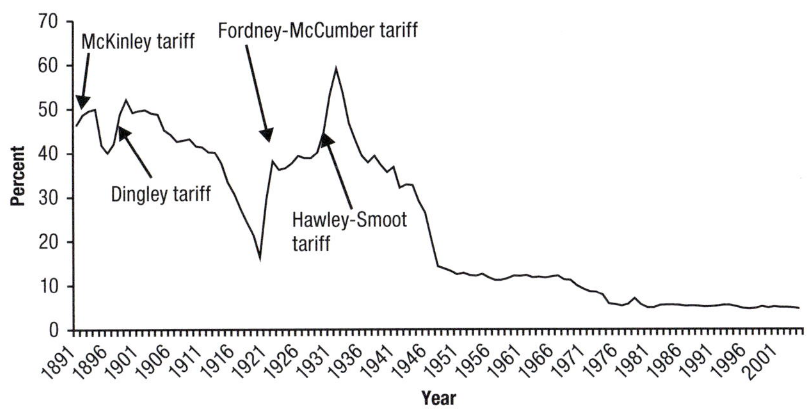

Source: USITC, n.d.

specific duties) for each reporter on each HS6 product every year and the frequency of tariff augmentation, defined as the number of MFN tariff augmentations divided by the product of 12 years and the number of HS6 lines.

As the AVE of specific tariffs may vary due to modification of unit values and as we focus on discretionary variations of import duties, and not on variations of import duties induced by price inflation (or deflation), we neutralize

TABLE 6.1 Frequency of most favored nation (MFN) tariff augmentation, 1995–2006 (%)

Country or region	Nonagricultural market access (NAMA) (%)	Agricultural market access (AMA) (%)	All (%)
Sudan	32.6	32.1	32.6
Qatar	24.8	20.2	24.2
Kuwait	24.7	20.1	24.1
Madagascar	21.4	21.1	21.4
Switzerland	19.2	26.0	20.1
Rwanda	19.5	10.2	18.3
Uzbekistan	17.5	20.4	17.9
Kyrgyzstan	17.4	20.4	17.8
Argentina	17.3	15.6	17.1
Nicaragua	15.3	18.9	15.7
Sri Lanka	14.3	24.6	15.7
Paraguay	15.4	10.8	14.7
Morocco	14.3	17.1	14.6
Uruguay	15.4	9.0	14.5
Bhutan	11.5	24.0	13.2
Lebanon	12.7	13.3	12.8
Democratic Republic of Congo	12.4	14.4	12.7
Afghanistan	11.0	16.9	11.8
India	11.2	15.3	11.8
Czech Republic	11.8	3.4	10.7
Republic of Moldova	10.1	13.3	10.5
Nigeria	10.7	9.0	10.4
World	**4.5**	**6.1**	**4.7**
United States	2.1	13.3	3.6
EU15	1.8	14.6	3.5
Japan	0.7	8.1	1.7
China	1.2	1.8	1.3

Source: TRAINS and authors' calculations.

Note: The frequency of most favored nation (MFN) tariff augmentation should be defined as the number of augmentations/(12 years . number of HS6 products). EU15 = Austria, Belgium, Denmark, Finland, France, Germany, Greece, Ireland, Italy, Luxembourg, Netherlands, Portugal, Spain, Sweden, United Kingdom.

the effect of unit value variations by assessing the AVE of specific duties, based on the 2004 year unit value, for every year from 1995 to 2006. Table 6.1 identifies 22 out of 164 countries in the database for which the frequency of tariff increase has been greater than 10 percent in all sectors. It also shows the

TABLE 6.2 **Percentage of most favored nation (MFN) tariff augmentation, 1995–2006, by groups of countries (%)**

Sector	WTO	Non-WTO	Least developed countries (LDCs)	Non-LDCs	Middle-income countries (MICs)	Non-MICs	Organisation for Economic Co-operation and Development (OECD)	Non-OECD
All sectors	4.7	5.3	4.1	4.9	5.2	3.8	3.3	4.9
Nonagricultural sectors (NAMA)	4.5	5.0	4.1	4.6	5.0	3.5	2.6	4.8
Agricultural sectors (AMA)	6.0	7.0	4.3	6.6	6.2	5.8	8.4	5.8

Source: TRAINS and authors' calculations.

Note: The WTO membership is here defined as the status observed in 2005. It would have been better to take into account the exact date of membership, but the final access to WTO is systematically preceded by a period of observer status.

frequency calculated for agricultural and nonagricultural products at the world level as well as at the national level for the United States, the EU15, Japan, and China.[7]

At the world level the frequency of tariff augmentation in all sectors is significant, even if not very large: close to 4.5 percent. While this frequency was higher than 20 percent in the case of 5 countries (Sudan, Qatar, Kuwait, Madagascar, and Switzerland), it was 0 during this period for 11 countries: Cyprus, Eritrea, Gambia, Guinea, Haiti, Hong Kong, Macau, Mayotte, Palau, Slovakia, and Syria. In general, tariff augmentations are more frequent in the agricultural sector.[8] But this is particularly true in rich countries like the EU15, the United States, Japan, but also Norway, and in middle-income countries, like Poland and Ukraine. In Norway, for example, from 1995 to 2006, while annual tariff augmentations occurred in only 0.2 percent of all nonagricultural cases, they were noted in 22 percent of agricultural cases.

Table 6.2 displays the frequency of MFN tariff augmentation from 1995 to 2006 for countries based on whether they are WTO members (WTO) or not (non-WTO), whether they are classified as least developed countries (LDC) or not (non-LDC), middle-income countries (MICs) or not (non-MICs), or OECD (OECD) or not (non-OECD). Finally, these ratios are calculated for all sectors (All), and for nonagricultural sectors (NAMA) or agricultural sectors (AMA).

7 The EU15 is Austria, Belgium, Denmark, Finland, France, Germany, Greece, Ireland, Italy, Luxembourg, Netherlands, Portugal, Spain, Sweden, and the United Kingdom.

8 Due to the volatility in agricultural prices, governments adjust trade policies more frequently. Let us notice that this fact is consistent with the political economy model used when we design trade policy scenarios (Jean, Laborde, and Martin 2008).

The propensity to augment MFN tariffs is lower among WTO members than among non-WTO countries, as it is lower in industry than in agriculture. It appears that LDCs raise their MFN tariffs less frequently than the world average, while MICs do so more often.[9] The propensity of OECD countries to augment their MFN tariffs is significantly low in industry but is relatively high in agriculture—higher than in MICs and LDCs.

Economic Crisis, Trade Wars, and Retaliations

The financial crisis ostensibly fostered demand for protectionism and could have led to new trade barriers, as occurred after the October 1929 crisis. A parallel can easily be drawn between the 2008 situation and the one that existed then. In the early 1930s, unemployment was rising, fear of deflation prevailed, and a lack of public resources (which was more pronounced in countries that paid war reparations) prevented governments from remedying the economic crisis. Moreover, in 2008 as in 1930, the context of decreasing prices could have mechanically reinforced protection, as specific duties (defined as monetary amounts by physical units), which are numerous in agriculture, become more and more restrictive when world prices are down. In this type of economic context, protectionism is a tempting policy instrument for policy makers—it shortsightedly increases domestic prices and supports domestic activity, and it provides new public revenue. In the Republican platform of the 1928 presidential election, the tariff was presented as the "household remedy" (Isaacs 1948): that is to say, a policy that leads to higher domestic prices and increased economic activity.

But the role of the Smoot-Hawley Tariff Act and the subsequent tariff retaliations in the decline of trade after 1930 should not be overestimated: recent evaluations (Irwin 1998; Madsen 2001) show that discretionary increases in tariff rates explain only a minor part of the post-1929 contraction of trade. For example, Madsen (2001) estimates that real world trade declined from 1929 to 1932 by approximately 14 percent because of decreasing national incomes, 8 percent because of discretionary augmentations of tariffs, 5 percent because of deflation-induced tariff increases, and 6 percent as a result of nontariff barriers.

It is theoretically and empirically proven that trade openness is employment-creating and income-supporting in sectors in which an economy has a

9 These findings are consistent with previous works (Laborde 2008) that emphasize the fact that LDCs have less sophisticated trade policies than more developed economies, in particular due to the lack of administrative capacity.

comparative advantage, but has a negative impact on employment and incomes in sectors where the economy has a comparative disadvantage. This implies that trade openness leads to a restructuring of an economy that can be costly, and trade openness is more popular in times of economic growth. During economic recession, the job market provides fewer opportunities and any threat on existing jobs is negatively perceived—in particular, in countries with a limited social protection net and where adjustment costs are large. In time of stagnation, lobbying to increase protection above usual levels in sectors without comparative advantage tends to be strong, especially when sectors are small and geographically/socially homogenous (Olson 1965). This explains why demand for protection is so strong in the US sectors of automobile and textile and apparel, in the European sectors of agriculture and automobile, in the Japanese agricultural sector, and so on.

The interdependence of trading partners should increase the probability of a trade war, thanks to the adoption of retaliatory measures: governments do not correctly anticipate that protectionism will initiate a cycle of world retaliation and counterretaliation, as was the case with the United States in 1930 and also in 2007–2008 when, in the middle of the food crisis, governments implemented export bans and export restrictions in successive rounds of retaliation and counterretaliation. There exists an economic theory of retaliation and two of its conclusions are worthwhile:

- Large countries can benefit from a trade war while small countries always lose (Johnson 1953). This point has been recently raised by Soesastro (in Baldwin and Evenett 2009) when he states that the largest economies will likely be more tempted by protectionism than small ones. Small countries are more dependent on international trade and could be severely damaged by a trade war. Large economies like the EU or the United States are much more independent and can benefit from the adoption of import tariffs that could substantially decrease the world prices of their imports.
- Trade wars may be long and damaging when countries do not identify who is at the origin of the process; and conversely, countries have to be "nice" in order to reestablish trade cooperation as quickly as possible (Axelrod 1981).

Finally, there is another factor that should contribute to rising protectionism. The failure of the DDA mainly comes from disagreements between rich and emerging countries: between India and the United States on the Safeguard Special Mechanism (SSM) in agriculture, between the United States and West Africa on cotton, and between the EU and Brazil on tariff reduction in agriculture, to name a few examples. This clearly defines a line of demarcation that could be the basis of future trade disputes. While there is no strong evidence of rising protectionism today, trade policies can still be changed by policy makers as a reaction to a particular economic situation. Current economic conditions could contribute to a complete change of mood in terms of trade policies implemented. In fact, even the post–World War II period, which is a remarkable period of history in terms of trade policies becoming freer and freer, trading partners, including WTO members, frequently augmented tariff protection when needed. This is especially true for middle-income countries in all sectors and OECD countries in agriculture.

Alternative Scenarios and Methodology

Based on this background, this chapter aims to compare the gains of trade cooperation with protectionist alternatives and to examine how a negotiated DDA can protect the world trading system from a rise in protectionism. With this objective, we implement different scenarios and compare the following:

- the implementation of the December 2008 package with different protectionist scenarios (elimination of binding overhang; and implementation of the highest MFN tariff applied during the 1995–2006 period for each importing country at the product level); and
- the implementation of these protectionist scenarios in a situation where the DDA is not implemented and the implementation of these scenarios in a situation where the DDA is implemented. This element shows how a new trade negotiation will prevent the world trading system from trade wars.

These assessments are carried out using the MIRAGE CGE model of the world economy, with protection data coming from the MAcMapHS6 database and a new historical database on MFN applied protection. The remainder of this section offers a methodological overview followed by a detailed description of each scenario.

Methodology

Data treatment

Tariff reform is implemented at the disaggregation level of the MAcMap-HS6v2.1 database with bound and applied tariff data for 2004 (including

5,113 products, 170 importing countries, and 208 exporting countries) at the HS6 product level.[10] We add several updates to take into account all major changes that occurred up to 2008, including major regional trade agreements (RTAs), new WTO members (such as Ukraine), but also the trade policy consequences of ongoing domestic reforms (such as the EU sugar trade reform). The TRAINS database was used to investigate tariff changes since 1995, and a special procedure was adopted to ensure comparability of MFN tariff rates between MAcMapHS6 and TRAINS. For ensuring intertemporal comparison of nominal protection, all specific tariffs are converted using the reference group unit values from MAcMapHS6v2.[11]

However, WTO published detailed guidelines in order to know which reduction coefficient has to be applied on specific duties.[12] Therefore, in our design of the policy scenario and for the purpose of tariff reduction formula classification, the official guidelines to compute unit values are used. Simultaneously all trade policy scenarios are implemented on a yearly basis following relevant timelines in each case. The Doha scenario and the free trade agreements (FTAs) that are included in the baseline give countries the freedom to select products eligible to certain clauses: these are either the "sensitive products" or the "special products" clauses that allow rich and developing countries to choose a list of products that will be less liberalized, or the "exception" clause included in the duty-free quota-free (DFQF) regime that will be given by OECD countries to LDCs (this clause implied that OECD countries will have the right to exclude 3 percent of tariff lines from this regime), or the binding rules under which countries have to define a list of unbound tariff lines that have to be bound at the end of the round. As the rule is "no rule," we have to define a criterion of selection of these products in our modeling. We

10 Slight modifications have been made on the MAcMapHS6v2.1 dataset: Malaysia's tariffs on tobacco products are updated (lowered), marginal protection on Chinese cereal TRQs are reduced, and protection faced on sugar and bananas by ACP (Africa, Caribbean, and Pacific) countries in the EU market is modified to better capture preference erosion mechanisms.

11 This method (exporter's reference group unit value) implies that the unit value taken for the AVE calculation of specific tariffs is the median unit value of world exports by a group of countries similar—from the point of view of trade—to the exporting country. It is aimed at (1) reflecting the different restrictive impacts of a specific tariff on exporting countries according to their vertical specialization (the specific duty imposed by the EU on pork sausages, for example, has a different protectionist impact whether the partner exports low-price or high-price pork sausage); and (2) not exhibiting excessive volatility (see Bouët et al. 2008).

12 In agriculture WTO members negotiate on a reduction coefficient to be applied on tariffs defined by intervals: tariffs from x percent to y percent will be reduced by z percent. This does not specify by which extent specific duties (US$ per ton, for example) will be reduced. These official guidelines describe in particular how AVE of specific duties have to be calculated to select the right reduction coefficient.

use the idea of the model developed by Jean, Laborde, and Martin (2008). It is based on a political economy approach where the government (common agent) gives protection to economic sectors (multiprincipals) against financial transfers and maximizes a function that includes national welfare and these financial transfers.

Concerning exemption clauses, as a result of this model, the government is supposed to select lines that maximize a political economy indicator—in particular, depending positively on the height of the tariff and the magnitude of imports. An extension of this model is used to define the choice of tariff lines to be bound by developing countries in the DDA scenario. Indeed, for a particular scenario when we combine tariff increases with the DDA implementation, it is very important to have a theoretical based approach to define the new bound tariffs, especially for countries (SVEs, small and vulnerable economies; LDCs; and initially low binding countries) that benefit from wide flexibilities to achieve their new binding coverage goal.[13] The DDA modalities (WTO 2008) define in this case the overall constraints faced by each country. Finally, when WTO members liberalize under the DDA, we suppose that the market access remains unchanged for non-WTO members.

Tariffs are aggregated from the HS6 level to the model aggregation (see below) using the reference group weighting scheme methodology (Boumellassa, Laborde, and Mitaritonna 2009) and then implemented in the MIRAGE multicountry, multisector dynamic model.[14] We assume perfect competition across all sectors.[15] Based on standard and robust assumptions, it should be noted that the model may underestimate the positive effects of trade reform, particularly when such reform drives new investments, technology improvements, or important trade or production diversification. Macroeconomic data (such as world trade flows, production, consumption, and intermediate use of commodities and services) come from the Global Trade Analysis Project

---

13 The only difference with the approach defined in Jean, Laborde, and Martin (2008) is that in order to compute the political cost of any new commitments, we do not take into account the applied tariff in 2004 (the base year), but the highest tariff during the 1995–2006 period.

14 This weighting scheme (reference group) implies that we weight a tariff imposed by country *r* on a product *i* coming from *s* by the imports by a group of countries similar to *r*—from the point of view of trade—of product *i* coming from country *s*; it is aimed at (1) reflecting the structure of country *r*'s trade; (2) avoiding the endogeneity bias arising from a bilateral trade weighting scheme (see Bouët et al. 2008).

15 The MIRAGE model makes possible an imperfect competition assumption, and it has been used in previous quantitative assessments. However, this hypothesis requires information about sector markups, number of firms, and magnitude of fixed costs, which is difficult to gather for developing countries. This is the reason why we preferred here to adopt a perfect competition hypothesis in all sectors.

(GTAP) 7 database (see Narayanan and Walmsley 2008 for a full documentation). Identified in the model are 27 regions (8 high-income regions), which map the main trade blocks. The sectoral decomposition is highly detailed in terms of agriculture and agrifood business (12 sectors), since most of the protection is concentrated in this sector. All other sectors are nonagricultural, including 13 industrial sectors and 2 service sectors.[16]

A Snapshot of MIRAGE

In each country a representative consumer maximizes a CES-LES (Constant Elasticity of Substitution–Linear Expenditure System) utility function under a budget constraint to allocate her (his) income across goods. The origin of goods is determined by a CES (Constant Elasticity of Substitution) nested structure following the Armington assumption.[17] In addition, developed countries are supposed to produce high-quality industrial goods, as compared to those supplied by developing countries. On the production side, value-added and intermediate goods are complements under a Leontief hypothesis. The value-added is a CES function of unskilled labor and a composite of skilled labor and capital: it allows for including less substitutability between the last two production factors.

In agriculture and mining, production depends on land and natural resources. New capital is perfectly mobile across sectors while installed capital is immobile. Skilled labor is perfectly mobile across sectors, while unskilled labor is imperfectly mobile between agricultural sectors and nonagricultural sectors. Total employment is constant. Investment is savings-driven, and the real exchange rate is adjusted (through price adjustments) such that the current account is constant in terms of world gross domestic product (GDP). This last assumption is important in this study since tariff reductions (Doha scenario) and tariff increases (protectionist scenarios) will have positively correlated impacts on both imports and exports for every country.

Baseline

A baseline is implemented from 2008 to 2025, which depicts the world without a new multilateral agreement. Concerning trade reform, new agreements adopted since 2004 have been included in the baseline: they are listed in

16 Geographic decomposition is presented in Appendix 6.1. Sector decomposition is not given here as we do not make any comment on sector variables. This sector decomposition can be requested from the authors.

17 The MIRAGE model is based on GTAP Armington elasticities, which are low as compared to those used in other models (the World Bank's LINKAGE model, for example).

Appendix 6.2.[18] This baseline serves as a point of comparison with all the scenarios. The results are reported for the year 2025. Results are presented as the difference for a macroeconomic variable in 2025 between the baseline and the scenario. Therefore this variation represents the unique impact of the policy shock described in the scenario. The analysis does not account for the surge in world prices of energy and food products between 2004 and 2008. However, exogenous increases in active populations are included in the model and each country's global factor productivity is affected such that GDP evolution, as described by the model, corresponds to the World Bank's GDP predictions.

Describing Alternative Scenarios

The five scenarios analyzed here include the Doha compromise, as decribed by the December 2008 modalities, and four protectionist alternatives. These are:

1. DDA: December 2008 modalities;
2. Up to Bound: Non–Free Trade Agreements (FTA) applied tariffs increased to existing bound levels;
3. Bound & DDA: Implementation of December 2008 modalities plus non-FTA applied tariffs increased to new, post-DDA, bound level;
4. Up to Max: Non-FTA applied tariffs increased to their last 10 years maximum level, capped by existing bound tariffs; and
5. Max & DDA: Implementation of December 2008 modalities plus non-FTA applied tariffs increased to their last 10 years maximum level, capped by new, post-DDA, bound tariffs.

The DDA Scenario

The first scenario represents a successful Doha outcome based on December 2008 modalities. After seven years of trade talks, market access modalities have reached a high level of sophistication. Even if the general philosophy is simple, with progressive tariff-cut formulas for both agricultural and nonagricultural goods, many flexibilities have been introduced with different degrees of special and differential treatment for different groups of developing countries. Following previous research (Laborde, Martin, and van der Mensbrugghe 2008; Berisha et al. 2008), this scenario implements all the details of these modalities in terms of market access including tariff-cutting

18 These "new" FTAs are additional to those already present in the GTAP 7 database.

formulas, country and product flexibilities (sensitive and special products), as well as special provisions for tariff escalation, tropical products, and long-standing preferences.[19] The scenario does not account for any changes on the sectoral initiative due to the lack of agreement on this issue. For the duty-free quota-free market access initiative for least developed countries (LDCs) and OECD countries (excluding South Korea [Republic of Korea] but including Mexico and Turkey), we assume a 3 percent exemption clause in terms of products.[20] Export subsidies are phased out by 2013 for developed countries.

Concerning domestic support, this scenario includes the constraint on overall trade-distorting support (OTDS) for the United States and the EU. In contrast to most traditional exercises where domestic support commitments are translated in *ad valorem* or specific subsidy caps for current applied policies, we explicitly introduce the OTDS as an overall limit for domestic support spending for each year. In the dynamic context and due to the growth of production in the baseline, the initial agricultural subsidy rates, based on 2004 prices, may lead to a violation of the new commitments. In our simulation, it appears that only the United States will face a real constraint forcing it to modify its production distortive programs.[21] With the reduction scheme of the OTDS on one hand, and the increasing production on the other, we estimate that subsidy rates of production and on some primary factors should start to decrease by 2011 and will have to be halved by 2025 down to the final US$16.4 billion limit. Any domestic support reduction will impact all sectors in a uniform way. Since this chapter focuses on tariffs and tariff changes across scenarios, we have introduced neither a program-specific modeling of domestic support policies, nor a political economy model aimed to explain how domestic support reduction across commodities will be handled. Our goal here is to show that the new OTDS commitments, even if they do not drive domestic support reduction today, have a real value on the medium run. The consequences of this treatment are discussed in Appendix 6.3.

Due to the complexity of integrating other elements of the DDA agenda in the simulations, other sources of potential gains are omitted, such as liberalization in services, WTO rules, trade facilitation, and intellectual property rights.

19 A full description of the modalities implemented in this study is provided in Laborde, Martin, and van der Mensbrugghe (2008). This scenario is based on the December 2008 Modalities.

20 This scenario mimics Scenario F in Berisha et al. (2008).

21 The recent Common Agricultural Policy (CAP) reform allows the EU to largely reallocate domestic program funds to the Green Box.

Up to Bound Scenario

Two protectionist scenarios are analyzed to offer a contrasting picture with the DDA. The first option, the Up to Bound scenario, examines the possibility for WTO countries to increase their tariffs up to their Uruguay Round (UR) bound level in a five-year period (2009–2014). It assumes that the entire binding overhang will be eliminated. For unbound lines the existing average binding overhang is applied to compute new tariff targets.[22] In this scenario, only MFN-applied rates and nonreciprocal, preferential rates are modified. The only nonreciprocal program that is maintained is the EU "Everything but Arms" initiative due to the way this program has been implemented and renewed in the EU legislation. Other nonreciprocal preferences given by rich countries to poor countries are removed.[23]

This scenario represents a strong increase in protection by eliminating all unilateral liberalization but does not represent an open trade war between WTO members. Existing commitments are still respected.[24] On the one hand, this scenario may appear extreme since many developing countries bound their tariffs during the Uruguay Round, using a ceiling option, to levels that they have never and may never apply. Countries also apply zero tariffs on a large selection of raw materials and imported inputs even if the existing bound tariffs are strictly positive. On the other hand, Up to Bound is not the worst scenario that can be anticipated. Many countries have not bound their import tariffs yet and are not constrained today by any upward limitation. In our scenario, applying bound duties can underestimate in some cases the desire for high protection on some specific products. Moreover, antidumping duties and safeguard mechanisms can be activated and can restrict trade even in rich countries where binding overhang is inexistent or limited.

Bound & DDA Scenario

Two scenarios intend to measure the extent by which the implementation of the December 2008 package could reduce the potential cost associated with a

---

22 We estimate a linear relation for each country relating bound duties to MFN applied duties (Bound_Rate = a MFN_rate + b), where Bound_Rate is an MFN bound duty and MFN_rate a MFN applied duty. Then we apply estimated parameters *a* and *b* on applied MFN rate to build theoretical bound tariffs for the unbound lines.

23 Examples of preferences removed are the US African Growth Opportunity Act, the US Caribbean Basin Initiative, the European GSP (given to non-LDCs), other GSPs from Japan, Norway. EPAs are supposed to be a reciprocal agreement: therefore they are not removed.

24 Even while adhering to their commitments, we may imagine that countries will use additional tools to increase their protection above bound levels by using contingent protection and by initiating litigation cases that would allow them to retaliate.

new trade war by lowering bound duties. Scenario Bound & DDA combines the DDA scenario and the Up to Bound scenario, but the bound duties that are used here are those derived from the December 2008 package. Therefore the difference between this scenario and the Up to Bound one represents the extent by which the DDA could reduce the capacity of WTO members to augment MFN tariffs. The treatment of unbound tariffs is very different in this scenario from the treatment in the Up to Bound case. Contrarily to the previous case, where an average binding margin was applied in a uniform way based on the existing binding overhang, in this scenario we apply the new DDA constraints in terms of binding rules based on the Jean, Laborde, and Martin (2008) political-economy approach combined with past trade policy behavior (see discussion elsewhere in this chapter). As previously, only MFN applied rates and nonreciprocal preferential rates are modified.

Up to Max Scenario

To adopt a more realistic protectionist scenario, historical data were used to determine the highest MFN applied protection rate implemented by every country during 1995 through 2006. In order to take into account bound tariffs implemented during the Uruguay Round (UR), the minimum between the historical maximum level and the existing bound tariffs was selected and applied to all relevant regions of origin, those for which no preference exists or for which we decided to remove a preference. This Up to Max scenario corresponds to a case whereby governments apply the most adverse trade policies of the past 10 years but still respect their UR commitments. On a historical basis, tariffs evolve as a response to changes in world prices, domestic production structure, and political pressures. In that sense this scenario is politically realistic. It is important to note that in all scenarios with increasing tariffs, the preferential tariffs protected by bilateral or regional agreements are unchanged.

Max & DDA Scenario

In this scenario the same combination (DDA plus a protectionist option) is adopted but the DDA scenario is combined with the Up to Max scenario. As new bound duties have been defined in the December 2008 package and as the tariff applied is the minimum between the highest duty applied during the 1995–2006 period and the newly defined bound duty, this scenario differs from the Up to Max scenario. The difference between them can represent the benefit from the DDA as a "preventive" scheme against trade wars. As previously, only MFN applied rates and nonreciprocal preferential rates are modified.

Results

Impact on Protection and Market Access

Figure 6.3 displays the consequences of these five scenarios on average world tariffs (the baseline is also represented).

The Doha scenario will reduce world protection by 22 percent, from 4.6 percent to 3.6 percent. Moving to bound tariffs (the Up to Bound scenario) will nearly double the level of protection on average. The elimination of unilateral tariff reductions enacted during the past 10 years (the Up to Max scenario) has a more limited impact but still represents an increase of 41 percent in world tariffs compared to the baseline (from 4.6 percent to 6.4 percent). The implementation of the December 2008 package has a significant impact on potential future trade wars. If the DDA is not implemented, current protection can be doubled when countries resort to bound levels, while it increases by only 41 percent in case the DDA is implemented. Under the Max & DDA scenario, world protection increases by only 5 percent while it increases by 41 percent under the Up to Max scenario. These comparisons show the extent to which the implementation of the December 2008 package could avoid costly protectionism. World agricultural protection decreases by 23 percent if the December 2008 package is implemented, while it becomes 1.8 times higher if bound duties are applied. Comparison of world agricultural protection under a DDA (12.6 percent) and under a global resort to bound duties (29.4 percent) provides a scale of 1 to 2.33. When the reference is maximum duties applied in the 1995–2006 period, it is 1 to 1.63.

Table 6.3 displays the results in terms of protection applied on imports by group of countries. The DDA scenario will cut the applied protection by one-third for HICs (from 3.0 percent down to 1.9 percent in all sectors, but from 15.6 percent to 10.3 percent in agriculture) and one-tenth for MICs (from 8.5 percent down to 7.8 percent in all sectors), a significant achievement when compared to previous GATT (General Agreement on Tariffs and Trade) rounds. It will also lock existing market access due to unilateral liberalization on an MFN or nonreciprocal preferences basis. Indeed, under the Up to Bound scenario, protection could increase by 48 percent in HICs, 132 percent in MICs, and 270 percent in LDCs compared to the current levels. Under the Up to Max scenario, protection in the same three groups of countries will increase by 23 percent, 56 percent, and 67 percent, respectively.

At the same time, the December 2008 package gives world exporters a "preventive" scheme against a potential rise in applied protection by MICs

FIGURE 6.3 World average tariffs by scenario, 2025 level

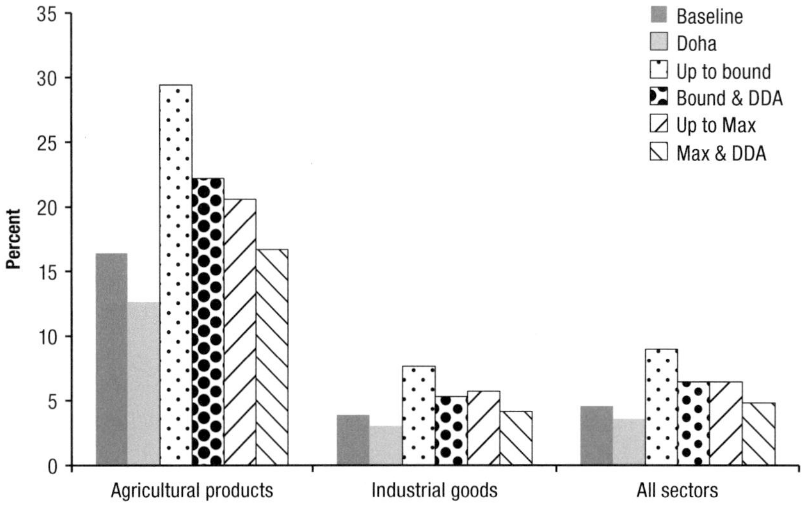

Source: MAcMapHS6v2.1, TRAINS, and authors' calculations (reference group weighting scheme).

TABLE 6.3 Protection applied by category of countries (%)

Category	Baseline	DDA	Up to Bound	Bound & DDA	Up to Max	Max & DDA
High-income countries (HICs)						
Agricultural products	15.6	10.3	22.9	15.6	18.5	13.6
Industrial goods	2.2	1.4	3.3	2.1	2.8	1.6
All sectors	*3.0*	*1.9*	*4.4*	*3.1*	*3.7*	*2.3*
Middle-income countries (MICs)						
Agricultural products	18.3	17.6	40.8	33.4	24.9	23.0
Industrial goods	7.9	7.0	17.9	12.2	12.9	10.2
All sectors	*8.6*	*7.8*	*19.8*	*14.0*	*13.3*	*10.9*
Least developed countries (LDCs)						
Agricultural products	11.6	11.6	65.3	65.5	20.0	20.0
Industrial goods	9.2	9.2	31.4	34.2	16.5	14.3
All sectors	*9.8*	*9.8*	*36.1*	*38.6*	*16.3*	*14.6*
World						
Agricultural products	16.4	12.6	29.4	22.2	20.6	16.7
Industrial goods	3.9	3.0	7.6	5.3	5.7	4.2
All sectors	*4.6*	*3.6*	*9.0*	*6.4*	*6.4*	*4.8*

Source: MAcMapHS6v2.1, TRAINS, and authors' calculations (reference group weighting scheme).

and LDCs: in the case of MICs, while protection can be augmented from 8.6 percent up to 14.0 percent (bound level) in case of implemented DDA, it can be augmented up to 19.8 percent today. As far as LDCs are concerned, if we compare the case of Up to Bound and Bound & DDA scenarios, we can see that tariffs will increase more in the latter case. Indeed, the flexibilities granted by the DDA modalities to bind tariffs will provide more freedom to increase tariffs than the homogenous binding overhang rate applied to build the Up to Bound scenario. By combining the political economy model in binding tariffs with the new rules, governments can achieve higher levels of protection than using a homogenous rate of binding overhang computed on existing bound tariff lines. This is consistent with the idea that the most sensitive products are the unbound ones.

Table 6.4 displays how access to foreign markets is modified under the baseline and the various scenarios. It calculates an average duty faced when a group of countries (or the world) exports to the rest of the world, either in all sectors, or only in agriculture or in industry.

In relative terms, the Doha scenario manages to deliver homogeneous market access gains with an average decrease of about 20 percent in the tariffs faced by three groups of countries: from 4.6 percent to 3.6 percent for both HIC and MIC countries, and from 4.0 percent to 3.2 percent for LDCs. The other scenarios, however, have significantly different results. Though the two protectionist scenarios have similar effects for HICs and MICs (90 percent or exactly 97 percent and 93 percent, respectively under the Up to Bound scenario, and 40 percent or exactly 42 percent and 37 percent, respectively under the Up to Max scenario), the LDCs are more severely affected due to losses of nonreciprocal preferences (except on the EU market, where the EBA program is maintained), in particular, in the United States and Japan: protection faced by LDCs is nearly tripled. Consequently, the implementation of a DDA is of great interest for LDCs not only because it improves access to foreign markets (even if the price of that improved access is an erosion of preferences), but also because it locks unilateral schemes and in particular the most recent initiatives. It will forbid a potential rise of protection faced by their exports: based on the maximum protection faced during the 1995–2006 period, protection faced by LDCs' exports can raise from 4.0 percent to 7.3 percent if DDA is not implemented while it can increase up to only 4.7 percent if DDA is implemented.

Economic Impacts

The MIRAGE CGE model is used to assess the economic impacts of these different tariff and domestic support scenarios up to 2025.

TABLE 6.4 Protection faced by category of countries (%)

Category of country	Baseline	DDA	Up to Bound	Bound & DDA	Up to Max	Max & DDA
High-income countries (HIC)						
Agricultural products	16.1	11.9	28.5	21.1	20.3	16.1
Industrial goods	3.8	3.0	7.7	5.4	5.6	4.2
All sectors	*4.6*	*3.6*	*9.0*	*6.4*	*6.5*	*5.0*
Middle-income countries (MIC)						
Agricultural products	17.1	13.8	30.6	23.7	21.2	17.7
Industrial goods	4.0	3.0	7.5	5.0	5.9	4.0
All sectors	*4.6*	*3.6*	*8.9*	*6.4*	*6.3*	*4.6*
Least developed countries (LDC)						
Agricultural products	9.9	8.2	30.2	24.0	14.6	12.6
Industrial goods	3.9	2.7	9.4	6.2	9.0	4.5
All sectors	*4.0*	*3.2*	*11.7*	*8.5*	*7.3*	*4.7*
World						
Agricultural products	16.4	12.6	29.4	22.2	20.6	16.7
Industrial goods	3.9	3.0	7.6	5.3	5.7	4.2
All sectors	*4.6*	*3.6*	*9.0*	*6.4*	*6.4*	*4.8*

Source: MAcMapHS6v2.1, TRAINS, and authors' calculations (reference group weighting scheme).

ECONOMIC IMPACTS AT THE GLOBAL LEVEL

Table 6.5 indicates the global results of all scenarios for the world economy in 2025. Under the Doha scenario considered here, world trade is augmented by a mere 1.9 percent (US$363 billion) and world real income by US$59 billion in 2025. This confirms the findings of other studies (see Decreux and Fontagné 2006 or Bouët, Mevel, and Orden 2006), except that here the gains are slightly lower mainly because the baseline includes numerous RTAs that already reduce applied tariffs before the DDA implementation. However, these numbers are driven by the assumption that no major political shock will take place if the DDA is not signed. Such an assumption should be considered carefully.

In the case of the Up to Bound scenario, world trade would contract by 9.9 percent (US$1,899 billion) and world real income by US$353 billion. In the case of the less damaging Up to Max scenario, world trade would decline less, by 4.2 percent (US$808 billion). While the increase in duties under the Up to Max scenario would especially impact agricultural exports (−9.4 percent), particularly harming developing countries' agricultural exports (−11.5 percent), the exports of industrial goods could also face a substantial reduction of 4.4 percent. In case of an implementation of the December 2008

TABLE 6.5 Global results led by tariffs and domestic support changes, change compared to the 2025 baseline

	DDA	Up to Bound	Bound & DDA	Up to MAX	Max & DDA
World exports in goods and services (%)[a]	**1.90**	**−9.93**	**−5.70**	**−4.23**	**−1.19**
Agrofood	5.47	−20.26	−13.42	−9.36	−4.52
Industry	1.96	−9.77	−5.07	−4.36	−0.95
World welfare (%)	**0.09**	**−0.51**	**−0.25**	**−0.19**	**−0.04**
North	0.07	−0.32	−0.20	−0.14	−0.08
South	0.13	−1.00	−0.35	−0.32	0.06
World exports in goods and services (US$ billions)[a]	**363**	**−1,899**	**−1,090**	**−808**	**−227**
Agrofood	73	−269	−178	−124	−60
Industry	279	−1,389	−721	−621	−135
World welfare (US$ billions)	**59**	**−353**	**−169**	**−134**	**−26**
North	33	−156	−100	−70	−37
South	26	−197	−69	−64	11

Source: Authors' calculations; MIRAGE simulations.
Note: Welfare changes are computed as the equivalent variation. Export volumes are defined using a Fisher index.
[a]intra-EU trade flows are excluded.

package and a subsequent augmentation of protection to Up to Bound levels, the decrease of world exports would be only US$1,090 billion, while it would be US$1,899 billion if the DDA is not applied. In other words, according to this assessment, the DDA implementation can prevent a potential reduction of US$809 billion of trade. If the rise in protectionism is the maximum protection applied during the 1996–2006 period, the DDA can prevent the potential reduction of US$581 billion of trade.

ECONOMIC IMPACT AT THE COUNTRY LEVEL

Here we focus on the impact of various scenarios on countries' macroeconomic variables. To simplify the presentation, we focus on 17 countries/zones instead of 27. Table 6.6 illustrates how various scenarios affect countries' exports in value. The impact of the Doha Agreement does not provide any surprising effect as compared to previous assessments. A look at the protectionist scenarios, without the DDA implemented, reveals how some countries could be greatly affected by a global resort to protectionism. Brazil, for example, is particularly affected by an augmentation of protection: let us recall that the Up to Bound scenario implies an increase in world agricultural protection by 13 percentage points, while protection in industry increases only

TABLE 6.6 Variations in exports (value—intratrade excluded) by countries led by tariffs and domestic support changes, percentage of change compared to the 2025 baseline

Country or region	DDA	Up to Bound	Bound & DDA	Up to Max	Max & DDA
ASEAN LIC	2.1	−18.7	−30.8	−10.7	−5.3
ASEAN MIC	2.2	−16.3	−8.0	−8.1	−3.8
ANZCERTA	3.3	−9.4	−1.0	−3.0	1.4
Bangladesh	5.8	−51.8	−52.5	−9.6	−10.8
Brazil	4.0	−25.6	−7.4	−5.9	−0.7
Canada	0.5	−1.9	−1.7	−0.8	0.1
Central Africa	0.1	−28.9	−26.9	−7.1	−7.1
China–Hong Kong	4.7	−3.3	−1.2	−1.5	3.9
EU	2.9	−10.4	−5.4	−8.6	−4.6
India	1.8	−38.9	−12.7	−12.7	−3.1
Japan	3.2	−3.0	1.1	−1.7	2.1
Mexico	0.6	−13.2	−5.2	−3.6	−2.0
MENA	4.4	−11.8	−1.4	−5.1	−0.2
Pakistan	2.1	−42.0	−35.3	−27.6	−20.9
Turkey	0.6	−12.4	−7.8	−5.7	−4.7
United States	1.9	−2.9	−0.5	−1.0	1.0

Source: Authors' calculations; MIRAGE simulations.

Note: ASEAN LIC = ASEAN low-income countries, ASEAN MIC = ASEAN middle-income countries, ANZCERTA (Australia New Zealand Closer Economic Relations Trade Agreement) = Australia and New Zealand group, MENA = Middle East and North African countries.

3.7 percentage points (see Table 6.3). Brazil's exports are especially reduced (−25.6 percent) under the Up to Bound scenario. If the DDA is agreed on, would Brazil be less hurt by a potential rise of protectionism? According to the findings here, if the DDA is implemented, Brazil's exports would be reduced by only 7.4 percent if bound duties were adopted after this agreement. The same mechanism is in play under the Up to Max and Max & DDA scenarios, but the magnitude is smaller.

Traditionally, assessments of the Doha Agreement conclude on a small effect for the EU and the United States. Our study leads to the same conclusion (for example, the increase in EU exports in 2025 is only 2.9 percent), but here we also assess the benefit of the DDA by comparing the cooperative scenario (DDA) with the protectionist one (the Up to Bound scenario, for example, results in a 10.4 percent decline of EU exports and 2.9 percent decline of US exports), or by comparing how the trade agreement prevents a reduction of exports related to increased protection (the difference between Up to

Bound and the Bound & DDA scenarios: 5 percent for the EU, 2.4 percent for the United States). Table 6.6 illustrates that this new evaluation amplifies the importance of the DDA for these large economies.

Variation in exports is also explained by the macroeconomic closure of the model, which supposes that each current account has to remain constant. Under the Up to Bound and Up to Max scenarios, each country augments applied protection such that its imports decrease. This can imply an appreciation of the real exchange rate in order to keep the current account constant. While the DDA increases Bangladesh's overall exports by 3.7 percent (in value terms), they decrease toward the European Union (erosion of preferences) but increase substantially toward the United States (+10 percent), Japan (+514 percent), and Brazil (+33 percent). Concerning the protectionist scenarios, reductions in Bangladesh's exports are mainly explained by the substantial increase in protection applied on imports and the macroeconomic closure.

Table 6.7 points out the welfare impacts of various scenarios. The Doha scenario implies gains for all regions except Mexico.[25] This loss can be explained by an erosion of preferences toward the United States and Canada in case of an agreed multilateral liberalization. In general, under the DDA scenario welfare gains are small; they are more significant for Brazil, Bangladesh, and the ASEAN MIC zone.

A rise of protectionism would mainly hurt MICs and LDCs. As already pointed out, in the case of the Up to Bound scenario, the relative loss of welfare is three times larger for developing countries than for developed countries (see Table 6.5). Asian developing countries are particularly affected (see the case of Bangladesh, India, and Pakistan in Table 6.6). The implementation of the DDA is important for these countries as a "preventive" action against the risk of trade wars—in particular, as far as India is concerned. We also note a few cases where increasing protectionism is beneficial. For instance, Canada takes advantage of increased preferential margins into the NAFTA markets while limited increases of its own tariff improve its terms of trade (optimal tariff argument) and imply small domestic distortions.

As illustrated by the Canadian case, tariff changes either implied by a country's own policy reform or by other countries' reform may have different, even opposite, effects on welfare. Decomposing the mechanisms that affect welfare is crucial to understanding the results. In particular, assessing the strength of the "what I do is what I get" argument is important. Indeed, in a context of global trade policy changes, a country will be affected by both

25 Nigeria and the rest of eastern Africa are also affected by a slight decrease in welfare.

TABLE 6.7 Variations in countries' welfare led by tariffs and domestic support changes, percentage of change compared to the 2025 baseline

Country or region	DDA	Up to Bound	Bound & DDA	Up to Max	Max & DDA
ASEAN LIC	0.4	−1.7	−1.3	−1.2	−0.1
ASEAN MIC	0.6	−1.3	−0.2	−0.4	−0.1
ANZCERTA	0.1	−0.2	−0.1	−0.1	0.0
Bangladesh	0.7	−2.0	−2.0	−0.6	−0.6
Brazil	0.3	−0.4	0.1	−0.1	0.2
Canada	0.0	0.0	0.1	0.1	0.1
Central Africa	0.0	−0.0	0.2	0.8	0.8
China–Hong Kong	0.1	−0.5	0.2	−0.2	0.1
EU	0.1	−0.5	−0.4	−0.3	−0.2
India	0.0	−1.8	−0.8	−0.4	−0.1
Japan	0.2	−0.3	0.0	−0.1	0.1
Mexico	−0.1	−1.7	−0.6	−0.2	−0.1
MENA	0.1	−0.6	−0.2	−0.2	−0.0
Pakistan	0.2	−2.1	−2.2	−2.0	−1.7
Turkey	0.1	−0.6	−0.3	−0.4	−0.3
United States	0.0	−0.2	−0.1	−0.1	−0.0

Source: Authors' calculations; MIRAGE simulations.

Note: ASEAN LIC = ASEAN low-income countries, ASEAN MIC = ASEAN middle-income countries, ANZCERTA (Australia New Zealand Closer Economic Relations Trade Agreement) = Australia and New Zealand group, MENA = Middle East and North African countries. Welfare changes are computed as the equivalent variation.

changes in its own tariffs (domestic policy effect) and in its partner tariffs (foreign policy effect). Due to intracountry reallocation of resources, imported inputs, and model closure (fixed current account), it is difficult to distinguish "import-led effects" from "export-led effects." Both domestic and foreign policy effects have negative and positive outcomes.[26] As previously stated, the main effects are as follows:

1. for domestic tariff increase:
    a. positive effect on welfare related to the "optimal tariff" argumentation;
    b. negative effect on welfare led by increasing distortions in domestic economy;

26 Countries can also be affected by the tariffs of countries they do not trade with because these changes may affect world prices. This effect is taken into account in the "foreign tariff" increase and is less important than other effects.

2. for foreign tariff increase:
    a. positive effect for exporters benefiting from preferences on increasingly protected markets;
    b. negative effect for exporters facing increased barriers.

We use a new methodology aimed to decompose consistently these welfare effects (Laborde 2009), and we compute normalized relative effects of "domestic" and "foreign" reform. As is clear from Figure 6.4, in the case of Up to Max scenario, we see that different countries respond differently to these conflicting effects. Several large countries (Canada, ASEAN, Brazil, India, EU27, and others) can benefit from their own tariff increases, as opposed to small countries for which a resort to high tariffs will be negative. For most exporters, tariff increases on destination markets will have drastic negative effects and will dominate the welfare changes. This is particularly true for Asian countries (China and Japan, for instance) that have no preferential access. But for a few countries benefiting from large preferential access (Canada and Mexico), the overall rise in protection at the global level still delivers positive effects: the increased value of existing preferences outweighs the loss of market access in third countries.

Finally, we examine how factors' real remuneration is modified under three scenarios: Doha, Up to Bound, and Bound & DDA (Table 6.8). The objective is only to illustrate how some productive factors are affected differently by a further liberalization of a country's economy or a global resort to protectionism.

In agricultural countries like Australia/New Zealand or Brazil, productive factors related to agriculture (land, agricultural unskilled labor) should be clearly supportive of a Doha agreement and opposed to a global augmentation of protection to Up to Bound levels. In Brazil, for example, the real remunerations of land and agricultural unskilled labor increase by 4.8 percent and 4.2 percent, respectively, if a Doha agreement is signed, while they decline by 10.3 percent and 8.5 percent if the Up to Bound scenario is implemented. The DDA agreement also plays a valuable role for land and unskilled agricultural labor in these countries since under the Bound & DDA scenario their remuneration declines but to a lesser extent (1.6 percent and 1.8 percent in the case of Brazil). The same mechanism works in Asian MICs and Central Africa. In these poor countries, the WTO Doha agreement is also a beneficial scheme for poor people.

On the other side, in rich countries such as Japan, Korea, and the European Free Trade Area (EFTA) countries, land and agricultural unskilled

FIGURE 6.4 Relative impacts of foreign and domestic policies on welfare results, Up to Max scenario

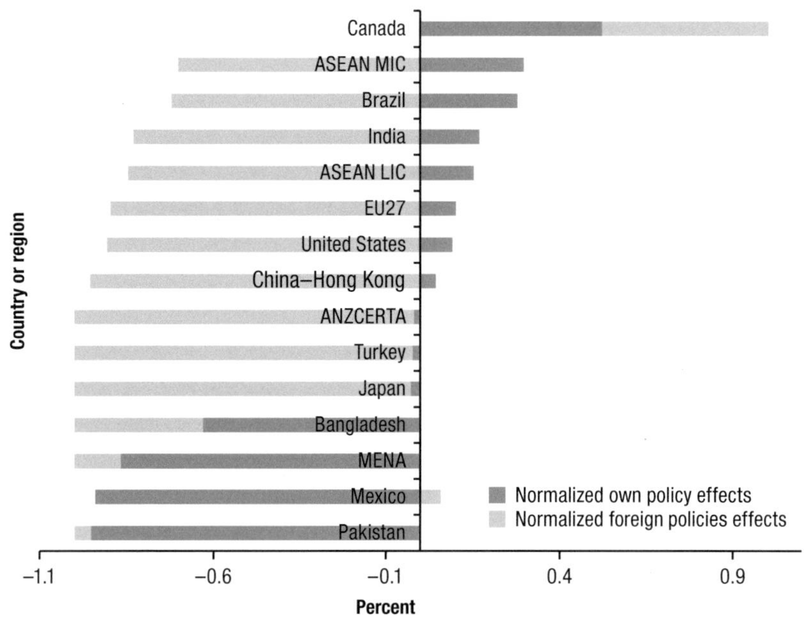

Source: Authors' calculations; MIRAGE simulations.

Note: ASEAN LIC = ASEAN low-income countries, ASEAN MIC = ASEAN middle-income countries, ANZCERTA (Australia New Zealand Closer Economic Relations Trade Agreement) = Australia and New Zealand group, MENA = Middle East and North African countries.

labor should be supportive of increased protectionism while opposed to further liberalization.[27] In the case of the EU and the United States, any reform leads to a decline in the real remuneration of these factors. Indeed, for the agricultural sector in both regions, the Doha Round will have adverse effects (reduction in subsidies or protective tariffs), but a global resort to protectionism will also hurt their agricultural interests. In the case of the Up to Bound and the Bound & DDA scenarios, the negative effects are smaller. It is noteworthy that in rich countries (Australia/New Zealand, Canada, the EU, Japan, and the United States), skilled labor and capital should generally support increased multilateral trade openness as it increases their real remuneration and oppose increased protectionism as it reduces their real remuneration.

27 EFTA and Korea are not included on Table 6.8. These results can be requested from the chapter authors.

TABLE 6.8 Variations in factor remunerations by countries led by tariffs and domestic support changes, percentage of change compared to the 2025 baseline

	Real return to capital			Real return to land			Skilled real wages			Unskilled real wages in agriculture			Unskilled real wages in nonagriculture		
Country or region	DDA	Up to Bound	Bound & DDA	DDA	Up to Bound	Bound & DDA	DDA	Up to Bound	Bound & DDA	DDA	Up to Bound	Bound & DDA	DDA	Up to Bound	Bound & DDA
ASEAN LIC	−0.2	−4.3	−8.8	0.9	−7.2	−8.8	0.4	−4.1	−7.6	0.8	−6.6	−8.9	0.4	−5.5	−9.4
ASEAN MIC	0.3	−5.4	−3.2	1.9	−6.7	−5.4	1.0	−6.1	−2.1	1.6	−7.5	−5.4	0.8	−7.4	−3.4
ANZCERTA	0.2	−0.4	0.1	3.3	−5.4	−1.6	0.2	−0.8	−0.2	3.3	−4.3	−0.8	0.1	−0.8	−0.2
Bangladesh	−0.5	−4.7	−4.8	6.8	10.8	10.8	−0.5	−6.0	−6.2	4.7	6.0	6.0	−0.9	−6.2	−6.3
Brazil	0.3	−2.0	−1.0	4.8	−10.3	−1.6	0.1	−0.5	0.2	4.2	−8.5	−1.8	−0.1	−2.0	−0.8
Canada	0.3	−0.2	−0.1	3.0	−3.8	−1.6	0.1	−0.2	0.1	1.9	−2.0	−0.2	0.1	−0.2	−0.1
Central Africa	0.0	−8.3	−8.1	−0.1	−4.5	−4.1	−0.0	1.4	1.8	0.0	−5.7	−5.1	−0.0	−2.6	−2.4
China–Hong Kong	0.1	−0.1	−0.6	0.7	−0.1	0.0	0.5	−0.9	−0.2	0.6	−0.2	−0.0	0.5	−0.6	−0.2
EU	0.2	−0.3	−0.1	−1.8	−0.1	−1.1	0.2	−0.8	−0.5	−1.9	−0.6	−1.3	0.2	−0.4	−0.2
India	−0.1	−2.9	−2.2	0.3	2.8	3.7	0.0	−5.3	−2.0	0.2	0.1	1.6	0.0	−4.4	−2.0
Japan	0.3	−0.0	0.0	−6.5	1.0	−2.4	0.5	−0.4	0.0	−5.2	0.8	−2.6	0.4	−0.3	0.0
Mexico	0.2	0.4	0.3	1.9	−1.1	−0.1	−0.1	−3.4	−1.2	1.3	−1.5	−0.3	−0.1	−2.6	−1.0
MENA	0.3	−1.6	−0.4	2.5	1.5	1.7	0.3	−2.4	−0.5	2.0	0.6	1.2	0.2	−2.0	−0.4
Pakistan	−0.2	−3.1	−1.9	0.7	0.8	1.1	0.1	−6.6	−7.6	0.6	−1.5	−1.2	0.1	−6.8	−6.7
Turkey	0.0	−2.9	−2.0	0.4	−0.0	−0.7	0.1	−1.4	−0.5	0.4	−0.6	−0.8	0.1	−2.0	−1.2
United States	−0.2	0.0	0.2	−5.8	−1.4	−0.6	0.1	−0.3	−0.2	−2.7	−0.7	−0.2	0.1	−0.2	−0.1

Source: Authors' calculations; MIRAGE simulations.

Note: ASEAN LIC = ASEAN low-income countries, ASEAN MIC = ASEAN middle-income countries, ANZCERTA (Australia New Zealand Closer Economic Relations Trade Agreement) = Australia and New Zealand group, MENA = Middle East and North African countries. Real returns to factor are computed as the nominal return deflated by the representative household price index.

The variations of real remuneration on labor and capital implied by these trade policies are less than those concerning land and agricultural unskilled labor: this is explained by differences in the degree of intersectoral mobility. These results are consistent with the traditional Heckscher-Ohlin-Samuelson framework.

What Is Really At Stake?

These figures allow for a clear reassessment of what is really at stake. A disagreement among WTO countries over the DDA would signal a failure of international cooperation. If countries subsequently implement protectionist policies, the reduction could be much greater. This exercise clearly gives an insight of what could be lost as a result of the failure of the DDA. A simple comparison reveals a potential reduction of US$1,171 billion in world trade. The failure of the DDA would not only prevent an increase of US$363 billion in world trade, as a result of new commitments on tariffs and domestic support, but a worldwide move toward protectionism would contract world trade by US$808 billion if we consider that the implementation of the highest duties applied during 1995 through 2006 is the realistic scenario to which countries would resort. If an implementation of bound duties is the relevant reference point, a failed Doha Development Agenda could mean that the "potential cost" of a trade war would be higher by US$2,262 billion, in volume of annual trade by 2025.

Moreover, the DDA will not only increase trade; it will also reinforce binding commitments and reduce existing bound duties. In so doing, it will play its international public good role by making the trade environment more secure and decreasing the costs associated with potential trade wars. We concretized this idea by comparing the application of bound duties based on their current levels to the same policy based on the level of bound duties implied by the DDA: in that case this difference is up to US$809 billion in terms of trade volume and US$184 billion in terms of real income.[28] Strikingly, these conclusions are especially true for poor countries. In terms of real income, if we consider that the real value of DDA is measured by the "preventive" role that it plays, from a global value of US$184 billion, US$128 billion (about two-thirds) represent the benefits to developing countries (see Table 6.5). This explains why the DDA should be finally considered as a Development Round.

Conclusion

Recent studies assessing the potential impact of the DDA have concluded that there would be modest augmentation in world trade and world real income. This study, which is limited to tariffs and domestic support, does not invalidate such conclusions, but it examines the situation from a different perspective. The failure of a WTO agreement would be a clear sign of international noncooperation; it would launch trade conflicts and litigations (especially between high-income and emerging countries) and would be the first

28 Calculation is as follows: 184 = −169 − (−353) and 809 = −1090 − (−1899).

unsuccessful round despite the fact that it is the first to focus on development and the first launched by the WTO. In a period of economic stagnation, the risk is high that this failure would give WTO members the incentive to pursue protectionist policies. In that case, international trade will face a dreadful iceberg: the most visible consequence of not concluding the DDA, an opportunity cost of US$363 billion of trade, will be outweighed by the immersed part—namely, a potential reduction of at least US$1,171 billion in world trade if countries fail to reach an agreement and were to implement protectionist policies. Therefore, stakes in Geneva are very high and a WTO agreement is the best "preventive" scheme if world trade risks colliding with a protectionist reef. Finally, the DDA appears to be the closest and most promising step toward a global development agenda for a world in turmoil.

Bibliography

Anderson, K., W. Martin, and D. van der Mensbrugghe. 2005. "Market and Welfare Implications of Doha Reform Scenarios." In *Agricultural Trade Reform and the Doha Development Agenda*, edited by K. Anderson and W. Martin, 333–399. London: Palgrave Macmillan; Washington, DC: World Bank.

Axelrod, R. 1981. "The Evolution of Cooperation." *Science* 211 (4489): 1390–1396.

Bairoch, P. 1995. *Economics and World History: Myths and Paradoxes*. Chicago: University of Chicago Press.

Baldwin, R. E., and S. Evenett, eds. 2008. *What World Leaders Must Do to Halt the Spread of Protectionism?* London: Center for Economic Policy Research.

———. 2009. *Murky Protectionism and the Crisis*. Center for Economic Policy Research. Accessed 2009. www.voxeu.org/reports/Murky_Protectionism.pdf.

Berisha, V., A. Bouët, D. Laborde, and S. Mevel. 2008. "The Development Promise: Can the Doha Development Agenda Deliver for Least Developed Countries?" IFPRI Briefing Note. Washington, DC: International Food Policy Research Institute.

Bouët, A. 2008. *The Expected Benefits from Trade Liberalization: Opening the Black Box of Global Trade Modeling*. IFPRI Food Policy Review 8. Washington, DC: International Food Policy Research Institute.

Bouët, A., Y. Decreux, L. Fontagné, S. Jean, and D. Laborde. 2008. "Assessing Applied Protection across the World." *Review of International Economics* 16 (5): 850–863.

Bouët, A., and D. Laborde. 2010. "Assessing the Potential Cost of a Failed Doha Round." *World Trade Review* 9 (2): 319–351.

Bouët, A., S. Mevel, and D. Orden. 2006. "More or Less Ambition in the Doha Round: Winners and Losers from Trade Liberalization with a Development Perspective." *The World Economy* 30 (8): 1253–1280.

Boumellassa, H., D. Laborde, and C. Mitaritonna. 2009. *A Picture of Tariff Protection across the World in 2004: MAcMap-HS6, Version 2*. IFPRI Discussion Paper 903. Washington, DC: International Food Policy Research Institute.

Decreux, Y., and L. Fontagné. 2006. *A Quantitative Assessment of the Outcome of the Doha Development Agenda*. CEPII Working Paper. Paris: Centre d'Etudes Prospectives et d'Information Internationale.

Decreux, Y., and H. Valin. 2007. "MIRAGE, Updated Version of the Model for Trade Policy Analysis: Focus on Agriculture and Dynamics." CEPII Working Paper. Paris: Centre d'Etudes Prospectives et d'Information Internationale.

Gamberoni, E., and R. Newfarmer. 2009. "Trade Protection: Incipient but Worrisome Trends." Accessed 2009. www.voxeu.org/index.php?q=node/3183.

Global Trade Alert. 2009. Accessed September 16, 2009. www.globaltradealert.org/.

Hufbauer, G. C., and J. J. Schott. 2009. "Buy American: Bad for Jobs, Worse for Reputation." PIIE Policy Brief N. PB09-2. Washington, DC: Peterson Institute for International Economics.

INTAL (Instituto para la Integración de América Latina y el Caribe). 2009. "Recession and Protectionism 'Within the Rules': Risks to the Multilateral Trade System." INTAL Monthly Newsletter 150.

Irwin, D. A. 1992. "Multilateral and Bilateral Trade Policies in the World Trading System: An Historical Perspective." In *New Dimension of Regional Integration*, edited by de J. de Melo and A. Panagarya, 90–119. London: Center for Economic Policy Research.

———. 1998. "The Smoot-Hawley Tariff: A Quantitative Assessment." *Review of Economics and Statistics* 80: 326–334.

Isaacs, A. 1948. *International Trade: Tariffs and Commercial Policy*. Chicago: Richard Irwin.

Jean, S., D. Laborde, and W. Martin. 2008. *Choosing Sensitive Agricultural Products in Trade Negotiations*. IFPRI Discussion Paper No. 788. Washington, DC: International Food Policy Research Institute.

Johnson, H. G. 1953. "Optimum Tariff and Retaliation." *Review of Economic Studies* 21: 142–153.

Laborde, D. 2008. "Mesures et détermination endogène des droits de douane." PhD thesis, Université de Pau et des Pays de l'Adour, France.

———. 2009. "Decomposition of Multilateral Trade Policy Shocks in a CGE." Unpublished, International Food Policy Research Institute, Washington, DC.

Laborde, D., W. Martin, and D. van der Mensbrugghe. 2008. "Implications of the 2008 Doha Draft Modalities for Developing Countries." Global Trade Analysis Project conference paper, Helsinki, June 12–14, 2008.

Lamy, P. 2009. Speech delivered at the Lowy Institute for International Policy. March 2. Accessed 2009. www.wto.org/english/news_e/sppl_e/sppl117_e.htm.

Madsen, J. B. 2001. "Trade Barriers and the Collapse of World Trade during the Great Depression." *Southern Economic Journal* 67 (4): 848–868.

Martin, W., and P. Messerlin. 2007. "Why Is It So Difficult? Trade Liberalization under the Doha Agenda." *Oxford Review of Economic Policy* 23 (3): 347–366.

Messerlin, P. 1985. "Les Politiques Commerciales et leurs Effets en Longue Periode." In *Le Protectionnisme*, edited by B. Lassuderie-Duchene and J.-L. Reiffers, 71–89. Paris: Economica.

Narayanan, B. G., and T. L. Walmsley, eds. 2008. Global Trade, Assistance, and Production: The GTAP 7 Data Base. Center for Global Trade Analysis, Purdue University, West Lafayette, IN, US.

Olson, M. 1965. *The Logic of Collective Action*. Cambridge, MA, US: Harvard University Press.

UNCTAD (United Nations Conference on Trade and Development). 2016. Trade Analysis Information System. Accessed 2009. http://r0.unctad.org/trains_new/index.shtm.

USITC (United States International Trade Commission). n.d. Database. Accessed 2009. https://dataweb.usitc.gov/.

WTO (World Trade Organization). 2008. Revised Draft Modalities for Agriculture. TN/AG/W/4/Rev.3, WTO Secretariat, Geneva.

———. 2009. Report to the TPRB from the Director-General on the Financial and Economic Crisis and Trade-Related Developments, January, JOB(09)/2. Geneva.

Appendix 6.1 Geographic Decomposition

TABLE 6.A1 Regional aggregation

Country or region	GTAP7 code
Australia/New Zealand	nzl, aus
Bangladesh	bgd
Brazil	bra
Canada	can
Central Africa	xac, xcf
China and Hong Kong	hkg, chn
EU	roa, bgr, gbr, swe, esp, svn, svk, prt, pol, nld, mlt, lux, ltu, lva, ita, irl, hun, grc, deu, fra, fin, est, dnk, cze, cyp, bel, aut
ASEAN MIC (middle-income countries)	tha, phl, mys
India	ind
Indonesia	idn
Japan	jpn
Republic of Korea	kor
ASEAN LIC (low-income countries)	xse, vnm, mmr, lao, khm, xea
Mexico	mex
MENA (Middle East and North African countries)	xnf, tun, mar, egy
Nigeria	nga
Pakistan	pak
Rest of eastern Africa	xec, uga, eth
Rest of Latin America	xcb, xca, pan, nic, gtm, cri, xsm, ven, ury, per, pry, ecu, col, chl, bol, arg
Rest of OECD	xef, nor, che
Rest of the world	xws, irn, geo, aze, arm, xsu, kgz, kaz, xer, xee, ukr, rus, hrv, blr, alb, xna, xoc
Rest of South Asia	xsa, lka
Rest of SADC (Southern Africa Development Community)	zwe, zmb, tza, moz, mus, mdg
Rest of ECOWAS (Economic Community of West African States)	xwf, sen
South African Custom Unions	xsc, zaf, bwa, mwi
Taiwan, China, and Singapore	sgp, twn
Turkey	tur
United States	usa

Source: Authors.

Appendix 6.2 Recent Trade Agreements Included in the Baseline

1. Full free trade agreements (FTA) for ASEAN (Association of South East Asian Nations), CEMAC (Communauté Economique et Monétaire de l'Afrique Centrale for Monetary and Economic Community of Central Africa), COMESA (Common Market for Eastern and Southern Africa), and SADC (Southern Africa Development Community).
2. Economic Partnership Agreements (EPAs) between ACP (Africa, Caribbean, Pacific) countries and the EU.
3. Implementation of the EU-India, EU-ASEAN, US-Colombia, US-Oman, US-Bahrain, US-Morocco, US-Australia, Mercosur-Colombia, and China-Chile FTAs.
4. All ongoing WTO accession commitments, including those of most recent members (Ukraine, Cape Verde, Viet Nam).
5. Updated GSP (generalized system of preference) scheme of Japan in favor of LDC countries.
6. Modified bound tariffs on EU poultry.
7. EU enlargement to Romania and Bulgaria in 2007.
8. The end of the EU EBA ("Everything but Arms") transitory regime is implemented for protocol products (sugar, banana, and rice).

Appendix 6.3 Modeling the OTDS Constraint in a Dynamic Setting

As discussed in the chapter, we introduce OTDS capping in the dynamic model. Under the standard approach, domestic support is computed from base-year level and converted to an *ad valorem* equivalent (AVE).[29] This approach is unrealistic as the WTO constraint involves limiting the payments made in overall support expressed in US dollars. Taking into account the growth of production value in the agricultural sector will lead to a reduction in subsidy rates to respect the new WTO commitments.

29 Since the current US domestic support is below new OTDS limits, it does not lead to reduction of current policies.

Table 6.A2 illustrates the consequences of this treatment. Focusing on agricultural production and exports, we see that:

- The EU is almost not affected by subsidy reduction thanks to the recent CAP reform and the large share of Green Box payments in the overall EU domestic support. US farmers are in the opposite situation, as the OTDS limits applied to the US farmers will benefit the EU producers and exporters. Overall, the EU production is less reduced by the DDA tariff reduction combined with the OTDS treatment than when it is not combined with the OTDS treatment (–1.17 percent versus –1.27 percent);
- The situation of Brazil is magnified compared to the EU one. In this case, the Brazilian production increases more with the OTDS treatment (+4.03 percent to +3.78 percent);
- US production is directly affected by domestic support reduction (–1.5 percent in agricultural and agribusiness production instead of +0.1 percent). We can even see that for some sectors, the gaps are reversed: from an expansion of the sugar (+1 percent) and wheat (+1.4 percent) sectors, we have a decline in production (respectively –4 percent and –5.5 percent).

TABLE 6.A2 **Agricultural export and production variations under the Doha scenario, with and without dynamic OTDS constraints**

	Brazil		EU		United States	
	Doha with constraint on OTDS	Doha without constraint on OTDS	Doha with constraint on OTDS	Doha without constraint on OTDS	Doha with constraint on OTDS	Doha without constraint on OTDS
	Exports – Volume – 2025: % deviation from the baseline					
Agriculture and Agrofood	**2.69**	**2.65**	**0.69**	**0.69**	**1.73**	**1.96**
Beverage and tobacco	3.90	4.05	1.58	1.57	5.69	5.74
Cereals	–1.76	–3.93	–0.19	–0.87	–8.80	1.91
Food products	4.35	4.30	1.34	1.19	6.90	7.40
Cattle	–4.38	–5.97	2.50	1.67	–16.06	–0.32
Meat products	31.35	31.41	–1.75	–2.05	11.62	13.25
Milk and dairy products	69.66	68.54	–2.59	–3.06	–21.57	–15.70
Other agricultural products	1.46	0.09	4.18	2.99	–5.52	4.27
Paddy and processed rice	17.10	14.90	–7.38	–7.69	–6.21	2.96
Sugar	3.70	3.80	–25.58	–25.72	15.53	12.48

(continued)

TABLE 6.A2 *(continued)*

	Brazil		EU		United States	
	Doha with constraint on OTDS	Doha without constraint on OTDS	Doha with constraint on OTDS	Doha without constraint on OTDS	Doha with constraint on OTDS	Doha without constraint on OTDS
	Exports – Volume – 2025: % deviation from the baseline					
Vegetables and fruit	−1.28	−3.11	−0.29	−0.74	−6.27	2.74
Wheat	−5.80	−7.30	6.42	4.63	−6.84	1.23
	Production – Volume – 2025: % deviation from the baseline					
Agriculture and Agrofood	**4.03**	**3.78**	**−1.17**	**−1.27**	**−1.50**	**0.10**
Beverage and tobacco	−1.85	−1.69	0.02	0.03	0.17	−0.05
Cereals	0.43	0.45	0.28	0.28	−0.07	−0.04
Food products	3.88	3.30	−0.63	−0.86	−6.59	0.26
Cattle	0.98	0.92	−0.15	−0.18	0.17	0.41
Meat	12.07	12.07	−0.96	−1.11	−1.98	1.07
Milk and dairy products	14.40	14.43	−5.38	−5.49	1.00	1.26
Other agricultural products	1.94	1.90	−1.82	−1.89	−3.62	−2.57
Paddy and processed rice	0.79	0.15	−0.13	−0.56	−5.67	0.03
Sugar	0.30	0.21	−9.66	−9.99	−4.09	1.07
Vegetables and fruit	−0.14	−0.14	−0.00	−0.01	0.11	−0.04
Wheat	0.17	−1.79	1.59	1.12	−5.47	1.35

Source: Authors' calculations based on MIRAGE simulation.
Note: OTDS = overall trade-distorting support.

Chapter 7

DOMESTIC AND TRADE POLICIES AFFECTING THE WORLD COTTON MARKET

Fousseini Traoré

While not a food item in and of itself, cotton is important for food security in many developing countries. The cotton sector is also subject to a lot of controversy regarding its role in development, poverty alleviation, North–South trade, and environmental destruction (Mancini et al. 2005); the crop has been successively depicted as increasing or decreasing poverty and as worsening countries' public deficits because of mismanagement (Moseley and Gray 2008). Yet a closer look at the topic shows that cotton is a major source of cash income for millions of people, particularly in Africa, where it is also a source of foreign exchange earnings for more than 15 countries (Tschirley, Poulton, and Labaste 2009). For example, in Mali (a least developed country, or LDC) three million people make their livelihoods directly off cotton production (Sanogo, Keita, and Sanogo 2009). In addition to providing producers with cash income, cotton also appears to be a key product for fighting rural poverty and achieving food security for several other reasons.

First, by providing cash income, cotton allows farmers to acquire more nutritious and diversified foods for household consumption, such as meat and milk (Fortucci 2002). On the macroeconomic side, cotton exports add to the food import potential of various countries, contributing more than 80 percent of agricultural exports for countries like Benin and Uzbekistan and more than 50 percent for many other African countries (Fortucci 2002; Tschirley, Poulton, and Labaste 2009).[1] Second, although the organization of the cotton sector differs from country to country, it appears that well-integrated sectors have been succesful in providing input credit and agricultural extension to farmers, particularly in Africa (Tschirley, Poulton, and Labaste 2009). This allows farmers to obtain equipment and productive inputs that can also be used for other crops. In addition, the knowledge acquired from extension

1 Including Burkina Faso, Central African Republic, Mali, Togo, Tajikistan, and Turkmenistan.

services can be used for growing other crops such as cereals, which are sometimes grown in rotation with cotton. As a result, and contrary to popular beliefs that cotton production is detrimental to other crops, cereal yields and consumption per capita tend to be higher in cotton-growing areas compared to other places in Africa (FAO 2008; Delarue et al. 2009; Traoré 2010).[2]

Despite these potential benefits, however, cotton remains a contentious commodity. Since the 2003 Cancun Ministerial Conference, cotton has been at the heart of agricultural negotiations, with no concrete measures agreed upon except for the removal of export subsidies in the United States. These debates led in 2004 to the creation of a special cotton subcommittee under the WTO Agriculture Committee's Special Sessions (see the detailed historical perspective on this later in the chapter). The negotiations have been subject to ongoing controversies between the United States, the EU, and developing countries; agreements have been stymied by the United States, due to the United States's desire to extend the discussion to tariff and nontariff barriers, synthetic fibers, and textiles in general, and by China, due to the huge tariff concessions that country may face.[3] Domestic support for the cotton sector is also still important in many countries (including the United States, the EU, and China; discussed further in the next section). A final agreement on cotton cannot be achieved without a broader global Agreement on Agriculture, for which there are still many obstacles, including the recent tough discussions led by India between developing and developed countries regarding a special safeguard mechanism (SSM) in agriculture for developing countries.

To a certain extent, the cotton issue provides a good example of developed countries refusing to reform a sector that is not essential for their own economies—although it is highly important for some developing countries—because of political lobbying by small interest groups. In the United States, the number of cotton growers has been decreasing significantly since the late 1990s. According to the USDA censuses, 18,605 farms were producing cotton in 2012, compared to 24,805 in 2002 (USDA 2012). This change is even more apparent when considering only farms that specialize in cotton production (8,915 in 2012 compared to 14,176 in 2002). However, although they are

2 See also the experience of India, where the introduction of new varieties yielded a 15 percent increase in income and food (calorie) and animal products consumption and reduced food insecurity by 15 to 20 percent among poor farm households (Qaim and Kouser 2013).

3 China's domestic policy is also a matter of discussion (see later in the chapter for more on this). However, China commited to grant duty-free quota-free (DFQF) market access for cotton produced and exported by LDCs as part of the Nairobi Ministerial Decision of December 19, 2015.

based on a very small number of farmers, cotton growers associations in the United States remain effective in defending their interests. Various government programs (that is, farm bills) are often the subject of intense lobbying on the part of farm groups in Congress (Smith 2014). Among these groups is the National Cotton Council of America and its related organizations, which represent the interest of the cotton sector and lobby in favor of farm bills agreeable to the cotton industry.

In Europe, only Bulgaria, Greece, Portugal, and Spain produce cotton, with the vast majority of production (more than 90 percent) coming from Greece and Spain (NCC 2015).[4] Data on cotton production and areas in Europe is easily available but relatively scarce when it comes to the number of farmers engaged in cotton production; however, the few sources available report that there are 79,000 cotton farmers in Greece and 9,500 in Spain (LMC International 2007). The value of cotton production represents less than 10 percent of total agricultural output in Greece and 1 precent in Spain. The economic share of this sector is thus clearly of limited importance in the EU compared to cotton-exporting developing countries.[5]

To many observers, the consistent decline of cotton prices from 1995 to 2005 appears to be due to the subsidies granted by developed countries (the EU and the United States) to their cotton producers. Global cotton subsidies averaged US$4 billion annually between 1997 and 2004 (Baffes 2006), with the United States and the EU making up the largest share. During this period, the United States was the largest exporter and the largest subsidizer of cotton, while the EU was the top region in terms of the per unit subsidy granted to its producers. However, the large amount of studies that have tried to assess the impact of these subsidies have not yielded converging results. According to the research, the positive impact of the removal of these subsidies on global cotton prices could range from 3 percent to 17 percent. Cotton prices today are at a low level, mainly due to China's expanded subsidy policy; meanwhile, the level of subsidies in the United States continues to decline due to new Farm Bill provisions, and subsidy levels are on a stable trend in the EU due to the reforms put forth by the EU's Common Agricultural Policy (CAP).

---

4 Production almost ceased in Portugal after the 2006 reform.

5 This is similar to the banana sector, where a few producers benefit from support in Cyprus, Spain, Greece, and French Overseas Departments and Teritorries, although some efforts have been recently made by the EU particularly on the import regime side.

At the global level, after a decade of WTO talks, cotton still remains an issue for developing countries. While the United States–Brazil case has been definitively settled (see Schnepf 2014) and both the United States and the EU have changed their support toward decoupled payments, new actors have emerged as major cotton subsidizers. Most important, China has replaced the United States as the top country in terms of the amount of support given to its cotton sector, although it has promised to grant duty-free and quota-free market access for cotton produced and exported by LDCs. In terms of market access, developing-country exports still face tariff barriers, particularly for above-quota quantities; the most important of these barriers are in other developing countries. As a consequence, and contrary to the situation that existed in the late 1990s, the main challenge now seems to be among developing countries themselves. This new scenario will shape future negotiations; under the larger umbrella of agricultural negotiations, the talks on cotton in the coming years will focus on facilitating market access for developing-country exports and reducing domestic support for cotton at a higher rate and a shorter implementation period compared to other agricultural products. Cotton talks will also focus on development issues with aid-for-trade-related measures.

Overview of the World Cotton Market

The Supply Side: Production and Exports

From 1990 to 2014, global cotton production increased by 40 percent; it is now estimated at 25 million tons.[6] After being the top cotton producer for many years, China has now been overtaken by India, whose production was estimated at 6.7 million tons in 2014, representing 26 percent of global production. Still, China's production has also increased by 47 percent since 1990, making it the second largest global cotton producer, at 6.6 million tons (Table 7.1). The United States follows China, with 3.5 million tons (14 percent of global production), and Pakistan is fourth, accounting for 9 percent of global production. As highlighted in Table 7.1, global cotton production is highly concentrated, with these four largest producers accounting for 75 percent of total production.

6 All measurements in tons in this chapter are metric tons.

TABLE 7.1 World cotton production, 1990 and 2014

1990			2014		
Country or region	Production (in 1,000 tons)	Share	Country or region	Production (in 1,000 tons)	Share
China	4,554	0.25	India	6,710	0.26
United States	3,411.1	0.18	China	6,600	0.26
India	2,009.7	0.11	United States	3,538.48	0.14
Pakistan	1,654.84	0.09	Pakistan	2,288	0.09
Uzbekistan	1,609.74	0.09	Brazil	1,540	0.06
Brazil	724.46	0.04	Uzbekistan	880	0.03
Turkey	661.54	0.04	Turkey	704	0.03
Turkmenistan	441.54	0.02	Australia	484	0.02
Australia	437.58	0.02	Turkmenistan	319	0.01
Egypt	303.16	0.02	Burkina	276.1	0.01
Argentina	298.1	0.02	Mexico	268.4	0.01
Paraguay	264.66	0.01	Greece	264	0.01
WCA	430.54	0.02	WCA	4,627	0.18
World	18,499.14	1.00	World	25,826.02	1.00

Source: NCC (2015).
Note: WCA = West and Central Africa (Mali, Benin, Côte d'Ivoire, Burkina Faso, and Chad).

In addition, with the exception of the United States and Australia, cotton production occurs mainly in developing and emerging countries (more than 80 percent of global production comes from these two groups). However, West African and Central African countries, which are part of the Franc Zone and at the heart of the Cotton Initiative, account for only 2 percent of global production. Brazil also presents an interesting case. From 1990 to 2014, Brazillian cotton production more than doubled to 6 percent of the global total, making Brazil the fifth largest cotton producer in the world today, as well as a key exporter.

One-quarter of the cotton produced in the world is exported, totaling 6 million tons. With the exception of China, the main cotton producers are also the main cotton exporters. The global cotton market is thus concentrated around a few actors: the top five exporters make up 71 percent of total exports (Table 7.2). While accounting for 14 percent of global production, the United States is by far the largest exporter, with 32 percent of global exports in 2014 (Table 7.2). The US market share has been relatively stable (around one-third)

TABLE 7.2 World cotton exports, 1990 and 2014

1990			2014		
Country or region	Exports (in 1,000 tons)	Share	Country or region	Exports (in 1,000 tons)	Share
United States	1,714.46	0.28	United States	2,354.00	0.32
Uzbekistan	1,186.46	0.19	India	924.00	0.13
Turkmenistan	383.46	0.06	Brazil	748.00	0.10
Australia	301.84	0.05	Australia	660.00	0.09
Pakistan	298.54	0.05	Uzbekistan	506.00	0.07
China	204.16	0.03	Burkina	247.50	0.03
Paraguay	197.12	0.03	Greece	203.50	0.03
Tajikistan	181.28	0.03	Mali	181.50	0.02
Turkey	165.66	0.03	Malaysia	176.00	0.02
Brazil	157.52	0.03	Côte d'Ivoire	154.00	0.02
India	155.76	0.03	Turkmenistan	132.00	0.02
Argentina	142.12	0.02	Pakistan	132.00	0.02
WCA	394.24	0.06	WCA	875.60	0.12
World	6,217.42	1.00	World	7,378.80	1.00

Source: NCC (2015).
Note: WCA = West and Central Africa (Mali, Benin, Côte d'Ivoire, Burkina Faso, and Chad).

since the 1990s; this high market share is often highlighted by opponents of US cotton policies, which have been accused of depressing world prices (see the United States-Brazil case discussed later in this chapter). India and Brazil are also large cotton exporters, making up 13 percent and 10 percent of the global market, respectively. Three African countries also appear in the top 10 global exporters. Although making up only a marginal share of global production, when it comes to exports, West and Central African countries account for 12 percent of the total; this makes the region the world's third largest exporter, falling just behind India and before Brazil. Burkina Faso and Mali account for 3 percent of the world's exports. Exports from West and Central Africa go mainly to Asia, where they face competition from the United States.

The Demand Side: Consumption and Imports

Global cotton consumption has regularly increased alongside cotton production and global population and is now estimated at 24 million tons (Table 7.3). In general, the largest consumers of cotton are also the main producers because production in these countries goes primarily to the domestic market. There is a huge concentration of cotton consumption in Asian

TABLE 7.3 World cotton use, 1990 and 2014

	1990			2014	
Country	Mill use (in 1,000 tons)	Share	Country	Mill use (in 1,000 tons)	Share
China	4,400.00	0.26	China	7,810.00	0.33
India	1,971.64	0.12	India	5,280.00	0.22
United States	1,904.54	0.11	Pakistan	2,310.00	0.10
Pakistan	1,242.56	0.07	Turkey	1,408.00	0.06
Russian Federation	1,203.18	0.07	Bangladesh	957.00	0.04
Brazil	730.62	0.04	Brazil	880.00	0.04
Japan	665.94	0.04	United States	803.00	0.03
Turkey	545.60	0.03	Viet Nam	781.00	0.03
Republic of Korea	440.22	0.03	Indonesia	704.00	0.03
Taiwan	349.58	0.02	Mexico	407.00	0.02
Thailand	331.32	0.02	Uzbekistan	330.00	0.01
Indonesia	328.46	0.02	Thailand	319.00	0.01
Italy	323.40	0.02	Republic of Korea	279.40	0.01
World	17,005.12	1.00	World	23,881.00	1.00

Source: NCC (2015).

countries: the three largest consumers (China, India, and Pakistan) account for 66 percent of global consumption, with China alone accounting for one-third. This high concentration is naturally explained by the relocation of textile industries to Asia as a result of rising labor costs in developed countries, particularly in Europe, after World War II. The end of the Agreement on Textiles and Clothing in 2005 has accelerated this phenomenon.

Asian countries account for more than 75 percent of global cotton imports, with one-fifth going to China (Table 7.4). Chinese imports have multiplied by 30 since 2000 (Figure 7.1), largely boosted by the liberalization of the country's textile market. This growth has made China a key player in the international market and a major determinant of global cotton prices (Traoré 2014). Both global consumption and global imports declined slightly in 2007–2008 due to the global economic crisis and have started increasing again as the economy has recovered.

Global Prices

Global cotton prices are usually approximated by the A Index of Cotlook Ltd, based in Liverpool, UK. This index is an average of the five cheapest

TABLE 7.4 World cotton imports, 1990 and 2014

	1990			2014	
Country	Imports (in 1,000 tons)	Share	Country	Imports (in 1,000 tons)	Share
Russian Federation	1,163.8	0.19	China	1,606.00	0.22
Japan	648.78	0.11	Bangladesh	979.00	0.13
China	485.10	0.08	Viet Nam	836.00	0.11
Korea	451.44	0.08	Turkey	792.00	0.11
Thailand	357.28	0.06	Indonesia	715.00	0.10
Italy	336.38	0.06	Thailand	324.50	0.04
Indonesia	327.80	0.05	Republic of Korea	280.50	0.04
Taiwan, China	325.38	0.05	Malaysia	253.00	0.03
Hong Kong	225.50	0.04	Indla	242.00	0.03
Germany	218.24	0.04	Mexico	209.00	0.03
Ukraine	176.88	0.03	Taiwan, China	187.00	0.03
Portugal	170.50	0.03	Pakistan	176.00	0.02
World	6,011.50	1.00	World	7,371.10	1.0

Source: NCC (2015).

quotations from a selection of 18 varieties of upland cottons most frequently traded internationally (Figure 7.2). The base quality of the Index is *MIDDLING* 1-1/8″. Like many commodity prices, cotton prices exhibit a trend of long-run declines coupled with large, short-run fluctuations. The long-term falling prices can be explained by technological progress, which increases yields and reduces production costs. In the early 1990s, a fall in Latin American production allowed global prices to reach a peak of 92 US cents per pound, followed by a sharp decline to an unprecedented level of 41 cents per pound in 2001. This decline was exacerbated by an increase in global production combined with a decrease in demand due to the East Asia crisis and to China's placement of an important part of its stocks on the international market as part of its new national pricing policy.

Developed countries' active support prices also play a key role in determining the evolution of world cotton prices. The declining trend observed between 1995 and 2005 is viewed by many authors as largely due to these support measures (see the next section). Cotton prices, like many other commodity prices, started rising in 2009; in fact, 2011 saw unprecedented prices (Figure 7.2). In addition to the continuing economic recovery, China's net imports and the low level of both global and Chinese stocks were the main

FIGURE 7.1 China cotton statistics (in 1,000 metric tons), 1990–2014

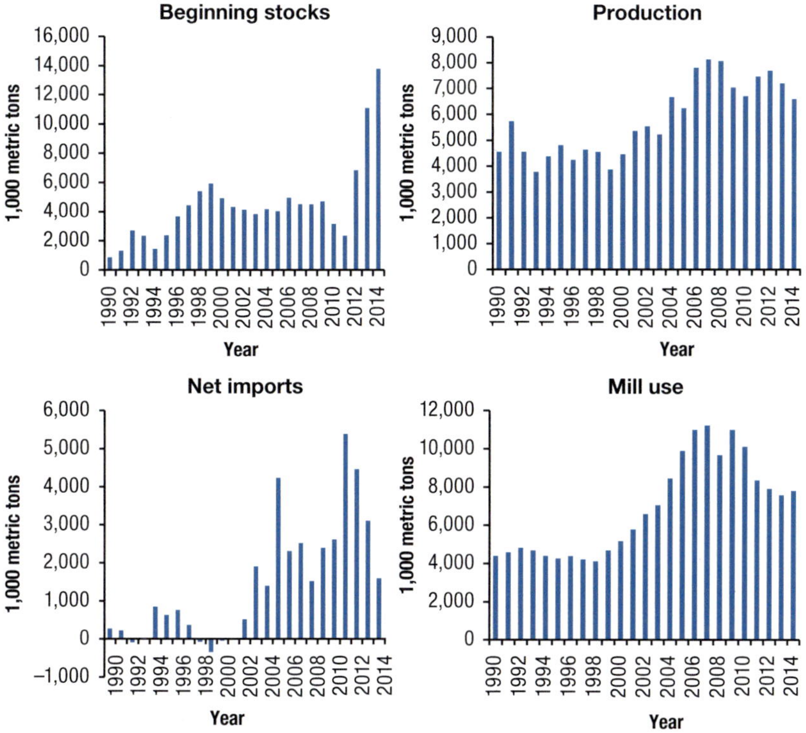

Source: NCC (2015).

determinants of this price increase (Figure 7.3).[7] This changed in 2012, however, when global stocks rose and China began accumulating large stocks; since that time, global prices have declined. Although it is hard to guess what Chinese policy will be in terms of handling its reserve stocks in the coming years, it is expected that the country will mainly rely on its stocks and will thus need fewer imports, depressing both domestic and international prices (ICTSD 2013).

7 Although stocks are endogenous (for speculative reasons, for instance) and as a consequence are part of the simultaneous model determining world prices, they participate in the formation of world prices and price expectations (see ICAC price model). However, the effect and its significance cannot be determined in the framework of this bivariate correlation analysis. A simultaneous equations framework (which will be nonrecursive here) is needed for that, and the structural coefficients can be determined using an appropriate estimator and restrictions as long as the model is identified (Cameron and Trivedi 2005).

FIGURE 7.2 Evolution of global cotton prices, 1975–2013

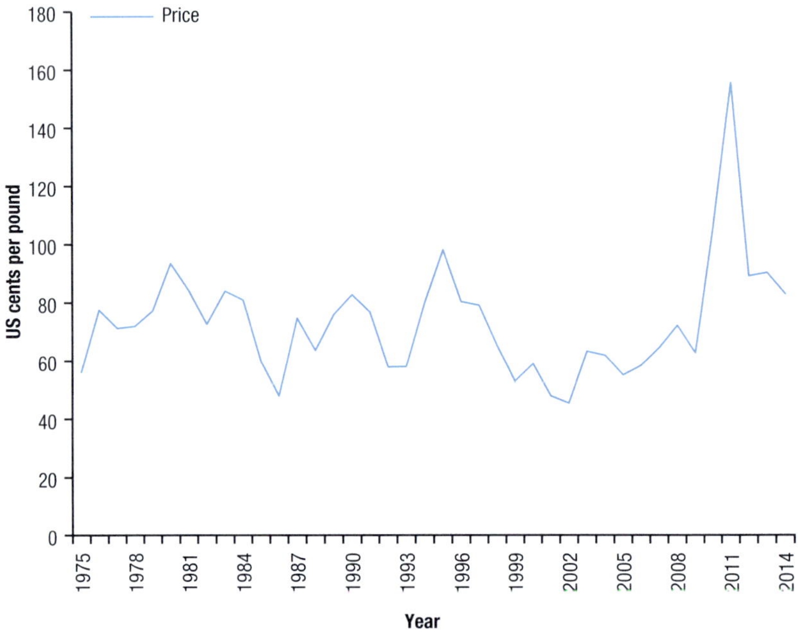

Source: NCC (2015).

FIGURE 7.3 Evolution of world price and stocks, 1975–2013

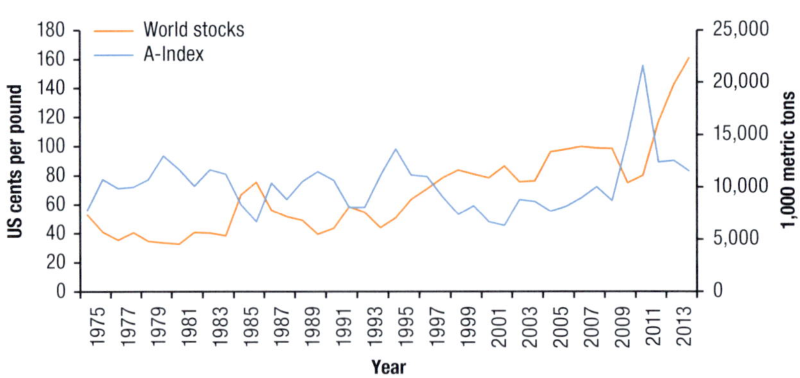

Source: NCC (2015).

Domestic and Trade Policies in Major Countries

Policies in the United States

The United States supports its cotton growers through many mechanisms aimed at stabilizing farm incomes.[8] These support measures are defined under the various farm bills passed by the US Congress every four or five years. Our focus here is on the principal measures based on the 2002 Farm Security and Rural Investment Act and the 2008 Food, Conservation, and Energy Act.[9] We also briefly describe the new Agricultural Act of 2014. These assistance programs include various measures of direct support to production, border protection, and insurance subsidies. Most of the subsidies apply to upland cotton, the main type of cotton that is traded globally. The US considers these subsidies to be decoupled from production and market prices, but to many observers, they in fact distort the global market and harm producers in developing countries.

POLICIES PRIOR TO 2008

It is important to start with a complete analysis of the policies in force before 2008, as the subsequent debate was focused on these measures. Also, most of the studies that assessed the impact of the subsidies cover this period.

Direct Payments (DPs)

Direct payments are designed to support producers' incomes. They are fixed payments that are a priori independent of market prices and based on past production; this system replaces the production flexibility contracts in use under the 1996 Fair Act. Under direct payments, eligible producers receive a payment based on their farm's base acreage (a historical average), the payment yield, and the direct payment rate, set at US$0.0667 per pound of upland cotton. The annual limit on payments directly attributed to one person for direct payments was US$40,000.

Since direct payments are not tied to current production and prices, they are less distortionary and thus fit into the WTO Green Box. However, the historical "base acres" are usually updated; in this way, direct payments encourage farmers to increase their acreages and their production, as they expect a new

8 This goes back to the commodity programs established during the Great Depression (Baffes 2006).

9 The other mechanisms are relatively few and are nonmonetary. See the Farm Security and Rural Investment (FSRI) Act of 2002 for more details.

updating mechanism from one period of legislation to another (Young and Westcott 2000). Furthermore, direct payments increase farmers' incomes and wealth. As a consequence, farmers may become less risk-averse (Pratt 1964; Arrow 1965; Binswanger 1981) and may continually increase their production (Hennessy 1998). By increasing farmers' wealth, these payments may then lead to further investment by reducing farmers' credit constraints (Westcott, Young, and Price 2002).

Countercyclical Payments (CCPs)

The countercyclical payments program is another income support mechanism based on historical acreages and yields. These payments are designed to protect farmers from low market prices. Unlike direct payments, countercyclical payments are tied to market prices. Payments are triggered when the effective price is lower than the target price. The effective price is the sum of the direct payment rate and the higher of the national season-average market price or the marketing year or the national loan rate (US$0.52 per pound). The effective price for cotton was set at US$0.7240 per pound. The payment rate is given by the amount by which the target price exceeds the effective price. The payments' base acres are the same as for direct payments, but many options are available to producers regarding payment yields. The annual limit on payments directly attributed to one person for countercyclical payments was US$65,000. As countercyclical payments are related to current prices, they can be viewed as fully coupled. In addition, the updatings of the base acres and yields raise the same issue as that raised by direct payments: namely, the potential to increase farmers' wealth.

Marketing Loans (MLs) and Loan Deficiency Payments (LDPs)

The marketing loans provisions cover both marketing assistance loans and loan deficiency payments. Marketing assistance loans consist of nonrecourse loans that producers can benefit from by pledging their harvested production as collateral. The program thus provides farmers some cash flow when prices are low so that they do not have to sell their production. The loan rate was set at US$0.52 per pound. As an alternative, the loan deficiency program gives producers a cash option by allowing them to sell their harvest in response to market signals without putting their commodity under loan while benefiting from the program. The payment limit for the marketing loan was US$75,000 per producer and per campaign; however, this limit was eliminated under the 2008 Act.

The marketing loans program works as a minimum price mechanism that gives producers a floor price and is not independent of current production.

As such, these loans could increase the production of risk-averse farmers who would have otherwise produced less. It has been shown that when they are above the market price, marketing loans can be viewed as output subsidies; in this case, if the export demand for cotton is more price-elastic than the domestic demand, exports will increase more than production, strengthening world price declines (Hertel 1989; Houck 1992; Westcott and Price 2001). As a consequence, marketing loans were included in the WTO Amber Box.

The Step 2 Mechanism

The so-called Step 2 mechanism consisted of subsidizing exporters and domestic cotton consumers when the US cotton price on the world market exceeded the world reference price (A-Index). This program aimed at keeping US cotton competitive on the world market without damaging domestic mills. Given the share of US exports in the global market, the United States can be viewed as a large country (a price maker). Thus, introducing an export subsidy would tend to depress world prices (Tweeten 1992). However, since it is coupled with a consumer subsidy, the Step 2 mechanism is equivalent to a producer subsidy. This mechanism was at the heart of Brazil's complaint against the United States in 2003; it was condemned by the World Trade Organization and eliminated in 2006.

Insurance Subsidies

Cotton growers can benefit from insurance subsidies under the federal crop insurance program in order to recover part of the premium they have settled. The goal of the program is to cover producers against climatic risks or diseases likely to lower yields. The program is administered by the USDA's Risk Management Agency. According to Sumner (2003), the average rate of the subsidy was US$19 per acre in 2002, and the International Cotton Advisory Committee estimates the cost of the support at 0.4 cents per pound (Guitchounts 2008). In 2009 the total upland cotton premiums paid by the US government were US$212 million.

Policies under the 2008 Farm Bill

In June 2008 the Food, Conservation, and Energy Act entered into force for the 2008–2012 period. This new law kept most of the previous provisions, with some minor changes. Regarding cotton, the main changes include the elimination of the payment limit for marketing loans, a new countercyclical target price set at US$0.7125 per pound, and the introduction of three new mechanisms (the ACRE, the SURE, and the Economic Adjustment Assistance to Users of Upland Cotton).

AVERAGE CROP REVENUE ELECTION PROGRAM (ACRE)

The ACRE program aims to address some of the shortcomings of the countercyclical program, mainly the strong focus on price that could lead to insufficient support when prices are high and yields are low (due to natural disaster, for instance). In these circumstances, producers do not benefit from countercyclical payments (Monke 2008). ACRE is a revenue-based program relying on statewide revenue data. Payments are made when actual revenues are less than a market-based, moving average guaranteed revenue. Two conditions must be met to trigger the payment: (1) the actual state revenue for cotton during the campaign must be less than the state-level guaranteed revenue amount; and (2) the actual individual farm revenue must be less than the farm's benchmark revenue. To be eligible for ACRE payments, producers must give up their countercyclical payment. They may still benefit from direct payments, but at a rate of US$0.05336 per pound instead of US$0.0667 (a 20 percent reduction). Producers may also benefit from the marketing loans at a lower rate: US$0.364 per pound instead of US$0.52 (a 30 percent reduction). Unlike countercyclical payments, the ACRE program is based on planted acres; in that sense, it is not decoupled from production and provides market-based revenue insurance for producers when market prices fall.

SUPPLEMENTAL REVENUE ASSISTANCE PAYMENTS (SURE) PROGRAM

The SURE program is designed to assist producers suffering from crop losses due to natural disasters. To receive the payment, eligible producers must have at least a 10 percent production loss due to a disaster in a disaster-affected county, provided that cotton is a crop of economic significance. Producers outside a disaster-affected county may also qualify for the program, provided that their production loss is greater or equal to 50 percent of the expected revenue of all crops on the farm (normal production on the farm). Payments are based on the difference between the SURE Disaster Program Guarantee and the Total Farm Revenue.

THE ECONOMIC ADJUSTMENT ASSISTANCE TO USERS OF UPLAND COTTON

This program, usually refered to as the Cotton Users Payment, is a measure designed to replace the former Step 2 mechanism and is targeted toward domestic cotton consumers. Unlike the Step 2 measure, the new program is valid for both domestic and foreign cotton. The payment must be used to modernize production technology and consists of 4 cents per pound.

Policies under the 2014 Farm Bill

The Agricultural Act of 2014 (otherwise known as the 2014 Farm Bill) was signed on February 7, 2014, and will remain in force through 2018. The aim of this Act was to progressively move from price and income support meaures to risk management measures. The Farm Bill brought major changes in commodity programs and added new crop insurance options, particularly for cotton. The main changes consist of the suppression of the direct and countercyclical payment programs, as well as the ACRE program. For cotton, additional changes consist of the introduction of a new insurance program (the Stacked Income Protection Plan, or STAX) and a modification of the marketing loan rate. With the elimination of the direct and countercyclical payments, producers now have the choice between the Price Loss Coverage (PLC) program and the Agricultural Risk Protection (ARP) program.

STAX was introduced in the wake of the United States–Brazil case. The program provides producers with additional protection against losses due to natural disasters or price declines. STAX is a revenue insurance program that producers can use in combination with the federal crop insurance program. It covers revenue losses of not less than 10 percent and not more than 30 percent of expected county revenue. The program premium is subsidized at 80 percent and pays for 70 to 90 percent of losses in farm yields relative to countywide area yield. It is clear that the STAX program is a coupled payment, given that subsidies are based on changes in market revenues (prices, yields, and planted acres) and not on past base or harvested acres.

The 2008 Farm Bill set the marketing loan rate at US$0.52 per pound. The new law uses a moving average of the two immediately preceding marketing years; thus the new rate is the simple average of the adjusted prevailing world price for the two immediately preceding marketing years, but not less than US$0.45 per pound or more than US$0.52 per pound. With this rule the loan rate is supposed to better reflect prevailing market prices. It is also worth noting that although the conservation of the Green/Blue Box direct payments was not politically viable because it gave producers subsidies on a historical basis, the more market-oriented marketing loan scheme and the introduction of the STAX will put more pressure on the US Current Total AMS and de minimis provisions in the 2008 draft modalities should prices fall (Blandford and Josling 2011; Smith 2014).

Trade Policies

In terms of export policies, the Step 2 program was eliminated in 2006 as a consequence of the case with Brazil. This program was not officially notified by the United States as an export subsidy, but it was considered so by the

TABLE 7.5 US average most favored nation (MFN) applied tariffs

Product heading (Harmonized System, HS)	Product name	Average MFN
52.01	Cotton, not carded or combed	0
52.02	Cotton waste (including yarn waste and garneted)	1.43
52.03	Cotton, carded or combed	4.77

Source: WTO (2015).

Note: In general, the term "cotton" in the public debate and the negotiations refers to headings 52.01, 52.02, and 52.03. See also WTO (2014).

WTO panel in the case. The same goes for the export credit guarantees for cotton.[10] On the import side, the United States has bounded all its tariff lines for cotton and provides preferential tariffs for countries with which there is a free trade agreement or to which it has granted a unilateral preference, such as African countries under the African Growth Opportunity Act (AGOA). The average MFN applied tariff is relatively low (Table 7.5); in addition, the United States has both *ad valorem* tariffs and four separate tariff-rate quotas (TRQs) for cotton, with in-quota tariffs ranging between 0 and 4.4 cents per kilogram. Cotton imports exceeding the TRQ face import tariffs of 31.4 cents per kilogram.

US Assistance to the Cotton Sector

Table 7.6 summarizes the United States's support to its cotton sector for the marketing years for which detailed data are available. From 2002 to 2007, the amount of support averaged US$2.3 billion, with large fluctuations (from US$1.1 billion to US$4.4 billion) due to the countercyclical nature of the mechanism. When world prices are low, the support is maximum (2002–2003 and 2004–2005) and vice versa. A detailed study shows that the most fluctuating amounts concern countercyclical payments and marketing loans. For the marketing years 2006–2007 and 2007–2008, the amount of these two assistances were relatively low.[11] Since 2009, global prices have increased; one can postulate a decrease in assistance since then. This trend can be approximated by looking at the evolution of the product-specific AMS for cotton as notified by the United States at the WTO (Figure 7.4).[12] According to the International Cotton Advisory Council (ICAC), the level of assistance averaged US$1.1 billion for

10 At least not until 2014.

11 Cotton marketing years start at August N and terminate at July N+1.

12 Green Box measures are excluded.

TABLE 7.6 Evolution of US subsidies (US$ millions)

	1998–1999	1999–2000	2000–2001	2001–2002	2002–2003	2003–2004	2004–2005	2005–2006	2006–2007	2007–2008
Subsidies/production										
Loan deficiency payments and marketing loans	561	1,547	541	2,245	697	154	1,736	116	85	15
Forfeitures	3	1	17	0	—	—	—	—	—	—
Direct payments[a]	637	614	575	474	645	645	645	464	464	464
Countercyclical payments[b]	316	614	613	524	1,372	402	1,372	955	955	447
Insurance	155	223	216	266	265	262	262	263	242	199
Step 2	214	486	253	125	358	260	470	—	—	—
Total	**1,790**	**3,179**	**2,048**	**3,706**	**3,336**	**1,722**	**4,484**	**1,798**	**1,746**	**1,125**
Production (1,000 metric tons)	2,934	3,548	3,658	4,268	3,599	3,881	4,752	5,201	4,700	4,183
Subsidy: US$ per kilogram	0.61	0.90	0.56	0.87	0.93	0.44	0.94	0.35	0.37	0.27
Unit subsidy: % of world price	42	77	43	82	91	32	69	28	49	44

Source: Araujo Bonjean, Calipel, and Traoré (2006) based on Baffes (2004), USDA and ICAC data.

Note: — = not available; [a]production flexibility contracts before 2002; [b]market loss assistances before 2002.

FIGURE 7.4 US Aggregate Measurement of Support (AMS) for cotton

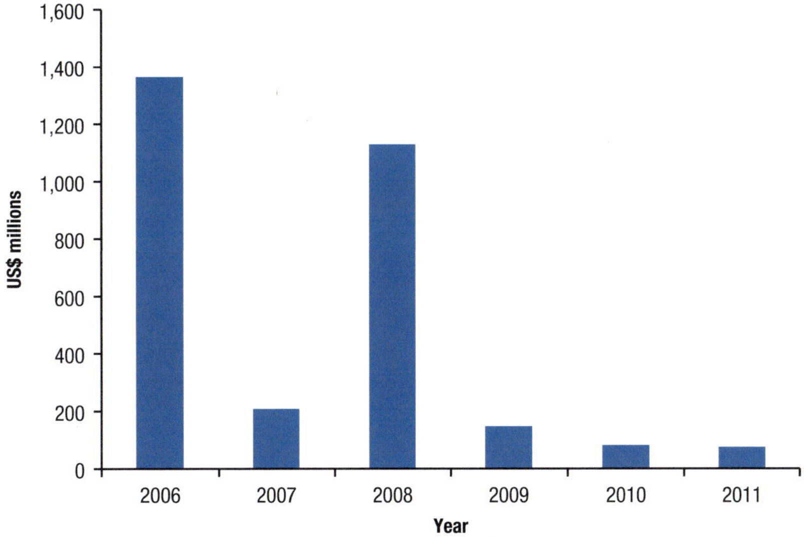

Source: WTO (2014).

the 2012–2013 marketing year. The new 2014 Farm Bill also aims to reduce the level of overall support to reach similar levels.

The EU Policy

The European Union accounts for 4 percent of global cotton production and 4.5 percent of cotton exports. However, on a per unit basis, the region is first in terms of support granted to cotton growers. The EU support mechanism (the Common Market Organization for cotton) started in 1981 when Greece joined the EU, followed by Spain and Portugal in 1986 and Bulgaria in 2007. Three successive regimes governed the sector.

The Support Mechanism before 2005–2006

The EU system was based on a floor price and an objective price determined by the European Commission. The floor price was 1,009.9 euros per metric ton and the objective price 1,063 euros per ton. The subsidy was given to cotton ginners provided that they had paid the producers at least the floor price. In order to fix the budget of the program, a stabilizer mechanism involving national quotas (the maximum quantity guaranteed, MQG) and a co-responsibility levy was established. The MQG for Greece was 782,000 tons; it was 249,000 tons for Spain and 1,500 tons for Portugal. If these MQG were reached, a step-by-step degressive mechanism would reduce both the objective and the floor price in order to keep the budget constant; the penalty would be accelerated when production in Greece and Spain exceeded 1,500,000 tons. The overall objective of the stabilizer mechanism was to contain the budget in the 770 million euro limit.

The 2003 Reformed Policy Regime

In 2003 the policy regime governing the cotton sector was reformed to further comply with WTO rules and to minimize the impact on world prices. The objective was to move toward more decoupled payments that could be put in the WTO Green Box. The new mechanism was designed to be budgetary neutral, not exceeding 800 million euros. It consisted of a mix of coupled and decoupled (Green Box) measures. The decoupled component consisted of a fully decoupled single farm payment scheme, similar to the US direct payment program and based on past areas. On average, the eligible areas for Greece were 380,436 hectares with a support of 795 euros per hectare; for Spain, the eligible area was 89,023 hectares with a support level of 1,285 euros per hectares (Karagianis 2004; Araujo Bonjean, Calipel, and Traoré 2006).

The direct payment accounted for 65 percent of the budget. The remaining budget (35 percent) was devoted to an area payment based on actual areas. As in the previous policy regime, a maximum area per member state was established in order to contain the budget. The repartition of the maximum area per country was 370,000 hectares for Greece, 70,000 hectares for Spain, and 360 hectares for Portugal. The amount of the support was as follows:

- Greece: 594 euros for the first 300,000 hectares and 342.85 euros for the remaining 70,000 hectares;
- Spain: 1,039 euros; and
- Portugal: 556 euros.

Following the stabilizer mechanism, whenever the actual areas exceeded the maximum guaranteed, the amount of the aid per hectare would be reduced proportionally. However, in Greece, this was applied only to the last 70,000 hectares.

The 2008 Revision

Spain argued that this policy regime violated the proportionality principle regarding the area payment; the court acknowledged that production costs had not been sufficiently taken into account in the calculations made by the Commission and suspended the regime. As a consequence, a new regime entered into force in January 2009. It maintained the decoupled payment, changed the maximum areas, and introduced fixed reference yields for the area payment. The new maximum areas were 250,000 hectares for Greece, 48,000 hectares for Spain, 3,342 hectares for Bulgaria, and 360 hectares for Portugal. The reference yields were set at 3.2 tons per hectare for Greece, 3.5 tons per hectare for Spain, 1.2 tons per hectare for Bulgaria, and 2.2 tons per hectare for Portugal.

The new aid amounts are determined by the product of the fixed yields and the reference amounts, which are country-specific: 251.73 euros for Greece, 400 euros for Spain, 671.33 euros for Bulgaria, and 252.73 euros for Portugal. As previously, the amount of aid per hectare would be reduced proportionally if the base areas were exceeded. For Spain the aid per hectare moved from 1,039 to 1,400 euros. The revision of the CAP that took place in 2013 changed the reference amounts as follows: Greece (234.18 euros), Spain (362.15 euros), Portugal (228 euros), and Bulgaria (584.88 euros in 2015 and 649.45 euros for 2016 and onward).

Analysis of EU Support

One significant feature of EU aid to its cotton sector is its stability (Table 7.7). Fluctuations are moderate, with an average of 825 million euros (about US$1 billion). Unlike the US aid mechanism, the gap between the lowest and highest amounts represents only 25 percent of the former (Table 7.7). The stability of European aid is due to the nature of its support programs; the total amount of European support is "guaranteed" by its stabilizer mechanism. Compared to the United States, the level of aid appears modest because of Europe's low level of production; however, the unit amount is actually much higher in the EU than in the United States. On a per unit basis, the European Union is the top region for the amount of assistance granted to its producers. Regarding the new mechanism, the area payment for cotton amounted to 247 million euros in 2011 and 245 million euros in 2012 (EC 2013). The high level of per unit subsidy for the EU must also be considered with regard to its weight on the world market.

Trade-Related Measures

Unlike the United States, the EU market is completely open; there are *no import duties or export subsidies* on cotton (Chapters 5201, 5202, and 5203). The bound rate is 0 percent for these three chapters. For the remaining related products (Chapters 5203 through 5212), the applied and bound rates are all set at 4 percent.

China's Cotton Policy

China occupies a central place in the global cotton market; it is the largest player so far in terms of production, consumption, and stocks (see Figure 7.1). In recent years China has also risen to be the world's largest cotton importer, giving it huge influence on world prices (Traoré 2014). However, China's imports are expected to decline in the coming years due to the release of its national reserves. The country maintains a national cotton reserve that serves as a national buffer stock and is managed by the China National Cotton Reserve Corporation (CNCRC).

An overall assessment of China's support to its cotton sector is tricky, as data are rarely available and often contested by the country. The cotton sector used to be highly subsidized with guaranteed prices and input subsidies before the domestic liberalization in 1999 and the country's accession to WTO in 2001. The consensus is that subsidies went mainly to the industry when the government managed the liquidation of its stocks (Sumner 2006). Recently

TABLE 7.7 EU support to its cotton sector

Support/production	1995–1996	1996–1997	1997–1998	1998–1999	1999–2000	2000–2001	2001–2002	2002–2003	2003–2004	2004–2005
Millions in euros	740	800	761	903	855	733	804	872	835	952
US$ millions	972	1,026	855	1,004	911	675	720	820	941	1,181
Production (1,000 tons)	484	417	488	494	572	535	563	469	426	500
Aid in euros per kilogram	1.53	1.92	1.56	1.83	1.49	1.37	1.43	1.86	2.00	1.71
Aid in US$ per kilogram	2.01	2.46	1.75	2.03	1.59	1.26	1.28	1.75	2.26	2.12
USA Index in US$ per kilogram	2.17	1.78	1.75	1.44	1.17	1.30	1.06	1.02	1.40	1.37
Unit aid in % of world price	93	139	100	141	136	97	121	171	161	155

Source: DG AGRI and Araujo Bonjean, Calipel, and Traoré (2006).

the government started implementing a new system of minimum support price, which consists of direct purchases from producers in order to rebuild the country's strategic reserves. According to the ICAC (2014), estimating China's support as the difference between domestic and imported prices adjusted for quality, the subsidies amounted to US$2.7 billion in 2003 and US$5.5 billion in 2012–2013. In addition to the price support, since 2007, the government has also provided subsidies to producers who used so-called high-quality varieties. According to these figures, China could be the largest provider of support to its cotton sector. However, the official notifications made by China to the WTO under the AMS are much lower, ranging from US$140 million in 2006 to US$655 million in 2007 (Figure 7.5). But even with these low figures that exclude Green Box payments, China appears to be the top country in terms of trade-distorting domestic support in recent years.

Although many countries apply a tariff on cotton imports, China is the only country other than the United States to practice a tariff-rate quota (TRQ) system. Since its accession to the WTO in 2001, China has established a calendar year tariff-rate quota with a 1 percent quota rate. Imports above the annual 894,000 tons may be taxed at a range of 5 percent to 40 percent. The additional quotas are released based on the country's needs, and the 894,000 tons have very often been exceeded since 2004. China's trade policy is also of great importance for African countries since it is the main destination for their exports. Many actors claim that China should grant duty-free quota-free (DFQF) market access to cotton from the LDCs, as it imports more cotton annually than these countries can deliver (Imboden 2014). As a consequence, following the Nairobi Ministerial Conference in 2015, China

FIGURE 7.5 China Aggregate Measurement of Support (AMS) for cotton

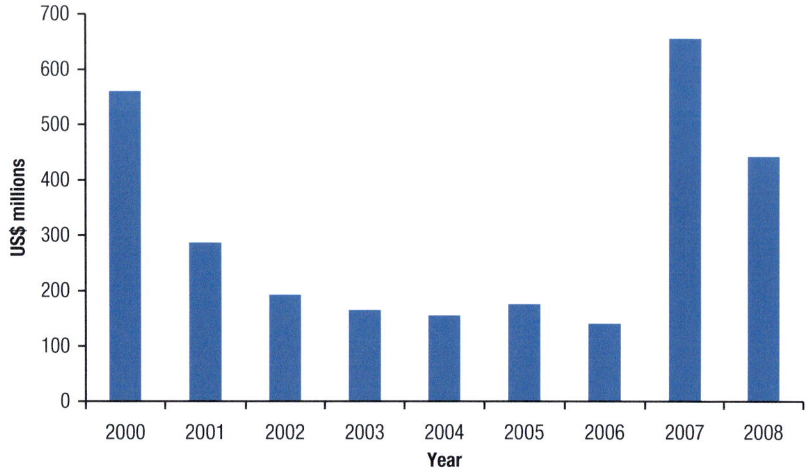

Source: WTO (2014).

declared that it may grant duty-free and quota-free market access for cotton exports from LDCs.

Policies in Other Countries

In addition to the United States, the EU, and China, many other countries support their cotton sector. It is difficult, however, to precisely estimate these supports, largely because of a lack of data. According to the CERI (2009), in addition to the United States and the European Union, more than a dozen countries worldwide (including Argentina, Australia, Brazil, Burkina Faso, Colombia, India, Mali, and Mexico) have support programs. In African countries these programs mainly consist of guaranteed prices. Other countries (such as Egypt, Turkey, and Uzbekistan) also subsidize inputs (fertilizers or irrigation) at favorable prices. In its last compilation in 2014, the WTO Secretariat identified six countries in addition to the United States, China, and the EU that practiced domestic support in the 2000–2010 period, according to their notifications (Brazil, Columbia, India, Mexico, Peru, and Viet Nam) (WTO 2014).

The most significant amounts were for Brazil (US$341 million in 2007 and US$325 million in 2008), India (US$94 million in 2002 and US$140 million in 2003), and Colombia (US$25 million in 2010).

TABLE 7.8 Bound and applied average tariffs in selected countries

Country	Year of applied tariff	Bound (%)	Applied (%)
India	2012	110	6
Indonesia	2012	37.4	4
Mexico	2012	39.4	0
Pakistan	2012	13	7
Viet Nam	2012	14	6
Colombia	2012	75.8	5
Brazil	2012	55	6.9
South Africa	2012	60	4.6
Japan	2012	0	0
Bangladesh	2011	200	3.5
Russian Federation	2012	0	0
Thailand	2011	4.5	0
Morroco	2012	22	2.5

Source: WTO (2014).
Note: This includes *ad valorem* equivalents.

Nonetheless, the support measures in these other countries must be analyzed with regard to the weight of these countries in global trade. With regard to trade-related measures, in the past decade, only India and the United States have notified export subsidies at the WTO. In addition to domestic support, import tariffs are also present in many countries. As highlighted in Table 7.8, these applied tariffs are higher in developing countries than in developed ones, although they remain low in general. The bound rates are set at high levels. Like China and the United States, South Africa and Colombia are the only countries to use TRQs.

Impact of Global Subsidies on the World Cotton Market

Since the cotton initiative launched by the C4 countries and the United States–Brazil case, a lot of studies have attempted to assess the impact of global cotton subsidies on the world cotton market and on individual countries. Some of these studies even try to estimate the likely compensation for which developing countries may ask. This section presents the differing results of these studies.

The Contrasted Effects of the Removal of Distortions

Table 7.9 summarizes the results of the various studies that have tried to address the impact of cotton subsidies.[13] One can observe a wide variety of results. According to the first study to attract a lot of attention (Sumner 2003), the removal of US subsidies would have a positive impact (12 percent) on global prices. The smallest impact was found by Pan et al. (2004), and the largest one by the Overseas Development Institue (ODI 2004). The same variability is observed for production and exports. This wide range of results can be explained by many factors related to the nature of the model used, the reference periods, the databases used, the nature and the amount of aids examined, and the values of the parameters used to simulate the scenarios.

Why So Many Numbers?

Type of Modeling

Most of the models used to simulate the impact of global cotton subsidies are partial equilibrium models, the only exception being the one used by Reeves et al. (2001). This latter study also simulates a full liberalization of the market for textiles, along with the removal of subsidies. Surprisingly, this model does not yield the greatest impacts. Among the partial equilibrium models, a distinction can be made between single commodity and multicommodity. Introducing substitution possibilities on the demand and supply sides make the supply and demand functions for cotton more elastic. As a consequence, for countries that practice subsidies, the reactions to a cut in subsidies are more accentuated.

It is also worth noting that the multicommodity aspect is important since it is reasonable to assume that subsidies would be cut for all commodities (including those competing with cotton). In that case, cotton's supply elasticity will be lowered and the impact on world markets will be less important. Finally, in terms of modeling strategy, there is a fundamental difference between the FAPRI (2002) model (the one by used Sumner [2003] and Pan et al. [2004]) on the one hand and the other models on the other hand. The former uses the producer's expected net income as the decision variable, not the price. In this configuration it is assumed that producers would stop planting when the expected net income from cotton becomes negative. This

13 This section is mainly based on Araujo Bonjean, Calipel, and Traoré (2006; 2007) and Traoré (2010).

TABLE 7.9 Summary of the main studies on the impact of cotton subsidies

Author(s)	Model type	Simulated scenario	Impact on world price in %
ICAC (2002)	Partial equilibrium		26.30
Goreux (2003)	Partial equilibrium	Removal of subsidies in the United States, the EU, and China	[7.5; 11.4]
Reeves et al. (2001)	General equilibrium (GTAP)	Removal of subsidies and all import barriers	10.70
Tockarick (2003)	Partial equilibrium	Removal of subsidies in the United States	2.80
ODI (2004)	Partial equilibrium	Removal of subsidies in the United States, the EU, and China	[18; 28]
Poonyth et al. (2004)	Partial equilibrium	Removal of subsidies and tariffs	[3.1; 5]
Sumner (2003)	Partial equilibrium	Removal of subsidies in the United States	12.60
FAPRI (2002)	Partial equilibrium	Multilateral liberalization of all agri-cultural commodities	11.40
Pan et al. (2004)	Partial equilibrium	Removal of subsidies in the United States	2.43
Araujo Bonjean, Calipel, and Traoré (2006)	Partial equilibrium	Removal of subsidies in the United States and the EU	

Source: Traoré (2010).

introduces a discontinuity that is absent from the classic supply curve models. As a consequence, the impacts are greater for the former group of models, all other things being equal.

The Choice of Supply and Demand Elasticities

As in almost all modeling exercises, the choice of parameters is a crucial one. In a supply and demand type model, the elasticities are the parameters that most drive the results, and all studies use their own elasticities. On the demand side, the range goes from −0.10 (Goreux 2003; ICAC 2002) to −1.25 (Poonyth et al. 2004); on the supply side, the range is from 0.14 (Sumner 2003) to 1.25 (Poonyth et al. 2004). On the demand side, a low elasticity is equivalent to assuming that there are no close substitutes to cotton. Thus studies that assume a low value tend to have greater impacts on the world price following the removal of subsidies (Goreux [2003] and ICAC [2002]). The authors who use noneconometrically estimated low elasticities argue that the share of raw cotton in the cost of textile products is small. In addition, technology constraints on the production side and the low substitutability between cotton and synthetic fibers is also mentioned by these authors.

On the supply side, the higher the supply elasticity in subsidizing countries, the higher the impact of the removal of subsidies on world price. In addition, the choice of the supply elasticity is also important for the potential gains in nonsubsidizing countries, such as African countries. In these countries an inelastic supply will lower the gains. This explains why Goreux (2003) finds a US$254 million gain for West and Central African countries using a supply elasticity of 0.90, while Sumner (2003) finds only US$116 million with a value of 0.3.

With regard to parameters, one can also mention the choice of the "decoupling" parameters used to reflect the decoupled nature of some measures, such as the direct payments in the United States. The choice of a particular value for these parameters plays a role in the supply response, and they are merely estimated in a consistent theoretical framework. These parameters are mainly found in studies using the expected net revenue approach.

The Transmission from International to Domestic Prices

When studying supply reactions in nonsubsidizing countries, it is important to have a good idea of the price transmission mechanism. The effect of the degree of transmission is related to the previous discussion about price elasticity: assuming a high or a perfect degree of transmission is equivalent to assuming a more elastic supply. However, in some countries (particularly in Africa), this transmission is far from perfect. In addition to the exchange rate effects (which is beyond the scope of the studies previously done), there are various price stabilization measures that could dampen the positive shock coming from the world market. Thus the study by de Poonyth et al. (2004) that assumes a full transmission surely overestimates the supply response in African countries, while the scenario put forth by Pan et al. (2004) and Araujo Bonjean, Calipel, and Traoré (2006) are closer to the real situation.

The Choice of Base Years and Databases

In a fluctuating environment, the choice of the base year is important. Since subsidies tend to be countercyclical (mainly in the United States), the base year may impact the final results. When global prices are low, subsidies are high and so is their impact on world prices (ICAC 2002). Sometimes, however, the choice of the reference period is driven by the availability of data; one of the differences between the various studies on the impact of subsidies is related to the database used. For instance, there is a difference between FAO and ICAC data regarding cotton production. The former uses the agricultural campaign, while the latter retains the civil year. With regard to subsidies, authors have gathered data on the United States from WTO, ICAC, or USDA. However, the data from ICAC are highly contested since they are not official and are generally higher than the official notifications. For instance, Poonyth et al. (2004) find an impact on global prices of 3.1 percent using WTO data but only 7 percent using ICAC data.

The Number of Countries Included in the Study

In the debate surrounding the subsidy issue, the United States has appeared to be the largest cotton exporter and thus a key actor. This situation explains why some studies focus only on US subsidies (ICAC 2002; Sumner 2003; Pan et al. 2004). Thus, all other things being equal, the authors who simulate the removal of subsidies only in the United States should find a lower impact than those who simulate a global removal. The difference in the modeling strategy, base year, parameters, and data used make this comparison tricky. Nevertheless, in studies that simulate a removal in the United States followed by a removal at the global level in a sequential way, the dominant effect of US subsidies appears clearly.

The Role of International Stocks

World cotton stocks now represent 86 percent of production and thus play an important role in the specification of the models used to study cotton subsidies. The role of stocks in commodity markets has been highlighted by Deaton and Laroque (1996). However, among all the studies mentioned in Table 7.9, only Pan et al. (2004) and Araujo Bonjean, Calipel, and Traoré (2006) include stocks in their modeling strategy. Taking stocks into account should yield smoother price fluctuations; however, if speculators' expectations are nonrational, expectation errors will accentuate the fluctuations.

The Takeaway Message

There are a lot of reasons explaining why the numbers vary so much. However, it is worth noting that despite the diverging numbers, most studies yield the same conclusion: domestic policies most impact global prices. Trade measures are limited and have less of an impact. One final limitation could be raised regarding the models used to address this issue. With the exception of Araujo Bonjean, Calipel, and Traoré (2006), none of the models incorporate risk and instability issues on the supply side.

New Initiatives and the Future of Global Trade Negotiations

The cotton issue is an important part of the WTO agricultural package and has been a key topic in the negotiations. In 2004 a special cotton subcommittee was created under the Agriculture Committee's Special Sessions. Most developed countries argue that the removal of subsidies will benefit emerging countries, such as India and Brazil, rather than poorer African countries. Under this argument, emerging countries appear to be "free riders" in the negotiations, pushing some developing countries to highlight the damage they themselves face without acknowledging that other developing countries are also a source of distortions while being major beneficiaries of the developed countries' reform. However, since the launch of the Doha Round, the negotiations have not produced a conclusive result and the question of cotton subsidies is still pending.

The Cotton Initiative and Its Consequences

In 2003 four African countries (Benin, Burkina Faso, Chad, and Mali, known as the C4 countries) raised a sectoral initiative in favor of cotton. These countries comprise the main cotton producers and exporters in Africa south of the Sahara; they argued that their economies heavily rely on cotton and cannot support the negative impact of developed countries' subsidies. The initiative aimed to push developed countries (specifically the United States and the EU) to first set up a plan to reduce production and export subsidies within three years and then establish transitory financial compensation for developing countries until the complete elimination of the subsidies.

The Cancun and Hong Kong Ministerial Conferences were not a great success for the C4 countries, due in large part to the diverging views of the United States and the EU regarding subsidies. However, the Cancun Ministerial did shed light on the issue and led to the creation of a specific subcommittee for cotton in 2004 and a Consultative Framework Mechanism on Cotton, a development forum chaired by the Director-General. In this forum, actors can exchange their views, notify their activities regarding cotton subsidies, and get briefed on the latest developments in the negotiations and the latest market conditions. The United States and the EU also committed themselves to supporting developing countries' cotton sectors in order to dampen the potential negative impact these countries may face from continued subsidies. These initiatives could be seen as a kind of "second best" solution, eluding the question of suppressing all subsidies.

In 2006 the United States also set up a new initiative called the West Africa Cotton Improvement Program (WACIP), designed for the C4 countries (Benin, Burkina Faso, Chad, and Mali).[14] The program aimed to improve cotton growers' yields and incomes by 15 percent. Initiated through USAID and given an initial budget of US$27 million, the program was executed by the International Fertilizer Development Center (IFDC) with the involvement of various national consultative committees and private US collaborators (Abt Associates Inc. and Aid to Artisans) and universities (Auburn University, Michigan State University, and Tuskegee University). The program mainly consisted of technical assistance to farmers, researchers, agrodealers, private enterprises, and interprofessional associations, as well as grants to allow producers' organizations to attend international conferences. Although the program seems to have worked in terms of productivity according to IFDC (2015), there was no independent scientific evaluation provided.

The EU also established a new partnership, but unlike the WACIP this partnership covered all cotton-producing African countries. The EU-Africa Partnership on Cotton was launched in 2004 in Paris and was included in the "All ACP Agricultural Commodities Programme" with a 15 million euro budget for the period 2007–2012. The program focused on trade and development, emphasizing increased competitiveness of cotton value chains, improved technical assistance (capacity building, reinforcement of producers' associations, technological innovation, and so on), and the facilitation of the coordination of local, regional, and international actors and states regarding international negotiations. The program started slowly; during the first review in 2009, only 1.06 million euros were disbursed by the European Community (COS 2009). In 2012 a new program took the place of this previous one, committing 11 million euros from 2012 to 2016. According to the program management, 257 million euros were used by the EU (European Community and Member States) between 2004 and 2012 for the program (COS 2014), the main contributors being France and Germany. As with the WACIP, however, there is no independent evaluation of the impact of the EU program. The remaining question is whether these measures could compensate for the potential losses that African countries may experience due to subsidies.

14 It was later extended to Senegal.

The United States-Brazil Case and Its Settlement

The question of the impact of subsidies granted to American and European cotton producers was first introduced in the public debate during a dispute between Brazil and the United States in 2003. In an initial consultation request made in September 2002, Brazil argued that the main support measures in effect in the United States were inconsistent with the obligations of that country and incompatible with the provisions of the Agreement on Agriculture and of the GATT.[15] US subsidies were condemned as promoting US exports and contributing to depressed global prices. After the failure of the initial consultation and a second request put forth by Brazil, a panel was established in March 2003 to examine the question. During this panel's proceedings, many countries reserved their third-party rights to participate in the process. These entities included Argentina; Australia; Benin; Bolivia; Canada; Chad; China; European Communities; India; Japan; New Zealand; Pakistan; Paraguay; Taiwan, China; Thailand; and Venezuela.

In its decision in March 2005, the Dispute Settlement Unit (DSU) estimated that direct aid and production flexibility contracts are not truly decoupled and thus eligible for the Green Box and that the Step 2 mechanism is an export subsidy inconsistent with the Agreement on Agriculture. The resolution also acknowledged that countercyclical payments and marketing loans were inconsistent with the United States' WTO commitments. The United States appealed the decision, but the Appellate Body confirmed the 2005 decision of the DSU in June 2008. Meanwhile, the only measure that was subject to an amendment by the United States was the Step 2 mechanism, which was abolished in August 2006. In 2009, as a consequence of the Appellate Body's decision, WTO arbitrators decided the level of countermeasures that Brazil could impose against US trade. However, in order to avoid these countermeasures, which would have affected approximately US$800 million in trade, the two parties signed an agreement in June 2010 providing a framework for regular discussions on the issue. The United States also provided the Brazil Cotton Institute with technical assistance and capacity-building activities.

At the expiration of this framework in February 2014, the two countries intensified discussions and on October 16, 2014, after 10 years of disputes, the United States and Brazil notified the DSU of a mutually acceptable solution on implementation. The two parties concluded a Memorandum

15 More precisely Articles 5(c), 6.3(b), (c), and (d), 3.1(a) and (b), and 3.2 of the SCM Agreement; Articles 3.3, 7.1, 8, 9.1, and 10.1 of the Agreement on Agriculture; and Article III:4 of GATT 1994.

of Understanding and agreed that the dispute was terminated. Under the terms of the new agreement, Brazil agrees not to bring new WTO actions against US cotton support programs while the current US Farm Bill is in force and to give up its rights to countermeasures against US trade or any further proceedings in this dispute. In turn, the United States will provide more technical assistance and undertake more capacity-building activities to support the Brazil Cotton Institute through a onetime final contribution of US$300 million.

Future of Trade Negotiations

The Situation before the Bali Conference

Cotton remains at the heart of current agricultural trade negotiations. The WTO Ministerial held in Cancun in 2003 marked a turning point in the negotiations, granting specific treatment to the cotton issue. The issue was put on the table through the joint proposal of the C4 countries with the support of other developing countries, who felt that US and European subsidies were detrimental to world prices. The European Union was willing to make efforts to address its subsidies, specifically through a reform of its Common Agricultural Policy; however, the United States's position favored the status quo and proposed to expand the discussion to include tariff and nontariff barriers, synthetic fibers, and textiles. As the negotiations failed over the "Singapore issues," the conference ended with no solution to the agricultural issues.[16]

It was hoped that the 2005 WTO Conference in Hong Kong would avoid the scenario that had ended in a stalemate in Cancun. The issue of cotton was raised again by the C4, supported by other developing countries (Brazil, Cameroon, India, and others) who reiterated their request to see the dismantling of all cotton support measures by the year 2009. As in Cancun, the United States reaffirmed the need to expand the question to the textile industry in general, while indicating the possibility of exempting African cotton from tariffs if all other countries agreed to do so. This measure, which would have required significant tariff concessions by China, was rejected. However,

16 The "Singapore issues" refers to the decision adopted in the WTO Ministerial meeting in Singapore in 1996 to establish working groups to study investment, competition, and transparency in government procurement and trade facilitation in WTO. The decision was controversial since many developing countries had not participated in the discussion that led to the text and the ones who participated did not want them to be introduced in the WTO.

the principle of the elimination of export subsidies by the end of 2006 was accepted, resulting in the removal of the Step 2 program in the United States in August 2006. As for domestic support, the text of the Ministerial Declaration contained only a broad statement that support should be reduced ambitiously in a relatively short period. Finally, in terms of market access, developed countries agreed to allow cotton from LDCs to enter their territory duty-free and quota-free, subject to a final Agreement on Agriculture.

Bali and Beyond

The Ministerial Conference of Bali in 2013 tried to shape a new agenda for future negotiations. In October 2013, before the Conference took place, the C4 countries introduced a draft text calling for duty-free and quota-free access for their cotton to developed- country markets, as well as to developing markets able to do so. For developing countries that are not able to open their makets, the text called for ways to improve market access for exports from LDCs. It also again raised the issue of export subsidies and domestic support (particularly support systems that distort trade, such as coupled payments). Finally, the proposal higlighted the need to strengthen development assistance for cotton by linking it to the Aid for Trade initiative. The talks led to a compromise draft text in which ministers reaffirmed their commitments to reform the global cotton trade according to the 2005 objectives, while leaving the modalities (that is, the size of the cuts and the time span in which they will be implemented) to the larger global negotiations on agriculture. One initiative particularly worth noting is the commitment to meet twice a year to discuss the latest cotton issues in terms of market access, domestic support, and export subsidies.

The Bali conference came to a decision consisting of eleven points. After stressing the importance of cotton for LDCs, ministers regretted the failure to achieve the 2005 Hong Kong trade-related objectives and reaffirmed their commitment to "ambitiously, expeditiously, and specifically" address the cotton issue within agricultural negotiations. Most of the concerns raised by the C4 were deemed relevant and were reaffirmed, particularly in terms of market access, domestic support, and export subsidies. The biannual sessions mentioned above were enacted and, most important, the Conference agreed on the so-called 2008 revised draft agricultural modalities as the reference point for future negotiations (WTO 2008). These modalities call for a reduction in domestic support for cotton that is more significant than the general reduction in AMS, as well as for a shorter period of implementation (one-third of the implementation period), particularly for trade-distorting domestic support. This special and differential treatment allows developing countries that subsidize their cotton sectors, but that also have relevant AMS and Blue Box commitments, to apply a one-third lower rate of reduction and for a longer period.

Looking ahead, we face a new environment marked by the rise of China, India, and Viet Nam in the international cotton market. In addition to being the world's top cotton producer and consumer, China appears to be the largest cotton subsidizer in the world, applying a high level of out-quota tariff. However, China declared that it is in the position to grant duty-free and quota-free market access for exports by LDCs as part of the Nairobi Ministerial Decision of December 19, 2015. The United States and the EU have also changed their support measures toward more decoupled payments. The remaining support measures in the United States are expected to be low in the future, given the actual level of world prices. Unlike the situation in 2003, when the C4 countries first raised the cotton issue, the main challenge now exists among developing countries themselves.

Conclusion

Cotton is a major commodity that provides export earnings to many developing countries and provides a source of income for millions of people, particularly in Africa south of the Sahara. The global cotton market has been characterized by huge subsidies in developed countries, particularly in the late 1990s; most of these subsidies have consisted of domestic support measures. While subsidies are declining in developed countries, new developing countries have emerged, potentially providing more subsidies than developed countries did previously and offering less market access for least developed countries. Since the United States and the EU have partially reformed their support measures and since US production is expected to fall in the future, the burden has now shifted to these emerging countries, such as China, which is also the main destination for African cotton. This creates a new environment for future negotiations and calls for a new approach that LDCs, particularly African countries, seem not to take into account (Imboden 2014).

Since the 2003 WTO Conference in Cancun, no concrete measures have been taken in terms of support reduction, with the exception of the removal of export subsidies in the United States. Cotton is still considered a key commodity that deserves specific treatment. It is now expected that the reduction of cotton subsidies will be more important than reductions for other commodities and that these reductions will be implemented over a shorter period of time. Developing countries that still provide subsidies could benefit from lower reduction rates and longer implementation periods. However, a formal agreement on cotton still relies on the overall negotiations on agriculture.

For developing countries, particularly in Francophone Africa, one should not necessarily expect a huge impact from the removal of cotton subsidies or from improved market access. In an influential study, Goreux (2003) estimates the loss incurred by developing countries due to global cotton subsidies to be US$250 million. However, these countries face many constraints on the supply side that may prevent them from taking advantage of a reduction in subsidies. Price-setting mechanisms often lead to an imperfect transmission from world markets to domestic markets; on the other hand, some developing countries peg their currency to the euro so that any appreciation of the euro relative to the US dollar is automatically transmitted to the national currency. Developing countries also often experience very low levels of crop yields, including for cotton. Due to these factors, major reforms of the global cotton sector are still required; otherwise, the majority of the gains from reduced cotton subsidies could go to emerging countries rather than to LDCs.

Bibliography

Agricultural Act of 2014. Pub. L. 113-79, 128 Stat. 649-1005. February 7, 2014.

Araujo Bonjean, C., S. Calipel, and F. Traoré. 2006. "Impact des aides américaines et européennes sur le marché international du coton." Research Report for the French Ministry of Agriculture, Paris, France.

———. 2007. "L'impact des aides américaines et européennes sur le marché du coton : résultats d'un modèle d'équilibre partiel dynamique." *Notes et Etudes Economiques* 27: 57–89.

Arrow, K. 1965. "The Theory of Risk Aversion. Lecture 2 in Aspects of the Theory of Risk-Bearing." Yrjo Jahnsson Lectures. Yrjo Jahnssonin Saatio, Helsinki, Finland.

Baffes, J. 2004. *Cotton: Market Setting, Trade Policies, and Issues.* World Bank Policy Research Working Paper 3218. Washington, DC: World Bank.

———. 2006. "Cotton and the Developing Countries: Implication for Development." In *Trade, Doha, and Development: A Window into the Issues*, edited by R. Newfarmer, 119–128. Washington, DC: World Bank.

Binswanger, H. 1981. "Attitudes Toward Risk: Theoretical Implications of an Experiment in Rural India." *Economic Journal* 91: 867–890.

Blandford, D., and T. Josling. 2011. "The WTO Agricultural Modalities Proposals and Their Impact on Domestic Support in the EU and the United States." In *Unfinished Business? The WTO's Doha Agenda*, edited by W. Martin and A. Matoo, 69–114. Washington, DC: World Bank.

Cameron, A. C., and P. K. Trivedi. 2005. *Microeconometrics: Methods and Applications*. Cambridge, UK: Cambridge University Press.

CERI (Cotton Economic Research Institute). 2009. "Crop Subsidies in Foreign Countries: Different Paths to Common Goals." Staff Report 09-02, Texas Tech University, Lubbock, TX, US.

COS (Comité d'Orientation et de Suivi) coton. 2009. *Mise à jour relative au Partenariat Union Européenne—Afrique sur le coton*. Brussels.

———. 2014. *Mise à jour relative au Partenariat Union Européenne—Afrique sur le coton*. Brussels.

Deaton, A., and G. Laroque. 1996. "Competitive Storage and Commodity Price Dynamics." *Journal of Political Economy* 104: 896–923.

Delarue, J., S. Mesple-Somps, J. D. Naudet, and A. S. Robilliard. 2009. "Le paradoxe de Sikasso: Coton et pauvreté au Mali." Document de Travail DT/2009-09. DIAL, Paris.

European Commission (Commission Européenne). 2004. "Le secteur du coton." Document de travail de la Direction Générale de l'Agriculture. Accessed 2016. http://europa.eu.int/comm/agriculture/markets/cotton/reports/rep_fr.pdf.

FAO (Food and Agricultural Organization of the United Nations). 2008. *The State of Food and Agriculture*. Rome: FAO.

FAPRI (Food and Agricultural Policy Research Institute). 2002. "The Doha Round of the World Trade Organization: Appraising Further Liberalization of Agricultural Markets." Working Paper 02-WP 317, Unpublished, FAPRI. Iowa State University and University of Missouri–Colombia.

Fortucci, P. 2002. "The Contributions of Cotton to the Economy and Food Security in Developing Countries." Mimeo. FAO, Rome.

Goreux, L. 2003. "Prejudice Caused by Industrialised Countries' Subsidies to Cotton Sectors in Western and Central Africa: Background Document to the Submission Made by Benin, Burkina Faso, Chad and Mali to the WTO." TN/AG/GEN/4. World Trade Organization, Geneva.

Guitchounts, A. 2008. "Cotton Subsidies and Beyond." Communication at the International Cotton Conference: Rationales and Evolution of Cotton Policies, CIRAD, May 13–17. Centre International en Recherche Agronomique pour le Developpement, Montpellier.

Hennessy, D. 1998. "The Production Effects of Agricultural Income Support Policies under Uncertainty." *American Journal of Agricultural Economics* 80: 46–57.

Hertel, T. W. 1989. "Negotiating Reductions in Agricultural Support: Implications of Technology and Factor Mobility." *American Journal of Agricultural Economics* 71: 559–573.

Houck, J. P. 1992. *Elements of Agricultural Trade Policies*. Prospect Heights, IL: Waveland Press, Inc.

ICAC (International Cotton Advisory Committee). 2002. *Reports on Injury due to Low Cotton Prices*. Washington, DC.

ICTSD (International Center for Trade and Sustainable Development). 2013. "Cotton: Trends in Global Production, Trade and Policy." Information Note. ICTSD, Geneva.

IFDC (International Fertilizer Development Center). 2015. *Annual Report*. Muscle Shoals, AL, US: International Fertilizer Development Center.

Imboden, N. 2014. "How to Re-invigorate the Cotton Issue at the WTO: Gin Ideas, Spin Proposals, Weave Solutions, and Avoid Stocks." In *Tackling Agriculture in the Post-Bali Context: A Collection of Short Essays*, edited by R. Meléndez-Ortiz, C. Bellmann, and J. Hepburn, 195–203. Geneva: ICTSD.

Karagiannis, G. 2004. *The EU Cotton Policy Regime and the Implications of the Proposed Changes for Producer Welfare*. FAO Commodity and Trade Policy Research Working Paper 9. Rome: FAO.

LMC International. 2007. "Study on the Cotton Sector in the European Union." Final report prepared for the Directorate General of Agriculture and Rural Development of the European Commission, Brussels.

Mancini, F., A. Van Bruggen, J. Jiggins, A. Ambatipudi, and H. Murphy. 2005. "Acute Pesticide Poisoning among Male and Female Cotton Growers in India." *International Journal of Occupational Health* 11 (3): 221–232.

Monke, J. 2008. "Farm Commodity Programs in the 2008 Farm Bill." Congressional Research Service report for Congress, Washington, DC.

Moseley, W., and L. C. Gray. 2008. *Hanging by a Thread: Cotton, Globalization, and Poverty in Africa*. Athens, OH, US: Ohio University Press.

NCC (National Cotton Council of America). 2015. World Cotton Database. Accessed April 2015. www.cotton.org/econ/cropinfo/cropdata/index.cfm.

ODI (Overseas Development Institute). 2004. *Understanding the Impact of Cotton Subsidies on Developing Countries and Poor People in Those Countries*. London: ODI.

Pan, S., S. Mohanty, D. Ethridge, and M. Fadiga. 2004. "The Impacts of U.S. Cotton Programs on the World Market: An Analysis of Brazilian WTO Petition." Working Paper, Texas Tech University, Lubbock, TX, US.

Poonyth, D., A. Sarris, R. Sharma, and S. Shui. 2004. *The Impact of Domestic and Trade Policies on the World Cotton Market.* Commodity and Trade Policy Research Working Paper. Rome: FAO.

Pratt, J. W. 1964. "Risk Aversion in the Small and in the Large." *Econometrica* 32: 122–136.

Qaim, M., and S. Kouser. 2013. "Genetically Modified Crops and Food Security." *PLoS ONE* 8 (6): e64879. DOI:10.1371/journal.pone.0064879.

Reeves, G., D. Vincent, D. Quirke, and S. Wyatt. 2001. *Trade Distortions and Cotton Markets: Implications for Global Cotton Producers.* Canberra, Australia: Cotton Research and Development Corporation, Centre for International Economics.

Sanogo, B., S. Keita, and S. Sanogo. 2009. Contribution du coton a la croissance economique au Mali. Unpublished, Ministere du Developpement Social, de la Solidarite et des personnes Agees et Observatoire du Developpement Humain Durable et de la Lutte Contre la Pauvrete, Bamako, Mali.

Schnepf, R. 2014. "Status of the WTO Brazil-U.S. Cotton Case." CRS Report R43336. Congressional Research Service, Washington, DC.

Smith, V. 2014. "The 2014 US Farm Bill: Implications for the WTO Doha Round in a Post-Bali Context." In *Tackling Agriculture in the Post-Bali Context: A Collection of Short Essays*, edited by R. Meléndez-Ortiz, C. Bellmann, and J. Hepburn, 153–157. Geneva: International Centre for Trade and Sustainable Development (ICTSD).

Sumner, D. 2003. "A Quantitative Simulation Analysis of the Impacts of U.S. Cotton Subsidies on Cotton Prices and Quantities." Paper presented to the WTO Cotton Panel, October, Geneva.

———. 2006. "Reducing Cotton Subsidies: The DDA Cotton Initiative." In *Agricultural Trade Reform and the Doha Development Agenda*, edited by K. Anderson and W. Martin, 271–292. Washington, DC: World Bank.

Tockarick, S. 2003. *Measuring the Impact of Distortions in Agricultural Trade in Partial and General Equilibrium Models.* IMF WP/O3/110. Washington, DC: International Monetary Fund (IMF).

Traoré, F. 2010. "Les aides americaines et europeennes au coton: Impact sur le marche mondial et consequences pour l'economie malienne." PhD dissertation, Centre d'Etudes et de Recherche sur le Developpement International, University of Auvergne.

———. 2014. "Assessing the Impact of China Net Imports on World Cotton Price." *Applied Economics Letters* 21 (15): 1031–1035.

Tschirley, D., C. Poulton, and P. Labaste, eds. 2009. *Organization and Performance of Cotton Sectors in Africa: Learning from Reform Experience.* Washington, DC: World Bank.

Tweeten, L. 1992. *Agricultural Trade: Principle and Policies*. Boulder, CO, US: Westview Press.

USDA (United States Department of Agriculture). 2012. *2012 Census of Agriculture, National Agricultural Statistics Service*. Washington, DC: USDA.

Westcott, P. C., and J. M. Price. 2001. "Analysis of the U.S. Commodity Loan Program with Marketing Loan Provisions." AER-801, USDA, Economic Research Service, Washington, DC.

Westcott, P. C, C. E. Young, and J. M. Price. 2002. "The 2002 Farm Act: Provisions and Implications for Commodity Markets." *Agriculture Information Bulletin* 778. Washington, DC: United States Department of Agriculture.

WTO (World Trade Organization). 2008. Revised Draft Modalities for Agriculture. TN/AG/W/4/Rev.4. Committee on Agriculture Special Session, December, Geneva.

———. 2014. "Cotton." Background paper by the Secretariat. TN/AG/GEN/34, TN/AG/SCC/GEN/13. Committee on Agriculture Special Session Sub-Committee on Cotton, Geneva.

———. 2015. Tariff Analysis Online facility. Accessed April, 2015. https://tao.wto.org/welcome.aspx?ReturnUrl=%2f.

Young, C. E., and P. C. Westcott. 2000. "How Decoupled Is US Agricultural Support for Major Crops?" *Amercan Journal of Agricultural Economics* 82 (3): 762–767.

SECTION 2

Successful and Failed Trade Instruments for Managing Price Volatility

Chapter 8

FOOD SECURITY STOCKS: ECONOMIC AND OPERATIONAL ISSUES

Eugenio Díaz-Bonilla

The use of public food stocks for food security purposes is a hotly debated topic in international trade negotiations on agriculture within the World Trade Organization (WTO). Regardless of the legal standing of food stocks under the WTO legal framework, however, one must also consider the more substantive issue of whether public food stock programs make sense in terms of food security. This chapter discusses several economic and operational factors relevant to the design and use of public stocks for food security purposes in developing countries. Chapter 9 focuses on the legal issues related to the WTO agreements. Chapter 8 contains four sections. First is the consideration of several new circumstances in which these food security programs would operate, including changes in the world's general economic and weather conditions, agricultural markets and policies, and food and nutrition security circumstances. The second section discusses general policy concepts related to food security and how food security stocks may fit into that policy framework. The third section covers different economic and operational issues specifically related to public food stocks and domestic food aid. A fourth and final section concludes the chapter.

A New Context for Food Security

General Economic and Climate Conditions

Although food security concerns are not a new topic in global trade negotiations (see Chapter 9), the general context for those negotiations has changed in recent years. Since agricultural and food prices (along with other commodities) began to increase in the mid-2000s, with price spikes in 2008 and 2011, food security has been analyzed against a backdrop of higher nominal prices and higher price volatility, in contrast to the previous context of lower global food prices seen during the mid-1980s and the 1990s. During these decades, agricultural trade negotiations focused on policies that either artificially expanded supply in some countries through subsidies or reduced demand in other countries through protection (thus lowering global prices). In more recent years, however, there has been larger interest in disciplining policies that may artificially restrict supply or distort demand in ways that contribute to higher world prices. In other words, whereas previous trade negotiations focused on agricultural producers, more recently there has been increased preoccupation with consumers as well (see Meyer and Schmidhuber 2013; Bureau and Jean 2013; Díaz-Bonilla 2013a; Tangermann 2013).

Figure 8.1 shows nominal world food prices in US dollars; these are clearly above those seen in previous decades (data from the IMF/IFS database; IMF 2014). At the same time, real (that is, inflation-adjusted) prices are not as high as they were in the 1960s and 1970s, even though the trend of declining prices seen during the 1980s and 1990s has been reversed.[1]

Among other things, high prices in nominal terms may reflect the well-known fact that global commodity prices (which are usually quoted in current and nominal US dollars) move in opposite directions from the value of the US dollar against other currencies (Mundell 2002). In other words, if the US dollar appreciates against other currencies, then the US dollar price of commodities declines, and vice versa: if the US dollar devalues, the prices of commodities increases. One very clear example of this reverse relation was the jump in nominal commodity prices seen in the early 1970s when the US dollar was devalued after the breakdown of the fixed exchange arrangements of Bretton Woods (see Figure 8.1). Then, another part of the reason why global commodity prices in nominal US dollars were high between 2007 and 2011 was that the US dollar dropped in value against other currencies during that time. In fact, if the index is measured in nominal Special Drawing Rights (or SDRs, a basket of currencies that evens out the fluctuations of the US dollar against other currencies), then recent prices in nominal terms do not seem as high as when measured in US dollars (Figure 8.2).[2] In any case, with any measure, the 2000s trend toward higher prices has stopped since 2011, opening

1 The inflation deflator is the manufacturing unit value of exports from the category of "advanced countries" as defined by the IMF.

2 The SDR is an international reserve asset, created by the IMF in 1969 to expand the official reserves of member countries. Its value is based on a basket of four key international currencies: the euro, Japanese yen, pound sterling, and US dollar. Starting in October 2016, the SDR will also include the Chinese renminbi. The SDR is not a currency per se but can be exchanged for freely usable currencies at a parity calculated by the IMF, using the market value of the four currencies mentioned and the weights they have in the basket. Because, in general, the market values of those currencies tend to move opposite to each other (that is, if the US dollar depreciates, then the euro appreciates), the market value of the SDR is more stable than each currency separately.

FIGURE 8.1 Food price indexes in US nominal and real values (US$)

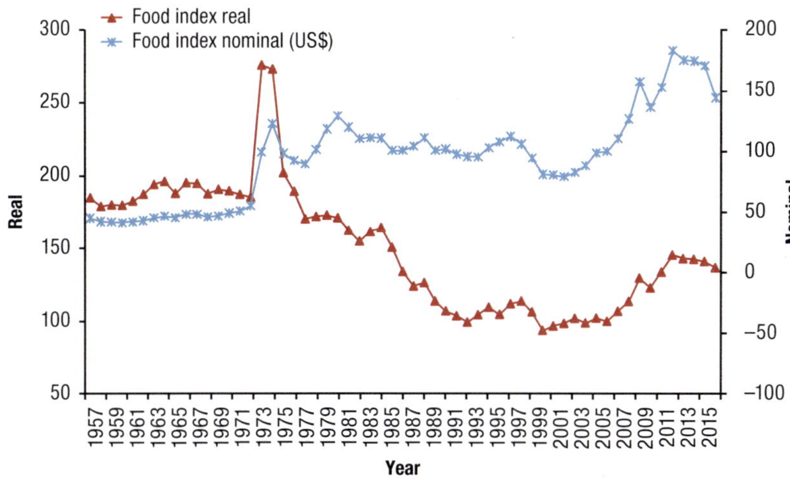

Source: Author calculations based on IMF (2016).

Note: (2005 = 100)

FIGURE 8.2 Food price indexes in US$ and Special Drawing Rights (SDRs) nominal values

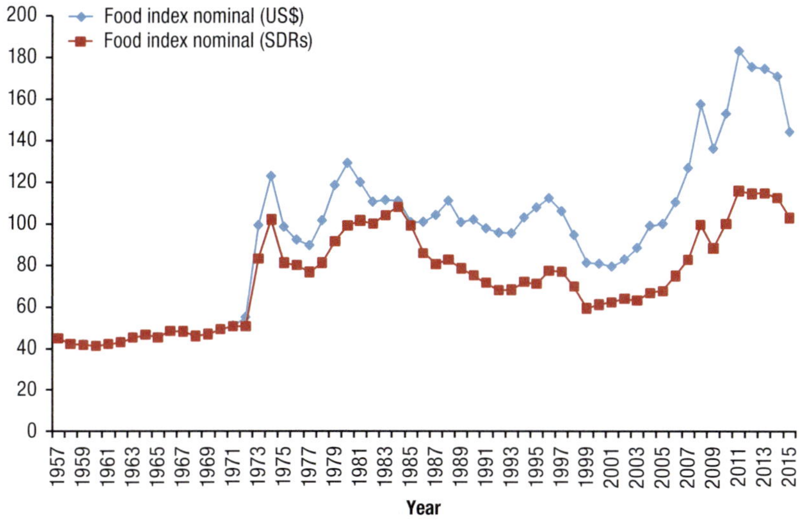

Source: Author calculations based on IMF (2014).

Note: (2005 = 100).

the possibility of a reversion to the previous secular decline in food prices (Díaz-Bonilla 2013a).

As discussed in greater detail in Chapter 9, the current high global commodity prices, measured in nominal US dollars, have implications for the calculation of domestic support according to the WTO Agreement on Agriculture (AoA), which uses international prices from 1986 through 1988 as a benchmark. Today's high nominal prices may persist into the future, but there may not necessarily be further increases; such a flat trend for nominal prices implies a decline of inflation-adjusted prices (a discussion of the potential scenarios stemming from this trend can be found in Díaz-Bonilla et al. 2013). This changed food price scenario is just one of a larger set of new circumstances for agriculture and food production that must be considered when analyzing the legal, economic, operational, and social aspects of food security stocks.

Another important change is that developing countries have been expanding their global economic presence as measured by several indicators, such as their share of global gross domestic product (GDP), particularly when measured in purchasing power parity (PPP). According to the IMF World Economic Outlook database, the world share of global GDP (at PPP values) of developing and emerging countries grew from 36 percent in 1980 to almost 58 percent in 2015, surpassing developed countries' share.[3] This increase in GDP, and the concomitant increase in developing-country incomes, has led to a reduction in poverty levels and to improvements in various health, nutrition, and food security indicators, although with important variations across developing countries and regions. A further implication of growing incomes in developing countries is that additional public-sector revenues have facilitated the expansion of agricultural domestic support, as discussed in the next section.

Another much-discussed aspect of the new global food security context is the expanded link between food prices and developments in the energy sector. The growth of biofuel mandates has been singled out as one factor behind the price spikes affecting corn and oilseeds in the second part of the 2000s (see OECD-FAO 2011, 2012, 2013; Schnepf 2013; Laborde and Msangi 2012;

3 The IMF identifies three categories of countries that are called "advanced economies," "emerging markets," and "developing economies." Using solely the "developed/developing" dichotomy, advanced economies would correspond to developed countries; the other two categories comprise developing countries in the broader, traditional sense. Measured in current dollars instead of PPP values, advanced countries still make up a larger percentage of the world economy, at somewhat more than 60 percent against less than 40 percent for developing and emerging countries.

Torero 2012; Headey and Fan 2010). Going forward, OECD-FAO (2013) estimates that without significant policy changes, global production of ethanol (mainly from coarse grains and sugar) and biodiesel (mainly from oilseeds) will require 12 percent of the world's coarse grains, 29 percent of the world's sugarcane, and 15 percent of the world's vegetable oil production by 2022. Simulations by the International Food Policy Research Institute (IFPRI) (see Rosegrant et al. 2013; Al-Riffai, Dimaranan, and Laborde 2010) suggest that biofuel policies, if maintained in their current state, will imply higher prices for food products in the coming decades; this link may be crucial because the global energy market is far larger than the global food market.[4] Developments in energy markets may thus drive outcomes in agricultural markets, adding another source of volatility for food production, demand, and prices.

A final widely noted development that affects food security is climate change. There are two aspects to consider in this regard: the longer-term trend and the shorter-term variability around that trend. With respect of the first aspect, and whatever the uncertainties about the overall and geographical medium- and long-term impact on agriculture and food production, it is important to consider the probability that the world may be on its way to surpassing the 2°C temperature increase threshold in the coming years (IPCC 2014; Rosegrant et al. 2014). Such an increase will affect agriculture and food production and will require sustained research and development (R&D) investments in both climate change adaptation and mitigation. This topic warrants a more careful review of domestic support within the WTO, considering the implications for the AoA (including issues of distortionary and Green Box domestic support) and for other WTO legal texts, such as the Agreements on Subsidies and Countervailing Measures and Technical Barriers to Trade (Blandford 2013).

The second and shorter-term aspect, of more immediate importance for agricultural production, is increased weather volatility. Atmospheric warming seems to have already increased the frequency of extreme weather events such as droughts and floods (Hansen, Sato, and Ruedy 2012; IPCC 2014). Along with the links between energy and food, this shorter-term weather variability

---

4 Estimates for 2006 (Díaz-Bonilla and Robinson 2010) suggest that the market for food energy amounted to about 28 exajoules, whereas the market for nonfood energy was approximately 460 exajoules for a population of about 6.4 billion people at that time. In other words, the market for nonfood energy was about 16 times larger than the market for food energy. Projections only increase this disparity in the future; for instance, for 2050, the nonfood energy market is forecast to be 21 times bigger than the food energy market (Díaz-Bonilla and Robinson 2010; see also Meyer and Schmidhuber 2013) (1 exajoule = about 239,000,000,000,000 cal; 1 joule = 0.000239 cal, and 1 exajoule = 1 joule times 10^{18}).

is increasing the volatility of food quantity and prices. All of these developments add further urgency to the consideration of the food security stocks and domestic food issues discussed in this and the following chapter (Murphy 2010; IATP 2012).

Changes in Agricultural Markets and Policies

General economic advances in developing countries have been accompanied by changes in agricultural production, trade, and policies; these changes have modified the landscape for the political economy of global trade negotiations (Díaz-Bonilla 2013b). In terms of global production, developing countries now represent about 75 percent of total agricultural production (as measured in constant international dollars by FAO/FAOSTAT [FAO 2014]). The increase in developing countries' share in production since the 1960s (almost 29 percentage points [pps]) can be explained mostly by Asia's expanded production (23 pps, of which China represents about 14.6 pps and India almost 2 pps). The global share of agricultural production in Latin America and the Caribbean (LAC) has also increased (3.5 pps), as has Africa's production share (1.2 pps). Looking at trade data for individual countries, the composition of the group of net agricultural exporters has also changed significantly since the mid-1990s, when the Uruguay Round of trade negotiations was finished. Table 8.1 shows the evolution of net agricultural exporters (FAO 2014).[5]

During the 1990s, only one developing country (Argentina) was in the top-five net agricultural exporters by value; only two more (Brazil and Thailand) were in the top ten. By 2010–2013, Brazil and Argentina had displaced the United States and the Netherlands as the top-two net exporters; with the addition of Thailand, Indonesia, and India, there were now five developing countries in the top-ten net exporters. It can also be noted that although China has dropped from the list, India has been climbing the ranks as a significant net agricultural exporter. In fact, in recent years, India has become a main global exporter of rice, beef, and cotton (see USDA 2014a, 2014b). Despite this growth, however, India's agricultural sector is still composed of a large number of small farmers who continue to be affected by poverty and vulnerability. In recent trade negotiations, India has emphasized this latter situation, while its trading partners have instead focused on the country's increasing presence in global food and agricultural exports. This duality plays a significant role in the legal debate on public food stocks analyzed in Chapter 9.

5 Net exports are total exports minus total imports. Of course, the ranking would be different if gross or total exports were considered.

TABLE 8.1 Net agricultural exports (current US$ millions)

Rank of countries	Average 1990s	Rank of countries	Average 2000s	Rank of countries	2010–2013
United States	19,951	Brazil	26,618	Brazil	66,826
Netherlands	14,054	Netherlands	20,250	Argentina	37,330
France	11,309	Argentina	17,641	United States	34,358
Australia	10,804	Australia	13,925	Netherlands	30,910
Argentina	8,008	France	11,620	Australia	22,505
Brazil	7,662	United States	11,384	Thailand	21,519
Denmark	5,313	Thailand	9,175	Indonesia	20,042
Thailand	4,864	New Zealand	8,033	France	16,406
New Zealand	4,681	Indonesia	6,209	India	15,899
Ireland	3,819	Denmark	5,784	New Zealand	15,073
China, mainland	3,563	Canada	5,760	Malaysia	12,603
Canada	3,455	Malaysia	5,726	Canada	10,209
Malaysia	3,065	Spain	4,319	Spain	10,078
India	2,104	India	3,588	Ukraine	7,867
Colombia	1,951	Ireland	3,448	Denmark	7,391

Source: FAO (2014).

While developing countries as a whole have advanced in production and global trade, they have also increased their agricultural support. Thus the old notion that the policy framework in developing countries is biased against agriculture needs to be significantly revised, as can be seen from the recent evolution of such indicators as the nominal rate of assistance (NRA) (calculated by a World Bank project reported in Anderson 2009), the producer support estimate (PSE) (computed by the Organisation for Economic Co-operation and Development [OECD]), and the categories of domestic support, as defined in the AoA (which will here be called WTO domestic support, or WTO DS).[6] Increases in the values of these indicators broadly signify

6 PSE and NRA are economic measures of support to agricultural producers, whereas WTO DS is an indicator for trade negotiations. These measures differ among themselves, particularly when comparing the first two with WTO DS. Among other things, the PSE and NRA consider a broader notion of support that includes border protection and use current world market prices, while the WTO measure focuses on domestic support as separate from issues of market access and export competition and uses a 1986–1988 fixed external reference price (see the discussion in Chapter 9). Broadly speaking (and drastically simplifying the issue), the PSE and the NRA consider support to farmers coming from taxpayers and consumers, while the WTO measure does not include transfers from consumers. For the calculation of the NRA, see Anderson (2009). Comparisons of PSE and different WTO measures of domestic support can be found in Effland (2011); see also Brink (2009).

that a country is expanding support to agricultural producers while decreases mean reduced support.

Figure 8.3 shows the NRA for the agricultural sector in several developing regions; the figure suggests that support for the agricultural sector in those countries has clearly been increasing. The shift from taxing the agricultural sector (a negative number in Figure 8.3) to supporting the sector through different measures (a positive number) becomes particularly clear in the developing countries in Asia and Europe and Central Asia (ECA). In these regions the NRA moved from a tax equivalent of about 10 percent to 20 percent of the value of total agricultural production for 1955 through 1989 to a positive transfer to agriculture since the 1990s, reaching about 15 percent to 20 percent of total agricultural production in the 2000s. LAC countries also shifted from taxing agriculture in the 1950s through the 1980s to supporting the sector since the 1990s; however, the NRA in this region has stayed below 10 percent and declined even further in the 2000s, although it is still in positive territory. Africa, however, continues to tax agriculture but at smaller rates, moving from an NRA of about −10 percent to somewhat less than −5 percent in the 2000s.

While the NRA calculated by the World Bank covers only developing countries, the PSEs calculated by the OECD provide a comparative view of the support in developed countries and a sample of developing countries (see also Bureau and Jean 2013). Table 8.2 shows the value of the PSEs in billion dollars for selected countries covered in the OECD database.[7] PSEs in the developed countries considered (particularly the combination of the European Union, Japan, and the United States) show large values of support (about US$213 billion in 2010–2015) and have remained relatively stable since the 1990s. However, the developing countries included have significantly increased their PSEs, from about US$20 billion in the 1990s to some US$300 billion in recent years. While this has been mainly driven by the large increase in China's support, the value of PSEs in the developing countries considered without counting China still reaches almost US$81 billion. This is about 40 percent of the level of the group of developed countries, but still almost a fivefold increase since the 1990s.

As mentioned, the WTO DS, and the aggregate measurement of support (AMS) within it, is a different measure than either the NRA or the PSE.[8]

7 See data in OECD (2016). India is not covered in the database.

8 See Chapter 9 for a more detailed discussion of the WTO measures of domestic support.

FIGURE 8.3 Nominal rate of assistance (NRA) total (%)

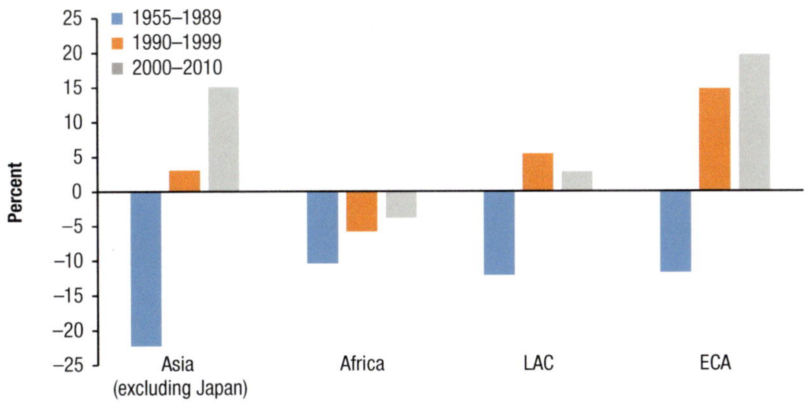

Source: Data are from Anderson and Nelgen (2013).

Note: ECA = developing countries in Europe and Central Asia; LAC = Latin America and the Caribbean; the data was produced as a part of a World Bank study covering a large number of developing countries.

TABLE 8.2 Producer support estimates, 1995–2015

Variable	1995–2000	2000–2005	2005–2010	2010–2015
Developed countries[a]				
Total US$ billions	216.5	210.0	216.2	211.8
without EU	106.7	104.4	93.5	104.6
EU % total	49.3	49.7	43.3	49.4
Japan % total	25.3	22.3	20.3	24.3
United States % total	17.4	20.4	15.0	16.6
Developing countries[b]				
Total US$ billions	19.9	52.1	122.8	300.1
without China	16.9	30.6	57.7	80.9
China % total	15.2	41.3	53.0	73.0

Source: OECD (2016).

Note: [a]See data in OECD (2016). India is not covered in the database. The developed countries included are Australia, Canada, the European Union (EU), Japan, New Zealand, Norway, Switzerland, and the United States. [b]The developing countries included are Brazil, Chile, China, Colombia, Indonesia, Kazakhstan, Mexico, the Russian Federation, South Africa, Turkey, Ukraine, and Viet Nam.

The AMS' capacity to measure the economic extent and impact of domestic support has been questioned (Orden, Blandford, and Josling 2011), in particular because in the WTO framework, the comparison uses fixed reference prices from 1986 to 1988 (which would not provide an interpretable economic measure of the effective domestic support at a point in time). As discussed before, the NRA and PSE use current market prices instead. The careful calculations in Orden, Blandford, and Josling (2011) for 1995 to 2008–2009 show that when using WTO categories, the developing countries considered in the study (Brazil, China, India, and the Philippines) have increased their domestic agricultural support in recent years; India in particular has moved from about 6 percent of the total value of agricultural production in the 1990s to a level above 18 percent in 2008–2009 (or more than 11 percent if the domestic food aid program and related public stockholding are not counted). China moved from 6.5 percent to 9.6 percent in the same period. Domestic support in Brazil and the Philippines, however, stayed relatively flat, at somewhat less than 6 percent and 4 percent of the value of agricultural production, respectively. Still, the levels of domestic support in these developing countries clearly remained below the levels seen in developed countries. In 2008–2009 the comparable percentages of domestic agricultural support over total value of agricultural production were 33 percent in the United States, 29.1 percent in Japan, and 28.7 percent in the European Union.[9]

Orden, Blandford, and Josling (2011) also provide calculations of the levels of what the 2008 Modalities call overall trade-distorting support (OTDS).[10] According to those estimates, China and India would be allowed OTDS levels that are comparable with or above the levels permitted for developed countries: China (US$85.5 billion), the EU (US$33.1 billion), India (US$25.6 billion), and Japan and the United States, each with about US$14 billion. The political economy of the WTO negotiations under such a domestic support scenario may change significantly. Developing countries that do not have the fiscal space to grant higher levels of support and developed countries that may

---

9 The PSEs of Japan and the European Union are far larger than those of the United States because their calculation includes a market protection component through border measures that is not part of the WTO measure of domestic support.

10 The "Revised Draft Modalities for Agriculture" (TN/AG/W/4/Rev.4, December 6, 2008), which are usually called "the 2008 Modalities," included very detailed language for the potential text of an agricultural agreement. This was the last attempt to reach an agreement on agriculture before the general Doha talks collapsed in 2008 (see Chapter 2). The OTDS, however, does not include all domestic support, distortionary or not. Therefore, the potential levels of domestic support under the 2008 Modalities are larger than the numbers mentioned in the text. For the intricacies of those calculations, see the chapters in Orden, Blandford, and Josling (2011), in particular Brink (2011).

have the money but are legally constrained under the WTO rules embedded in the 2008 Modalities may join forces against those large developing countries that have both the financial resources and the legal space under the SDT provisions of the 2008 Modalities (see Brink 2011). WTO members may also be less willing to accept at prima facie the food security concerns of countries that are large exporters in the global food market and that use significant amounts of domestic subsidies to support their agriculture.

Changes in Food Security and Nutrition Conditions

Although there is a large heterogeneity of food (in)security conditions among developing countries, it is clear that there have been overall improvements in food security at the global level.[11] Figure 8.4 shows the evolution of food security indicators in different developing regions based on the Global Hunger Index.[12] South Asia and Africa south of the Sahara (SSA) show the worst indicators (a higher number implies worse hunger conditions), with the countries in the Near East and North Africa, LAC, and Eastern Europe and Central Asia on the other extreme. Overall, however, there has been a general decline of the Global Hunger Index over time, implying improvements in hunger conditions in developing countries, though with important differences across regions and countries.

At the same time, the world now suffers from a "triple burden" of malnutrition (Pinstrup-Andersen 2007): undernutrition, the traditional focus on insufficiencies in calories and proteins; overnutrition, particularly the overconsumption of fat, sugar, and salt, leading to problems of obesity, diabetes, and cardiovascular disease; and micronutrient deficiency, which has a variety of negative consequences for nutrition and human development. In developing countries, both undernutrition and overnutrition may coexist, even within the same family (see Garret and Ruel 2003). Important changes in consumption patterns in developing countries are linked to increasing incomes, urbanization, and structural modifications in the processing and marketing of food products—all of which have led to a diversification of diets and a decline in the percentage of calories and proteins consumed from the usual staple crops considered in

11 See Díaz-Bonilla et al. (2000) and Díaz-Bonilla and Thomas (2016) for a typology of countries based on food security indicators.

12 Welthungerhilfe, IFPRI, and Concern Worldwide developed the Global Hunger Index to reflect the multidimensional nature of hunger, combining three equally weighted indicators into one index: (1) the proportion of undernourished people as a percentage of the population, (2) the proportion of children younger than age five who have low weight for their age, and (3) the mortality rate of children younger than age five (see von Grebmer et al. 2013).

FIGURE 8.4 Contribution of components to 1990, 1995, 2000, 2005, and 2013 Global Hunger Index scores, by region

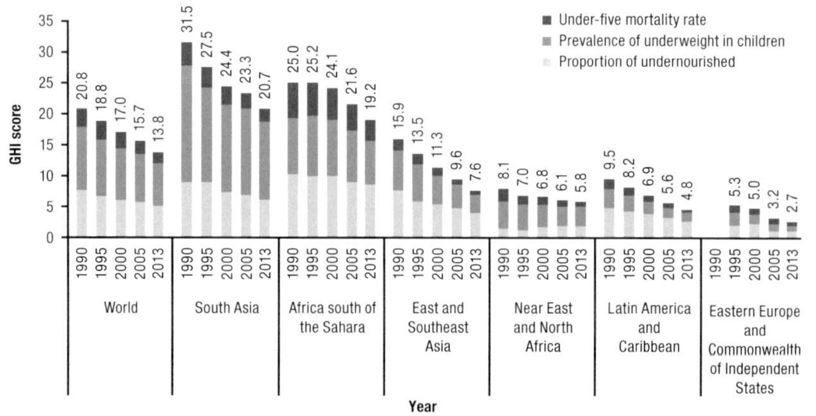

Source: von Grebmer et al. (2013).

Note: For the 1990 GHI, data on the proportion of undernourished are for 1990–1992; data on child underweight are for the year closest to 1990 in the period 1988–1992 for which data are available; and data on child mortality are for 1990. For the 1995 GHI, data on the proportion of undernourished are for 1994–1996; data on child underweight are for the year closest to 1995 in the period 1993–1997 for which data are available; and data on child mortality are for 1995. For the 2000 GHI, data on the proportion of undernourished are for 1999–2001; data on child underweight are for the year closest to 2000 in the period 1998–2002 for which data are available; and data on child mortality are for 2000. For the 2005 GHI, data on the proportion of undernourished are for 2004–2006; data on child underweight are for the year closest to 2005 in the period 2003–2007 for which data are available; and data on child mortality are for 2005. For the 2013 GHI, data on the proportion of undernourished are for 2010–2012; data on child underweight are for the latest year in the period 2008–2012 for which data are available, and data on child mortality are for 2011. For Eastern Europe and the Commonwealth of Independent States, most countries in this region became independent after 1990 GHI scores were calculated.

food security stocks. Some of these changes are due to improved infrastructure and integration of markets (Rashid, Gulati, and Cummings 2008); for example, Reardon et al. (2012) document the modernization of rice and potato value chains in four Asian countries that resulted from the expansion of roads, electricity, and government support to small traders and processors.

Reardon and Timmer (2012) review the expanding literature regarding the important changes occurring in many developing countries' processing, wholesale, and retailing sectors. The authors document the different waves of transformation that have taken place at different points along the value chain, from processing to marketing, and focus particularly on the advance of supermarkets. Although the expansion of supermarkets started earlier and has gone further in LAC, the "retail revolution" has also expanded in Asia and more recently in Africa. Modern food retail in many developing countries is spreading, or has already spread, beyond the upper and middle classes into low-income markets, small cities, and rural towns through a combination of small formats, cheap prices, and flexible inventories. While these transformations have not advanced equally throughout Africa, where landlocked areas still lack the modernized marketing chains that are present in other countries, the overall tendencies point in the same direction (see also Reardon, Timmer, and Berdegue 2004).

In summary, along with improvements in more traditional indicators of food and nutrition security in developing countries, new concerns regarding overnutrition and its related health problems have emerged. At the same time, there are clear changes toward more diversified diets (although whether these new diets are healthier depends on their composition), and new marketing channels for food delivery have been evolving, even in poor urban and rural areas. These changes in nutrition concerns, consumer demand, and retail channels suggest that food security approaches that are limited to a reduced number of staple crops distributed by a public system (the type of program that is the focus of much of the legal debates discussed in Chapter 9) may become less and less relevant in many developing countries.

General Policy Considerations and Food Security

The previous section discussed significant changes in global economic, social, nutritional, energy, and climate conditions that have set the context for food security concerns. Those changes notwithstanding, some of the policies advocated to address food security concerns still seem similar to those put forth in the past under very different conditions. A clear example is the changed situation in agricultural and food prices. In many countries, alarm about high food prices and high food price volatility has led to proposals to increase self-sufficiency using import barriers and distortionary domestic support; this method is similar to what was done in the past to try to help producers affected by low prices. While many policy makers and observers in civil society suggest protection (and distortionary support) as their preferred policy option to deal with either low or high prices, other standard advice recommends trade liberalization in all circumstances. Here, as in other things, a more nuanced approach is required.

Food Security: A Multidimensional Concept

It is always useful to remember the multidimensional definition of food security adopted at the World Food Summit in 1996: (1) availability (which depends on domestic production, stocks, and trade); (2) access (which is influenced by income, employment, and poverty patterns related to economic growth and development); (3) utilization (which depends on food quality as well as on other factors such as health services, water and sanitation infrastructure, education, and women's empowerment); and (4) stability (the fact that physical and economic access to and proper utilization of food should take place "at all times" and that many factors can affect this stability). It is widely recognized that food (in)security is strongly correlated with poverty, which is also a multidimensional concept affected by many factors.[13] For instance, Sinha, Lipton, and Yaqub (2002) consider that poverty, its severity at a point in time, its persistence at the individual level, and its intergenerational transmission are all associated with what they call "damaging fluctuations." This is a general concept that goes beyond risks or shocks and encompasses changes over time that potentially harm people's welfare. The authors identified six major damaging fluctuations affecting the poor: (1) violence (wars, civil strife, community violence, and domestic violence); (2) natural disasters; (3) harvest failure; (4) disease or injury; (5) unemployment or underemployment; and (6) shocks that worsen the relative price of food when compared with income.

For poor and food-insecure households, the main challenges lie in exposure and vulnerability to these damaging fluctuations. However, typically only a part of such events is related to food price variability; most of the negative impacts on poor and vulnerable households are caused by other factors, such as weather shocks, health events, and the spread of conflict and war. In addition, macroeconomic crises with subsequent drops in production and employment, chaotic currency devaluations, and high inflation are also major contributors to poverty and food insecurity (Díaz-Bonilla 2008). Although the current period of higher and more volatile prices in global food markets has led to increased attention on the impact of those factors on poverty and food security, economic access to food is not solely a problem of food prices. Access to food also depends on the relationship between household incomes (broadly defined), on the one hand, and the cost of the minimum household food requirements (MHFRs), on the other. Both income and costs involve

13 There is also a definitional relation between *food insecurity* and *poverty* considering that the general poverty line is usually the cost of minimum household food requirements (MHFRs), with an additional markup representing other expenditures; the line for indigence is usually the cost of MHFRs without any additional expenditures. Therefore, poverty and food insecurity measures should move closely together by statistical construction (although there may be some differences due to the diverse data sources used to construct the indicators). One implication of this is that if a policy measure increases the cost of MHFRs, keeping other things constant, this would then increase both the poverty headcount and the number of food-insecure households among those that are net food buyers. However, other things may not be constant (more on this below).

prices, wages, employment, and other variables; it is not just a matter of a simple comparison of food prices with wages. Therefore, to truly assess economic access to food, the proper equations (Sinha, Lipton, and Yaqub 2002; Díaz-Bonilla and Ron 2011) to consider are as follows:

Incomes = wages . employment (or prices . quantity of goods and services sold by the poor)[14] + subsidies or taxes from the government + other transfers and public services to the poor

Costs = food prices . MHFR + costs of complementary goods and services needed to properly use food

In short, a more multidimensional view of the problem is needed because a single policy intervention will not address the multiplicity of factors affecting food security (see below).

Differentiated Impacts of Policies

In terms of the general economy, the impact of a policy intervention depends on its interactions with other policies and structural factors. Therefore the same policy intervention may have different impacts depending on the context in which it is implemented. For example, a reduction of agricultural tariffs will have different impacts on a country depending on, among other things, whether the tariffs are reduced unilaterally or as a result of a multilateral exercise and whether the adjustment only includes agricultural products or applies to other products and services as well. Structural aspects, such as land distribution and rural infrastructure, are also crucial to determining the effects of a policy; following the previous example, reducing (or increasing) agricultural tariffs in a country with relatively equal land distribution and good infrastructure will have different impacts than those policies would have in a country with unequal landholdings and poor infrastructure.

It is also widely accepted that because households are diverse, any policy with economywide impacts will have differentiated impacts on households. Such heterogeneity needs to be considered because food security issues take concrete form at the household and individual levels. For instance, it is obvious that the impact of changes in food prices on households will be different depending on whether a household is a net food buyer or a net food seller. Urban households are typically net buyers; however, an important number of rural families are also net buyers, including landless rural workers and a

---

14 Obviously, taxes enter with a negative sign.

significant percentage of small farmers, some of whom may experience seasonal variations as net sellers/buyers. Only poor families that are net food sellers (which may not necessarily be the largest percentage of rural families in many developing countries) would benefit from higher food prices.

Table 8.3 shows a general typology of African households and the price issues that may affect those households. (It should be noted that category 3 is nested into category 2, which in turn is nested into category 1; category 4 is separate; see also World Bank [2005].)[15]

An example of how this heterogeneity influences food security outcomes can be found in the analysis of the 2010–2011 food price shock by Ivanic, Martin, and Zaman (2011). They show that poverty increased in 27 of the 28 countries studied but that in Viet Nam it actually decreased. Viet Nam's situation was different mainly because of the large size of its rural population and the more egalitarian structure of landholdings in rural areas, where more poor people were net producers of food. This meant that the higher food prices led to an aggregate reduction in poverty in that country.

Prices: Trends, Cycles, Volatility, and Extreme Lows and Highs

Both price levels and price variability have an effect on food production and consumption, but they are two different concepts that require some clarifications. In the context of monetary policies, the idea of *price stability* has traditionally taken into account inflation in the range of 0 percent to 2 percent per year. More recently, it has been suggested that the definition of price stability could be expanded to include annual inflation of up to 4 percent (Blanchard, Dell'Ariccia, and Mauro 2010). Obviously, "stable" inflation of 2 percent per year means that the nominal price level is permanently increasing: at 2 percent per year the price level increases almost 50 percent in nominal terms in 20 years, while at 4 percent it more than doubles during the same period. In other words, stability in terms of price level is one concept, while stability in terms of the rate of change of those levels (that is, the stability of inflation) is another. In the case of food and agricultural prices, the notion of (in)stability refers mainly to what happens to price levels.

Furthermore, it is important to distinguish among *price trends*, potential changes in those trends, and variability or volatility around those trends,

15 World Bank (2005) presents the following estimates of the percentages of rural households that are net sellers: Zambia (maize), 24 percent; Mozambique (maize), up to 25 percent; Kenya (maize), 27 percent; Ethiopia (maize and teff), 25 percent; Indonesia (rice), 29 percent; Viet Nam (rice), 43 percent; and Mexico (maize), 25 percent.

TABLE 8.3 Who is affected by food price instability and how?

Affected Group	Significance	Problem	Interseasonal or intraseasonal variability the bigger issue?
1. Poor consumers	Majority of both rural and urban population; includes nearly all poor households	High prices reduce real incomes, especially in years of low harvest	Peaks in both
2. Net deficit producers	70–80% of rural households	As in 1, but high prices also discourage investment in high-value crops	Peaks in both
3. Net deficit sellers	10–15% of rural households, including some of the poorest	As in 2, but low prices immediately after harvest also reduce real incomes	Intraseasonal troughs
4. Surplus producers	20–30% of rural households; often non-poor, but important to food security of poor	Price collapse at bumper harvest and (to a lesser extent) low prices immediately after harvest reduce real incomes and depress initiatives for investment in intensification	Troughs in both, particularly interseasonal troughs

Source: Poulton et al. (2006).

which may take several forms (see a discussion in Díaz-Bonilla and Ron [2010] and Díaz-Bonilla [2016], where other methodological issues are discussed). The impacts of changes in price trends on food production and food consumption are different from the impacts of changes in volatility around those trends (cycles and spikes). The following paragraphs briefly discuss both aspects (price levels on the one hand and cycles and spikes on the other).

Prices levels affect producers' profits (and therefore their incentives to produce) and consumers' costs (and consequently their economic access to food). Therefore, much of the debate regarding different food security policies usually revolves around a traditional policy dilemma: what contributes more to generating food security: high prices for producers or low prices for consumers (Timmer, Falcon, and Pearson 1983)? High food prices benefit food producers (other things being equal), whereas low food prices help consumers, at least in the short run. However, in the medium to longer term, there may be positive dynamic effects from higher prices that may help net food buyers as well. For example, higher agricultural and food prices may lead to increased investments by the private and public sectors in agricultural production and in rural areas; these investments can generate positive employment and wage effects, particularly among the poor, which may compensate for the higher cost of food.[16] Those investments may also lead to increases in productivity that may reduce production costs and prices in the medium term.

Of course, the opposite may also happen. Farmers shielded by high protection and pampered by subsidies may not need to incur additional costs and investments in order to attain their desired profit levels; therefore, protection and subsidization may lead to fewer investments and slowed productivity. Mogues et al. (2012) conducts an extensive review of the impact of public-sector expenditures on agriculture and shows that subsidies have limited impact in terms of their contribution to agricultural productivity in India and several other countries. In the case of LAC, López (2007) estimates that public agricultural expenditures labeled "nonsocial subsidies" or "private goods" (export subsidies, forestry subsidies, targeted rural production subsidies, and so on) have a negative impact on per capita agricultural GDP, as opposed to the positive impact of "public goods" (such as investment in R&D, plant and animal disease control, and environmental protection).

In summary, both high prices and low prices result in adjustment processes if markets operate normally and if signals are transmitted properly to producers and consumers. Higher prices should eventually lead to more production and less consumption; these effects push prices lower (and vice versa, in the case of a low-price policy). Therefore, as mentioned, a good part of the debate about food security in developing countries revolves around how to solve this policy dilemma: high (low) food prices should normally lead to more (less) food production, improving (worsening) the physical availability of food, while at the same time making food consumption more (less) costly and reducing (increasing) "economic access."

Those who take the perspective of poor producers prefer high prices, arguing that agriculture's multiplier effect has important benefits for employment and poverty alleviation; many of these arguments tend to gravitate toward protection and price support. Those who take the perspective of poor consumers, however, emphasize the importance of low prices because of the impact on urban and rural poverty and malnutrition. They usually suggest lower levels

16 Looking specifically at poverty impacts, some empirical studies have found strong and statistically significant links between higher real food prices and increases in the prevalence and depth of undernourishment as well as in the incidence of poverty (Warr 2013). Other studies have suggested that while higher food prices negatively affect the poor in the short term, this impact may be reversed in the medium term, depending on the size of the price shock and how domestic wages evolve after the price shock (Ivanic and Martin 2014). Headey (2014) also estimates a positive medium- to long-term impact of higher food prices on poverty reduction. Agricultural and food prices typically go up when growth picks up at the global and national levels (Díaz-Bonilla and Robinson 2010); therefore it may be interesting to separate the impact of growth on poverty reduction from the impact of higher food prices.

of protection and the use of consumption subsidies. In the end, governments need to consider the welfare of both producers and consumers as well as the fiscal costs of the possible interventions. The attempts at harmonizing these concerns have led to a diversity of policy measures, with mixed results.

The debate about price volatility, cycles, and spikes differs from that about price levels. It has been argued that price instability generates uncertainty about the "true" price level for producers and consumers; this can lead to suboptimal production and consumption decisions compared with what would have been the case under more stable price conditions. For producers, price volatility may reduce investments and shift production toward lower risk, but also less productive, technologies (although World Bank [2005] estimates that these effects may not be that large). High and variable food inflation and price spikes affect consumers negatively through reduced, or at least uncertain, access to food. This is particularly true for poor and vulnerable households whose incomes do not adjust with inflation and who do not have the assets needed to stabilize consumption patterns. There may also be negative macroeconomic impacts, such as inflation and balance-of-payment and public deficits, as well as a decline in total investment (due to uncertainties about the macroeconomic framework), with adverse second-round effects on poverty and food security (Timmer 1989). It is also important to consider the political impacts linked to social unrest and riots caused by increases in food prices; however, it has been noted that what seems to contribute most to the occurrence of political riots and unrest are high price shocks rather than volatility per se (see Barrett and Bellemare 2011). Persistent food inflation also tends to generate political problems; in many cases, however, sustained inflation (as opposed to price shocks) results from macroeconomic difficulties, which may not be related to developments in food markets.

Prices are not the only factor influencing food security, and obviously a variety of policies affects prices. As argued earlier, a one-dimensional analysis looking only at a specific policy's impacts on price levels or price volatility would leave a significant part of the causes of, and potential solutions to, food security out of the picture.

Protectionism and Food Security

The current period of price volatility has led to increased interest in food self-sufficiency. Clearly, developing countries would be well advised to invest more in the expansion and stabilization of their domestic agricultural production. The issue then becomes what are the best policies through which to accomplish this goal. The instinctive reaction of some policy makers and civil society advocates, both in the previous context of low world food prices and in the new context of higher prices, has been to resort to protectionist measures. However, usually other measures linked to different types of investments in agricultural R&D, human capital, and infrastructure are the ones that provide the real basis for competitiveness and productivity.

Díaz-Bonilla, Thomas, and Robinson (2003) discuss the argument, offered by some nongovernmental organizations during the WTO negotiations, that such investments "cost money and are difficult to administer." This argument implies that protectionist measures do not cost money and are easier to implement (see the references in Díaz-Bonilla, Thomas, and Robinson 2003); however, in fact, protectionism does cost money. It operates as a privately collected and regressive tax on food, the costs of which are paid relatively more by poor consumers (given the incidence of food in their total expenditures) and the benefits of which accrue relatively more to large producers (considering that protection is an additional markup on individual prices that accrues per unit produced). High tariffs and related import restriction measures also increase the price of agricultural inputs to other sectors, negatively affecting production and employment in those other activities. Higher costs for staple goods may lead to demands for higher salaries, affecting other labor-intensive export industries. Large trade protection also tends to overvalue the real exchange rate, with negative implications for other tradable sectors. On the other hand, increased trade, rather than protectionism, seems to have greater positive effects on technological advancement, investments, and productivity (see the literature review on total factor productivity by Isaksson [2007]).

Import barriers and related interventions are usually less-than-optimal, and potentially costly, ways to try to insure against price volatility. Self-sufficiency approaches must consider the fact that domestic production in individual countries is far more volatile than global and regional aggregates (see, for example, Díaz-Bonilla, Thomas, and Robinson 2003; World Bank 2005). Thus, using international trade to supplement domestic production should, in fact, stabilize domestic food availability. Although some developing countries have successfully managed external volatility, there are likely more examples in which efforts to shield domestic markets from global volatility led to increased internal volatility. For instance, Minot (2011, 2012) shows that (1) food price volatility in several SSA countries (Africa south of the Sahara) seems more prevalent in domestic markets than in international markets; (2) such domestic food price volatility has not changed much with recent increases in international price volatility; (3) commodities that are more traded internationally have lower volatility than those that are less globally traded; and (4) volatility is higher in countries and for commodities in which governments actively intervene in markets through state-owned enterprises.[17] Chapoto and Jayne (2009) also illustrate the destabilizing results of government interventions aimed at stabilizing maize prices in several SSA countries (see also Hazell, Shields, and Shields [2005]).[18]

So far, this analysis has argued against the use of protectionism as the preferred policy option to deal with both high and low prices. However, there is also a mirror-image case to be considered: the argument that proposes trade liberalization irrespective of the context of low or high prices. Proponents of this approach must consider that slow or no mobility in labor, capital, and land implies that any reallocation of factors and resources will take time and would include potentially significant transition costs. In particular, small and vulnerable producers may not be able to adjust to the new policy environment and may see a definitive negative impact on their livelihoods.[19] Thus there is the need for carefully modulated policies that also consider both fiscal impacts and the fact that any intervention may displace other public expenditures that have more positive impacts on production and poverty (see Fan [2008] and Mogues et al. [2012] on public expenditures and Díaz-Bonilla [2015] for a general discussion of the macroeconomic and trade policies involved).

What Are the Outlines of an Adequate Policy Approach?

Two general policy rules must always be considered when aligning objectives and instruments. One is the Tinbergen rule (Tinbergen 1952), which indicates the need to have as many instruments as objectives. If there are two policy objectives, then there need to be at least two policy instruments. Proposals in favor of just one policy or targeting one intermediate variable (such as high or low prices) will not effectively ensure the welfare of both producers and consumers and would most likely not deliver the multifaceted results called for in increasingly complex societies.

---

17 For our analysis of patterns of volatility, the dataset uses wholesale and retail food prices compiled from local statistical agencies by the Famine Early Warning System Network (FEWS NET) for ten staple foods (beans, bread, cooking oil, cowpeas, maize, millet, rice, sorghum, teff, and wheat) in 15 countries (Chad, Ethiopia, Guinea, Kenya, Malawi, Mali, Mauritania, Mozambique, Niger, Nigeria, Rwanda, Uganda, United Republic of Tanzania, Zambia, and Zimbabwe).

18 Hazell, Shields, and Shields (2005) show that the domestic prices of food products tend to be more volatile than the respective world prices, although the period of analysis does not cover the recent global price spikes.

19 In trade theory, this would apply to models with "specific factors of production"—that is, those that cannot be converted easily or at all into other activities.

A second policy imperative can be called the Bhagwati rule, following the pioneer article on distortions and welfare (Bhagwati 1971). This analysis emphasizes the need to tailor policy interventions to the source of the problem as closely as possible to prevent potential second-round problems. For example, if a country wants to help its poor and vulnerable people, targeting specific food products is an indirect, and at times inefficient and inequitable, way to reach the intended objectives of poverty reduction and food security. In addition, if the income of small and poor producers is the concern, trying to increase the price of some agricultural products would be an indirect mechanism that, by necessity, would benefit larger producers more than smaller ones. Here, as in other cases in which food security concerns are invoked, the focus of the policy analysis should be on people rather than on crops or food products.

Overall, the most effective way out of this policy dilemma is through interventions that increase production efficiency and reduce costs, such as agricultural R&D, infrastructure, and related investments allowed in the Green Box of the Agreement on Agriculture. All of these interventions increase profits and incomes for food producers and contribute to reducing prices and expanding food availability for consumers. The challenges faced by poor and vulnerable populations can also be addressed through properly designed and funded safety nets and cash transfer programs (Hidrobo et al. 2012; Hoddinott et al. 2013). An overall adequate policy framework for food security and poverty alleviation would include good governance; macroeconomic stability; a relatively neutral trade policy; investments in infrastructure, R&D, and human capital (health, nutrition, and education) with a focus on the poor and vulnerable; policies and investments that ensure the adequate functioning of product and factor markets; land and water policies that favor a more equitable agrarian structure and that facilitate access to the sustainable use of natural resources by poor rural households and small and family farmers; women's empowerment programs; support for community organization and participation, particularly for the poor and vulnerable; and maintenance of law and order in rural areas.[20]

20 It was already mentioned that Sinha, Lipton, and Yaqub (2002) identify violence and conflict (wars, civil strife, community violence, and domestic violence) as one of the "damaging fluctuations" that deeply affect the poor and vulnerable. This fact is corroborated by the World Bank study titled "Voices of the Poor" and summarized in Narayan et al. (1999), which suggests the importance of effective and noncorrupt public law and order for the poor. Therefore the maintenance of public safety in rural areas is crucial for food security.

The specific debate about the economic and operational aspects of food security stocks, which is the topic of the next section, must be placed in the general food security context and policy considerations outlined previously.

Food Security Stocks and Domestic Food Aid

The design of food stocks for food market stability and domestic food aid needs to take into account a variety of economic and operational issues. The operational problems and costs involved are likely more important in developing countries than the issue of policy space within the WTO framework discussed in Chapter 9.[21]

Food Stocks: Unidimensional and Multidimensional Approaches

The analysis of public food stocks must be placed in the general context of food security policies. It should be reiterated that prices are not the only variable impacting food security, nor are they even always the main one. At the same time, it is important to remember that many different policy instruments, not just public food stocks, affect the level and volatility of prices. Therefore a unidimensional approach that only traces the link from food stocks to price stability to food security would be highly constraining; rather, a multidimensional analysis is needed (Figure 8.5).

Furthermore, while public food stocks are intended to address price instability, they could in fact generate broader macroeconomic problems (such as those associated with fiscal deficits) that may damage food security more than the price instability they tried to solve (see, for instance, Timmer 1989; Dorosh 2008). That being said, because food stocks are often discussed in the context of price stabilization, this section mainly highlights prices as the intervening variable of interest for food security. Galtier and Vindel (2013) identify a variety of policies within four broad strategies resulting from a two-by-two

21 The long list of theoretical and empirical studies on food stocks cannot be reviewed here. Different evaluations of the uneven experiences of food stocks for stabilization of prices in developing countries can be found in Islam and Thomas (1996), Hazell (1993), and Knudsen and Nash (1990). Recent analyses include Galtier and Vindel (2013), who are more supportive of the use of food stocks for price stabilization. Less sanguine assessments can be found in World Bank (2005, 2012) and Gilbert (2011). A detailed treatment of commodity price stabilization can be found in Newbery and Stiglitz (1981). Townsend (1977) and Salant (1983) present theoretical models, arguing about the impossibility of price stabilization. Gouel (2013) provides a review of different approaches, including simulations with dynamic optimizing models. See also HLPE (2011). This section focuses on domestic food stocks; discussions about regional and international food stocks can be found in World Bank (2005, 2012), von Braun and Torero (2009), and Tangermann (2011).

FIGURE 8.5 Unidimensional versus multidimensional policy approaches

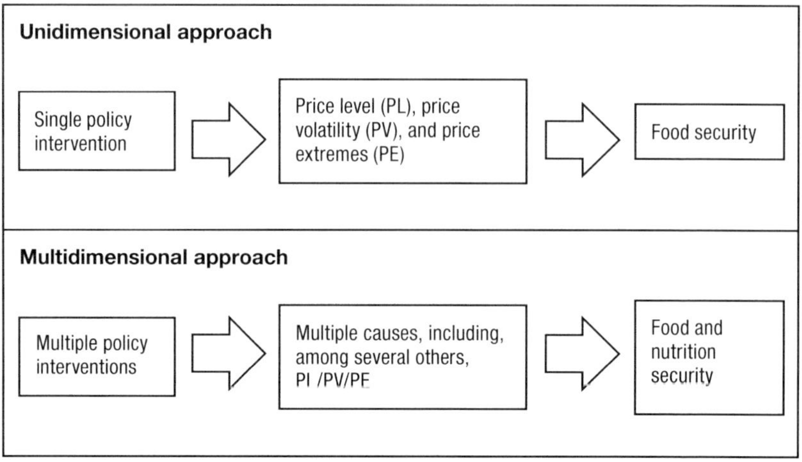

Source: Author.

matrix that combines markets and governments, with the goal of stabilizing prices or managing and coping with the consequences of price volatility. The four quadrants of the matrix define what the authors call strategy A (the use of market-based policies to stabilize prices), strategy B (the use of market-based policies to cope with volatility), strategy C (direct interventions by governments to stabilize prices), and strategy D (direct interventions by governments to cope with volatility). The authors emphasize strategy C, which in their view is often missing from the advice given to developing countries.[22]

Table 8.4, taken from the report by the High Level Panel of Experts on Food Security and Nutrition of the Committee on World Food Security (HLPE 2011), expands on the ABCD framework by defining a three-by-three matrix. The left column identifies policies and interventions operating through markets and the private sector, directly implemented by the governments or carried out by the civil society; the top row distinguishes policies and interventions that focus on stabilizing prices or that assume that price volatility and shocks will occur and thus try to manage those problems ex ante or to

22 Timmer (1989), who consistently highlights the importance of price stabilization in the successful expansion of agricultural production in Asian countries such as Indonesia, also wrote the preface to Galtier and Vindel (2013). In that introduction, Timmer argues, "It is not easy to stabilize food prices, but it is not impossible either. We just need to stop arguing that stable food prices are a bad thing and get on with the tough analytical and empirical work to learn how to do it effectively, efficiently, and honestly."

TABLE 8.4 ABCD framework

Policies and Programs	Reduce the eventuality and size of price shocks	Ex ante interventions relative to price shocks	Ex post interventions relative to price shocks
Programs	**Reduce price volatility**	**Manage price volatility**	**Cope with price volatility**
Interventions through markets and with the private sector	**A. Make markets work better in time and space** • Information systems • Transport and communication infrastructure • Increase competition in domestic market and trade • Private sector storage development through improved access to financing • Grades and standards	**B1. Financial products** • Crop/livestock insurance (index-based) • Credit and savings associations **B1. Investment in agriculture** • Increase domestic food production • Diversification and resilience of food systems • Growing local crops • Food storage systems at all levels including community storage	**B2. Emergency loan programs** • Access of importers to trade loans • Loans to producers and consumers
Direct state interventions	**C. Intervene in markets** • Public stocks • Price bands schemes • Price stabilization	**D1. Enhance productivity in smallholder farming** • Resilience of farming systems • Targeted input subsidies (seeds, fertilizer) • Production for home consumption **D1. Employment in the rural nonfarm economy** • Decentralization • Small and medium rural enterprise programs	**D2. Social protection for vulnerable households** • Case and food transfers • School feeding programs • Taking into account human life cycle
Interventions through and with civil society		**E1. Negotiated ex ante social protection** • Minimum wage, right to food **E1. Producer organizations' services to members** • Rotating credit schemes • Group insurance • Local purchases for food distribution systems (e.g., WFP's P4P)	**E2. Community-driven productive social protection** • Workfare (coping) with community-driven development projects (management)

Source: HLPE (2011).

Note: WFP = Word Food Programme; P4P = Purchase for Progress.

cope with them ex post. The HLPE classification in Table 8.4 also includes a useful list of possible policies and interventions in all the ABCD strategies, including food stocks as part of strategy C (direct government interventions to try to stabilize prices). The point here, rather than trying to discuss and rank all the possible policies and interventions, is simply to note that policy makers have an extensive array of options available to them and that all of these potential interventions must be analyzed and deployed in an integrated framework for food security. Public stocks for food security purposes are just one potential component of that framework.

Objectives and Types of Food Stocks

A common operational problem for food stocks is that they lack clear objectives or have multiple and sometimes conflicting objectives (NEPAD 2004; Dorosh 2009). Those objectives may include coping with emergencies, helping populations suffering from chronic hunger, stabilizing prices for producers at profitable levels, and providing food to urban populations at prices that are stable and affordable (NEPAD 2004). Such varying objectives can result in food stocks of an inadequate size (too high or too low), confusing decision-making and management structures that are prone to political interference and short-term horizons, high costs and operational inefficiencies, and inappropriate levels of funding and misallocation of resources (NEPAD 2004). A basic starting point, therefore, is to properly define the objectives of the food stocks using three general categories (NEPAD 2004; World Bank 2005, 2012).

First, emergency food stocks try to cope with natural disasters and other disruptions in the domestic or international food supply. These stocks are usually small and are supposed to bridge the supply gap until the arrival of commercial supplies or food aid. Hazell (1993) suggests that relatively small percentages of total consumption (which he estimates at 5 percent of total consumption in the case of SSA countries) may suffice to act as an insurance mechanism. NEPAD (2004) calculates that such stocks should be able to cover two to three months of consumption, which amounts to 17–25 percent of total consumption.

A second category can be called *food redistribution stocks*, which serve as a rotating stock that backs up the distribution of food through a variety of programs; these programs can include targeted safety nets to help the poor and vulnerable, school lunch programs, supplementary feeding programs for women and children, food-for-work (FFW) schemes, semitargeted public distribution systems (such as fair price shops and *ration* shops), or even nontargeted public systems (although this option has generally been discontinued because of its high cost). Food redistribution stocks may also be used like the previous type of food stocks to cover emergencies, such as natural disasters, that disrupt food supply.

Food redistribution stocks are typically bigger than emergency stocks, depending on the coverage and scope of the food distribution system of which they are a component. For instance, India's Targeted Public Distribution System (TPDS) is the largest food system of this type in the world (Dorosh 2008). The system reached some 600 million food-vulnerable or undernourished people in the early 2000s, but India's National Food Security Act, 2013 increased this coverage to about 800 million people. Such a large system obviously requires large inventories; and to achieve the needed level of these inventories, the government has purchased up to one-third of the wheat and rice produced in the country in recent years (Hoda and Gulati 2013). Although additional consumption may not increase one-to-one with the rations distributed (see Rashid and Lemma 2011), the people receiving food support represent an additional level of demand that would not have existed without the domestic food security and domestic aid program. This additional demand tends to support the prices of the food products involved.

At the same time, different studies show that at different points over the past two decades, India has accumulated inventories far in excess of the amounts needed for its food stock program, generating large fiscal costs for the government and leading to subsidized exports (Dorosh 2008). The direct costs of the current TPDS were estimated at about 0.9 percent of India's GDP in 2009–2010 and 2010–2011 (Hoda and Gulati 2013). If the increase in coverage leads to a proportional increase in costs, the fiscal cost of the new scheme may reach close to 1.2 percent of the country's GDP. That cost, however, may not necessarily translate into equivalent support to poor consumers because of waste and losses due to inadequate storage, handling, and transportation, leakages of funds and products, and diversion of food away from the poorest members of the society. Hoda and Gulati (2013) estimate leakages and diversion of the TPDS to be between one-fifth and one-third of the subsidy on food grains. The program's operation may also have been pro-cyclical during recent episodes of global price increases, through further stock accumulation that may have exacerbated the spikes. India also appears to have exported some of the products from its public food security stocks. Both interventions would not have helped poor Indian consumers (Gouel 2013).

Access to food from public stocks is another challenge for poor populations. In their analysis of rice distribution in several Asian countries, Reardon et al. (2012) found that, according to the surveys conducted in New Delhi, fair price shops were closed during business hours in about two-thirds of the cases. This finding is consistent with other studies about the inefficiency of the TPDS. However, it must be noted that since India started procuring cereals domestically for its public distribution system in the mid-1970s, the country has avoided a major food crisis, even though several instances of sharp declines in production have occurred (for instance, in 1976, 1979, 1982, 1986–1987, 2002, and 2009, there were declines of more than 7 percent in cereal production). Furthermore, the country has been able to maintain reasonable stability in the domestic price of major food products, even in the face of important exogenous price shocks in recent years (although at a cost to other countries due to the shift of India's domestic volatility to global markets) (Gouel 2013). The issue here then becomes how to design a more efficient, equitable, and cost-effective scheme to support competitive agricultural production, provide a safety net for the poor, and insure against food shocks. It should be noted, however, that improving and modernizing such an enormous program, which reaches hundreds of millions of poor producers and consumers, may take many years, and the country must be given enough time to find its way to do so.[23]

The third category of food stocks is buffer stocks, the purpose of which is to stabilize prices.[24] These stocks generally tend to handle larger quantities of food than the other two categories; they may even carry enough food to serve as emergency relief and as a backup for the operation of a public distribution system (World Bank 2005, 2012). This is true in India, where the large public purchase and distribution system appears to have helped stabilize domestic prices, although at a significant cost compared with other countries in the region that have followed more market-based strategies (Dorosh 2008).

Stabilization stocks differ in their definition of price targets—that is, single price, symmetric price bands of different widths, and extreme values (as discussed below). If the real objective of the food stock program is price stabilization (as opposed to subsidizing producers with above-market prices or taxing them with below-market prices), then the target levels for single prices or for price bands should be updated to track mean trend values over the period of stabilization, such as a three-to-five year rolling average (Timmer 1989). However, historical examples show that these stabilization stock policies tend to drift into being subsidized price support policies to producers, to

23 It must be recalled that the process of reform of the Common Agricultural Policy of the European Union, which started in 1992 with the McSharry Program, is far from finished after more than two decades. In the United States, agricultural policy reform has shifted across different approaches over the years; the current 2014 Farm Bill, if anything, is a movement away from WTO disciplines on trade- or production-distorting support (Orden 2014).

24 Several theoretical models show that buffer stocks to maintain fixed prices (or fixed bands) fail with a probability of one in finite time (see the pioneer article by Townsend [1977]), particularly in the presence of speculators (Salant 1983). Typically, real-life buffer stocks do not attempt to defend a permanently fixed price but rather try to smooth market fluctuations, perhaps by using rolling averages. The properties of these buffer stocks are mostly an empirical matter, depending on the specific price rules and circumstances, as discussed further in the text.

the detriment of consumers and taxpayers, or into taxing producers with low prices to help consumers. Analyses of the welfare effects of price stabilization have generally found small positive effects for consumers (Gouel 2013) as well as some small efficiency gains for producers (World Bank 2005), but usually with significant fiscal costs.

The more important gains may come not from symmetric stabilization per se but from preventing large upward spikes (which may affect poor consumers irreversibly by hurting their health and nutritional status) and downward price busts (which may force small and vulnerable producers into bankruptcy or a fire sale of assets). At the macroeconomic and political level, these large upward or downward spikes may affect political stability and the general economy in ways that are not captured in the smaller values of the more limited welfare and efficiency measures mentioned before (Timmer 1989). However, there are different views regarding whether the political and macroeconomic benefits of avoiding price spikes are as large as postulated (see World Bank 2005).

Both food redistribution stocks (which, in principle, try to help specific poor and vulnerable consumers) and buffer stocks (which are not targeted in their effects on consumption) may be more relevant when a country's consumption depends on a reduced number of basic products and when those products are more storable (World Bank 2005). According to the food balance sheets calculated by FAO (2014), Indonesia (highlighted by Timmer [1989, 2013] as a positive example of price stabilization) provides a clear example in which a product that is storable (rice) represents around 48 percent of the calories and 40 percent of the proteins consumed on average (using 2009 data; these values were 56 percent and 53 percent, respectively, in 1980).

However, many African countries have a more diversified structure that uses some products (such as cassava and yams) that are difficult and/or costly to store. In western Africa in 2009, for example, the percentage of average calorie consumption was distributed as follows: 5.4 percent wheat and wheat products, 12.6 percent rice, 9.1 percent maize and maize products, 10 percent millet and millet products, 9.1 percent sorghum and sorghum products, 8.7 percent cassava and cassava products, and 7.9 percent yams.[25] Although India is closer to Indonesia, it is still more diversified, with 21 percent of the total average calories consumed in 2009 coming from wheat and wheat

25 Including Benin; Burkina Faso; Cabo Verde; Gambia; Ghana; Guinea; Guinea-Bissau; Liberia; Mali; Mauritania; Niger; Nigeria; Saint Helena, Ascension and Tristan da Cunha; Senegal; Sierra Leone; and Togo.

products and about 29 percent coming from rice. Therefore policy makers face different challenges when trying to stabilize just one widely consumed, easily storable product (as in Indonesia) and when dealing with a variety of products of diverse degrees of storability.

Another aspect that determines the usefulness of public stocks for food security is a country's level of advancement, because development is broadly associated with the quality and extension of infrastructure and the scope of the operation of the private sector, among other factors.[26] A country's geographical position also matters. A landlocked country with infrastructural limitations will face more challenges than a country with easy access to maritime routes; thus the former may benefit from holding emergency food stocks.

In summary, emergency and redistributive food stocks can play an important role in food security arrangements, depending on the number and storability of the products involved, the country's geographical position, the quality of its infrastructure, and how advanced its private sector is. However, carrying stocks as an insurance mechanism or as a component of safety nets is different from using stocks to stabilize domestic grain prices, which, as noted, usually requires larger stocks and may be expensive and more prone to failure. Although it has been argued that some stabilization schemes seem to have worked better in Asia, the same cannot be said about many of the schemes used in African countries (see Galtier and Vindel 2013; NEPAD 2004). This last observation coincides with the findings in Minot (2011, 2012) about the destabilizing effects of domestic policies in several SSA countries. Developing countries in LAC, which tend to have relatively diversified diets and more developed private systems for food processing and distribution, have in general moved away from public food stocks and have instead linked their domestic food programs to general safety nets, mostly using cash transfers. Instability in LAC countries also tends to be associated with macroeconomic factors; thus, trying to stabilize the price of one or several food products would not address the main problem. However, in countries such as Indonesia, where macroeconomic policies have historically been more stable than in LAC and where rice

26 For instance, Galtier and Vindel (2013) argue that the price stabilization scheme could be adjusted according to the level of a country's development: a less developed country, where agriculture may be in a pre–Green Revolution stage, may need price bands that are not too narrow but not too wide; developing countries with more productive agricultural and market institutions may reduce and even eliminate the lower support price but may maintain the upper part of the band to avoid shocks to consumers; finally, developed countries, where producers are competitive and food has a smaller incidence in consumers' expenditures, may abandon the stabilization stock.

dominates food consumption, then stabilizing the price of that product may also help to stabilize economic and political conditions.

As discussed in Chapter 9, neither emergency stocks nor food redistribution stocks should conflict with WTO disciplines if the products are purchased at market prices.[27] The only additional conditions mentioned in Annex 2, paragraph 3 are that stocks must be an integral part of a food security program identified in national legislation, must correspond to predetermined targets related solely to food security, and must include a financially transparent process for stock accumulation and disposal. These reasonable conditions can help increase transparency and limit opportunities for corruption and misallocation. The main issue, both operationally and in terms of the AoA (as discussed in Chapter 9), is the purchasing price of those stocks.

Purchasing Prices

Stabilization stocks may focus on single prices, defend price bands (mostly symmetrically), or center on preventing price extremes (this last focus may have an asymmetric definition, such as preventing price spikes that hurt consumers). This section discusses some operational aspects of these different approaches. It has been argued that the single-price approach may be costly and may eliminate all incentives for private-sector traders to offer storage, which in turn forces the public sector to undertake a larger role and incur more costs (Gouel 2013).[28] In addition, if the level at which food prices are stabilized is higher on average than what it would have been without stabilization, this would help producers but hurt consumers, particularly poorer ones (Sumner 2000). Thus there may be a trade-off between price stability and price levels, with price stabilization schemes at higher price levels possibly driving more people into food insecurity (Sumner 2000).

Purchasing prices above market-clearing prices can also lead to excessive accumulation of stocks. These stocks will eventually have to be disposed of on domestic and/or international markets, which would in turn depress domestic or world prices. Furthermore, in the case of exports (which, to be competitive in world markets, may have to receive an explicit or implicit subsidy with respect to the purchasing price), this disposal of surpluses on global markets will most likely generate trade frictions with other countries (see Dorosh 2008,

27 The source of food for these food stocks may be food aid or international purchases, both of which raise other issues. However, these issues are unrelated to the problem of domestic support discussed here.

28 As mentioned before, Townsend (1977) and Salant (1983), for example, develop models in which price stabilization is impossible.

2009). Gouel (2013) shows that structuring purchases to defend a price band (to avoid excessively high or low prices) will lead to better prices for producers during the buildup of stocks but would put downward pressure on prices (although with less volatility as well) once those levels have been reached, provided the stocks are not exhausted to defend certain levels and then permanently replenished. This latter approach will keep prices higher at significant fiscal costs (Thompson and Tallard 2010). Gouel (2013), in line with other literature, also disputes the notion that wider price bands lead to lower costs (supposedly because the government buys low and sells high and does not have to intervene too often) because this idea does not take into account the carrying costs of such policies, which increase with wider price bands because of the longer time that stocks have to be immobilized and maintained (see also World Bank 2012).

Thompson and Tallard (2010) analyze asymmetric interventions, which are used only when prices are excessively high. Their simulations focus on the problem of sharp upward price spikes, such as were seen in 2007–2008 and 2011, and illustrate many of the trade-offs related to the high/low food price policy dilemma highlighted earlier. Thompson and Tallard use the OECD's Aglink-Cosimo economic model (documented in OECD-FAO 2015) of global agricultural markets to simulate three policies to confront a sudden price increase in the global wheat and rice markets: (1) trade measures (that is, increases in export taxes or reductions of import taxes) to prevent domestic prices from going above 35 percent of the pre-shock level; (2) consumer subsidies that limit the increase in consumer prices by 20 percent to 40 percent; and (3) additional public stocks of up to one-third of domestic consumption that are built and then released on domestic markets, if domestic prices rise by at least 40 percent in a specified period.

These policies are assumed to be implemented by a group of ten countries (Argentina, Brazil, Chile, China, India, Indonesia, the Russian Federation, South Africa, Ukraine, and Viet Nam) but not in the rest of the world (which nonetheless suffers the consequences of the policies implemented in the core group).[29] The new policies are in addition to any existing measures that these countries may have already had in place. Wheat and rice prices are simulated to jump a sizable 70 percent over the previous year (which the authors argue was similar to what happened during the 2007–2008 price shock) and then

29 The countries selected represented about half the world's population and about two-thirds of rice consumption and production, 45 percent of world wheat consumption for food, and 43 percent of world wheat production in 2010–2011.

revert to trend levels. The simulations calculate the levels of producer and consumer prices in these countries, the fiscal costs of the policies, changes in the per capita consumption of wheat and rice, and the impacts on world prices. The baseline (without the price surge or the new policies) and the simulated paths with the new policies cover a total of 10 years, with the price shock taking place somewhat before the midpoint of that period and the consequences of the shock and policies playing out until the tenth year.

The simulation in Thompson and Tallard (2010) show that world prices are higher than the baseline when food stocks are being built and are obviously lower than the counterfactual during the year of the price shock when food stocks are released (about 20 percent to 25 percent lower than world prices would have been with the shock alone). Prices are then higher again if stocks are rebuilt. Producers benefit and consumers lose while the stocks are being built; during the price shock, the reverse happens. Producers in the rest of the world (outside the 10 core countries considered) also benefit during the buildup and rebuild from the higher prices (underlining the fact shown in simulations by Gouel and Jean [2012] that additional trade measures are needed to keep the economic effects of building and releasing food stocks within the country). If the stocks are built and the price shock does not then take place, prices will have been maintained at a higher level during the buildup and will then return to the baseline once the desired level is achieved, all at a significant fiscal cost.

It is important to look at the results in terms of rice and wheat consumption, which is a main variable for measuring food security. During the 10-year period of the simulations, consumption of both products is lower in the countries using the simulated policies for food stocks as well as in the rest of the world. To understand these results, the following pair of scenarios must be considered: first, how a world without a price surge and without new policies related to food stocks would compare with a world without a price surge but with new food stocks; and second, how a world with a price surge and with new food stock policies would compare with a world with a price surge and without new food stock policies. In the first scenario, the result is obvious: food stocks have been built for no purpose (that is, there was no price shock), leading only to price increases while stocks are built and thus to a reduction in consumption. The result in the second scenario is a combination of the period of the shock, when prices are lower and consumption is higher due to the release of stocks, and the rest of the years, which show higher prices and lower consumption during the periods of stock buildup. In this second scenario, the positive effect in consumption during the price shock (when the increase is mitigated by releasing stocks) is more than compensated for by the negative effect in the rest of the years.[30]

Thus the old dilemma of high/low prices cannot be avoided. In these simulations producers in the 10 countries (and in the rest of the world) benefit from higher prices, while consumers, both in those countries and in the rest of the world, lose on average (although they suffer less during the price shock). In addition, the whole scheme implies significant fiscal costs.[31] This final problem highlights another point made earlier. If, as shown in Hazell, Shields, and Shields (2005), a significant part of domestic price variability is related to macroeconomic crises, then fiscal deficits caused by food price stabilization schemes may lead to macroeconomic problems and may destabilize domestic prices through other channels (as recognized in Timmer 1989). More generally, macroeconomic crises lead to increases in poverty, with negative effects on food security, nutrition, and health (see, for example, Díaz-Bonilla 2008).

It is also important to note that in these simulations, the buildup of stocks only goes up to a fixed level of consumption (one-third) and is then firmly maintained at that level. However, experience shows that farmers' pressure to maintain high prices (or to increase prices further) once stocks have been built may lead to excessive accumulation of stocks (Dorosh 2008, 2009). Therefore food stocks may need to be designed with a strict limit (see Gouel 2013). These results are based on food stock operations in which purchases are made at market prices. As discussed in the next section, however, in many cases the objective may be to provide further price support to farmers.

Additional Price/Income Support to Farmers

During recent WTO negotiations, a group of developing countries suggested changes in the language of the Agreement on Agriculture that would have allowed them to buy food for public food security stocks at prices higher than those prevailing in the market when those purchases came from low-income or resource-poor producers (LIRP producers) (see Chapter 9). The proposal seemed to consider that making purchases for food security stocks or domestic food aid at market prices may be ineffective in attaining developing countries'

---

30 The simulations are conducted in quantity units (not in monetary welfare metrics), and the results are not discounted over time.

31 It is also interesting to note that the other simulated policies (trade measures and consumer subsidies) increase the level of wheat and rice consumption in the 10 countries when compared with a counterfactual of a price surge but no new policies; consumption also increases more with consumer subsidies than with trade measures. However, in the rest of the world, both policies lead to smaller consumption in addition to the decline caused by the price shock—although with consumption subsidies, that additional decrease is small.

food security objectives. Therefore those countries suggest exempting purchases from LIRP producers from domestic support limits in the Agreement of Agriculture.

It is not clear, though, why buying at market prices should be an ineffective way to help with food security. Certainly, to build food security stocks for emergencies and to provide domestic food aid for poor consumers, governments in developing countries would be far better off financially if they bought at market prices (especially in a context of high food prices). On the one hand, it does not make sense for poor countries to add to the costs of the food security program by using above-market administered prices, which generate further losses through buying high to support farmers and selling low to subsidize consumers. On the other hand, conducting the operations at market price will ensure that the program is part of the domestic support allowed under the Agreement on Agriculture (see Chapter 9).

If the objective is to pay LIRP producers above the prevailing market price, then obviously the previous arguments do not apply. Still, it is important to note that even when purchases are made at market prices, the program would nonetheless offer support to farmers (as noted in the simulations of Thompson and Tallard [2010]).[32] This impact is reinforced if the food stocks are used annually and rotated as part of social safety nets or other public systems of food distribution targeting the poor and needy. As noted earlier, this type of redistributive program expands "effective demand" (that is, demand backed by purchasing power, in this case intermediated by government purchases) and leads to higher prices for producers than would have been the case otherwise. Although this cost would be borne by those consumers who do not receive food aid and by the taxpayers, it would allow poor people to attain higher levels of food consumption.

It should be further noted that even without the government having to physically purchase food and distribute food aid, an income-redistribution program with discounted food vouchers for poor consumers would also lead to higher demand and therefore higher prices for farmers when compared

32 See also Islam and Thomas (1996), who argue that if a government buys, say, 10 percent of the production of a crop at harvest time, paying market prices to achieve a stock-to-consumption ratio defined for food security reasons, then that operation would increase prices compared with the counterfactual of no intervention. As discussed before, this results from the fact that at least part of the products from those stocks goes to support food consumption for families and individuals that would not have been able to afford it without the program.

with the counterfactual of no program.[33] Of course, this assertion depends on the existence of a private sector that can adequately cover the national territory, that operates reasonably efficiently (that is, with no large losses in the physical handling of the products), and that behaves competitively along the procurement and marketing chain (meaning that there are no intermediate actors with dominant market positions that may retain a larger share of the benefits of the redistribution, charging lower prices to farmers and higher prices to consumers). In this situation the comparison is between the quality and efficiency of the coverage, efficiency, and competitive behavior of the private sector, on one hand, and the performance of the public bureaucracy distributing food, on the other.

However, if a government is still focused on providing additional income support to LIRP producers (which is a separate objective from food security and nutritional support to consumers), developing countries can use direct payments to producers (paragraph 5, Annex 2, of the AoA; this is in addition to the investment and input subsidies of Article 6, paragraph 2; see Chapter 9 for more on this).[34] These payments should not be more difficult to implement and monitor (particularly with the extension of national identity cards in many countries and with the detailed household records kept under conditional or unconditional cash transfer programs) than a system of public purchase solely from LIRP producers, in which the problems of properly identifying appropriate sellers and avoiding leaks and abuses will also be present.

If reducing poverty is the concern, providing income support to LIRP producers goes directly to the heart of the matter. This is another application of the Bhagwati rule, noted earlier, regarding the need to target policies as closely as possible to the source of the problem in order to prevent second-round problems that may occur if the policy focuses only on a proxy for the desired objective. As argued earlier, if a country wants to help its poor and vulnerable populations, then targeting crops or livestock production is an indirect, and many times inefficient and inequitable, way to achieve poverty reduction and food security. When food security concerns are invoked, the focus of the policy analysis should be on people rather than on crops or food products.

---

33 In the case of the United States, the political economy of the farm bills has always featured the alliance of farmers with social advocates who support food vouchers and similar redistributive programs. That alliance was maintained in the 2014 Farm Bill (Orden 2014).

34 Article 6, paragraph 2, has the advantage, from the equity viewpoint, of encouraging developing countries to design specific programs for rural development or alleviation of rural poverty, instead of resorting to general and nontransparent subsidy schemes that may benefit richer farmers or be wasted in corruption (see Chapter 9).

If there are sharp downward price spikes because of international shocks (including import surges, perhaps due to unfair trade practices in other countries), trade measures such as safeguards and countervailing duties can be used as well, and developing countries, many of which have applied tariffs below bound ones, can also adjust the value of those import taxes (see Chapter 9).[35] The drawback to this approach is that it would force the adjustment onto the rest of the world and would be self-defeating if other countries did the same, as argued by Martin and Anderson (2012). In many cases, problems stemming from competitiveness in the farming sector (that is, imports coming at low prices) may result from overvalued exchange rates due to macroeconomic mismanagement. In this case, the right approach is to correct the overvaluation, which will help all tradable sectors, not just agriculture.

Consumer Issue 1: Impact and Delivery Mechanisms

For poor consumers it may be more efficient to use cash transfers or food vouchers and to let the private sector manage the physical handling of food products (see Hoddinott et al. 2013). The argument that managing cash transfers or food vouchers is far more cumbersome than the physical distribution of the food items seems incorrect. If the government has a system to identify poor households and to distribute the physical product, it can do the same with food vouchers. The administrative costs and the possibility for corruption and misallocation are also similar in both schemes; with food vouchers, however, the government avoids losses stemming from handling the grain through bureaucratic structures (although those losses need to be compared with the ones affecting potentially ineffective and underdeveloped private-sector channels). The other challenge stems from the possibility of the abuse of market position by private-sector operators, which must be compared with the possibility of corruption and abuse by the public staff operating governmental schemes.

The simulations in Thompson and Tallard (2010) also show that consumer subsidies seem to have more beneficial food security effects (as measured by wheat and rice consumption) for the countries applying them than does the use of trade measures and food stocks to avoid price peaks (which reduce

35 WTO members declare maximum tariffs as part of the trade agreements, called "bound" tariffs. The values applied may be lower. Galtier and Vindel (2013) argue that such adjustments should not be ad hoc but should rather follow a rule, such as variable levies and price bands. These mechanisms, which basically force adjustments onto the rest of the world on a permanent basis, have been banned in the WTO.

consumption over the decade simulated because of the higher prices resulting from the buildup of stocks). Furthermore, consumer subsidies in these simulations have smaller negative impacts on the quantities of wheat and rice consumed in the rest of the world than using food stocks to counter price spikes; however, they carry an important fiscal cost (which may be more or less than the buildup of public stocks, depending on the prices at which those stocks are released). Of course, there is still the issue of how to ensure the physical delivery of food products to isolated areas, which cannot be guaranteed by simply handing out vouchers. The expansion of a private-sector delivery network is something that evolves along with general economic development and supportive government policies. In this scenario the question of whether the government or the private sector is better equipped to handle physical distribution becomes an empirical issue.

Consumer Issue 2: Public Food Security or Nutrition Security?

The triple burden of malnutrition also poses new challenges when considering food security stocks. Each of the components of the triple burden (undernutrition, overnutrition, and micronutrient deficiency) has different negative impacts on human health and may be affected differently (or not at all) by the policies negotiated under the AoA, particularly by the operation of food security stocks and domestic food aid. For instance, a food security program centered on a limited number of products selected mainly because of their caloric content will not address the fact that a lack of dietary diversity appears more correlated with the prevalence of child stunting and wasting and with underweight mothers than simply the average consumption of calories (Arimond and Ruel 2006).

More generally, changes in consumption patterns linked to increasing incomes in developing countries, which have led to the expanded use of products other than the usual staple crops considered in food security stocks, bring the limited focus of these programs into question (see, for instance, Hoda and Gulati [2013], who criticize India's National Food Security Act, 2013 for being "cereal centered"). In addition, except for the decreasing number of countries in which a significant proportion of calories and nutrients depends on only one or two products, food price inflation and upward price spikes are associated with a larger basket of goods; when such spikes do occur, they are mostly related to macroeconomic imbalances. Thus food security stocks may not have the product breadth to address these problems and may actually contribute to creating macroeconomic imbalances through high fiscal costs.

Other Concerns

Additional concerns have been mentioned as justification for the need to build public-sector food distribution systems. One is the potential for monopoly power exercised by private operators, which may push down prices for farmers and increase prices for consumers. If such a problem exists, it is important to understand the causes. Monopolies of commonly consumed food products may exist due to the presence of policies such as discretionary import licenses or domestic trade licenses and restrictions. However, if the monopoly (or monopsony) power has its origin in market imperfections, as opposed to a policy-induced imperfection, then the persistence of the problem may be related to government failure to implement adequate regulations to eliminate abuses of market power. Therefore a better approach would be to eliminate any policy-induced monopolies/monopsonies and to establish adequate competition regimes to avoid anticompetitive practices, rather than trying to establish a governmental distribution system to counterbalance the potential abuses of the private sector.

Conclusion

This chapter has discussed some economic and operational issues related to public food security stocks, noting the changing world context within which food security concerns are being debated. One aspect of this new context has been the presence of higher (in nominal terms) and perhaps more volatile food prices, in part associated with expanding links among energy markets and food production, supply and prices, and greater weather variability associated with climate change. Since 2011, however, price levels have been decreasing, perhaps signaling a return to the historical decline in real prices for agricultural and food products.

While some approaches seem to focus on price volatility or price extremes as the main cause of food insecurity (a unidimensional approach), this chapter has mentioned a variety of damaging fluctuations and governance and macroeconomic problems that are also crucial, and in many cases more relevant, determinants of poverty and food insecurity. Therefore the chapter argues for the need to take a multidimensional approach and develop an integrated framework for food security and poverty alleviation; this approach includes, but clearly goes beyond, the potential link between high and volatile prices and food security. For example, inadequate monetary, fiscal, and monetary policies may have more relevance for inflationary pressures in food markets than product-specific policies, including food stocks. Thus research and policy dialogue must consider a multidimensional, integrated framework for food security and poverty alleviation; within this general framework the problems of price volatility and price extremes, as well as the possible contribution of food security stocks, can be discussed as just one component among several. In that context the contribution of food stocks to national welfare varies significantly with consumption diversification, the perishability of the main food products, the level of the country's development (which, among other things, defines the quality and extension of infrastructure and the operation of the private sector), and the country's geographical position.

The recent period of higher nominal prices has also led to more interest in food self-sufficiency. Clearly, developing countries would be well advised to invest more in the expansion and stabilization of their domestic agricultural production. The instinctive reaction of some policy makers and civil society advocates (both in the previous context of low world food prices and in the new context of higher prices) has been to resort to protectionist measures; however, investments in public goods, human capital, and related measures are the true basis for competitiveness and productivity. Overall, in developing countries, the most important constraints to designing and implementing adequate trade and nontrade policies to ensure food security continue to be the limitations of those countries' financial and human resources and institutional capabilities. It must also be remembered that general trade policies are not necessarily the main factor affecting food security and that, in any case, trade policies are blunt instruments with which to address the challenges of poverty and hunger. Therefore special and differential treatment defined at the national and crop level may not focus on the main problem; rather, well-targeted safety nets for the poor, both consumers and producers, are needed.

The best policy approach would include a relatively neutral trade policy; support for land and water ownership by small producers and landless workers; investments in human capital, infrastructure, climate change adaptation and mitigation, and agricultural R&D; appropriate management of natural resources (including fisheries); strengthened safety nets for the poor and vulnerable (such as conditional cash transfers, school lunches, women and infant nutrition programs, and food-for-work programs); women's empowerment programs; community organization and participation, particularly for the poor and vulnerable; adequate functioning of product and factor markets; macroeconomic stability; and overall good governance, including strong efforts to reduce corruption and ensure public safety.

Considering that the debate that almost derailed the Bali negotiations focused on food security stocks, several economic and operational issues do merit analysis. In line with other analyses, this chapter distinguishes food stocks for emergencies (type 1) and redistribution (type 2) from stocks for price stabilization (type 3). Based on a country's conditions, emergency food stocks (type 1) and food redistribution stocks that are part of safety nets and targeted food programs (type 2) may help to achieve food security objectives. Governments of landlocked countries, which display concentrated consumption patterns of some less perishable food products and have difficulty gaining access to international markets, may find it necessary to maintain food security stocks to help prevent potential breakdowns in supply. If that food is procured domestically, those purchases, if well-timed at harvest, will provide some price support for farmers, even if those purchases follow prevailing market prices.

Depending on the conditions prevalent in the country, a food redistribution stock (type 2) could also be a useful component of that country's social safety nets and targeted food programs. It is important to have such safety nets (conditional cash transfers, nutritional programs for women and children, school lunches, Food for Work programs, and so on) in place so that they can be scaled up if and when a sharp upward price spike occurs. But again, buying at market prices is the best option with which to build these stocks: if a developing country is buying food above market prices to provide farmers with high price support and selling below market prices to help poor and vulnerable populations, it will most likely get into severe fiscal problems long before other WTO members consider the possibility of bringing a trade case against that country. Along with the extension of safety nets for poor consumers, governments should also consider establishing safety nets for poor and vulnerable agricultural producers; these safety nets could provide income support and may be scaled up in emergencies, such as when harvests fail or in the case of sharp downward price spikes.

This chapter also notes that food stocks that are for emergency purposes and operate as redistributive devices backing up safety nets and other targeted food aid programs (if the stocks are purchased domestically) expand domestic food demand and support prices, as compared with the counterfactual that no such program exists. Still, in the case of redistributive food stocks plus food aid, it is necessary to evaluate the development and competitive operation of markets by the private sector against the costs and benefits of having the government perform the purchasing and distribution functions. With the continuous expansion and integration of markets in LAC and Asia, and the slower but nonetheless similar process going on in Africa, the cost-benefit analysis of these different options should be reassessed in countries with large governmental intervention in food markets. Reardon et al. (2012) note that fair price shops in India's public distribution system handle about 15 percent of the rice consumed in New Delhi, whereas the incipiently expanding supermarkets are already reaching 7 percent of consumption (although it may be the case that customers at those two types of retail outlets differ).

The discussion on the new context for food security also notes the challenges posed by the triple burden of malnutrition; recent studies show that increases in dietary diversity, rather than in caloric availability, are more closely related with declines in stunting and wasting in children and underweight in mothers. Thus food security stocks based on a limited number of staple crops, usually selected only for their calorie content, may not be the best approach for tackling the multiple challenges of malnutrition. Also, food price inflation and price extremes would be better managed by a combination of macroeconomic, trade, and investment policies, combined with safety nets that supplement the incomes of the poor. If public food stocks are built, they must operate with clear objectives and rules, as well as with strong financial, accounting, and audit safeguards. They must also be adequately sized and properly located (with the necessary transport, storage, and communications infrastructure). Finally, there should be adequate funding arrangements with properly trained staff (NEPAD 2004; World Bank 2005, 2012).

Whatever type of public food stocks is implemented, it will be important to consider additional policies, such as credible early warning and food security information systems about harvest prospects, potential food shortages, and emergency needs; in addition, governments should embed the operation of stocks in an integrated policy framework for food security. This framework should consider a full array of policies to support production, ensure market development, invest in infrastructure (transport, storage, and communications), help farmers and farmer associations create and expand their own stock-holding facilities (including traditional on-farm options) through warehouse receipts and credit, adequately use trade to enhance food security, expand safety nets for the poor and vulnerable, support women's empowerment and community participation, avoid ad hoc policy interventions, and ensure good governance and macroeconomic stability (NEPAD 2004).

The debate about the treatment of public food stocks within the WTO legal framework will continue in the coming years (see Chapter 9), keeping food security concerns at the center of future negotiations. This debate will require a full consideration of the legal, economic, and diplomatic issues involved and will benefit from ongoing efforts to revisit the topic of the operation of food stocks (for emergencies, food security, and stabilization) and to understand what has worked and what has not (as suggested by Timmer 2013). More generally, WTO members need more precise analyses of the quantitative impacts of all the different options available, not just food stocks, in order to define food security policies that are equitable and efficient. This analysis, to which this chapter tries to contribute, is separate from the legal issues related to how to treat the operation of public food stocks within the WTO, which is the topic of the next chapter.

Bibliography

Al-Riffai, P., B. Dimaranan, and D. Laborde. 2010. *European Union and United States Biofuel Mandates: Impacts on World Markets.* Technical Notes IDB-TN-191. Washington, DC: Inter-American Development Bank.

Anderson, K. 2009. *Distortions to Agricultural versus Nonagricultural Producer Incentives.* Washington, DC: World Bank.

Anderson, K., and S. Nelgen. 2013. *Updated National and Global Estimates of Distortions to Agricultural Incentives, 1955 to 2011.* Washington, DC: World Bank.

Arimond, M., and M. Ruel. 2006. "Dietary Diversity Is Associated with Child Nutritional Status: Evidence from 11 Demographic and Health Surveys." *Journal of Nutrition* 134: 2579–2585.

Barrett, C., and M. Bellemare. 2011. *The G-20's Error: Food Price Volatility Is Not the Problem.* Ithaca, NY, US: Cornell University Press.

Bhagwati, J. 1971. "The Generalized Theory of Distortions and Welfare." In *Trade, Balance of Payments, and Growth,* edited by J. Bhagwati, R. Jones, R. Mundell, and J. Vanek, 1–42. Amsterdam: North-Holland Publishing.

Blanchard, O., G. Dell'Ariccia, and P. Mauro. 2010. "Rethinking Macroeconomic Policy." Unpublished document, IMF Staff Position Note 10/03, International Monetary Fund, Washington, DC.

Blandford, D. 2013. "International Trade Disciplines and Policy Measures to Address Climate Change Mitigation and Adaptation in Agriculture." In *Agriculture and Food Security Group Proposals and Analysis.* Electronic book prepared by the E-15 Initiative. Bali: International Centre for Trade and Sustainable Development, World Economic Forum, and International Policy Council.

Brink, L. 2009. "WTO Constraints on Domestic Support in Agriculture: Past and Future." *Canadian Journal of Agricultural Economics* 57: 1–21.

———. 2011. "The WTO Disciplines on Domestic Support." In *WTO Disciplines on Agricultural Support,* edited by D. Orden, D. Blandford, and T. Josling, 23–59. Cambridge, UK: Cambridge University Press.

Bureau, J.-C., and S. Jean. 2013. "Do Yesterday's Disciplines Fit Today's Farm Trade?" In *Agriculture and Food Security Group Proposals and Analysis.* Electronic book prepared by the E-15 Initiative. Bali: International Centre for Trade and Sustainable Development, World Economic Forum, and International Policy Council.

Chapoto, A., and T. Jayne. 2009. "The Impact of Trade Barriers and Market Interventions on Maize Price Unpredictability: Evidence from Eastern and Southern Africa." MSU International Development Draft Working Paper 102. Michigan State University. East Lansing, MI, US.

Díaz-Bonilla, E. 2008. *Global Macroeconomic Developments and Poverty.* IFPRI Discussion Paper 766. Washington, DC: International Food Policy Research Institute.

———. 2013a. "Agricultural Trade and Food Security: Some Thoughts about a Continuous Debate." In *Agriculture and Food Security Group Proposals and Analysis.* Electronic book prepared by the E-15 Initiative. Bali: International Centre for Trade and Sustainable Development, World Economic Forum, and International Policy Council.

———. 2013b. "Lost in Translation: Why WTO Negotiations Seem to Go Nowhere." Food Security Portal Food for Thought blog, November 4. Accessed 2015. www.foodsecurity portal.org/lost-translation-why-wto-negotiations-seem-go-nowhere.

———. 2015. *Macroeconomics, Agriculture, and Food Security: A Guide to Policy Analysis in Developing Countries.* Washington, DC: International Food Policy Research Institute (IFPRI).

———. 2016. "Volatile Volatility: Some Conceptual and Measurement Issues Related to Price Trends and Volatility." Chapter 2 in *Food Price Volatility and Its Implications for Food Security and Policy,* edited by M. Kalkuhl, J. von Braun, M. Torero, 35–57. Cham, Switzerland: Springer.

Díaz-Bonilla, E., and S. Robinson. 2010. "Macroeconomics, Macrosectoral Policies, and Agriculture in Developing Countries." In *Handbook of Agricultural Economics,* vol. 4, edited by R. E. Evensen and P. Pingali, 3033–3211. Amsterdam: North-Holland.

Díaz-Bonilla, E., and J. Ron. 2010. *Food Security, Price Volatility, and Trade: Some Reflections for Developing Countries.* ICTSD Issue Paper 28. Geneva: International Centre for Trade and Sustainable Development.

Díaz-Bonilla, E., E. Saini, B. Creamer, G. Henry, and E. Trigo. 2013. *Better to Be Foresighted Than Myopic: A Foresight Framework for Agriculture, Food Security, and R&D in Latin America and the Caribbean.* Cali, Colombia: Centro Internacional de Agricultura Tropical (CIAT).

Díaz-Bonilla, E., and M. Thomas. 2016. *Why Some Are More Equal Than Others: Country Typologies of Food Security*. IFPRI Discussion Paper 1510. Washington, DC: International Food Policy Research Institute.

Díaz-Bonilla, E., M. Thomas, and S. Robinson. 2003. "Trade, Food Security, and the WTO Negotiations: Some Reflections on Boxes and Their Contents." In *Agricultural Trade and Poverty: Making Policy Analysis Count*. Proceedings of the OECD Global Forum, Paris, May 23–24, 2002.

Díaz-Bonilla, E., M. Thomas, S. Robinson, and A. Cattaneo. 2000. *Food Security and Trade Negotiations in the World Trade Organization: A Cluster Analysis of Country Groups*. IFPRI Trade and Macroeconomics Working Paper 59. Washington, DC: International Food Policy Research Institute.

Dorosh, P. 2008. "Food Price Stabilisation and Food Security: International Experience." *Bulletin of Indonesian Economic Studies* 44 (1): 93–114.

———. 2009. "Price Stabilization, International Trade, and National Cereal Stocks: World Price Shocks and Policy Response in South Asia." *Food Security* 1: 137–149.

Dorosh, P., and S. Rashid. 2012. *Bangladesh Rice Trade and Price Stabilization: Implications of the 2007/08 Experience for Public Stocks*. IFPRI Discussion Paper 1209. Washington, DC: International Food Policy Research Institute.

Effland, A. 2011. "Classifying and Measuring Agricultural Support Identifying Differences between the WTO and OECD Systems." *Economic Research Service Economic Information Bulletin* 74. Washington, DC: Economic Research Service. Accessed 2015. www.ers.usda.gov/media/129064/eib74.pdf.

Fan, S., ed. 2008. *Public Expenditures, Growth, and Poverty: Lessons from Developing Countries*. Baltimore: Johns Hopkins University Press.

FAO (Food and Agriculture Organization). 2014. FAOSTAT database. Rome: FAO. Accessed 2015. http://faostat3.fao.org/faostat-gateway/go/to/home/E.

Galtier, F., and B. Vindel. 2013. *Managing Food Price Instability in Developing Countries: A Critical Analysis of Strategies and Instruments*. Paris: Centre de coopération internationale en recherche agronomique pour le développement (CIRAD); Paris: Agence Française de Développement (AFD).

Garret, J., and M. Ruel. 2003. *Stunted Children–Overweight Mother Pairs: An Emerging Policy Concern?* IFPRI Discussion Paper 148. Washington, DC: International Food Policy Research Institute.

Gilbert, C. 2011. *Food Reserves in Developing Countries: Trade Policy Options for Improved Food Security*. ICTSD Issue Paper 37. Geneva: International Centre for Trade and Sustainable Development.

Gouel, C. 2013. *Food Price Volatility and Domestic Stabilization Policies in Developing Countries.* NBER Working Paper 18934. Cambridge, MA, US: National Bureau of Economic Research.

Gouel, C., and S. Jean. 2012. *Optimal Food Price Stabilization in a Small Open Developing Country.* World Bank Policy Research Working Paper 5943. Washington, DC: World Bank.

Hansen, J., M. Sato, and R. Ruedy. 2012. *Perceptions of Climate Change: The New Climate Dice.* New York: Columbia University Press.

Hazell, P. 1993. "Implications of Grain Trade Liberalization for LDC Food Security." In *Managing Food Security in Unregulated Markets,* edited by D. Roberts, 41–47. San Francisco: Westview.

Hazell, P., G. Shields, and D. Shields. 2005. "The Nature and Extent of Domestic Sources of Food Price Instability and Risk." Paper presented to the international workshop on Managing Food Price Instability in Low-Income Countries, Washington, DC, February 28–March 1.

Headey, D. 2014. *Food Prices and Poverty Reduction in the* Long Run. IFPRI Discussion Paper 1331. Washington, DC: International Food Policy Research Institute.

Headey, D., and S. Fan. 2010. *Reflections on the Global Food Crisis: How Did It Happen? How Did It Hurt? And How Can We Prevent the Next One?* IFPRI Research Monograph 165. Washington, DC: International Food Policy Research Institute.

Hidrobo, M., J. Hoddinott, A. Peterman, A. Margolies, and V. Moreira. 2012. *Cash, Food, or Vouchers? Evidence from a Randomized Experiment in Northern Ecuador.* IFPRI Discussion Paper 1234. Washington, DC: International Food Policy Research Institute.

HLPE (High Level Panel of Experts). 2011. *Price Volatility and Food Security: A Report by the High Level Panel of Experts on Food Security and Nutrition*. Rome: Committee on World Food Security.

Hoda, A., and A. Gulati. 2013. *India's Agricultural Trade Policy and Sustainable Development.* ICTSD Issue Paper 49. Geneva: International Centre for Trade and Sustainable Development.

Hoddinott, J., D. Gilligan, M. Hidrobo, A. Margolies, S. Roy, S. Sandström, B. Schwab, and J. Upton. 2013. *Enhancing WFP's Capacity and Experience to Design, Implement, Monitor, and Evaluate Vouchers and Cash Transfer Programmes: Study Summary.* IFPRI Project Summary. Washington, DC: International Food Policy Research Institute.

IATP (Institute for Agriculture and Trade Policy). 2012. *Grain Reserves and the Food Price Crisis: Selected Writings from 2008–2012.* Washington, DC: IATP.

IMF (International Monetary Fund). 2014. International Financial Statistics. Accessed 2015. https://www.imf.org/en/Data.

———. 2016. International Financial Statistics. Accessed June 2016. http://data.imf.org/?sk=5DABAFF2-C5AD-4D27-A175-1253419C02D1.

IPCC (Intergovernmental Panel on Climate Change). 2014. *Climate Change 2014: Impacts, Adaptation, and Vulnerability: IPCC WGII AR5 Summary for Policymakers.* IPCC Phase I Report. Geneva: IPCC. Accessed 2015. www.ipcc.ch/pdf/assessment-report/ar5/wg2/ar5_wgII_spm_en.pdf.

Isaksson, A. 2007. *Determinants of Total Factor Productivity: A Literature Review.* UNIDO Research and Statistics Branch Staff Working Paper 02/2007. Vienna: United Nations Industrial Development Organization.

Islam, N., and S. Thomas. 1996. *Food Grain Price Stabilization in Developing Countries: Issues and Experiences in Asia.* IFPRI Food Policy Review 3. Washington, DC: International Food Policy Research Institute.

Ivanic, M., and W. Martin. 2014. *Short- and Long-Run Impacts of Food Price Changes on Poverty.* Policy Research Working Paper 7011. Development Research Group, Agriculture and Rural Development Team. August. Washington, DC: World Bank.

Ivanic, M., W. Martin, and H. Zaman. 2011. *Estimating the Short-Run Poverty Impacts of the 2010–11 Surge in Food Prices.* World Bank Policy Research Working Paper 5633. Washington, DC: World Bank.

Knudsen, O., and J. Nash. 1990. "Domestic Price Stabilisation Schemes in Developing Countries." *Economic Development and Cultural Change* 38 (3): 539–558.

Laborde, D., and S. Msangi. 2012. "Biofuels, Environment, and Food: The Story Gets More Complicated." In *2011 Global Food Policy Report.* Washington, DC: International Food Policy Research Institute (IFPRI).

López, R. 2007. "Fiscal Policies in Highly Unequal Societies: Implications for Agricultural Growth." *eJADE Electronic Journal of Agricultural and Development Economics* 4 (1): 123–145.

Martin, W., and K. Anderson. 2012. "Export Restrictions and Price Insulation during Commodity Price Booms." *American Journal of Agricultural Economics* 94 (2): 422–427.

Meyer, S., and J. Schmidhuber. 2013. "Has the Treadmill Changed Direction?" In *Agriculture and Food Security Group Proposals and Analysis.* Electronic book prepared by the E-15 Initiative: International Centre for Trade and Sustainable Development (ICTSD), World Economic Forum, and International Food & Agricultural Trade Policy Council. Geneva: ICTSD.

Minot, N. 2011. *Transmission of World Food Price Changes to Markets in Sub-Saharan Africa.* IFPRI Discussion Paper 1059. Washington, DC: International Food Policy Research Institute.

———. 2012. *Food Price Volatility in Africa: Has It Really Increased?* IFPRI Discussion Paper 1239. Washington, DC: International Food Policy Research Institute.

Mogues, T., B. Yu, S. Fan, and L. McBride. 2012. *The Impacts of Public Investment in and for Agriculture: Synthesis of the Existing Evidence.* IFPRI Discussion Paper 1217. Washington, DC: International Food Policy Research Institute.

Mundell, R. 2002. "Commodity Prices, Exchange Rates, and the International Monetary System." Presentation at the Consultation on Agricultural Commodity Price Problems, organized by the Commodities and Trade Division, Food and Agriculture Organization, Rome, March 25–26.

Murphy, S. 2010. *Grain Reserves: A Smart Climate Adaptation Policy.* Washington, DC: Institute for Agriculture and Trade Policy.

Narayan, D., R. Chambers, M. Shah, and P. Petesch. 1999. *Global Synthesis: Consultations with the Poor.* World Bank Working Paper 45350. Washington, DC: World Bank.

NEPAD (New Partnership for Africa's Development). 2004. *NEPAD Study to Explore Further Options for Food-Security Reserve Systems in Africa.* Rome: NEPAD, with technical support from the United Nations World Food Programme.

Newbery, D. M. G., and J. Stiglitz. 1981. *Theory of Commodity Price Stabilization: Study in the Economics of Risk.* Oxford, UK: Oxford University Press.

OECD (Organisation for Economic Co-operation and Development). 2016. OECD Producer and Consumer Support Estimates database. Accessed 2015. www.oecd.org/tad/agricultural-policies/producerandconsumersupportestimatesdatabase.htm.

OECD-FAO (Organisation for Economic Co-operation and Development—Food and Agriculture Organization of the United Nations). 2011. *Agricultural Outlook.* Geneva.

———. 2012. *Agricultural Outlook.* Geneva.

———. 2013. *Agricultural Outlook.* Geneva.

———. 2014. Producer and Consumer Support Estimates database. Accessed 2015. www.oecd.org/agriculture/agricultural-policies/producerandconsumersupportestimatesdatabase.htm#summary.

———. 2015. "Aglink-Cosimo Model Documentation: A Partial Equilibrium Model of World Agricultural Markets." Accessed 2015. www.agri-outlook.org/abouttheoutlook/Aglink-Cosimo-model-documentation-2015.pdf.

Orden, D. 2014. "New U.S. Farm Bill Reaffirms Support to Producers." Food Security Portal Food for Thought blog, February 6. Accessed 2015. www.foodsecurityportal.org/new-us-farm-bill-reaffirms-support-producers.

Orden, D., D. Blandford, and T. Josling, eds. 2011. *WTO Disciplines on Agricultural Support*. Cambridge, UK: Cambridge University Press.

Pinstrup-Andersen, P. 2007. "Agricultural Research and Policy for Better Health and Nutrition in Developing Countries: A Food Systems Approach." *Agricultural Economics* 37 (s1): 187–198.

Poulton C., J. Kydd, S. Wiggins, and A. Dorward. 2006. "State Intervention for Food Price Stabilization in Africa: Can It Work?" *Food Policy* 31: 342–356.

Rashid, S., A. Gulati, and R. Cummings Jr., eds. 2008. *From Parastatals to Private Trade Lessons from Asian Agriculture*. Baltimore: Johns Hopkins University Press.

Rashid, S., and S. Lemma. 2011. *Strategic Grain Reserves in Ethiopia: Institutional Design and Operational Performance*. IFPRI Discussion Paper 1054. Washington, DC: International Food Policy Research Institute.

Reardon, T., K. Chen, B. Minten, and L. Adriano. 2012. *The Quiet Revolution in Staple Food Value Chains: Enter the Dragon, the Elephant, and the Tiger*. Manila, Philippines: Asian Development Bank and International Food Policy Research Institute. Accessed 2015. www.adb.org/sites/default/files/pub/2012/quiet-revolution-staple-food-value-chains.pdf.

Reardon, T., and C. P. Timmer. 2012. "The Economics of the Food System Revolution." *Annual Review of Resource Economics* 4: 14.1–14.40.

Reardon, T., C. P. Timmer, and J. Berdegue. 2004. "The Rapid Rise of Supermarkets in Developing Countries: Induced Organizational, Institutional, and Technological Change in Agrifood Systems." *Journal of Agricultural and Development Economics* 1 (2): 168–183.

Rosegrant, M., J. Koo, N. Cenacchi, C. Ringler, R. Robertson, M. Fisher, C. Cox, K. Garrett, N. Perez, and P. Sabbagh. 2014. *Food Security in a World of Natural Resource Scarcity: The Role of Agricultural Technologies*. Washington, DC: International Food Policy Research Institute (IFPRI).

Rosegrant, M., C. Ringler, T. Zhu, S. Tokgoz, and P. Bhandary. 2013. "Water and Food in the Bioeconomy: Challenges and Opportunities for Development." *Agricultural Economics* 44 (s1): 139–150.

Salant, S. 1983. "The Vulnerability of Price Stabilization Schemes to Speculative Attack." *Journal of Political Economy* 91 (1): 1–38.

Schnepf, R. 2013. "Agriculture-Based Biofuels: Overview and Emerging Issues." Congressional Research Service R41282. Washington, DC: Congressional Research Service.

Sinha, S., M. Lipton, and S. Yaqub. 2002. "Poverty and Damaging Fluctuations: How Do They Relate?" *Journal of Asian and African Studies* 37 (2): 186–243.

Sumner, D. A. 2000. "Agricultural Trade Policy and Food Security." *Quarterly Journal of International Agriculture* 39 (4): 395–409.

Tangermann, S. 2011. *Policy Solutions to Agricultural Market Volatility: A Synthesis.* ICTSD Issue Paper 33. Geneva: International Centre for Trade and Sustainable Development.

———. 2013. "A Post-Bali Food Security Agenda: The E-15 Initiative. Strengthening the Multilateral Trading System." Report prepared for ICTSD Agriculture and Food Security Group, Bali. Accessed 2015. www.ictsd.org/sites/default/files/research/AG_Policy_ok.pdf.

Thompson, W., and G. Tallard. 2010. *Potential Market Effects of Selected Policy Options in Emerging Economies to Address Future Commodity Price Surges.* OECD Food, Agriculture, and Fisheries Papers 35. Paris: Organisation for Economic Co-operation and Development.

Timmer, C. P. 1989. "Food Price Policy: The Rationale for Government Intervention." *Food Policy* 14 (1): 17–27.

———. 2013. Preface. In *Managing Food Price Instability in Developing Countries: A Critical Analysis of Strategies and Instruments,* edited by F. Galtier and B. Vindel, 9–16. Paris: Centre de coopération internationale en recherche agronomique pour le développement (CIRAD); Paris: Agence Française de Développement (AFD).

Timmer, C. P., W. Falcon, and S. Pearson. 1983. *Food Policy Analysis.* Baltimore: Johns Hopkins University Press.

Tinbergen, J. 1952. *On the Theory of Economic Policy.* Amsterdam: North-Holland.

Torero, M. 2012. "Riding the Rollercoaster." In *2011 Global Food Policy Report.* Washington, DC: International Food Policy Research Institute.

Townsend, R. 1977. "The Eventual Failure of Price Fixing Schemes." *Journal of Economic Theory* 14 (3): 190–199.

USDA (United States Department of Agriculture). 2014a. *Livestock and Poultry: World Markets and Trade.* FAS World Production, Markets, and Trade Reports. Washington, DC: USDA. Accessed 2015. http://apps.fas.usda.gov/psdonline/circulars/livestock_poultry.pdf.

———. 2014b. *World Agricultural Supply and Demand Estimates.* Washington, DC: USDA. Accessed 2015. www.usda.gov/oce/commodity/wasde/latest.pdf.

von Braun, J., and M. Torero. 2009. *Implementing Physical and Virtual Food Reserves to Protect the Poor and Prevent Market Failure.* IFPRI Policy Brief 10. Washington, DC: International Food Policy Research Institute.

von Grebmer, K., D. Headey, T. Olofinbiyi, D. Wiesmann, H. Fritschel, S. Yin, Y. Yohannes, C. Foley, C. von Oppeln, B. Iseli, C. Béné, and L. Haddad. 2013. *2013 Global Hunger Index—The Challenge of Hunger: Building Resilience to Achieve Food and Nutrition Security.* Bonn, Germany: Welthungerhilfe; Washington, DC: International Food Policy Research Institute; Dublin: Concern Worldwide.

Warr, P. 2013. *Food Security, Agriculture, and Poverty in Asia*. ReSAKSS Asia Working Paper 1. Washington, DC: IFPRI. Accessed 2015. www.ifpri.org/sites/default/files/publications/resakssasiawp1.pdf.

World Bank. 2005. *Managing Food Price Risks and Instability in an Environment of Market Liberalization*. Agriculture and Rural Development Department Report 32727-GLB. Washington, DC: World Bank.

———. 2012. *Using Public Foodgrain Stocks to Enhance Food Security*. World Bank Report 71280. Washington, DC: World Bank.

Chapter 9

FOOD SECURITY STOCKS AND THE WTO LEGAL FRAMEWORK

Eugenio Díaz-Bonilla

The international trading system's ability to operate adequately is important for global economic development, poverty alleviation, and food security. Of particular importance to the global trading system is the set of multilateral trade rules first defined under the General Agreement on Trade and Tariffs (GATT) in 1948 and later expanded during the different rounds of trade negotiations and the agreements reached in the Uruguay Round in 1995, which established the World Trade Organization (WTO). This round, however, left unresolved several critical issues regarding appropriate rules for global agriculture and other topics of importance for developing countries, and WTO members have been trying to settle these remaining questions ever since. The Doha Round, launched in 2001 during the fourth WTO Ministerial Conference, focused specifically on the development agenda.[1]

From the viewpoint of many developing countries, the Doha negotiations were needed to better balance what those countries considered to be the excessive concessions that industrialized countries received under the Uruguay Round. These concessions related not only to the introduction of new topics in the legal commitments, such as intellectual property rights and services, but also to the legal room allowed to protect and subsidize industrialized countries' agriculture and to use export subsidies for agricultural products (such subsidies have been prohibited for industrial products under the GATT

1 The Ministerial Conference is the supreme authority of the WTO, composed by WTO members' Ministers of Trade or equivalent positions. The Conference usually meets every two years. The next level of authority is the General Council, which meets regularly in Geneva to carry out WTO operations. It is subordinated to the Ministerial Conference, but it has the authority to act on behalf of the Ministers, who then can confirm or change what has been done in Geneva. The General Council is composed of representatives from WTO members (usually ambassadors or the equivalent). The list of WTO Ministerial Conferences since the creation of the organization is as follows: Singapore, December 9–13, 1996 (first); Geneva, May 18–20, 1998 (second); Seattle, November 30–December 3, 1999 (third); Doha, November 9–13, 2001 (fourth); Cancun, September 10–14, 2003 (fifth); Hong Kong, December 13–18, 2005 (sixth); Geneva, November 30–December 2, 2009 (seventh); Geneva, December 15–17, 2011 (eighth); Bali, December 3–6, 2013 (ninth); and Nairobi, December 15–19, 2015 (tenth).

and the WTO agreements and have been only recently prohibited for agricultural products in the 2015 WTO Ministerial at Nairobi). In recognition of developing countries' concerns about these issues, the Doha Ministerial Declaration put out an ambitious negotiating package called the Doha Development Agenda (DDA).[2] The DDA included specific instructions for the discussion of agriculture; services, electronic commerce, and market access for nonagricultural products; intellectual property, investment, and competition policy; and government procurement, trade facilitation, WTO rules for regional trade agreements, the Dispute Settlement Understanding, and environmental issues.

After one final, sustained push to complete the trade talks collapsed in 2008, the Doha negotiations have stalled, in large part because of disagreements between developed and developing countries regarding an adequate balance across the agricultural and nonagricultural commitments being negotiated, market access requests by developed countries, and differing opinions about special and differential treatment (SDT) for developing countries.[3] Two agricultural issues in particular played a major role in derailing the 2008 negotiations. One was related to the operation of a special safeguard mechanism (SSM) to increase protection for selected staple products under specific conditions. Several developing countries presented SSM as a food security issue linked to the market-access component of the agricultural negotiations.[4] The second factor was a controversy over cotton trade involving the United States and several cotton-producing African countries.

Given the difficulties in completing the Doha negotiations, WTO members subsequently decided to refocus their talks on a more limited number

2 The Doha Ministerial also addressed some of the problems created by the original agreement on trade-related intellectual property rights (TRIPs): the Declaration on the TRIPs Agreement and Public Health (WT/MIN(01)/DEC/2, November 20, 2001), recognizing "the gravity of the public health problems afflicting many developing and least-developed countries, especially those resulting from HIV/AIDS, tuberculosis, malaria, and other epidemics," made some of the requirements in the original text more flexible for developing countries.

3 SDT refers to the notion that developing countries may need special considerations under trade rules, differentiated from the legal obligations of developed countries.

4 The three pillars of the agricultural negotiations within the WTO are domestic support, market access, and export competition. The debate about the SSM focused on whether tariff increases on products affected by import surges could, under certain circumstances, go above the levels previously negotiated and bound. However, whether the SSM really addressed developing countries' food security concerns was a matter of debate. Simulations in a global model suggested that if the protection afforded by the SSM were sustained over time, developing countries using that safeguard would have been worse off in terms of food security (measured as food consumption) and in other dimensions, such as employment, production, and exports (Díaz-Bonilla, Diao, and Robinson 2004).

of issues that seemed to have a better chance of being agreed upon; a smaller list of topics were discussed at the ninth Ministerial Conference in Bali, Indonesia, and at the tenth Ministerial Conference in Nairobi, Kenya. However, negotiating smaller deals has not eliminated all of the challenges faced by WTO members. For instance, during the frantic final days of the Bali negotiations, even the more circumscribed package being considered was at risk of stalling. Once again, food security concerns were a major reason for the disagreements.

The food security debate at Bali shifted from the market-access issue that had derailed talks in 2008 to the pillar of domestic support for agriculture; in particular, the problem was the WTO's legal treatment of the use of administered prices to build public food security stocks in developing countries. This time, however, failure was temporarily averted through the establishment of a mechanism dubbed a *peace clause*, which provided additional time for members to resolve their disagreements over these food security issues. The wording of this clause, which itself brought negotiations to the verge of a breakdown and led to a one-day extension of discussions, was finally included in the Ministerial Decision on Public Stockholding for Food Security Purposes (to be discussed in detail later). Thanks to this last-minute peace clause, the Bali Agreements were concluded, representing the first comprehensive multilateral trade package negotiated since the creation of the WTO in 1995 (see Díaz-Bonilla and Laborde [2015] for an overview and analysis of what was agreed upon at Bali).

However, further differences about the interpretation of the peace clause held up implementation of the Bali Agreements and the establishment of a post-Bali work program, which was supposed to take place during 2014. Crucially, the wording and definition of the final legal steps of the Agreement on Trade Facilitation (ATF) needed one last review before being sent to the WTO members for approval by their legislatures.[5] These wording and legal issues were scheduled to be resolved during a meeting of the WTO General Council in July 2014, which was also supposed to focus on the definition of the future work program. However, that meeting broke down in disarray when India made the implementation of the ATF's final legal steps contingent on clarifications about the wording of the peace clause, which had supposedly

5 The Bali Package had been agreed upon by representatives of the executive branches of the WTO members. However, the ATF, being a new WTO agreement, required the additional approval by the legislative branches of many WTO members.

been agreed upon several months before in Bali. The dispute (discussed below in detail) centered on the fact that the Ministerial Decision on Public Stockholding for Food Security Purposes still contained wording with alternative interpretations. Therefore, India decided to hold up negotiations on the ATF until the text of the peace clause was clarified to its satisfaction. Only on November 27, 2014—almost a year after the original Bali Ministerial—was the wording about the peace clause applying to public food stocks finally agreed upon at the WTO General Council meeting (WT/L/939). The Nairobi Conference approved a Ministerial Decision on the same topic (WT/MIN[15]/44 —WT/L/979), which reaffirmed the decision by the WTO General Council regarding the peace clause.[6] Still, as discussed below, a permanent solution to the issue of public food stocks is still pending.

This chapter focuses on the legal issues posed by the WTO texts on public stockholding for food security purposes. It is aimed at policy makers, development practitioners, and the general public in developing countries who are interested in these issues but who have not necessarily followed WTO and related debates closely. Therefore, I present these legal texts in detail to provide a basic reference. The chapter is organized into five sections. The first section provides an introduction to the topics being debated. The chapter then presents a short background on the discussions of food security in the WTO. The third section analyzes in detail the legal aspects of the texts on food security stocks approved in Bali (the Ministerial Decision on Public Stockholding for Food Security Purposes, WT/MIN[13]/W/10) and the modifications agreed upon in November 2014 (WT/L/939). Next, the chapter discusses potential options to reach a final agreement on the operation of food security stocks in the WTO framework. A final section concludes the chapter.

Background

Food Security as a Trade Concern

Food security is not a new concern for either developing or developed countries. It has appeared as a key issue during several rounds of trade negotiations.

6 The approval by the ministers of the decision by the WTO General Council was considered necessary to provide legal support, to the extent that the latter WTO organ is subordinated to the Conference of Ministers, but it had modified language that had been originally approved by ministers.

For example, during the Uruguay Round, several developing and developed countries invoked food security concerns to justify barriers to food imports and higher levels of domestic support (even though, under any metric, the notion of food insecurity in richer countries was clearly very different from the conditions in developing countries that warrant such a label). At the conclusion of the Uruguay Round, food security was reflected in the Marrakesh Declaration and the establishment of the Net Food-Importing Developing Countries (NFIDCs) category; these countries, along with least developed countries (LDCs), were supposed to receive financial aid and other help in case food prices increased as a result of trade negotiations.[7] Article 20 of the Agreement on Agriculture (AoA) also mentioned that "nontrade concerns" (food security being among them) had to be taken into account in the continuation of negotiations on agriculture, which were still unfinished after the closing of the Uruguay Round.

Subsequently, several developed countries included food security as a component of the notion of multifunctionality, which argued (1) that agriculture created positive externalities for society (one being food security) beyond the direct market value of food and fiber, and (2) that these effects were inseparable from production. From this standpoint, barriers to food imports and higher levels of domestic support were justified to expand the agricultural sector.[8] Some of these countries attempted to use that notion (which, as noted, included food security as part of the positive externalities) to build alliances with developing countries for the WTO negotiations. However, it was obvious that no developed country fit the profile of "food insecure" according to comparable indicators of food consumption, production, and exports (Díaz-Bonilla et al. [2000] and Díaz-Bonilla and Thomas [2016]). It also became clear that if developed countries expanded their agriculture using protection and domestic support on account of the potential multifunctionality effects, other countries (mostly developing ones) would have seen their agriculture

7 Whereas NFIDC is a WTO category, LDC is a group defined by the United Nations based on development indicators. There are currently 48 LDCs determined by the United Nations, 35 of which have become WTO members. There are 7 other LDCs that are negotiating to join the WTO, one of which, Afghanistan, completed the negotiations during the Nairobi Ministerial and, as of this writing, is proceeding with the internal ratification.

8 Díaz-Bonilla and Tin (2006) noted that a similar notion of positive externalities, with a comparable debate about appropriate policies, was behind the drive toward industrialization in developing countries after World War II. However, the GATT legal system put stronger disciplines on subsidization and protection of industry, whereas agriculture was largely exempted for several decades until some disciplines were introduced with the conclusion of the Uruguay Round.

contract (for a given level of global demand); therefore their assumed multifunctionality would have declined (Díaz-Bonilla and Tin 2006). In the end, the use of multifunctionality as the foundation for the protection and subsidization of agriculture in developed countries did not gain much traction in trade negotiations.

Developing countries, however, clearly have stronger grounds for claims of food security concerns. In the early 2000s these claims were manifested in the request by several developing countries for a Food Security Box, which included more options to maintain high levels of protection and support for some agricultural products. Several of those proposals were incorporated in the "Revised Draft Modalities for Agriculture" (TN/AG/W/4/Rev.4, December 6, 2008). This document, which included very detailed language for the potential text of an agricultural agreement, is usually called "the 2008 Modalities, Rev 4" (sometimes shortened to "Rev.4") and was the last attempt to reach an Agreement on Agriculture before the general Doha talks collapsed in 2008. Although the 2008 Modalities were not agreed upon, part of the language from this document reemerged in some proposals in the process leading up to the ninth and tenth Ministerial Conferences and in the agreements reached in these two WTO conferences related to agriculture.[9]

New Circumstances

Although food security issues are not new in trade negotiations, these concerns have more recently appeared against a background of higher nominal prices and volatility, whereas formerly they were postulated in a context of lower food prices (discussed in Chapter 8; see Meyer and Schmidhuber 2013; Bureau and Jean 2013; Díaz-Bonilla 2013a; Tangermann 2013). For the legal issues discussed in this chapter, the main point is the evolution of nominal food prices, shown in Table 9.1, when compared to the WTO benchmark of 1986 to 1988. The table shows six indexes (2005 = 100) and several individual products in market prices (all in nominal dollars) and includes historical values and IMF projections until 2020 as a reference.

Nominal food prices are clearly above the 1986–1988 prices in US dollars. This has implications for the calculations of domestic support according

9 For instance, two other Ministerial Decisions at Bali (General Services, WT/MIN[13]/W/9 and the Understanding on Tariff-Rate Quota Administration Provisions of Agricultural Products, WT/MIN[13]/W/11) were also based on language from the 2008 Modalities. At Nairobi the Ministerial Decision on "Export Competition" (WT/MIN[15]/45—WT/L/980) also reflected several aspects of the 2008 Modalities (see Díaz-Bonilla and Hepburn 2016).

TABLE 9.1 Nominal prices: Indexes and individual commodities

Nominal Prices	1986–1988	2014–2015	2016–2020 (Projections)	2014–2015 (% above 1986–1988)	2016–2020 (% above 1986–1988)
Food and Beverage Price Index	105.4	157.9	140.3	49.8	33.1
Food Price Index	102.3	156.7	139	53.2	35.9
Cereals Price Index	82.6	161	143.3	94.9	73.5
Oilseeds Price Index	83.8	173.7	149.7	107.3	78.6
Meat Price Index	100.8	152.4	141.5	51.2	40.4
Sugar Price Index	76.3	134.3	134.8	76.0	76.7
Wheat	124.3	240.3	202.1	93.3	62.6
Maize (corn)	90.1	177.6	169.9	97.1	88.6
Rice	229.1	415.6	351.2	81.4	53.3
Soybeans	221.4	409.3	353.7	84.9	59.8
Soybean meal	203.7	413.1	349.6	102.8	71.6
Soybean oil	420.3	756	723.6	79.9	72.2
Beef	105.8	220.6	206.6	108.5	95.3
Poultry (chicken)	42.9	114.1	125.9	166.0	193.5
Sugar, free market	7.7	15.5	15.7	101.3	103.9
Cotton	62.1	73	56.5	17.6	−9.0

Source: IMF 2015.
Note: Wheat, No.1 Hard Red Winter, ordinary protein, FOB Gulf of Mexico, US$ per metric ton
Maize (corn), US No. 2 Yellow, FOB Gulf of Mexico, US price, US$ per metric ton
Rice, 5 percent broken milled white rice, Thailand nominal price quote, US$ per metric ton
Soybeans, US soybeans, Chicago Soybean futures contract (first contract forward) No. 2 yellow and par, US$ per metric ton
Soybean meal, Chicago Soybean Meal Futures (first contract forward) Minimum 48 percent protein, US$ per metric ton
Soybean oil, Chicago Soybean Oil Futures (first contract forward) exchange approved grades, US$ per metric ton
Beef, Australian and New Zealand 85% lean fores, FOB US import price, US cents per pound
Poultry (chicken), whole bird spot price, Georgia docks, US cents per pound
Sugar, free market, Coffee Sugar and Cocoa Exchange (CSCE) contract no.11 nearest future position, US cents per pound
Cotton, Cotton Outlook A Index, Middling 1-3/32 inch staple, CIF Liverpool, US cents per pound

to the AoA, which requires comparisons with some fixed external reference prices for those years (more on this later). Conceivably, if a government is buying food products from that country's producers at predetermined prices that are in line with national and global market prices, the government may appear to be offering additional price support to producers under the WTO legal definition; however, from an economic point of view, that would not be true. This is a crucial issue in the legal debate.

Public Stockholding for Food Security Purposes: Existing Legal Texts

Background

The AoA (WTO 2008b) has four categories of domestic support.[10] The first three are exempted from disciplines under certain conditions; they include those considered in (1) Annex 2, the so-called Green Box (although no colored boxes are mentioned in the AoA); (2) Article 6.4 (also known as the Blue Box); and (3) Article 6.2 (which applies to developing countries only).[11] The remaining domestic support measures not included in these three categories are a residual category, usually called the Amber Box. These measures must be added up in an aggregate measurement of support (AMS) for each product (that is, product-specific AMS) and for agricultural producers in general (non-product-specific AMS) (Brink 2011), which were capped and reduced in the AoA, as discussed below.

Product-specific support includes an estimation of market price support (MPS), which "shall be calculated using the gap between a fixed external reference price and the applied administered price multiplied by the quantity of production eligible to receive the applied administered price" (Annex 3, paragraph 8).

$$\text{MPS} = (\text{administered price} - \text{fixed external reference price}) \cdot \text{eligible production}$$

10 This section draws significantly from Díaz-Bonilla (2014) and Díaz-Bonilla and Laborde (2015). For a detailed discussion of these topics, see Brink (2011), particularly Figure 2.1. See also the explanations in WTO (2008b).

11 Article 6.4 allows certain payments directly linked to area or animal numbers but operating under mechanisms that also limit production to be exempted from the general rule that all subsidies linked to production must be maintained below a de minimis level or reduced. Because of the importance of Article 6.2 for developing countries, it is quoted here in full as reference:

> In accordance with the Mid-Term Review Agreement that government measures of assistance, whether direct or indirect, to encourage agricultural and rural development are an integral part of the development programs of developing countries, investment subsidies which are generally available to agriculture in developing country Members and agricultural input subsidies generally available to low-income or resource-poor producers in developing country Members shall be exempt from domestic support reduction commitments that would otherwise be applicable to such measures, as shall domestic support to producers in developing country Members to encourage diversification from growing illicit narcotic crops. Domestic support meeting the criteria of this paragraph shall not be required to be included in a Member's calculation of its Current Total AMS.

It should be noted that in the accession negotiations, China agreed to limit the subsidies covered by this article 6.2 to 8.5 percent of the value of farm output.

It is important to note three crucial concepts—the fixed external reference price (FERP), the applied administered price (AP), and the eligible production—because they feature prominently in the legal issues discussed in this chapter.

Product-specific AMS also must include other nonexempt production-related payments and support to producers. The sum of MPS and other nonexempt payments is then compared with the value of production; if the sum is more than a de minimis level (5 percent of production value for developed countries and 10 percent for developing countries), then the value is included in its entirety (that is, not only the excess over the de minimis) in the current total aggregate measurement of support (CTAMS).[12] The non-product-specific support (usually measured through budgetary data) also needs to be compared to the entire agricultural production; if it exceeds the de minimis value, it must be added to the CTAMS. Finally, the CTAMS is compared to, and cannot exceed, the ceiling commitment (sometimes called the Final Bound Total AMS, or FBTAMS), which is a value negotiated during the Uruguay Round or defined later during the accession process for new WTO members (Brink 2011).

Two things should be noted. First, most developing countries have not declared domestic support (that is, the amount considered in the FBTAMS) in the negotiations; therefore the 10 percent de minimis limits these countries' levels of domestic support.[13] Yet a small number of developing countries have declared domestic support. Therefore they have the possibility of offering domestic support up to the FBTAMS; however, the value of that domestic support is small compared to the allowances negotiated by developed countries during the Uruguay Round.[14] Second, as noted, the notion of special and differential treatment in Article 6.2 allows developing countries to exempt both general investment support for agriculture and input subsidies for low-income or resource-poor farmers from the AMS, despite the fact that these domestic measures can be considered trade-distorting.

The debate before and during the Bali Ministerial revolved around two sections of Annex 2 of the AoA (Green Box): food security stocks (AoA,

---

12 Some countries have accepted a different de minimis as part of their accession agreement. For instance, in China's case, this level is 8.5 percent.

13 The relevant text in Article 7(b) reads: "Where no Total AMS commitment exists . . . the Member shall not provide support to agricultural producers in excess of the relevant de minimis level set out in paragraph 4 of Article 6."

14 A total of 33 countries have FBTAMS, but Canada, the European Union, Japan, Norway, Switzerland, and the United States represent 87 percent of the total value declared by WTO members (the European Union alone represents about 49 percent of the total).

Annex 2, paragraph 3) and domestic food subsidies (AoA, Annex 2, paragraph 4). Prior to the Ministerial, a group of developing countries (known at the WTO as the G33) presented a proposal based on the 2008 Modalities that included new language for paragraph 3 (Public Stockholding for Food Security Purposes) and paragraph 4 (Domestic Food Aid).[15] To understand the suggested modifications, it is necessary to look first at the current language of Annex 2. The opening paragraph indicates the conditions that the different measures listed in the Green Box must meet to be exempted from the AMS. First, support programs must meet "the fundamental requirement that they have no, or at most minimal, trade-distorting effects or effects on production." They must also "conform to the following basic criteria: (a) the support in question shall be provided through a publicly-funded government program (including government revenue foregone) not involving transfers from consumers; and, (b) the support in question shall not have the effect of providing price support" (WTO 2008b, Annex 2, paragraph 1).

The specific language related to food security stocks (Annex 2, paragraph 3) declares "expenditures (or revenue foregone) in relation to the accumulation and holding of stocks of products which form an integral part of a food security program identified in national legislation" to be Green Box measures, provided they comply with the fundamental requirement and basic criteria mentioned before. Those expenditures must also comply with other conditions such as "the volume and accumulation of such stocks shall correspond to predetermined targets related solely to food security" and "the process of stock accumulation and disposal shall be financially transparent." However, a footnote simplifies the criteria for developing countries: food security stocks are considered in conformity with Annex 2, paragraph 3, if the operation "is transparent and conducted in accordance with officially published objective criteria or guidelines."

Annex 2, paragraph 3 also indicates that "food purchases by the government shall be made at current market prices and sales from food security stocks shall be made at no less than the current domestic market price for the

15 As is the case with many international groups, the G33 has a different number of members than the name suggests. As of the time of this writing the countries in that group, according to WTO information, were Antigua and Barbuda; Barbados; Belize; Benin; Bolivia; Botswana; China; Côte d'Ivoire; Cuba; Democratic Republic of the Congo; Dominica; Dominican Republic; Ecuador; El Salvador; Grenada; Guatemala; Guyana; Haiti; Honduras; India; Indonesia; Jamaica; Kenya; Madagascar; Mauritius; Mongolia; Mozambique; Nicaragua; Nigeria; Pakistan; Panama; Peru; Philippines; Republic of Korea; Saint Kitts and Nevis; Saint Lucia; Saint Vincent and the Grenadines; Senegal; Sri Lanka; Suriname; Taiwan, China; United Republic of Tanzania; Trinidad and Tobago; Turkey; Uganda; Venezuela; Zambia; and Zimbabwe.

product and quality in question." On that basis, some observers have argued that governments are not allowed to subsidize consumers (that is, sales must be made at market prices). This ignores the fact that the text is again modified for developing countries; footnotes 5 and 6 (a combined footnote so numbered) applies to both Public Stockholding for Food Security Purposes (Annex 2, paragraph 3) and Domestic Food Aid (another Green Box measure in Annex 2, paragraph 4) and allows the selling of products at subsidized prices "with the objective of meeting food requirements of urban and rural poor in developing countries on a regular basis." Although this stipulation allows developing countries to offer subsidies in the selling price, footnote 5 to the food security stock provision does not permit purchases made at anything other than market prices to be part of the Green Box. If purchases are at "administered prices" (different from market prices), then the "difference between the acquisition price and the external reference price is accounted for in the AMS."

The section on domestic food aid (Annex 2, paragraph 4), in addition to allowing the provision of subsidized food through domestic aid, establishes some reasonable criteria for the operation of these aid programs, such as that "eligibility to receive the food aid shall be subject to clearly-defined criteria related to nutritional objectives" and that "the financing and administration of the aid shall be transparent." It also allows domestic food aid to be in-kind or other means "to allow eligible recipients to buy food either at market or at subsidized prices."

Some developing countries, particularly India, believed that if they had to account for the gap between administered prices and fixed external reference prices, they would bump against, and probably exceed, the product-specific limit of 10 percent de minimis of total production in some key products.[16] Further, they argued that, given the current high international prices, it did not make sense to compare current buying prices to the external reference prices that were defined under the AoA as those prevailing in 1986–1988. In fact, if purchases were made at administered prices that closely tracked current world prices (and therefore would not be distortionary in an economic sense), the AoA comparison with the 1986–1988 values would still show (largely imaginary) margins of market price support, as can be inferred when comparing the nominal values in the different columns of Table 9.1 (the indexes in the table are just a general reference because the FERP must be defined by each individual product in the respective country).

16 This limit does not affect other options, such as the rest of the Green Box measures, Blue Box measures of support, and, for developing countries only, those considered in Article 6.2.

Based on these concerns, the language proposed by the G33 exempted the difference between administered prices and the FERPs from the obligation of being included in the AMS when developing-country governments have purchased products for food security stocks (paragraph 3) and domestic aid (paragraph 4) from a specific type of producer—those that are "low income or resource poor" (LIRP; this category is already considered by the AoA for some special treatment in Article 6.2).[17]

This approach generated two basic objections. First, it appeared to go against the conditions established for the Green Box (Annex 2, paragraph 1), particularly the second basic criteria (point b) which indicates that "the support in question shall not have the effect of providing price support" (Annex 2, paragraph 1). The G33 proposal clearly allowed for the provision of price support, at least to a certain type of producer; therefore there was the fear that once a loophole was created in the Green Box general criteria and conditions, anything could happen with the rest of the programs listed there. Furthermore, other developing countries were concerned about the leeway already granted under the current Annex 2 to provide income support that is, in theory (but not clearly in fact), decoupled from prices. According to this objection, offering price support to LIRP producers would significantly undermine the possibility of disciplining those other Green Box measures that are currently used mostly by industrialized countries and that may create more than minimal trade distortions.[18]

Second, some countries worried that the stocks allegedly accumulated for food security reasons would end up being sold on world markets, affecting their own domestic or export markets. WTO members that provide price support to LIRP producers could potentially accumulate products in excess of domestic consumption and then decide to sell those surpluses in external markets to help finance the program's fiscal cost.[19] In fact, during 2011–2012 and 2012–2013,

17 Note that the relevant section of Article 6.2 of the AoA says to refer to "investment subsidies," which are "generally available" to LIRPs. An issue to be considered is whether "generally available" means only for LIRP producers. Also, the wording refers to "low-income *or* resource-poor producers" (emphasis added), which seems to expand the scope of the category when compared to "low-income *and* resource-poor producers" (Lars Brink, personal communication; emphasis added).

18 Some developing countries, such as China, have been fast increasing their use of that type of support.

19 In general, any public stockholding programs involving administrated prices, or at least price management within some range, may require the use of variable trade policy instruments (such as, export subsidies or restrictions for exported commodities or import duties adjustments for imported commodities), as demonstrated in the previous version of the EU Common Agricultural Policy (CAP). These operations may create large negative effects for their trade partners if there are no strict rules limiting those operations.

about 20 percent of Indian wheat exports were drawn from public stocks.[20] Negotiators therefore looked at other options, including the possibility of changing the 1986–1988 FERPs, adjusting the definition of the production eligible to receive administered prices, and imposing a temporary standstill to challenges under the WTO Dispute Settlement Unit (DSU) that may arise if a country breached its allowed levels of domestic support because of government procurement of products for food security stocks at administered prices.

However, changing the FERPs would have opened an entirely new set of difficult issues (such as the valuation of the commitments by countries with declared domestic support in the base year). The notion of eligible production, as noted earlier, was also a key variable because, according to the AoA, the gap between the administered price and the FERP for 1986–1988 must be multiplied by the quantity of all production that is eligible to be bought at the administered prices. The interpretation of the term was clarified by the dispute about Korean beef (WTO 2000b); although the ruling left out other options to define eligible production (discussed below), this line of negotiation was considered too complicated to be sorted out in time for the Bali Ministerial Declaration. In the end, the peace clause was implemented in Bali as an interim solution.[21]

The Bali Ministerial Decision (WT/MIN[13]/W/10)

The draft of the Ministerial Decision establishing the peace clause went through several iterations before a final text was approved (although, as the July 2014 dispute in the General Council showed, India was still not completely in agreement). To understand these disagreements, it is useful to distinguish three different issues: (1) the substance and coverage of the peace clause, (2) the conditions for its application, and (3) the period and conditions under

---

20 Some countries, such as Pakistan, argued during the Bali negotiations that India was exporting rice from food stocks, thus affecting global rice markets and their own domestic markets and food security. India has become an important world exporter of rice in recent years (see Chapter 8). However, it could be argued that the rice exported by India and the rice used in its food security stocks are of different qualities (basmati rice being the exported product and common rice the one for domestic consumption); therefore, in this line of analysis, the postulated impact on global markets of domestic food stocks would be nil. However, Dorosh and Rashid (2012) showed that rice prices in Bangladesh and subsidized prices for that product from India's public stocks appear highly correlated. This correlation was the result of the operation of private-sector importers that helped stabilize the operation of the rice market in Bangladesh to the benefit of poor consumers but with negative impact on producers.

21 There is a nontrivial difference between *temporary* (which seems to imply a specific date as deadline) and *interim* (which does not necessarily have a specific termination date). Although in common parlance, people tend to refer to the Ministerial Decision as a "temporary" solution, the decision uses the word *interim* (Lars Brink, personal communication).

which the peace clause is operational. The original language of the peace clause regarding the substance and coverage (point 1) and conditions (point 2) did not change much during the negotiations in Bali. What did change was the definition of the period during which the peace clause was operational (point 3).

SUBSTANCE AND COVERAGE

The basic point of the peace clause is defined in paragraph 2 of the Ministerial Decision; it states that WTO members cannot challenge developing-country members regarding compliance with their obligations not to exceed the AMS (Article 6.3) or the de minimis (Article 7.2b) when all the following circumstances apply:

- If it is "support provided for traditional staple food crops in pursuance of public stockholding programs for food security purposes."
- If the programs existed as of the date of the decision.
- If those programs are consistent with the rest of the criteria of Annex 2 for food security stocks (other than the issue of price support; see the earlier discussion).
- If they comply with other conditions established in the Ministerial Decision (analyzed below).[22]

One footnote to the Bali Ministerial Decision indicates that if and when a permanent solution is found, it will apply to all developing countries. Another footnote mentions that developing countries can initiate new programs that comply with Annex 2, paragraph 3; however, as mentioned earlier, only programs existing as of the date of the decision are covered by the peace clause.[23]

---

22 The complete language is as follows:

> 2. In the interim, until a permanent solution is found, and provided that the conditions set out below are met, Members shall refrain from challenging through the WTO Dispute Settlement Mechanism, compliance of a developing Member with its obligations under Articles 6.3 and 7.2 (b) of the AoA in relation to support provided for traditional staple food crops in pursuance of public stockholding programs for food security purposes existing as of the date of this Decision, that are consistent with the criteria of paragraph 3, footnote 5, and footnote 5 & 6 of Annex 2 to the AoA when the developing Member complies with the terms of this Decision.

23 Matthews (2014) identified 16 developing countries (under the self-designation permitted in the WTO and GATT before) that had public food stocks at the time of the decision: Botswana, Brazil, China, Costa Rica, India, Indonesia, Israel, Kenya, Republic of Korea, Namibia, Nepal, Pakistan, Philippines, Saudi Arabia, South Africa, and Sri Lanka. Note the presence of Israel and Republic of Korea, which, according to the WTO rules, have defined themselves as developing countries for the purposes of the AoA.

The new language may have somewhat changed the product scope. The language in the original draft referred to the products bought as part of the food security program that can thus be covered by the peace clause as "traditional staple food crops" (note the word *crops*, suggesting that livestock products are not included). The new language agreed upon in Bali includes a footnote by the word *crops* that says, "This term refers to primary agricultural products that are predominant staples in the traditional diet of a developing Member." This definition can be interpreted as a tightening of the definition of *staple food crops* through the use of the word *predominant* (which suggests that some significant percentage of consumption must be used to determine what crops are covered). However, it could also be argued that by using the word *products* rather than *crops*, this change may have expanded coverage to include other, noncrop products. Another question remains as to whether *primary agricultural products* is different from the *basic agricultural products* in the agreement's definition of the AMS.

CONDITIONS

The Ministerial Decision establishes additional conditions in paragraphs 3, 4, and 5 for those developing countries that currently operate food stock programs and that want to be protected from legal challenges by the peace clause. Those conditions did not change from the original draft and are in addition to the relevant conditions in Annex 2, paragraph 3 of the AoA. To benefit from this decision, developing countries must do the following:

1. Notify the Committee on Agriculture "that it is exceeding or is at risk of exceeding either or both of its aggregate measurement of support (AMS) limits (the Member's Bound Total AMS or the de minimis level)" (paragraph 3 a).
2. Stay current on notifications of its domestic support (paragraph 3 b).
3. Provide timely information regarding each public stockholding program maintained for food security purposes, plus other related information according to a template included in the annex of the decision (paragraph 3 c and d).
4. Ensure that stocks procured under food security programs do not distort trade or adversely affect the food security of other members (this latter reference was also an addition to the original language, which referred only to trade distortions) (paragraph 4).

5. Make sure that the potential increase in domestic support in excess of the allowed levels is only to the amount notified to the Committee on Agriculture (see the first point mentioned above) (paragraph 5).
6. Accept requests for consultations by any other WTO member countries that may be interested in the operation of the notified public stockholding program or programs (paragraph 6).

The decision also instructs the Committee on Agriculture to monitor the information submitted under this decision (paragraph 7) and indicates that WTO members must agree to establish a work program in which the committee can make recommendations for a permanent solution. The recommendations for a solution should be made no later than the eleventh Ministerial Conference. Advances will be reported to the General Council during the tenth Ministerial Conference (paragraphs 8, 9, and 10).

PERIOD OF APPLICATION OF THE PEACE CLAUSE

In the original draft the peace clause had a specific end—the tenth WTO Ministerial (about two years from Bali, considering the usual time between Ministerial meetings); after that time the clause would lapse and WTO members would decide on next steps. With the final language "members agree to put in place an interim mechanism . . . and to negotiate on an agreement for a permanent solution . . . for adoption by the eleventh Ministerial Conference" (paragraph 1). The new language thus changed the period covered by the peace clause (the eleventh Ministerial would take place four years after the Bali Ministerial); the peace clause will also remain in place "until a permanent solution is found," which changed the conditions to end this mechanism as well.

However, there was still some ambiguity in the Bali text. On the one hand, it ostensibly defined a deadline (the eleventh Ministerial), but on the other, it referred to the peace clause as being in effect until a "permanent solution is found," without specifying when that may happen. By the first interpretation, the day of reckoning was extended from the two years in the original language to the four years in the final text; after that, the protection of the peace clause would lapse, and challenges in the dispute settlement mechanism may take place.[24] The second interpretation, on the other hand, strengthened the protection of the countries involved to the extent that the country would avoid

24 WTO members could still mount challenges under other legal texts.

challenges under the AoA until a permanent solution was found. This ambiguity was clarified in the General Council of November 2014.

The Decision at the November General Council (WT/L/939)

As noted, the breakdown in the WTO process at the July 2014 General Council was related to India's discomfort with this ambiguity regarding whether the peace clause was operational for a specified time limit (determined to be until the eleventh Ministerial Conference, that is, about four years) or for an undefined period until a permanent solution is found. The latter was India's preferred interpretation, and this is what was approved in the Ministerial Decision on Public Stockholding for Food Security Purposes of November 27, 2014 (document WT/L/939). The first paragraph of this document states:

> Until a permanent solution is agreed and adopted, and provided that the conditions set out in paragraphs 3 to 6 of the Bali Decision are met, Members shall not challenge through the WTO Dispute Settlement Mechanism compliance of a developing Member with its obligations under Articles 6.3 and 7.2(b) of the Agreement on Agriculture (AoA) in relation to support provided for traditional staple food crops in pursuance of public stockholding programmes for food security purposes existing as of the date of the Bali Decision, that are consistent with the criteria of paragraph 3, footnote 5, and footnote 5 and 6 of Annex 2 to the AoA.

To make things even clearer, the second paragraph indicates that

> if a permanent solution for the issue of public stockholding for food security purposes is not agreed and adopted by the eleventh Ministerial Conference, the mechanism referred to in paragraph 1 of the Bali Decision, as set out in paragraph 1 of this decision, shall continue to be in place until a permanent solution is agreed and adopted.

With this language the "peace clause" is operational until a "permanent solution" is "agreed and adopted." Note that the permanent solution has to be not only "agreed" upon but "adopted" as well. Note, also, that under the WTO's consensus approach, potential solutions may be blocked until there is one that all countries consider acceptable.

Finally, it must be noted that the peace clause refers only to challenges under the AoA, not to other legal texts, such as the Agreement on Subsidies and Countervailing Measures (ASCM), which may be the basis for other disputes. The decision also urges that "the negotiations on a permanent solution on the issue of public stockholding for food security purposes shall be pursued on priority" (paragraph 3). To ensure that this happens, it sets out a proposed deadline (December 31, 2015), defines the institutional framework for the negotiations (the Committee on Agriculture in Special Session, "in dedicated sessions and in an accelerated time-frame"), and clarifies that these talks must take place as "distinct from the agriculture negotiations under the Doha Development Agenda." In paragraph 5 it establishes that the "General Council shall regularly review the progress of these dedicated sessions." While the Bali Ministerial Decision instructed WTO members to establish a work program in the Committee on Agriculture (CoA) to make recommendations for a permanent solution no later than the eleventh Ministerial Conference (paragraphs 8, 9, and 10), the November decision shortens the timeframe by about two years (December 2015) and creates a distinct institutional track (the CoA in special sessions) and a separate conceptual negotiating framework (different from the Doha Negotiations on Agriculture).

The Ministerial Decision at Nairobi (WT/MIN[15]/44—WT/L/979)

At the Nairobi Ministerial the ministers reaffirmed the General Council Decision of November 27, 2014 (WT/L/939), thus providing legal backing to the text. The Ministerial Decision also reiterated that the negotiations will be held in the Committee on Agriculture in Special Session and separate from the agriculture negotiations under the Doha Development Agenda. Considering that the Nairobi Ministerial did not find consensus on the continuation of the negotiations within the DDA, the language allows the talks about public food stocks to proceed whether or not other negotiations take place.

Final Comments

First, the peace clause does not solve the basic debate surrounding the use of public stocks for food security reasons, but now that the ambiguity of the 2013 Bali Decision has been eliminated, it is clear that the peace clause will be operational until a permanent solution is agreed upon and adopted. As noted, it remains to be seen whether challenges under other legal texts, such as the Agreement on Subsidies and Countervailing Measures, could be mounted by countries believing that they are affected by the operation of governmental purchases under this scheme.[25] Second, the peace clause's notification

---

25 Whatever the legal issues involved, there is always the public relations issue of challenging a developing country on a program that is allegedly aimed at helping the poor.

and transparency requirements are not mere formalities when one considers that many WTO members—including India and other developed and developing countries—have usually been behind schedule in their notifications under the current AoA obligations (see the discussion in Orden, Blandford, and Josling [2011] in general and Gopinath [2012] for the case of India). To invoke the peace clause, therefore, WTO members will have to complete their notifications of domestic support and be open to consultations and questions regarding the actual operation of their food stock programs. Doing so would allow for more transparency and would facilitate closer scrutiny and monitoring of the different domestic support programs in countries using the peace clause option.

Third, in general, the debate has centered on the prices at which food products for food security stocks are procured (which could be done by subsidizing producers through "administered prices"), rather than on the prices at which those food products are sold to domestic consumers (which could be done by subsidizing those products through below-market prices). However, these two aspects have been conflated in some discussions, confusing the terms of the debate. It should be clear that WTO members can provide subsidized food to their own population under paragraph 4 of Annex 2 of the AoA (more on this below). Finally, finding a permanent solution is now on an accelerated time frame and separate institutional and conceptual frameworks. The WTO work program in the coming years will therefore include activities dedicated to finding a permanent solution. This solution could take multiple different forms, including some of the options discussed in the pre-Bali negotiations that were discarded because of a lack of time to complete adequate negotiations. The next section discusses these possible options.

Potential Options for a "Permanent Solution"

This section discusses the different legal options available to address the food security objectives for both producers and consumers, starting with those approaches that are already available using current legal texts and then moving to others that may require further negotiations to change or expand the language in the AoA.[26] The focus here is only on what can be done in legal terms under the WTO Agreement, without judging whether those options make sense in economic or social terms (for this discussion, see Chapter 8).

26 Further analysis can be found in Díaz-Bonilla (2013b), Matthews (2014), Montemayor (2014), and Glauber (2016).

Domestic Food Aid

It is clear that any developing country can provide subsidized food to its own population under paragraph 4 of Annex 2 of the AoA. The claim by some observers (see, for instance, OWINFS 2013) that it is unfair for the United States to have a food stamp program while denying India the right to have a similar program is thus mistaken. In fact, the combined footnote 5 and 6 indicates "the provision of foodstuffs at subsidized prices with the objective of meeting food requirements of urban and rural poor in developing countries on a regular basis at reasonable prices shall be considered to be in conformity with the provisions of this paragraph." This footnote is in Annex 2, paragraphs 3 and 4, which means it covers both sales from food security stocks and any other sale of subsidized food by developing countries to help the urban or rural poor. Therefore, the question is not whether a country can give subsidized food to poor and needy people, which they can under the AoA; the question is how governments may procure that food. More generally, the issue is whether a country's policies to support food stocks may affect that country's trading partners; there should be some type of guarantee that such programs will not lead to ad hoc adjustments in export and import policies that generate instability and other negative externalities for the rest of the world. The following options thus focus on the purchasing side of public food stocks.

Buy at Market Prices

One possibility is for countries to build food security stocks simply by buying food products at *market prices*; this approach is compliant with Annex 2, paragraph 3, of the AoA. The United States, Brazil, and other countries do buy food for their domestic food security programs at market prices. Buying at market prices will not further increase the program's procurement costs (although other operational costs and the sales subsidy still remain). In addition, some countries, such as Brazil, have determined that a specific percentage of the food purchased must come from small farmers as defined in national legislation (Krivonos 2013), which is one of the aspects highlighted by the G33's original proposal focusing on LIRP producers. A country buying food at market prices to build public food stock could decide that the purchases must come from LIRP producers. India, on the other hand, uses *administered prices* announced in advance by the government, which may trigger Annex 2, paragraph 3, footnote 5. Those administered prices, however, seem to have been in line with market prices, at least until 2012 (Hoda and Gulati 2013). A country that buys significantly above market prices and then wants to sell below market prices to poor and vulnerable populations will soon get into fiscal difficulties. However, although selling at below-market prices imposes a fiscal cost, it may still be justified in the case of assisting the poor and needy (if properly targeted), while buying above market prices will help mostly large producers that have more product to sell.

It should be noted that, as discussed in Chapter 8, even when buying at market prices, such programs offer some support to farmers compared to the counterfactual without the domestic food aid programs; in this latter case, poor consumers would not represent the same level of actual demand. With the program, however, the recipients of food aid increase their effective demand as actual consumers of food through the intermediation of the domestic food aid program. Furthermore, that impact is reinforced if the food stocks are used annually and are rotated as part of social safety nets or other public systems of food distribution targeting the poor and needy.[27]

Provide Indicative Prices, Use Trade Measures to Guide Prices, but Still Buy at Market Prices

In the absence of futures markets in many developing countries, farmers' expectations about market conditions, and their subsequent production decisions, are often based on preannounced government prices (or "administered prices"). If governments simply buy at spot market prices without previously announcing future buying prices, they may fail to provide forward guidance to farmers and there may not be other mechanisms to provide adequate information to form expectations; therefore governments in these conditions may conclude that they need to announce "administered prices" in advance to producers. However, if the aim is simply to give producers some future anchor for their expectations and calculations, this can be done without necessarily committing to buying all or part of the production.[28] Similarly, even if government purchases do occur, they can be done at market prices. Furthermore,

27 It should be further noted that an income redistribution program with discounted food vouchers for poor consumers would also lead to higher demand and therefore higher prices for farmers when compared with the counterfactual of no program, without the government having to physically intermediate the purchase of food and the distribution of food aid (as, for instance, in the case of food stamps in the United States).

28 An example would be the approach applied by COTRISA (Comercializadora de Trigo S.A.), a public agency in Chile whose role is to ensure adequate functioning of the country's wheat market. The country is a net importer but also produces about three-quarters of its total domestic wheat consumption. The government estimates and announces an import parity price, and COTRISA stands ready to buy or sell if the domestic price deviates much from the government estimated value. Usually COTRISA does not have to actually trade in the wheat market; the perceived possibility that such intervention may happen appears to be enough to align domestic prices with the market-based price guidance provided by the government.

in the case of developing countries that have room between the bound and applied tariffs, if the country is an importer, the government can use those tariffs to ensure that the domestic price follows the preannounced price without violating WTO commitments, as long as the prices stay below the bound tariffs. Such an approach must consider some legal and economic aspects. In legal terms, the changes in tariffs under the bound levels must take into account the WTO case against Chile regarding its "price band" system, which clarified the options and limits to those practices under the current agreements (WTO 2007). In economic terms, trying to achieve some desired level of domestic prices through changes in import tariffs will force a larger adjustment in price and quantities in the world market than would have been the case without such a manipulation of tariffs, with potentially negative effects on other countries (Bouët and Laborde 2010).[29]

Provide Indicative Prices, Buy at Market Prices, but Offer Income Support using Annex 4 of the AoA

A government may (1) announce an indicative price to give producers an anchor for their expectations, (2) inform producers that there will be public purchases at market prices, and (3) inform producers that the difference will be covered if the market price ends up being below the indicative price. It could be argued that this approach would fall under the Equivalent Measure of Support (EMS), Annex 4 of the AoA's "Domestic Support: Calculation of Equivalent Measurement of Support." Paragraph 1 of this Annex indicates that "equivalent measurements of support shall be calculated in respect of all basic agricultural products where market price support as defined in Annex 3 exists but for which calculation of this component of the AMS is not practicable." Paragraph 2 states that "equivalent measurements of market price support shall be made using the applied administered price and the quantity of production eligible to receive that price or, where this is not practicable, on budgetary outlays used to maintain the producer price."

29 A related current discussion has focused mainly on export taxes. However, there is a symmetry of effects for the following pairs of trade actions (when equivalently scaled): (1) increasing export taxes or reducing import taxes, (2) reducing export subsidies or increasing import subsidies, (3) reducing production subsidies or increasing consumption subsidies, (4) using export tax differentials or import tax differentials (tariff escalation), (5) imposing an export quota or eliminating an import quota, and (6) an export ban or anticipatory hoarding by an importer. Even though all those measures that try to stabilize domestic prices may lead to destabilizing effects on world prices and may thus affect other countries, they are treated differently (or not at all) in the current WTO framework (see Díaz-Bonilla 2013a).

The key point here is that using actual budgetary outlays would amount to a measure of support that is usually far smaller than what is determined applying the normal method (that is using market prices, administrative prices, and the eligible production), significantly reducing the possibility of violating the de minimis (or other allowed maximum for domestic support). A central issue in this approach would be to show that the normal calculation method explained in Annex 3 "is not practicable" and therefore that the EMS approach based on budgetary outlays can be used (paragraph 2 in Annex 4). It remains a question, then, as to why the calculation of the MPS in the procurement of food security stocks at administered prices is "not practicable."

Define Eligible Production in a Way That Focuses More Closely on Quantities Actually Bought

The calculation of the MPS that has to be counted in the AMS includes both prices and quantities. In the previous examples, procurement has taken place at the market price, thus complying with Annex 2, paragraph 3. However, if the government is using administered prices (APs) rather than market prices, then footnote 5 kicks in and the AP must be compared to the FERP of 1986–1988. If the AP is higher than the FERP, this positive gap has to be multiplied by the "eligible quantity" (not the quantity actually bought) and then compared with the de minimis. If the former value is more than the de minimis, it must be counted as part of the AMS in its entirety. Obviously, if the gap between the AP and the FERP is more than 10 percent above the market price used to value current production and if the eligible production is the total production, then the de minimis will be exceeded. If a developing country has a final AMS commitment (the FBTAMS), then the whole amount (not only the value of production bought) will have to be counted as part of the product-specific AMS and will have to be compared to, and must not exceed, the FBTAMS. If the country does not have a FBTAMS, then it is prohibited by Article 7.b of the AoA from exceeding the de minimis.

The key here is the definition of *eligible production*. This topic was clarified in the Korean beef case (WTO 2000b), which considered claims that the Korean government was violating the AoA by only using the amount of production it actually bought in its WTO notifications, when the amount of eligible production defined by the government was larger. By not notifying the total eligible production but rather the smaller amount that was actually purchased, the value counted within the AMS was reduced. This practice was challenged, and the WTO DSM ruled that the Korean government should notify the production defined as eligible and not the amount actually purchased. Because of this ruling, some observers appear to assume that *eligible* production is always the *total* production. However, this interpretation is not correct. Because the Korean government had established a maximum amount to be bought, the *eligible production* was less than the total production. Therefore the ruling in the case considered only the capped amount and not the total production. The appellate body left open the possibility that eligible production can be more limited in cases in which the eligibility criteria identifies a specific region or in which there is another type of limit on the quantity purchased.[30] In fact, in an example of what would be the appropriate calculation, the appellate body uses only up to the maximum amount the Korean government said it was going to buy as *eligible quantity*, which, as mentioned, was less than the total production but more than the amount that it actually bought.

So if a government plans to buy, say, 30 percent of production (perhaps because that is the amount needed to run a food distribution system for the poor and needy), it may declare only that volume as eligible production, which would be far less than total production. Typically, developing countries running food stocks buy only a fraction of total production. For example, Montemayor (2014) shows that purchases of rice and wheat stay largely below one-third of total production in the five countries analyzed between 2008 and 2011. Hoda and Gulati (2013) estimate that in India, procurement for rice was, on average, about 32 percent of total production; for wheat, it was close to 27 percent during 2007–2008 and 2010–2011 (these are national averages, but the percentage varies significantly across states). Governments can make

30 The relevant wording of the appellate body report in paragraph 827 reads:

> "In general, with market price support programmes, all producers of the products which are subject to the market price support mechanism enjoy the benefit of an assurance that their products can be marketed at least at the support price. Therefore, the minimum price support will be available to all marketable production of the type and quality to which the administered price support programme relates, including where actual market prices are above the administered minimum price level. There may, of course, be circumstances where eligible production may be less than total marketable production, as for example where the minimum price support is only available to producers in certain disadvantaged regions. Another possible example would be where there is a legislatively predetermined, non-discretionary, limitation on the quantity of marketable production that a governmental intervention agency could take off the market at the administered price in any year. In the latter case, the particular design and operation of the price support mechanism would have to be taken into account in determining eligible production, since even governmental purchases at a level below the legislatively predetermined quantity limit could, depending on market conditions, suffice to maintain market prices at above the minimum levels for all marketable production. Hence, with these qualifications, eligible production for the purposes of calculating the market price support component of current support should comprise the total marketable production of all producers which is eligible to benefit from the market price support, even though the proportion of production which is actually purchased by a governmental agency may be relatively small or even nil."

such quantity limits clear in the definition of *eligible production*. It should be noted, though, that the panel added the qualification that in such a case "the particular design and operation of the price support mechanism would have to be taken into account in determining eligible production."

In the G33 proposal, purchases were limited to food produced by "low-income or resource poor producers" (LIRPs) in Article 6.2. The appellate body in the Korean beef case also used language related to the eligibility of certain producers in disadvantaged regions. Therefore, another way to ensure that eligible production is less than total production is to require that it come from LIRP producers. The issue then becomes how to define that category of producers and how to establish the operational safeguards to ensure that the production effectively comes from that group.[31] One possible way to identify the farmers who would qualify for assistance is to apply the usual poverty line used for international comparisons of US$1 (or US$2) a day or to use a relative measure of poverty within the country (for instance, producers with less than 40 percent of national income per capita; Díaz-Bonilla, Thomas, and Robinson 2003). In practice, the use of the LIRP category in WTO notifications seems to have been relatively elastic and variable over time, even within the same country. For instance, India has moved from declaring about 80 percent of its producers as LIRP in the WTO notifications for 1995–1997 (based on a survey that showed that 80 percent of the farmers had fewer than 2 hectares) to basically considering all of its producers in that category (based on a subsequent survey that calculated that close to 99 percent of Indian producers were LIRPs; Gopinath 2012). Such an extension of the LIRP concept may test the limits of the notion that support should only be given to a specific type of producer.[32]

(Re)Define Fixed External Reference Price in US Dollars or in Special Drawing Rights

Now we move to the other variable in the equation used to calculate MPS: the fixed external reference price. Article 1(a)(ii) of the AoA indicates that the current AMS has to be "calculated *in accordance* with the provisions of Annex 3 of this Agreement and *taking into account* the constituent data and methodology used in the tables of supporting material incorporated by reference

31 Obviously, the administrative controls needed to ensure that purchases from the type of farmers targeted are not trivial. An (imperfect) proxy to those controls may be to establish a fixed cap on the quantity that can be bought from each individual farmer.

32 As noted before, Article 6.2 refers to "investment subsidies," which are "generally available" to "low-income or resource-poor producers," and therefore a point to be considered is whether "generally available" means *only* for LIRP producers.

in Part IV of the Member's Schedule" (emphasis added). Annex 3, in turn, indicates in paragraph 9 that "the fixed external reference price shall be based on the years 1986 to 1988 and shall generally be the average f.o.b. [freight on board] unit value for the basic agricultural product concerned in a net exporting country and the average c.i.f. [cost, insurance, and freight] unit value for the basic agricultural product concerned in a net importing country in the base period." In the tables and calculations submitted as constituent data and methodology, some countries presented the FERP in domestic currency, whereas others presented it in a foreign currency. This difference occurred because the Annex does not specify which currency is to be used; the only requirements are that the FERP be "fixed," "external," and refer to the base period of 1986–1988.

For example, in a background paper prepared by the WTO Secretariat (WTO 2000a), one example shows the use of FERPs in dollars.[33] This document notes that it obviously makes a big difference if the nominal variables for the commitments on domestic support and the relevant parameters (such as the external reference price) have been originally notified in the domestic currency of the reporting country or in a foreign currency. In the latter case, there is an automatic adjustment for domestic inflation to the extent that the devaluation of the exchange rate follows the evolution of internal prices. Certainly, considering that developing countries usually have a domestic inflation rate and a pace of devaluation that make 1986–1988 values in domestic currency outdated, those that notify the FERPs in foreign currency (say, US dollars) will have fewer problems comparing current APs with the FERPs than if they notify the FERPs in their domestic currency. It is true that given the current high commodity prices in nominal US dollars (see Table 9.1), a 1986–1988 FERP in that currency will still show a gap with current APs, even if the latter follow market prices. But that gap would be substantially higher for most developing countries if the comparison were between current APs and 1986–1988 FERPs in domestic currency. This is why some countries, including India, switched the original 1986–1988 FERPs from domestic currency to US dollars. The FERP is still fixed (in US dollars), external, and refers to the 1986–1988 base period, but it is now no longer affected by the impact of devaluation.

It has been argued, however, that this switch may violate at least two WTO obligations (Brink 2014). First, because the "constituent data and

33 It should be noted that documents by the Secretariat are just opinions by the WTO international staff and are not meant to interpret the legal texts negotiated by the WTO members.

methodology" was part of the commitments and was presented in domestic currency, such currency denomination cannot be changed afterward. As also clarified by the Korean beef case, there is a hierarchy of obligations: the AMS has to be "calculated *in accordance* with the provisions of Annex 3 of this Agreement and *taking into account* the constituent data and methodology" (emphasis added). The appellate body in the Korean beef case noted that the ordinary meaning of *accordance* is "agreement, conformity, harmony," while *taking into account* is defined as "take into consideration, notice." Therefore the appellate body held that Article 1(a)(ii) accorded "higher priority" to the provisions of Annex 3 than to the "constituent data and methodology" contained in a member's schedule and that the term *in accordance with* reflects a more rigorous standard than the term *taking into account.* Therefore, by using the equivalent in US dollars of the 1986–1988 FERP that had been presented in domestic currency in the members' schedule, the constituent data and methodology has been "taken into account"; in fact, it is the same economic value for the reference year. To insist that the FERP must be denominated in the same currency as presented originally in the constituent data and methodology would be to use the other criteria ("in accordance"), which the panel indicated was not the standard for the supporting data.

The second objection is that if the FERP that was presented originally in domestic currency is transformed into foreign currency for the base period and then is transformed back every year into domestic currency to be compared with the respective annual AP (also in domestic currency), then the FERP is no longer "fixed" (that is, it would change every year in *domestic currency* according to the annual exchange rate). However, this objection assumes that the APs and FERPs will be presented every year in domestic currency, when it is also possible (1) to redefine the respective FERP into foreign currency (which is maintained fixed), (2) to transform the corresponding AP into the equivalent foreign currency every year using the annual exchange rate, or (3) to calculate the gap in foreign currency (as in example 5 of WTO [2000b], mentioned earlier).

An interesting exercise by Montemayor (2014) uses the case of five countries and several staple products to estimate whether those countries and products would stay within their actual de minimis under different assumptions of adjustments in key variables—basically, variations of the definitions of FERPs and eligible quantity. The simulations show that if eligible production is defined as being capped by some fixed quantity (that is, if the government announces purchases of a certain quantity for food stocks or only from LIRP producers), which is then not exceeded, *and* if the 1986–1988 FERP is defined in US dollars, then all cases analyzed stay below the de minimis. Therefore, applying the adjustments discussed in this and the previous section would go a long way toward solving most of the problems that developing countries may encounter in complying with their WTO obligations.

Although changing the 1986–1988 FERP to US dollars is one way to deal with the differential inflation between developing countries and the United States, there are two other aspects to be considered: one is the erosion of the value of the US dollar due to US inflation and other factors; and the other is the influence of the US dollar on commodity prices. As discussed in Chapter 8, high prices may reflect the well-known fact that nominal global commodity prices (which are usually quoted in US dollars) move in opposite directions from the US dollar (Mundell 2002). In other words, if the dollar appreciates against other currencies, then the dollar price of commodities declines and vice versa. Therefore, part of the reason why global commodity prices in nominal dollars have been high in recent years is because the US dollar has been dropping in value against other currencies during that period.

In fact, as shown in Chapter 8, if the food price index is measured in nominal Special Drawing Rights (SDRs) instead of US dollars, the differences shown in Table 9.1 above the prices prevailing in 1986–1988 are significantly reduced (see Figure 8.2 in Chapter 8; the average for 2013–2015 in nominal US dollars would be 55 percent above the 1986–1988 average, while measured in SDRs, it would be higher by 33 percent, which is still higher than the reference period but significantly less than it is in US dollars).[34] Therefore, using the same reasoning as before, an option that would make values even more comparable across periods, smoothing out both inflation in developing countries and fluctuations in the US dollar, would be to define the FERPs in SDRs for the base period (which would be fixed, external, and from 1986 to 1988).

Consider Adjustments Due to Domestic Inflation

Estimates for India by Hoda and Gulati (2013, see Table A-4) show that administered prices for wheat and rice in that country have been largely below the 1986–1988 FERPs in domestic currency if the calculations take inflation into account. Hoda and Gulati (2013) justify the use of inflation-adjusted measures based on Article 18, paragraph 4 of the AoA, which says: "In the review process, Members shall give due consideration to the influence of

34 As discussed in Chapter 8, the SDR is an international reserve asset based on a basket of key international currencies. Therefore the market value of the SDR is more stable than each currency separately.

excessive rates of inflation on the ability of any Member to abide by its domestic support commitments." Other analysts, however, believe this text does not allow individual members to consider "excess inflation" and adjust their notifications to it (see Brink 2014). Rather, they argue that Article 18.4 should be read literally as guidance to the rest of the WTO members so that those other countries reviewing the notifications (and not the member presenting the data) are the ones to "give due consideration to the influence of excessive rates of inflation" on the ability "to abide by its domestic support commitments."

However, *excessive inflation* has not been defined; therefore it is not clear how WTO members could take that phenomenon into account in the notifications presented by others, let alone how they should adjust for it in their own notifications. These questions have not been raised in the DSM; as a consequence, the proper interpretation of those concepts remains unsettled. Several factors can be noted regarding this issue—some that seem to lend some support in favor of allowing for inflationary adjustments and some that seem to go in the opposite direction. First, some countries have used constant prices in the tables and calculations submitted as constituent data and methodology. For instance, Mexico used "constant 1991 pesos" for its Bound Total AMS. Again, Annex 3 does not specify which currency should be used to value the commitments and, apparently, no one has contested the use of constant prices (that is, inflation adjusted) in the example cited. Therefore, conceivably, if a country had notified its FERP in constant 1986–1988 domestic prices, it would be legally valid to use the inflation adjustments such as those used in Hoda and Gulati (2013) for India.

Second, another document by the WTO Secretariat (WTO 1999) indicates in paragraph 43 that "the advice consistently provided to delegations has been that, for the purposes of the Review Process and Article 18.4 of the Agreement, the relevant Domestic Support (DS) Tables should be submitted concurrently on both an unadjusted and an inflation-adjusted basis." However, as mentioned before, the opinions of the WTO Secretariat cannot officially interpret WTO legal texts. In fact, the background paper prepared by the WTO Secretariat on inflation and exchange rate (G/AG/NG/S/19, October 23, 2000) presents an example that uses a FERP in domestic prices but that does not adjust for inflation.

A conclusion one can draw from these factors is that determining whether a member is in compliance by using inflation adjustment methods that are simply based on how that member defined its nominal variables in the base period (domestic currency, foreign currency, or, as in the case of some countries, constant domestic prices) appears to lack a proper economic rationale.

However, from a legal viewpoint, some analysts and negotiators feel that countries have had plenty of time to consider how to present their commitments and that once they have presented them in a particular way, they cannot keep changing them. Still, the need to "take into account" the "constituent data and methodology used in the tables of supporting material," but not necessarily to be "in accordance" with them, may require further clarification.

It has also been noted (Matthews 2014) that if the objective of the WTO disciplines is to eliminate distortionary practices, then the approach of defining the commitments associated with the AMS and related variables in nominal terms helps reduce or eliminate trade-distorting practices over time simply through inflationary erosion. In this view, recasting commitments in inflation-adjusted terms would thwart the implicit correction of undesirable trade practices simply by the evolution of inflation. However, it can be argued that what may be a gentle adjustment process for industrialized countries with low inflation rates could become a drastic cut in inflation-prone developing countries, without much of an economic or social rationale to justify those reductions in agricultural support. One final point is that the de minimis, which is calculated using the current value of production, automatically adjusts for inflation. Thus there is an automatic, but partial, built-in safeguard against inflation that operates for all countries (see WTO 2000a).

Clarify the Link between Administered Prices and Market Prices

The options discussed thus far have focused on adjusting some of the variables for the calculation of the MPS, or the use of the EMS of Annex 4. The alternative presented now, which builds on Díaz-Bonilla (2013b), takes a different approach. This section starts by noting that the estimates for India by Hoda and Gulati (2013, Table A-4) show that administered prices for wheat and rice in that country have been largely below both international market prices and domestic market prices, in addition to being below inflation-adjusted FERPs in domestic currency.[35] Figure 9.1 and Figure 9.2 show the international price, the domestic price, and MPSs for rice and wheat, as calculated by Hoda and Gulati (2013).

In economic terms it seems odd that if products for food security stocks are purchased at prices that track market prices, such a purchase price is still presumed to be distortionary simply because it is called "administered price"

35 It can be argued that those are average annual prices, when in fact (1) the government buys only during a specific period of time and (2) during that period the administered price is above the temporary lower market price. The counterargument is that the AoA has always been interpreted and applied as average prices over a whole producing and marketing year, without getting into the complexities of intraseasonal pricing.

FIGURE 9.1 Price of rice: International, domestic, and MPS (US$)

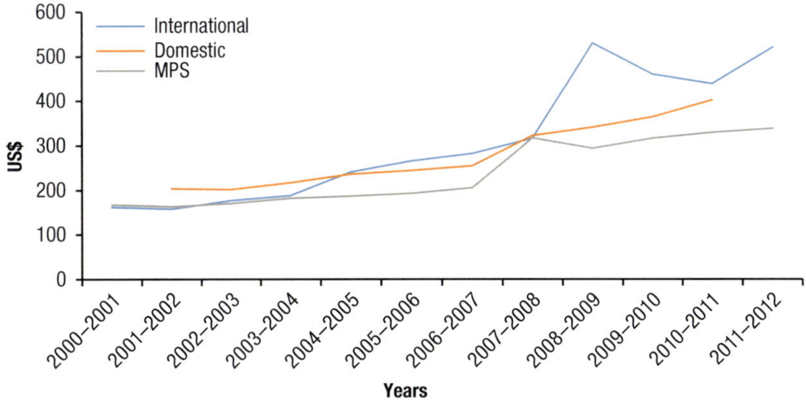

Source: Based on data from Hoda and Gulati (2013).
Note: MPS = market price support.

FIGURE 9.2 Price of wheat: International, domestic, and MPS (in US$)

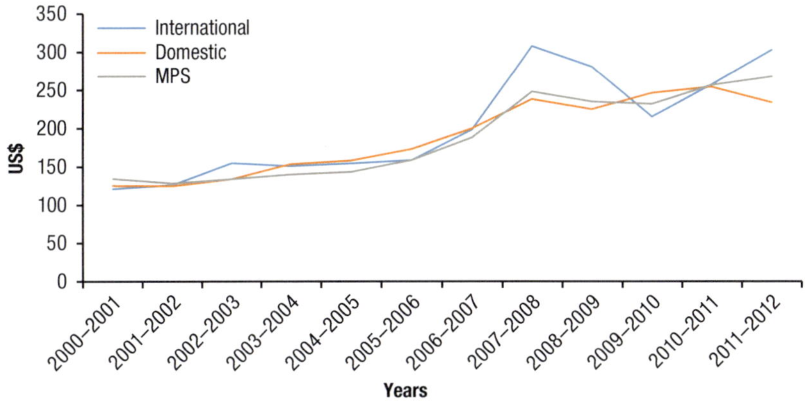

Source: Based on data from Hoda and Gulati (2013).
Note: MPS = market price support.

and, as a consequence, has to be compared to an outdated 1986–1988 FERP, measured in domestic currency, and counted in the AMS. Developing countries, which saw the domestic programs of the United States and the European Union protected by carefully crafted language during the Uruguay Round, may consider it unfair that they have to redesign their own domestic programs just because of the possible legal interpretation of terms such as administered prices, FERPs, and the like. India's impatience with the idea of a temporary peace clause and its insistence on a more permanent solution should be seen in this context.

As mentioned before, in the absence of futures markets, the only coordinating device for developing-country farmers' expectations about market conditions and production decisions may be preannounced government prices. In such cases, to analyze compliance with the AoA, one must consider whether the announced administered prices for food security products are in line with relevant market prices. One approach would be to try to clarify the relationship between the language in Annex 2 regarding market prices and administered prices. For example, footnote 5 of paragraph 3 on food stocks could be updated to state that a country may be considered "rebuttably presumed in compliance" with the price support requirement (and therefore it does not have a price gap that must be counted in the AMS) if the administered price does not exceed the appropriate domestic market price (or, if there are no clear domestic references, the import or export parity equivalent, depending on the net trading position of the country and based on the world market price of the product considered). Market protection in the form of tariffs, tariff-rate quotas (TRQs), or similar measures that comply with WTO obligations must be considered in the calculation of the import parity price. In this way, domestic price support would be separated from market access measures, which have a different treatment under the AoA.

This approach is based on the notion expressed in paragraph 3 of Annex 2 of the AoA—to qualify as a Green Box measure (and therefore be exempted from the AMS), "food purchases by the government shall be made at current market prices." If the administered prices largely coincide with market prices, then it seems reasonable that those purchases should be considered in compliance with paragraph 3.[36] In addition, if a WTO member decides to challenge another member's food security program, the former would need to show that the administered price is above the relevant market prices in ways that would offer price support to producers and thus distort trade.

Regarding the concern that food security stocks might be accumulated in excess of food security requirements and end up being exported to other countries, thus disrupting their domestic markets, additional language could

36 It is true that some language in the Korean beef case reads, "The minimum price support will be available to all marketable production of the type and quality to which the administered price support programme relates, *including where actual market prices are above the administered minimum price level*" (paragraph 827; emphasis added). But this is just a commentary that seems to question the very notion that buying at market prices does not violate Annex 2, paragraph 3. Of course, any government's purchase, even at market prices, may provide an implicit support compared to the counterfactual of no purchases, but this is allowed in Annex 2, paragraph 3.

also be added to strengthen the current Ministerial Decision on Food Stocks. This document, as noted before, asks only that the developing country availing itself of this option ensure that its food security stocks "do not distort trade or adversely affect the food security of others." Additional language could require that food security stocks be used only for domestic consumption purposes linked to food security and that any exports be prohibited. If exports do occur, the administered prices will have to be compared with the reference prices and counted against the AMS, as applicable. The only possible exception to this language would be if a country with food security stocks were asked by the appropriate UN agency to release part of its accumulated stocks into world markets due to a global, regional, or national food security emergency. This approach would provide stricter disciplines than the weaker language currently included in the peace clause (as noted in Matthews [2014]).[37]

In summary, this approach tries to align the economic rationale and the legal intent of the AoA by ensuring that administered prices used to build food security stocks are treated as market prices under the meaning of Annex 2, paragraph 3, when they stay at or below market prices and when products from food security stocks do not affect trade flows and, potentially, the food security of other WTO members. It could be argued that this proposal would still offer price support, particularly if market prices drop below the administered price. Of course, the suggested wording uses the phrase "rebuttably presumed," which means that in the case of market prices falling below the administered prices, the program can be brought to the dispute settlement process, in addition to whatever challenges may be presented under the ASCM.

It can also be claimed that the proposal may lead to circular reasoning, considering that once a government announces a price, that price may become the "market price." In addition, the expectation of more certain future prices would reduce uncertainty and expand production. Still, to the extent that the administered price is required to be within the export or import parity band, and with the application of the prohibition on exporting from food security stocks (except in the case of global or regional food emergencies), the potential

37 It was noted that Pakistan complained during the Bali negotiations about rice exports from India potentially disrupting its market, whereas Bangladeshi consumers may have benefited (and producers may have been negatively affected) from exports of Indian rice (Dorosh and Rashid 2012). This is another manifestation of the constant debate about whether food security is better attained by high food prices that benefit producers or by low prices that help consumers (see Chapter 8).

for countries' domestic support to distort global trade beyond what is already built into countries' market access commitments would be largely absent.[38]

Other Options?

In addition to the suggestions outlined in the previous sections, WTO member countries also discussed other potential permanent solutions to the problem of food security stocks in the context of the AoA. One option that has been debated is to change the 1986–1988 base period for FERPs to more recent values, for a fixed period or for rolling averages (say, three to five years). Although from an economic viewpoint, the need to update the external reference prices may seem obvious, developing countries should be very careful with this option in legal or negotiating terms because industrialized countries currently have a large legal allowance to grant domestic support under the permitted levels of AMS. If reference prices are updated to the current values (and that will most likely apply to all WTO members), the difference to be charged against the AMS is reduced but the overall allowed AMS does not change. This change could potentially expand developed countries' margins to offer distortionary domestic support.

Other ideas discussed include expanding the de minimis and exempting MPS from the AMS if the actual procurement is less than a certain percentage of total production (see, for instance, the enumeration in Montemayor [2014]). All of these options, however, seem less adequate than, or are already incorporated in, the alternatives presented in previous sections. Expanding the de minimis would be a temporary solution and would go against the goal of reducing or eliminating distortionary support, while exempting a percentage of production from the MPS may be better addressed, in economic and legal terms, if "eligible production" is handled as discussed in the previous section.

Glauber (2016) offers two additional options. One is to exempt LDCs from the obligations of counting expenditures for public stockholding programs in the calculations of domestic support. It should be noted that

38 Public stockholding programs involving administrated prices that exceed world prices would require the use of variable trade policy instruments (such as export subsidies or restrictions for exported commodities or import duties adjustments for imported commodities) to maintain the level of domestic support desired when the latter is clearly out of line with global market values. But if the possibility of exporting from food security stocks is banned (except in the cases of food emergencies in other countries) and import measures other than those already part of the market access commitments are not allowed, then such programs would not much affect global markets. For instance, assuming that there is an independent domestic market price and the government is buying clearly above it, but that price is still below the import parity value, then there will not have been imports in that case; with the export prohibition, there will not be exports either.

excluding LDCs from these obligations would cover mainly countries with a very food-insecure profile (see the cluster typologies in Díaz-Bonilla et al. [2000] and Díaz-Bonilla and Thomas [2016]). Still, if the reason for excluding LDCs is food insecurity, then this research also shows that there are countries with comparable profiles but that have not been named LDCs by the United Nations (which is a procedure unrelated to food security issues). The other option was to transform the interim solution into a permanent one and to extend it to all developing countries. These countries would still be required to provide detailed information about the operation of their programs, which then could be challenged under the ASCM, as discussed before.[39] Both options are worth considering.

Conclusion

The chapter began with an explanation of the background of the debate over food security stocks and the interim solution (the peace clause) agreed upon at Bali. Two interpretations of the duration of the peace clause were discussed; one suggested that countries complying with the conditions will be protected from challenges under the AoA until a permanent solution is found (which seems to leave the duration open-ended), while the other specified that the period in which to find a permanent solution would last until the eleventh WTO Ministerial (four years after Bali). The November 2014 decision supported the first interpretation but also encouraged members to find a permanent solution earlier.

In either case, WTO members that want to be protected by the peace clause will face more stringent notification and transparency requirements regarding domestic support, forcing those that are extremely behind schedule in their notifications to become current in their obligations under the AoA. This requirement will facilitate closer scrutiny and monitoring of the different programs of domestic support in the countries using the peace clause option. The Bali Ministerial Decision also instructed WTO members to establish a work program in the Committee on Agriculture to make recommendations for a permanent solution, and the Nairobi Ministerial Decision established a procedure to complete those negotiations.

39 It may also be argued that this second option of making the peace clause permanent but allowing challenges under the ASCM would have similar effects to the option of making administrative prices rebuttable presumed to be in compliance if they are below a maximum market price defined by the import parity, while prohibiting exports from those stocks.

I then focused on a variety of options for a permanent solution, starting with those that seem to be already available under the current texts and then moving to other options that may require further negotiations. Carefully defining "eligible production" (perhaps by capping the percentage of production to be bought, by restricting purchases to come only from a certain type of producer such as LIRP ones, or by other similar approaches) and allowing the FERP to be defined in US dollars (or a basket of currencies, such as the SDRs) may go a long way toward preventing developing countries from exceeding the de minimis. To align the economic and legal aspects of the operation of food stocks, I also discussed the proposal (based on Díaz-Bonilla 2013b) to clarify the relationship between "administered prices" and "market prices"; the intention would be to not penalize schemes in which the former basically do not exceed the latter, as such schemes would basically comply with the requirement that food stocks should be purchased at (no more than) market prices in order to be considered within the Green Box. Exempting LDCs and making the peace clause permanent are also options to be considered (Glauber 2016). Even if a permanent solution is found under the WTO legal framework, it may not necessarily solve the main issues regarding the use public food stocks to solve food security concerns in developing countries. Economic and operational considerations, as discussed in Chapter 8, may be more relevant for food security in poor countries than the legal debates covered here.

Bibliography

Bouët, A., and D. Laborde. 2010. *Economics of Export Taxation in a Context of Food Crisis: A Theoretical and CGE Approach Contribution.* IFPRI Discussion Paper 994. Washington, DC: International Food Policy Research Institute.

Brink, L. 2011. "The WTO Disciplines on Domestic Support." In *WTO Disciplines on Agricultural Support,* edited by D. Orden, D. Blandford, and T. Josling, 23–58. Cambridge, UK: Cambridge University Press.

———. 2014. *Support to Agriculture in India in 1995–2013 and the Rules of the WTO.* IATRC Working Paper 14-01. St. Paul, MN, US: International Agricultural Trade Research Consortium.

Bureau, J.-C., and S. Jean. 2013. "Do Yesterday's Disciplines Fit Today's Farm Trade?" In *Agriculture and Food Security Group Proposals and Analysis.* Electronic book prepared by the E-15 Initiative. Bali: International Centre for Trade and Sustainable Development, World Economic Forum, and International Policy Council.

Díaz-Bonilla, E. 2013a. "Agricultural Trade and Food Security: Some Thoughts about a Continuous Debate." In *Agriculture and Food Security Group Proposals and Analysis.* Electronic book prepared by the E-15 Initiative. Bali: International Centre for Trade and Sustainable Development, World Economic Forum, and International Policy Council.

———. 2013b. "Some Ideas to Break the Stalemate on Agricultural Issues at Bali." Food Security Portal Food for Thought blog, December 5. Accessed 2015. www.foodsecurityportal.org/some-ideas-break-stalemate-agricultural-issues-bali.

———. 2014. *On Food Security Stocks, Peace Clauses, and Permanent Solutions after Bali.* IFPRI Discussion Paper 1388. Washington, DC: International Food Policy Research Institute.

Díaz-Bonilla, E., X. Diao, and S. Robinson. 2004. "Thinking Inside the Boxes: Alternative Policies in the Development and Food Security Boxes." In *Agricultural Policy Reform and the WTO: Where Are We Heading?* edited by G. Anania, M. Bohman, C. Carter, and A. McCalla. Cheltenham, UK; Northampton, MA, US: Edward Elgar Publishing

Díaz-Bonilla, E., and J. Hepburn. 2016. "Export Competition Issues after Nairobi." In *Evaluating Nairobi: What Does the Outcome Mean for Trade in Food and Farm Goods?,* edited by J. Hepburn and C. Bellmann, 19–36. ICTSD Programme on Agricultural Trade and Sustainable Development. Geneva: International Centre for Trade and Sustainable Development.

Díaz-Bonilla, E., and D. Laborde. 2015. *Bali and Beyond: Some Considerations from the Perspective of Developing Countries.* IFPRI Discussion Paper. Washington, DC: International Food Policy Research Institute.

Díaz-Bonilla, E., and M. Thomas. 2016. *Why Some Are More Equal Than Others: Country Typologies of Food Security.* IFPRI Discussion Paper 1510. Washington, DC: International Food Policy Research Institute (IFPRI).

Díaz-Bonilla, E., M. Thomas, and S. Robinson. 2003. "Trade, Food Security, and the WTO Negotiations: Some Reflections on Boxes and Their Contents." In *Agricultural Trade and Poverty: Making Policy Analysis Count.* Proceedings of the OECD Global Forum, Paris, May 23–24, 2002.

Díaz-Bonilla, E., M. Thomas, S. Robinson, and A. Cattaneo. 2000. *Food Security and Trade Negotiations in the World Trade Organization: A Cluster Analysis of Country Groups.* IFPRI Trade and Macroeconomics Working Paper 59. Washington, DC: International Food Policy Research Institute.

Díaz-Bonilla, E., and J. Tin. 2006. "That Was Then but This Is Now: Multifunctionality in Industry and Agriculture." In *WTO Negotiations and Agricultural Trade Liberalization: The Effect of Developed Countries' Policies on Developing Countries,* edited by E. Díaz-Bonilla, S. Frandsen, and S. Robinson, 235–260. Wallingford Oxfordshire, UK: CABI (Centre for Agriculture and Biosciences International).

Dorosh, P., and S. Rashid. 2012. *Bangladesh Rice Trade and Price Stabilization: Implications of the 2007/08 Experience for Public Stocks*. IFPRI Discussion Paper 1209. Washington, DC: International Food Policy Research Institute.

Glauber, J. W. 2016. "After Nairobi: Public Stockholding for Food Security." In *Evaluating Nairobi: What Does the Outcome Mean for Trade in Food and Farm Goods?*, edited by J. Hepburn and C. Bellmann, 69–82. ICTSD Programme on Agricultural Trade and Sustainable Development; Geneva: International Centre for Trade and Sustainable Development.

Gopinath, M. 2012. "WTO Disciplines on Agricultural Support Update: A Comparison of India's WTO Domestic Support Notifications with Shadow Measurements." Unpublished. Oregon State University, Corvalis, OR, US.

Hoda, A., and A. Gulati. 2013. *India's Agricultural Trade Policy and Sustainable Development*. ICTSD Issue Paper 49. Geneva: International Centre for Trade and Sustainable Development.

IMF (International Monetary Fund). 2015. World Economic Outlook database. Accessed July 2015. www.imf.org/external/pubs/ft/weo/2015/01/.

Krivonos, E. 2013. "Public Food Procurement Programmes in Latin America." Presentation at the Bali Trade and Development Symposium, organized by the International Centre for Trade and Sustainable Development, Bali, December 3–5.

Matthews, A. 2014. *Food Security and WTO Domestic Support Disciplines Post-Bali*. ICTSD Programme on Agricultural Trade and Sustainable Development Issue Paper 51. Geneva: International Centre for Trade and Sustainable Development.

Meyer, S., and J. Schmidhuber. 2013. "Has the Treadmill Changed Direction?" In *Agriculture and Food Security Group Proposals and Analysis*. Electronic book prepared by the E-15 Initiative: International Centre for Trade and Sustainable Development (ICTSD), World Economic Forum, and International Food & Agricultural Trade Policy Council. Geneva: ICTSD.

Montemayor, R. 2014. "An Evaluation of Possible Elements of a 'Permanent' Solution to the Public Stockholding Issue." Presentation at the Dialogue on Public Stockholding for Food Security Purposes: Towards a "Permanent Solution?," organized by the International Centre for Trade and Sustainable Development and the Food and Agriculture Organization of the United Nations, Geneva, March 18.

Mundell, R. 2002. "Commodity Prices, Exchange Rates, and the International Monetary System." Presentation at the Consultation on Agricultural Commodity Price Problems, organized by the Commodities and Trade Division, Food and Agriculture Organization, Rome, March 25–26.

Orden, D., D. Blandford, and T. Josling, eds. 2011. *WTO Disciplines on Agricultural Support*. Cambridge, UK: Cambridge University Press.

OWINFS (Our World Is Not for Sale). 2013. "Stand Firm on Defending India's Food Security: Nothing Less Will Do for India!" Letter published on December 6. Accessed 2015. www.ourworldisnotforsale.org/en/article/stand-firm-defending-india-s-food-security-nothing-less-will-india.

Tangermann, S. 2013. "A Post-Bali Food Security Agenda. The E-15 Initiative. Strengthening the Multilateral Trading System." Report prepared for ICTSD Agriculture and Food Security Group, Bali. Accessed 2015. www.ictsd.org/sites/default/files/research/AG_Policy_ok.pdf.

WTO (World Trade Organization). 1999. "Notification Issues." G/AG/W/45, June 18. Background Note by the Secretariat of the Committee on Agriculture. Geneva.

———. 2000a. "Inflation and Exchange Rate Movements in the Context of Domestic Support Commitments." G/AG/NG/S/19. Committee on Agriculture Special Session. Geneva.

———. 2000b. "Korea: Measures Affecting Imports of Fresh, Chilled, and Frozen Beef." WT/DS161/R, WT/DS169/R. Geneva.

———. 2007. Case DS207: "Chile—Price Band System and Safeguard Measures Relating to Certain Agricultural Products." Accessed February 22, 2017. https://www.wto.org/english/tratop_e/dispu_e/cases_e/ds207_e.htm.

———. 2008a. "Revised Draft Modalities for Agriculture." TN/AG/W/4/Rev.4. Geneva.

———. 2008b. The WTO Agreements Series 3: Agriculture. Geneva. www.wto.org/english/res_e/booksp_e/agrmntseries3_ag_2008_e.pdf.

Chapter 10

AGRICULTURAL INSURANCE AND THE WTO

Joseph W. Glauber

Insurance programs have become an increasingly popular method for providing support to agricultural producers.[1] Mahul and Stutley (2010) reported that in 2007 more than 100 countries had agricultural insurance programs available. In the United States multiple-peril crop insurance was available on a limited basis as early as the late 1930s; more recently, insurance has become the dominant safety-net program in the United States in terms of government outlays, overshadowing more traditional price and income support programs (Glauber 2012). Recent reforms in the European Community (EC) could potentially expand insurance programs there as well (European Commission 2013).

Nor is interest in insurance programs confined to the developed world. There has long been interest in the potential of crop insurance to help smallholder agricultural producers manage production risks and improve food security in developing countries (Hazell, Pomareda, and Valdes 1986). Crop insurance has often been touted as a means to reduce production risk, encourage adoption of improved seed varieties, or foster more sustainable production practices (Carter et al. 2014). Early work by Hazell, Pomareda, and Valdes (1986) pointed out that the experience with insurance programs in developing countries was disappointing due to the high program costs. Individual insurance coverage is expensive to monitor due to the presence of classic insurance problems like moral hazard and adverse selection, and most programs have failed in the absence of providing producers with large subsidies. More recently, there has been considerable interest in weather-based and other index insurance measures that can provide protection but whose administrative costs are lower because they minimize moral hazard and adverse selection issues (Miranda and Farrin 2012; Hatch et al. 2012; Kalra 2013). Critics such as Binswanger-Mkhize (2012) and Smith (2016) charge that the subsidy costs remain high for such products.

1 Acknowledgments to John Dyck, Anne Effland, Pam Cooper, Lars Brink, David Orden, Vince Smith, and Tim Josling.

The scope of agricultural insurance programs has grown rapidly among developing countries, particularly among the larger emerging economies like China and India. For example, in 2014, China had a program with a total liability second in size only to that of the United States. India's weather-based program is targeted at millions of producers. An often-cited impetus for the growth in insurance programs is the potential exemption of such programs from World Trade Organization (WTO) reduction commitments (Roberts 2005; Mahul and Stutley 2010). Under Annex 2 of the Uruguay Round Agreement on Agriculture (AoA), domestic support measures that have no, or at most minimal, trade-distorting effects or effects on production are excluded from reduction commitments. Paragraph 7 of Annex 2 includes criteria that identify qualifying income insurance and income safety-net programs, while paragraph 8 includes criteria that identify qualifying natural disaster assistance programs, including crop insurance (WTO 2003). Yet, although WTO rules shield so-called Green Box policies from reduction, few developed countries have notified agricultural insurance policies under Annex 2 (Smith and Glauber 2012). There are also questions as to how crop insurance programs have been notified by larger developing countries (Glauber 2015). Moreover, crop insurance programs have been challenged in recent WTO dispute settlement cases and domestic countervailing duty investigations (Schnepf 2005, 2010).

This chapter examines the treatment of agricultural insurance under the WTO. The section "The Growth of Agricultural Insurance" discusses the growth of insurance programs since the launch of the Uruguay Round in 1986, with a particular focus on the growth over the past 10 years in developed and developing countries. "Agricultural Insurance and the Uruguay Round Agreement on Agriculture" presents the negotiating history of Annex 2 in the AoA; of particular significance is that many countries, including the United States, had originally argued that crop insurance subsidies should be disciplined. Next is a detailed examination of the criteria in paragraphs 7 and 8 of Annex 2 in the AoA, followed by an analysis of how countries have notified their insurance programs to the WTO. The chapter then turns to a discussion of how subsidies are measured, including those subsidies provided in order to deliver insurance to producers. The following section presents a literature review of how agricultural insurance affects production decisions and an analysis of the treatment of agricultural insurance in trade disputes, including Brazil's WTO challenge to US support programs for upland cotton. Lastly, proposed changes to Annex 2 are discussed, including recent proposals under the Doha Development Agenda negotiations. Conclusions are offered in the final section.

FIGURE 10.1 Growth of world agricultural insurance premium volume, 1980–2015

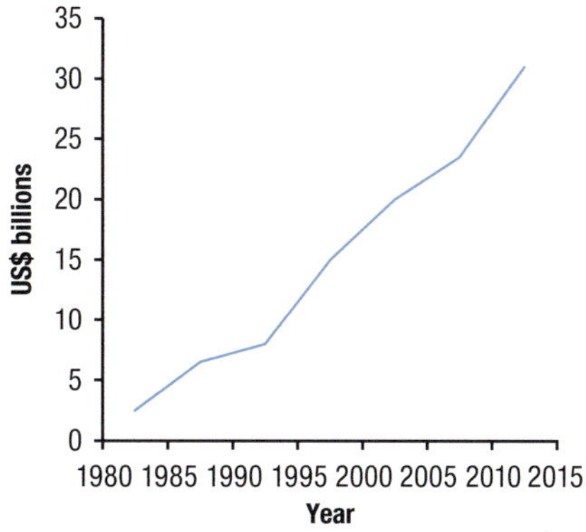

Source: Roberts (2005); Dick and Wang (2010); Mahul and Stutley (2010); and Boissande (2015).

The Growth of Agricultural Insurance

Although privately offered insurance to protect livestock and crops from hail was sold before 1800 (Munich RE 2011), the growth in agricultural insurance truly began in the first half of the twentieth century with the establishment of government-sponsored insurance programs. In the United States, Canada, and Japan, such programs date to the late 1930s. Initially those programs were operated on a pilot basis with limited crop and regional coverage; however, with additional government subsidies, participation grew (Hazell, Pomareda, and Valdes 1986). By the time the Uruguay Round was launched in 1986, total agricultural insurance premiums for these three countries totaled about US$1.6 billion.[2] Although a number of other countries' insurance programs date to the second half of the twentieth century, these were small, with total premium volume likely less than $1.0 billion in 1986 (FAO 1991).

Figure 10.1 shows the growth of agricultural insurance programs since 1986. Because the premium estimates are taken from a variety of sources (Roberts 2005; Dick and Wang 2010; Mahul and Stutley 2010; Kalra 2013; Boissonade 2015), exact intertemporal comparisons are not possible; nonetheless, the estimates suggest that premium volumes increased at an annual rate of about 16 percent between 2004 and 2013, about twice the annual growth seen between 1986 and 2004.

The rapid growth in agricultural insurance markets since 2004 is attributable to several factors, including the appreciation in commodity prices;

2 Unless otherwise indicated, all dollar amounts in this chapter refer to US dollars.

FIGURE 10.2 Growth of China and US agricultural insurance premiums since 2001

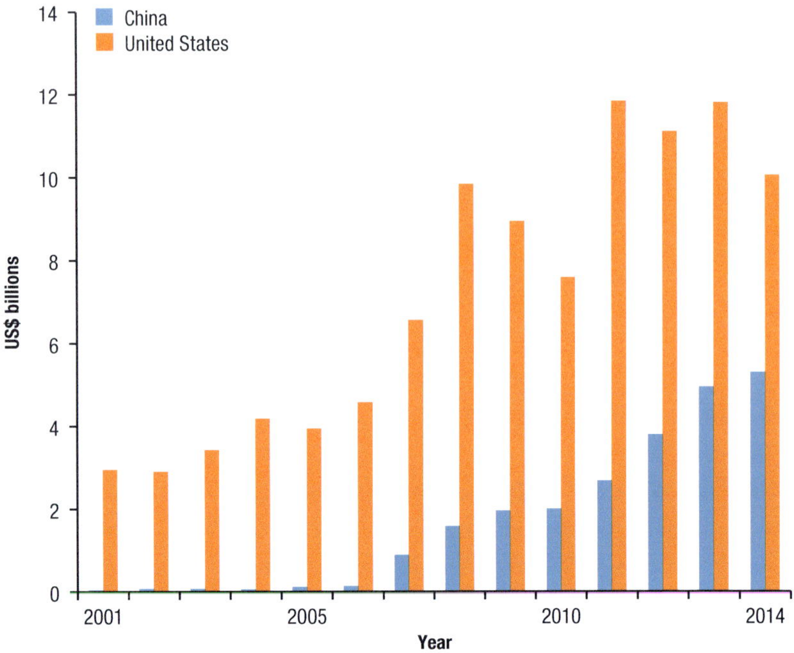

Source: USDA RMA (2015); Li (2014).

increased government subsidies, resulting in higher coverage levels in the US market; and growth of agricultural insurance in emerging economies, particularly China. Figure 10.2 shows the growth of China and US crop insurance markets since 2001. In that year, the average coverage level in the United States was 63 percent, with 48 percent of enrolled area insured at 70 percent coverage or higher. By 2013, because of increased subsidies, the average coverage level was 72 percent, with 78 percent of crop area insured at coverage levels of 70 percent or higher (USDA RMA 2015). China's agricultural premiums remained at relatively low levels in 2007, when premium subsidies were introduced, which resulted in premium volumes increasing from $300 million in 2007 to almost $5 billion in 2013 (Li 2014).

In developed economies such as the United States, Japan, Canada, and Europe, agricultural insurance is generally characterized by indemnity-based programs that provide crop and livestock coverage against named perils, multiple perils, and, more recently, price and revenue risks. Individual-based coverage is expensive because of the high cost of administering contracts and adjusting losses. Moreover, individual-based policies are prone to moral hazard and adverse selection problems, which add to the monitoring costs (Kalra 2013). Because of those costs and in the absence of subsidies, demand for insurance products is low, which is why private unsubsidized markets for multiple peril insurance have generally failed (Wright and Hewitt 1994; Goodwin and Smith 1995) and why the larger insurance programs in the United States, Canada, and Japan are generally highly subsidized. In their comprehensive review of agricultural insurance programs, Mahul and Stutley (2010) found that almost two-thirds of the countries surveyed reported that they subsidized premium costs. Those countries accounted for more than 90 percent of total premiums, at an average subsidy rate of 47 percent. For example, the public costs of the US program, which are estimated at about one-third of 2014 total global premium volume, are projected to exceed $8.5 billion annually over the next 10 years, an expenditure of almost 90 cents for every $1 premium written (CBO 2015).

With such high costs, it is little wonder that the larger agricultural insurance programs are generally found in developed countries. The high costs of contracting with large numbers of dispersed smallholders when there are fixed costs to contracting and poorly developed legal institutions for enforcing contracts have led many to conclude that conventional, indemnity-based insurance does not work for smallholder farmers in developing countries (Hazell 1992). To address these concerns, index-based insurance products based on specific perils or events (for example, regional yield loss, drought, or flood) and recorded at a regional level (for example, by regional weather stations) have been promoted. Examples of such products include area-yield insurance, where premiums and indemnities are based on the average yield in a region, or weather-based indexes, such as rainfall insurance, where producers receive a payment if rainfall in the region falls below a designated level (Skees, Hazell, and Miranda 1999; Carter 2012). Such contracts typically minimize moral hazard and adverse selection issues (Miranda 1991) and can be provided at lower costs because loss adjustment and monitoring costs are so much lower.

Index insurance schemes have been piloted in a number of developing countries, with somewhat limited success (see Miranda and Farrin 2012; Carter et al. 2014). Participation in pilot programs has been generally limited (Binswanger-Mkhize 2012). Smith (2016) points out that small-holder farmers already have ways of mitigating risk, including informal community-based initiatives, enterprise diversification, and off-farm employment. Another drawback is the existence of basis risk—that is, the degree to which the regional yield or weather variable is correlated with the individual farm yield.

Producers whose yields are poorly correlated with the aggregate index may find such insurance offers to provide insufficient risk protection; thus, basis risk can act to limit demand. One exception is India's Weather Based Crop Insurance Scheme (WBCIS), an index-based insurance program that has grown considerably since its introduction in 2007 to include more than nine million Indian producers in 2010 and 2011, with a combined commercial premium volume of about $260 million (Clarke et al. 2012; Mahul, Verma, and Clarke 2012). However, the program is heavily subsidized, and participation is mandatory if producers participate in government credit programs.

Some believe that the potential market for weather-based insurance products is more likely limited to insuring relatively large groups of farmers, either directly or indirectly through aggregators such as input providers, credit providers, or buyers in contract farming situations (Binswanger-Mkhize 2012; Smith 2016). Another potential use of weather-based contracts would be by national governments to mitigate widespread emergencies like droughts (Miranda and Farrin 2012). Agricultural insurance has witnessed dramatic growth since the launch of the Uruguay Round, but that growth has largely been the result of substantial government support measures, which are subject to discipline under the Uruguay Round AoA.

Agricultural Insurance and the Uruguay Round Agreement on Agriculture

A landmark achievement of the 1986 Uruguay Round, and specifically of the AoA, was the full inclusion of agriculture in a system of multilateral rules and disciplines, including disciplines governing agricultural support.[3] With the launch of the Uruguay Round, trade negotiators in Geneva began to debate how best to "achieve greater liberalization of trade in agriculture and bring all measures affecting import access and export competition under strengthened and more operationally effective GATT [General Agreement on Tariffs and Trade] rules and disciplines" by "improving the competitive environment by increasing disciplines on the use of all direct and indirect subsidies and other measures affecting directly or indirectly agricultural trade, including the phased reduction of their negative effects and dealing with their cause" (GATT 1986).

In 1987 the Organisation for Economic Co-operation and Development (OECD) published its seminal study measuring and analyzing the effect of

3 For a detailed history of the negotiations, see Josling, Tangermann, and Warley (1996).

select members' domestic support measures on agricultural trade.[4] The OECD report put forward the concept of the producer support estimate (PSE), developed in the 1970s (see Tangermann, Josling, and Pearson 1987). The PSE distinguished among *market price supports,* covering policies that raise market prices received by producers (and consumers); *direct income supports,* which raise the effective prices of producers through transfers rather than raising the price paid by consumers; *indirect income support,* which reduces the producers' costs; and *other support measures,* which cover measures that reduce the cost to the agricultural sector as a whole and which are of general benefit to the society but have no direct effect on producer or consumer prices (OECD 1987). Significantly, the study recognized that although the PSE represented an aggregate measurement of distortion, various policy measures did not have the same relative impact on production and trade as they did on farmers' income. In particular, measures in the last category ("other support") were seen as potentially less distorting than the other three categories.

The OECD study had a large impact on subsequent negotiations (Stancanelli 2009). Initial proposals by the United States and the Cairns Group broadly endorsed the concept of the PSE and called for elimination of trade-distorting subsidies (GATT 1987a, 1987c). In line with OECD research, which classified crop insurance subsidies as indirect income support, the US proposal explicitly called for the elimination of "policies such as subsidized crop insurance" (GATT 1987a, 3). In GATT parlance, subsidies were identified by boxes, which were given the color of traffic lights: Green (permitted policies that would be exempt from reduction), Amber (to be reduced), and Red (prohibited policies) (Josling, Tangermann and Warley 1996).[5] Both the United States and the Cairns Group proposals would exempt from reduction any income support policies that were decoupled from production and marketing, including those that provided a safety net against natural disaster. Canada, a Cairns Group member, put forward a technical discussion paper on domestic support measurement that would classify crop insurance subsidies as "partially distorting measures" subject to discipline (GATT 1988). Like the US proposal, Canada considered disaster payments as nondistorting measures (that is, Green Box). Similarly, Japan's initial proposal would have exempted

4 The countries included Australia, Austria, Canada, the EC10, Japan, New Zealand, and the United States.

5 The concept of Red Box policies was later discarded in the agricultural negotiations. In addition, a Blue Box was defined in Article 6.5 of the AoA for Amber Box policies that limit production. Under the AoA, Blue Box policies are exempt from reduction (Josling, Tangermann, and Wharley 1996).

"subsidies related to disaster relief," but it was unclear whether those were to include crop insurance subsidies (GATT 1987d). Finally, the EC's proposal allowed for domestic support reforms but did not mention insurance programs or disaster assistance (GATT 1987b).

Thus, at the outset of the negotiations, two of the world's largest agricultural insurance programs—Canada and the United States—were willing to put crop insurance subsidies on the table for reduction and elimination. In contrast, there was general agreement among negotiating members that bona fide disaster measures should be exempt from reduction commitments. By 1989, contracting parties to the GATT began to contemplate the inclusion of crop insurance in the list of permitted policies. In its comprehensive proposal, put forward in the fall of 1989, the United States distinguished among (1) policies to be phased out, (2) policies to be disciplined, and (3) permitted policies. Permitted policies included "disaster assistance keyed to bona fide production losses, including disaster payments, *crop insurance*, disaster relief, etc." (GATT 1989, 20; emphasis added).

In July 1990, Aart de Zeeuw, chair of the agriculture negotiating group, put together the first attempt at a unifying draft proposal (Josling, Tangermann, and Warley 1996). In its discussion of internal support measures exempted from reduction commitments, the de Zeeuw text included crop insurance and bona fide disaster assistance as well as income safety-net programs. The text called upon contracting parties to develop specific criteria as necessary. Although the measures were not subject to "progressive and substantial reduction," they were to remain subject to the overall ceiling on support as well as to surveillance and review (GATT 1990a).[6] Inclusion of safety-net programs in the Green Box was supported by the United States, the Cairns Group, and Canada, while the EC favored treating those programs as Amber and hence subject to reduction (GATT 1990b).

In 1991 a series of technical discussions were held on the Green Box.[7] The new chairman, Arthur Dunkel, circulated language laying out the basis for exemption from reduction as well as criteria that defined exempt government service programs as those that provided indirect benefits to producers and consumers, such as research and other general services, domestic food

---

6 Stancanelli (2009, 30) asserted that there was "no indication as to a ceiling or limit to overall support," but in a technical note circulated by the chair in March 1991, it is clear that the issue of whether the Green Box would be capped was still not settled (GATT 1991a). However, by the time the Dunkel Draft was published in December 1991, Green Box spending was uncapped.

7 I am particularly grateful to Pam Cooper for her helpful insights and excellent memory concerning the development of Green Box language during AoA discussions in 1991.

aid, and public stockholding programs (GATT 1991c, 1991d). Criteria for support provided through direct payments, such as decoupled income support, income safety-net programs, crop insurance, and disaster programs, were debated in the fall of 1991 and captured in the Draft Final Act (the Dunkel Draft) of December 1991 (GATT 1991e). Although the negotiations were not to conclude until December 1993, the language for Annex 2 (the Green Box) remained essentially unchanged from the Dunkel Draft. One significant change in the AoA (not in Annex 2, but that had implications for Annex 2 policies) was whether Annex 2 policies would be exempt from countervailing duty challenges. Under Article 7.3 of the Dunkel Draft ("General Disciplines on Domestic Support"), policies conforming to Annex 2 would be considered exempt from such challenges. That protection was dropped in the final AoA, although Green Box policies were protected from challenge during the AoA implementation period under the so-called peace clause provisions of the AoA (Article 13, "Due Restraint").

Agricultural Insurance in the Green Box

Under Annex 2, domestic support measures that claim Green Box status must meet the general criteria of paragraph 1, as well as the policy-specific criteria articulated in 11 separate paragraphs.[8] Although the AoA includes special and differential treatment for reduction commitments for developing countries, Annex 2 criteria are the same for both developed and developing countries. Paragraph 1 states that to be exempt from reduction commitments, domestic support measures "shall meet the fundamental requirement that they have no, or at most minimal, trade-distorting effects or effects on production" (WTO 2003). Paragraph 7 of Annex 2 includes criteria that identify qualifying income insurance and income safety-net programs, while paragraph 8 includes criteria that identify qualifying natural disaster assistance programs, including crop insurance. Thus, to claim Green Box status, agricultural insurance programs must meet all criteria in a specific paragraph as well as the more general criteria in paragraph 1.

The development of the language for paragraphs 7 and 8 gives some sense of the evolution and refinement of the final language. In a technical note by the Secretariat circulated in early May 1991, qualifying payments for disaster relief, including crop insurance, would include "the payments of premiums and/or the settlement of claims under *financially sound* crop (including

8 The relevant paragraphs of Annex 2 are presented in the chapter appendix.

livestock) insurance programmes designed to compensate for the effects of natural disasters" (GATT 1991b; emphasis added). Given that average indemnities paid under the Canadian, Japanese, and US crop insurance programs generally exceeded premiums (including subsidies) during the 1980s (Sigurdson and Sin 1994; Glauber 2004), it is perhaps not surprising that the phrase "financially sound" was dropped in subsequent drafts; however, it is interesting that, at least in early deliberations, the concept of a financially sound insurance program was envisioned.

Natural disasters were defined in the May document as including "the damage resulting from *unexpected or unusually severe* climatic events" (GATT 1991b; emphasis added). In a paper circulated in November 21, 1991, eligibility for losses under either paragraph 7 (income insurance and income safety-net programs) or paragraph 8 (crop insurance and disaster assistance) was to be confined to covering "catastrophic" losses (GATT 1991d). What constituted a "catastrophic" loss? At the time of negotiations, the Canadian program allowed producers to insure up to 80 percent of their expected yields (Sigurdson and Sin 1994). Although the US program allowed participants to insure up to 75 percent of their expected yield, almost 75 percent of area, representing 70 percent of premiums, was insured at coverage levels of 65 percent or lower (USDA RMA 2015). Moreover, US disaster programs in the 1980s required losses of 35 percent before producers could receive payment (Glauber and Collins 2002). In the Draft Final Act, the catastrophic loss threshold was defined as losses in excess of 30 percent of average production or income.

A striking feature of paragraphs 7 and 8 is the prescriptive criteria that are often at odds with good insurance principles. The prescriptive language grew out of concern about allowing some kind of support to deal with production and income losses beyond a producer's control but not allowing unlimited support that would presumably result in market distortions. For example, both paragraphs use a three-year or five-year "Olympic average" (that is, an average in which the highest and lowest entries are discarded) as the base period for determining losses in a current year. When Annex 2 criteria were being debated, both the United States and Canada had established yield guarantees (that is, the level of yield used as benchmark for the insurance) for their crop insurance programs that were based on yield histories of up to 10 years (Sigurdson and Sin 1994; Skees and Reed 1986). From an actuarial perspective, longer time series produced a more accurate yield estimate that was thought to minimize adverse selection problems caused by producers who might buy insurance when an average based on three-year yield histories was high relative to their expected yield and not buy insurance when the three-year average was lower than their expected yield (Skees and Reed 1986).

This led to an interesting question: why did the negotiated criteria not reflect a more actuarially appropriate time period? A primary concern for the United States was ensuring that its ad hoc disaster programs qualified under paragraph 8. US disaster programs typically used a three-year average or a five-year Olympic average to establish production losses. Moreover, in the late 1980s and early 1990s, the George H. W. Bush administration had been critical of the US crop insurance program and had even proposed eliminating crop insurance and replacing it with a standing disaster program in its 1990 Farm Bill proposal (Glauber and Collins 2002; Glauber 2012). Similarly, criteria in paragraph 8 would seem to bias reporting toward natural disaster programs rather than insurance programs. For example, paragraph 8(a) states that eligibility "shall arise only following a formal recognition by government authorities that a natural or like disaster . . . has occurred or is occurring"; however, such language is less appropriate for insurance programs. Indemnity-based insurance losses are, by their nature, idiosyncratic; indeed, even in years with bumper crops, individual farms may suffer losses. Thus requirements for a public declaration of disaster would seem to preclude insurance programs from qualifying under paragraph 8.

Last, and perhaps most important, after the release of the Dunkel Draft, there was effectively no opportunity for negotiators to make changes to Annex 2. The text was considered "locked down" while discussions were stalled around the larger issues of total versus product-specific aggregate measurement of support (AMS) disciplines and export subsidy reduction percentages (Josling, Tangermann, and Warley 1996). In the end, only minor changes were made to Annex 2, none of which affected paragraphs 7 or 8 (Stewart 1999).

WTO Members' Use of Annex 2 to Notify Agricultural Insurance Programs

Under the AoA, members are required to make annual notifications to the WTO on the extent of their domestic support measures. Given the differences between Annex 2 criteria and the provisions of selected WTO member insurance programs, how have WTO members notified their agricultural insurance programs? Paragraph 7 has been little used by WTO members. Through 2012–2013, only Australia, Canada, and the European Union (EU) had made consistent use of the provisions, and this use has largely been for safety-net

TABLE 10.1 Notification of income safety-net programs under Annex 2, paragraph 7, select countries (US$ millions)

Notification year	Australia	Canada	EU	Russian Federation
2008–2009	78.0	523.2	23.8	n.a.
2009–2010	59.5	641.2	22.4	n.a.
2010–2011	30.9	698.4	30.4	n.a.
2011–2012	237.9	555.8	40.3	n.a.
2012–2013	144.8	522.0	37.8	171.8
Average	**110.2**	**588.1**	**30.9**	**171.8**

Source: WTO (2015b).
Note: n.a. = not applicable.

programs rather than true insurance schemes. Australia notifies tax savings from its whole farm–based Farm Management Deposits scheme, a tax shelter–based savings account on which farmers may draw in times of natural disasters (Commonwealth of Australia 2015). Outlays averaged $110 million from 2008–2009 through 2012–2013 (Table 10.1).

Canadian income safety-net programs have undergone several changes since the late 1990s but, like Australia's program, function as a producer-funded savings account in which producers receive matching deposits from the federal and provincial governments (Antón, Kimura, and Martini 2011). Federal and provincial outlays under Canada's AgriInvest program (and its predecessors) averaged $588 million from 2008–2009 through 2012–2013. The EU is the only other WTO member to consistently notify some support under paragraph 7, but the values notified have been small, averaging less than $30 million annually from 2008 through 2012. The Russian Federation began notifying an income safety-net scheme under paragraph 7 in 2012–2013, with reported outlays totaling $172 million.[9]

The United States has offered revenue insurance since the mid-1990s; in 2014 revenue products accounted for two-thirds of total area insured and more than 80 percent of total premiums (USDA RMA 2015). However, most of the US revenue insurance policies are crop specific and pay when producers have either a production or revenue loss. Criteria in paragraph 7(c) state that

9 It is unclear whether the reported measure is an income insurance scheme or a yield-related crop insurance scheme (see Bobojonov, Götz, and Glauben [2014] for a discussion of Russian insurance schemes).

TABLE 10.2 Notification of agricultural insurance, select countries (US$ millions)

	United States	Japan	Canada	EU	China	India	Brazil
How reported	Amber	Green/ Amber	Amber	Amber	Not reported	Green	Green
2008–2009	5,691	626	699	770	1,148	174	65
2009–2010	5,426	682	771	548	1,473	330	181
2010–2011	4,711	695	748	550	1,571	693	302
2011–2012	7,461	779	881	583	2,080	n.a.	78
2012–2013	6,926	736	1,002	n.a.	2,949	n.a.	455
Average	**6,043**	**704**	**820**	**613**	**1,844**	**399**	**216**

Source: WTO (2015b).
Note: n.a. = not available.

payments "shall not relate to the type or volume of production," which would seemingly preclude product-specific revenue schemes and programs that pay on production losses, even if those losses are offset by a rise in prices (as can be the case under the US program).

The Australian and Canadian programs appear to provide whole farm–based income safety nets, yet it is less clear whether their provisions are fully consistent with paragraph 7. Under Australia's Farm Management Deposits scheme, producers can withdraw funds whenever there is a disaster, but neither the disaster designation nor the size of the withdrawal appears to be tied to the 70 percent criteria laid out in paragraph 7(a). Similarly, under the Canadian AgriInvest program, producers can withdraw the funds at any time for risk mitigation or other investments. Little detail is known about the EU or Russian programs.

Many WTO members have notified support under paragraph 8 for disaster assistance; however, the main issue surrounding these notifications is a lack of transparency. Few of the programs notified appear to be agricultural insurance–type programs; rather, they are programs responding to ad hoc disasters. Based on the numerous questions and answers exchanged during the review process of the WTO Committee on Agriculture's regular meetings, however, it is not clear that many countries actually meet all the criteria.[10] Most developed countries that have notified crop insurance outlays to the WTO,

10 Agriculture-related information notified by WTO members and questions and responses provided in the context of the review process carried out by the Committee on Agriculture can be found at http://agims.wto.org/.

including the United States, Canada, and the European Union (which notifies for all its member states), have notified those outlays as Amber Box outlays (Table 10.2). The exception is Japan, which notifies subsidies for those insurance policies at coverage levels of 70 percent or less under paragraph 8 (Green Box). For policies with coverage levels in excess of 70 percent, Japan notifies the subsidies as Amber (Ito and Dyck 2002).

As discussed earlier, the past several years have seen significant growth in agricultural insurance markets in developing countries. Based on recent WTO notifications, Brazil, India, and the Philippines have notified agricultural insurance programs under paragraph 8. Chile notifies its insurance program under paragraph 6 (decoupled support payments), and Mexico has notified its subsidies under paragraph 6.2 (developmental measures that are exempt from reduction). The Republic of Korea has notified its subsidies as Amber Box outlays. China, which paid premium subsidies totaling almost $3 billion in 2012–2013, has yet to include agricultural subsidies as part of its domestic support notifications. The WTO criteria have become even more out of step in light of changes in agricultural insurance programs, especially those in the United States. In addition to revenue products, the United States has developed area-based products using average county yields and livestock and dairy margin products based on the difference between input and output prices. Index insurance products are also available, based on weather or vegetative growth indexes. These new products are even further removed from the WTO criteria developed more than 20 years ago.

In light of the incompatibility of WTO Green Box criteria and the actual operation of crop insurance programs, two conclusions can be drawn. One is that the criteria have adequately prevented abuse of crop insurance programs. This is revealed by the fact that practically all developed-country programs notify as part of the Amber Box (Smith and Glauber 2012). However, the second conclusion is that the criteria are overly restrictive and ill-structured to allow for the establishment of even a modest and actuarially sound crop insurance program designed to protect producers from catastrophic losses. The latter conclusion would seem to demand the development of new WTO Green Box criteria that would allow for minimally trade-distorting crop insurance programs, while still reigning in production-distorting elements.

Measurement of Agricultural Insurance Subsidies

Annex 3 of the AoA specifies guidelines for calculating the aggregate measurement of support, which is calculated as budgetary outlays including "revenue foregone by governments or their agents" (paragraph 2) minus "specific agricultural levies or fees paid by producers" (paragraph 4). Support is measured at both the national and subnational levels (paragraph 3). In addition, the AoA provides guidance for non–price support measures, including input subsidies and other measures such as marketing-cost reduction measures; it states that "the value of such measures shall be measured using government budgetary outlays or, where the use of budgetary outlays does not reflect the full extent of the subsidy concerned, the basis for calculating the subsidy shall be the gap between the price of the subsidized good or service and a representative market price for a similar good or service multiplied by the quantity of the good or service" (paragraph 13).

Perhaps the most straightforward method of calculating insurance outlays is to simply take the difference between indemnities paid and premiums collected for the reporting year. The United States reported insurance subsidies in that manner from 1995 to 2008. Due to the nature of the risks incurred, crop insurance indemnities can be highly variable. For example, net indemnity payments under the US crop insurance program have varied from $121.0 million in 2007 to more than $13.3 billion in 2012 (Table 10.3). Due to this variability, such ex post measures may give little insight into the level of subsidy provided by the insurance program.[11]

A more accurate measure of the ex ante benefits of a subsidized insurance program would be the producer's expected net indemnity payment at the time the planting decision was made. The expected benefit would equal the expected indemnity payment minus the premium paid by the producer, which is the premium charged minus any premium subsidy:

$$\text{E(benefit)} = \text{E(indemnity)} - (\text{premium} - \text{premium subsidy}) \qquad (1)$$

Assuming premiums are set at actuarially fair rates, the premium will equal the expected indemnity. In this case, the expected benefit will be equal to the premium subsidy:

$$\text{E(benefit)} = \text{premium subsidy} \qquad (2)$$

Many countries, including the United States, the EU, Japan, and Canada, currently report premium subsidies to the WTO. However, if premiums do not accurately reflect underlying risks, premium subsidies may underestimate

11 From 1995 to 2002, Canada also reported an ex post measure of support calculated by multiplying indemnities paid in that year by the "long run contribution from government," given as 56 percent of the total contribution. Canada began reporting premium subsidies in the 2003 reporting period (WTO 2015b).

TABLE 10.3 Net indemnities paid versus premium subsidies, US crop insurance program, 1995–2014 (US$ millions)

Year	Indemnity	Total premium	Premium subsidy	Producer premium	Net indemnity
1995	1,567.7	1,543.3	889.5	653.8	913.9
1996	1,492.7	1,838.6	982.1	856.4	636.3
1997	993.6	1,775.4	903.1	872.3	121.3
1998	1,677.5	1,875.9	947.6	928.4	749.1
1999	2,434.7	2,310.1	1,394.0	916.2	1,518.5
2000	2,594.8	2,540.2	951.2	1,589.0	1,005.9
2001	2,960.1	2,961.9	1,771.7	1,190.1	1,770.0
2002	4,066.7	2,915.9	1,741.4	1,174.5	2,892.2
2003	3,260.8	3,431.4	2,042.0	1,389.3	1,871.5
2004	3,209.7	4,186.1	2,477.4	1,708.7	1,501.0
2005	2,367.3	3,949.2	2,343.8	1,605.4	761.9
2006	3,503.6	4,579.5	2,682.0	1,897.5	1,606.1
2007	3,547.6	6,562.1	3,823.4	2,738.8	808.8
2008	8,679.9	9,851.3	5,690.9	4,160.4	4,519.5
2009	5,228.8	8,950.7	5,426.9	3,523.9	1,705.0
2010	4,251.4	7,594.4	4,711.3	2,883.1	1,368.3
2011	10,809.6	11,841.1	7,366.0	4,475.2	6,334.5
2012	17,441.9	11,113.6	6,977.3	4,136.3	13,305.6
2013	12,073.6	11,805.2	7,295.1	4,510.1	7,563.5
2014	9,057.3	10,061.4	6,208.1	3,853.3	5,203.9
Average 1995–2014	**5,061.0**	**5,584.4**	**3,331.2**	**2,253.1**	**2,807.8**

Source: USDA RMA (2015).

the benefits provided to producers. In that case, expected benefits equal the premium subsidy plus expected excess losses, defined as total indemnities minus total premiums:

$$E(\text{benefit}) = \text{premium subsidy} + E(\text{indemnity} - \text{premium}) \tag{3}$$

Glauber (2004) showed that the historical loss ratio for the US crop insurance program from 1981 to 1993 was more than 150 percent (that is, total indemnities exceeded total premiums, including premium subsidies, by 50 percent). Over that period, net indemnities averaged $411 million annually, while the average premium subsidy was only $130 million. With rate reforms initiated in the early 1990s and broader participation stemming from increased premium subsidies, loss ratio performance improved considerably over the past 20 years. From 1995 to 2014 the average loss ratio for the US crop insurance program was 91 percent.[12] Annual premium subsidies averaged \$3.3 billion over the period, compared with annual net indemnity payments that averaged only \$2.8 billion (Table 10.3).

A related issue is how delivery costs are notified. Countries provide varying degrees of support to agricultural insurance programs (Mahul and Stutley 2010; Smith and Glauber 2012). Some countries, such as the United States, develop insurance products for producers and then separately provide reinsurance and delivery expense reimbursements to private companies to deliver such insurance to producers. In other countries, such as France, private companies develop insurance products and include delivery expenses in the insurance premiums. The government then provides subsidies to producers to cover a portion of the total premium costs. Delivery of agricultural insurance can be quite costly (Hazell 1992; Goodwin and Smith 1995). In a 2008 World Bank survey, Mahul and Stutley (2010) found that in 29 sampled countries with subsidized insurance programs, delivery costs averaged about 25 percent to 30 percent of the gross (unsubsidized) premium. Delivery costs include marketing and acquisition costs (including commissions paid to agents and brokers), administrative expenses, and loss adjustment expenses. In his 1992 paper, Hazell measured the full economic cost of subsidized insurance to governments as the ratio of the sum of total indemnities plus delivery costs, divided by premiums paid by producers:

$$\text{Hazell ratio} = (\text{indemnities} + \text{delivery costs})/\text{producer premium} \qquad (4)$$

Table 10.4 presents the full costs of the US crop insurance program for 1995–2014. Recall from Table 10.3 that indemnities paid equaled 91 percent of total premiums collected over the period (including subsidies). On average, producers received \$2.25 in indemnity payments for every \$1.00 they paid in premiums. However, once delivery costs are included, the government paid an average \$3.00 for every \$1.00 received in producer premiums.

Clearly, if agricultural insurance were delivered by the private sector in the absence of any government subsidies, delivery costs would be fully loaded into premium costs. As such, delivery cost subsidies constitute a subsidy to

12 The United States began notifying crop insurance support using premium subsidies (rather than net indemnity payments) in the 2008 reporting year, arguing that because the 2008 Farm Bill required crop insurance premiums to be set on an actuarially fair basis (that is, where the expected loss ratio is equal to 100 percent), premium subsidies were a more accurate estimate of the subsidy (WTO 2015a).

TABLE 10.4 Total economic costs of US crop insurance program, 1995–2014 (US$ millions)

Year	Indemnity	Producer premium	Net indemnity	Delivery costs	Total insurance outlays	Producer loss ratio[a]	Hazell ratio[b]
1995	1,567.7	653.8	913.9	509.3	1,423.2	2.40	3.18
1996	1,492.7	856.4	636.2	714.0	1,350.2	1.74	2.58
1997	993.6	872.3	121.3	793.1	914.3	1.14	2.05
1998	1,677.5	928.4	749.2	715.5	1,464.7	1.81	2.58
1999	2,434.7	916.2	1,518.5	770.3	2,288.9	2.66	3.50
2000	2,594.8	1,589.0	1,005.9	824.8	2,245.3	1.63	2.91
2001	2,960.1	1,190.1	1,770.0	994.1	2,764.2	2.49	3.32
2002	4,066.7	1,174.5	2,892.2	616.0	3,508.2	3.46	3.95
2003	3,260.8	1,389.3	1,871.5	1,117.0	2,988.5	2.35	3.15
2004	3,209.7	1,708.7	1,501.0	1,590.0	3,091.0	1.88	2.81
2005	2,367.3	1,605.4	761.9	1,748.0	2,509.9	1.47	2.56
2006	3,503.6	1,897.5	1,606.1	1,787.0	3,393.1	1.85	2.79
2007	3,547.6	2,738.8	808.8	2,909.0	3,717.8	1.30	2.36
2008	8,679.9	4,160.4	4,519.5	3,111.0	7,630.5	2.09	2.83
2009	5,228.8	3,523.9	1,705.0	3,896.0	5,601.0	1.48	2.59
2010	4,251.4	2,883.1	1,368.3	3,300.0	4,668.3	1.47	2.62
2011	10,809.6	4,475.2	6,334.5	3,049.0	9,383.5	2.42	3.10
2012	17,441.9	4,136.3	13,305.6	94.0	13,399.6	4.22	4.24
2013	12,073.6	4,510.1	7,563.5	2,056.0	9,619.5	2.68	3.13
2014	9,057.2	3,853.3	5,203.9	3,324.0	8,527.9	2.35	3.21
Average 1995–2014	**5,061.0**	**2,253.1**	**2,807.8**	**1,695.9**	**4,524.5**	**2.25**	**3.00**

Source: Glauber (2004); USDA RMA (2015).
Note: [a]Indemnities divided by producer premium; [b]Indemnities plus delivery costs divided by producer premium.

producers. However, as pointed out by Mahul and Stutley (2010), the Hazell ratio may overstate benefits because the measure does not take into account the insurance company's performance as a financially viable or nonviable entity. The US crop insurance program, for example, has been heavily criticized for providing excessive subsidies to the private sector that have largely been captured by crop insurance agents and others (GAO 2009; Babcock 2012). Thus for programs that subsidize delivery costs, the actual benefit to the producer expressed as a ratio of benefits to premium paid likely falls between the producer loss ratio and the Hazell ratio. For countries where producers receive subsidies to cover a portion of fully loaded premiums (such as France), the full subsidy is captured by the premium subsidy. Where delivery costs are provided separately, they have typically not been reported to the WTO. The United States began reporting delivery costs in its 2009 WTO notification but, under paragraph 2 (general services) of Annex 2, not as an Amber Box subsidy.

Last, there is the issue of whether Amber Box agricultural insurance subsidies should be notified as a product-specific subsidy (for example, corn crop insurance subsidies) or as a non-product-specific subsidy (such as water subsidies that may be generally available for all crops). WTO members have generally notified Amber Box crop insurance subsidies as non-product-specific.[13] For example, responding to a question raised by the European Union concerning insurance subsidies, the United States defended notifying them as non-product-specific by saying, "Since the parameters are uniform by commodity and such a wide range of commodities are covered, this programme is notified as 'non-product specific'" (WTO 1999). Canada made similar arguments defending crop insurance subsidies as non-product-specific, stating that insurance is "available to almost all commercially grown commodities (more than one hundred) across Canada. Any producer in Canada is eligible to participate in the programme for agricultural products eligible for coverage" (WTO 2008a).

Yet although crop insurance may be available for "almost all crops," subsidy levels vary markedly across crops. Table 10.5 shows premium subsidy levels for selected US crops in 2014. Subsidies are calculated on a per-insured-acre basis as well as a percentage of the value of production. While the average insured acre received a per unit subsidy of $21.00, among the crops considered, subsidies ranged from $15.12 per acre for barley to $45.65 for upland cotton. On a value of production basis, premium subsidies for barley, corn, peanuts, rice, and soybeans were less than 5 percent in 2014, whereas premium subsidies for upland cotton, grain sorghum, and wheat all exceeded 7.5 percent.

The United States began notifying crop insurance subsidies on a product-specific basis with its 2012 domestic support notification. The country noted

13 Notifying crop insurance subsidies as non-product-specific Amber dates to 1992, when the United States, Japan, Canada, and other contracting parties submitted schedules of commitment (WTO 1995). At the time, comprehensive records of crop-specific insurance data were not readily available, and it seems likely that the lack of data may have been an important factor in the decision to notify subsidies as non-product-specific.

TABLE 10.5 US crop insurance subsidies for selected crops, 2014

Commodity	Acres (millions)	Value of production (US$ millions)	Subsidy (US$ millions)	Average subsidy per acre ($/acre)	Subsidy as percentage of value of production (%)
Barley	2.2	869.7	33.0	15.12	3.8
Corn	79.0	52,372.2	2,187.7	27.70	4.2
Cotton	10.4	4,625.8	473.1	45.65	10.2
Grain sorghum	5.3	1,670.4	134.4	25.35	8.0
Peanuts	1.2	1,122.3	38.2	30.72	3.4
Rice	2.7	3,104.6	57.3	21.51	1.8
Soybeans	73.8	40,288.5	1,391.8	18.85	3.5
Wheat	47.9	11,923.9	918.3	19.16	7.7
All crops	294.5	223,867.2	6,209.7	21.09	2.8

Source: USDA RMA (2015).

that questions had been raised by various WTO members regarding US classification of crop insurance as non-product-specific:[14]

> In preparing its 2012 notification the United States undertook a review of its notification of its crop insurance program. As a result of that review, the United States decided that because crop insurance premiums are based on production histories and expected prices of specific commodities, and because crop insurance policies are priced according to the actual crop planted and contain crop specific terms and features, and thus the associated premium support has similar crop-specific associations, the U.S. crop insurance program is more appropriately classified as product-specific support. (WTO 2015a)

Impact of Agricultural Insurance Subsidies on Production

Recall that the general criteria for Green Box measures require that such measures must have no, or at most minimal, trade-distorting effects on production. Insurance generally improves welfare for risk-averse producers (Just, Hueth, and Schmitz 2005), because in the presence of contingency markets

14 The United States indicated that it would submit corrected notifications reflecting the new reporting method for 2008 through 2011 (WTO 2015a).

like crop insurance, these producers will grow more. However, empirical evidence for US producers suggests that these effects are likely small. Just, Calvin, and Quiggin (1999) found that for producers participating in the US federal crop insurance program, risk aversion was a minor part of the incentive to participate. Rather, the decision to participate was largely driven by the size of the expected benefit (due to premium subsidies). Recent papers by Babcock (2015) and Du, Feng, and Hennessy (2014) pointed out that if producers are participating in the crop insurance program primarily to "harvest" subsidies, they are not acting optimally (that is, they are not choosing optimal levels of coverage to maximize subsidies). These studies concluded that farmers' decisions about how much crop insurance to buy are not generally consistent with either expected profit or utility maximization. Farmers do not pick coverage levels that maximize expected subsidies, nor do they demand full insurance coverage. Over time, however, producers have tended to sign up for higher coverage levels when the per unit subsidies tend to be higher. Glauber (2012) showed that the average coverage levels for most row crops have grown significantly and continuously since the late 1990s, when subsidies were increased for higher coverage levels.

Empirical work on insurance has focused primarily on the effects of the US crop insurance program on planted area and the effects of insurance on input use. In an analysis of Nebraska corn producers, Wu (1999) concluded that farms that purchased insurance were more likely to produce soybeans and less likely to produce forage crops. Using a simulation model with regional acreage supply equations, Young, Vandeveer, and Schnepf (2001) found that planted acreage for major field crops was only 0.4 percent higher due to subsidized insurance. Increased plantings of wheat and cotton accounted for about three-fourths of the increase. Goodwin, Vandeveer, and Deal (2004) examined Midwestern corn and soybean producers and wheat and barley producers in the Northern Plains and found that a 30 percent decrease in premium costs was likely to increase barley acreage by about 1.1 percent and corn acreage by less than 0.5 percent; soybean and wheat acreage showed no statistically significant impact. Ligon (2012) analyzed the impact of crop insurance on specialty crops and concluded that the introduction of crop insurance had a large and positive impact on tree crops but a negligible impact on nontree crops.

Although no studies have directly analyzed the effects of crop insurance on yield, much research has been done on the effects of crop insurance on input use (Horowitz and Lichtenberg 1993; Quiggin, Karagiannis, and Stanton 1993; Babcock and Hennessy 1996; Smith and Goodwin 1996; Goodwin and Smith 2003; Goodwin, Vandeveer, and Deal 2004). With the exception

TABLE 10.6 Average subsidies, 1993 versus 2014

	US$ per acre		Subsidy as percentage of premium	
Crop	1993	2014	1993	2014
Barley	1.41	15.12	26.9%	62.0%
Wheat	1.33	19.16	27.2%	63.2%
Corn	2.12	27.70	25.7%	60.0%
Soybeans	1.71	18.85	25.8%	61.6%

Source: USDA RMA (2015).

of Horowitz and Lichtenberg, these studies concluded that the effects of crop insurance on input use are negative, suggesting that the resulting effect on yields is also likely negative. Whether this effect is large enough to offset any positive effect on crop acreage remains an open question. Although research on the production effects of insurance programs outside the United States is limited, similar conclusions have been drawn. Garrido, Bielza, and Sumpsi (2003) found that crop insurance subsidies had minimal effects on Spanish producers' planting decisions. In an analysis of Indian rice producers, Varadan and Kumar (2012) found that crop insurance encouraged crop specialization among Tamil Nadu farmers; however, it was unclear whether all crops were provided insurance or just rice.

Goodwin and Smith (2012) questioned whether the results of earlier studies continue to be relevant, given that subsidy levels are much higher now than when earlier research was conducted and that revenue policies have largely replaced yield coverages. For example, Goodwin, Vandeveer, and Deal (2004) examined the effects of insurance subsidies from 1986 to 1993, prior to the enactment of major legislation in 1994 and 2000, which dramatically increased subsidy levels and the introduction of revenue insurance (Glauber 2004). In 1993 government subsidies as a percentage of total premium costs averaged 25–27 percent for the crops examined in the study, compared with 60–63 percent for those crops in 2014 (Table 10.6). Average subsidies ranged from \$1.33 to \$2.12 per acre in 1993, compared with \$15.12 to \$27.70 per acre in 2014.

Recent studies by Walters et al. (2012) and Claasen, Langpap, and Wu (2015) found negligible effects of crop insurance on land use, though the latter found more significant impacts on crop choice and crop rotation. Yet, although the levels of support for insurance products have increased substantially, the relative share of subsidies across crops has remained largely the same, at least for those crops that are offered similar types of insurance products. With improvements in rate making, due in part to the wealth of farm-level data, premium rates are more in line with underlying risks, which means that relative rates should not favor one insured crop over another (Glauber 2012). Further complicating analyses is the fact that because price elections for most of the major row crops are now based on futures market prices, per acre premiums (and subsidies) are highly correlated to harvest price expectations.

The general conclusions from this body of research are mixed and are largely based on US experience. Studies mostly indicate that crop insurance subsidies have had minimal effect, at least in areas where insurance is broadly available across crops. In addition, crop insurance likely has larger impacts on crop choice when insured crops compete against uninsured crops or when crops with available revenue products compete against crops for which only yield products are available.[15] Such distortions may become even larger with the development of new products, such as margin insurance and supplemental coverage, particularly if such products are not widely available across crops.

Treatment of Crop Insurance in Trade Disputes

Crop insurance has been subject to investigation in various trade disputes, including Brazil's WTO challenge to US cotton subsidies (US–Upland Cotton) and several countervailing duty investigations (see Schnepf 2005; Johnson and Becker 2010). Although the international rules differ, each case addressed similar issues: (1) the crop specificity of the program, (2) the treatment of producer benefits, and (3) the treatment of company benefits.

US–Upland Cotton

The US crop insurance program was part of Brazil's WTO challenge to US support programs for upland cotton. Brazil objected to US domestic support programs based on two factors: (1) those programs provided support to upland cotton and thus needed to be included as part of the peace clause analysis, and (2) subsidies for upland cotton distorted US cotton production, which depressed world cotton prices (price suppression).

The first part of Brazil's challenge concerned Article 13 of the AoA (the so-called peace clause), which protected domestic support measures from challenge under the WTO Subsidies and Countervailing Duties Agreement if all

15 Under the US program, revenue products are mostly available for crops for which there are viable futures markets for price discovery purposes (for example, corn, wheat, and cotton).

non–Green Box support from those measures did not exceed support granted "to a specific commodity in excess of that decided during the 1992 marketing year" (WTO 2003). The peace clause determination was thus a threshold decision that determined whether Brazil could bring a price-suppression case against US cotton subsidies. Brazil included crop insurance and other price and income support programs for cotton in the peace clause calculation and used premium subsidies for upland cotton as the measure of that support. The United States argued that support for crop insurance should be excluded from the peace clause calculation—not because subsidies were Green (indeed, as presented previously, subsidies had been notified as Amber), but because the insurance subsidies were not specific to cotton but were generally available for all insured crops. The United States did not contest the use of premium subsidies as measurement, even though it had been notifying net indemnities as a measure of support.[16]

A WTO compliance panel sided with Brazil, determining that crop insurance subsidies were specific to cotton and accepting Brazil's original data on premium subsidies for upland cotton as the measure of support. Thus premium subsidies to upland cotton were included in total support to cotton during the 1999–2002 period of investigation. The panel found that the support exceeded cotton support in 1992 and thus ruled that US cotton programs were not exempt from challenge. Once the panel concluded that US support programs were not exempt from challenge under the peace clause, all the programs—including crop insurance—were exposed to Brazil's serious prejudice challenge. Brazil claimed that the combined US programs, by paying out large subsidies, encouraged excess US production and exports, thus driving down world prices to the disadvantage of Brazil's cotton producers.

To evaluate Brazil's claims, the panel examined the nature of the US subsidy to determine whether payments under the various programs were price contingent (WTO 2004, para. 7.1290). The panel considered it highly relevant that certain US subsidies were directly linked to world market prices, including marketing loan payments, Step 2 payments, and countercyclical payments: "We consider that the nature of the United States subsidies at issue—in terms of their structure, design, and operation—is relevant in assessing whether or not they have price suppressing effects. We see before us two

16 The difference in measures would have had little material difference in the calculation. Upland cotton premium subsidies for 1999–2002 averaged $197 million, compared with $27 million in 1992 (a difference of $170 million). Net indemnities averaged $373 million for 1999–2002, compared with $224 million in 1992 (a difference of $149 million). Thus the difference in the measures would have been about $21 million.

general types of United States subsidies: those that are directly price-contingent, and those that are not" (WTO 2004, para. 7.1289). The panel concluded that crop insurance—along with direct payments and their predecessor, production flexibility contract payments—was not price contingent. The panel noted that subsidized crop insurance reduced costs, affected risk considerations, and heightened economic security, all of which could have positive ramifications for producer wealth and investment and economic stability (WTO 2004, para. 7.1306). However, the panel concluded that crop insurance subsidies were more in the nature of income support and therefore did not need to be included in the final analysis of price suppression.

The panel's serious prejudice ruling for crop insurance seemingly ignores the fact that revenue insurance was available to US cotton producers and thus, arguably, was price contingent.[17] In its review of crop insurance, the panel noted that the major plan type, which was available for more than 100 commodities, was "actual production history" and that other plan types, such as area plans and revenue plans, were available for only a small number of commodities. Thus crop insurance was viewed mainly as a program that insured crop yields.

During the period of investigation (1999–2002), revenue policies never exceeded more than 14 percent of cotton area enrolled in the program. Since revenue policies were first introduced in the mid-1990s, they have grown in popularity and now dominate US crop insurance choices.[18] In 2014 revenue policies accounted for about 80 percent of enrolled cotton area and 90 percent of cotton insurance premium subsidies. In addition, the 2014 Farm Bill replaced cotton income support programs with a supplemental area-based revenue insurance program for cotton producers; this was called the Stacked Income Protection Plan (STAX).[19] Lau, Schropp, and Sumner (2015) pointed out that recent case law from the WTO Appellate Body ruling in *US–Large Civil Aircraft* clarified that panels are to include in serious prejudice findings any subsidies with an identifiable impact on production or pricing decisions. Under the new jurisprudence, panels would arguably have to take subsidies

17 Brazil did not appeal the panel's decision on crop insurance, presumably because crop insurance subsidies were small relative to the other price-based programs.

18 Revenue insurance for upland cotton was introduced in 1998.

19 The primary motivation for the STAX program was to resolve the WTO case with Brazil. On October 16, 2014, Brazil and the United States notified the WTO Dispute Settlement Unit (DSU) that, in accordance with Article 3.6 of the Dispute Settlement Understanding, they had concluded a memorandum of understanding and agreed that this dispute was terminated (Schnepf 2014).

into account, even if those subsidies are not price contingent but could be shown to have an impact on production or pricing decisions.

Crop Insurance and Countervailing Duty Challenges

In a countervailing duty (CVD) challenge, a country claims that the effect of subsidized imports of a product harms its domestic industry. US support programs for several commodities have been challenged on several occasions, and some of those challenges have involved crop insurance. The cases reviewed here include three challenges that Canada made to US programs for corn as well as China's challenge to US chicken exports based on subsidies to corn and soybeans as feed ingredients that passed through to chicken prices. The rules for CVD investigations are different from those involved in the *US–Upland Cotton* case or in domestic support notifications to the WTO. In general, the aim of these investigations is to determine whether a subsidy is specific to a product and, if so, to determine a subsidy rate, such as dollars per bushel. (Whether the subsidized imports damage the domestic industry is a separate analysis.) The treatment of crop insurance in these investigations provides interesting insight into how different countries have measured and analyzed those programs.

Canada–US Corn Cases

Canada challenged US corn programs three separate times under its Special Import Measures Act for the marketing years 1985, 1998–1999, and 2003–2004. In each case, crop insurance was included as an actionable subsidy specific to corn. The subsidy was measured differently each time, and unlike in the *US–Upland Cotton* case, benefits to the companies were included. In the 1985 case, the Canadian authorities found: "The program is considered to be targeted in that, while the program is apparently available to all persons engaged in agriculture, in fact it is not" (cited in GATT 1992, 14). The amount of the subsidy was equal to the amount of indemnities paid to corn, plus the administration and operating expenses allocated to corn, minus the producer-paid premiums. The subsidy was divided by total corn production to give a subsidy per bushel of $0.003345 (GATT 1992).

In the 1998–1999 case, Canada estimated the crop insurance subsidies as total net indemnities and expenses for all crops and then allocated a portion of that total to corn based on corn's percentage of the value of all insurance (based on liabilities) and divided that by total corn production. This method resulted in a subsidy of $0.043 per bushel for 1998 and $0.056 per bushel for 1999 (Canada Border Services Agency 2001). Similar to its arguments in *US–Upland Cotton*, the United States argued that crop insurance subsidies were not specific to corn, noting the number of products insured and the large share of all crops that were insured in various states. In addition, the United States argued that Canada should use net indemnities for corn only, claiming that corn had lower loss ratios than the combined book of business. To calculate corn's share of underwriting gains and delivery expenses, the United States proposed using corn's share of total premiums, noting that underwriting gains and delivery expenses were based on premiums, not liabilities.

In its final determination, Canada rejected the US arguments about specificity, noting that three crops (corn, wheat, and cotton) received a "disproportionate share of the subsidy granted by the US Government for the Federal crop insurance program" (Canada Border Services Agency 2001, 22). On the question of method, Canada accepted the US argument that actual government costs for corn (premium subsidies and net indemnities) should be used. Canada also accepted the US method of allocating administrative and operating expenses and underwriting gains based on corn's share of total premiums. The total expenses were divided by total corn production for a subsidy of $0.051 per bushel for 1998 and $0.065 per bushel for 1999 (Canada Border Services Agency 2001). In the 2003–2004 challenge, Canada calculated the benefit from crop insurance as the sum of premium subsidies plus administrative and operating expenses minus administrative fees paid by producers under the catastrophic insurance (CAT) program.[20] Unlike in the 2001 determination, underwriting gains were not included in the calculation of insurance subsidies (Canada Border Services Agency 2006).

China–US Poultry Case

In 2009 the Ministry of Commerce of China launched antidumping and antisubsidies investigations into chicken meat produced in the United States (Johnson and Becker 2010). China claimed that US subsidies to corn and soybeans resulted in lower feed prices, which were in turn passed through to poultry producers, resulting in lower chicken prices for exports and harming the Chinese chicken industry. Crop insurance subsidies for corn and soybeans were included with other price and income support subsidies. China calculated insurance subsidies based on premium subsidies for corn and soybeans

20 Under the CAT program, producers receive free 50 percent yield coverage in exchange for a nominal signup fee.

as well as administrative costs for delivery of corn and soybean policies. The United States argued that the most appropriate method was to use net indemnities for corn and soybeans.[21] China did not change its method in its final determination, which resulted in a subsidy of $0.22 per bushel for corn and $0.61 per bushel for soybeans.

In both the *US–Upland Cotton* case and the four antisubsidy cases in which crop insurance was investigated, the authorities found that US programs conferred a specific subsidy. In no case have US arguments that its crop insurance program does not confer benefits to a specific crop prevailed. In contrast to the treatment of crop insurance in the *US–Upland Cotton* case, the investigating authorities in the CVD cases always included government support to insurance companies in some fashion as well as the benefits to producers, either in the form of premium subsidies or net indemnities.[22]

Efforts to Reform Green Box Criteria Relating to Agricultural Insurance

Given the evolution and growth of agricultural insurance programs, questions have arisen as to whether such programs are compatible with current Green Box criteria and whether those criteria should be modified to more closely match the structure of current insurance programs or to meet the needs of developing countries (Nassar et al. 2009). In this light, the Doha Development Agenda negotiations have put forth various proposals to amend paragraphs 7 and 8 in Annex 2.[23]

---

21 US premium subsidies for corn and soybeans totaled $3.2 billion in 2009, compared with total net indemnities of –$417 million (USDA RMA 2015).

22 In the broader issue of injury determination, the Canadian Import Trade Tribunal ruled that US corn subsidies injured producers in the 1985 case. The finding was challenged by the United States under the Subsidies and Countervailing Measures provisions of the GATT and overturned (GATT 1992). In the other two corn CVD cases brought by Canada, the Canadian Import Trade Tribunal failed to find injury. In the China poultry case, China found injury as a result of corn and soybean subsidies. However, the United States challenged the ruling in the WTO; the determination was overturned in a WTO dispute settlement ruling in 2014 (WTO 2013).

23 Under the Agreed Framework adopted by WTO members on August 1, 2004, it was agreed that "Green Box criteria will be reviewed and clarified with a view to ensuring that Green Box measures have no, or at most minimal, trade-distorting effects or effects on production. Such a review and clarification will need to ensure that the basic concepts, principles, and effectiveness of the Green Box remain and take due account of non-trade concerns. The improved obligations for monitoring and surveillance of all new disciplines foreshadowed in paragraph 48 below will be particularly important with respect to the Green Box" (WTO 2004).

Reforming Criteria for Defining Eligible Losses

Under paragraphs 7 and 8, eligible insurance programs must require a 30 percent loss threshold before losses are paid. Presumably, contracting parties agreed that a 30 percent loss threshold defined a "catastrophic loss" for production and income losses. However, for area-indexed policies and weather derivatives, a 30 percent loss threshold may be more stringent than the threshold established for indemnity-based individual losses. Given the interest of area-based and weather-based insurance products, loss thresholds are particularly of interest. Research on area- and weather-indexed products suggests that producers must typically carry insurance with higher coverage levels in order to obtain similar protection to indemnity-based products (Miranda 1991; Smith, Chouinard, and Baquet 1994; Skees, Black, and Barnett 1997). The Revised Draft Modalities for Agriculture, circulated by the chair of the agriculture negotiations in December 2008, included changes to allow developing countries to establish loss thresholds of less than 30 percent for compensation for income or production losses under paragraphs 7 and 8. That variance would not apply to developed countries.

Reforming Criteria for Determining Yield and Revenue Guarantees

Current criteria for establishing production and revenue guarantees are based on the previous three years or the previous five years, excluding high and low entries. Many countries, such as Canada and United States, base guarantees on longer time series, arguing that doing so gives a more accurate estimate of a producer's expected yield or revenue. In the Revised Draft Modalities, paragraph 8 is modified to allow members to base production guarantees on "a period demonstrated to be actuarially appropriate" (WTO 2008b, 41). However, that change applied to paragraph 8 only; no comparable changes are proposed for paragraph 7.

Reforming Criteria in Paragraph 7 Concerning Revenue Insurance

Currently, use of paragraph 7 has largely been confined to income safety-net programs such as those used in Australia and Canada. Although revenue insurance programs exist, most are incompatible with the current criteria. For example, under the US program, most revenue insurance policies are offered on an individual crop basis, not on a whole farm basis as called for in paragraph 7.[24] Moreover, in the US program, revenue products are based on futures prices that are arguably more reflective of planting time expectations for harvest prices as compared with guarantees based on historical prices under current criteria.

Another issue concerns whether loss thresholds for gross income should necessarily be the same as for insurance products based on net income. Current criteria in paragraph 7 call for thresholds to be made on an "equivalent" basis but do not specify how that should be done. Given the growth and interest in income margin insurance, the cost of production insurance, and other net income schemes, more research would seem warranted in this area. The Revised Draft Modalities are silent on paragraph 7, perhaps reflecting members' concerns about exempting revenue insurance schemes from domestic support disciplines.

Increased Transparency

An important goal of the Doha Development Agenda negotiations has been to enhance monitoring to ensure full transparency (WTO 2004, 2008b). Agricultural insurance programs are particularly complicated, and detailed data on program operation (participation data, premiums, indemnities, subsidies, delivery costs, and so on) are often difficult to obtain. Increased reporting requirements would enhance transparency and allow members a better understanding of how those programs may affect production and trade.[25]

Conclusion

Agricultural insurance programs have grown considerably over the past 25 years and now make up an integral part of many domestic support programs in developed countries and important emerging markets. There is considerable interest in the use of insurance products, including weather derivatives, as important tools to promote risk-management strategies in developing economies. The AoA seemingly encourages the development of insurance programs in lieu of more trade- and production-distorting programs, such as price supports or production-linked subsidies. However, criteria in paragraphs 7 and 8 of Annex 2 appear to be poorly fitted for most modern insurance

24 The United States offers whole farm revenue insurance, but uptake has been limited. Changes in the 2014 Farm Bill were aimed at making whole farm insurance policies more attractive.

25 As the section on trade disputes shows, improved transparency is important not just for the AoA but also for the Agreement on Subsidies and Countervailing Measures and the AoA (see Josling 2015).

programs. That said, the overarching criterion of Annex 2—for programs to "have no, or at most minimal, trade-distorting effects or effects on production"—requires that care and consideration be given to any proposed changes to guard against introducing potential distorting subsidies under the guise of safety-net programs.

Recent papers suggest that insurance subsidies could come under renewed scrutiny in potential WTO cases against countries with large insurance programs, such as the United States (Lau, Schropp, and Sumner 2015) and China (DTB Associates 2014; Hudson 2015). Recent WTO cases, such as *US–Upland Cotton,* provide a ready blueprint for such challenges (Andersen and Taylor 2009–2010). This record may imply that the use of such programs to countervail price volatility may be less effective if they will be increasingly challenged at the WTO. In this vein, Josling (2015) recently suggested that a future scenario for reform could be to abandon the AoA altogether and subsume domestic support rules in the category of actionable subsidies under the Agreement on Subsidies and Countervailing Measures. Such a move would require increased transparency and monitoring of the growing variety of agricultural insurance programs around the world.

Bibliography

Andersen, S., and M. Taylor. 2009–2010. "Brazil's Challenge to U.S. Cotton Subsidies: The Road to Effective Disciplines of Agricultural Subsidies." *Business Law Brief* (Fall–Winter): 2–10.

Antón, J., S. Kimura, and R. Martini. 2011. *Risk Management in Agriculture in Canada*. OECD Food, Agriculture, and Fisheries Paper 40. Paris: OECD Publishing.

Babcock, B. 2012. "The Politics and Economics of the U.S. Crop Insurance Program." In *The Intended and Unintended Effects of U.S. Agricultural and Biotechnology Policies,* edited by J. Graff Zivin and J. Perloff, 83–112. Chicago: University of Chicago Press.

———. 2015. "Using Cumulative Prospect Theory to Explain Anomalous Crop Insurance Coverage Choice." *American Journal of Agricultural Economics* 97: 1317–1384.

Babcock, B., and D. Hennessy. 1996. "Input Demand under Yield and Revenue Insurance." *American Journal of Agricultural Economics* 78: 416–427.

Binswanger-Mkhize, H. 2012. "Is There Too Much Hype about Index-based Agricultural Insurance?" *Journal of Development Studies* 48 (2): 187–200.

Bobojonov, I., L. Götz, and T. Glauben. 2014. "How Well Does the Crop Insurance Market Function in Russia?" Paper prepared for presentation at the European Association of Agricultural Economists 2014 Congress, Ljubljana, Slovenia, August 26–29.

Boissonade, A. 2015. "New Frontiers in Agricultural Insurance." *The Actuary*, March 5. Accessed June 24, 2015. www.theactuary.com/features/2015/03/new-frontiers-in-agriculture/.

Canada Border Services Agency. 2001. "Final Determination—Grain Corn." Investigation No. 4237-88 AD/1242; 4218-10 CV/91. February, Ottawa.

———. 2006. "Concerning the Making of a Final Determination of Dumping and Subsidizing Respecting Unprocessed Grain Corn, Excluding Seed Corn (for Reproductive Purposes), Sweet Corn, and Popping Corn, Originating in or Exported from the United States of America." Investigation No. 4214-10 and 4218-20. March, Ottawa.

Carter, M., 2012. "Designed for Development Impact: Next Generation Approaches to Index Insurance for Smallholder Farmers." *MunichRe Microinsurance Compendium* 2.

Carter, M., A. de Janvry, E. Sadoulet, and A. Sarris. 2014. "Index-Based Weather Insurance for Developing Countries: A Review of Evidence and a Set of Propositions for Up-scaling." La Fondation pour les Études et Recherches sur le Développement International. Accessed on September 28, 2015. www.ferdi.fr/sites/www.ferdi.fr/files/evenements/presentations/wp_ferdi_working_paper_on_index_insurance_june_19_kl.pdf.

CBO (Congressional Budget Office). 2015. *2015 Baseline for Farm Programs*. March, Unpublished, Washington, DC.

Claassen, R., C. Langpap, and J. Wu. 2015. "Impacts of Federal Crop Insurance on Land Use and Environmental Quality." Selected paper presented at the 2015 Agricultural and Applied Economics Association, San Francisco, CA, July 26–28.

Clarke, D., O. Mahul, K. Rao, and N. Verma. 2012. *Weather Based Crop Insurance in India*. Policy Research Working Paper 5985. Washington, DC: World Bank.

Commonwealth of Australia. 2015. "Agricultural Competitiveness." White Paper. Canberra.

Dick, W., and W. Wang. 2010. "Government Interventions in Agricultural Insurance." *Agriculture and Agricultural Science Procedia* 1: 4–12.

DTB Associates. 2014. "Agricultural Subsidies in Key Developing Countries: November 2014 Update." Washington, DC: DTB Associates, LLP.

Du, X., H. Feng, and D. Hennessy. 2014. "Rationality of Choices in Subsidized Crop Insurance Markets." Center for Agricultural and Rural Development Working Paper 14-WP 545. February. Accessed September 28, 2015. www.card.iastate.edu/publications/DBS/PDFFiles/14wp545.pdf.

European Commission. 2013. "Overview of CAP Reform 2014–2020." *Agricultural Policy Perspectives Brief* 5, December.

FAO (Food and Agricultural Organization). 1991. *A Compendium of Crop Insurance Programmes*. Rome.

GAO (Government Accountability Office). 2009. *Crop Insurance: Opportunities Exist to Reduce the Costs of Administering the Program*. GAO-09-445. Washington, DC.

Garrido, A., M. Bielza, and J. M. Sumpsi. 2003. "The Impact of Crop Insurance Subsidies on Land Allocation and Production in Spain." AGR/CA/APM(2002)16/Final. *OECD Report*. Unpublished, OECD, Paris.

GATT (General Agreement on Tariffs and Trade). 1986. "Punta del Este Declaration." BISD 33S/40. Unpublished. Geneva.

———. 1987a. "United States Proposal for Negotiations on Agriculture." MTN.GNG/NG5/W/14. Unpublished. July 7. Geneva.

———. 1987b. "European Communities Proposal for Multilateral Trade Negotiations on Agriculture." MTN.GNG/NG5/W/20. Unpublished. October 26. Geneva.

———. 1987c. "Cairns Group Proposal to the Uruguay Round Negotiating Group on Agriculture." MTN.GNG/NG5/W/21. Unpublished. October 26. Geneva.

———. 1987d. "Japanese Proposal for Negotiations on Agriculture." MTN.GNG/NG5/W/39. Unpublished. December 26. Geneva.

———. 1988. "A Framework for Agricultural Reform Submitted by the United States." MTN.GNG/NG5/W/83. Unpublished. November 9. Geneva.

———. 1989. "Submission of the United States on Comprehensive Long-Term Agricultural Reform." MTN.GNG/NG5/W/118. Unpublished. October 25. Geneva.

———. 1990a. "Framework Agreement on Agriculture Reform Programme—Draft Text by the Chairman (de Zeeuw Draft)." MTN.GNG/NG5/W/170. Unpublished. July 11. Geneva.

———. 1990b. "Draft Final Act Embodying the Results of the Uruguay Round of Multilateral Trade Negotiations." MTN.TNC/W/35/Rev.1. Unpublished. December 3. Geneva.

———. 1991a. "Technical Work on Domestic Support—Suggested Checklist of Issues by Art Dunkel for the Consultations on Agriculture." Unpublished. March 11–15. Geneva.

———. 1991b. "Domestic Support: Policies That Shall Be Excluded from the Reduction Commitment—Technical Note by the Secretariat." Unpublished. May 8. Geneva.

———. 1991c. "Options in the Agricultural Negotiations—Notes by the Chairman." MTN.GNG/AG/W/1. Unpublished. June 24. Geneva.

———. 1991d. "Draft Working Papers on Agriculture." Unpublished. November 21. Geneva.

———. 1991e. "Draft Final Act Embodying the Results of the Uruguay Round of Multilateral Trade Negotiations." MTN.TNC/W/FA. Unpublished. December 20. Geneva.

———. 1992. "Report of the Panel on Canadian Countervailing Duties on Grain Corn from the United States." SCM/140 and Corr.1-39S/411. Unpublished. Geneva.

Glauber, J. 2004. "Crop Insurance Reconsidered." *American Journal of Agricultural Economics* 86 (6): 1179–1195.

———. 2012. "The Growth of the Federal Crop Insurance Program, 1990–2011." *American Journal of Agricultural Economics* 95 (2): 482–488.

———. 2015. *Agricultural Insurance and the World Trade Organization*. IFPRI Discussion Paper 1473. Washington, DC: International Food Policy Research Institute.

Glauber, J., and K. Collins. 2002. "Crop Insurance, Disaster Assistance, and the Role of the Federal Government in Providing Catastrophic Risk Protection." *Agricultural Finance Review* 62: 81–102.

Goodwin, B., and V. Smith. 1995. *The Economics of Crop Insurance and Disaster Relief.* Washington, DC: AEI Press.

———. 2003. "An Ex Post Evaluation of the Conservation Reserve, Federal Crop Insurance, and Other Government Programs: Program Participation and Soil Erosion." *Journal of Agricultural and Resource Economics* 28: 201–216.

———. 2012. "What Harm Is Done by Subsidizing Crop Insurance?" *American Journal of Agricultural Economics* 95 (2): 489–497.

Goodwin, B., M. Vandeveer, and J. Deal. 2004. "An Empirical Analysis of Acreage Effects of Participation in the Federal Crop Insurance Program." *American Journal of Agricultural Economics* 86 (4): 1058–1077.

Hatch, D., M. Nunez, F. Vila, and K. Stephenson. 2012. "Agricultural Insurance in the Americas: A Risk Management Tool." Inter-American Institute for Cooperation on Agriculture. San Jose, Costa Rica. Accessed September 28, 2015. http://test-iica-web-dev.pantheon.io/es/content/los-seguros-agropecuarios-en-las-am%C3%A9ricas.

Hazell, P. 1992. "The Appropriate Role of Agricultural Insurance in Developing Countries." *Journal of International Development* 4: 567–581.

Hazell, P., C. Pomareda, and A. Valdes. 1986. *Crop Insurance for Agricultural Development: Issues and Experience.* Baltimore: Johns Hopkins University Press.

Horowitz, J. K., and E. Lichtenberg. 1993. "Insurance, Moral Hazard, and Chemical Use in Agriculture." *American Journal of Agricultural Economics* 75: 926–935.

Hudson, D. 2015. *Statement before the U.S. House of Representatives, Committee on Agriculture, Public Hearing on Review of Agricultural Subsidies in Foreign Countries.* 114th Congress. Washington, DC, June 3.

Ito, K., and J. Dyck. 2002. *Vegetable Policies in Japan.* Economic Research Service VGS-293-01. November. Washington, DC: USDA (US Department of Agriculture), Economic Research Service.

Johnson, R., and G. Becker. 2010. *China-U.S. Poultry Dispute*. Congressional Research Service Report R40706. Washington, DC: Congressional Research Service.

Josling, T. 2015. *Rethinking the Rules for Agricultural Subsidies*. E15 Initiative. Geneva: International Centre for Trade and Sustainable Development (ICTSD) and World Economic Forum. February.

Josling, T., S. Tangermann, and T. Warley. 1996. *Agriculture in the GATT*. London: MacMillan Press.

Just, R. E., L. Calvin, and J. Quiggin. 1999. "Adverse Selection in Crop Insurance: Actuarial and Asymmetric Information Incentives." *American Journal of Agricultural Economics* 81: 834–849.

Just, R., D. Hueth, and A. Schmitz. 2005. *The Welfare Economics of Public Policy: A Practical Approach to Project and Policy Evaluation*. Cheltenham, UK: Edward Elgar Publishing.

Kalra, A. 2013. "Partnering for Food Security in Emerging Markets." Swiss RE. *Sigma* 1. Accessed September 28, 2015. http://media.swissre.com/documents/sigma1_2013_en.pdf.

Lau, C., S. Schropp, and D. Sumner. 2015. *The Economic Effects on the World Market for Cotton of US Cotton Subsidies under the 2014 US Farm Bill*. Geneva: International Centre for Trade and Sustainable Development.

Li, X. 2014. "The Development of Agricultural Insurance in China." Presentation to the CAS Reinsurance Seminar, New York, May 21–22.

Ligon, E. 2012. "Supply and Effects of Specialty Crop Insurance." In *The Intended and Unintended Effects of U.S. Agricultural and Biotechnology Policies*, edited by J. Graff Zivin and J. Perloff, 113–142. Chicago: University of Chicago Press.

Mahul, O., and C. Stutley. 2010. *Government Support to Agricultural Insurance: Challenges and Opportunities for Developing Countries*. Washington, DC: World Bank.

Mahul, O., N. Verma, and D. Clarke. 2012. *Improving Farmers' Access to Agricultural Insurance in India*. Policy Research Working Paper 5987. Washington, DC: World Bank.

Miranda, M. 1991. "Area-Yield Crop Insurance Reconsidered." *American Journal of Agricultural Economics* 73 (May): 233–242.

Miranda, M., and K. Farrin. 2012. "Index Insurance for Developing Countries." *Applied Economic Perspectives and Policy* 34 (3): 391–427.

Munich RE. 2011. *Crop Insurance for the Wealthy*? Munich RE. Accessed September 28, 2015. www.munichre.com/site/corporate/get/documents_E-2053940859/mr/assetpool.shared/Documents/0_Corporate%20Website/2_Reinsurance/Business/Non-Life/Systemagro/systemagro-crop-insurance-for-the-wealthy_en.pdf.

Nassar, A., M. Rodriguez-Alcala, C. Costa, and S. Nogueia. 2009. "Agricultural Subsidies in the Green Box: Opportunities and Challenges for Developing Countries." In *Agricultural Subsidies in the WTO Green Box,* edited by R. Melendez-Ortiz, C. Bellmann, and J. Hepburn, 329–368. Cambridge, UK: Cambridge University Press.

OECD (Organisation for Economic Co-operation and Development). 1987. *National Policies and Agricultural Trade*. Paris.

Quiggin, J., G. Karagiannis, and J. Stanton. 1993. "Crop Insurance and Crop Production: Empirical Study of Moral Hazard and Adverse Selection." *Australian Journal of Agricultural Economics* 37: 95–113.

Roberts, R. 2005. *Insurance of Crops in Developing Countries*. FAO Agricultural Services Bulletin 159. Rome: Food and Agriculture Organization of the United Nations.

Schnepf, R. 2005. *U.S.-Canada Wheat and Corn Trade Disputes*. Washington, DC: Congressional Research Service.

———. 2010. *Brazil's WTO Case against the U.S. Cotton Program*. Washington, DC: Congressional Research Service RL35271.

———. 2014. *Status of the WTO Brazil-U.S. Cotton Case*. Washington, DC: Congressional Research Service R43336.

Sigurdson, D., and R. Sin. 1994. "An Aggregate Analysis of Canadian Crop Insurance Policy." In *Economics of Agricultural Crop Insurance: Theory and Evidence,* edited by D. Hueth and W. Furtan, 45–72. Boston, MA, US: Kluwer Academic Publishers.

Skees, J., J. Black, and B. Barnett. 1997. "Designing and Rating an Area Yield Crop Insurance Contract." *American Journal of Agricultural Economics* 79 (May): 430–438.

Skees, J., P. Hazell, and M. Miranda. 1999. *New Approaches to Crop Yield Insurance in Developing Countries*. EPTD Discussion Paper 55. Washington, DC: International Food Policy Research Institute.

Skees, J., and M. Reed. 1986. "Rate Making for Farm-Level Crop Insurance: Implications for Adverse Selection." *American Journal of Agricultural Economics* 68 (3): 653–659.

Smith, V. 2016. "Producer Insurance and Risk Management Options for Smallholder Farmers." *The World Bank Observer*. Advance Access, March 29.

Smith, V., H. Chouinard, and A. Baquet. 1994. "Almost Ideal Area Yield Crop Insurance Contracts." *Agricultural and Resource Economics Review* 23 (April): 75–83.

Smith, V., and J. Glauber. 2012. "Agricultural Insurance in Developed Countries: Where Have We Been and Where Are We Going?" *Applied Economic Perspectives and Policy* 34 (3): 363–390.

Smith, V., and B. Goodwin. 1996. "Crop Insurance, Moral Hazard, and Agricultural Chemical Use." *American Journal of Agricultural Economics* 78: 428–438.

Stancanelli, N. 2009. "The Historical Context of the Green Box." In *Agricultural Subsidies in the WTO Green Box,* edited by R. Melendez-Ortiz, C. Bellmann, and J. Hepburn, 19–35. Cambridge, UK: Cambridge University Press.

Stewart, T. 1999. *The GATT Uruguay Round: A Negotiating History (1986–1994).* Vol. 4, *The End Game.* The Hague, Netherlands: Kluwer Law International.

Tangermann, S., T. Josling, and S. Pearson. 1987. "Multilateral Negotiations on Farm-support Levels." *The World Economy* 10 (3): 265–282.

USDA RMA (US Department of Agriculture, Risk Management Agency). 2015. *Summary of Business.* Washington, DC.

Varadan, R., and P. Kumar. 2012. "Impact of Crop Insurance on Rice Farming in Tamil Nadu." *Agricultural Economics Research Review* 25 (2): 291–298.

Walters, C., C. Shumway, H. Chouinard, and P. Wandscheider. 2012. "Crop Insurance, Land Allocation, and the Environment." *Journal of Agricultural and Resource Economics* 37 (2): 301–320.

Wright, B., and J. Hewitt. 1994. "All-Risk Crop Insurance: Lessons from Theory and Experience." In *Economics of Agricultural Crop Insurance: Theory and Evidence,* edited by D. L. Hueth and W. H. Furtan, 73–114. Boston: Kluwer Academic Publishers.

WTO (World Trade Organization). 1995. "Supporting Tables Relating to Commitments on Agricultural Products in Part IV of Schedules." G/AG/AGST. Unpublished. Geneva.

———. 1999. "US Response to Question by the European Union in Connection with Individual Notifications." Committee on Agriculture, September 29. Available through the WTO Agricultural Information Management System, ID no. 20117. Geneva.

———. 2003. *Agriculture.* The WTO Agreements Series. Vol. 3. Geneva.

———. 2004. "Doha Work Program: Decision Adopted by the General Council on 1 August 2004." WT/L/579. August 2. Unpublished. Geneva.

———. 2008a. "Canada Response to Question by Australia in Connection with Individual Notifications." Committee on Agriculture, March 18. Available through the WTO Agricultural Information Management System, ID no. 51009. Geneva.

———. 2008b. "Revised Draft Modalities for Agriculture." TN/AG/W/4/Rev.4. December 6. Unpublished. Geneva.

———. 2013. "China Antidumping and Countervailing Duty Measures on Broiler Production from the United States: Report of the Panel." WT/DS427/R. Unpublished. Geneva.

———. 2015a. "US Response to Question by India in Connection with Individual Notifications." Committee on Agriculture, March 4. Available through the WTO Agricultural Information Management System, ID no. 76045. Geneva.

———. 2015b. WTO Documents on line Search Facility. Accessed September 28, 2015. https://docsonline.wto.org/dol2fe/Pages/FE_Search/FE_S_S001.aspx?language=1.

Wu, J. 1999. "Crop Insurance, Acreage Decisions, and Nonpoint-Source Pollution." *American Journal of Agricultural Economics* 81: 305–320.

Young, C., M. Vandeveer, and R. Schnepf. 2001. "Production and Price Impacts of U.S. Crop Insurance Programs." *American Journal of Agricultural Economics* 83 (5): 1196–1203.

Appendix 10.1 Provisions in Annex 2 Encompassing Insurance Programs

Annex 2

DOMESTIC SUPPORT: THE BASIS FOR EXEMPTION FROM THE REDUCTION COMMITMENTS

1. Domestic support measures for which exemption from the reduction commitments is claimed shall meet the fundamental requirement that they have no, or at most minimal, trade-distorting effects or effects on production. Accordingly, all measures for which exemption is claimed shall conform to the following basic criteria:
   (a) the support in question shall be provided through a publicly-funded government programme (including government revenue foregone) not involving transfers from consumers; and
   (b) the support in question shall not have the effect of providing price support to producers;

   plus policy-specific criteria and conditions as set out below.

. . .

5. Direct payments to producers
   Support provided through direct payments (or revenue foregone, including payments in kind) to producers for which exemption from reduction commitments is claimed shall meet the basic criteria set out in paragraph 1 above, plus specific criteria applying to individual types of direct payment as set out in paragraphs 6 through 13 below. Where exemption from reduction is claimed for any existing or new type of direct payment other than those specified in paragraphs 6 through 13, it shall conform to criteria (b) through (e) in paragraph 6, in addition to the general criteria set out in paragraph 1.

. . .

7. Government financial participation in income insurance and income safety-net programmes
   (a) Eligibility for such payments shall be determined by an income loss, taking into account only income derived from agriculture, which exceeds 30 per cent of average gross income or the equivalent in net income terms (excluding any payments from the same or similar schemes) in the preceding three-year period or a three-year average based on the preceding five-year period, excluding the highest and the lowest entry. Any producer meeting this condition shall be eligible to receive the payments.
   (b) The amount of such payments shall compensate for less than 70 per cent of the producer's income loss in the year the producer becomes eligible to receive this assistance.
   (c) The amount of any such payments shall relate solely to income; it shall not relate to the type or volume of production (including livestock units) undertaken by the producer; or to the prices, domestic or international, applying to such production; or to the factors of production employed.
   (d) Where a producer receives in the same year payments under this paragraph and under paragraph 8 (relief from natural disasters), the total of such payments shall be less than 100 per cent of the producer's total loss.

8. Payments (made either directly or by way of government financial participation in crop insurance schemes) for relief from natural disasters
   (a) Eligibility for such payments shall arise only following a formal recognition by government authorities that a natural or like disaster (including disease outbreaks, pest infestations, nuclear accidents, and war on the territory of the Member concerned) has occurred or is occurring; and shall be determined by a production loss which exceeds 30 per cent of the average of production in the preceding three-year period or a three-year average based on the preceding five-year period, excluding the highest and the lowest entry.
   (b) Payments made following a disaster shall be applied only in respect of losses of income, livestock (including payments in connection with the veterinary treatment of animals), land or other production factors due to the natural disaster in question.

(c) Payments shall compensate for not more than the total cost of replacing such losses and shall not require or specify the type or quantity of future production.

(d) Payments made during a disaster shall not exceed the level required to prevent or alleviate further loss as defined in criterion (b) above.

(e) Where a producer receives in the same year payments under this paragraph and under paragraph 7 (income insurance and income safety-net programmes), the total of such payments shall be less than 100 per cent of the producer's total loss.

Chapter 11

A QUANTITATIVE ANALYSIS OF TRADE POLICY RESPONSES TO HIGHER WORLD AGRICULTURAL COMMODITY PRICES

T. Edward Yu, Simla Tokgoz, Eric Wailes, and Eddie C. Chavez

From 2007 through mid-2008, world prices of major agricultural commodities, such as cereals, oilseeds, and their by-products, experienced unprecedented surges since World War II (Baffes and Haniotis 2010).[1] The world food price indexes produced by the Food and Agricultural Organization (FAO) of the United Nations increased by 56 percent between 2006 and 2008, while cereals and vegetable oils price indexes doubled during the same period (FAO 2010). Although price pressure for these commodities was temporarily relieved in late 2008 and 2009, the world price indexes for food, grains, and vegetable oils have rebounded in 2011 to their former high levels again (Figure 11.1). The sudden price spikes of agricultural and food commodities in 2007–2008 quickly caught worldwide attention because cereal grains such as rice and wheat are staples in many developing economies, while corn is an important feedstock for the growing livestock sector in both developed and developing countries. For some food-deficit developing economies that rely heavily on imports for food consumption, drastic increases in the prices of these crops threatened the nutritional needs and social stability of these economies. Moreover, in major Asian rice-producing and rice-consuming countries, rice availability and affordability is a focus of national food security and policies (Wailes 2005).

In order to insulate domestic food prices from global price increases, a number of key grain exporting countries, primarily developing economies, adopted policies that included export bans or at least partial export restrictions in an attempt to provide enough domestic production for local consumption. Meanwhile, some major grain importing nations reacted by tendering larger-than-anticipated import bids, reduced preexisting import restrictions such as tariffs, and relaxed tariff-rate quotas. Export restrictions, as well as lowering import tariffs, can reduce domestic prices in the short-term, but these trade policy adjustments are generally considered as inadequate responses

1 This chapter was originally published as an article in *Food Policy* (Yu et al. 2011).

FIGURE 11.1 Annual world food price indexes, 1990–2010

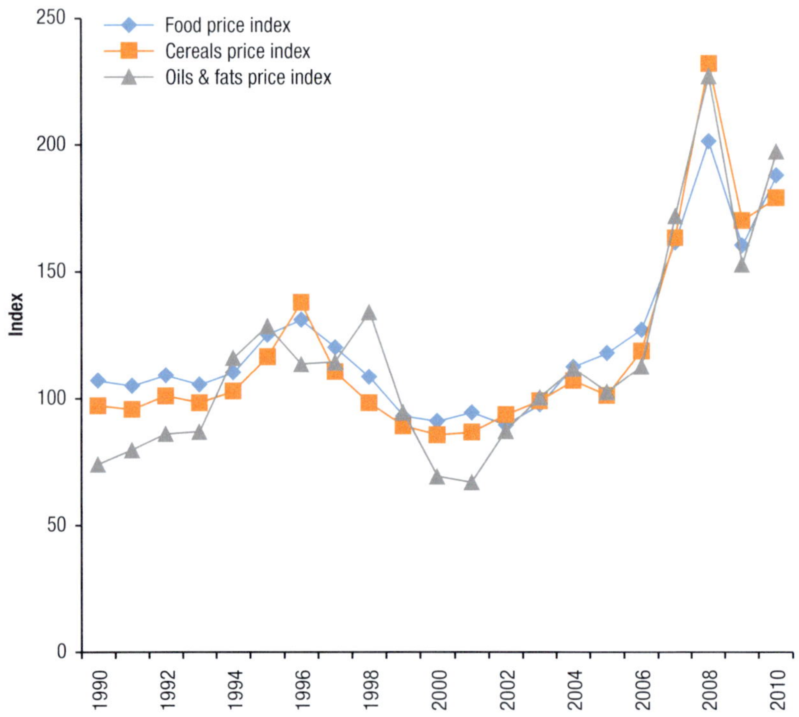

Source: FAO (2010).
Note: 2002–2004 = 100

to high commodity prices (Trostle 2008; Von Braun 2008; Rapsomanikis 2009). Export bans will eventually discourage producers in exporting countries from expanding production, while lowering import tariffs will stimulate the consumers' demand in importing countries. The combination of these two polices will ultimately push the world commodity prices even higher, transferring more price pressure to consumers in the poorest food-deficit countries. However, these two polices are usually the most commonly used means to control domestic prices by large trading countries since the desired short-term effect of lowering domestic prices is hard to resist. As of May 2008, there were 66 countries that adopted various trade and consumption policies to mitigate domestic price pressures, of which 18 economies (27 percent) chose to reduce import tariffs and 17 countries (26 percent) increased export restrictions (FAO 2008).

To date, few studies have attempted to explore the impacts of policy interventions on mitigating the recent price spike in agricultural and food commodities. Rapsomanikis (2009) made a qualitative analysis of the consequences of various consumption and trade policy responses in eastern and southern Africa to the 2007–2008 price surges. The author observed that both import tariff reductions and export bans exercised by a number of countries in that region had limited success in stabilizing domestic food prices. Moreover, the study argued that adopting policy interventions without caution may negatively affect private traders and investors in agribusiness. Sugden (2009) analyzed the factors driving the food commodity price boom in 2007–2008 and discussed the policy responses adopted by Asian Pacific governments at the global, regional, and national levels, respectively. This study concluded that coordinated elimination of trade restrictions such as export bans is considered as the most sensible action to control surging commodity prices at the regional level. Nouve and Wodon (2008) studied the upward pattern in Mali's rice price starting from 2004 and simulated the impact of reducing the import tariff and increasing productivity on the rice market using a dynamic general equilibrium model. Results showed that a reduction in the tariff would have only a limited effect on mitigating price pressures and on reducing the poverty rate in Mali. Coady, Dorosh, and Minten (2009) examined the soaring rice price issue in Madagascar and applied a partial equilibrium model to evaluate the net household and social welfare impacts of lowering the rice tariff and introducing targeted transfers for the rice sector. Their analysis suggested that tariff reductions allocated more gains to the better-off households and reduced the welfare of poor rice sellers. Bouët and Laborde (2010) used a Computable General Equilibrium (CGE) model to illustrate the impacts of export taxes and import duties on world wheat prices and national real incomes (their measure of welfare). They ran scenarios where there is a demand shock that increases the world wheat price by 10 percent, and countries change export taxes and/or import duties to maintain the constant real domestic price of wheat. They found that the world wheat price increased by 20.6 percent to 41.0 percent under the scenarios of changes in export taxes and import duties. These studies undoubtedly improve our knowledge on the impacts of trade policy responses on commodity markets. However, they focus typically on a single commodity market in one particular country or region. Thus the intermarket and intercountry links are usually ignored in these analyses.

This chapter aims to investigate the potential effects of trade policy responses on the prices and trade of major crops in the world and in different countries. In contrast to previous studies, this chapter generates a more comprehensive analysis of the trade policy impacts on various commodity markets over a wider coverage of countries and regions. The consequences of reactive trade policies on the welfare of producers and consumers in these countries are also analyzed. The relevant export and import policy changes in major exporting and importing countries that affected various crops in 2007–2008 are used for the policy impact analysis.

The remainder of the chapter is organized as follows: "Method of Analysis" describes the analytical tool and the policy scenario analyzed in this chapter. A discussion of the simulated price and trade impacts of policy interventions is presented in "Simulated Impacts of Trade Policy Responses on World Grains and Oilseeds Markets," while the section "Distributions of Welfare Gains and Losses from Trade Policy Responses" provides the associated welfare changes for producers and consumers. The final section offers conclusions and a discussion of policy implications.

Method of Analysis

In order to capture the inclusive impact of trade policy modifications on agricultural commodity markets, a broad modeling system of the world agricultural sector is used. The models are a set of multimarket, partial-equilibrium, and nonspatial models of agricultural crops. The models cover major crops, such as wheat, corn, barley, sorghum, rice, soybeans, rapeseed, and sunflower for all major country producers and consumers and are calibrated on the most recently available data. Each model is a homogenous product model such that the same product produced in different countries is viewed indifferently by the buyers. The structure of this modeling system—including the exogenous drivers, historical agricultural data, endogenous variables, commodities, and major trade countries/regions—is summarized in Table 11.1. Macroeconomic variables, such as GDP, population, and exchange rates, are exogenous variables that drive the projections of the model. The country/region coverage varies by commodity group, and we present the country coverage for all crops in Table 11.1.

Extensive market links exist in these models (rice, grains, and oilseed sector) with the symmetric cross-price elasticities, reflecting competition for land in production and consumer substitution possibilities for close substitutes such as oilseed meals and vegetable oils. The model structure and the elasticities used in the model are based on analysis of historical data, current academic research, and a reliance on accepted economic and agronomic relationships in the agricultural markets. The price elasticities of supply and demand and income elasticities in the grain sector are summarized in Table 11.A1 (in the

TABLE 11.1 Structure of the multicommodity and multicountry model

Exogenous drivers	Historical agricultural data	Endogenous variables (by commodity and country)	Commodities
Population	Area harvested	World prices	Grains: Rice, corn,
GDP	Yield	Domestic prices	wheat, sorghum,
GDP deflator	Production	Production (area harvested, yield)	barley
Exchange rate	Consumption	Consumption by use (food, feed, biofuel, crush)	
Population	Exports	Net trade	Oilseeds (seeds and beans, meal, and oil): Soybeans, rapeseed, sunflower, palm, peanuts
Policy variables	Imports	Beginning stocks	
	Ending stocks	Ending stocks	Biofuels: Ethanol, Biodiesel
	Domestic prices		
	World prices		
Major countries or regions: Algeria; Argentina; Australia; Bangladesh; Brazil; Canada; China; Commonwealth of Independent States (CIS); Côte d'Ivoire; Egypt; EU27; India; Indonesia; Iran; Iraq; Israel; Japan; Malaysia; Mexico; Myanmar; Morocco; Nigeria; other Africa; other Asia; other CIS; other eastern Europe; other Latin America; other Middle East; Pakistan; Paraguay; Philippines; rest of the world; the Russian Federation; Saudi Arabia; South Africa; South Korea (Republic of Korea); Taiwan, China; Thailand; Tunisia; Turkey; Ukraine; United States; Uruguay; Viet Nam.			

Source: Authors.
Note: Country coverage varies by commodity. EU27 = European Union—27 countries.

appendix), while the elasticities of supply, crush demand, food demand, and income for the oilseed sector are provided in Table 11.A2 (in the appendix).[2] In general, for each commodity sector, the economic relationship that supply equals demand is maintained by determining a market-clearing price for the commodity. The models include behavioral equations for arca harvested and yield on the supply side, and feed use, per capita consumption, stocks, and net exports on the demand side. Specifically, the supply, demand, and stock equations of each commodity in a country/region are functions of market prices, while the net exports equation is the difference between supply and utilization by commodity in each country. The models solve for representative world crop prices by equating excess supply and excess demand across countries. To generate domestic prices of crops for each country, price transmission equations are used that link the representative world price to domestic prices by using

2 More information regarding the set of models used in this study is provided at www.fapri.iastate.edu/models.

TABLE 11.2 List of policy scenarios

Export policies in selected countries by commodity	Units	Baseline	Scenario
Rice			
China: Export tax	%	0	5
China: Export tax rebate	%	13	0
Egypt: Export tax	EGP/metric ton	200	300
Egypt: Export restriction (estimate)	%	0	30
India: Export restriction	%	0	14
India: Export tax (basmati rice)	US$/metric ton	0	200
India: Minimum export price (basmati rice)	US$/metric ton	0	1,000
Pakistan: Minimum export price (super basmati)	US$/metric ton	0	1,500
Pakistan: Minimum export price (medium grade basmati)	US$/metric ton	0	1,300
Pakistan: Minimum export price (IRRI-6)	US$/metric ton	0	750
Pakistan: Export restriction (estimate)	%	0	10
Viet Nam: Export tax	US$/metric ton	0	176
Viet Nam: Export restriction (estimate)	%	0	10
Wheat			
Argentina: Export tax	%	20	28
China: Export tax	%	0	20
Russian Federation: Export tax	%	0	40
Corn			
Argentina: Export tax	%	20	25
China: Export tax	%	0	5
Barley			
China: Export tax	%	0	20
Russian Federation: Export tax	%	0	30
Soybeans			
Argentina: Export tax	%	27.5	35
Soy meal			
Argentina: Export tax	%	24	32
Soy oil			
Argentina: Export tax	%	24	32
Sunflower seed			
Argentina: Export tax	%	23.5	32
Sun meal			
Argentina: Export tax	%	20	30
Sun oil			
Argentina: Export tax	%	20	30

Export policies in selected countries by commodity	Units	Baseline	Scenario
Palm oil			
Indonesia: Export tax	%	1.5	15
Import policies in selected countries by commodity	**Units**	**Baseline**	**Scenario**
Rice			
Indonesia: Import tariff	Rp/kg	550	450
Japan: Import makeup	Yen/metric ton	154,023	152,004
Japan: Special safeguard duty	Yen/metric ton	374,162	351,486
Japan: Specific import tariff	Yen/metric ton	281,325	264,275
Nigeria: Import tariff	%	100	2.7
Philippines: (Milled rice) In-quota tariff	%	50	7
Turkey: Import tariff	%	35	25
Wheat			
India: Import tariff	%	50	0
Republic of Korea: Import tariff	%	2	0
Corn			
India: In-quota import tariff	%	15	0
India: Out-of-quota import tariff	%	50	0
Republic of Korea: Import tariff	%	428.7	0
Barley			
Republic of Korea: Import tariff	%	406.4	0
Soybeans			
China: Import tariff	%	3	1
Soy meal			
China: Import tariff	%	5	2
Soy oil			
India: Import tariff	%	45	0
Sunflower oil			
CIS: Import tariff	%	15	5
Palm oil			
India: Import tariff	%	80	46.5
Rapeseed oil			
CIS: Import tariff	%	15	5
India: Import tariff	%	75	0
Peanut oil			
India: Import tariff	%	100	92.7

Source: Authors.

exchange rates and other price policy wedges. The models incorporate major agricultural and trade policies in each country since they affect the supply and demand decisions of the producers and the consumers.

In this chapter, the analysis is based on a 2008 baseline (FAPRI 2008) modified by specifying the 2007 export and import policy regimes that existed before the commodity price inflation. The baseline projections include supply, utilization, and prices for grains, rice, and oilseeds, including applicable by-products. In the scenario the modified export restrictions and import policies that were adopted by major trading countries in response to the price inflation in the 2007–2008 marketing year are incorporated for three years (2008–2009 through 2010–2011). Since the other parameters remain unchanged between the baseline and scenario models, the difference (in absolute quantity and percent) between the baseline and scenario captures the impact of the trade policy changes. Changes in export and import policy restrictions in the major grain and oilseed exporting and importing countries used for the scenario are summarized in Table 11.2.

Simulated Impacts of Trade Policy Responses on World Grains and Oilseeds Markets

Figure 11.2 presents the world price and net trade changes for the trade policy scenario relative to the baseline for 10 selected agricultural commodities. Results are presented as the three-year average of the annual percentage changes between the marketing years of 2008–2009 and 2010–2011.[3] It is clear that the world prices for selected grains and oilseed products all increased due to higher export restrictions and lower import restrictions in the global market. The world rice price increased the most since rice is a thinly traded commodity in the global market, where less than 7 percent of the production enters international markets. Also, trade is highly concentrated with only six countries accounting for 90 percent of the global rice exports. Increases in grain prices were generally higher than the increase in prices of oilseeds and oilseed-derived products, as more policy adjustments were executed in the grain markets.

3 We also simulate the impact of trade policy interventions on the total price rise between 2007 and 2008 by imposing the policy shocks in the 2007–2008 marketing year alone. The output, presented in Table 11.A3, suggests that trade policy interventions accounted for about 26 percent of the rice price increase between 2007 and 2008. Trade policy changes also increased the price of other coarse grains by 15 percent to 23 percent and moved the oilseed sector prices up by 5 percent.

FIGURE 11.2 Impact of trade policy changes on world prices and net trade of agricultural commodities

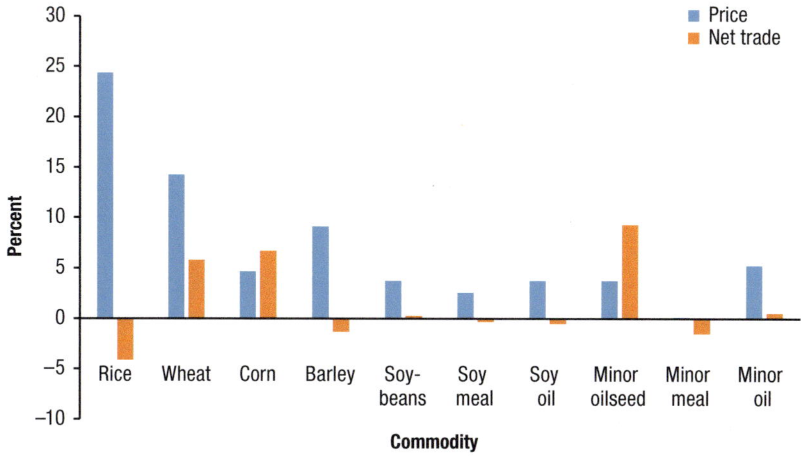

Source: Authors' calculations.

Changes in aggregate world net trade varied by commodity: trade of wheat, corn, soybeans, minor oilseeds (sunflower and rapeseed), and minor oil expanded; while rice, barley, soybean meal and oil, and minor meal markets experienced a trade reduction. The difference depended mostly on which policy was primarily used in each market. For instance, export tax and restrictions were heavily utilized in primary rice exporting countries, which consequently reduced the trade in the international rice market.

Following is a detailed discussion associated with the impact of trade policy by major commodity markets. We focus on the major food and feed commodities in the detailed discussion. To better understand the variations in the trade policy impacts among commodities and countries, a summary of the results by commodity and by country group (that is, developed and developing) is presented in Table 11.3. The developing-country group is further categorized based on whether the country implemented trade policy responses or not, both for the net exporters and net importers subgroups. The average price change in each group is an aggregate average price change weighted by consumption quantities in the baseline.[4]

4 The details of the average impact of the scenario on trade, production, and consumption by individual country are not included here due to limited space but are available from the authors upon request.

TABLE 11.3 Impacts of trade policy responses on price, production, consumption, and net trade, by commodity

	Price/metric ton US$ (%)	Production	Consumption	Net trade
		1,000 metric ton (%)		
Rice				
Developed-country net exporters	+94 (+20.10)	+993 (+15.71)	−104 (−2.54)	+1111 (+50.49)
Developed-country net importers	+30 (+3.83)	+288 (+1.90)	−321 (−1.67)	−163 (−4.01)
Developing-country net exporters	+94 (+15.03)	+4800 (+1.64)	−1229 (−0.46)	−2249 (−8.73)
Implemented trade policy	+32 (+10.72)	+4684 (+1.80)	−1187 (−0.48)	−2264 (−15.77)
Did not implement trade policy	+828 (+18.33)	+116 (+0.36)	−43 (−0.20)	+15 (+0.13)
Developing-country net importers	+38 (+7.94)	+938 (+1.03)	+468 (+0.45)	−352 (−2.68)
Implemented trade policy	−13 (−2.05)	+148 (+0.31)	+873 (+1.61)	+866 (+15.40)
Did not implement trade policy	+93 (+23.19)	+790 (+1.84)	−405 (−0.81)	−1218 (−16.24)
World	+88 (+24.02)	+7340 (+1.70)	−2689 (−0.62)	−1561 (−5.01)
Wheat				
Developed-country net exporters	+13 (+5.11)	+3050 (+1.26)	−3067 (−2.06)	+7636 (+12.41)
Developed-country net importers	+35 (+13.61)	+13 (+1.45)	−1397 (−13.28)	−1476 (−15.08)
Developing-country net exporters	−21 (−8.80)	−1362 (−1.21)	+1059 (+1.29)	−2554 (−8.69)
Implemented trade policy	−69 (−29.59)	−1728 (−2.60)	+1488 (+3.45)	−3421 (−15.04)
Did not implement trade policy	+33 (+13.86)	+366 (+0.80)	−429 (−1.11)	+866 (+13.00)
Developing-country net importers	−3 (−0.87)	−5262 (−1.80)	+1517 (+0.41)	+6557 (+8.16)
Implemented trade policy	−50 (−16.24)	−7013 (−3.91)	+6254 (+3.49)	+13726 (+2679.40)
Did not implement trade policy	+11 (+3.76)	−1079 (−0.99)	−3830 (−2.01)	−3138 (−3.93)
World	+35 (+14.29)	−3561 (−0.55)	−2488 (−0.39)	+5320 (+5.80)
Corn				
Developed-country net exporters	+9 (+3.43)	+3410 (+1.01)	−2080 (−0.74)	+6471 (+11.32)
Developed-country net importers	−67 (−17.69)	+178 (+0.26)	+5160 (+4.76)	+5435 (+14.05)
Developing-country net exporters	+3 (+1.52)	−211 (−0.18)	+384 (+0.44)	−509 (−1.16)
Implemented trade policy	−15 (−8.10)	−289 (−0.44)	+509 (+2.22)	−816 (−4.23)
Did not implement trade policy	+9 (+4.63)	+78 (+0.15)	−124 (−0.19)	+247 (+2.31)
Developing-country net importers	+5 (+2.23)	−232 (−0.08)	+325 (+0.10)	+509 (+1.16)
Implemented trade policy	−1 (−0.46)	−409 (−0.26)	+180 (+0.12)	+620 (+138.16)
Did not implement trade policy	+6 (+2.45)	+177 (+0.14)	+145 (+0.08)	−111 (−0.26)
World	+9 (+4.71)	+3189 (+0.41)	+3795 (+0.47)	+5953 (+6.75)
Barley				
Developed-country net exporters	+6 (+2.59)	+163 (+0.19)	−178 (−0.24)	+440 (+4.07)
Developed-country net importers	+13 (+9.15)	+1 (+0.52)	−91 (−0.72)	+120 (+1.41)
Developing-country net exporters	−16 (−9.88)	−254 (−0.77)	+344 (+1.31)	−659 (−11.90)
Implemented trade policy	−35 (−23.58)	−302 (−1.76)	+416 (+2.63)	−795 (−66.12)

	Price/metric ton US$ (%)	Production	Consumption	Net trade
		1,000 metric ton (%)		
Did not implement trade policy	+12 (+7.32)	+48 (+0.31)	−72 (−0.69)	+136 (+3.13)
Developing-country net importers	+13 (+7.95)	+88 (+0.01)	+21 (+0.02)	−1041 (−2.43)
Implemented trade policy	−18 (−12.37)	−66 (−2.02)	+143 (+2.75)	−213 (+10.85)
Did not implement trade policy	+14 (+8.67)	+154 (+0.02)	−122 (−0.14)	−828 (−1.85)
World	+13 (+9.16)	−2 (0.00)	+96 (+0.07)	−219 (−1.34)
Soybeans				
Developed-country net exporters	+15 (+4.42)	−617 (−0.73)	−313 (−0.53)	−270 (−1.08)
Developed-country net importers	+17 (+3.36)	+11 (+0.91)	−69 (−0.29)	−91 (−0.40)
Developing-country net exporters	+1 (+0.85)	−2 (0.00)	−540 (−0.58)	+506 (+1.05)
Implemented trade policy	−0.07 (−0.09)	−495 (−0.94)	−696(−1.59)	+127 (+1.49)
Did not implement trade policy	+0.04 (+0.02)	+493 (+0.55)	+156 (+0.31)	+378 (+0.95)
Developing-country net importers	+5 (+1.88)	+20 (+0.09)	+354 (+0.48)	+327 (+1.39)
Implemented trade policy	+0.02 (+0.01)	+60 (+0.40)	+390 (+0.76)	+326 (+0.89)
Did not implement trade policy	+0.04 (+0.02)	−39 (−0.50)	−36 (−0.17)	+1 (+0.01)
World	+19 (+3.81)	−587 (−0.23)	−562 (−1.66)	+236 (+0.32)
Soybean Meal				
Developed-country net exporters	+15 (+3.88)	−168 (−0.40)	+89 (+0.27)	−255 (−2.94)
Developed-country net importers	+8 (+2.33)	−30 (−0.18)	−193 (−0.41)	−174 (−0.58)
Developing-country net exporters	+6 (+3.56)	−63 (−0.06)	−301 (−0.61)	+235 (0.47)
Implemented trade policy	+6 (+3.98)	−224 (−0.34)	−187 (−0.56)	−48 (−0.15)
Did not implement trade policy	+4 (+2.53)	+162 (+0.48)	−114 (−0.72)	+283 (1.56)
Developing-country net importers	+5 (+3.24)	+8 (+0.06)	+168 (+0.42)	+153 (+0.57)
Implemented trade policy	n.a.	n.a.	n.a.	n.a.
Did not implement trade policy	+5 (+3.24)	+8 (+0.06)	+168 (+0.42)	+153 (+0.57)
World	+9 (+2.59)	−252 (−0.15)	−237 (−0.14)	−188 (−0.32)
Soybean Oil				
Developed-country net exporters	+43 (+3.90)	−40 (−0.40)	−81 (−0.86)	+56 (+7.39)
Developed-country net importers	+42 (+3.83)	−7 (−0.18)	+3263 (+64.43)	+710 (+58.03)
Developing-country net exporters	+14 (2.78)	−133 (−0.91)	−31 (−0.54)	−106 (−1.19)
Implemented trade policy	−22 (−7.11)	−136 (−1.69)	+17 (+1.26)	−159 (−2.36)
Did not implement trade policy	+24 (+2.08)	+3 (+0.05)	−48 (−1.08)	+53 (+2.51)
Developing-country net importers	+6 (+0.77)	+112 (+0.93)	+99 (+0.49)	−1 (−0.01)
Implemented trade policy	−155 (−15.90)	+34 (+2.09)	+152 (+5.28)	+136 (+10.84)
Did not implement trade policy	+33 (+1.15)	+78 (+0.75)	−54 (−0.31)	−138 (−1.99)
World	+50 (+3.82)	−68 (−0.17)	−68 (−0.17)	−50 (−0.52)

Source: Authors' calculations.

Note: n.a. = not available.

Rice

The scenario results for rice contribute to our understanding of why international rice prices increased dramatically in the 2007–2008 marketing year. Major exporting countries that adjusted export policies included China, Egypt, India, Pakistan, and Viet Nam. The combination of export restrictions by these nations exerted significant pressure on the rice supply in the global market. Importing countries that grew anxious with the price inflation responded by lowering import tariffs or with larger than normal import tenders. Particularly important were the Philippines and Nigeria, which implemented significant cuts in import tariffs. The aggregate global changes show that the international reference price increased by US$88 per metric ton (24.0 percent), production increased by 7.3 million metric tons (1.7 percent), consumption declined by 2.7 million metric tons (0.62 percent), and net trade declined by 1.6 million metric tons (5.0 percent). The net exports were reduced, particularly in the key exporting countries of Egypt, India, Pakistan, and Viet Nam.

The impact of policy changes by country subgroups show on average that *developed-country net exporters* (represented solely by the United States) experienced a weighted price increase of 20.1 percent, a gain in production of 993,000 metric tons (15.7 percent), an increase in trade of 1.1 million metric tons (50.5 percent), and a decline in domestic consumption of 104,000 metric tons (2.5 percent). In contrast, the weighted average price in the *developed-country net importers* increased by 3.8 percent, with production gaining 288,000 metric tons (1.9 percent), and both domestic consumption and net imports declining by 321,000 metric tons (1.7 percent) and 163,000 metric tons (4.0 percent), respectively.

In developing countries, the net exporters group exhibited a relatively weaker weighted average price increase of 15.0 percent, with production increasing by 4.8 million metric tons (1.6 percent), and consumption and net trade declining by 1.2 million metric tons (0.5 percent) and 2.2 million metric tons (8.7 percent), respectively. However, decomposing the impact shows that there is a higher price shock for countries that did not implement a policy that insulated their domestic prices from the international price, at 18.3 percent, compared to those that implemented the trade-insulating policies, at only 10.7 percent. Rice prices in the subgroup of countries that imposed export constraints still increased because the impact of the higher world price outweighed the effect of the policy interventions on domestic price in some countries—for example, China, where the aggregate rice production then increased, while consumption declined. Net exports in this group declined, primarily as a result of significant cuts in India's exports because of its export ban, higher export taxes, and higher minimum export prices.

The *developing-country net importers* group also experienced a weighted average price increase of 7.9 percent, and an increase in average production and consumption of 938,000 metric tons (1.0 percent) and 468,000 metric tons (0.5 percent), respectively. Net imports declined by 352,000 metric tons (2.7 percent). As in the case of the net exporters' group, the subgroup impacts show that the price increase for those countries that did not implement the policy, at 23.2 percent, is much higher than for those countries that implemented the trade-insulating policies (for example, Philippines, Nigeria, and Turkey) at 2.1 percent.

The model results demonstrate that much of the export supply response over a three-year period comes from Western Hemisphere net exporters including Argentina, the United States, and Uruguay. Inelastic supply and demand throughout much of Asia, where rice is the dominant food staple, thus explains why the trade policy adjustments in the politically sensitive rice sector can induce a large price movement.

Wheat

Exporters such as Argentina, China, and the Russian Federation implemented export-restrictive policies and decreased their export supply to the world market. Moreover, China switched to being a net importer of wheat due to these policy changes. Significant decreases in the import tariffs in India led to a higher domestic demand. Countries that did not adjust their import policy regimes in this environment decreased their imports of wheat due to higher prices in the world market. The increases in Indian and Chinese wheat net imports were more than enough to offset the declines in wheat imports of other countries. The overall changes in the world show that the international reference price of wheat increased by US$35 (14.29 percent), production decreased by 3.56 million metric tons (0.55 percent), consumption declined by 2.48 million metric tons (0.39 percent), and net trade increased by 5.80 percent.

Taking a closer look at the market changes by country groupings, we see that *developed-country net exporters* experienced a weighted price increase of 5.11 percent, a gain in production of 3.05 million metric tons (1.26 percent), an increase in trade of 7.6 million metric tons (12.41 percent), and a decline in consumption of 3.07 million metric tons (2.06 percent). In contrast, the weighted average price in the *developed-country net importers group* increased by 13.61 percent, with production gaining 13 thousand metric tons (1.45 percent). As a result, consumption and net imports declined by 1.39 million metric tons (13.28 percent) and 1.47 million metric tons (15.08 percent), respectively.

For the *developing-country net exporters*, the weighted average price decreased by 8.80 percent, as production decreased by 1.36 million metric tons (1.21 percent), and net trade declined by 2.55 million metric tons (8.69 percent). Consumption increased by 1.06 million metric tons (1.29 percent) for this group. However, the price impacts were different between developing-country net exporters that implemented the policy responses and those that did not. Those countries that implemented trade policy responses successfully lowered their price by 29.59 percent; however, countries that did not adjust their trade policy experienced an average price increase of 13.86 percent.

The *developing-country net importers* group experienced a weighted average price decline of 0.87 percent, with weighted average production decreasing by 5.26 million metric tons (1.80 percent) and consumption increasing by 1.51 million metric tons (0.41 percent). Net imports dropped by 6.55 million metric tons (8.16 percent). Similarly, decomposing the impact showed that those countries that did not implement the policy interventions encountered an increase in wheat price of 3.76 percent, while those that implemented policies saw a price decline of 16.24 percent.

Coarse Grains

In the corn market, Argentinean net exports decreased because of the higher export tax for corn. China implemented export-restrictive policies for corn, resulting in a decline in corn production and higher corn net imports. India eliminated its import tariffs for corn, which increased domestic consumption and imports. Higher world corn prices led some major exporters to increase their exports to meet the growing demand, including Brazil, the United States, and South Africa. In response to higher world corn prices, many countries and regions decreased their net imports since they did not implement any changes in their tariff policies. The overall changes in the world show that the international reference price for corn increased by US$9 per metric ton (4.71 percent), production increased by 3.19 million metric tons (0.41 percent), consumption by 3.79 million metric tons (0.47 percent), and net trade by 5.95 million metric tons (6.75 percent).

On average, *developed-country net exporters* experienced a weighted price increase of 3.43 percent, a gain in production of 3.41 million metric tons (1.01 percent), an increase in trade of 6.47 million metric tons (11.32 percent), and a decline in consumption of 2.08 million metric tons (0.74 percent). In contrast, the weighted average price in the *developed-country net importers* decreased by 17.69 percent due to the removal of import tariffs in South Korea (Republic of Korea), with production gaining 0.26 percent. Consumption and net imports consequently increased by 5.16 million metric tons (4.76 percent) and 5.4 million metric tons (14.05 percent), respectively.

The *developing-country net exporters* as a group exhibited a weighted average price increase of 1.52 percent, with production decreasing by 211 thousand metric tons (TMT) (0.18 percent), and net trade declining by 0.5 million metric tons (1.16 percent). Consumption increased by 0.38 million metric tons (0.44 percent) for this group. However, the price impacts were different for *developing-country net exporters* that implemented the policy shocks and those that did not. Local corn prices decreased 4.63 percent for *developing-country net exporters* that adopted trade policy responses. Countries that did not exercise trade policy responses experienced higher domestic prices.

The *developing-country net importers* experienced a weighted average price increase of 2.23 percent. Production decreased by 232 thousand metric tons (0.08 percent) and consumption increased by 325 thousand metric tons (0.10 percent). As a group, net imports increased by 509 thousand metric tons (1.16 percent). Those countries adopting trade policy responses experienced a lower local corn price and more imports while the countries that did not implement policy interventions had a price increase of 2.45 percent.

In the barley market, the changes are partially due to modifications in trade policies and partially in response to movements in the wheat and corn markets. The Russian Federation introduced an export tax for barley, which led to lower domestic production and a consequent decline in its net exports. Other barley exporters, such as the EU and Canada, responded to the increase in world barley prices by increasing their net exports. A Chinese barley export tax reduced barley production, thus increasing its net imports. Other barley importers decreased their net imports due to higher prices in the world market. Overall changes in the international reference price of barley showed an increase of US$13 per metric ton (9.16 percent).

Average results of the policy changes in the barley market show that *developed-country net exporters* experienced a weighted price increase of 2.59 percent. Also, the weighted average price in the *developed-country net importers* group increased by 9.15 percent. The *developing-country net exporters* group exhibited a decrease of 9.88 percent in world average price. However, decomposing the average impact shows that the price impact was different for each group: price increased 7.32 percent for the countries that did not implement the policy shocks, and declined 23.58 percent for the ones that implemented policy responses. The *developing-country net importers* experienced a weighted average price increase of 7.95 percent. Again, price increased 8.67 percent in those countries that did not adopt policy shocks while those using policy tools pushed local prices down by 12.37 percent.

Soybean Sector

Changes in the world trade and price of soybeans and derived products were relatively smaller than those in the trade and price of grains, as policy modifications were less intensive in this sector. Argentina increased the export tax for soybeans and derived products (soybean meal and oil), while China lowered the import tariffs for soybeans and meal. India also reduced the tariffs for soybean oil. The other two major soybean exporters, Brazil and the United States, reacted to the policy shocks differently. Brazil's net exports for soybeans, meal, and oil rose, while the US soybean exports decreased as soybean area shifted to other commodities with stronger prices, such as wheat. The overall change in the three-year average soybean world price increased by US$19 per metric ton (3.8 percent), partially driven by the changes in trade policies and partially by the response to area competition from corn and wheat. World production decreased modestly while consumption declined by 562 thousand metric tons (1.7 percent). The aggregate trade remained stagnant, although the trade flows changed among countries.

On average, *developed-country net exporters* (represented by the United States and Canada) encountered a higher weighted soybean price of US$15 per metric ton (4.42 percent) and consequently a reduction in consumption of 313 thousand metric tons (0.53 percent). Although the price increased, production declined by 617 thousand metric tons (0.73 percent) because the soybean areas in the United States shifted to other more profitable crops. As a result, net trade declined by 1.08 percent. The group of *developed-country net importers* encountered a price increase of US$17 per metric ton (3.36 percent) and reduced net imports by 91 thousand metric tons (0.40 percent).

Soybean prices in the *developing countries net exporters* slightly increased by 0.85 percent and the net exports also gained by 506 thousand metric tons (1.05 percent). However, decomposing the impact shows that countries without trade policy interventions experienced a price increase of 0.02 percent, while the group of countries that manipulated trade policies (solely represented by Argentina) lowered the local price by 0.09 percent. The consumption in these countries decreased due to a lower crush margin after the policies imposed on both soybeans and derived products.

The *developing-country net importers* of soybeans also experienced a higher weighted average price by 1.88 percent, driven by rising net imports of 327 thousand metric tons (1.39 percent). Similar to other commodities, the increase of net imports in this group was primarily contributed by those countries that lowered their import tariffs. The increasing demand offset the impacts of lower tariffs and increased the local price only slightly in those countries that adopted policy changes (0.01 percent). Net importing countries without policy distortions had a slightly higher price increase of 0.02 percent.

In the soybean meal market, the overall policy changes show that the international reference price increased by US$9 per metric ton (2.59 percent) and net trade declined by 188 thousand metric tons (0.32 percent). The average results of the policy impacts show that *developed-country net exporters* encountered an increase in weighted price of US$15 (3.88 percent), while the weighted average price in *developed-country net importers* increased by 2.33 percent. The weighted average prices also rose by US$6 (3.56 percent) and US$5 (3.24 percent) for *developing-country net exporters* and *developing-country net importers*, respectively. A similar pattern was observed in the soybean oil market, where a US$50 (3.82 percent) gain in the international reference price and a reduction in net trade of 50 thousand metric tons (0.52 percent) occurred. The weighted average soybean oil prices increased in all groups, up to 3.9 percent, except for developing countries that implemented trade policy interventions.

Distributions of Welfare Gains and Losses from Trade Policy Responses

Estimates of the welfare distribution among trading countries in the world due to trade policy interventions imposed by major countries can provide a more comprehensive understanding of the effects of those policies. Timmer (2010) considered the aggregate global welfare in the rice market and believed that trade policy interventions employed by larger trading countries (that is, India and Indonesia) may be an effective way to mitigate a domestic food crisis even if the consequent pecuniary externality of higher global price volatility will exacerbate poverty in those small countries that rely on food imports. In contrast, the main focus of this study is to illustrate the consequences of trade policy interventions adopted by some major exporting and importing countries on the welfare changes in individual countries, including those food-deficit countries that have little power in manipulating their trade policies.

To explore the impacts of increasing export constraints and lowering import tariffs in individual countries, a welfare analysis consisting of the

FIGURE 11.3 Welfare effects of an import tariff decline for a net importer

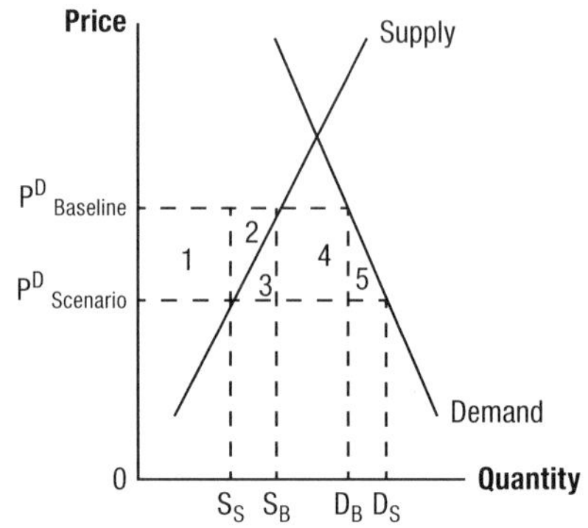

Source: Authors.

changes in the producer surplus (PS), consumer surplus (CS), and tariff and tax revenues (TR) was conducted for the evaluated countries. The three-year average production, consumption and real price (in 2000 US dollars) of commodities were used to calculate the changes in PS, CS, and TR for each country in the model. The changes in trade policies by various countries affect consumers and producers as well as the revenue for the government. The net impact of a trade policy depends on various factors, such as whether the country is a net exporter or a net importer. The final change in the price of a commodity determines whether consumers and producers will lose or gain.

To illustrate the computation of welfare measures in our study, we include two examples: one for an import tariff decline and one for an export tax increase. Figure 11.3 depicts the change in welfare in a country that is a net importer of a commodity where the trade policy change is an import tariff decline. The domestic price of the commodity is $P^D_{Baseline}$ in the baseline and $P^D_{Scenario}$ after the shock. The change in consumer surplus in this country for this particular commodity is represented by sum of the areas (1, 2, 3, 4, and 5). The change in producer surplus is represented by sum of the areas (1 and 2). The change in government revenue due to tariff decline is represented by area 4. In contrast, Figure 11.4 shows the change in welfare in a country that is a net exporter of a commodity where the trade policy change is an export tax increase. In Figure 11.4, $P^D_{Baseline}$ is the domestic price of the commodity in the baseline, while $P^D_{Scenario}$ represents the price after trade policy interventions. The change in consumer surplus in this country for this particular commodity is represented by sum of the areas (1 and 2). The change in producer surplus is

FIGURE 11.4 Welfare effects of an export tax increase for a net exporter

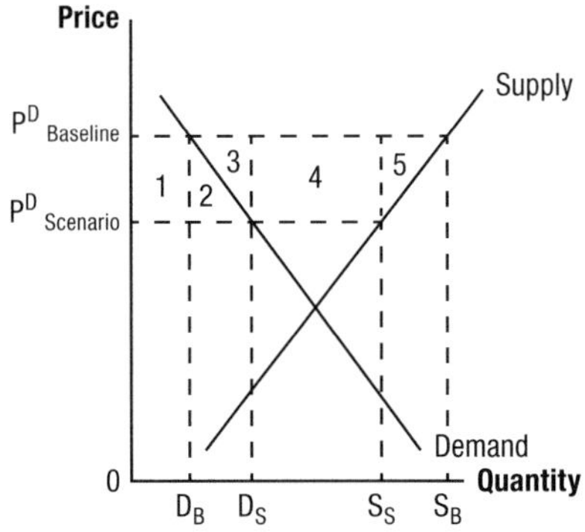

Source: Authors.

represented by sum of the areas (1, 2, 3, 4, and 5). The change in government revenue due to export tax increase is represented by area 4.

The change in the domestic price of a commodity in a country reflects not only the change in the representative world price of that commodity but also the trade policy changes implemented in that country. Since policy changes were implemented for multiple commodities in many countries, the final change in the domestic price for a given crop in one country is affected not only by the trade policy changes in this country, but also by the dynamics of world agricultural markets. To demonstrate the welfare changes in different country groups, Table 11.4 presents welfare changes for producers, consumers, and government for developing countries and regions included in the model, while Table 11.5 summarizes the distribution of welfare gains and losses in developed countries. Comparison of net welfare changes among countries is made difficult by the difference in commodity coverage in each country.

As seen in Table 11.4, developing countries that imposed higher export restrictions (tax or quota) experienced significant gains in consumers' surplus and government tax revenues but had adverse effects on the producers' welfare. These countries include Argentina (corn, wheat, soybeans and products, and sunflower and products), Egypt (rice), Pakistan (rice), the Russian Federation (wheat and barley), and Viet Nam (rice). Also, some developing countries in Table 11.4 only reduced import tariffs.[5] These countries include Commonwealth of Independent States (CIS) (sunflower oil and rapeseed oil),

(text continues on page 393)

5 Pakistan raised the minimum export price for rice instead of imposing tax or quota, so the government did not receive any direct tax revenue from the policy response.

TABLE 11.4 Welfare effects of trade policy scenario on major crops in evaluated developing countries and regions

	Average 2008–2010 (2000 US$ [1,000])			
Country/Commodity	Change in producer surplus[a]	Change in consumer surplus[b]	Change in tax revenue[c]	Net welfare change
Countries with trade policy responses				
Argentina				
Rice	15,499	−6,019	n.a.	9,480
Wheat	15,680	−4,277	295,928	307,331
Corn	−60,183	4,705	170,974	115,496
Barley	9,606	−4,733	n.a.	4,873
Sorghum	14,172	−824	n.a.	13,348
Soybeans, meal, and oil	−341,351	1,035	1,669,843	1,329,527
Sunflowers, meal, and oil	−65,296	8,982	213,994	157,680
Peanuts, meal, and oil	−2,684	−518	n.a.	−3,202
Total 14 commodities	−414,558	−1,649	2,350,739	1,934,533
China				
Rice	8,803,477	−8,530,384	60,354	333,447
Wheat	−1,748,017	1,641,231	38,042	−68,744
Corn	−111,344	32,511	5,694	−73,139
Barley	−48,043	60,668	259	12,884
Soybeans, meal, and oil	316,722	−309,675	−286,400	−279,353
Rapeseeds, meal, and oil	163,269	−303,008	n.a.	−139,739
Sunflowers, meal, and oil	22,802	−16,465	n.a.	6,337
Palm oil	0	−51,762	n.a.	−51,762
Peanuts, meal, and oil	−56,541	18,346	n.a.	−38,195
Total 17 commodities	7,342,325	−7,458,538	−182,051	−298,264
CIS				
Corn	22,511	−3,169	n.a.	19,342
Barley	62,885	−10,798	n.a.	52,087
Soybeans, meal, and oil	−949	−68,834	n.a.	−69,783
Rapeseeds, meal, and oil	9,624	−2,153	n.a.	7,471
Sunflowers, meal, and oil	−77,095	44,078	n.a.	−33,017
Total 11 commodities	16,976	−40,876	0	−23,900
Egypt				
Rice	195,782	−152,586	4,612	47,808
Wheat	250,048	−482,679	n.a.	−232,631

Country/Commodity	Average 2008–2010 (2000 US$ [1,000])			
	Change in producer surplus[a]	Change in consumer surplus[b]	Change in tax revenue[c]	Net welfare change
Corn	45,784	–15,817	n.a.	29,967
Total 3 commodities	491,614	–651,082	4,612	–154,856
India				
Rice	–2,191,983	2,094,043	1,201,667	1,103,727
Wheat	–5,394,185	5,757,943	–126,939	236,819
Corn	–267,543	139,601	0	–127,943
Sorghum	52,634	–43,806	n.a.	8,828
Soybeans, meal, and oil	–160,437	24,672	–604,200	–739,965
Rapeseeds, meal, and oil	114,186	–95,156	–15	19,015
Palm oil	–3,808	326,925	–1,195,119	–872,002
Peanuts, meal, and oil	–176,585	–89,094	95,590	–170,089
Total 14 commodities	–8,027,721	8,115,128	–629,017	–541,610
Indonesia				
Rice	1,030,853	–1,081,115	–394	–50,656
Corn	98,329	–53,001	n.a.	45,328
Palm oil	–77,807	0	1,861,095	1,783,288
Total 3 commodities	1,051,375	–1,134,116	1,860,701	1,777,960
Nigeria				
Rice	–696,146	1,120,933	–497,552	–72,765
Sorghum	141,977	–139,637	n.a.	2,340
Total 2 commodities	–554,169	981,296	–497,552	–70,425
Pakistan				
Rice	–93,550	42,995	n.a.	–50,555
Wheat	742,219	–712,931	n.a.	29,287
Corn	10,730	–5,984	n.a.	4,746
Barley	3,000	–3,000	n.a.	0
Sorghum	1,575	–1,119	n.a.	456
Total 5 commodities	663,974	–680,040	0	–16,066

(continued)

Source: Authors' calculations.

Note: n.a. = not applicable; [a]For oilseeds, change in producer surplus is computed for seed and bean producers and for crushers; [b]For oilseeds, change in consumer surplus is computed for oil consumers and for consumers where there is food consumption of seeds; [c]Change in tax revenue refers to the change in tax revenue of countries that applied an export tax change or to the change in tariff revenue of countries that applied an import tariff change.

TABLE 11.4 *(Continued)*

	Average 2008–2010 (2000 US$ [1,000])			
Country/Commodity	Change in producer surplus[a]	Change in consumer surplus[b]	Change in tax revenue[c]	Net welfare change
Philippines				
Rice	−511,151	617,153	−219,571	−113,569
Corn	61,188	−16,543	n.a.	44,646
Total 2 commodities	−449,963	600,610	−219,571	−68,923
Russian Federation				
Corn	29,158	−4,667	n.a.	24,491
Wheat	−3,018,480	1,460,809	625,015	−932,656
Barley	−474,444	132,733	15,810	−325,901
Total 3 commodities	−3,463,766	1,588,875	640,825	−1,234,066
Turkey				
Rice	17,460	−28,282	−1,798	−12,620
Total 1 commodity	17,460	−28,282	−1,798	−12,620
Viet Nam				
Rice	−220,660	178,679	1,556,442	1,514,461
Corn	35,016	−7,988	n.a.	27,027
Total 2 commodities	−185,644	170,691	1,556,442	1,541,489
Group Welfare Changes	**−3,512,097**	**1,462,017**	**4,883,330**	**2,833,252**
Countries without trade policy responses				
Algeria				
Wheat	79,788	−226,908	n.a.	−147,119
Corn	7	0	n.a.	7
Barley	7,418	−1,727	n.a.	5,691
Total 3 commodities	87,213	−228,634	0	−141,422
Bangladesh				
Rice	2,566,741	−2,639,077	n.a.	−72,336
Total 1 commodity	2,566,741	−2,639,077	0	−72,336
Brazil				
Rice	580,763	−642,970	n.a.	−62,208
Wheat	98,304	−300,021	n.a.	−201,718
Corn	382,943	−47,757	n.a.	335,186
Barley	3,872	−7,639	n.a.	−3,766
Soybeans, meal, and oil	406,577	−56,171	n.a.	350,406
Total 7 commodities	1,472,459	−1,054,558	0	417,901

Country/Commodity	Average 2008–2010 (2000 US$ [1,000])			
	Change in producer surplus[a]	Change in consumer surplus[b]	Change in tax revenue[c]	Net welfare change
Côte d'Ivoire				
Rice	60,591	−99,687	n.a.	−39,095
Total 1 commodity	60,591	−99,687	0	−39,095
Iran				
Rice	106,133	−143,001	n.a.	−36,868
Wheat	729,136	−729,312	n.a.	−176
Total 2 commodities	835,269	−872,313	0	−37,044
Iraq				
Rice	65,549	−348,931	n.a.	−283,381
Total 1 commodity	65,549	−348,931	0	−283,381
Malaysia				
Rice	131,276	−207,958	n.a.	−76,682
Corn	654	−1,166	n.a.	−513
Palm oil	136,384	−6,153	n.a.	130,231
Total 3 commodities	268,313	−215,276	0	53,037
Mexico				
Rice	15,852	−67,243	n.a.	−51,391
Wheat	111,578	−183,217	n.a.	−71,639
Corn	171,133	−119,195	n.a.	51,938
Barley	10,029	−951	n.a.	9,078
Sorghum	40,109	−707	n.a.	39,402
Soybeans, meal, and oil	17,607	−18,734	n.a.	−1,127
Peanuts	−1,536	4,253	n.a.	2,717
Total 9 commodities	364,771	−385,793	0	−21,022
Morocco				
Wheat	169,427	−326,983	n.a.	−157,555
Total 1 commodity	169,427	−326,983	0	−157,555
Myanmar				
Rice	13,394,692	−13,394,405	n.a.	287
Total 1 commodity	13,394,692	−13,394,405	0	287

(continued)

Source: Authors' calculations.

Note: n.a. = not applicable; [a]For oilseeds, change in producer surplus is computed for seed and bean producers and for crushers; [b]For oilseeds, change in consumer surplus is computed for oil consumers and for consumers where there is food consumption of seeds; [c]Change in tax revenue refers to the change in tax revenue of countries that applied an export tax change or to the change in tariff revenue of countries that applied an import tariff change.

TABLE 11.4 *(Continued)*

Country/Commodity	Average 2008–2010 (2000 US$ [1,000])			
	Change in producer surplus[a]	Change in consumer surplus[b]	Change in tax revenue[c]	Net welfare change
Paraguay				
Soybeans, meal, and oil	36,158	–555	n.a.	35,603
Total 3 commodities	36,158	–555	0	35,603
Saudi Arabia				
Rice	0	–26,008	n.a.	–26,008
Barley	0	–103	n.a.	–103
Total 2 commodities	0	–26,111	0	–26,111
South Africa				
Rice	0	–44,174	n.a.	–44,174
Corn	75,902	–31,947	n.a.	43,955
Barley	2,202	–1,629	n.a.	573
Sorghum	1,439	–1,193	n.a.	246
Total 4 commodities	79,543	–78,943	0	600
Tunisia				
Wheat	73,588	–123,614	n.a.	–50,026
Total 1 commodity	73,588	–123,614	0	–50,026
Ukraine				
Corn	56,775	–4,192	n.a.	52,583
Wheat	246,471	–146,748	n.a.	99,723
Barley	76,657	–14,234	n.a.	62,423
Total 3 commodities	379,903	–165,174	0	214,730
Uruguay				
Rice	–26,018	–4,738	n.a.	–30,755
Total 1 commodity	–26,018	–4,738	0	–30,755
Other African countries				
Corn	250,500	–232,129	n.a.	18,371
Wheat	1,097,378	–1,676,675	n.a.	–579,297
Barley	48,753	–37,913	n.a.	10,840
Total 3 commodities	1,396,631	–1,946,718	0	–550,087
Other Asian countries				
Wheat	226,001	–702,291	n.a.	–476,290
Corn	38,256	–29,344	n.a.	8,912
Barley	23,568	–24,398	n.a.	–831
Total 3 commodities	287,825	–756,033	0	–468,208

	Average 2008–2010 (2000 US$ [1,000])			
Country/Commodity	Change in producer surplus[a]	Change in consumer surplus[b]	Change in tax revenue[c]	Net welfare change
Other CIS countries				
Wheat	951,828	−669,559	n.a.	282,269
Total 1 commodity	951,828	−669,559	0	282,269
Other Eastern European countries				
Wheat	53,299	−72,329	n.a.	−19,030
Corn	26,656	−3,841	n.a.	22,815
Barley	5,843	−2,456	n.a.	3,387
Total 3 commodities	85,798	−78,626	0	7,172
Other Latin American Countries				
Wheat	168,634	−595,349	n.a.	−426,715
Corn	220,932	−104,639	n.a.	116,292
Barley	16,230	−21,790	n.a.	−5,560
Total 3 commodities	405,796	−721,778	0	−315,983
Other Middle Eastern countries				
Corn	42,721	−16,209	n.a.	26,512
Barley	125,761	−23,658	n.a.	102,104
Total 2 commodities	168,483	−39,867	0	128,616
Rest of the world				
Wheat	122,798	−152,001	n.a.	−29,203
Corn	83,493	−31,708	n.a.	51,785
Barley	19,599	−4,586	n.a.	15,013
Sorghum	166,235	−134,969	n.a.	31,266
Soybeans, meal, and oil	51,019	−202,172	n.a.	−151,153
Rapeseeds, meal, and oil	30,118	−79,721	n.a.	−49,603
Sunflowers, meal, and oil	94,359	−154,096	n.a.	−59,737
Palm oil	−74,474	−224,888	n.a.	−299,362
Peanuts, meal, and oil	−451,313	328,758	n.a.	−122,555
Total 17 commodities	41,835	−655,385	0	−613,550
Group welfare changes	**23,253,979**	**−24,854,020**	**0**	**−1,600,038**

Source: Authors' calculations.

Note: n.a. = not applicable; [a]For oilseeds, change in producer surplus is computed for seed and bean producers and for crushers; [b]For oilseeds, change in consumer surplus is computed for oil consumers and for consumers where there is food consumption of seeds; [c]Change in tax revenue refers to the change in tax revenue of countries that applied an export tax change or to the change in tariff revenue of countries that applied an import tariff change.

TABLE 11.5 Welfare effects of trade policy scenario on major crops in evaluated developed countries and regions

	Average 2008–2010 (2000 US$ [1000])			
Country/Commodity	Change in producer surplus[a]	Change in consumer surplus[b]	Change in tax revenue[c]	Net welfare change
Countries with Trade Policy Responses				
Japan				
Rice	–339,345	346,242	91,019	97,917
Wheat	27,713	–173,344	n.a.	–145,630
Corn	7	–35,561	n.a.	–35,554
Barley	2,086	–3,197	n.a.	–1,111
Soybeans, meal, and oil	–5,606	–46,466	n.a.	–52,072
Rapeseeds, meal, and oil	92	–59,621	n.a.	–59,529
Total 10 commodities	–315,052	28,054	91,019	–195,979
Republic of Korea				
Rice	348,145	–363,561	n.a.	–15,416
Wheat	123	50,967	–13,234	–64,078
Corn	–40,941	1,679,754	–6,281,674	–4,642,861
Soybeans, meal, and oil	630	–18,052	n.a.	–17,422
Total 6 commodities	307,957	1,247,173	–6,294,908	–4,739,777
Group Welfare Changes	**–7,095**	**1,275,227**	**–6,203,889**	**–4,935,756**
Countries without Trade Policy Responses				
Australia				
Rice	14,626	–29,822	n.a.	–15,196
Wheat	476,755	–54,789	n.a.	421,966
Corn	3,113	–1,028	n.a.	2,086
Barley	77,342	–9,880	n.a.	67,462
Sorghum	15,873	–36	n.a.	15,838
Rapeseeds, meal, and oil	11,847	–7,693	n.a.	4,154
Total 8 commodities	599,557	–103,247	0	496,310
Canada				
Rice	0	–18,749	n.a.	–18,749
Wheat	575,451	–129,237	n.a.	446,214

Country/Commodity	Average 2008–2010 (2000 US$ [1000])			
	Change in producer surplus[a]	Change in consumer surplus[b]	Change in tax revenue[c]	Net welfare change
Corn	72,930	–29,302	n.a.	43,628
Barley	126,564	–14,598	n.a.	111,966
Soybeans, meal, and oil	27,754	–8,903	n.a.	18,851
Rapeseeds, meal, and oil	136,014	–15,564	n.a.	120,450
Peanuts	0	6,061	n.a.	6,061
Total 11 commodities	938,713	–210,293	0	728,420
European Union				
Rice	160,133	–269,391	n.a.	–109,257
Wheat	522,658	–254,656	n.a.	268,003
Corn	186,021	–48,729	n.a.	137,292
Barley	153,261	–40,563	n.a.	112,699
Soybeans, meal, and oil	16,551	–182	n.a.	16,369
Rapeseeds, meal, and oil	436,797	–169,255	n.a.	267,541
Sunflowers, meal, and oil	156,566	–153,989	n.a.	2,577
Palm oil	0	–40,699	n.a.	–40,699
Peanuts, meal, and oil	3,284	38,459	n.a.	41,743
Total 17 commodities	1,635,272	–939,005	0	696,267
Hong Kong				
Rice	0	–3,245	n.a.	–3,245
Total 1 commodity	0	–3,245	0	–3,245
Israel				
Corn	0	3	n.a.	3
Barley	0	–115	n.a.	–115
Sorghum	0	–33	n.a.	–33
Total 3 commodities	0	–145	0	–145

(continued)

Source: Authors' calculations.

Note: n.a. = not applicable; [a]For oilseeds, change in producer surplus is computed for seed and bean producers and for crushers; [b]For oilseeds, change in consumer surplus is computed for oil consumers and for consumers where there is food consumption of seeds; [c]Change in tax revenue refers to the change in tax revenue of countries that applied an export tax change or to the change in tariff revenue of countries that applied an import tariff change.

TABLE 11.5 *(Continued)*

	Average 2008–2010 (2000 US$ [1000])			
Country/Commodity	Change in producer surplus[a]	Change in consumer surplus[b]	Change in tax revenue[c]	Net welfare change
Taiwan, China				
Rice	76,585	−86,718	n.a.	−10,133
Wheat	0	−32,396	n.a.	−32,396
Corn	600	−2,804	n.a.	−2,204
Barley	0	−322	n.a.	−322
Soybeans, meal, and oil	−323	−20,627	n.a.	−20,950
Total 7 commodities	76,862	−142,868	0	−66,006
United States				
Rice	519,745	−308,124	n.a.	211,621
Wheat	1,698,892	−808,809	n.a.	890,082
Corn	2,472,644	−261,715	n.a.	2,210,930
Barley	55,301	−34,755	n.a.	20,546
Sorghum	66,644	−5,629	n.a.	61,015
Soybeans, meal, and oil	922,653	−322,910	n.a.	599,743
Rapeseeds, meal, and oil	1,440	−32,979	n.a.	−31,539
Sunflowers, meal, and oil	19,098	−15,737	n.a.	3,361
Peanuts, meal, and oil	12,722	−14,524	n.a.	−1,802
Total 17 commodities	5,769,139	−1,805,182	0	3,963,956
Group Welfare Changes	**9,019,543**	**−3,203,985**	**0**	**5,815,557**

Source: Authors' calculations.

Note: n.a. = not applicable; [a]For oilseeds, change in producer surplus is computed for seed and bean producers and for crushers; [b]For oilseeds, change in consumer surplus is computed for oil consumers and for consumers where there is food consumption of seeds; [c]Change in tax revenue refers to the change in tax revenue of countries that applied an export tax change or to the change in tariff revenue of countries that applied an import tariff change.

Nigeria (rice), Philippines (rice), and Turkey (rice).[6] Consumers' welfare in those countries typically gained from price reduction, while producers' welfare and government revenues dropped. Moreover, a number of countries took a mixed strategy of export restrictions and import tariff reductions for different commodities to alleviate the price pressure in their domestic markets, such as China, India, and Indonesia. Those mixed policy distortions created various impacts on each of those countries. In general, producers in the developing countries implementing trade policy responses endured the largest loss in welfare, while most revenues switched to governments through tax collections. The welfare changes in this group totaled US$2.8 million, including a loss of US$3.5 million in PS, a gain of US$1.5 million in CS, and an increase of TR of US$4.9 million.

For other developing countries and regions that made no adjustments in trade policies, consumers typically suffered from the higher food and agricultural commodity prices, while producers gained in terms of their welfare (see Table 11.4). Except for some countries that are major exporters of agricultural and food commodities (such as Brazil, Malaysia, Paraguay, and Uruguay), the high commodity prices caused by the trade restrictions in other countries resulted in a significant net adverse effect on net importing countries. This situation is particularly significant in many developing countries in Africa, the Middle East, and Latin America that have less opportunity of being self-sufficient in agricultural production and rely heavily on imports for domestic food demand. Most of the countries/regions (75 percent) in this group experienced net welfare losses. The aggregate gains of US$23.2 million in PS were offset by the reduction in CS (US$24.8 million), resulting in a net welfare loss of US$1.6 million.

Most developed countries did not adopt any trade policy adjustments during this period, except Japan (rice) and Republic of Korea (wheat and corn). In Table 11.5, Japan's aggregate loss in PS outweighed the total gain in CS and TR, and caused a net welfare loss of US$0.2 million. In the Republic of Korea, loss in tax revenue dominated the gain in both PS and CS of six selected commodities, resulting in nearly a US$5 billion loss in net welfare. Hence those two countries together endured about a US$4.9 billion loss in welfare, primarily shared by the Republic of Korea's government. For developed countries that did not impose modifications in trade policy, the distribution of welfare between producers and consumers is consistent: PS increases while CS decreases

---

6 Since CIS is a net exporting region of sunflower and rapeseed oils, changes in the government revenue of import tariffs were not considered in this study. This suggests the estimate of the loss in total net welfare in CIS is conservative.

(see Table 11.5). Net welfare in dominant exporting countries (for example, Australia, Canada, the European Union, and the United States) increases since the significant gain in PS surpassed the loss in CS. As expected, developed countries relying on imports of grains and oilseeds (for example, Taiwan [China] and Israel) experienced a loss in net welfare as loss in CS dominated a slight gain in PS. In this group the total PS gain, US$9.0 million, outweighed the reduction in CS, US$3.2 million, creating a net welfare gain of US$5.8 million.

Conclusions

It is generally believed that inefficient trade policies, such as export restrictions or import tariffs, can create a short-term impact of mitigating the upward pressure on domestic commodity prices, but ultimately will tend to have an adverse impact on domestic prices. Moreover, trade policies implemented by those major trading countries will usually create more price pressure on the poorer food-deficit countries/regions that are less capable of manipulating their trade policies. Unfortunately, most policy makers focus on the short-term impacts and adopt these polices as a way to combat price inflation. We use a set of multimarket, partial-equilibrium, and nonspatial models of agricultural commodities to investigate the impacts adopting these trade policies will have on the world agricultural commodity prices and trade. The policy scenario is based on the relevant policy parameters utilized by the major exporting and importing countries by July 2008 in a period when these countries attempted to slow down the price hikes in their domestic markets.

The scenario results suggest a consistent world price behavior, but a heterogeneous trade pattern impact, among agricultural commodities. The international reference prices of the major agricultural commodities increased, ranging between 0.1 percent and 25.0 percent, due to the trade policy responses by various countries. Rice price experienced the largest increase, at 24.0 percent, as major exporting countries imposed export bans and restrictions, negatively impacting supplies on the global rice market. Considerable increases in the world prices of wheat (14.3 percent) and barley (9.2 percent) were also observed due to the additional export taxes and lower import tariffs. Similar to the rice market, world net trade of barley fell. However, wheat and corn world net trade expanded as higher demand was encouraged by the lower import tariffs. Oilseed prices reacted moderately to the policy modifications, as fewer trade policies had been exercised in these markets. However, vegetable oil price responses were larger as India eliminated or cut the typical high import tariffs.

Decomposing the price and trade impact of policy interventions by country type, the results show that the group of developing countries implementing trade policy responses lowered their domestic price and consequently reduced their net exports (the exporting countries) or increased their net imports (the importing countries). However, the group of developing countries with less power in manipulating their trade policies faced higher prices from the world market and had to lower their imports of agricultural and food commodities.

Welfare analyses of these trade policies show that the negative net welfare is observed particularly in many developing countries in Africa and Latin America that rely on imports for their domestic consumption and have little power to introduce any trade policy changes. This group experienced a total US$1.6 million net welfare loss as estimated in this study. For these countries the higher world commodity prices brought about by trade policy modifications generate more challenges in attaining food security. This suggests that the "costs" of major trading countries imposing trade restrictions on small countries relying on food imports are important and should not be neglected. In contrast, developing countries that increased export taxes or lowered/eliminated import tariffs enjoyed total net welfare gains. However, the welfare gain primarily goes to the government in the form of higher revenue; and the producers' losses in these countries actually outweighed the gains in consumers' welfare. The distribution of the additional tax revenue is beyond the scope of our analysis, but the efficiency of compensating producers and consumers with those extra tax revenues is crucial in this group.

The findings of this study are consistent with literature. FAO (2009) discusses the various trade policy responses adopted by countries in response to higher food prices and argues that by maintaining prices at artificially low levels, these countries may experience lower production. It also warns that export restrictions will lower supplies in world markets, leading to even higher prices. Von Braun et al. (2008) raise similar concerns and note that "policy responses such as export bans or high export tariffs may reduce risks of food shortages in the short term for the relevant country, but they are likely to backfire by making the international market smaller and more volatile. At the country level, price controls can also backfire by reducing farmers' incentives to produce more food and diverting resources away from those who need them most." Results of our study show the adverse effects of export bans/restrictions on the production of agricultural commodities in countries that implement them.

In terms of the price and welfare impact of trade policy adjustments, von Braun et al. (2008) conclude that the elimination of export bans would reduce price levels by as much as 30 percent. Bouët and Laborde (2010) also suggest that the world wheat price increases by 20.6 percent to 41.0 percent in the scenarios of raising export taxes. The welfare analysis in Bouët and Laborde finds that under policy interventions wheat net exporters' welfare increases while the net importers' welfare decreases. Those findings are in line with the direction of price and welfare impacts estimated in this study. The price impacts of trade policy adjustments in those studies are relatively higher than the commodity price changes in this study (2.6 percent to 25.0 percent among different commodities), which could be due to scenario definition and modeling differences. Although it is difficult to make a direct comparison of the magnitude of price impacts, the directions of price changes in those studies are similar to the percentage price changes in this study.

This chapter provides an illustration of the adverse impacts of exercising inefficient trade policies to mitigate the price pressure in domestic commodity markets. In order to stabilize the price of agricultural and food commodities, governments can rely on minimizing the policy distortions in markets and focusing on investment in infrastructure, information diffusion, and research in the agricultural sector (Cummings et al. 2006). As suggested by von Braun (2009) and illustrated by Nouve and Wodon (2008), policies that encourage productivity improvements that boost the supply would be much more beneficial and provide a long-term solution for the higher price problem of today's agricultural markets.

Bibliography

Baffes, J., and T. Haniotis. 2010. "Placing the 2006/08 Commodity Price Boom into Perspective." Policy Research Working Paper 5371. Development Prospects Group, World Bank, Washington, DC.

Bouët, A., and D. Laborde. 2010. "Economics of Export Taxation in a Context of Food Crisis." Discussion Paper 994. Washington, DC: International Food Policy Research Institute.

Coady, D., P. Dorosh, and B. Minten. 2009. "Evaluating Alternative Policy Responses to Higher World Food Prices: The Case of Increasing Rice Prices in Madagascar." *American Journal of Agricultural Economics* 91 (3): 711–722.

Cummings, R. Jr., S. Rashid, and A. Gulati. 2006. "Grain Price Stabilization Experiences in Asia: What Have We Learned?" *Food Policy* 31: 302–312.

FAO (Food and Agricultural Organization of the United Nations). 2008. "The State of Food and Agriculture." Rome. Accessed March 2011. www.fao.org/docrep/011/i0100e/i0100e00.htm.

———. 2009. "The State of Food Insecurity in the World 2008." Rome. Accessed March 2011. www.fao.org/docrep/011/i0291e/i0291e00.htm.

———. 2010. "World Food Situation." Rome. Accessed March 2011. www.fao.org/worldfood situation/FoodPricesIndex/en/.

FAPRI (Food and Agricultural Policy Research Institute). 2008. "FAPRI 2008 US and World Agricultural Outlook." Iowa State University, Ames, IA.

Nouve, K., and Q. Wodon. 2008. "Impact of Rising Rice Prices and Policy Responses in Mali: Simulations with a Dynamic CGE Model." World Bank Policy Research Working Paper 4739, WPS4739. Washington, DC: World Bank.

Rapsomanikis, G. 2009. "The 2007–2008 Food Price Episode: Impact and Policies in Eastern and Southern Africa." FAO Commodities and Trade Technical Paper. Trade and Markets Division. Unpublished. Food and Agricultural Organization of the United Nations, Rome.

Sugden, C. 2009. "Responding to High Commodity Prices." *Asian-Pacific Economic Literature* 23 (1): 79–105.

Timmer, C. P. 2010. "Reflections on Food Crises Past." *Food Policy* 35 (1): 1–11.

Trostle, R. 2008. "Global Agricultural Supply and Demand: Factors Contributing to the Recent Increase in Food Commodity Prices." USDA Economic Research Service Report WRS-0801. Washington, DC: United States Department of Agriculture.

von Braun, J. 2008. "Rising Food Prices: What Should Be Done?" Policy Brief. Washington, DC: International Food Policy Research Institute (IFPRI).

———. 2009. "Addressing the Food Crisis: Governance, Market Functioning, and Investment in Public Goods." *Food Security* 1: 9–15.

von Braun, J., A. Ahmed, K. Asenso-Okyere, S. Fan, A. Gulati, J. Hoddinott, R. Pandya-Lorch, M. W. Rosegrant, M. Ruel, M. Torero, T. van Rheenen, and K. von Grebmer. 2008. "High Food Prices: The What, Who, and How of Proposed Policy Actions." Policy Brief. Washington, DC: International Food Policy Research Institute (IFPRI). www.ifpri.org/sites/default/files/publications/foodpricespolicyaction.pdf.

Wailes, E. J. 2005. "Rice Global Trade, Protectionist Policy, and Impact of Trade Liberalization." In *Global Agricultural Trade and Developing Countries*, edited by M. Ataman Aksoy and John C. Beghin, 177–194. Washington, DC: World Bank.

Yu, T.-H., S. Tokgoz, E. Wailes, and E. Chavez. 2011. "A Quantitative Analysis of Trade Policy Responses to Higher World Agricultural Commodity Prices." *Food Policy* 36 (5): 545–561.

Appendix

TABLE 11.A1 International grains model supply and demand elasticities

Commodity/Country	Supply elasticity	Price elasticity of demand	Income elasticity of demand
Rice			
Australia	0.19	–0.44	2.31
Bangladesh	0.16	–0.00	0.41
India	0.09	–0.04	–0.16
Indonesia	0.10	–0.13	–0.09
Malaysia	0.15	–0.30	0.09
Myanmar	0.15	–0.10	0.13
Philippines	0.04	–0.25	0.15
Thailand	0.15	–0.05	–0.16
Viet Nam	0.01	–0.20	–0.23
China	0.22	–0.10	–0.14
Hong Kong	n.a.	–0.16	–0.19
Japan	0.29	–0.11	–0.26
South Korea (Republic of Korea)	0.24	–0.66	–0.32
Taiwan, China	0.17	–0.02	–0.29
Argentina	0.24	–0.07	0.11
Brazil	0.08	–0.10	–0.05
Canada	n.a.	–0.21	0.47
Mexico	0.10	–0.05	0.46
Uruguay	0.21	–0.17	0.50
Iran	0.00	–0.35	0.20
Iraq	2.18	–0.04	0.53
Pakistan	0.29	–0.18	0.10
Saudi Arabia	n.a.	–0.25	0.10
Egypt	0.161	–0.15	0.30
South Africa	n.a.	–0.20	0.47
Côte d'Ivoire	0.57	–0.55	0.14
Nigeria	0.10	–0.15	0.25
European Union	0.10	–0.08	1.63
Turkey	0.05	–0.01	1.41
United States	(0.39,0.81)[a]	–0.12	0.37

Commodity/Country	Supply elasticity	Price elasticity of demand	Income elasticity of demand
Wheat			
India	0.27	−0.26	n.a.
China	0.33	−0.08	−0.06
Argentina	0.31	−0.28	−0.11
Brazil	0.32	−0.25	0.04
Canada	0.35	−0.24	0.01
European Union	0.02	−0.22	−0.03
United States	(0.13,0.44)[a]	−0.08	n.a.
Australia	0.27	−0.26	−0.21
Corn			
India	0.34	−0.21	0.00
China	0.27	−0.15	0.05
Argentina	0.60	−0.42	n.a.
Brazil	0.33	−0.14	0.01
Canada	0.31	−0.31	0.07
European Union	0.03	−0.24	−0.03
United States	(0.17,0.52)[a]	−0.07	n.a.
Australia	0.20	−0.25	0.05
Barley			
China	0.43	−0.30	0.05
Argentina	0.31	−0.36	−0.08
Brazil	0.16	−0.36	0.11
Canada	0.33	−0.35	0.01
European Union	0.05	−0.31	−0.06
United States	(0.19,0.59)[a]	−0.09	n.a.
Australia	0.28	−0.33	0.01
Sorghum			
India	0.22	0.25	0.01
Australia	0.22	−0.35	0.02
Argentina	0.39	−0.28	−0.35
United States	(0.16,0.28)[a]	−0.49	n.a.

Source: Authors.

Note: n.a. = not applicable.

[a]The ranges of the elasticities for the 9 subregions in the US crops model are presented. The regions include the Corn Belt, the Central Plains, the Delta States, the Far West, the Lake States, the Northeast, the Northern Plains, the Southeast, and the Southern Plains.

TABLE 11.A2 International oilseeds model supply and demand elasticities

Commodity/Country	Supply elasticity	Revenue elasticity of crush demand	Price elasticity of food demand	Income elasticity of food demand
Soybeans				
India	0.33	0.15	−0.30	0.85
China	0.30	0.21	−0.20	0.60
Japan	0.34	0.25	−0.34	0.45
Taiwan, China	n.a.	0.04	−0.30	0.43
Argentina	0.26	0.20	n.a.	n.a.
Brazil	0.33	0.10	n.a.	n.a.
Paraguay	0.18	0.08	n.a.	n.a.
Mexico	0.22	0.23	n.a.	n.a.
Canada	0.31	0.25	n.a.	n.a.
European Union	0.30	0.20	−0.25	0.40
United States	(0.16,0.33)[a]	0.08	n.a.	n.a.
Rapeseed				
India	0.34	0.25	n.a.	n.a.
China	0.22	0.24	n.a.	n.a.
Canada	0.25	0.20	n.a.	n.a.
CIS	0.34	0.25	n.a.	n.a.
Japan	0.24	0.17	n.a.	n.a.
European Union	0.24	0.26	n.a.	n.a.
United States				
Australia	0.25	0.10	n.a.	n.a.
Sunflower				
China	0.33	0.20	−0.17	0.01
Argentina	0.19	0.23	n.a.	n.a.
European Union	0.25	0.20	n.a.	n.a.
CIS	0.32	0.20	n.a.	n.a.
United States	(0.47, 0.48)[a]	0.34	−0.17	n.a.
Peanuts				
India	0.36	0.25	−0.20	0.20
China	0.20	0.30	−0.03	0.50
Argentina	0.25	0.20	−0.20	0.20
Canada	n.a.	n.a.	−0.40	0.20
United States	(0.28,0.60)[a]	0.48	−0.19	n.a.
Palm				
Indonesia	0.01	0.20	n.a.	n.a.
Malaysia	0.01	0.22	n.a.	n.a.

Source: Authors.

Note: n.a. = not applicable.

[a]The ranges of the elasticities for the 9 subregions in the US crops model are presented. The regions include the Corn Belt, the Central Plains, the Delta States, the Far West, the Lake States, the Northeast, the Northern Plains, the Southeast, and the Southern Plains.

TABLE 11.A3 Simulated price impacts of policy shocks in 2007–2008

Commodity	Simulated price impact of trade policy shocks in 2007/2008 (%)	Actual price growth between 2006/2007 and 2007/2008 (%)	Share of policy shocks on the total price change (%)
Rice	19	72	26
Wheat	13	70	19
Corn	6	40	15
Barley	9	37	23
Soybeans	3	64	5
Soymeal	3	70	5
Soyoil	1	72	1
Minor oilseeds	0	79	1
Minor oil meals	3	65	4
Minor oils	1	80	1

Source: Authors' calculations.

Note: The second column represents the price impacts of trade policy shocks imposed in the 2007/2008 marketing year. It is computed as the percentage change in commodity prices in scenario and baseline. The third column is the actual growth rate of commodity prices between 2006/2007 and 2007/2008 marketing years. Therefore the impact of trade policy responses on the actual price increase from 2006/2007 to 2007/2008 is the ratio of the simulated price growth rate over the actual price growth rate, which is presented in the fourth column.

Chapter 12

FOOD CRISIS AND EXPORT TAXATION: THE COST OF NONCOOPERATIVE TRADE POLICIES

Antoine Bouët and David Laborde

Export restrictions are trade measures that are permanently adopted by countries throughout the world.[1] Piermartini (2004) noted that approximately one-third of World Trade Organization (WTO) members impose export duties. Examples are export taxes implemented by Indonesia on palm oil, by Madagascar on vanilla, coffee, pepper, and cloves, by Pakistan on raw cotton, by the Philippines on copra and coconut oil, by Indonesia on palm oil, and by the European Union on wheat (Bouët and Laborde 2010; OECD 2010). What are the effects of such policy measures? And why do governments restrict exports in times of food crisis?

As the section "The Economics of Export Taxation in the Context of a Food Crisis" shows, economic analysis provides several rational justifications for using these restrictions—in particular, in terms of changes in international terms of trade and the impact on domestic prices of final and intermediate goods and public receipts. Moreover, it appears that countries have a relatively large degree of freedom in the implementation of such taxes, as the WTO does not prohibit export taxes and other forms of export restrictions. More precisely, as stated by Crosby (2008, 3), "general WTO rules do not discipline Members' application of export taxes," but "they can agree—and several recently acceded countries, including China, have agreed—to legally binding commitments in this regard." In addition, the Uruguay Round Agreement on Agriculture (AoA) stipulates that when implementing a new export restriction, a WTO member must (1) consider the implications of these policies on food security in importing countries, (2) give notice to the Committee on Agriculture, and (3) consult with WTO members that have an interest in the country's export policies. This agreement does not, however, impose

1 This chapter was originally published as an article in the *Review of World Economics* (Bouët and Laborde 2012). The authors would like to thank the participants of a workshop organized at OECD on October 30, 2009, and of a seminar organized at IFPRI-MTID in Washington, DC, on April 10, 2010, and in particular Jeonghoi Kim, David Tarr, Franck van Tongeren, and Maximo Torero for useful comments on an earlier version. Two anonymous reviewers have also been very helpful.

any penalty on countries that ignore the rules. Finally, this form of trade policy does not receive a great deal of attention from the public or the academic establishment.

This chapter provides a theoretical and empirical background that contributes to a better understanding of export taxes in the context of food crises. The 2006–2008 food crisis has shown that governments may be tempted by these policies at a time when their use is not regulated by international cooperation. As we show, these instruments may amplify the surge in world agricultural commodities prices—in particular when they are combined with a reduction of import tariffs by large net food-importing countries. This amplification effect is the result of a noncooperative game between large net food-importing countries and large net food-exporting countries; small net food-importing countries do not have the capacity for reaction and are hurt by this game equilibrium. We illustrate this process through a Computable General Equilibrium (CGE) model that quantifies these mechanisms. This modeling exercise clearly shows that when world food prices spike, both the implementation of new export restrictions and the reduction of import tariffs on agricultural commodities feed augmentation of world prices and harm small net food-importing countries. Such outcomes represent a clear lack of international coordination; we argue that international institutions should promote more cooperation in this area.

The next section provides an analytical framework that can help better explain these trade policies. In particular, in the section "A General Equilibrium Analysis," we develop a theoretical model under general equilibrium that (1) describes what the consequences are of adopting import taxes in large and small net-food importing countries and export taxes in large and small net food-exporting countries and (2) derives optimal policies when the objective of a government is to maximize the country's real income. In the section "An Illustration of the Adoption of Export Taxes on Agricultural Commodities and Their Effects Using the MIRAGE Model of the World Economy," we use the MIRAGE model to illustrate the potential impact of world price shocks and how countries may react using either increased export taxes and/or reduced import taxes, emphasizing the effects of noncooperative trade policies in this context.[2] In this modeling exercise, the objective of the government is to keep domestic prices constant in the case of an external

2 The MIRAGE model was initially developed at the Centre d'Etudes Prospectives et d'Informations Internationales (CEPII) in Paris. Full description of the model is available in Bchir et al. (2002) and Decreux and Valin (2007).

shock that implies a surge in world food prices. The rationale of this behavior is explained at the beginning of the next section. A final section concludes.

The Economics of Export Taxation in the Context of a Food Crisis: A General Equilibrium Analysis

The objective of this section is to provide a more complete theoretical framework to explain the effects of export taxation in a general equilibrium. It might be helpful to present a list of the purported objectives of export taxation as stated officially by various governments. This list can be then compared to the actual impact of export restrictions as revealed by economic analysis. Kim (2010) provides a list that was revealed by WTO members during their Trade Policy Review. It includes: (1) noneconomic reasons related to security issues, such as chemical weapons and nuclear nonproliferation, (2) noneconomic reasons related to life, public health, safety, and environmental issues (for example, transboundary movement of hazardous waste), (3) economic reasons in accordance with international or bilateral agreements (for example, international commodities agreements on sugar, coffee, and petroleum), and (4) maintenance of an adequate supply of essential products or promotion of downstream industries. The economic analysis of export taxation provides other economic reasons.

We develop a general model of international trade between four countries (two large and two small). The purpose of this exercise is to understand that, as far as a food crisis is concerned, there is a distinction to be made between (1) large food-exporting countries that can increase the world price of the commodity they export while decreasing the domestic price of this commodity, (2) large food-importing countries that can also have an impact on world prices and accept a deterioration in their terms of trade in order to decrease the domestic price of an agricultural commodity, (3) small net food-importing countries that cannot affect world prices and are harmed by the policies of large countries, and (4) small net food-exporting countries that cannot affect world prices and benefit from the policies of large countries. The entire process is a "trade game" with strategic interdependence on import tariffs and export taxes.

A Partial Equilibrium Analysis

The partial equilibrium framework provides several insights (Figure 12.1). Consider first the case of a small country (left graph on Figure 12.1) imposing an export tax t (defined in specific terms). The initial domestic price is p_0,

FIGURE 12.1 A partial equilibrium analysis of an export tax

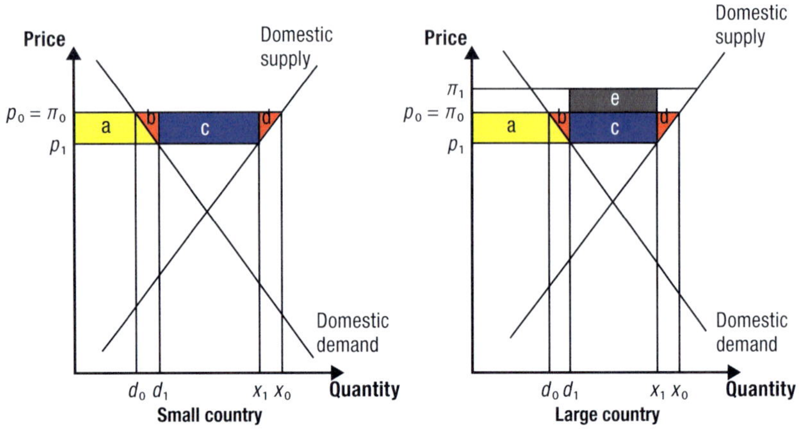

Source: Authors' investigation.

while the initial world price is π_0. At these initial prices, domestic demand is d_0 and is less than domestic supply, x_0, the difference being exported on the world market. As these exports are now taxed, at the initial prices, domestic producers prefer offering their supply on the local market (untaxed) rather than on the world market (taxed). On the domestic market, the supply is increased, reducing the domestic price until $p_1 + t = \pi_0$, while the world price is, by definition, unchanged (small country). At this level of prices, domestic producers are indifferent between selling their products on local markets and exporting them.

Domestic consumers benefit from this policy, as they consume more ($d_1 > d_0$) at a lower price ($p_1 < p_0$); their gain is here measured by area a. Domestic producers are hurt by this policy, as they produce and sell less ($x_1 < x_0$) at a lower price ($p_1 < p_0$); their loss is here measured by (a + b + c + d). Finally, the export tax increases public revenues (area c). Clearly, policy makers should not implement such a policy if it is assumed that one dollar of consumers' surplus has the same value as one dollar of producers' surplus and one dollar of public revenue. Nevertheless, if policy makers have a food security objective that implies a decrease in domestic prices, export taxes may be justified in the sense that they augment domestic consumption and reduce the local consumer price. They increase the surplus of food consumers. In such a case, a consumption subsidy is a first-order instrument (meaning it is more efficient), but it may have a cost for the government: if we assume that the government has difficulties raising taxes on other products and/or sources of income (for example, a tax on firm profits), an export tax may be preferred to a consumption subsidy.[3] Both arguments explain why one dollar of increase in consumers' surplus or in public revenue is more important for the government than one dollar of loss in terms of producers' surplus.

The case of a large country (see right graph on Figure 12.1) differs in the sense that the world price is affected by the export tax. The reason is that a large country is assumed to export a significant share of world exports, such that if these exports are reduced, world exports would be significantly reduced and the world price would increase. Consumers' and producers' surpluses are identically affected, but public revenues are augmented as the world price is raised up to π_1; the post-tax level of exports is still the difference between x_1 and d_1, but the unit tax is now $\pi_1 - p_1$. This is all the more important, as the implementation of this policy can lead to an augmentation of domestic welfare if the area denoted by e is larger than the sum of the areas (b + d). While b + d represents welfare losses coming from these new distortions, e represents an improvement in national terms of trade. Final exports $(x_1 - d_1)$ are sold at π_1 and not π_0, with the difference $(\pi_1 - \pi_0)$ representing a gain in terms of trade for each unit exported.

Simultaneously, the same political elements are still in play, as domestic consumers and the public budget are favored and domestic producers are hurt by this decision. Therefore economic analysis provides several justifications for the implementation of export taxes.

1. **Terms of trade.** This is perhaps the most important justification. By restricting its exports, a country that supplies a significant share of a particular commodity in the world market can raise the world price of that commodity. This implies an improvement in that country's terms of trade. The reasoning behind this argument is very similar to the optimum tariff argument (Bickerdike 1906; Johnson 1953), which states that by implementing a tariff on its imports, a "large" country can significantly decrease the demand for a commodity that it imports; this therefore leads to a decrease in the commodity's world price.

3 It has also been argued that export taxes on commodities (cocoa, oil) have been administrated in a very convoluted way in several developing countries (for example, Côte d'Ivoire) and have fostered corruption, as this resource is less monitored than other taxes paid by local customers/constituencies.

2. **Food security and final consumption price.** By creating a wedge between the world price and the domestic price, a government can lower the latter by reorienting domestic supply toward the domestic market. Piermartini (2004) provides an example in which the Indonesian government imposed export taxes on palm oil products, including crude and palm cooking oil, in 1994 because it considered cooking oil an "essential" commodity. This rationale was often used by governments during the food crisis of 2006–2008 to justify the implementation of export taxes and other forms of export restrictions.

3. **Intermediate consumption price.** Export taxes on primary commodities (especially unprocessed ones) work as an indirect subsidy to higher-value-added manufacturing or processing industries by lowering the domestic price of inputs compared with those inputs' world—nondistorted—price. While the previous justification addresses the use of export taxes to lower prices for final consumption, this one is concerned with decreasing prices for intermediate consumption. This justification follows a reasoning similar to the theory of effective protection and is noted by Corden (1971), who considers that an export tax on an exportable input protects the using industry. For example, in 1988, Pakistan imposed an export tax on raw cotton in order to stimulate the development of the yarn cotton industry. This kind of degressive export tax structure (greater than zero for the raw commodity; zero or close to zero for the processed good) also exists in China (for steel products, metal ore sand, and ferro-alloys) and Indonesia and Malaysia (for palm oil/biodiesel and cooking oil; see Amiruddin 2003).

4. **Public receipts.** Export taxes provide revenues for developing countries that have limited capacity for domestic taxation. This is a lesser argument because in order to raise a given amount of revenue, the imposition of lump-sum taxes is the best policy (Ramsey 1927; Diamond 1975). Deardorff and Rajaraman (2005) demonstrate that for a country exporting a (primary) product under monopsony's power, the best available policy may be to tax exports so as to extract some of the profits of the monopsonist; doing so worsens the distortion but increases domestic public receipts to the detriment of monopsony's rents.

5. **Income redistribution.** Like import tariffs, export taxes are measures that imply redistribution of income to the detriment of the domestic

producers taxed and to the benefit of domestic consumers and public revenues.

6. **Stabilization of domestic prices.** In order to stabilize domestic prices for export producers, some developing countries use variable tax rates. Piermartini (2004) provides the example of Papua New Guinea, which established an export tax/subsidy rate for cocoa, coffee, copra, and palm oil equal to one-half the difference between the reference price—calculated as the average of the world price in the previous 10 years—and the actual price for the year.

It is worth noting that in the long run, consequences could be different because, as noticed by Mitra and Josling (2009, 11), "producers in the rest of the world will increase their supply in response to higher prices. As a result of increased supply the price adjusts downward from the short-run level, but still remains above the pre-restriction level." Therefore it is quite possible that export restrictions could be beneficial in the short run while having negative consequences in the long run due to adjustments in the terms of trade. Evidently the partial equilibrium approach does not provide a rigorous and consistent framework, as it does not account for income effects and all interdependent links that exist in the world economy. A general equilibrium analysis is required.

A General Equilibrium Analysis

We consider a model of international trade between four countries: two are large (1 and 2), meaning that they are price makers on the world market, and two are small (3 and 4), meaning that they are price takers. These countries produce and trade two commodities, an agricultural commodity (A) and an industrial commodity (I). Countries 1 and 4 have a comparative advantage in A: they export the agricultural good and import the industrial one. In contrast, countries 2 and 3 have a comparative advantage in I: they export the industrial good and they import the agricultural good. Country i's welfare function is denoted as U_i, and the local demand of country i for good k is D_i^k, $\forall i = 1, 2, 3, 4$; $\forall k = A, I$. Let X_i^k, $\forall i = 1, 2, 3, 4$ and $\forall k = A, I$, the production of good k in country i. The variable π^k is the nominal world price of good k, and p_i^k is the nominal local price of good k in country i. The variable π is the relative price of good A on the world market in terms of industrial goods, p_i is the relative price of good A within country i. Variable y_i indicates the real income in country i, and Y_i is the nominal income in country i.

Let us assume the following:

1. Technology is accounted for by “well-behaved” production functions.
2. Competition is perfect in each country in both product and factor markets.
3. Welfare depends only on local consumption of both goods:

$$U_i = U_i(D_i^A, D_i^I) \text{ with: } \frac{\partial U_i}{\partial D_i^k} > 0, \forall i, \forall k. \quad (1)$$

4. Governments select either an import tariff/subsidy or an export tax/subsidy on good A in order to maximize the national welfare function.[4]
5. Trade is balanced in each country:

$$X_i^I - D_i^I = \pi \,.\, (D_i^A - X_i^A) \quad (2)$$

Both sides are positive for $i = 2$ and 3 and negative for $i = 1$ and 4.

6. There is no transportation cost.
7. The tariff/export tax revenue is redistributed totally to local agents without losses.

We first analytically derive the effects of an import tariff in countries 2 and 3 and of an export tax in countries 1 and 4. We then determine the optimal policy for each country.

AN IMPORT TARIFF IN THE LARGE FOOD-IMPORTING COUNTRY

Let us first consider the traditional case of the impact of an import tariff on demand. In the case of 2, t_2 is a tariff on agricultural imports. The demand for imports is:

$$M_2^A = D_2^A(p_2, y_2) - X_2^A(X_2^I(p_2)). \quad (3)$$

Total differentiation brings:

$$dM_2^A = \frac{\partial D_2^A}{\partial p_2}(p_2, y_2)dp_2 + \frac{\partial D_2^A}{\partial y_2}(p_2, y_2)dy_2 - \frac{dX_2^A}{dX_2^I}\frac{dX_2^I}{dp_2}dp_2. \quad (4)$$

We have:

$\sigma^c{}_2 = -\frac{p_2}{M_2^A}\frac{\partial D_2^A}{\partial p_2}(p_2, y_2)$ is the compensated relative price elasticity of demand for agricultural imports in country 2; $m_2 = p_2 \frac{\partial D_2^A}{\partial y_2}(p_2, y_2)$; m_2 is the marginal

4 The main reason is that we are interested in what happens to demand for the agricultural good. There are some equivalence theorems that show that in a two countries/two goods model, the imposition of an export tax is equivalent to an import tax (Lerner 1936). We could also consider that import tariffs on the industrial good are bound at 0.

propensity to spend on agricultural goods in country 2; $e_2 = -\frac{p_2}{E_2^I}\frac{dX_2^I}{dp_2}$; e_2 is related to a relative price elasticity of supply for industrial products in country 2.

Let us find an expression of dy_2. If $V_2 = V_2\,(p_2, Y_2)$ is the maximum utility that can be attained by 2 when the domestic price is p_2 and nominal income is Y_2, Roy's theorem gives:

$$D_2^A = -\frac{\partial V_2(p_2,Y_2)}{\partial p_2} \Big/ \frac{\partial V_2(p_2,Y_2)}{\partial Y_2} = -V_{2p_2} / V_{2Y_2} \tag{5}$$

Therefore:

$dy_2 = \frac{dV_2}{V_{2Y_2}} = dY_2 - D_2^A.dp_2 = dX_2^I + p_2.dX_2^A + X_2^A.dp_2 + d(\pi t_2 M_2^A) - D_2^A.dp_2.$
Since perfect competition ensures that the economy is located on the production frontier: $dX_2^I + p_2.dX_2^A = 0$, we have

$$dy_2 = -M_2^A.dp_2 + M_2^A\,d(p_2 - \pi) + \pi t_2\,dM_2^A = -M_2^A.d\pi + \pi t_2\,dM_2^A \tag{6}$$

Equation (6) states that in this international trade model, a country's real income is affected either by a change in world prices ($d\pi < 0$ means that the world price for the agricultural good decreases; this is the good that country 2 imports) or a variation in quantities traded (real income increases when trade increases, other things being equal).

Integrating equation (6) and the previous definitions inside (4)[5], we obtain:

$$\frac{dM_2^A}{M_2^A} = \left\{-\sigma^c{}_2.\frac{dp_2}{p_2} - \frac{m_2}{1+t_2}\frac{d\pi}{\pi} - \frac{e_2}{1+t_2}\frac{dp_2}{p_2}\right\}/d_2 \tag{7}$$

where:

$$d_2 = 1 - [m_2 t_2 / (1 + t_2)].$$

RESULT 1. IN THE LARGE FOOD-IMPORTING COUNTRY, WHEN IMPOSING A TARIFF, FOUR MECHANISMS ARE AT PLAY.

1. A substitution effect on domestic consumption: under constant real income, a tariff increase leads to a domestic agricultural price increase, which reduces domestic consumption of the agricultural good in favor of other goods.

2. A substitution effect on domestic production: under constant real income, a tariff increase leads to a domestic agricultural price increase,

5 In particular to obtain equation (7), remember that: $p_2 = \pi(1+t_2)$ and $E_2^I = \pi M_2^A$.

which expands domestic production of the agricultural good to the detriment of other goods.

3. The imposition of a tariff on the country's imports of the agricultural good reduces the world price of this good, which implies that terms of trade are improved for this country.

4. A multiplier effect: an increase in real income increases demand for imports, which in turn increases tariff receipts, which increases real income, and so on. Starting from free trade (that is, a situation in which no tariff is imposed) ($t_2 = 0$), this effect is nil.

AN EXPORT TAX IN THE LARGE FOOD-EXPORTING COUNTRY

We turn now to the case of country 1, which may consider the implementation of a tax t_1 on its agricultural exports. Its supply of agricultural exports is:

$$E_1^A = X_1^A\,(X_1^I(p_1)) - D_1^A(p_1,y_1) \tag{8}$$

Total differentiation brings:

$$dE_1^A = \frac{dX_1^A}{dX_1^I}\frac{dX_1^I}{dp_1}dp_1 - \frac{\partial D_1^A}{\partial p_1}(p_1,y_1)dp_1 - \frac{\partial D_1^A}{\partial y_1}(p_1,y_1)dy_1 \tag{9}$$

$\sigma^c_1 = -\frac{p_1}{E_1^A}\frac{\partial D_1^A}{\partial p_1}(p_1,y_1)$ is the compensated relative price elasticity of supply of agricultural exports in 2, $m_1 = p_1\frac{\partial D_2^A}{\partial y_2}(p_1,y_1)$ is the marginal propensity to demand agricultural goods in 1, and $e_1 = -\frac{p_1}{M_1^I}\frac{\partial X_1^I}{\partial p_1}$ is the relative price elasticity of the supply of industrial goods in 1. Let us find an expression of dy_1. As for $i = 2$, $V_1 = V_1\,(p_1,Y_1)$ is country 1's indirect utility and Roy's theorem is:

$$D_1^A = -\frac{\partial V_1(p_1,Y_1)}{\partial p_1}\Bigg/\frac{\partial V_1(p_1,Y_1)}{\partial Y_1} = -V_{1p_1}\Big/V_{1Y_1} \tag{10}$$

Therefore:

$$dy_1 = \frac{dV_1}{V_{1Y_1}} = dY_1 - D_1^A.dp_1 = dX_1^I + p_1.dX_1^A + X_1^A.dp_1 + d(p_1t_1E_1^A) - D_1^A.dp_1$$

$p_1t_1E_1^A$ is country 1's public revenue from taxation of exports ($\pi = p_1(1+t_1)$). Following similar manipulations, we obtain:

$$dy_1 = E_1^A.d\pi + p_1t_1dE_1^A \tag{11}$$

Equation (11) is important because it states that country 1's real income is affected either by a change in world prices (terms of trade effect; $d\pi > 0$ means that the agricultural good's world price increases; this is the good that country 1 exports) or a variation in quantities traded (real income increases when trade increases, other things being equal). The terms-of-trade effect is proportional to the amount of country 1's agricultural exports. Integrating equation (11) and the previous definitions inside (9), we obtain:

$$\frac{dE_1^A}{E_1^A} = \left\{\sigma^c_1 . \frac{dp_1}{p_1} - m_1(1+t_1)\frac{d\pi}{\pi} + (1+t_1).e_1\frac{dp_1}{p_1}\right\}/d_1 \qquad (12)$$

where:

$$d_1 = 1 + m_1 t_1.$$

RESULT 2. IN THE LARGE FOOD-EXPORTING COUNTRY, WHEN IMPOSING A TAX ON ITS AGRICULTURAL EXPORTS, FOUR MECHANISMS ARE AT PLAY.

1. A substitution effect on domestic consumption: under constant real income, a tax on agricultural exports leads to a domestic agricultural consumer price decrease, which in turn augments the domestic consumption of the agricultural good ("food security effect").
2. A substitution effect on domestic production: under constant real income, a tax on agricultural exports leads to a domestic agricultural producer price decrease, which decreases domestic production of the agricultural good ("antifarmer effect").
3. As this is a large country, the imposition of a tax on exports of an agricultural good increases the world price of that good, which implies that the country's terms of trade are improved.
4. A divisor effect: an increase in real income increases demand for the agricultural commodity, which decreases export supply of the agricultural commodity, which in turn reduces export tax receipts, which decreases real income. Starting from free trade (t = 0), this effect is nil.

TARIFFS AND TAXES IN SMALL COUNTRIES

As far as country 3 is concerned, the problem is similar to country 2 in that it has a comparative disadvantage in the production of the agricultural good; country 3 imports this good. The only difference is that it is a small country, so that a change in its real income is expressed as:

$$dy_3 = \pi t_3 dM_3^A \qquad (13)$$

Concerning country 4, the problem is similar to country 1 in that it has a comparative advantage in the production of the agricultural good; country 4 exports this good. The only difference is that it is a small country, so that a change in its real income is expressed as:

$$dy_4 = p_4 t_4 dE_4^A \tag{14}$$

For small countries, the higher the level of trade, the higher the real income. Concerning country 3, welfare is maximized with $\pi = p_3$; that is, domestic price equal to world price $t_3 = 0$, as $p_3 = \pi(1+t_3)$. The same policy conclusion applies for country 4: $t_4 = 0$ is the optimal policy, and any other policy does not maximize real income.

A TRADE WAR OF IMPORT TARIFFS AND EXPORT TAXES

If country 3 implements a tariff on its agricultural imports, it decreases its traded imports and its real income is negatively affected. Country 3's reaction function is:

$$t_3 = 0 \tag{15}$$

Similarly, country 4's reaction function is:

$$t_4 = 0 \tag{16}$$

As far as country 2 is concerned, its program consists of selecting a production structure and a world price that maximize real income:

$$Max_{X_2^I,\pi} U_2 = U_2(D_2^A; D_2^I) = U_2(X_2^A + M_2^A; X_2^I - E_2^I)$$

Under:

$$E_2^I(\pi) = \pi M_2^A \tag{17}$$

$$X_2^I = -p_2 X_2^A + constant \tag{18}$$

$$p_2 = \pi(1 + t_2) \tag{19}$$

Equation (17) defines trade balance, (18) defines production frontier, and (19) defines the relation between world and domestic prices. This program can be rewritten as:

$$Max_{X_2^I,\pi} U_2 = U_2\left(-\frac{X_2^I}{p_2} + \frac{E_2^I(\pi)}{\pi}; X_2^I - E_2^I(\pi)\right) \tag{20}$$

Solving (20) yields country 2's reaction function:

$$t_2 = \frac{1}{\sigma_2^* - 1} \tag{21}$$

where $\sigma_2^* = \frac{\pi}{E_2^I} \frac{\partial E_2^I}{\partial \pi} > 0$ is the reciprocal demand elasticity facing 2. It is a general equilibrium elasticity that measures how much the rest of the world is willing to trade agricultural goods against country 2's industrial goods. In this elasticity, substitution effects (on both the consumption and production side), real income effects, and multiplier effects are embedded.[6]

As far as country 1 is concerned, the same approach gives:

$$Max_{X_1^A,\pi}\ U_1 = U_1\ (D_1^A;D_1^I) = U_1\ (X_1^A - E_1^A;X_1^I + M_1^I) \tag{22}$$

Under:

$$M_1^I = \pi E_1^A(\pi) \tag{23}$$

$$X_1^I = -p_1 X_1^A + constant \tag{24}$$

$$\pi = p_1(1 + t_1) \tag{25}$$

This can be rewritten as:

$$Max_{X_I^A,\pi} U_I = U_I(X_I^A - E_I^A(\pi); -p_I X_I^A + \pi E_I^A(\pi)) \tag{26}$$

Solving (26) yields country 1's reaction function:

$$t_1 = \frac{1}{\sigma_1^* - 1} \tag{27}$$

where $\sigma_1^* = \frac{\pi}{E_I^A} \frac{\partial E_I^A}{\partial \pi} > 0$ is the reciprocal demand elasticity facing country 1. Under the conditions that countries 1 and 2 are large countries, these elasticities are greater than unity, and optimal taxes (on imports for country 2 and on exports for country 1) are strictly positive.[7]

6 We can easily derive a relation between the reciprocal demand elasticity and the parameters s_2^C, e_2, m_2, and d_2 defined previously.

7 The design of optimal export taxes requires the estimation of consumption, production, and trade elasticities. Broda, Limao, and Weinstein (2006) find evidence that non-WTO members have market power and implement relatively high tariffs compared to WTO members. Warr (2001) concludes that available econometric estimates for the world demand elasticity of rice facing Thailand imply optimal export taxes ranging from 25 percent to 100 percent. This assessment may lead to false interpretations; Bautista (1996) gives an example in which the Philippine government implemented an export tax on copra and coconut oil based on the principle that the country represented a large share of the world market for these products and faced a "negative elasticity" in world export demand. In fact, this evaluation did not take into account substitutability with other vegetable oils and the Philippines' consequent low share of the world market. Moreover, demand and supply elasticities may change over time; consequently a country may gain in the short run while losing in the longer run.

RESULT 3. UNDER THESE ASSUMPTIONS, FOUR CONCLUSIONS MAY BE DERIVED FROM THE "IMPORT TARIFF-EXPORT TAX" GAME.

1. Each time either the large food-importing country or the large food-exporting country increases its tax, this move has a double effect. The first is the terms-of-trade effect, which consists of an improvement in the terms of trade for the country that implements the tax increase and a deterioration in the terms of trade for the other large country. The second effect is a traded volume effect, which consists of a decrease in traded volume for the country that implements the policy and its partners. A change in the small country's trade policy does not have an impact on its terms of trade and affects only traded volume.
2. Concerning large countries (1 and 2), as any policy change in this context has these two effects, at a given stage a country may decide to decrease its tax and accept a deterioration in its terms of trade while benefiting from an increase in trade volumes.
3. If the government's objective is to maximize real income, the Nash equilibrium is the intersection of reaction functions (15), (16), (21), and (27). This Nash equilibrium implies a loss of real income for country 3, a gain of real income for country 4, and a reduction in world real income. At equilibrium, a large country may also benefit from augmented real income as compared to free trade.
4. If the objective of a government is to decrease the domestic price of the agricultural good, the policy to be implemented is a decrease in the import tax in the large food-importing country and an increase in the export tax in the large food-exporting country. Both policies will have the effect of increasing the world price of the agricultural good and therefore hurting country 3, while increasing country 4's real income.

Point (i) comes from the expression of the changes in real income as stated by equations (6), (11), (13), and (14). Point (ii) is implied by the fact that moving from free trade to autarky, other things being equal, will bring about an initial increase in a large country's real income followed by a decrease; as a consequence, it is possible that, due to excessive taxation of trade flows, trade may be too small and a country may try to increase it by reducing the distortion that the tax caused. As far as Point (iii) is concerned, from the two effects under play, one being positive and one negative, the improvement in the terms of trade for one large country means deterioration for the other, while the reduction of trade is negative for both large countries; at Nash equilibrium involving a positive export tax in country 1 and a positive import tax in country 2, trade volumes are reduced. Therefore, either both large countries are worse off than under free trade or one is better off and the other is worse. Concerning Point (iv) an increase of the world price for the agricultural good deteriorates country 3's (small net food-importing country) terms of trade while improving country 4's (small net food-exporting country) terms of trade. If these countries do not tax either imports or exports, they maximize the quantities they trade. Consequently, country 3's real income is reduced while country 4's real income is augmented as compared to the initial situation of world free trade.

We thus see the possibility that governments may engage in a trade war for food security purposes, through which they respond to increases in world agricultural prices by increasing export taxes in agriculture-exporting countries and decreasing import taxes in agriculture-importing countries. This is illustrated in Figure 12.2a.

Figure 12.2a illustrates the case of an agriculture-importing country (A is the agricultural good and is located on the vertical axis) whose aim is to maintain the domestic agricultural price at p_0. Initially, the world price is at π, which leads this country to impose a tariff of *tm* on agricultural imports, such that $\pi.(1 + tm) = p_0$ (this accounts for the impact of *tm* on π). If an increase in the agricultural world price occurs, from π to π', this country must reduce its import tariff to *tm*′, such that $\pi'.(1 + tm') = p_0$. It must be noted that the agriculture-importing country's real income is decreased from y_0 to y_1.

Figure 12.2b depicts the case of an agriculture-exporting country that also aims to maintain the domestic agricultural price at p_0. Initially, the world price is at π which leads this country to impose a tax of *tx* on agricultural exports, such that $p_0\,(1 + tx) = \pi$ (this accounts for the impact of *tx* on π). If an increase in the world agricultural price occurs, from π to π', this country must augment its export tax up to *tx*′, such that $\pi'/(1 + tx') = p_0$. While its two trading partners are hurt by this price shock and subsequent policy reaction, it is worth noting that the agriculture-exporting country's real income is increased from y_0 to y_1. Let us note also that with the imposition of this import tariff, the country does not maximize the international value of its production; if it were maximized, the international price lines (π or π') would be tangential to the production-possibility frontier and domestic production would adjust to a change in international prices.

FIGURE 12.2 A general equilibrium analysis of import and export taxes

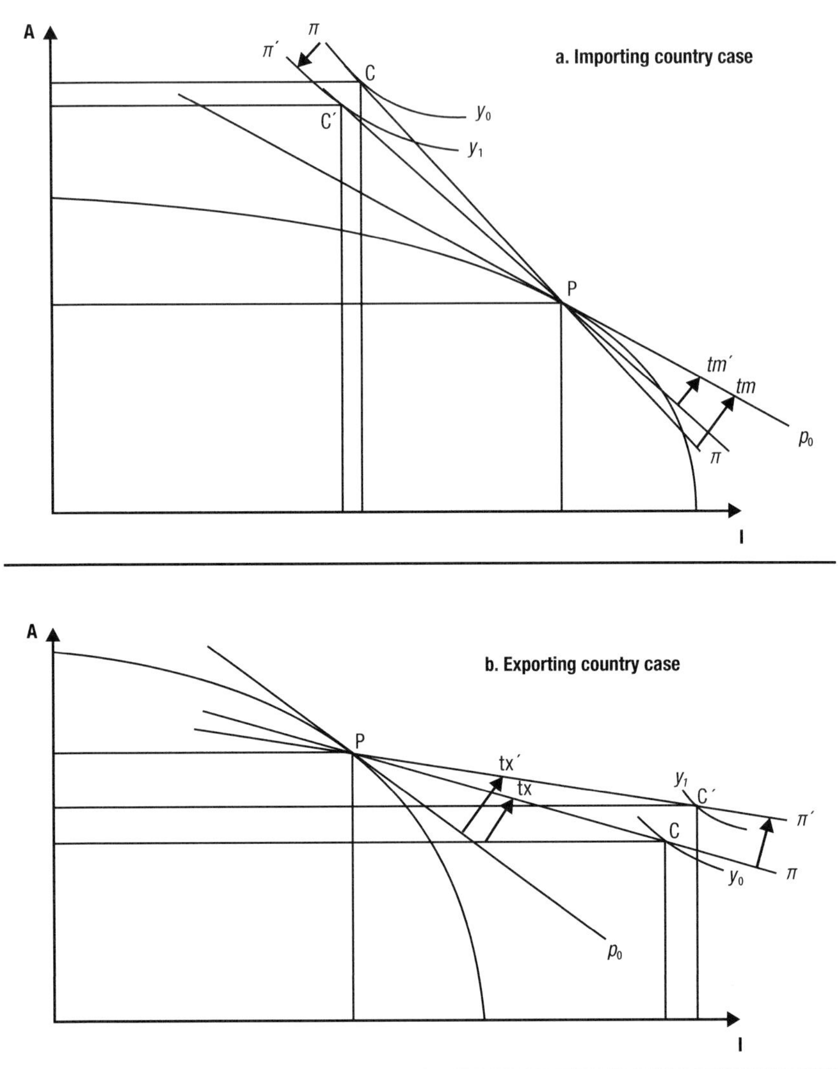

Source: Authors' investigation.

As stated previously, the WTO does not really limit the use of export restrictions, especially export taxes; however, WTO members are committed to "bind" import duties. Consequently, WTO members are authorized to increase export taxes and reduce import duties. As we have shown, this is exactly the sequence of policy options that large countries may implement in the case of upward food price spikes when their aim is to maintain domestic food prices at a maximum level. This clearly entails a lack of international coordination that can harm trading partners—in particular small net food-importing countries. The only option available for small net food-importing countries in this scenario is to decrease import tariffs or implement import subsidies, which has a cost in terms of public revenues and does not have any impact on terms of trade.

Finally, it must be emphasized that if under free trade, a country (either 1 or 2 in our example) has an interest in implementing an export tax or an import tariff because such a policy will increase its real income (or decrease domestic agricultural prices), this does not mean that at the end of the process (when all countries have implemented their respective policies) each country is better off than it would be under free trade. In particular, each country's real income could be reduced as compared to free trade; this is the classical "prisoner's dilemma." Nonetheless, a country can win from a trade war in the sense that its real income can be greater than it was initially (Johnson 1953).

An Illustration of the Adoption of Export Taxes on Agricultural Commodities and Their Effects Using the MIRAGE Model of the World Economy

This section uses the MIRAGE model of the world economy to assess the economic consequences of various trade policies. These simulations rely on low supply and demand elasticities.[8] They are compatible with a short-run situation. We simulate a demand shock that implies a 10 percent increase of the world price of wheat as well as various trade policies implemented to react to this shock and maintain domestic food security. We use short-term elasticities to generate the price increase; our objective is to understand the mechanisms that take place in the short run and explain the adoption of policies that preserve food security at home but generate negative consequences for trading partners.

In this modeling exercise, all countries are pursuing domestic price stability. The rationale for this objective is that governments are now striving to prevent a significant increase in the prices of necessary goods (food) for

8 The model is also based on low Armington elasticities (these are GTAP elasticities, see Hertel et al. 2007) as compared to other models like LINKAGE from the World Bank. A sensitivity analysis has been undertaken in order to conduct the same analysis with higher elasticities. These results are given in footnote 13.

low-income households. Policy makers have recently increased statements about the need to decrease food price volatility.[9] Recent economic studies show that the implications of upward food price spikes are substantial, not only in terms of short-term household welfare but also in terms of nutrition and loss of capital (long-term perspective; see Headey and Fan 2010; Hoddinott et al. 2008).

It remains to explain why policy makers choose to use trade policy instruments to pursue their objective. This may be a second-rank policy compared to cash transfers to low-income households or consumption subsidies. However, both these policy options are costly in terms of public revenues, while export taxes or restrictions are not and may even increase public receipts. Moreover, cash transfers may be difficult and take a long time to implement. Consumption subsidies (or de-taxations) are also costly in terms of public receipts and support all households, not only low-income households. Finally, we have to account for the differentiation of local and foreign goods: when a shock comes from world markets, governments may think that they have to change the prices of internationally traded goods without affecting the prices of domestically produced goods.

The Model

The MIRAGE model is a multinational, multisector Computable General Equilibrium (CGE) model (Bchir et al. 2002; Decreux and Valin 2007). We use the MIRAGE model under its static version, with a perfect competition hypothesis and without modeling foreign direct investment. We use perfect competition instead of imperfect competition because the latter framework necessitates supplementary data (number of firms, markup, and magnitude of scale economies) for calibration purposes that are difficult to gather for many regions. Moreover, we focus on agriculture, which is usually characterized by strong competition. The use of the static version is also justified by the fact that we are not interested in the dynamics of reform.

The first source of data is GTAP7 (see Narayanan and Walmsley 2008 for full documentation), which provides world macroeconomic accounts and trade flows for the year 2004. The market access data come from the MAcMapHS6 version 2.1 database (Boumellassa, Laborde, and Mitaritonna 2009), which measures protection in 2004 and includes all regional

9 See the statements made during G20 Seoul meetings in November 2010 (Kim 2010).

agreements and trade preferences existing to this date.[10] The geographic decomposition is a key element of the methodological design of the study. On the basis of the GTAP7 database, we select countries that are net wheat exporters and net wheat importers.[11] In the Appendix, Table 12.A1 presents the geographic and sectoral decomposition. The sectoral decomposition focuses on agriculture and identifies 25 sectors, 13 of which are agricultural.

We design and study scenarios in order to evaluate the impact of trade policies (implemented through either a variation of import duties or a variation of export taxes) on world prices and national real incomes. We suppose that these trade policies are aimed at keeping the domestic price of an agricultural commodity constant when the world price of that commodity suffers a shock. In other words, these are clearly food security policies. Our objective is to understand the international implications of these policies for world prices and national real income—in particular for small countries.

We implement six scenarios (Table 12.1). The first is called "Base" and represents a demand shock in the wheat sector. We assume that the demand from oil-exporting countries increases, such that the world price of wheat is augmented by about 10 percent. Similar results could be driven by alternative assumptions, such as an increased demand for wheat for biofuel (ethanol production in Europe) or increased demand from large Asian countries (such as India and China). We have chosen to locate the demand increase in oil-exporting countries due to the diversity of their suppliers and our desire not to blur the results for other important importing regions.

We then endogenize export taxes in net wheat exporters, such that the real domestic price of wheat remains constant (scenario ET). The next scenario is an endogenization of import taxes (scenario IT) under the same objective in net wheat importing countries. As scenario IT implies the adoption of import subsidies, we implement another scenario in which the decision to decrease import taxes is limited by 0 (free trade); this scenario is called IT0. Finally, we study two scenarios that cumulate two political situations described earlier:

10 This does not represent an evaluation of the analysis conducted in subsections 2.2 to 2.5 since we do not assess the consequences of the implementation of increased export taxes and reduced import duties starting from free trade. The objective of this section is to evaluate the economic consequences of trade policies (either through increased export taxes or reduced import taxes designed to keep domestic prices constant) on countries' real income, since we think that these policies have been adopted during the food crisis. In that sense, we add new distortions to a world trading system with initial distortions. We could study how close initial policies are to their optimal level, but it would represent a new object of research.

11 In the GTAP7 database (base year 2004), the EU27 position on wheat is atypical with a balanced position. Therefore we do not treat the European Union as a net exporter (or a net importer).

TABLE 12.1 Six scenarios

Scenario	Description
Base	Base demand shock.
ET	Implementation of export taxes in countries that are net wheat exporters, such that the real domestic price of wheat is constant.
IT	Implementation of import taxes (or import subsidies) in countries that are net wheat importers, such that the real domestic price of wheat is constant.
ITO	Implementation of import taxes (import subsidies are forbidden) in countries that are net wheat importers such that the real domestic price of wheat is constant; the domestic price is not constant if the strategic rigidity (no import subsidies) is binding.
ETIT	Implementation of IT import taxes in countries that are net wheat importers and of export taxes in countries that are net wheat exporters, such that the real domestic price of wheat is constant.
ETITO	Implementation of ITO import taxes in countries that are net wheat importers and of export taxes in countries that are net wheat exporters, such that the real domestic price of wheat is constant (import subsidies are forbidden).

Source: Authors' investigation.

(1) import taxes are fixed at the level of scenario IT and export taxes are endogenous, such that the real domestic price of wheat remains constant (scenario ETIT), and (2) import taxes are fixed at the level of scenario IT0—no import subsidy—and export taxes are endogenous, such that the real domestic price of wheat remains constant (scenario ETIT0).[12] In scenarios ET, IT, IT0, ETIT, and ETIT0, each of the exporting or importing countries applies their new trade tax simultaneously.

Results

Table 12.2 presents the import taxes required by net wheat importers to keep the domestic price of wheat constant.[13] Variations of import tariffs are substantial—in particular in the Middle East and North Africa and the "rest of

12 In a scenario in which export and import taxes are both endogenous, countries enter a spiral of never-ending escalation of export taxes and import subsidies because on the importing countries' side, the governments have no fiscal constraints and can finance the subsidies using a lump-sum transfer from households.

13 A sensitivity analysis has been carried out. It focuses on the ET scenario under which wheat-exporting countries impose an export tax in order to maintain domestic price constant. Two options are considered: either Armington elasticities are doubled, or supply elasticities are doubled. Results are not much modified. Evolution of world prices and countries' real incomes are very close to our central scenario. Export taxes that governments have to implement in order to keep domestic price constant are slightly different, but only differ from taxes in the central scenario by 0.6 to 4.6 points. The maximum difference occurs in the case of the Russian Federation's export tax (24.9 percent in the central scenario) when Armington elasticities are doubled. Detailed results of this sensitivity analysis may be requested from the authors.

TABLE 12.2 Additional import taxes

Country or region	Import taxes (%)
Rest of Asia	–20
China	–30
Thailand	–28
Viet Nam	–13
Bangladesh	–19
Pakistan	–29
Rest of South Asia	–19
Mexico	–27
Rest of Europe	–32
Rest of Latin America	–30
Brazil	–25
Rest of Commonwealth of Independent States	–30
Middle East and North Africa	–42
Egypt	–26
West Africa	–21
East Africa	–24
Southern Africa	–19
South Africa	–28

Source: Authors' calculation.

Europe" region. For instance, Egypt and Thailand may be obliged to implement an import subsidy in order to keep the domestic price of wheat constant.

Table 12.3 presents the augmentations of export taxes needed to keep the domestic price of wheat constant in net exporting countries under three scenarios. When only export taxes are implemented in net wheat exporters, the changes in export taxes are systematically less than 6 percent, while they are always higher than 45 percent when import taxes are also implemented in net wheat importers. This illustrates the interdependence of trade policies and how a process of retaliation and counterretaliation may worsen the whole process of policy decision making. If no import subsidies are implemented (column ETIT0), which may be a more realistic scenario, the changes in export taxes (from 19 percent to 50 percent) may be much less important but may remain substantial—in particular as compared to the scenario ET.

TABLE 12.3 Additional export taxes

Country	ET (%)	ETIT (%)	ETITO (%)
Australia	16	47	19
India	19	46	21
Canada	18	52	25
United States	20	52	27
Argentina	19	50	25
Russian Federation	25	57	37
Ukraine	20	50	50

Source: Authors' calculations.

Table 12.4 indicates how world prices on traded quantities of agricultural goods may be affected in various scenarios. Almost all agricultural prices may be positively affected by various shocks due to substitution effects on the demand and supply sides; however, according to this modeling exercise, wheat is by far the commodity that is most exposed to world price shocks. While the world price of wheat may increase by 10.8 percent due to the demand shock, it may increase by 16.8 percent when net wheat exporters react by increasing export taxes. Therefore this policy reaction is typically a beggar-thy-neighbor decision, as it is a rational decision from the single-country point of view but it amplifies the negative global aspects of the initial shock. The effects may be even larger when net importing countries implement reductions in import tariffs (27.3 percent). When no import subsidies are implemented, the impact of import taxes on world prices (12.6 percent) is much more comparable to the impact of export taxes. Finally, the combination of increased export taxes in net wheat exporters and reduced import taxes in net wheat importers may cause a dramatic increase in this commodity's world price (41.1 percent when import subsidies are implemented; 20.6 percent when they are not), as the disconnection between domestic and world prices is fueled by these border distortions.

Figure 12.3 indicates how the national real income of a few countries is affected by these various policy shocks. In the previous section, it was expected that net wheat exporters' welfare would be positively affected by the initial shock and their subsequent policy response (increased export taxes), while net wheat importers' welfare would be negatively affected. That is clearly confirmed by this modeling exercise. Argentina's welfare may significantly increase under all shocks, in particular under one that combines endogenous export taxes and import tariffs with allowed import subsidies (scenario ETIT); its

TABLE 12.4 World prices (percentage of change compared to reference situation)

Sector	Base	ET (%)	IT (%)	ITO (%)	ETIT (%)	ETITO (%)
Wheat	10.84	16.76	27.31	12.62	41.10	20.58
Dairy products	0.04	0.05	0.00	0.02	0.03	0.04
Livestock	0.19	0.21	0.18	0.13	0.24	0.17
Meat	0.07	0.08	0.06	0.06	0.07	0.07
Oilseeds	0.09	0.06	0.09	0.08	0.05	0.04
Other crops	0.16	0.17	0.18	0.12	0.18	0.13
Other food	0.04	0.08	−0.04	0.00	0.04	0.04
Paddy and processed rice	0.21	0.13	0.32	0.20	0.10	0.11
Plant fiber	0.13	0.11	0.14	0.10	0.13	0.09
Sugar	0.14	0.12	0.20	0.12	0.16	0.10
Vegetable and fruits	0.20	0.21	0.25	0.14	0.27	0.14
Vegetable oil	0.01	0.01	−0.01	0.00	0.00	0.00

Source: Authors' calculations.

real income may be increased by 0.6 percent. Australia (+0.23 percent under ETIT), Canada (+0.18 percent), and Ukraine (+0.07 percent) are other beneficiaries. On the other side, net wheat importers may be significantly harmed by these shocks in terms of real income: −0.85 percent in the case of Egypt under the ETIT scenario and −0.37 percent for eastern Africa.

These results rely on low supply and demand elasticities that are compatible with a short-run situation. In reality, these parameters can change over time; for instance, if agents expect that price changes will remain, both producers and consumers will change their behaviors. In case of a price augmentation, producers, including new producers, will invest more (in technology, irrigation, and so on), and world supply elasticity will increase in the long run.[14] Consumers will shift their demand to other products and/or new suppliers (increase in demand elasticity for wheat and in the Armington elasticities) and counteract initial real income benefits.

The case of Argentina also reveals how increased export taxes on a primary commodity can be used to encourage high-value processed sectors to buy this primary commodity as an intermediate good. When the demand shock augments the world price of wheat by about 10 percent, the Argentinean production of wheat may increase by 4.5 percent (in volume) while production of the "other food" sector, which includes milling industries and other flour-related

14 As explained previously, we used the static version of the MIRAGE model.

FIGURE 12.3 Welfare impact of various scenarios (percentage of change compared to reference situation)

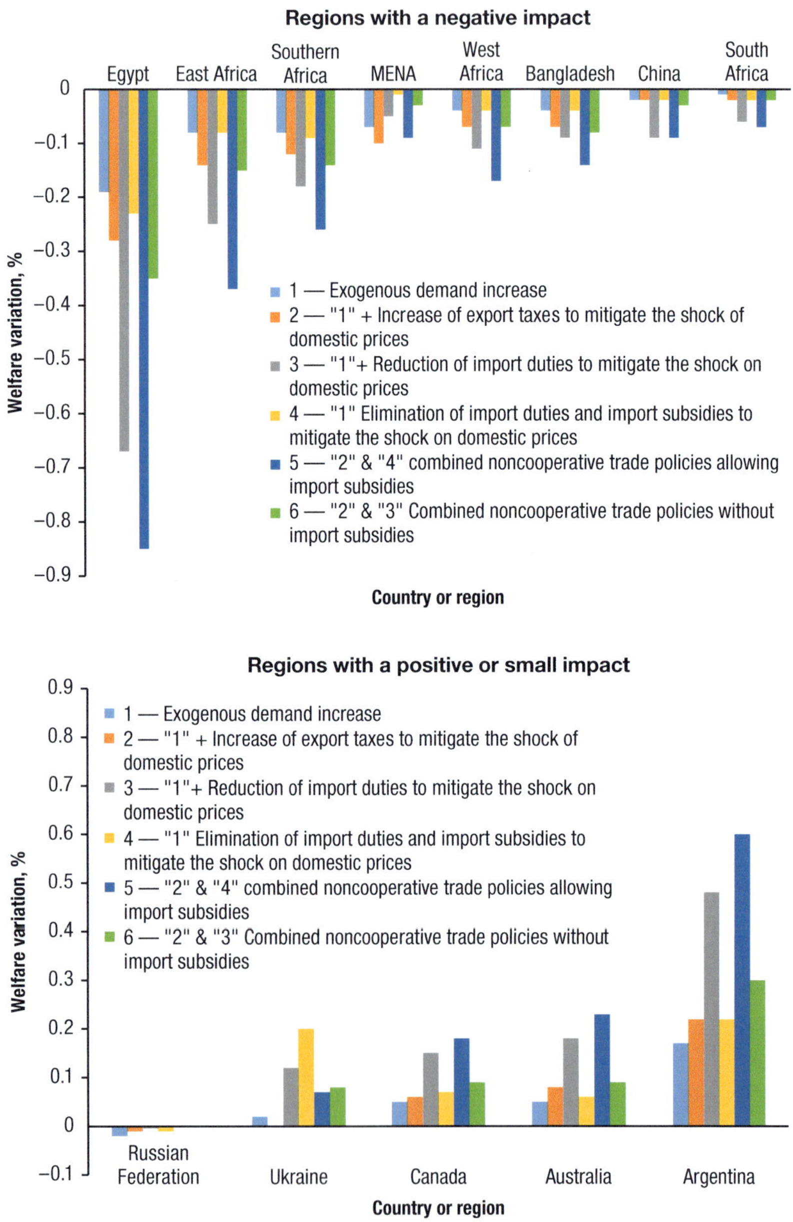

Source: Authors' calculation.

Note: MENA = Midde East and North Africa. For each country or region the columns represent successively the following scenarios: 1 - Base; 2 - ET; 3 - IT; 4 – ITO; 5 – ETIT; 6 – ETITO.

products, may be reduced by 0.6 percent. Under the ET scenario, in which governments of net wheat exporting countries increase their export taxes as a reaction to this world price shock, the production volumes of wheat and "other food" sectors are constant. An increased export tax on a primary commodity is clearly a way to promote the production of sectors using this commodity as an intermediate good.

Conclusion

This chapter provides an economic analysis of the use of export taxes and illustrates why these policies have been so popular during the food crisis. Several elements can justify the implementation of such trade practices: (1) export taxes can raise the world price of exports and therefore improve terms of trade; (2) export taxes can reduce the domestic price of the taxed commodity and benefit final consumers of this commodity (this may be an important policy issue when food security is at stake); (3) export taxes can reduce the domestic price of the taxed commodity and benefit intermediate consumption of this commodity (which is important when it is a primary commodity and expansion of the manufacturing sector that purchases it is at stake); (4) export taxes increase public revenue, which is beneficial in a country where domestic fiscal receipts are small; and (5) export taxes provide a means of redistributing income from domestic producers to domestic consumers and the public sector.

As a consequence, export taxes are attractive trade policy instruments. However, this chapter draws attention to one key element of the implementation of export taxes: these are typically beggar-thy-neighbor policies that deteriorate the terms of trade and real incomes of some trading partners. This often leads to retaliation by partners whose terms of trade have been negatively affected by initial export taxes. We show that these trading partners can react by either reducing import tariffs or augmenting export taxes, depending on their status as either net importers or exporters of the commodity. The 2006–2008 food crisis clearly illustrates this point about retaliation and counterretaliation in response to either reduced import duties or augmented export taxes. Evidence of such government reactions during the 2006–2008 food crisis have been largely documented in terms of increased export taxes and adoption of export restrictions (such as export bans), as well as in terms of a reduction of import duties and government-to-government panic purchases (Polovinkin 2010; Headey 2010; Headey and Fan 2010). In that sense, our predictions in terms of tariffs and export duties changes were supported by reality.

Several policy conclusions are worth noting. First, this process implies the implementation of a noncooperative policy equilibrium that lessens world welfare; as a consequence, this calls for international cooperation. Second, although large countries can implement beggar-thy-neighbor policies that increase national welfare at the expense of trading partners, small countries do not have this option; changes in their own policies neither improve their own welfare nor harm their partners' situation. Finally, there is a key asymmetry between net exporters and net importers of an agricultural commodity during a food crisis, as net exporters can benefit from increases in world prices while net importers are hurt and have no capacity to retaliate efficiently.

Another topic of interest is to analyze government responses to a downward price spike; for example, Martin and Anderson (2010, 2) state that "intensified import restrictions and export subsidies played a significant role in downward price spikes in 1986." Obviously there are some similarities between upward versus downward price spikes and their implications on economic agents and government responses. First, governments can react to downward price spikes in international markets by either increasing import duties (in net food importing countries) or reducing export taxes (in net food exporting countries) in order to increase domestic prices; both reactions lead to reduced world demand by the first group of countries and increased world supply by the second one, with both reactions feeding into the downward price spikes. Second, this could magnify the harm done to small net food-exporting countries. This is another example of a lack of international coordination in the trade policy area.

But there are also some strong differences between these economic phenomena. First, increasing import duties may not be an option, as many countries impose import duties equal to bound duties (no binding overhang). Second, export taxes are implemented more frequently in developing countries and also serve as an important source of public revenue.[15] Therefore, reducing export taxes is a more difficult policy option than increasing export taxes. Simultaneously reducing export taxes in a large net food-exporting developing country contributes to deteriorating terms of trade and increasing the price of input for domestic manufacturers. Third, in the case of upward price spikes, the rationale for intervention is obviously to protect low-income consumers, while reducing export taxes in the case of downward price spikes is aimed at supporting domestic producers. This is a completely different political

15 Kim (2010) states that among WTO members imposing export duties, 21 are least developed countries, 40 are middle-income countries, and only 4 are rich countries.

context. Moreover, in the case of low world food prices, policy alternatives may be easier to implement, such as public storage (it is always possible to buy crops for public storage when prices are low, while selling crops in the case of high food prices may not be feasible if public storage is zero) or cash transfers (it may be more difficult to give cash transfers to many low-income consumers in developing countries when prices are high than to give cash transfers to a limited number of farmers when prices are low).

Today, the European Union, the United States, and Mexico have already filed a case at the WTO on China's export restrictions on raw materials. In 2008, China raised export taxes on some metal resource products, such as parts of steel products, metal ore sand, and ferro-alloys. From this article we may understand that the objective of this policy was to reorient the supply of these goods on the domestic market in order to decrease the price of intermediate goods for domestic manufacturing sectors. Under these conditions, it is understandable that the European Union has proposed to discipline such practices.[16] Although this proposal has been well received by countries such as Canada, the United States, Switzerland, and the Republic of Korea, it has been highly criticized by some developing countries such as Argentina (which also confirms what was expected from our analytical framework), Brazil, Cuba, India, Indonesia, Malaysia, Pakistan, and Venezuela, with Argentina leading the opposition. The reasons advanced by this group of countries is that "export taxes are a right and a legitimate tool for developing countries; they help increase fiscal revenue and stabilize prices; there is no legal basis for a negotiation; there is no explicit mandate for a change in WTO rules on this issue" (Raja 2006). It is worth noting that the European Union makes a distinction between trade-distorting taxes and "legitimate" export taxes such as those applied in the context of balance-of-payments imbalances. The European Union proposes a full prohibition of trade-distorting export taxes. The European Union and the United States frequently implement bans of export taxes when they negotiate bilateral agreements.

Under the Doha Development Agenda, the European Union has been very active in demanding substantive commitments by all WTO members to eliminate or reduce export taxes. This chapter shows that export taxes and import tariffs exhibit strong similarities and can even be equivalent in terms of their impact on domestic and foreign welfare. Taking commitments on export taxes into the WTO context may be justified, as these commitments exist in the domain of import tariffs. Moreover, another justification for this is the

16 The European Union's proposal is available on the WTO website (WTO 2006).

consideration of small net food-importing countries that can be harmed in the event of a food crisis and by the escalation of export taxes throughout the world and that do not have many policy instruments with which to address this kind of issue. Export taxes and export restrictions could clearly become a new and major bone of contention between high-income countries and agri-food-exporting middle-income countries in trade negotiations.

Bibliography

Amiruddin, M. N. 2003. "Palm Oil Products Exports, Prices and Export Duties: Malaysia and Indonesia Compared." *Oil Palm Industry Economic Journal* 3 (2): 15–20.

Bautista, R. M. 1996. "Export Tax as Income Stabiliser under Alternative Policy Regimes: The Case of Philippine Copra." In *Choice, Growth, and Development: Emerging and Enduring Issues*, edited by E. de Dios and R. V. Fabella, 235–252. Quezon City, Philippines: University of the Philippines Press.

Bchir, H., Y. Decreux, J.-L. Guerin, and S. Jean. 2002. *MIRAGE, A Computable General Equilibrium Model for Trade Policy Analysis*. CEPII Discussion Paper 2002-17. Paris: Centre d'Etudes Prospectives et d'Informations Internationales.

Bickerdike, C. F. 1906. "The Theory of Incipient Taxes." *Economic Journal* 16 (64): 529–535.

Bouët, A., and D. Laborde. 2010. *The Economics of Export Taxation in the Context of a Food Crisis: A Theoretical and CGE-Approach Contribution*. IFPRI Discussion Paper 994. Washington, DC: International Food Policy Research Institute.

———. 2012. "Food Crisis and Export Taxation: The Cost of Non-cooperative Trade Policies." *Review of World Economics* 148 (1): 209–233.

Boumellassa, H., D. Laborde, and C. Mitaritonna. 2009. *A Picture of Tariff Protection across the World in 2004: MAcMap-HS6, Version 2*. IFPRI Discussion Paper 903. Washington, DC: International Food Policy Research Institute.

Broda, C., N. Limao, and D. Weinstein. 2006. *Optimal Tariffs: The Evidence*. NBER Working Paper 12033. Cambridge, MA, US: National Bureau of Economic Research.

Corden, W. M. 1971. *The Theory of Protection*. Oxford, UK: Clarendon Press.

Crosby, D. 2008. "WTO Legal Status and Evolving Practice of Export Taxes." *Bridges* 12 (5): 3–4.

Deardorff, A. V., and I. Rajaraman. 2005. *Can Export Taxation Counter Monopsony Power?* RSIE (Research Seminar in International Economics) Discussion Paper 541. Ann Arbor, MI, US: University of Michigan.

Decreux, Y., and H. Valin. 2007. *MIRAGE, Updated Version of the Model for Trade Policy Analysis: Focus on Agriculture and Dynamics.* CEPII Discussion Paper 15. Paris: Centre d'Etudes Prospectives et d'Informations Internationales.

Diamond, P. A. 1975. "A Many-Person Ramsey Rule." *Journal of Public Economics* 4 (4): 335–342.

Headey, D. 2010. *Rethinking the Global Food Crisis: The Role of Trade Shocks.* IFPRI Discussion Paper 958. Washington, DC: International Food Policy Research Institute.

Headey, D., and S. Fan. 2010. *Reflections on the Global Food Crisis: How Did It Happen? How Has It Hurt? And How Can We Prevent the Next One?* Washington, DC: International Food Policy Research Institute.

Hertel, T., D. Hummels, M. Ivanic, and R., Keeney. 2007. "How Confident Can We Be of CGE-based Assessments of Free Trade Agreements?" *Economic Modelling* 24 (4): 611–635.

Hoddinott, J., J. A. Maluccio, J. R. Behrman, R. Flores, and R. Martorell. 2008. "Effect of a Nutrition Intervention during Early Childhood on Economic Productivity in Guatemalan Adults." *The Lancet* 371 (9610): 411–416.

Johnson, H. G. 1953. "Optimum Tariffs and Retaliation." *Review of Economic Studies* 21 (2): 142–153.

Kim, D. 2010. "G20 Leaders to Discuss Food Price Stabilization." *Korea Times.* Accessed February 22, 2017. www.koreatimes.co.kr/www/news/biz/2010/10/301_74514.html.

Kim, J. 2010. "Recent Trends in Export Restrictions on Raw Materials." In *The Economic Impact of Export Restrictions on Raw Materials,* 13–57. Trade Policy Studies. Paris: Organisation for Economic Co-operation and Development.

Lerner, A. P. 1936. "The Symmetry between Import and Export Taxes." *Economica* 3 (11): 306–313.

Martin, W., and K. Anderson. 2010. "Trade Distortions and Food Price Surges." Paper for the World Bank–UC Berkeley Conference on Agriculture for Development—Revisited, Berkeley, CA, October 1–2.

Mitra, S., and T. Josling. 2009. "Agricultural Export Restrictions: Welfare Implications and Trade Disciplines." IPC Position Paper, Agricultural and Rural Development Series. Unpublished, International Food and Agricultural Trade Policy Council, Washington, DC.

Narayanan, B. G., and T. L. Walmsley, eds. 2008. *Global Trade, Assistance, and Production: The GTAP 7 Data Base.* West Lafayette, IN, US: Center for Global Trade Analysis, Purdue University.

OECD (Organisation for Economic Co-operation and Development). 2010. "Policy Responses in Emerging Economies to International Agricultural Commodity Price Changes." TAD/CA/APM/WP(2010)13. OECD, Paris.

Piermartini, R. 2004. "The Role of Export Taxes in the Field of Primary Commodities." WTO Discussion Paper 4. World Trade Organization, Geneva.

Polovinkin, S. 2010. "Food Crisis and Food Security Policies in West Africa: An Inventory of West African Countries' Policy Responses during the 2008 Food Crisis [Internet]." Version 9. Knol. May 3. Accessed 2010. http://www.knol.google.com/k/sergey-polovinkin/food-crisis-and-food-security-policies/cju5lr97z6h4/32.

Raja, K. 2006. "Clash in NAMA Talks on Proposed Export-Tax Rules." SUNS, June 1. Accessed 2010. www.twnside.org.sg/title2/twninfo418.htm.

Ramsey, F.P. 1927. "A Contribution to the Theory of Taxation." *Economic Journal* 37 (145): 47–61.

Warr, P. G. 2001. "Welfare Effects of an Export Tax: Thailand's Rice Premium." *American Journal of Agricultural Economics* 83 (4): 903–920.

WTO (World Trade Organization). 2006. "Market Access for Non-agricultural Products." TN/MA/W/11/add. 6. Accessed February 22, 2017. http://trade.ec.europa.eu/doclib/docs/2008/september/tradoc_140481.pdf.

Appendix

TABLE 12.A1 Geographic and sectoral decomposition

Country/region	MIRAGE label
Australia	Paddy and processed rice
Rest of Asia	Wheat
China	Other grains
Thailand	Vegetable and fruits
Viet Nam	Oilseeds
Bangladesh	Sugar
India	Plant fiber
Pakistan	Other crops
Rest of South Asia	Livestock
Canada	Other natural resources
United States	Other food
Mexico	Fossil fuels
Rest of Europe	Meat
Argentina	Vegetable oil
Rest of LAC (Latin America and Caribbean)	Dairy products
Brazil	Textile
EU27 (European Union)	Wearing and apparel
Rest of CIS (Commonwealth of Independent States)	Leather
Russian Federation	Other manufacturing products
Ukraine	Chemical products
MENA (Middle East and North Africa)	Motor vehicles and transport equipment
Egypt	Capital goods
West Africa	Services
East Africa	Construction
Southern Africa	Transportation
South Africa	

Source: Authors' investigation.

Chapter 13

CONCLUSION: WHICH POLICY SPACE IN THE INTERNATIONAL TRADE ARENA CAN SUPPORT DEVELOPMENT AND FOOD SECURITY?

Antoine Bouët and David Laborde

In November 2001, seven years after the creation of the World Trade Organization (WTO) and only two months after the deadly terrorist attacks of September 11, 2001, trade ministers gathered in Doha, Qatar, to launch a new round of trade negotiations aimed at lowering trade barriers and establishing rules for those barriers remaining in place. The Doha Round was ambitious, both because it proposed to cover an extensive set of topics (agriculture, industry, services, intellectual property, rules, trade facilitation, environment, geographical indications, and so on) and because it included an expanded WTO membership (the number of countries involved in the WTO grew from 128 members at the signing of the Marrakesh Declaration in 1994 to 162 on November 30, 2015; see Chapter 2). Designing an agreement that satisfies so many countries has proven to be an almost impossible challenge, particularly since barriers to trade are unequally high among sectors in these countries (see Chapter 3).

The Doha Round was semiofficially titled the Doha Development Agenda (DDA) and was launched in a special political context. After the events of 9/11, the international community felt a need for increased multilateral cooperation. Policy makers saw global free trade as the solution to poverty and a way to fight terrorism. At the time, US President George W. Bush said, "By expanding trade, we spread hope and opportunity to the corners of the world, and we strike a blow against the terrorists who feed on anger and resentment" (G. W. Bush, September 14, 2005). Benjamin Mkapa, then president of the United Republic of Tanzania, stated, "It is futile, if not foolhardy, to think there is no link between poverty and terrorism" (B. Mpaka, February 23, 2003). Such statements raised developing countries' expectations for the Doha negotiations. Previous rounds of trade talks, under the aegis of the General Agreement on Tariffs and Trade (GATT), were often frustrating for these countries, as most of the agreements were negotiated between developed countries such as the United States and the European Union. Barriers to trade remained high in the agricultural sector, in which many developing countries have a comparative advantage. Not only were tariff barriers much higher in agriculture than in industry, but farmers in developed countries also benefited from substantial domestic support, which insulated them from market prices, distorted production decisions, and created commodity surpluses that depressed world prices. Even after the completion of the ambitious Uruguay Round, which brought agriculture under new trade disciplines, developing countries still felt largely left out of the discussion. The DDA promised to address developing countries' trade concerns.

Almost from the start, however, the negotiations were characterized by deep North–South disagreements. At the Cancun Ministerial Conference in September 2003, that tension resulted in developing countries' rejection of a proposal drafted by the European Union and the United States that was widely considered as tilted in their favor. The collapse of the Cancun Ministerial gave a clear signal that developing countries would be equal partners in any future agreement. At the Hong Kong Ministerial Conference in December 2005, there was some progress made on the development issue, such as the agreement to negotiate the phasing out of export subsidies, to address cotton subsidies in an ambitious and expeditious fashion, and to focus on granting duty-free quota-free (DFQF) market access to least developed countries (LDCs).

Nevertheless, a subsequent meeting of ministers in 2006 collapsed, resulting in a suspension of the talks by the WTO's Director-General. At a "mini-ministerial meeting" in Geneva in July 2008, negotiators again failed to reach an agreement. This time the discussions showed an irreconcilable gap between key agricultural exporters, led by the United States, and the G33, whose concerns were voiced by India over the special safeguard mechanism (SSM) in agriculture. The cotton issue also remained a topic of contention between developing and developed countries. Unfortunately, little progress has been made in the ensuing years. Fifteen years after the Doha Declaration, this round of trade negotiations is still not yet complete. The tenth WTO Ministerial that took place in Nairobi, Kenya, on December 15–18, 2015, did not change the overall situation, although some advances were made on specific topics such as administration of tariff-rate quotas and the agreement to definitively phase out export subsidies.

The first section of this book points out the potential gains of a successful DDA: increased global production of food and industrial goods, resulting in better access to cheaper (food) items and greater consumer welfare. Moreover, a successful DDA might lead to better trade infrastructure and more efficient customs procedures in developing countries, which would ease trade flows and lower the costs of trade. Finally, a successful DDA would result in lower tariff protection, reduced production-distorting domestic support, and elimination of export subsidies.[1] At a time of reduced worldwide economic growth and weakened international cooperation, these achievements would be important. However, the first section also illustrates the complexity of the international negotiation: more members, more complex trade issues, and potentially high political costs—all reasons to be concerned about the chance of success for the negotiation of the ambitious full agenda of the Doha Round.

Obviously, the failure of the Doha Round represents a failure of international cooperation in trade and development. However, this is not the only example of failure in international cooperation in this domain. In 2007–2008 global agricultural markets registered record growth in some commodity prices (see Chapter 8). While the main factors behind this evolution have been well identified (biofuel policies, energy prices, insufficient investment in the agricultural sector, and weather shocks, to name a few), the surge in global agricultural prices was exacerbated by misguided trade policies that attempted to address domestic concerns through beggar-thy-neighbor policies that increased price volatility for others. New export restrictions, increased export taxes, and decreased import duties on agricultural commodities reinforced the initial shocks to global agricultural prices (see Chapters 11 and 12). These are clearly uncooperative policies. The spikes in agricultural commodity prices in 2007–2008, 2010–2011, and 2012–2013 led many to ask whether agriculture is in a new paradigm, in which the concern is less over traditional issues like market access, export competition, and domestic support and is instead focused on export restrictions and food security reserves.

In such a case, is the WTO framework still relevant?[2] In this time of uncertainty and lack of cooperation in international trade, what is the policy space for enhancing development and food security through trade?

We conclude that for international trade to be most effective in improving food security worldwide, trade should be based on true comparative advantage *and* public and private instruments should be available to protect against risks and uncertainties at the economywide level (climate change, conflicts, disease, exchange rate and price variations, and so on) and at the household level (harvest failure, injury, unemployment or underemployment, and so forth). With this in mind, we provide six recommendations organized around three principles.

1 As noted, the latter goal was at least achieved during the Nairobi meeting in 2015 (see Díaz-Bonilla and Laborde [2016] for a quantification of this issue).

2 More recently, agricultural prices have fallen and traditional concerns about subsidies and trade barriers have been renewed.

Principle 1

The international community must promote a global trading system based on efficient and transparent markets in order to guarantee that international trade is based on true comparative advantage.

In a context in which climate change increases the pressure on the global food system, aiming for the optimal use of global resources is an important element in achieving sustainable food security in the long run. Such a global trading system should require the following:

BASIC WTO RULES SHOULD BE RESPECTED.

Regardless of the outcome of the Doha Round, the WTO remains an active international institution, providing benefits to its members in general and to developing countries in particular. The WTO offers an international public good, particularly through the organization's rules regarding nondiscrimination, which give countries an equal chance to compete; rules regarding national treatment, which ensure that commitments to open markets are not negated by behind the border measures that penalize foreign suppliers; rules regarding binding of tariffs (that is, a commitment not to increase a duty beyond an agreed level); and rules requiring transparency. It is true that there are many cases in which these principles are violated (including regional trade agreements and preferential regimes), but these exemptions are codified and give the trading system some flexibility. A world trading system without basic rules of the type set out by the WTO would obviously increase global uncertainty, reduce incentives to trade, and encourage trade conflicts. Trade rules especially benefit small and poorer countries that would otherwise be vulnerable to unilateral decisions by larger and more powerful countries. The global trading system already offers two instruments for protection against systemic risk: bound duties and the trade dispute settlement procedure. Their key roles should never be underestimated. Indeed, economic history has clearly shown that trade wars arising in the absence of such rules are very costly: disciplining retaliations and lowering the bound duties reduces the costs (see Chapter 6) and the probability of potential trade wars.

EFFORTS TO REDUCE DISTORTIONS SHOULD BE MAINTAINED.

International trade can still enhance food security even in the presence of some distortions, but policy-induced distortions at the border and/or distortions behind-the-border potentially create artificial comparative advantage.

These lead to the waste of environmental and financial resources and an overspecialized production pattern that increases the risk exposure of the food system and leads to underinvestment in agriculture in non-subsidizing countries. Three recent facts are important to illustrate the ongoing trends and challenges of agricultural distortions. First, for the past 20 years, rich countries, particularly the EU and the United States, have reduced their trade-distorting domestic support measures, although they have continued to provide relatively high levels of income support. Second, progress was made on tariff liberalization on a multilateral basis during the implementation, until 2004, of the Uruguay Round. Further progress was made between 2004 and 2013, partly through regional agreements but mainly through unilateral reforms that still need to be locked in at a multilateral setting. These are promising policy developments that deserve recognition.

Third, and unfortunately, there are also policy developments that raise concerns, such as the substantial increase in distorting domestic support in emerging economies like China and India (see Chapter 5). These may become a major source of inefficiency and conflict in the global trading system. One illustration is the cotton sector (see Chapter 7), in which China has recently expanded its subsidy policy even while the level of subsidies is declining in the United States and remains stable in the EU. China is now facing the delicate challenge of reforming its policies. This is clearly evidence of a political economy problem (see Chapter 4) in which a policy is implemented for the benefit of a few while the costs of that policy are either diluted among many or transferred to foreigners. To avoid undermining the global system, it is important to address China's increased economic power and role in the global market through the agreement on appropriate disciplines.

Principle 2

To achieve these two first targets, it is important that the WTO keeps a proactive role in trade liberalization dynamics.

Limiting the WTO's role to managing past achievements and addressing disputes will erode the long-term attractiveness of the institution. In addition, alternative approaches (like regional trade agreements) are inferior instruments. However, the WTO negotiation approach has to be adjusted and alternative negotiation forums used with parsimony:

MULTILATERAL TRADE NEGOTIATIONS SHOULD BE REVAMPED.

Many are of the opinion that the DDA is dead.[3] Indeed, world trade has changed so much since 2001 that it is possible to consider that (1) the initial point of departure (substantial cuts in rich countries' agricultural tariffs versus more modest cuts in emerging economies' industrial tariffs) of the Doha negotiations is no longer valid, and (2) some negotiation modalities have become less relevant. Baldwin (2012) goes so far as to propose a WTO 2.0 and emphasizes the increasing role of regional value chains and the importance of disciplines on supply-chain trade and foreign investment. Negotiations on these disciplines have until now been conducted outside the WTO through regional trade agreements and bilateral investment treaties.

In this context, a new basis for negotiation is needed. Two approaches are possible: the "small is beautiful" approach, prioritized by the current WTO Director-General Roberto Azevêdo and aimed at the negotiation of smaller packages, or the launching of a new round with new rules of negotiation.[4] Chapter 3 provides three directions that this latter approach could take.[5] First, the number of negotiating parties could be restricted, as it appears that the number of WTO members and the consensus rule are an obstacle. Either a few countries (including key representatives among developing countries) could decide for all (which would be difficult to implement), or a few countries could adopt a trade liberalization package and implement the agreement among themselves; this latter is the plurilateral approach already adopted by WTO members for some topics.[6] Second, the domain of the negotiations could be extended; this would make more deals possible since concessions could be found in new sectors. For example, rich countries could accept ambitious cuts in agricultural tariffs if trade negotiations include services and/or the adoption of disciplines on investment and regional value chains, domains

---

3 See Brandi 2015; Stewart 2015; Vyasan 2015; Donnan 2015; *New York Times* Editorial Board 2016.

4 The Bali Package, adopted in December 2013, contains a Agreement on Trade Facilitation that includes provisions to expedite the trade of goods and measures to ensure effective cooperation between customs authorities on customs compliance issues, with provisions for technical assistance and capacity-building efforts for LDCs. See a summary of this package in *The Bali Agreement: An Assessment from the Perspective of Developing Countries* (Díaz-Bonilla and Laborde 2015).

5 Chapter 3, "Why Is the Doha Development Agenda Failing? And What Can Be Done? A Computable General Equilibrium–Game Theoretical Approach," was published in 2010 in *The World Economy*, but a first version was written in 2004 for a European Commission project.

6 A recent example of this is the Information Technology Agreement; after 17 rounds of negotiations, more than 80 participants gathered at a meeting on July 24, 2015, and agreed to eliminate tariffs on a list of 201 products, representing annual trade of over $1.3 trillion per year.

in which they could benefit from concessions given by emerging economies. Third, side payments could be implemented in order to compensate countries that do not benefit from the trade deal and thus attain their approval.[7]

The "Aid for Trade" package, which, according to the WTO, means further assistance for developing countries "to increase their capacity to take advantage of more open markets," has been interpreted by some as financial compensation for countries that are expected to suffer losses under the agreement.[8] Chapter 3 also provides important suggestions about how market access negotiations should be conducted with simpler modalities and better compromises between efficiency gains and political costs.

REGIONAL AND BILATERAL TRADE NEGOTIATIONS SHOULD REMAIN A STEPPING STONE TOWARD MULTILATERAL OUTCOMES, NOT A SUBSTITUTE OR A DEFAULT CHOICE.

Outside the WTO's multilateral framework, regional trade agreements have multiplied in the past 15 years. All WTO members are currently involved in at least one RTA, and 281 agreements notified at the WTO are currently in force, of which 224 include at least one developing country and 103 are South-South agreements. However, these agreements vary a lot in terms of scope, ambition, and effective implementation. Therefore their effectiveness is quite heterogeneous and their relevance as a sustainable policy option for developing countries is unclear. A good example is the implementation of the Economic Partnership Agreements (EPAs) negotiated by the European Union with six groups of African-Caribbean-Pacific countries; the economic gains implied by this agreement are limited and sometimes negative, and asymmetry in bargaining power leads to real concerns. Another example of a North–South agreement is the Trans-Pacific Partnership Agreement (TPP). Currently this agreement incorporates 12 participants, including both rich countries like the United States and developing countries like Chile, Malaysia, Peru, and Viet Nam.[9] The TPP is ambitious, targeting not only the elimination of tariff and nontariff barriers but also the harmonization of trade rules on sensitive issues like labor, the environment, competition policy, investment, and state-owned enterprises as well as increased coherence on regulatory issues.[10]

---

7 In game theory, cooperative games with side payments are efficient since players can choose the deal that maximizes the "size of the cake" and use side payments to compensate losers and "buy" the agreement of each player.

8 See Stiglitz and Charlton (2006).

9 On January 23, 2017, President Trump signed a presidential memorandum to withdraw the United States from the agreement. However, TPP negotiations continue among other nations.

10 For information on TPP, see USTR (2017).

While there is a clear lack of ambition in the EPAs, implying that their implementation is relatively easy, there is real ambition in the TPP; consequently, the implementation of this agreement is politically more difficult. Developing countries can also implement regional agreements among themselves; these are usually called South-South regional agreements. For instance, in Africa, many regional agreements have been launched, but implementation of the majority of them has been delayed or downsized in terms of ambition. In June 2015 the African Union officially began negotiations on the establishment of a continentwide free trade zone by 2017. However, the likelihood of full implementation of this zone remains questionable, as such an agreement would require significant political commitment from signatory countries. Similarly, in the early 1990s Latin America showed a remarkable willingness to address trade integration through the construction of MERCOSUR; however, this trade agreement faces many difficulties today.[11]

In short, regional agreements may help, but they have serious limitations: lack of transparency during the negotiation process, overlapping and nonharmonized rules (for example, rules of origin), and by definition, discriminatory tariffs. Moreover, these agreements are unlikely to address key issues such as domestic subsidies in agriculture. More problematic are the political economy consequences of some RTAs: because exporters receive access to key markets, their incentives to lobby for a more open trade agenda are removed, or even reversed, by concerns about preference erosion. Therefore these arrangements reduce the counterbalancing force applied by exporters against the influence of protectionist interests from import-competing sectors. Thus the multilateral approach remains the best and more inclusive direction for trade integration in the long run. In this context a moratorium on mega-trade deals would be desirable until multilateral talks are redefined and restarted.

Principle 3

To address concerns regarding systemic risk and uncertainties, particularly for the poor and vulnerable, the global trading system must provide an institutional framework for efficient protection against risk at the macroeconomic or microeconomic levels.

The WTO also needs to address the export restriction issue and offer a clear and fair legal framework for different domestic measures implemented for food security (food reserves).

---

11 In 2011, Argentina decided to suspend automatic import licenses for 600 items; in 2012 it complicated import procedures from an administrative point of view. In 2012, Paraguay was suspended for one year for offending MERCOSUR's "democracy clause" (Economist 2012).

EXPORT RESTRICTIONS AND TAXES SHOULD BE DISCIPLINED AND ELIMINATED.

In case of high global food prices, export restrictions and taxes are an attractive policy instrument for policy makers in individual exporting countries. By taxing, restricting, or even banning exports, governments lower local food prices and improve the access of the local population to food products. Export taxes may also increase public revenues. However, as shown in Chapters 11 and 12, the application of export restrictions and taxes also increases world food prices and amplifies the initial shock on world markets. Today the WTO has no discipline on the use of export taxes by its members, and quantitative export restrictions are permitted as a means to avoid food shortages. This is an important issue that deserves to be addressed by the institution as soon as possible. Several directions can be followed.

Bouët and Laborde (2016) argue that the elimination of export taxes is politically impossible since too many countries do not currently have the proper domestic fiscal base and rely on export taxes to generate public revenues or enforce redistribution goals. Agreements on the binding of current export taxes, and perhaps the banning of new ones, can thus be negotiated on a plurilateral basis.[12] Such clauses on the regulation of export taxes currently exist in specific regional trade agreements. Second, a strong monitoring and notifications process should be enforced since export restrictions impose negative externalities on other countries in the rest of the world. Finally, it could be desirable to consider a Pigovian tax, meaning that when a country implements a new export restriction on food products, it would have to pay a fee. This could lead countries to internalize the negative consequences (on trading partners) of an export tax (Bouët and Laborde 2016) and create an international fund to help vulnerable countries pay their food import bill in time of crisis.

CASH TRANSFERS SHOULD BE FAVORED INSTEAD OF FOOD STOCKS, WHEN POSSIBLE.

Protection against risk can be achieved by domestic policies, particularly food stocks and cash transfers. The constitution of food reserves and food stocks has been another common policy response to recent global food crises. These policies have also been much criticized because they have too many objectives (emergency aid, helping poor consumers in times of food scarcity or in times of high prices, providing support to producers in order to keep prices at profitable levels, and so on) and because they are very costly (this is often related to the first reason; see Chapters 8 and 9). Cash transfers to urban and rural households based on poverty criteria may be one of the best alternative

12 Agreements on export restrictions on a plurilateral basis can take the form of quotas exempted from restrictions and also explicit provisions regarding any new multilateral export tax.

policies to implement to support food consumption.[13] Transfers will help poor households cope with higher food prices, allowing prices to remain higher and thus spurring local production in the medium term.

The problem comes not from high prices but from low incomes; some households do not have enough revenue to buy necessary goods, such as food. Consequently, an intervention that raises income levels is the first-best policy. Poverty-based cash transfers can also compensate for other negative shocks that poor households, both urban and rural, may suffer. Income support to poor producers may also be considered (see Chapter 8), especially when the price rise is associated with a negative production shock affecting smallholders (for example, in the case of El Niño). However, cash transfers may be difficult to implement in some poor countries because poor households need to be identified and a distribution system needs to be put in place. There is also the issue of how to finance those transfers. The international community should play a larger role in helping to set up these poverty-based safety nets.

Since 2001, world trade has deeply changed, with powerful new trading partners emerging, new forces like the emergence of global value chains shaping world trade, and a new economic environment putting different pressures on agricultural prices as well as new farm policies, energy policies, and trade policies. Obviously the stalemate in current multilateral discussions reflects this drastic modification of the world trade environment and the uncertainties regarding the new balance of responsibilities in the collective effort to support a healthy trading system. There is thus the significant need to revamp multilateral trade negotiations. We recommend that WTO officially announce the end of the Doha Development Agenda and the launch of new multilateral trade negotiations based on new principles. With this announcement it may be possible to capture recent progress, such as the elimination of export subsidies that was announced in Nairobi, and officially announce the updating of bound tariff schedules. This updating could lock in the last decade of unilateral tariff reduction.

Concerning new multilateral trade negotiations, there are a few general principles that should guide these negotiations, such as an extended domain of negotiation and the role of side payments and the plurilateral approach. Importantly, food security has to be positioned at the center of these negotiations, with a focus on the positive role that international trade can play in improving food security. This will reshape the content of the negotiations to focus more on: the elimination of traditional distortionary policies (import

---

13 See Ahmed et al. 2009; Hidrobo et al. 2012; Marshall and Hill 2015.

duties and trade-distorting domestic support in rich and emerging countries) hurting agricultural and food items; new disciplines on the use of export taxes and restrictions; and a strict definition of the role that food stocks can play at the national level in ensuring food security and of the associated operational issues.

Bibliography

Ahmed, A. U., A. R. Quisumbing, M. Nasreen, J. F. Hoddinott, and E. Bryan. 2009. *Comparing Food and Cash Transfers to the Ultra Poor in Bangladesh.* IFPRI Research Monograph. Washington, DC: International Food Policy Research Institute.

Baldwin, R. 2012. "WTO 2.0: Global Governance of Supply Chain Trade." *CEPR Policy Insight* 64. London: Centre for Economic Policy Research.

Bouët, A., and D. Laborde. 2016. "Food Crisis and Export Taxation: Revisiting the Adverse Effects of Noncooperative Aspect of Trade Policies." In *Food Price Volatility and Its Implications for Food Security and Policy*, edited by M. Kalkuhl, J. von Braun, and M. Torero, 167–179. Switzerland: Springer Open.

Brandi, C. 2015. "The Doha Round Is Dead—Long Live the WTO?" *The Current Column.* Bonn: German Development Institute.

Brenton, P., and G. Isik. 2012. *De-Fragmenting Africa Deepening Regional Trade Integration in Goods and Services.* Washington, DC: World Bank.

Díaz-Bonilla, E., and D. Laborde. 2015. *The Bali Agreement: An Assessment from the Perspective of Developing Countries.* IFPRI Discussion Paper. Washington, DC: International Food Policy Research Institute.

———. 2016. *Catastrophic Flood or Inoffensive Drizzle: Assessing the Impact of Countries Using the Existing Water in Export Subsidies.* IFPRI Discussion Paper. Washington, DC: International Food Policy Research Institute.

Donnan, S. 2015. "Trade Talks Lead to 'Death of Doha and Birth of New WTO.'" *Financial Times*, December 20.

Economist. 2012. "Mercosur RIP?" July 14. Accessed July 2016. www.economist.com/node/21558609.

Hidrobo, M., J. F. Hoddinott, A. Peterman, A. Margolies, and V. Moreira. 2012. *Cash, Food, or Vouchers? Evidence from a Randomized Experiment in Northern Ecuador.* IFPRI Discussion Paper 1234. Washington, DC: International Food Policy Research Institute.

Marshall, C., and P. S. Hill. 2015. "Ten Best Resources on Conditional Cash Transfers." *Health Policy and Planning* 30: 742–746.

New York Times Editorial Board. 2016. "Global Trade after the Failure of the Doha Round." *New York Times*, January 1.

Stewart, H. 2015. "Doha Is Dead. Hopes for Fairer Global Trade Shouldn't Die, Too." *Guardian*, December 20.

Stiglitz, J., and A. Charlton. 2006. "Aid for Trade: Report for the Commonwealth Secretariat." Accessed July 2016. http://unctad.org/sections/ditc_tncdb/docs/ditc_tncd_bpgeneva03-06_en.pdf.

USTR (Office of the United States Trade Representative). 2017. "The Trans-Pacific Partnership." Accessed February 22, 2016. https://ustr.gov/tpp/.

Vyasan, R. 2015. "Long Live the WTO—Doha Development Agenda Is Dead." *Morung Express*, December 27.

Glossary

aggregate measurement of support (AMS): The indicator on which the domestic support discipline for the Agreement on Agriculture is based; AMS calculates a market price support estimate for each commodity receiving support, plus non-exempt direct payments or any other subsidy not exempted from WTO reduction commitments, less specific agricultural levies or fees paid by producers.

Agreement on Agriculture (AoA): An international treaty aimed at reducing distortionary agricultural trade policies; the AoA was negotiated during the Uruguay Round of the General Agreement on Tariffs and Trade and entered into force with the establishment of the WTO on January 1, 1995.

Agreement on Trade Facilitation (ATF): Agreement concluded in December 2013 by WTO members at the Bali Ministerial Conference with provisions for facilitating the movement, release, and clearance of goods, including goods in transit.

agricultural market access (AMA): WTO negotiations focusing on the reduction or elimination of tariffs and tariff-rate quotas on agricultural commodities.

Amber Box: A classification of the AoA for domestic agricultural subsidies; the Amber Box subsidies include domestic support that is considered distortionary and are therefore subject to reduction commitments; technically calculated as the aggregate measurement of support (AMS).

These definitions are taken from the website of the World Trade Organization (https://www.wto.org/english/thewto_e/glossary_e/glossary_e.htm).

Bali Package: A trade agreement resulting from the ninth Ministerial Conference of the World Trade Organization in Bali, Indonesia, in December 2013; the package aims at lowering global trade barriers and is the first agreement reached through the WTO that was approved by all its members. The package includes provisions for lowering import tariffs and agricultural subsidies, and established the commitment for a final decision on the use of public food stocks for food security purposes in developing countries.

beggar-thy-neighbor policy: A trade policy that protects or helps the economy of one country at the expense of other countries.

Blue Box: A classification of the AoA for domestic agricultural subsidies; the Blue Box subsidies link to one product but do not increase according to production levels; aid that is linked to production limitation programs and calculated according to a fixed production data from an earlier period; and support that requires farmers to limit production. There are currently no limits on spending on Blue Box subsidies.

Bound Total AMS: A consolidated aggregate measurement of support above which WTO members are not authorized to implement their total AMS.

BRIC: Brazil, the Russian Federation, India, and China; a group of emerging economies typically grouped together.

Computable General Equilibrium (CGE) models: A class of economic models that use actual economic data to estimate how an economy might react to changes in policy, technology, or other external factors.

crop insurance: Insurance purchased by agricultural producers to protect against crop loss due to natural disasters, such as hail, drought, and floods, or revenue loss due to declines in the prices of agricultural commodities.

current total aggregate measurement of support (CTAMS): The sum of all domestic support provided during any year of the implementation period in favor of agricultural producers, calculated as the sum of all aggregate measurements of support for basic agricultural products, all non-product-specific aggregate measurements of support, and all equivalent measurements of support for agricultural products.

current total AMS: See current total aggregate measurement of support (CTAMS).

Development Box: A proposed set of special AoA provisions applicable only to developing countries, including exemptions from commitments on staple food products, the possibility of negotiating higher tariffs, the use of simple safeguards to protect staples, a ban on developed countries "dumping" agricultural products, an international food security fund, better market access to developed-country markets, and binding commitments on technical assistance for developing countries; this proposed special treatment remains controversial and is opposed by a number of both developed and developing countries.

Dispute Settlement Unit (DSU): A WTO body that provides a framework for litigating trade disputes.

Doha Declaration: Common statement made by WTO trade ministers concerning the launch of a new round of multilateral trade negotiations, made in Doha (Qatar) on December 2001.

Doha Development Agenda (DDA): The current trade-negotiation round of the WTO; the round commenced in November 2001 with the objective to lower global trade barriers and thus facilitate increased global trade, particularly for the benefit of developing countries. See also Doha Round.

Doha Round: The current trade-negotiation round of the WTO; the round commenced in November 2001 with the objective to lower global trade barriers and thus facilitate increased global trade, particularly for the benefit of developing countries. See also Doha Development Agenda.

domestic agricultural support: The annual monetary value of gross transfers to agriculture from consumers and taxpayers arising from government policies that support agriculture, regardless of their objectives and economic impacts.

Economic Partnership Agreements (EPAs): A scheme to create a free trade area (FTA) between the European Union and the African-Caribbean-Pacific countries (ACP).

fixed external reference price (FERP): Market price that serves as a reference to calculate the AMS, in comparison to the intervention price.

free trade agreement (FTA): Cooperation between at least two countries to reduce or eliminate trade barriers—import quotas and tariffs—and to increase trade of goods and services with each other.

General Agreement on Tariffs and Trade (GATT): A multilateral agreement regulating international trade designed to reduce tariffs and other trade barriers and eliminate preferential treatment; GATT was negotiated during the United Nations Conference on Trade and Employment and was signed by 23 nations in Geneva on October 30, 1947. It remained in force until 123 nations signed the Uruguay Round Agreements in Marrakesh on April 14, 1994, which established the World Trade Organization.

Green Box: A classification of the AoA for domestic agricultural subsidies; the Green Box includes policies that are not restricted by the WTO because they are not considered trade-distorting or are minimally distorting. Certain agriculture-related subsidies fall under the Green Box.

G10: Group of Ten; comprises Belgium, Canada, France, Germany, Italy, Japan, Netherlands, Sweden, Switzerland, the United Kingdom, and the United States.

G20 developing nations (G20+): A group of influential developing countries formed at the fifth Ministerial Conference in 2003 to ensure developing-country interests were represented; comprises Argentina, Bolivia, Brazil, Chile, China, Cuba, Ecuador, Egypt, Guatemala, India, Indonesia, Mexico, Nigeria, Pakistan, Paraguay, Peru, Philippines, South Africa, Thailand, United Republic of Tanzania, Uruguay, Venezuela, and Zimbabwe. It is different from the G20 macroeconomic forum gathering of representants from 20 major economies.

G33: Group of 33 developing countries; comprises Antigua and Barbuda, Barbados, Belize, Benin, China, Côte d'Ivoire, Cuba, Democratic Republic of the Congo, Dominican Republic, El Salvador, Grenada, Guyana, Guatemala, Haiti, Honduras, India, Indonesia, Jamaica, Kenya, Lao People's Democratic Republic, Mauritius, Madagascar, Mongolia, Mozambique, Nicaragua, Nigeria, Pakistan, Panama, Peru, Philippines, Saint Kitts and Nevis, Saint Lucia, Saint Vincent and the Grenadines, Senegal, Sri Lanka, Suriname, Trinidad and Tobago, Turkey, Uganda, United Republic of Tanzania, Venezuela, Zambia, and Zimbabwe.

least developed countries (LDCs): Countries that, according to the United Nations, exhibit the lowest indicators of socioeconomic development, with the lowest Human Development Index ratings of all countries in the world.

market price support (MPS): The annual monetary value of gross transfers from consumers and taxpayers to agricultural producers arising from policy measures creating a gap between domestic market prices and border prices of a specific agricultural commodity measured at the farm gate level.

MIRAGE model: Modelling International Relationships in Applied General Equilibrium, a multicountry, multisector dynamic model of the world economy used to study trade policy scenarios and assess bilateral and multilateral agreements.

most favored nation (MFN): Status of trade treatment accorded by one WTO member to another WTO member; the recipient must receive equal trade treatment as the "most favored nation" from the country granting it.

nonagricultural market access (NAMA): WTO negotiations focusing on the reduction or elimination of tariffs on manufacturing products, fuels and mining products, fish and fish products, and forestry products.

overall trade-distorting support (OTDS): Any domestic support measures considered to distort trade.

special and differential treatment (SDT): Provisions that exempt developing countries from the same strict trade rules and disciplines that apply to more industrialized countries.

special safeguard mechanism (SSM): In the Doha Round agricultural negotiations, a tool that will allow developing countries to raise tariffs temporarily to deal with import surges or price falls.

Trans-Pacific Partnership Agreement (TPP): North–South trade agreement that aims to eliminate tariff and nontariff trade barriers.

Uruguay Round: The eighth round of multilateral trade negotiations conducted within the framework of the GATT, spanning from 1986 to 1994 and comprising 123 countries; the round led to the creation of the World Trade Organization and expanded trade liberalization attempts to such new sectors as agriculture, textiles, and services.

World Trade Organization (WTO): The only global international organization dealing with the rules of trade between nations; it is based in Geneva and has 164 members as of January 2017.

Contributors

Antoine Bouët (a.bouet@cgiar.org) is a senior research fellow in the Markets, Trade, and Institutions Division of the International Food Policy Research Institute (IFPRI), Washington, DC, and a professor of Economics at the University of Bordeaux, France. His main fields of research are international trade, trade policy, and development economics. He earned a PhD in Economics from the University of Bordeaux, France.

Lars Brink (Lars.Brink@hotmail.com) is an independent agricultural and trade policy advisor. With many years of government experience, he focuses on understanding different countries' policy support to agricultural producers and the application of international trade rules.

Eddie C. Chavez (echavez@uark.edu) is a senior program associate at the Department of Agricultural Economics and Agribusiness at the University of Arkansas, Fayetteville, US. He currently manages the Arkansas Global Rice Model, one of a handful of internationally recognized models in existence that represent the world rice economy. His main research areas are the rice economies of the United States, the Association of Southeast Asian Nations, and African nations, as well as the global rice economy. In particular, he focuses on long-term modeling projections and market and policy impact analyses. He earned a bachelor's degree in Agricultural Engineering from the University of the Philippines at Los Baños, a master's of business administration from De La Salle University in Manila, and a master's degree in Agricultural Economics from the University of Arkansas, Fayetteville, US.

Giselle Datz (gdatz@vt.edu) is an associate professor at the School of Public and International Affairs, Virginia Polytechnic Institute and State University, Blacksburg, US. Her fields of research are Latin American politics, debt and financial crises, and pension reforms.

Eugenio Díaz-Bonilla (E.Diaz-Bonilla@cgiar.org) is the head of the Latin America and Caribbean Program at IFPRI, Washington, DC. He has represented his country, Argentina, as a senior diplomat and as executive director at the Inter-American Development Bank. He has worked for several international organizations, including the World Bank, the United Nations Development Programme, the Food and Agriculture Organization of the United Nations, the International Institute for Cooperation in Agriculture, and the Organization of American States. He earned a master's degree in International Relations and a PhD in Economics, both from Johns Hopkins University, Baltimore.

Joseph Glauber (j.glauber@cgiar.org) is a senior research fellow in the Markets, Trade, and Institutions Division of IFPRI, Washington, DC, and a former chief economist at the US Department of Agriculture, Washington, DC.

David Laborde Debucquet (d.laborde@cgiar.org) is a senior research fellow in the Markets, Trade, and Institutions Division and the theme leader on Macroeconomics and Trade for IFPRI, Washington, DC. His research interests include international trade, measurement and modeling of protectionism, and multilateral and regional trade liberalization, as well as environmental issues (climate change, biofuels). Prior to joining IFPRI, he was an economist at the Centre d'Etudes Prospectives et d'Informations Internationales (CEPII), Paris, between 2003 and 2007. He earned a PhD in Economics from the University of Pau in 2008.

Will Martin (w.martin@cgiar.org) is a senior research fellow in the Markets, Trade, and Institutions Division of IFPRI and president of the International Association of Agricultural Economists. He studied economics and agricultural economics at the University of Queensland, the Australian National University, and Iowa State University and worked at the Australian Bureau of Agricultural Economics, the Australian National University, and the World Bank before joining IFPRI in 2015.

David Orden (orden@vt.edu) is a professor and director of the Global Issues Initiative, Institute for Society, Culture and Environment, at Virginia Polytechnic Institute and State University, Blacksburg, US, and a former senior research fellow at IFPRI, Washington, DC. His research focuses on agricultural policy and trade.

Simla Tokgoz (s.tokgoz@cgiar.org) is a research fellow in the Markets, Trade, and Institutions Division of IFPRI, Washington, DC. She earned a PhD in Economics from North Carolina State University in 2003. Her main field of research is modeling and analysis of biofuels, energy, and agricultural markets, particularly the integration of agricultural and energy markets in developing countries.

Fousseini Traoré (Fousseini.Traore@cgiar.org) is a research fellow in the Markets, Trade, and Institutions Division of IFPRI, Washington, DC. His main fields of research are international trade and commodity markets. He earned a PhD in Development Economics from the University of Clermont-Ferrand I, France.

Eric Wailes (ewailes@uark.edu) is the L.C. Carter Endowed Chair in Rice and Soybean Marketing and a distinguished professor of Agricultural Economics and Agribusiness at the University of Arkansas, Fayetteville, US. His main fields of research are domestic and international agricultural marketing, trade policy, and development economics. He earned a PhD in Agricultural Economics from Michigan State University, East Lansing, US.

T. Edward Yu (tyu1@utk.edu) is an associate professor of Agricultural and Resource Economics at the University of Tennessee, Knoxville, US. His main fields of research are agricultural logistics, bioenergy economics, and international trade. He earned a PhD in agricultural economics from Texas A&M University, College Station, US.

Index

Made in the USA
Monee, IL
12 September 2026

62981000R00293